Mistakes, Errors and Failures across Cultures

Elisabeth Vanderheiden • Claude-Hélène Mayer
Editors

Mistakes, Errors and Failures across Cultures

Navigating Potentials

Springer

Editors
Elisabeth Vanderheiden
Catholic Adult Education of Germany
Römerberg, Germany

Claude-Hélène Mayer
Department of Industrial Psychology
and People Management
University of Johannesburg
Johannesburg, South Africa

Institut für Therapeutische Kommunikation
und Sprachgebrauch
Europa Universität Viadrina
Frankfurt (Oder), Germany

ISBN 978-3-030-35573-9 ISBN 978-3-030-35574-6 (eBook)
https://doi.org/10.1007/978-3-030-35574-6

This Springer imprint is published by the registered company Springer Nature Switzerland AG.
The registered company address is: Gewerbestrasse 11, 6330 Cham, Switzerland

Foreword

I was delighted that Elisabeth Vanderheiden and Claude-Hélène Mayer asked if I could provide a Foreword to their interesting book exploring the genesis of mistakes. Mistakes are perhaps the most common of human errors and often the least understood. My delight came from the fact that the invitation came just as I was completing the renewal of my Certified Instrument Flight Instructor (yes, researchers do have lives outside of the laboratory). To be sure, aviation has had an understandable concern with eliminating mistakes. For the layman, this concern has seemed to be focused on commercial operations. CRM (cockpit resource management) came about after the crash of a United Airlines DC-8 in the northwest which ran out of fuel shortly before landing at the airport. The analysis of the incident revealed that the crew depended too much on the captain as they tried to solve a problem all the while using precious fuel. That incident resulted in the airline, followed by the entire industry, to adopt training on how to delegate and integrate the resources of the crew, hence CRM. But in the public's mind, there seems to be less concern about general aviation in avoiding, if not eliminating, mistakes. Many of the mistakes in this domain may not result in the loss of life, though some do. One case I remember well was that of a doctor and his wife who set off in their single engine for a trip for a mid-south state to Texas. The pilot carefully calculated the amount of fuel he would need to easily reach an airport for refueling. However, for reasons unknown, he underestimated the strength of headwinds as they approached the airport. When on final approach, they ran out of fuel and hit trees just off the end of the runway. Both lives were lost. Another example is from my own early days as a pilot. We had just moved to a state in the Southern United States to a town about 50 miles away from the Mississippi River. On one of those perfect VFR days, we decided to fly over to the river and see the barges from a thousand feet. So, we flew up and down the river for a while and then headed back to the home base. Now, this was normally a 45-minute jaunt in our 172, but it seemed to drag on and on. And then I realized I was lost; all the land looked the same. The two lakes that bracketed the home airport were nowhere to be seen. Finally, I called for help from ATC, who found me, and I realized that we had drifted 50 miles south. Yes, a mistake in that as a new pilot is that I forgot to use the instruments in the plane to triangulate between two VORs and keep myself on course. But it was an unintentional mistake. But, one, if the weather had turned nasty, could have had undesirable consequence. The point being that there are intentional mistakes (usually accompanied by the optimism bias), such as scud running and unintentional errors. Over the years, the CFI training has significantly changed to a focus on risk assessment and mitigation. And I would suggest that the concept of risk assessment can be applied outside of the aviation community, e.g., in analyzing vehicular accidents such as starting a trip on an icy day without considering the probability of losing control.

What this book takes as its rationale is "are mistakes, errors, and failures culture bound?" To be sure, in aviation, we have known for some time that cultures that are highly hierarchical make for problems in the cockpit. For example, a Korean Airlines 747 crashed on approach to a landing because the first officer would not forcefully speak up when he realized that the captain was allowing the plane to drop below the glide slope. The analysis suggested that Korean culture vested almost god-like characteristics in the captain. As a result, Korean revamped its entire training and evaluation program. Of course, this issue is not confined to one airline or one country; similar events have occurred in many countries. But we tend to see these issues, at least before this book, as restricted to certain occupations and not generally spread throughout the culture and through many aspects of everyday living. For that reason, this book can serve as a guide to future research on mistakes, errors, and failures.

This is an important book; the chapters are written with care to the existing research and applications to real-world issues. The authors are to be commended for advancing our knowledge of this critical area.

Dan Landis completed his PhD in General-Theoretical Psychology from Wayne State University in 1963. He has held several academic and research positions. He is currently Affiliate Professor of Psychology at the University of Hawaii at Mānoa, Professor Emeritus of Psychology, and Dean Emeritus of the College of Liberal Arts, University of Mississippi. He is also Past Chair of the Department of Psychology, Indiana University-Purdue University Indianapolis, Research Psychologist at Educational Testing Service, Senior Research Psychologist at the Franklin Institute, and Visiting Research Professor at the East-West Center; Defense Equal Opportunity Management Institute (DEOMI); University of Illinois; Victoria University in Wellington, NZ; and Primate Laboratory, University of Wisconsin. He is the Founding Editor in Chief of the *International Journal of Intercultural Relations* (1977–2011), the Founding President of the International Academy for Intercultural Research, and the Coeditor/Author of *Ethnic Conflict: International Perspectives* (1985), of the three editions of the *Handbook of Intercultural Training* (1986, 1996, 2004), of the *Handbook of Ethnic Conflict: International Perspectives* (2012), and of *Neuroscience in Intercultural Contexts* (2015). A Mandarin translation of the 2004 Training Handbook was published by Peking University Press in 2010. He is an Elected Fellow of several organizations: American Psychological Association, Association for Psychological Science, Society for the Psychological Study of Social Issues, Division of International Psychology of APA, and

International Academy for Intercultural Research. He is listed in Who's Who and other biographical compendiums. In 2007, he was given a Lifetime Achievement Award by the International Academy for Intercultural Research and, in 2012, was honored by the American Psychological Association with its award for Distinguished Contributions to the Internationalization of Psychology.

Keaau, HI, USA

Dan Landis
danl@hawaii.edu

Acknowledgments

Elisabeth Vanderheiden and Claude-Hélène Mayer
We would also like to thank our colleagues who have so generously shared their knowledge in the chapters of this book.

The successful completion of this book was made possible with the continued support and encouragement of several individuals. Special thanks go to Ruth Coetzee who has language edited many of the chapters and thereby contributed to the language quality of this book.

Further thanks go to Professor Freddie Crous, Head of the Department of Industrial Psychology and People Management, University of Johannesburg, who has supported the preparation of this book on different levels and wherever possible.

Finally, we would like to thank our publisher, Springer International Publishing AG, for the continuous support and interest in our projects. Especially, we would like to thank Shinjini Chatterjee and Ameena Jaafar, Ram Prasad Chandrasekar and Nitesh Shrivastava and their teams for their commitment and support with regard to this book project.

Elisabeth Vanderheiden
Making mistakes, admitting errors, or experiencing failure is often initially associated with very painful experiences. It is often shameful, can trigger feelings of guilt, can cause great suffering and deep crises, and can have serious personal, professional, legal, or material consequences. But ideally, these events also initiate deep holistic learning opportunities, chances for reorientation, and manifold occasions to develop new visions as a person, organisation, collective, or society, to discover new skills and resources, and to take unknown paths at the crossroads of professional or private life decisions. In this sense, I thank all the people who have given me the opportunity to make mistakes and fail because these extraordinary learning opportunities and catalysts for my personal and professional development would not have existed without them. Above all, I thank those who stood by my side on these occasions, inspired me, and walked with me for a little while or longer on my way to new and sometimes unknown terrains of knowledge, action, and changed life practice.

Contents

Editors and Contributors

About the Editors

Elisabeth Vanderheiden is a Pedagogue, Theologian, Intercultural Mediator, and Managing Director of the Catholic Adult Education Rhineland-Palatinate, and the President of the Catholic Adult Education of Germany. Her publishing focus centers on the context of basic education for adults, in particular on trainings for teachers and trainers in adult education, as well as vocational and civic education, and edited books on intercultural opening processes and intercultural mediation. Her latest publications focused on shame as resource as well as mistakes, errors, and failures and their hidden potentials in the context of culture and positive psychology. She also works as an Independent Researcher. In a current project, she investigates life crises and their individual coping strategies from different cultural viewpoints. A topic that has also aroused her research interest is humor and how it appears in different cultural perspectives and from various scientific disciplines. She lives in Germany and Florida.

Claude-Hélène Mayer (Drhabil, PhD) is Professor of Industrial and Organizational Psychology at the Department of Industrial Psychology and People Management at the University of Johannesburg; an Adjunct Professor at the European University Viadrina in Frankfurt (Oder), Germany; and a Senior Research Associate at Rhodes University, Grahamstown, South Africa. She holds a PhD in Psychology (University of Pretoria, South Africa) and in Management (Rhodes University, South Africa), a Doctorate in Political Sciences focusing on sociocultural anthropology and intercultural didactics (Georg-August University, Germany), and a Habilitation in Psychology (European University Viadrina, Germany) with focus on work, organizational, and cultural psychology. She has published several monographs, text collections, accredited journal articles, and special issues on transcultural mental health and well-being, sense of coherence, shame, transcultural conflict management and mediation, women in leadership in culturally diverse work contexts, constellation work, coaching, and psychobiography.

Contributors

Umut Altunoz MD senior psychiatrist & psychotherapist, Wunstorf Psychiatric Clinic, Hannover Region Clinics, Wunstorf, Germany.

Alice Anderson Manager of Audience Research and Impact, Minneapolis Institute of Art, USA.

Thalita Camargo Angelucci Psychologist Federal University of São Carlos (UFSCar, Brazil), PhD Student at the National University of Rosario (UNR, Argentina).

Christine Bales Student of rehabilitation psychology B.Sc., occupational therapist, Stendal and Göttingen, Germany.

Paul Barach MD, MPH, anesthesiologist and critical care physician physician-scientist, Clinical Professor Wayne State University School of Medicine, and Children's Hospital of Michigan, USA.

Maria Belz Dr., Graduated psychologist and in training to become a certified behavioral psychotherapist, Göttingen, Germany.

Maike Baumann scientific associate University of Potsdam, Germany.

Katja Brinkmann student applied psychology B.Sc., Göttingen, Germany.

Jan S. Brommundt (Dr.) is medical doctor in anaesthesiology as well as international, humanitarian and disaster medicine, University Medical Center Groningen, The Netherlands.

Alessandro Carretta PhD, Full Professor in Economics and Management of Financial Intermediation, former Director of the Program in Banking and Finance at University of Rome Tor Vergata, Italy.

Franziska Carow student of health communication, Department of Population Medicine and Health Services Research at Bielefeld, Germany.

Clifford H. Clarke ABD, teaching intercultural communication at Stanford and the University of Hawaii, USA, Japan.

Hannah Eger BA health communication at Bielefeld, Germany.

Lucrezia Fattobene Assistant Professor in Financial Markets and Institutions at LUM Jean Monnet University, Bari, Italy.

Florian Fischer (Dr.) Postdoc researcher at Bielefeld University, Germany.

Saraswathie Govender Associate Professor, University of Limpopo, South Africa.

Zhi Guo research fellow in the Department of Industrial Engineering, Tsinghua University, China.

Mary Hallay-Witte certified religious pedagogue, research associate at Medical School Hamburg, Hamburg.

Jan U. Hagen (Prof. Dr.) associate professor at ESMT European School of Management and Technology in Berlin, Germany.

Bettina Janssen (Dr. iur.) solicitor, mediator (BM), supervisor (DGSV), coach (ECA), Cologne, Germany.

Klas-Göran Karlsson (Dr.) Professor of History, Lund University, Sweden.

James L. Kelley Researcher and writer, USA.

Aliraza Javaid BSc Criminology, MSc Clinical Criminology, MRes Social Sciences, PhD in Sociology and Social Policy, United Kingdom.

Dan Landis PhD, Affiliate Professor of Psychology University of Hawaii at Manoa, Professor Emeritus of Psychology, and Dean Emeritus of the College of Liberal Arts, University of Mississippi, USA.

Fernando Lanzer Pereira de Souza B.A. Clinical, Educational and Organisational Psychology, guest lecturer at business schools in Europe and Brazil, The Netherlands.

Xin Lei PhD student in the Department of Industrial Engineering, Tsinghua University, China.

Josua Leibrich student od psychology B.Sc., Göttingen, Germany.

Václav Linkov (PhD), researcher in transportation psychology, Brno, Czech Republic.

Adam V. Maltese (PhD) Associate Professor of Science Education at Indiana University and director of the MILL Makerspace, Indiana University, USA.

Lolo Jacques Mayer young author and public speaker. Germany and South Africa.

Kathryn Anne Nel (Prof. PhD), Industrial Psychology, University of Limpopo, South Africa.

Elmar Nass (Prof. Dr. Dr.), Professor of Economic and Social Ethics at the Wilhelm Loehe University Fürth, Germany.

Rudolf M. Oosthuizen DLitt, associate professor Department of Industrial and Organisational Psychology University of South Africa.

Ibrahim Özkan (Dr.) Graduated psychologist and certified psychological psychotherapist, Göttingen, Germany.

Bo Petersson Professor of Political Science and IMER (International Migration and Ethnic Relations), Malmö University, Sweden.

Wayne Petherick (PhD) Associate Professor of Criminology Bond University Queensland, Australia.

María Isabel Pozzo Professor, Licentiate and Doctor in Educational Sciences from the National University of Rosario (UNR, Argentina).

Nan Qie doctoral candidate at Tsinghua University, China.

Pei-Luen Patrick Rau Professor Industrial Engineering and Global Innovation Exchange Institute, Tsinghua University, China.

Paul C. Rosenblatt PhD Professor Emeritus Family Social Science at the University of Minnesota, USA.

Thomas Ryan (PhD), Associate Professor Philosophy and Theology of the University of Notre Dame Australia.

Amber Simpson Assistant Professor Department of Teaching, Learning, and Educational Leadership, Binghamton University, Binghamton, NY, USA.

Paola Schwizer Full Professor Financial Markets and Institutions University of Parma (Italy) and Professor at SDA Bocconi School of Management, Italy.

Chris P. Subbe (Dr.), Senior Clinical Lecturer at the School of Medical Sciences, Bangor University, United Kingdom.

Karel Stanz Professor Industrial Psychology University of Pretoria, South Africa.

Euisuk Sung (PhD), postdoctoral researcher at Indiana University, USA.

Naomi Takashiro (PhD), adjunct faculty at the Kyoto University of Foreign Studies and Junior college Kyoto, Japan.

Matita Tshabalala Industrial Psychologist, Aviation Psychologist, Pretoria, South Africa.

Jaco van der Westhuizen (PhD), Ex-Air Traffic Controller and Human Factor Specialist, Pretoria, South Africa.

Sofia von Humboldt (Prof. Dr.), Associate Professor and Principal Investigator, William James Center for Research at ISPA-Instituto Universitário, Lisbon, Portugal.

Janina Wesolowski B.Sc., student of psychology, Hannover Medical School, Germany.

Andong Zhang PhD student, Department of Industrial Engineering, Tsinghua University, China.

Petr Zámečník Head of Department of Traffic Psychology, Transport Research Centre, Brno, Czech Republic.

Chapter 1
"There Is a Crack in Everything. That's How the Light Gets in": An Introduction to Mistakes, Errors and Failure as Resources

Elisabeth Vanderheiden and Claude-Hélène Mayer

> *"I have often said that from the amoeba to Einstein there is only one step. Both work with the method of trial and error. The amoeba must hate error, for it dies when it errs. But Einstein knows that we can learn only from our mistakes, and he spares no effort to make new trials in order to detect new errors, and to eliminate them from our theories. The step that the amoeba cannot take, but Einstein can, is to achieve a critical, a self-critical attitude, a critical approach. It is the greatest of the virtues that the invention of the human language puts within our grasp. I believe that it will make peace possible."*
>
> Karl Popper, All Life is Problem Solving

Abstract To fail in a task, to misjudge a situation and to make wrong conclusions, or to be unable to achieve a desired goal, are basic human experiences that occur in everyday activities as well as in longer-term projects in the context of personal development. But the assessments of what is a mistake, an error, or a failure depend heavily on cultural as well as individual contexts. Errors, failures and mistakes do

---

"There is a crack in everything (there is a crack in everything) That's how the light gets in". *Leonard Cohen, Anthem*

E. Vanderheiden (✉)
Catholic Adult Education of Germany, Römerberg, Germany
e-mail: ev@keb-rheinland-pfalz.de

C.-H. Mayer
Department of Industrial Psychology and People Management, University of Johannesburg, Johannesburg, South Africa

Institut für Therapeutische Kommunikation und Sprachgebrauch, Europa Universität Viadrina, Frankfurt (Oder), Germany

E. Vanderheiden, C.-H. Mayer (eds.), *Mistakes, Errors and Failures across Cultures*, https://doi.org/10.1007/978-3-030-35574-6_1

not constitute objectively ascertainable facts, but are subject to the validity of certain rules within a context-dependent judgement. These rules can exist in various forms and degrees of explicitness and are adopted in the course of social negotiation processes. The aim of this book is to synthesise empirical research-based and theoretical perspectives on mistakes, errors, and failure in and across cultures, in order to provide a comprehensive view of contemporary research and practice which is accessible to researchers and practicing professionals internationally.

Mistakes or errors can, at the individual level, cause deep shame and embarrassment, and can lead to severe personal, organisational and collective crises. However, they can also be viewed as a resource for self-development and organisational, collective and societal change. At the organisational level, mistakes, errors and failure can have serious consequences for individuals such as employees or clients in the field of transportation, or in the context of medicine or chemistry, for example. At the same time, they can reveal inaccuracies in process chains, or weaknesses in a system, and they can also trigger contingent and sustainable improvement processes on all levels. Even in the political context, actual or perceived wrong decisions can have massive and long-lasting consequences for individuals, societal groups and subcultures, and for the society as such. Societal mistakes, errors and failures might then even be discussed in global contexts and in terms of their universal impact.

Keywords Mistakes · Error · Failure · Resource · Across cultures

1.1 Introduction

To fail in a task, to misjudge a situation and to make wrong conclusions, or to be unable to achieve a desired goal, are basic human experiences that occur in everyday activities as well as in longer-term projects in the context of personal development. But the assessments of what is a mistake, an error or a failure depend heavily on cultural as well as individual contexts (see Backert 2004; Pitta et al. 1999; Frese and Keith 2015; Mu et al. 2015; Chaps. 5, 11, 13, 23, 26 and 31). Errors, failures and mistakes do not constitute objectively ascertainable facts, but are subject to the validity of certain rules within a context-dependent judgement (Reason 1990, 1995, 2005; Lei 2018; Giolito and Verdin 2018). These rules can exist in various forms and degrees of explicitness and are adopted in the course of social negotiation processes (Heid 1999). The aim of this book is to synthesise empirical research-based and theoretical perspectives on mistakes, errors and failure in and across cultures, in order to provide a comprehensive view of contemporary research and practice which is accessible to researchers and practising professionals internationally.

Mistakes or errors can, at the individual level, cause deep shame and embarrassment and can lead to severe personal, organisational and collective crises. However, they can also be viewed as a resource for self-development and organisational, collective and societal change. At the organisational level, mistakes, errors and failure can have serious consequences for individuals such as employees or clients in the field of transportation, or in the context of medicine or chemistry, for example. At the same time, they can reveal inaccuracies in process chains, or weaknesses in a system, and they can also trigger contingent and sustainable improvement processes on all levels. Even in the political context, actual or perceived wrong decisions can have massive and long-lasting consequences for individuals, societal groups and subcultures and for the society as such. Societal mistakes, errors and failures might then even be discussed in global contexts and in terms of their universal impact.

In this book, the authors explore:

1. The handling of mistakes, errors and failure from different cultural perspectives.
2. Practical approaches to mistakes, errors and failure across cultures including models for working with mistakes, errors and failure in self-reflection, therapy and counselling as well on the individual, organisational and political level.
3. Mistakes, errors and failure as constructs which are seen as part of the human condition. The authors of this book aim to view all three concepts from a perspective which aims to highlight their positive functional aspects.

1.2 Defining Mistake, Error and Failure

Interestingly, there are no generally accepted definitions of the terms "mistake", "error" or "failure". Even scientific studies that deal with error prevention or error management in very different contexts often do so without a clear definition of the term. Nevertheless, in our view, having definitions or at least approximations of these terms is indispensable. What is regarded as a mistake, error or failure differs in the various disciplines; therefore, we approach the concepts from multiple scientific viewpoints. These are partly supplemented and deepened in the chapters of the book by additional scientific perspectives.

The definitions of mistake, error and failure are diverse and inconsistent. Some selected perspectives on these terms will be presented here. On one hand, they are fundamental approaches and points of view for research and scientific discourse; on the other hand, they are definitions of terms that are significant and relevant for the disciplines discussed in this book.

Generally, we understand:

- "Mistake" as a deviation from a norm or a standard
- "Error" as a wrong assumption, idea or behaviour
- "Failure" as lack of success in desired goals or values "due to complex situations and circumstances" (Mayer 2020; Chap. 26)

How individual scientific disciplines explain these terms in their respective contexts is examined in more detail below. The decisive factor in selecting disciplines to appear in this book was that the discipline had made a particularly intensive and extensive examination of and elaborate research into the topic, for example, in medicine, aviation but also pedagogy. These discussions are reflected in the various sections of this book.

1.2.1 Defining Mistake from an Interdisciplinary Perspective

What is commonly referred to as a mistake is a deviation from a standard, code of conduct or other requirement that jeopardises or obfuscates the achievement of a goal (Reason 1990, 1995, 2005; Senders and Moray 1991; Bauer 2008; Glendon et al. 2006).

Morgenroth and Schaller (2010, p. 1) extend this from a *psychological perspective* to the idea that, like failure, mistakes can only occur in the context of goal-orientated behaviour and constitutively involve the non-achievement of a goal or partial goal. In contrast to failure, one would speak of a mistake only if it was potentially avoidable.

According to Zapf et al. (1999), three criteria must be met for a mistake to exist:

1. Mistakes occur only in goal-orientated behaviour.
2. They mean the failure to achieve a goal or sub-goal.
3. Mistakes are potentially preventable.

This is confirmed in many psychological studies by Frese and colleagues (Frese 1993; Frese and Keith 2015). For example, when working with the computer:

> Mistakes can only be made by humans, because machines have no intentions … a mistake involves not reaching a certain goal and actually making it better. The latter is particularly problematic because it suggests blaming: those who make a mistake are often considered guilty. At least they are looking for a culprit: scientifically speaking, that does not make sense, because in reality the mistake is always due to a non-adaptation or a mismatch. If for example, if a glass shatters, one can never fully determine if this was due to the fragility of the glass or the clumsiness of the person. Both factors must work together so that it can break. (Frese 1993, p. 96, translated by Vanderheiden)

In the numerous experiments of systems psychologist Dietrich Dörner (1989) and engineering and medicine expert Bernhard Zimolong (1990; Zimolong and Trimpop 1993), the following errors have emerged, which are currently to be found in dealing with complex systems (Table 1.1).

Depending on the *language context* and on the understanding of the researchers, the terms "mistake" and "error" are often used synonymously in pedagogical contexts. In the German-language context, for example, in school research by Zander et al. (2014), the terms are used interchangeably. In other languages such as English or Spanish, a clear distinction may be made under certain circumstances (Chap. 20). A clearer nomenclature can be found in the language pedagogical perspective of second-language teaching. It will, according to Carl James (as cited by Kryeziu 2015), classically distinguish between various types, including:

Table 1.1 Types of mistakes (Vanderheiden based on Dörner 1989 and Zimolong 1990)

Mistake type	Example
Goal-setting mistake	An unrealistic goal is formulated and thus overloaded.
Assignment mistake	Decisions are made on the basis of prejudice or lack of information.
Forecasting mistake	Something is estimated wrongly, such as a required time window or required resources.
Mistake in reasoning	In the form of misjudgement in a hypothesis or experiment.
Recognition mistake	It is not recognised that a food is no longer edible.
Automation mistake	A slip, switching lanes in traffic.
Selection mistake	In the selection of stuff members, selection of partner or partner choosing a wrong product while shopping.
Memory and forgetting mistakes	During learning processes, when passing on information.
Judgement mistakes	A situation is wrongly judged.
Habitual mistakes	You drive a familiar route, forgetting to deviate slightly to run a particular errand.
Mistake by omission	Forget to fill up with petrol just before the car runs dry.

> *Slips* or lapses of tongue, pen and these can be detected and self-corrected. Then there are *mistakes* which can be corrected by their agent if the deviance is pointed out to the speaker. The third group are *errors* that cannot be self-corrected until further input has been provided to the learner to be able to correct that error. (Kryeziu 2015, p. 397)

Gartmeier (2009, p. 11) chooses a much broader approach to define mistakes as avoidable deviations from existing norms, which on one hand can never be completely eradicated but on the other hand represent significant opportunities for the initiation of learning activities (Gruber 1999, as cited in Gartmeier 2009, p. 11).

Various authors conclude that mistakes therefore can be regarded as useful starting points for individual competence development as well as for organisational innovation activities (Cannon and Edmondson 2005; Harteis et al. 2008; Harteis et al. 2006, translated by Vanderheiden).

Mistakes can describe actions as well as the results of actions. These may be deviations from context-specific, action-relevant action goals or objectives (Senders and Moray 1991; Gartmeier 2009, p. 17). In this case, a mistake can equally be seen as the omission of an action that would have been necessary in a certain situation (Meurier et al. 1997). At the same time, mistakes are not facts that can be objectively determined, but are judgements dependent on the validity of certain rules within a context (Reason 1990). These rules can exist in many different forms and degrees of explicitness and are adopted in the course of social negotiation processes (Heid 1999, cited in Gartmeier 2009, p. 17). However, mistakes offer opportunities for learning and enable awareness of potential deficits in one's own knowledge or action, which helps to identify appropriate fields of learning. Studies by Zander et al. (2014, p. 206) demonstrate that constructive handling of mistakes has a positive effect on the success of learning processes, reduces the fear of making mistakes and promotes a positive orientation towards learning from mistakes. Important factors in this context appear to be collaborative peer networks and the individual involvement of students in this structure, especially when linked to the experience of high general self-efficacy.

In the Institute of Medicine's publication "To Err is Human: Building a Safer Health System" (Kohn 1999) published in 1999, the terms "mistake" and "error" are used synonymously. This publication has substantially increased the attention paid to *errors and mistakes in health care*—especially in the USA and the UK (see also discussion in Schrappe 2015, p. 6 and Brommundt 2018, p. 170; Chaps. 15 and 28).

Many current medical studies prefer to use the term "error" (see next paragraph), although Kistler, Walter, Mitchell and Sloane (2010, p. 3) explicitly state that: "The term 'mistake' was chosen over 'medical error' as other studies have demonstrated patients' confusion around the term 'medical error' ". In their research, Kistler et al. (2010) identify mistakes as diagnostic and treatment mistakes. However, they do not offer a clear definition of the term, but instead derive error characteristics from the feedback of their study participants in order to come to the two relevant categories, i.e. mistakes in diagnosis and treatment.

These figures are quite impressive: in 2017 alone, a total of 13,519 suspected errors were reported by patients or doctors to the relevant conciliation body of German health insurance funds (Medizinischer Dienst des Spitzenverbandes Bund der Krankenkassen e.V., [MDS] 2018). An error is understood to mean that a treatment was not carried out appropriately, carefully, correctly or on time (treatment error). The term covers different types of medical misconduct: for example, if necessary medical treatment is omitted or carried out with insufficient care, an error in treatment is present, and also when, for example, an operation is performed which was not individually indicated. All areas of medical care—from examination, diagnosis, clarification to therapy and documentation—can be affected by a treatment error (MDS 2018, p. 6). Although this figure is already high, further scientific research suggests that the number of actual errors in medical treatment greatly exceeds the number of resulting allegations by a multiple of five ("litigation gap"). The so-called litigation gap describes the fact that only 3% of patients have an unwanted event clarified (Schrappe 2015). In this context, Schrappe (2015, p. 140) makes the following distinction important: there are undesirable events which must meet three conditions:

- The event is negative for the patient.
- It is treatment-related (and not the course of the disease).
- It occurs unintentionally.

A distinction is made between an avoidable unwanted event that can be traced back to an error—in the sense of a rule violation—and legal terms such as "treatment error" where, in addition, the lack of care can be proven according to the service term (Schrappe 2015, p. 26), and the term "misuse", which describes treatment methods that cause avoidable damage or where the damage potential exceeds the respective benefit (Schrappe 2015, p. 26).

In addition to the medical field, in certain *technical domains*, research regarding mistakes is intensive, as mistakes can have particularly far-reaching, often even fatal consequences, for example, in space research, aviation or traffic research (Helmreich 2000; Hagen 2018). Since the term "error" is predominantly used here in the international arena.

1.2.2 Defining Error from an Interdisciplinary Perspective

> Errors are not easily defined. (Senders and Moray 1991)

In the following section, we present different approaches to the term and concept of "error". We follow different disciplinary perspectives which have predominantly researched errors and taken them into account, such as psychology, organisational psychology, medical sciences, pedagogical and technically orientated sciences.

From a *psychological perspective*, error has been generally defined in the APA Dictionary of Psychology (2019) as "a deviation from true or accurate information (e.g., a wrong response, a mistaken belief)". From a psychological perspective as well, Rasmussen (1982, 1997; referring to it Grote 2018; Carroll 2018; Klement 2018) highlights the difficulty of providing a satisfying definition of human error, as it is often only retrospectively identified as such. For example, in terms of human–machine interaction, a system that functions less satisfactorily than normal owing to a human action or disorder that could have been counteracted by a reasonable human action is likely to be identified as human error. In the case of systematic or frequent miscasts, the cause is usually considered to be a constructional error. Occasional malfunctions are typically classified as system failures or human errors due to variability in part of the system or as man-made.

Rasmussen (1982, 1997) therefore strongly advocates seeing human variability as an important part of adaptation and learning. The human ability to adapt to the peculiarities of system performance and to optimise interaction is, in his view, the real reason that humans are in a system. In order to optimise performance and develop smooth and efficient skills, this author considers it crucial to have the ability to conduct experimental and error experiments and to regard human errors as unsuccessful experiments with unacceptable consequences (Rasmussen 1982, p. 3).

As constitutive of the error concept, Rasmussen (1982, p. 6) considers that:

> [e]rrors are related to variability of force, space or time coordination. The rule-based domain includes performance in familiar situations controlled by stored rules for coordination of subroutines, and errors are typically related to mechanisms like wrong classification or recognition of situations, erroneous associations to tasks, or to memory slips in recall of procedures. Since rule-based behavior is used to control skill-based subroutines, the error mechanisms related to skill-based routines are always active. Rule-based behavior is not directly goal-controlled, but goal oriented, and the immediate criteria for errors deal with whether the relevant rules are recalled and followed correctly or not. This is the case, unless the total task is considered explicitly as one integrated whole and ultimate error correction is included in the error definition.

Against this background he has developed a model for the classification of errors and their management, a model with a distinction between three levels of behaviour:

Table 1.2 Model for the classification of errors and their management with a distinction between three levels of behaviour (Vanderheiden based on Rasmussen 1982, p. 6)

Level of behaviour according to Rasmussen	Examples	Definition of error type
Skill-based performance	This is about errors in the context of certain sensory-motor coupling mechanisms in automatically running procedures, e.g. for experienced motorists, switching, flashing, etc. are largely automated.	Errors are related to variability of force, space or time coordination.
Rule-based performance	This is about errors in rather regular, schematic behavioural contexts such as simple turns at a crossroads or opening a document on the computer.	Criteria for errors deal with whether the relevant rules are recalled and followed correctly or not.
Knowledge-based performance	These are errors in more complex contexts or new unfamiliar actions, e.g. finding your way around a foreign city or setting up a new cell phone.	Errors in this domain can only be defined in relation to the goal of the task, and generic error mechanisms can only be defined from very detailed studies based on verbal protocols which can supply data on the actual process.

skill, rule and knowledge-based performance which is still an indispensable part of the current scientific discourse (see Goodman et al. 2011; Brüggemann 2009, p. 132) (Table 1.2).

In addition to these three types of errors, Rasmussen identifies errors of discrimination, referring to error mechanisms which are related to failure in selecting the proper level of behaviour in an abnormal situation (Rasmussen 1982, p. 7).

Reason's definition is still one of the most frequently used in the research literature on mistakes and errors. As referred to by Frese and Keith (2015), Carroll (2018), Edmondson and Verdin (2018), Lei (2018) and Glendon et al. (2006), Reason (1990, p. 9) defines human error as:

> a generic term to encompass all those occasions in which a planned sequence of mental or physical activities fails to achieve its intended outcome, and when these failures cannot be attributed to the intervention of some chance agency.

Following Reason (1990), Frese and Keith (2015, p. 664) point to an important difference between active and latent errors. Latent errors are associated with weak or omitted organisational defences and are related to management decisions, security procedures, organisational structure and cultural factors:

> [The] harmful consequences [of latent events] can rest for a long time, which only becomes apparent when they are combined with active errors and local triggers to break through the many defense mechanisms of the system. (Frese and Keith 2015, p. 664)

Examples given by Reason are the catastrophe of Bhopal (Reason 1990) and the death of mountaineers on Mount Everest (as cited in van Dyck et. al).

From an *organisational psychological perspective,* Goodman, Ramanujam, Carroll, Edmondson, Hofmann and Sutcliffe (2011, p. 151) distinguish organisational errors as a construct that differs from errors at the individual level. They understand errors to be essentially unintentional deviations from rules or procedures (e.g. non-verification of drugs prior to administration to patients, non-compliance with safety guidelines in a coal mine) that can lead to negative organisational results. Goodman et al. (2011) assume that mistakes can affect various aspects of our lives, such as physical security, the economy, the environment and the political domain. According to their research, individual and organisational errors differ fundamentally. Because an organisational error is constitutive, the structures and processes that have caused multiple people within an organisation to participate in that common behavioural pattern or deviation need to be analysed and identified. By contrast, individual errors indicate action deviations of a person that differ from the actions of other people within the organisation. Individual factors in particular must be taken into account for error analysis. Goodman et al. (2011) understand "organisational errors" to mean the behaviour of several organisational participants which deviates from the rules and procedures laid down in the organisation which can therefore potentially lead to negative organisational results. The conclusion reached by Goodman et al. (2011) is that the errors are essentially reflected in several organisational aspects. On one hand, they represent unintended deviations from the expectations of the organisation with regard to adequate methods for carrying out work activities. Second, they could be deviations at the action level of several persons who act in their formal organisational roles and work towards organisational goals. Third, the deviations may potentially lead to negative organisational outcomes, and finally, such deviations may be primarily attributable to organisational conditions (i.e. they cannot be explained solely by reference to specific characteristics of individuals). Thus, an organisational error differs from an individual error that occurs in an organisational context (Goodman et al. 2011, p. 161).

Frese and Keith (2015) choose a slightly different approach to errors in the organisational context and describe them as unintended and potentially avoidable deviations from the objectives and standards set by an organisation, which may have either negative or positive organisational consequences (this is essentially also confirmed by Frese and Keith 2015; Hofmann and Frese 2011; Lei et al. 2016; and Frese and Keith 2015, as cited in (Lei 2018, 2)). Also Giolito and Verdin (2018, p. 68) point out specific organisational errors which are:

> a double deviation from (a) organizationally specified rules or norms of action and (b) the organization's objectives and goals.

Frese and Keith (2015) emphasise the existence of so-called "latent" errors, which remain unrecognised and often show their consequences only in the medium or long term (see also Ramanujam 2003). Furthermore, Giolito and Verdin (2018, p. 69) offer an additional differentiation between lower- and higher-order errors, which essentially differ as follows:

> Lower-order errors refer to deviations from clear and concrete rules and norms. Higher-order errors refer to situations in which an organizational rule itself is 'wrong,' that is, it deviates from higher principles, which may range [from] legal principles to commonsense rules including safety of people and organizational survival.

In organisational contexts, strategic mistakes are often spoken of. These are usually high-order errors, even if they have begun at the low-order level. A characteristic feature of a strategic error is that it affects the strategic level of the organisation, i.e. its goals, resources and competitive advantages, but can also relate to strategic decisions such as those of the management and can also affect errors that may have initially arisen at a lower hierarchical level but then have consequences for the entire organisation or large parts of it (Giolito and Verdin 2018, p. 69).

Edmondson and Verdin (2018, p. 83) add further aspects of organisational errors that:

- Concern the actions of multiple organisational members
- Have the potential to result in adverse organisational outcomes
- Represent unintended discrepancies from goals and expectations
- Carry a risk of harm
- Are caused by organisational conditions such as rules and values.

Various authors distinguish an organisational error from an error that an individual makes in an organisational context, in that an organisational error is not caused by idiosyncratic characteristics of one or more persons (Russo and Schoemaker 1989; Kahnemann 2013; Roxburgh 2003), but results from the conditions existing in the organisation (Goodman et al. 2011). Organisational errors are not the result of simple human misconduct, but can be traced back to organisational conditions, policies and strategies (Edmondson and Verdin 2018, p. 83).

From a *medical point of view*, the notion of "error" is quite diverse, as noted by Elder et al. (2006), in a study examining the understanding of this term. Physicians have been asked to report errors from primary care, but little is known about how they apply the term "error". The study by Elder et al. (2006) qualitatively assessed the relationship between the variety of error definitions found in the medical literature and physicians' assessments of whether an error occurred in a series of clinical scenarios. Through qualitative analysis, Elder and colleagues found that three approaches may affect how physicians make decisions about error, namely, the process that occurred versus the outcome that occurred, rare versus common occurrences and system versus individual responsibility.

Rogers, Griffin, Carnie, Melucci and Weber (2017, p. 1) agree that there is no common understanding of the term "error" in the medical context. This is a critical problem with regard to the reporting of errors. Rogers et al. (2017, p. 1) identify human error, risk behaviour and reckless behaviour as relevant to error development, in that:

> [h]uman error involves unintentional and unpredictable behavior that causes or could have caused an undesirable outcome. Often there are faults within the system that allow the error to occur.

Table 1.3 Four error types (Vanderheiden based on Elder 2004, p. 128)

1	Office administration errors	Missing charts, laboratory or radiograph processing errors
2	Physician-related errors	Skill problems, time management problems (interrupted, feeling rushed)
3	Patient communication errors	Problems communicating with patient by physician, staff or other physicians; appointment and triage errors
4	Preventable adverse events	Missed diagnosis, misdiagnosis, delayed treatment, incorrect treatment

In the medical context, Elder (2004) substantiate this, identifying four types of error as indicated in Table 1.3.

As previously noted, the most basic definition goes back to Reason (1990) who defines errors from a *pedagogical perspective* (Chap. 18).

Also at the beginning of the 1990s, Senders and Moray (1991) correctly pointed out that such an understanding presupposes a normative dimension of error, insofar as an error can only be recognised as such if a norm does not cover this deviation (Harteis et al. 2008).

On the other hand, James (1998) observes a crucial difference in the context of language learning since error cannot be self-corrected, while mistakes can be self-corrected. According to James (1998, p. 78), who carried out significant basic research in this field, to which reference is still made today (see Kryeziu 2015; Amara 2019) a very clear distinction occurs between mistake and error:

> if the learner is inclined and able to correct a fault in his or her output, it is assumed that the form he or she selected was not the one he intended, and we shall say that the fault is a mistake. If, on the other hand, the learner is unable or in any way disinclined to make the correction, we assume that the form the learner used was the one intended, and that is an error.

Following this definition, in the context of language learning, an error is considered a deviance or discrepancy between what a learner tends to say and what a native speaker tends to say. According to James it is constitutively for errors that errors cannot be self-corrected until further input has been provided to the learner to be able to correct that error.

From another *pedagogical perspective*, Gartmeier (2009) defines errors even more broadly, as avoidable deviations from valid norms, which, although never completely eradicable, on the other hand represent significant opportunities for the initiation of learning activities. Gartmeier (2009) understands the concept of error as being applied to actions as well as the results of actions. He refers to deviations from context-specific or situation-specific relevant action goals (Senders and Moray 1991). Not only an action itself but also the renunciation of an action that would have been necessary in a certain situation can also be an error or a potential error (Meurier et al. 1997). It must be taken into account that errors are not objectively ascertainable facts, but are judgements that depend on the validity of certain rules in a context (Reason 1990). These rules can exist in various forms and manifestations and are located within the framework of social negotiation processes (Heid 1999; Gartmeier 2009, p. 17).

Amini and Mortazavi (2013, p. 1) (Chap. 28) point out:

> There is a certain component of risk in everything we do. Its relevance is based on the testimony that mistakes are inevitable in complex organizations. Errors can result in negative consequences (e.g., loss of time, faulty products) as well as in positive ones (e.g., learning, innovation).The scientific understanding of the negative effects of errors is much better developed than that of the potential positive effects of errors. Most of the research has supported the concept of error prevention—the effort to block erroneous actions whenever possible. The potential long-term positive consequences of errors, such as learning, innovation, and resilience, however, are less obvious, although people readily agree that they can learn from errors.

In a large-scale study involving aviation crews from 26 nations on 5 continents, Helmreich et al. (2000) have looked at error research in the *technical context* of aviation (Chaps. 30, 31 and 32). They point out that human error is a relevant critical factor in aviation, as it is in other sociotechnical fields such as space travel and medicine. Error is understood in this context:

> as action or inaction that leads to deviation from crew or organizational intentions or expectations (Helmreich et al. 2000, p. 6)

and is divided into five categories as shown in Fig. 1.1.

From a *technical-philosophical perspective*, Kiassat (2013) approaches the topic by touching on questions of automation, asserting that since all individuals are unique in their characteristics, it must be assumed that logically their positive and negative contributions to the performance of a system also differ. Therefore, Kiassat (2013) concludes that in any system that is not fully automated, the effect of the human participants must be taken into account if performance optimisation of a

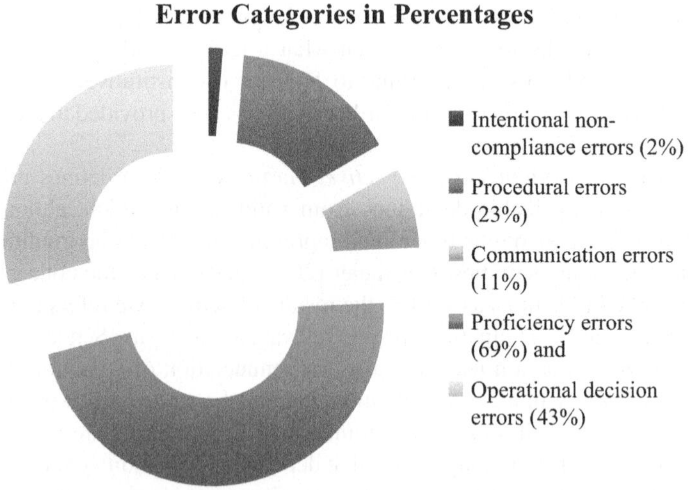

Fig. 1.1 Five categories of errors (Vanderheiden based on Helmreich 2000, p. 7 & p. 9)

system is intended. Although humans are intelligent, adaptable and adaptive, on the other hand—according to the author—they are also prone to error:

> Therefore, in situations where human and hardware have to interact and complement each other, the system faces advantages and disadvantages from the role the humans play. It is this role and its effect on performance that is the focus of this dissertation. (Kiassat 2013, p. 23)

This approach led Kiassat to understand "error" to mean "the incorrect performance of an operator as required for a particular task" (Kiassat 2013, p. 23). However Glendon, Clarke and McKenna (2006, p. 153) place less emphasis on the inevitability of making errors than on the necessity and positive implications of mistakes, affirming that:

> Errors are essential for learning because of the feedback that they provide and evidence suggests that we learn best if we are allowed to make errors.

1.2.3 Defining Failure from an Interdisciplinary Perspective

Having reviewed the terms "mistake" and "error", we now focus on the term "failure" and the meaning of the concept from different disciplinary perspectives.

Psychology (see Morgenroth and Schaller 2010, p. 1) understands failure as being unsuccessful in a special situation, failing to accomplish a task or being unable to achieve a desired goal, and understands it as a basic human experience that occurs in everyday activities as well as in longer-term projects in the context of personal development. Morgenroth and Schaller (2010) stress that failure is associated with a special tragic moment or event when it becomes clear to all involved that a person, group or organisation has missed a goal, for instance, termination at work, a failed relationship or the bankruptcy of a company. The unambiguity, but also the insight into the necessity of failure, can often only be experienced or realised afterwards (Morgenroth and Schaller 2010). This results from the fact that here it is primarily a question of context-bound subjective assessments and usually not of objective facts (Morgenroth and Schaller 2010, p. 3, translated by Vanderheiden).

According to these authors, the everyday usage of the concept of failure implies:

1. That there is a clearly defined goal
2. That objective criteria are available for assessing the success of the action
3. That the judgement is independent of the judgement or judgement context.

Morgenroth and Schaller (2010) emphasise that all three assumptions are problematic from a *psychological viewpoint* and suggest that judgements about success and failure are highly relative. Accordingly, these authors regard the common definition of failure as questionable from a scientific psychological perspective for the following reasons:

1. Targets are often ambiguous and not specifically defined. Furthermore, more than one indicator or criterion is often relevant in terms of target achievement, e.g. in terms of career success.
2. In judging success and failure, there is often a problem in obtaining objective yardsticks to evaluate outcomes that justify such a verdict. This measurability is dependent on the subject of the action and can greatly differ individually, for example, in judging when a relationship is considered by the parties to be failed.
3. Judgements are tied to the concrete context of judgement. This includes, for example, the perspective given by the individual who judges. This relativity is already clear in the fact that failures from the point of view of the actor are valued differently from the observer's viewpoint. This phenomenon is known in psychological attribution research as an actor–observer difference.

In addition, Morgenroth and Schaller (2010) highlight that the failure assessment may additionally depend on whether the person concerned is currently living through a life crisis (Chap. 2) or if stronger sanctions are to be expected. Furthermore, in line with Backert (2004), they stress that failure judgements are embedded in a cultural context that influences the social consequences of failure. Backert (2004) contends that, on the basis of economic failures in Germany compared to the USA and Japan, failure is assessed more negatively and is penalised with stronger sanctions.

Relevant factors here appear to be fear of failure and success orientations, which are interrelated and interact in many ways (see Martin and Marsh 2003; De Castella et al. n.d.). Martin and Marsh (2003) have classified three types of failure in terms of people's attitude towards failure: those who are success-orientated, those who are fail-avoidant and those who accept failure.

According to Martin (2012, p. 1), it is also important to distinguish between ways of handling failure, namely, between:

1. Students who deal with their fear of failure by hard work and/or success (referred to as over-strivers and sometimes as perfectionists)
2. Students who deal with their fear of failure

Meanwhile, many authors (Chaps. 2, 11, 12, 16, 18, 23, 26, 27, 28) emphasise that, as with errors, failure should be attributed with a positive function. In contrast or in addition to this, a positive consideration and evaluation of failure experiences not only optimises the regulation of action in a more or less limited area but is also about the personality as a whole, for example, concerning a person's values, goals, attitudes, self-concept and prospects for future self-development.

Sociology, too, is based on a rather broad understanding of failure. Ackroyd (2007, p. 3306) defines failure in terms of organisational contexts:

> By organizational failure is usually meant failure against some measure of performance, or failure to achieve a goal that is normally expected … But failure to perform against particular criteria is a customary or legal definition of failure, and may or may not indicate that there is some more fundamental problem of organization. Many writers on management have conveniently conflated the distinction between measured and substantive organizational failure.

Hans Braun (n.d.) first notes that failure is constitutively part of being human: "failure is part of the human condition" (Braun n.d., p. 38, translated by Vanderheiden) and correctly points out that failure is sociological perspective has many manifestations. First of all, he distinguishes failure from defeat, in that failure:

> affects the people or institutions concerned more or less essentially. (Braun n.d., p. 29)

People can fail in themselves and in the circumstances in which they act; they can also fail in relationships or in systems. In addition, a failure of the system itself is conceivable, for instance, in politics and economics (Braun n.d., p. 32). From a *sociological perspective*, this can be considered positive and systemically inherent, because failure of political processes in systems in which citizens participate in decision-making directly or through their elected representatives is not only inevitable but also in a positive sense can be seen as an expression of the functioning of democracy (Braun n.d., p. 32). The author goes even further in his positive assessment of failure when discussing the economic sector. Here, Braun (n.d., p. 32) assumes that it is appropriate for companies to fail if they do not produce cost-effectively or if they ignore customer preferences, because this is part of the nature of the market economy and constitutes its strength.

In addition to the individual and organisational dimension when dealing with failure processes, the cultural context is of particular importance:

> After all, cultural frameworks play a role in the processing of failures. It makes a difference whether people fail in an environment where everything depends on not losing their prestige, or whether this happens in an environment where failure, leaving personal relationships out of consideration, is an inevitable downside to being positively risk-tolerant and as a basis for a reboot. In this context we talk about "cultures of failure". (Backert 2004, p. 35 as cited in Braun, translated by Vanderheiden)

Braun emphasises another interesting dimension of failure, namely, the public. This is certainly the case in the context of economics and politics in a special way, as well as in reputation-related failure, such as in sports or science (Braun n.d., p. 37), but can also play a role in private contexts in many countries, such as in divorce proceedings, which people often experience as massive failures (Chaps. 2 and 12).

From *a medical research perspective*, Lingard et al. (2004, p. 332) distinguish four types of failure:

1. Occasion failures: Problems in the situation or context of the communication event
2. Content failures: Insufficiency or inaccuracy apparent in the information being transferred
3. Audience failures: Gaps in the composition of the group engaged in the communication
4. Purpose failures: Communication events in which purpose is unclear, not achieved or inappropriate

Table 1.4 Differences characteristics: mistake, error and failure

Mistake	"Mistake" can be applied to actions as well as the results of actions (Gartmeier 2009, p. 17).
	Mistakes may be deviations from context-specific, action-relevant action goals or objectives (Sender & Moray, 1991, as cited in Gartmeier 2009, p. 17).
	Mistakes are not facts that can be objectively determined, but are judgments dependent on the validity of certain rules within a context (Reason 1990, as cited in Gartmeier 2009, p. 17).
	These rules can exist in many different forms and degrees of explicitness and are adopted in the course of social negotiation processes (Heid 1999, as cited in Gartmeier 2009, p. 17).
	Mistakes offer opportunities for learning and enable awareness of deficits in one's own knowledge or action (Gartmeier 2009, p. 17).
	Mistakes are a deviation from a standard, code of conduct or other requirement that jeopardises or frustrates the achievement of a goal (Morgenroth and Schaller 2010).
	They occur only with purposeful behaviour and involve the failure to reach a goal or sub-goal (Morgenroth and Schaller 2010).
	The omission of an action that would have been necessary in a particular situation can equally be described as a mistake (Meurier et al. 1997).
	A mistake is potentially preventable (Morgenroth and Schaller 2010).
	Mistakes are performance-related and may occur even though a learner has the knowledge from a system safety perspective; it is important to report and learn from both errors and mistakes (Nassaji 2018, as cited in Chap. 30).
	A behaviour mistake describes a behaviour which is wrong in the current cultural environment and circumstances (Chap. 32).
	Mistakes have in common that an alternative behaviour would be preferable in each case and those responsible could have known or done it better. There are objective and technical mistakes, mistakes of estimation, strategic mistakes and moral mistakes (Chap. 15).
	They occur only with purposeful behaviour and involve the failure to reach a goal or sub-goal (Morgenroth and Schaller 2010).
Error	An error is a deviation from true or accurate information (APA Dictionary of Psychology 2019).
	It is related to variability of force, space or time coordination (Rasmussen 1982).
	Error involves unintentional and unpredictable behaviour that causes or could have caused an undesirable outcome (Rogers et al. 2017).
	Errors are "unintended—and potentially avoidable—deviations from organisationally specified goals and standards" (Frese and Keith 2015, as cited in Lei 2018, p. 2).
	Errors are avoidable deviations from valid norms, which, although never completely eradicable, on the other hand represent significant opportunities for the initiation of learning activities (Gartmeier 2009).
	An "error" is based on the premise that rules or regulations are incorrectly applied or executed, especially in an industry that is considered highly regulated. Errors are thus defined as deviations that are competence-based and occur as a result of a lack of knowledge (Nassaji 2018, as cited in Chap. 30).

(continued)

Table 1.4 (continued)

	Errors are defined as "mistakes" and can occur for different reasons, such as a result of ignorance, a personal decision or preference, a habit, forgetfulness, lack of awareness or similar psychological issues (defined in reference to Love et al. 2009, by Mayer and Mayer in Chap. 8).
	From a forensic point of view, four types of terror must be distinguished: practitioner error (refers to human error that may be related to negligence or incompetence), instrument error (occurs when instruments or technologies fail), statistical error (refers to an error in the algorithms used by the device providing the measurement) and method error (refers to limitations that have nothing to do with practising error and therefore would not be related to cognitive errors such as metacognition) (Chap. 25).
Mistakes and Errors	Mistakes can be understood as the most general term used in everyday situations, whereas error is more suitable for formal contexts. In addition, the term "error" might even be considered as more severe than a mistake. Mistakes can be thought of as accidental happenings, while errors are made due to a lack of knowledge, for example, not knowing the fitting answer to a question or the way of performing adequately (Chap. 29).
Failure	"Failure is part of the *conditio humana*" (Braun n.d., p. 38).
	Failure means failing some measure of performance, or to achieve a goal that is normally expected (Ackroyd 2007).
	Failure is the intended or use of a wrong plan to achieve an aim (Kohn et al. 1999).
	Failure is expected to occur only with purposeful behaviour and involves the failure to reach a goal or sub-goal (Morgenroth and Schaller 2010).
	It depends on individual judgement (Morgenroth and Schaller 2010).
	Failure can be influenced by the fact that a person is in crisis (Morgenroth and Schaller 2010, p. 2).
	Failure judgements are embedded in a cultural context that influences the social consequences of failure (Backert 2004).
	Failure is the result of individual poor decision-making or the consequence of personal misconduct (Chap. 2).
	Failure refers to a lack of success in communicating and/or in building relationships. Failure in intercultural communication situations combined with erroneous ascriptions of identity classification can easily lead to a failure in building trustful intercultural employee–client relationships (Chap. 8).
	Failure can be understood as a particular communicative and relationship-building activity (modelled after Lingard et al. 2004) which lacks success in communicating and/or building relationships with regard to a specific topic or content (Chap. 26).
	A "moral failure" is not a lapse in decorum or social practice. One sense of the term is as the equivalent of deliberate wrongdoing. There are certain forms of behaviour that are viewed, across cultures, as gravely damaging to individuals or the group, such as treason, murder, slavery, rape. These capture key moral boundaries that guide human life. Such come under the umbrella of the Universal Declaration of Human Rights to which every adult and child without exception is entitled (Chap. 16).

From an *engineering and philosophical perspective*, failure can be defined as:

> [t]he condition when the machine is unavailable for production due to an unplanned event. Within the context of failures caused by the operators, failure is the consequence of any operator-related mistake that takes the machine out of production. (Kiassat 2013, p. 23)

Table 1.4 summarises important differences between the terms "mistake", "error" and "failure" on the basis of the previous statements in this section.

1.3 Dealing with and Attitude Towards Mistakes, Errors and Failure

In most scientific studies and discourses, it is assumed that mistakes, errors and failure are unavoidable and negative. Ultimately, however, the question is not how to avoid them, but how to manage mistakes, errors and failures constructively and use them as resources (van Rooij 2015). The spectrum ranges from the most diverse methods of mistake or error prevention, to error management, to methods of error correction and to concepts of error-friendliness.

Frese (1993, p. 4) also considers mistakes and errors to be unavoidable—a consequence of the fact that humans are able to quickly integrate information into their thought and action system and to remain able to act in the face of uncertainty. In his studies in connection with the use of computer programs, Frese (1993, p. 4) found that, interestingly enough, experts make more mistakes than newcomers but at the same time discover and correct these errors more quickly. Against the background of the inevitability of errors, Frese (1993) and his colleagues instead of for the original concept of error management meanwhile for a concept of error avoidance.

Error management is prescriptively defined by Frese (1993, p. 4) as:

> a meaningful approach to an error with the goal
>
> - to avoid further errors or mistakes,
> - that the negative effects of errors do not arise, and
> - the consequences of errors can be quickly eliminated.

Amini and Mortazavi (2013) consider error management to be critical, observing that error prevention also potentially stops certain long-term positive effects of inevitable errors. These authors note that scientific understanding of the negative effects of errors is much better developed than that of the possible positive effects of errors. As a result, most of the research has been devoted to the concept of error avoidance in an attempt to prevent erroneous actions as far as possible. Amini and Mortazavi (2013, p. 1) advocate a greater focus on the potential long-term positive consequences of errors such as learning, innovation and resilience, even if these are less obvious.

Grout (2006, p. 1) also comments critically on the concept of error management and advocates the introduction of what he sees as the wider concept of mistake proofing, known by its Japanese slang buzzword as "poka-yoke":

> Mistake proofing uses changes in the physical design of processes to reduce human error. It can be used to change designs in ways that prevent errors from occurring, to detect errors after they occur but before harm occurs, to allow processes to fail safely, or to alter the work environment to reduce the chance of errors. Effective mistake proofing design changes should initially be effective in reducing harm, be inexpensive, and easily implemented. Over time these design changes should make life easier and speed up the process. Ideally, the design changes should increase patients' and visitors' understanding of the process. These designs should themselves be mistake proofed and follow the good design practices of other disciplines.

The author recommends mistake proofing since, from his point of view, it also includes the improvement of the work environment and helps in detecting mistakes, preventing mistakes and preventing the influence of mistakes.

Gartmeier (2009, p. 14), on the other hand, deals in particular with the concept of "error-friendliness" in his studies, in which a distinction is made between error-friendliness at the level of individual, error-related settings like attitude and error-friendliness in the sense of a knowledge-based ability to avoid errors. On the basis of the definition from von Weizsäcker and von Weizsäcker (1998, as cited in Gartmeier 2009, p. 19):

> [t]he concept of error-friendliness describes the attributes of biological systems that make it possible that system disturbances do not lead to their extinction, but that they can be used for their further development (von Weizsäcker and von Weizsäcker 1984, 1998). Organisms—as special forms of biological systems—have a variety of mechanisms that allow them to deal with negative environmental effects or to use them for their development.

This feature of error-friendliness can be an indispensable and central tool of human development. According to von Weizsäcker and von Weizsäcker (1984, as cited in Gartmeier 2009, p. 19), learning from mistakes, errors and failures helps to adapt to ever new environmental conditions and to solve the associated problems. In terms of learning from failure, mistakes plays a significant role (Chaps. 2, 11, 14, 16, 18, 23, 24, 26, 27, 28, 29, 30, 31, 32).

Von Weizsäcker and von Weizsäcker (1984, as cited in Gartmeier 2009, p. 20) point out in this context that, above all, long-term adaptation skills are necessary, at the level of cognitive structures, so that people can benefit from positive learning effects for further development.

Gartmeier (2009, p. 20) has been able to observe three aspects of error-friendliness in particular, which have proven particularly effective in this context:

1. A positive attitude towards mistakes
2. The knowledge-based ability to avoid mistakes and errors
3. Certain forms of experiential knowledge, especially negative knowledge.

A positive basic attitude to mistakes has been found to encourage people to show a greater willingness to act on their own initiative. This is important not only at the individual level of dealing with errors with regard to personal learning effects and further education but also on the systemic level. When certain errors are systemically conditioned, for example, if people are exposed to permanent demands or dangerous situations, then proactive action is required to deal with these systemic-related grievances.

Von Weizsäcker and von Weizsäcker (1984) explain that, in order to understand perceptions of their environment as deviations from a certain norm, individuals have to resort to past, memory-based experiences. Consequently, error-friendliness is an important resource for the further development of cognitive structures, so that, for example, judgement in relation to relevant categories such as "dangerous" and "safe", "relevant" and "irrelevant" is developed, as well as new action strategies. The specific knowledge developed when learning from mistakes can be linked to the long-term positive effects of error-related learning processes in the competence of people in the most diverse contexts.

An important concept in this context is the so-called negative knowledge (originally researched by Minsky 1997, followed by Oser and Spychiger 2005 and Parviainen and Eriksson 2006, as cited in Gartmeier 2009, p. 22). Negative knowledge is experience-based knowledge of what is not to be done in a particular situation, for instance, not placing bare hands into boiling water. Negative knowledge can also refer to misconceptions or ideas that exist in a particular context, such as that someone in England or South Africa should under no circumstances drive on the same side of the road as they should in the USA or Germany. The concept of negative knowledge thus makes a connection between experiencing and learning from mistakes and individual knowledge. On the other hand, it allows the explanation of long-term positive effects of the acquired knowledge on the competence and performance of the individual (Gartmeier 2009, p. 22). In exploring the relevance of negative knowledge especially in regard to workplaces, Gartmeier (2009, p. 55) found that:

> [p]rofound changes bring about situations where relevant and applicable knowledge becomes obsolete and is turned into non-viable or expired knowledge. In such situations, an individual awareness about knowledge that is to be reconsidered or updated is a crucial factor in developing and maintaining professional competence. The more precisely individuals manage to detect lacks of relevant know-how as well as of outdated knowledge being still "in use", the better it should be possible to recognize what is to be learned.

Negative knowledge in this context offers various beneficial effects, because it:

1. Supports certainty in how to proceed
2. Increases efficiency during actions
3. Improves the quality and depth of reflection processes on action.

Negative knowledge can be considered as the outcome of learning from errors but at the same time can be seen as a special case of experiential learning, because error-related learning employs the construction of knowledge from episodic events. Gartmeier (2009) emphasises errors have the potential to challenge individual mental models and thereby enable modifications of these models. Search processes of modification can happen in different modes, such as through differentiation of the underlying model of action, through replacement of parts of the model or through indexing false connections or weak areas within the model that bring about potential for errors which are relevant elements for the construction of negative knowledge.

Zander et al. (2014) emphasise that these norms are situation-specific or group-specific. The occurrence of errors can be an aversive affective experience. In their research, Spychiger et al. (2006) found that students can develop and be inhibited by fear of mistakes in learning or achievement situations if they assume that these could negatively influence their competences and abilities. This affective dimension of dealing with errors is fundamentally social in nature, since it implicitly involves an expected negative evaluation by others. On the other hand, Zander et al. (2014) were able to confirm that constructive handling of mistakes is conducive to successful learning processes and has both an affective and a cognitive dimension, which is reflected in a reduced fear of mistakes and a greater willingness to learn from mistakes.

These viewpoints can be supported by perspectives such as positive psychology, positive organisational psychology and positive scholarship which emphasise that aspects of positive and optimal functioning can significantly contribute to a positive handling of life situations and life and work challenges (see Seligman and Csikszentimihalyi 2000; Luthans 2002a, b; Luthans and Youssef 2007; Wong 2011). These are discussed in the following section.

1.4 Mistakes, Errors and Failure in the Context of Positive and Optimal Functioning Research

Several scientific approaches have affirmed that a positive and constructive viewpoint can change negative and challenging experiences (Seligman and Csikszentimihalyi 2000), such as mistakes, errors and failures. In order to deal constructively with mistakes, errors and failure from the perspective of positive and optimal functioning, it is crucial to overcome a destructive culture of error and transform it in favour of a constructive culture of error. Characteristic elements of a destructive error culture would be, for example, a threat or guilt culture (Löber 2012, pp. 232–238). Shame and shaming can also potentially be a component of this destructive culture of error if it is closely linked to fear and insecurity, misused as an instrument of power or not consciously used and perceived as a resource (Mayer et al. 2019). In order to use mistakes, errors and potential failure as a resource, a positive error culture is necessary and decisive. Important elements of such a culture can be a sense of security and support for learning from mistakes which opens spaces for experimental error-friendliness (Löber 2012, pp. 245–263; Frese and Keith 2015) as well as experimental possibilities (Gartmeier 2009, p. 126).

Within the concept of error-friendliness, the argument could be put forward that individuals with a pronounced tendency to experiment—whether mentally or in reality— get to know errors and dangers more playfully, thereby learning more about their own limitations and being in a better position to adapt to circumstances that are new and dynamic for them. Löber (2010) adds an interesting consideration to this idea, namely, that all employees must experience fair dealings with each other in order to tackle relevant problems with confidence in the freedom from sanctions.

This corresponds with the research results of management researcher Amy Edmondson (2004), who investigated how factors at the group and organisational level affected errors in administering medications to hospital patients. Edmondson (2004) discovered the particular relevance of a certain social climate, in that the results from patient care groups in two hospitals showed systematic differences not only in the frequency of errors but also in the probability that errors were recognised and learned from by the group members. It appears that the error rates depended on at least two influences: actual errors (related to particularly sensitive areas such as intensive care) and the willingness of the members of a team to report errors. In addition, it shows that there were positive correlations between error rates and nursing manager coaching, perceived unit performance and the quality of relationships between team members. There were higher error rates in teams with better average values in coaching nurses, a higher relationship quality between the team members. Edmondson (2004) attributes this finding to the members' perception of how safe it was to report and discuss errors in their unit. The readiness to report a mistake correlates with the assumed perception of the members of a team that a mistake in their unit was not directed against them (Edmondson 2004, p. 79). In her conclusion, Edmondson (2004, p. 86) underlines the importance of dealing constructively with errors, especially in the context of creating a trustworthy social climate, because the way in which mistakes have been dealt with in the past, as well as which mistakes have been made or reported, contributes to a climate of fear or openness that can amplify itself and that sustainably influences the ability and willingness to identify and discuss errors and problems. Decisive factors are thus the experience of psychological security, which makes it possible to express oneself openly, but also to hold different opinions—a climate which allows mistakes to be corrected and potential risks to be discussed openly (Edmondson and Verdin 2018, p. 81). (Chaps. 27 and 28)

It is also important that a system allows for a diversity of perspectives, without this becoming too great. Dahlin et al. (2018) as cited in Frese and Keith (2015, p. 669) explain:

> Thus, people need to be at ease to report errors, but their perspectives also need to be different enough to detect errors. If all people see the same situation in a similar way as wrong or right, chances to detect errors are lower. If people are too different, it may be difficult to persuade others where the error lies.

According to this statement, a variety of different perspectives is important, not to create a "think tank" of the analysis of mistakes, errors and failures, but to support and broaden the understanding and analysis of mistakes, errors and failures from different cultural perspectives.

1.5 Mistakes, Errors and Failure Across Cultures

Given the particular significance of this topic, there is a void of research on mistakes, errors and failure from diverse cultural perspectives. Most research refers to a selected cultural context, the direct comparison between one or two different cultural groups, and to a very specific field of application such as aviation, a certain medical or technical field, or a form of organisation. Various new investigations and conceptual considerations are presented in this book, and the following explanations will therefore initially deal with general, overarching considerations and basic research.

We provide a brief overview of existing research which focuses on the topic of mistakes, errors and failure within and across different cultural contexts.

1.5.1 Differences in the Understanding of Failure in the Economic Context of Japan, the USA and Germany

Important basic work on this topic was done at the beginning of the millennium by sociologist Wolfgang Backert. Backert (2004) deals in particular with the understanding of failure in the economic context of Japan (Chaps. 14 and 19), the USA and Germany. He assumes that there is a basic consensus in Germany to discredit the person who failed in the truest sense of the word: they will no longer be trusted in the future; their credibility and creditworthiness in the broadest sense are gone and very difficult to restore (Backert 2004, p. 65). The mistake or failure is attributed to the person individually. Failure in Japan occurs at the level of a highly organised form of individual irresponsibility: owing to particular emphasis on the organisation which places the individual in the background, failure of an individual in the larger context is not possible, because the organisation is regarded as a priority. At the same time, this can be connected with the fact that in the event of a crisis, an individual takes on the "victim role" symbolically, so to speak, in order to save the honour of the organisation, thus earning the community—at least according to the internal logic of the organisation—a merit. This symbolic failure, in the form of assuming external responsibility, can have very far-reaching consequences in Japan, including suicide. Backert (2004, p. 65) goes on to explain that the American variant of understanding failure focuses on the process of how failure could occur. The danger for the social reputation is then not to have made an effort and to have failed less in this respect. Defeat in the USA usually offers the chance to try again and, this time, to do it better. When forming new teams, the practice of taking on a member who has already failed at precisely this point can thus demonstrate experience of defeat in this sector that seems completely absurd from a German point of view but that makes sense according to American opinion. According to Backert (2004, pp. 67–68), the individual attribution of guilt is typical when dealing with mistakes or failure in the German context, possibly including public humiliation up to social death. For Japan, the author refers in the economic context to unilateralism, the organisation according to the *ie* principle (the company as a family, with clear hierarchies that are especially linked to seniority) and the far-reaching access of the company to the individual. According to this, processes of failure in such a context could actually have serious consequences for the failing individual, since ultimately this person is interwoven with the company, and the failure of the company consequently falls back on the individual. However, the principle of *uchi* and *soto*, by which in Japan the design of the organisational–environmental relationship is established, overrides exactly this point: *uchi* and *soto* describe, in essence, the separation of "inside" and "outside", "we and them" and "we against the others". The perception partly disintegrates into concerns which concern the company (the *ie*) in general and questions which concern the rest (the society). At this point failure becomes de facto impossible for an organisational member. The relevant structures within the organisation emphasise the internal cohesion; the social environment as a "judicial authority" in failure processes is largely ignored. It is important for the organisation to save face to the outside. A personalised form of guilt allocation, which actually falls back to the failing individual, does not result. Instead, according to Backert (2004, p. 69), in the Japanese model, responsibility is distributed among so many positions that it is not really possible to actually localise the person responsible: in case of doubt, the nominal top of the organisation assumes the duty of apology to the outside world, but above all this has a ritual function.

In contrast to the tendency towards personalisation and discrediting which can be observed in the German context, and the more ritualistic practice of assuming responsibility in Japan, Backert (2004, p. 71) describes failure as a chance for a new beginning as more typical for the American context than, for example, for the German context. The failure of a serious attempt is seen as an experience, broadening the horizon and not leading to the exclusion of the failed person. The reason for this is the notion that mistakes and experience of failure can be used as a resource to include someone in a team who has made certain mistakes or has failed in a particular context. This can mean that when a new attempt is made, precisely these wrong decisions can be avoided and can be adequately reacted to in advance. Backert (2004) cautions that this positive understanding of failure and making mistakes does not apply to everyone in the American context but only to those who "make an effort". This benevolent view does not apply to those who are unable or unwilling to do so, who are unable to adapt to this normative requirement (Backert 2004, p. 73).

Lewis et al. (2009, p. 1) come to similar conclusions in a study in which they observed the emotional responses to performance contexts of 149 preschoolers from three cultures. The children were Japanese (N = 32), African Americans (N = 63) and White Americans of mixed European descent (N = 54) (Chap. 19). The results showed that Japanese children differed from American children in that they expressed less shame, pride and sadness but more disclosure and evaluative embarrassment. African American and White American children obviously did not differ from each other. American children, however, showed more valuation as opposed to exposure of embarrassment. This finding supports the idea that success and failure are interpreted differently by Japanese children in the preschool years. The low level of sadness and shame expression and the limited number of different expressions observed in Japanese children agree with the general finding that East Asian infants and young children differ from Western infants and children mainly in the presentation of negative expressions. These results show that cultural differences, whether of temperament or direct socialisation of cultural values, influence how children respond to performance situations.

Lewis et al. (2009) found that differences could already be found in preschool children in their study, depending on the culture. They differed in the emotions expressed in response to failure and success and in the number of different expressions that appeared in response to failure. This suggests that cultural differences occur early, perhaps as soon as or shortly after the expression itself. In that study, culture was proven to be a factor that clearly influences the facial expression of emotions. Thus, small Japanese children showed less sadness and shame in response to failure and they were less likely than American children to show more than one type of expression in response to failure. In response to success, Japanese children expressed less pride and more embarrassment. In general, Japanese children appeared to show little shame or pride compared to American children (Lewis et al. 2009, p. 10).

While there were differences between American and Japanese children, no differences were found between White and African American children. There are few studies that show emotional differences between African Americans and White Americans of European descent. The difference between embarrassment after failure and embarrassment after success was much greater for American children than for Japanese children. American children, whether of White or African American descent, showed less embarrassment after success compared to embarrassment after failure, while Japanese children showed the same values under both conditions. The authors attribute the much greater embarrassment shown by Japanese children to the cultural differences associated with the fact that they are the subject of someone else's attention. Miyake and Kosuke (1995) have argued that it is probably frightening and embarrassing for Japanese children to be in the centre of attention and not be part of the group, whereas in American culture, it is much more frequent and socially desirable to be praised.

Lewis and his colleagues (2009) see here a connection between the Japanese culture of the "we-self" and the "I-self" of American culture (based on Kitayama and Markus 1999; Markus and Kitayama 1994, as cited in Lewis et al. 2009, p. 10). Here the authors see a clear contrast to the perspective on Japanese culture suggested by early anthropological literature. Instead of being a culture that socialises solely out of shame, the cultural goals of promoting a "we-self" orientation can lead to more differentiated, self-evaluative emotional responses that depend on the demands of the situation, age and goals of the child.

Kitayama and Markus (1999) observed self-confident, self-evaluating emotions in response to performance tasks and found differences in the cultural view of "we ourselves", "I myself" (Kitayama and Markus 1999; Kitayama et al. 1997). They describe how American children tend to orientate themselves towards an "I-self" view and feel more pride or shame when they are successful or fail. Japanese children who orientate themselves towards a "we-self" view are less likely to react to personal success or failure in an environment that reliably evokes this expression in American children. American children who are socialised in an "I-culture" respond to successes and failures in a way that is consistent with the perceived performance of the self. Japanese children, on the other hand, who are socialised in a "we culture" show patterns of expression that reflect their fearful ambivalence about being in a context in which their performance is shown to another.

In addition to cultural practices that can explain the differences in the self-confident emotional responses of American and Japanese children, there are also some indications that temperament may continue to play a role. Several studies have found early differences between East Asian and West European groups in the first 6–12 months of life that may be related to temperament. East Asian and European American infants differ in negative facial expressions (Camras et al. 1997, 1998, 2002). Japanese infants displayed less screaming and decreased eyebrow expressions, both of which are characteristic of negative emotions (Camras et al. 1998). In contrast, few differences in smiling behaviour between Japanese and American infants were found (Camras et al. 1998; Fogel et al. 1988). In summary, these studies suggest that Japanese children have fewer vocal and negative facial expressions than Americans of white European descent. Less expression of shame and sadness in the present study supports this general finding of less expression of negative emotions, although the results of less pride and more embarrassment do not.

Even these early differences in negative expression, often due to temperament, can be cultural. For example, Japanese care practices may increase children's tendency to be less expressive. Japanese mothers touch their infants more than American mothers and tend to react more selectively to infant voices, actions that could serve to inhibit or minimise infant expression (Fogel et al. 1988). In contrast to Japanese and South American emigrant mothers, Japanese–American mothers showed behavioural patterns consistent with Japanese cultural values of privacy, tranquillity and weakened verbal communication (Bornstein and Cote 2001). Such socialisation practices seem likely to reinforce less intense emotional expressions, especially negative emotions, in Japanese children. Thus, the tendency of Japanese children to express less sadness, shame and pride and a narrower range of expressions in response to failure in this study (Camras et al. 2002) is likely to reflect an interplay of early temperamental differences and socialisation practices. The study of the interplay between early individual differences in expression and cultural differences is a complex enterprise that probably requires a longitudinal study. The study shows that cultural differences in the self-evaluation of emotions are observable at least from the age of 4 years.

1.5.2 *Cultural Context and Differences in the Understanding of Failure Using the Example of Chinese and Western Cultures*

Pitta et al. (1999) have established in their research that cultural context plays a decisive role in the question of what is understood as failure, because culture is a relevant basis for ethical behaviour and determines what is ethical and what is unethical in the respective context. In China, *guanxi* (a set of connections or relationships) determines the context of the business in which a set of expectations and a certain degree of trust can be expected. Thus, when Chinese managers negotiate a contract, they rely less on the content of the contract than on the context in which it was negotiated. The relationship between the individuals is particularly important. When a conflict arises, Chinese managers believe that communication and relationships will solve it. There is less concern about compliance with the terms of the contract, as the contract is seen as a symbol of the relationship between the partners.

By contrast, Western managers consider the content of a contract to be very important. The concrete wording, the dates, the amounts and the responsibilities are clearly defined. For an American manager, negotiating the details implicitly means striving to meet the requirements of the contract. Failure to meet the terms of the contract will mean embarrassment in the American context, or in the worst case, a loss of face. The situation is even more pronounced for German managers. According to Pitta et al. (1999), German culture can be regarded as even more contract-orientated than American culture: Every single aspect of the contract is regarded as binding.

In the German, American and Chinese cases, different evaluations and assessments regarding errors and failures and the associated potential ethical conflicts can be derived solely from the different value systems of the cultures.

Differences between the American and Chinese contexts were also the focus of the psychological and neurobiological research of Mu et al. (2015). Starting from the fact that humankind is unique among all living beings in the ability to develop and enforce social norms, but noting that there are great differences in the strength of social norms between human societies, Mu et al. (2015) examine how violations of social norms are recognised at the neurobiological level. In the context of cultural neuroscience, they use non-invasive electroencephalography (EEG) to investigate the violation of social norms in order to investigate the neuronal mechanisms underlying the recognition of norm violations and how they differ between cultures. With the help of EEG recordings of Chinese and American participants ($n = 50$), Mu et al. (2015) were able to demonstrate a consistent negative deflection of the event-related potential by 400 ms (N400) across the central and parietal regions, which serve as cross-cultural neural markers for the recognition of norm violations. However, the N400 in the frontal and temporal range was observed only among Chinese, not among American participants, illustrating culture-specific neural substrates for the detection of norm violations. In addition, the frontal N400 predicted a variety of behavioural and attitudinal measurements related to the strength of social norms found including higher cultural superiority and self-control but lower creativity

(Mu et al. 2015, p. 15348). The authors began from the following contention: Although the existence of social norms is universal in all human cultures, there are great differences worldwide in the observance of social norms and the punishment of violators of norms. The question arose whether the neuronal basis of the recognition of violations of the social norm reacts to cultural differences. Mu et al. (2015) started from the premiss that human groups in countries such as China with a high level of territorial threats, national defence, low natural resources (e.g. food supply) and many natural disasters (e.g. floods, hurricanes and droughts) were confronted with societies that were more likely to develop into close relationships, in terms of having strong norms and less tolerance for deviant behaviour to coordinate their social action. Human groups in countries such as the USA that generally have lower levels of threat develop into loose groups with weaker norms and greater tolerance for deviant behaviour. Thus, individuals in close relationships tend to adhere to social norms and are more sensitive to injuries from others, compared to those living in loose cultures. Mu et al. (2015) also assumed that the N400 is a neuronal marker for the recognition of norm violations and that its amplitude will be greater in response to social norm violations in narrow (e.g. Chinese) cultures than in loose (e.g. American) cultures. The investigations of Mu et al. (2015) examined cultural differences and questioned whether such neurobiological differences are related to cultural differences in a variety of attitudes and behaviours. In comparison to loose cultures, the authors assumed that individuals in narrow cultures have more self-control, prefer standard to creative solutions for tasks, attach more importance to territorial defence (i.e. maintaining order in their own country) and are more ethnocentric (i.e. believe that their own culture is superior to others and reject deviations that threaten social order). These are human adaptations that always support and reinforce the strength of social norms (Mu et al. 2015). Such correlations of tightness and loosening have been found at the national and state levels of analysis, suggesting a compromise of more order, stability and cohesion in tight groups, but more creativity and openness in loose groups (Mu et al. 2015, p. 15349).

1.5.3 Cultural Dimensions as Relevant Factors for Error Understanding and Management

Helmreich and his colleagues (Helmreich and Davies 2004; Helmreich 2000; Helmreich et al. 2000) have been intensively researching errors and cultural differences in the context of aviation since the 1990s. In various large international studies, flight teams from 22 nations were examined, and the influences of three culture dimensions were identified as relevant for the cockpit regarding risk minimisation and error culture, namely, the professional cultures of pilots, the cultures of organisations and the national cultures surrounding individuals and their organisations (Helmreich 2000; Helmreich et al. 2000). This book presents in Part VIII several chapters that deal with aviation and cultural issues in more detail than is possible at this point, so only the research findings relevant to the cultural aspect are listed here.

Helmreich et al. (2000) found in their studies that there are significant differences in the way pilots carry out their work depending on national culture and that these differences affect safety. Their research design was based on Geert Hofstede's (1980, 1991) four-dimensional cultural model, in particular his survey on work attitudes (Chaps. 10, 13, 24, 29, 31, 32), which they then supplemented with a series of new questions relevant to the aviation environment. Their studies showed that three of the four dimensions of Hofstede proved to be conceptually relevant for team interaction in the cockpit: power distance, individualism collectivism and uncertainty avoidance

The first of these, power distance, reflects the acceptance of unequal power relations by subordinates and is defined by statements that younger people should not question the decisions or actions of their superiors and the nature of leadership (i.e. consultative versus autocratic). Crew members from 22 nations were examined. A high power distance score indicated the acceptance of a more autocratic type of leadership. Helmreich et al. (2000) found that cultures with a high power distance can suffer the certainty that people are not willing to contribute to the actions or decisions of executives. Countries such as Morocco, the Philippines, Taiwan and Brazil had the highest values, indicating the highest acceptance of unequally distributed power. At the other end of the power continuum were countries such as Ireland, Denmark and Norway, with the USA also positioned at the lower end of the distribution.

The second dimension, individualism collectivism, describes differences between individualistic cultures, where people define situations in terms of costs and benefits to themselves, and more collectivist cultures, where the focus is on harmony within their own primary work or family group. The concept of teamwork and communication can be achieved more easily by collectivists than by people with a more individualistic orientation. The USA and Australia performed best in individualism, while many Latin American and Asian cultures were considered highly collectivistic.

The third dimension, termed "uncertainty avoidance" by Hofstede (1980, 1991), was redefined by the researchers in that it was interpreted as requiring written procedures for all situations and that the rules of a company should never be broken, even if they might be in the best interest of the company. This dimension was described by Helmreich et al. (2000, Helmreich and Davis 2004) as "rules and order" and could have both positive and negative effects according to their understanding. Those who deal with it are perhaps the least inclined to deviate from procedures and rules, but they are less creative in dealing with new situations. These low levels may be more vulnerable to procedural breaches but may be better equipped to deal with conditions that are not covered by the procedures. On the newly defined scale, Taiwan, Korea and the Philippines performed best, while Anglo-Saxon cultures such as Great Britain, Ireland and the USA performed very poorly.

In view of the advance of automation and the 4th Industrial Revolution, the results of the research by Helmreich et al. (2000), Helmreich and Davis (2004) are particularly relevant in terms of the error aspect: They were able to demonstrate that there are significant cultural differences in attitudes towards automation—both preference for automation and opinions about its application (Helmreich et al. 2000, p. 7). In particular, pilots from high-performance groups proved to be particularly successful in terms of both automation and the likelihood that it would be used under all circumstances. The authors conclude that there are no "good" and "bad" national cultures in terms of the prevalence of human error and the goal of safety and error culture, because each specific culture includes elements with positive and negative effects on the effective group function, as it influences these universal goals. Helmreich et al. (2000) therefore attach particular importance to specific organisational cultures in actively promoting a safety culture and maximising the positive and minimising the negative aspects of professional and national cultures. Helmreich and Davis consider it crucial to develop culturally congruent organisational initiatives and at the same time increase safety, suggesting that this could be achieved, for example, by declaring error management a universally valued goal that can be accepted by individuals from all cultures. Under the two objectives of threat and error management, training programmes can be conducted that do not violate cultural values, but nevertheless lead to desired behaviours.

1.5.4 Cultural and Organisational Factors as Relevant Factors Influencing Each Other in Dealing with Errors

As described earlier in this chapter, from the point of view of error management, Frese and Keith (2015, p. 665) assume, on one hand, that it is pointless to try to prevent the occurrence of all errors and, on the other hand, that errors are omnipresent. Errors cannot be completely prevented because human cognitive equipment is designed for error-prone heuristic processing and not for potentially error-free algorithmic processing (Reason 1990). Frese and Keith assume a certain general validity here, even if they notice differences between sexes and cultures (Li et al. 2012; Roese and Vohs 2012). The boundaries between organisational and national factors are certainly fluid. Thus Frese and Keith (2015, p. 668) refer to the increased number of air accidents in South Korea in the 1970s, with a military background that was associated with an extraordinarily strong hierarchical orientation. They emphasise that for an appropriate perception and articulation of errors, a great difference is beneficial, because too great a similarity of participants reduces errors to detect and report. But even if diversity and multi-perspectivity are ensured, the interfaces must be optimally communicated. As an example, the authors refer to a NASA mission that ultimately failed because it was too late to notice that one partner used metric units and the other English units (Bell and Kozlowski 2002 as cited in Frese and Keith 2015, 669).

van Dyck et al. (2005) have conducted studies on the culture of organisational error management in two different European countries. They examined 65 Dutch companies and 47 German companies. This is interesting because Germany and the Netherlands belong to different clusters of leadership culture (Brodbeck et al. 2010, as cited in van Dyck et al. 2005, p. 8). The Netherlands is rated lower than Germany in terms of error intolerance (among 62 countries, the Netherlands ranks 12th in terms of error intolerance, while Western Germany ranks 2nd) and in terms of uncertainty avoidance (suggesting that the uncertainties caused by errors are less likely to have negative consequences). Van Dyck and her colleagues found that error management contributes positively to the performance and survivability of companies. Important factors include communication about errors, exchange of error knowledge, help in error situations and rapid error detection and analysis, effective troubleshooting and coordinated error handling. These elements of the error management culture can help avoid and reduce negative error consequences and develop better strategies for dealing with errors in the future (van Dyck et al. 2005). These results agree with those of Edmondson (1996) and Helmreich and Merritt (1998), who also emphasise the importance of free-flowing communication, the rewarding of error reporting (or at least its non-punishment) and a continuous reflexive and interactive learning approach to increase success and security in high-security organisations. No notable differences that could be attributed to cultural factors are mentioned by the authors; it is merely pointed out that:

> Despite this diversity in positions and departmental affiliations, managers tended to agree in their assessment of their company's error culture, indicating that error culture may indeed be a pervasive organizational characteristic. Nevertheless, it is still possible that managers and rank-and-file workers differ in their assessment of their company's culture. Future research should address this concern by collecting information from both managers and workers. (van Dyck et al. 2005, p. 1237)

New studies from the USA have added completely different findings regarding cultural implications in the perception of mistakes and how to deal with them.

1.5.5 Differences in Safety Culture and Risk Perception and Their Effects Using the Example of Latin American and Non-Latin Construction Workers in the USA

As Kane Bormann and colleagues (Bormann 2012; Bormann et al. 2013) have found in a large cross-sectional study conducted in the Denver Metro and Northern Colorado areas, there are major differences in safety culture and risk perception between Latin American and non-Latin construction workers. A number of factors have been shown to play a significant role in the errors and failures in these technically very complex contexts. The reason for the study was that in the USA construction industry, Latino workers currently suffer a disproportionately high number of injuries and deaths compared to non-Latino workers. Studies showed that potential Latin American construction workers with very little knowledge of health and safety, the ability to enforce safety regulations and little or no prior knowledge of the construction industry are entering the USA (Brunette 2004 as cited in Bormann 2012, p. 19).

Available educational resources seem to be of particular importance here. On one hand, there is a language barrier between Latin American and non-Latin construction workers. In order to avoid mistakes or to be able to communicate, linguistic communication must be possible, especially in complex contexts such as construction. However, according to a 2003 National Safety Council content survey (Vazquez and Stalnaker 2004), few Latinos speak English when entering the USA, and more than 71% of companies employ non-English-speaking workers or non-English-speaking workers. This is also the reason given to explain why Latino immigrants and Spanish-speaking workers often receive less training in occupational safety and health (Ruttenberg 2004). Also, it seems that native speakers are less willing to explain things to people with limited English, and foremen get frustrated when they try to explain to employees how to do a job safely and properly (Ruttenberg 2004).

Another educational resource proved to be relevant in this context: In 2010, the Morrison Institute (Vazquez and Stalnaker 2004) reported that Mexican immigrants had an average of less than 9 years of schooling and only about half of Latinos in the Western USA had high school education. The US Census Bureau (Vazquez and Stalnaker 2004) conducted a similar study and found that 27.3% of adult Latinos had less than a ninth grade education. As a result, many of these people are incompletely alphabetised in English. Bormann (2012) points out that for Latinos, learning opportunities such as written work instructions, safety briefings, observations and discussions between workers that could help supplement formal classroom training are not as useful or effective if the knowledgeable and experienced construction workers and managers speak only English (Vazquez and Stalnaker 2004).

In addition, there are other relevant factors, namely, that young workers are preferred for physically heavy work in the construction industry. They are particularly vulnerable to errors and hazards at these workplaces because they lack experience and training and are therefore less likely to be able to identify hazards (Williams Jr et al. 2010), lack educational resources and often have an unexplained legal status. Some authors also come to the conclusion that young workers in particular lack the physical strength to cope with some work tasks and lack the individual maturity to make correct judgements and the confidence to talk to their superiors about dangers (O'Connor et al. 2005).

Various authors refer in particular to socio-political factors influencing errors and failures, namely, the fear of immigration status and the strong economic pressure to remain employed (Brunette 2004). Criticism of grievances and the reporting of mistakes could lead to job loss or deportation, while the rejection of dangerous work conditions could mean that the money for the workers and their families can no longer be raised (Williams Jr et al. 2010). These barriers can all lead to unsafe working environments and the problem that Latinos do not fully report the number of nonfatal injuries in order to maintain positive relationships with employers (Brunette 2004).

Other studies focus more on the cultural differences between Latinos and non-Latinos to explain the significantly higher accident and death rates among Latinos. Both Brunette (2004) and Vazquez and Stalnaker (2004) point out that at the beginning of the century, Latinos immigrating to the USA, as well as workers, have different histories, cultural sensitivities, strong health beliefs and cultural backgrounds to non-Latin American workers. Brunette (2004) and Vazquez and Stalnaker (2004) conclude that some Latin American cultures and values could pose challenges and lead to safety problems on the construction site. For example, Vazquez and Stalnaker (2004) observes that Latin American culture teaches that authoritative personalities must be accorded the highest respect, which means that Latinos rarely disagree with superiors, even if they are wrong as superiors. This cultural value of respect would also prevent Latinos from asking questions or challenging instructions from superiors. Canales et al. (2009) confirm this by referring to the weak UA in Latin American culture that leads to excessive zeal being considered inappropriate (Canales et al. 2009). Canales et al. (2009) comment that this is shown by the phenomenon that people often prefer to remain silent rather than to tackle problems offensively. According to Canales et al. (2009), the Latinos attach great importance to the family, which often goes beyond the primary family members. In the workplace, Latinos often talk to each other and create close relationships but hesitate to discuss issues with non-Latinos or regulators. The development of trust in Latino culture therefore requires time to build personal relationships. Given the nature of construction and the constant movement around construction sites and relocations, it is unlikely that Latinos will develop these relationships with superiors, which is why they never really build trust with each other (Vazquez and Stalnaker 2004).

Bormann (2012), Arciniega et al. (2008) and Menzel and Gutierrez (2010) also refer to the concept of "machismo" as relevant in this context. Machismo refers to a standard of behaviour shown by men and understood as the male force that in one way or another influences all male behaviour both positively and negatively (Arciniega et al. 2008). In a study by Menzel and Gutierrez (2010), respondents stated that machismo plays a role in the higher injury rates of Latinos when it prevents Latino workers from wearing safety equipment (Menzel and Gutierrez 2010).

Differences in risk perception between Latinos and non-Latinos could also be observed in the studies mentioned above. Already in the late 1980s, sociological and anthropological studies were able to show that the social and cultural environment had a formative effect on risk perception and the acceptance of forms of risk (Slovic 1987), as well as on the way in which employees perceive these safety regulations and procedures and, in the process, also on the level of safety and the handling of errors at the workplace (Mohamed 2002). Menzel and Gutierrez (2010) investigated this in a qualitative study with Latino trade union workers in the south of Nevada, in which differences were determined, especially with regard to the perception of injury risks. Menzel and Gutierrez (2010) found that the level of professional qualification influenced the perception of responsibility for safety and accident prevention. Low-skilled workers saw responsibility primarily in the hands of the employer, while highly qualified workers preferred to place responsibility with themselves and their employees. Another identified factor affecting perceived risk was immigration status, where illegal immigrants seemed more prepared to take more risks at work (Menzel and Gutierrez 2010). English literacy has proven to be particularly significant, affecting the ability of Latino staff to read and understand security training and signs. The fourth decisive factor here was also the traditional Latin American culture.

1.6 The Contribution of This Book: Introducing the Content

This book adds to the literature on mistakes, errors and failures and takes various theoretical and methodological perspectives into account while drawing from a variety of focus points.

In the following section, we briefly introduce the content of the chapters to provide an overview of the varied subjects covered in this book. The book is divided into 8 parts, containing 32 chapters.

Part I focuses on mistakes, errors and failure on cultural and individual levels.

Elisabeth Vanderheiden begins the book by focusing on the topic of life crisis—which may be caused by the death of a loved one, serious illness or disability, the breakup of a relationship, a divorce, the loss of workplace, unemployment or even the impact of natural or technical disasters or political disasters like war, genocide, flight or structural suppression. Such life crises are often experienced by the person affected as an expression of failure, the result of individual wrong decision-making or as the consequences of personal misconduct, which can also lead to ill health. The chapter focuses on how to deal with these issues on an individual basis from a resource-orientated perspective.

This chapter is followed by **Paul C. Rosenblatt's** chapter on errors, mistakes and failures in love letters and written communication. The author analyses ten sets of published love letters from the 1820s to the 1940s, in which he discovers that most love-letter writers raise concerns about the meaning of gaps in communication and the brevity of explanations. The author points out strategies for addressing and avoiding failures, mistakes and errors in exchanging love letters and communication during the described contexts and times.

Further on, **James L. Kelley** investigates the life of Donald Fagen from a psychobiographical perspective. His psychobiographical examination of the subject with an object relations emphasis highlights that Fagen used his role as a successful musician to confer on himself a sense of legitimacy and to distance himself from the structures of conventional "bourgeois" existence. The chapter focuses on mistakes, errors and failures of the musician.

Part II refers to mistakes, errors and failure in society.

The author **Sofia von Humboldt** points out new and highly relevant aspects of age and longevity from global and cultural perspectives. Her chapter discusses mistakes, errors and failures in the cultural context of research, policy and interventions in old age. The chapter concludes with a discussion of future suggestions for research and policy interventions for dealing with longevity from cultural and cross-cultural perspectives.

From a sexuality research perspective, **Aliraza Javaid** explores possibilities for mistakes, errors and failures. Drawing upon his personal experiences of conducting what Janie M. Irvine aptly calls "dirty work", he sheds light on his different (sometimes presumed) mistakes, errors and failures when doing sexuality work. He locates these in their cultural and social contexts, delving into hindsight to resurrect memories of pain and loneliness when doing such work, with the assistance of research diary extracts. In his chapter, Javaid exposes his vulnerability as a researcher with regard to doing sexuality work and what this could mean for other and potential sexuality writers. He provides examples of his work and opens it up for further discussion on how to deal with "risky" research constructively.

Maike Baumann explores research on hierarchies across cultures and reasons to assign a leading role to one party in an interpersonal relationship which can include advanced knowledge or expertise, seniority, agreement and ownership or control of resources. The author reflects on expectations, including qualities of interaction, responsibilities, the other's value system and, consequently, the other's behaviour as well as assumptions concerning the other's expectations. She provides a new and original model for dealing with hierarchical relationships positively and resource-orientated. The proposed model helps analysing existing conflict dynamics and repeatedly occurring conflicts with the goal of enabling the development of understanding and a change of behaviour, by using insights from systemic theory, research on cognitive biases, sociolinguistics as well as motivational theory.

Claude-Hélène Mayer and **Lolo Jacques Mayer** present an ethnographic case study which refers to the experience of failure in intercultural communication and relationship-building for members of different cultural and racial groups within a specifically selected public space in South Africa. The authors focus on concepts of erroneous identity ascriptions, intersectionalities and power which respond to the question "Who am I?" in a specific sociocultural context. Findings show that failed intercultural communication and ascribing identities in intercultural contexts can lead to erroneous assumptions about "the other", interwoven in conscious and unconscious discourses of race, power and accessibility to resources—which contribute to the failure of employee–client relationship-building in intercultural public spaces.

Klas-Göran Karlsson and **Bo Petersson** provide outstanding new insights into the final stage of the history of the Soviet Union, from 1985 to 1991, when the last Communist Party and Soviet state leader Mikhail Gorbachev tried to reform his country by making economic life more effective, widening the scope of political participation, opening up history and culture for debate and introducing a new, peaceful thinking in international affairs. Gorbachev wanted to save the Soviet system but ended up destroying it. The chapter focuses on political mistakes which are often difficult to distinguish from failures caused by structural problems. The chapter deals with these difficulties and provides new insights into political decision-making.

In Part III, the authors focus on mistakes, errors and failure in organisations.

Alessandro Carretta, **Paola Schwizer** and **Lucrezia Fattobene** write about errors and failures in European banking from cultural perspectives, seeing misconduct as a result of errors in policies and procedures, of mistakes in individual behaviours, of failure in management and control systems. The researchers elaborate on a new theory of risk culture in banking and develop a general framework of errors and failures in banking while taking the existing literature and empirical evidence that is currently available into account. They further focus on the influence of national (banking) culture on risk and perception of errors and mistakes; the trade-off between risk appetite and control culture in decision-making; the impact on reputational risk of misconduct driven by errors in management practices; the role of media (traditional and social) in influencing public opinion about banks and enhancing the effects of errors on capital markets, risk management practices, compliance with law and regulation, individual behaviours and organisational structures; and the role of banking regulators and supervisors in the handling of errors and mistakes. Finally, the authors demonstrate that culture is one main driver of organisational and individual behaviours and consequently of errors, mistakes and failures in bank management.

Fernando Lanzer Pereira de Souza analyses how mistakes are handled in organisations across different cultures by looking at them through the prism of Huib Wursten's (Wursten and Lanzer 2013) mental images, a framework that takes Hofstede's four classic dimensions of value, reshaping them into six different styles of organisational culture. In addition, Japanese organisations provide a seventh and different style which is taken into account. The resultant seven business culture styles (contest, well-oiled machine, network, social pyramid, traditional family, solar system and Japanese) are described in terms of how they differ in the way that they identify and deal with mistakes. Several practical examples taken from real-life situations are provided and reflected on in this chapter.

Claude-Hélène Mayer provides an in-depth insight into ethnographic experiences of conflict and failure in a South African work context, perceived from the perspective of an individual with a European cultural origin. The author analyses and interprets conflict in work experiences and a specific work relationship from systems psychodynamic theory perspectives, to provide new and differentiated ideas on the in-depth complexity of conflict experiences in a specific cultural context. The purpose of this chapter is to offer insight into an intra- and inter-psychological conflict experience from an ethnographic perspective. A single individual's case is presented through interviews, field notes, contextual descriptions and interpretations. Recommendations for future theory and practice are offered.

Rudolf M. Oosthuizen writes in his chapter about perceptions of failure synthesised in studies investigating resilience factors to emotional distress resulting from the experience of failure in organisational settings. The author introduces the impact of failure experiences and conceptualises resilience-based approaches and concludes by discussing the implications for psychological resilience-building interventions in response to failure, error or mistakes for individuals and teams in organisations.

Elmar Nass reflects on credible corporate culture in value-based organisations with special regard to Christian companies. The author refers to Christian business ethics and provides a Christian image of humans which presupposes the defectiveness of mankind. He further hypotheses that lived error culture has yet to be researched and practised. A systematic approach to how the Christian image of humans is a basis of values, which should determine the error culture, is presented. The author proposes selected principles of Christian error culture as a normative compass for organisations.

Thomas Ryan also focuses on a Christian context and writes about the Catholic Church in Australia and its instance of gross moral failure in the final findings of the Royal Commission into Institutional Responses to Child Sexual Abuse of December 2017. This specific case study in moral failure is approached through the interplay of psychology and moral science. The author suggests a new approach on how to deal with the mistakes, errors and failure and offers grounds for hope in the task of cultural change.

Mary Hallay-Witte and Bettina Janssen write about sexual abuse in the Catholic Church in Germany and how this was being concealed and information withheld over years by church representatives. The authors emphasise in this chapter that up to the present day, victims testify scandalous mishandling of their cases. Mistakes and omissions made in the past continue to be repeated in the present. This chapter presents findings of the research project titled "Sexual abuse of minors by Catholic priests, deacons and male members of orders in the domain of the German Bishops Conference" and highlight relevant touchstones for future reappraisal and for future intervention into and protection from the sexual abuse of minors.

Part IV takes an educational perspective into account.

Amber Simpson, Euisuk Sung, Alice Anderson and Adam V. Maltese explore the terms "failure", "mistakes", "errors", "obstacles" and "struggle" which are often used interchangeably across disciplines and cultures. The purpose of this chapter is to synthesise and clarify how these terms are articulated and utilised in research studies and commentaries published between 1970 and 2017. Through a systematic literature review, the authors discuss similarities and differences in how researchers have defined these terms, as well as how these definitions differ by cultural context, discipline and age of participants. The authors also provide insight into their own research study including 500 youths and 150 educators situated in a variety of educational settings. The authors conclude with open questions and recommendations for the field to consider when conducting research around failures, errors and mistakes in educational contexts.

The authors **Naomi Takashiro** and **Clifford Clarke** include different ethnicities in their study of students with low socio-economic status and identify what factors contribute to their academic success following failure, in a systematic review of 19 qualitative studies, which were published between 2000 and 2018. Their findings are grouped under three themes: (a) family and others' support and influence, (b) motivation and (c) learning strategies. The authors also refer to the topic of culture shock and cultural adaptation to new cultures as motivation. The findings are of value to researchers, educators and school officials who are interested in educating disadvantaged students who manage to achieve academic success despite adversity, mistakes, errors and failure.

Thalita Camargo Angelucci and **María Isabel Pozzo** use a psychoanalytical perspective, associating the subjective development of human beings with their appropriation of the language of their environment. The authors affirm that the subject is structured in and on language while taking migration issues into account. With this focus, they highlight significant errors in processing teaching and learning languages by presenting theoretical reviews on polysemy and the plurality of meanings, within the concept of error in the field of foreign language teaching. Thereby, the sociolinguistic perspective of Marcos Bagno and the methodological approach of discourse analysis are adapted with regard to applying a positive and resource-orientated view of learners' mistakes and errors.

Part V focuses on mistakes, errors and failure in psychology, therapy and counselling.

Kathryn Nel and **Saraswathie Govender** investigate deficiencies in the use of therapeutic and theoretical models in psychology on the African continent, which stem from individualistic theories with Western philosophical underpinnings. The authors emphasise that the notion of "if the client does not speak, the therapist does not speak", might work for middle-aged to elderly persons from a Western cultural background, but is doomed to failure in an African setting. The chapter explores how the failures and misunderstandings brought about by using psychodynamic therapy cause therapeutic misunderstandings and failure. A brief overview of the key points in the work of Klein, Winnicott and Fairbairn is given, and culture-specific insights regarding African collectivism and caregiving are presented. The chapter provides insights into case-study examples, outlining how psychodynamic therapy failed in these settings.

Researchers **Christine Bales, Josua Leibrich, Katja Brinkmann, Ibrahim Özkan, Umut Altunoz, Janina Wesolowski** and **Maria Belz** demonstrate learning from treatment errors in transcultural psychiatry and psychotherapy and need for transcultural sensitivity in psychotherapeutic and psychiatric treatment of migrants, by both the patient and the therapist, based on mutual misunderstandings due to cultural differences. The chapter describes selected cultural differences, language barriers and different expressions of psychological stress and the experience of "othering". Therapists' insecurities might be anchored in fear of making mistakes, resulting in their avoidance of taking migrants as patients. The chapter takes processes of culturalisation and attribution errors into account which lead to treatment errors. Case descriptions present strategies to approach diversity phenomena successfully by avoiding errors and mistakes in transcultural psychiatry and psychotherapy. A case vignette offers an example of describing transcultural treatment processes.

Jung's archetypes have been subject to numerous research studies, as is the case in this research study by **Claude-Hélène Mayer**. In this chapter, the author reflects on the trickster archetype and its implications in the life of Michael Jackson, an American leader in the music industry, by using a psychobiographical approach. She offers an analysis of the behaviour of Michael Jackson within the context and expression of the trickster archetype, and his appeals to fluidly overcome boundaries of race, gender, generation and culture with ingenuity, creativity and positive leadership. In the end, however, it is assumed that the strength and power of the trickster archetype active in this celebrity's life led to failures, and ultimately to his premature death. It is argued that the trickster archetype needs to be recognised, seen, acknowledged and understood in its depth to maintain the success of the leader or to transform leadership stories from those of failure to stories of success.

Pei-Luen Patrick Rau, Zhi Guo, Qie Nan, Xin Lei and **Andong Zhang** present the theoretical framework and empirical research on cognitive bias in cross-cultural design, together with the integrative framework of training design. The authors discuss information processing and emotional biases as resources which help the human individual to survive and examine the relationships between mental models and user-centred designs. Further, the authors present empirical research in cross-cultural design, bias and the influence of cultural dimensions by providing practical insights into case studies in the design.

Part VI illuminates mistakes, errors and failure in law and justice.

Wayne Petherick describes errors and failures as critical within the forensic disciplines, such as forensic science, forensic psychology/psychiatry and forensic criminology, where they might have a profound negative impact on the life or liberty of the individuals concerned. Errors and failures can occur when experts do not avail themselves of all the evidence available in a given case or when they remain, at best, unaware that more evidence exists, when experts are unaware of their own limitations or where bias or cognitive distortion taints the expert's opinion even when the evidence may be voluminous. This chapter examines error from the perspective of forensic criminology, incorporating the evidentiary considerations of validity, reliability and sufficiency, followed by metacognition and cognitive bias. Case studies are used as examples throughout with some recommendations provided for how current and future generations of forensic psychologists can overcome the obstacles to effective forensic examination.

For those who are combatting failure in crime eradication, this chapter by **Claude-Hélène Mayer** describes the common attempts to combat and eradicate wildlife crime by examining examples of wildlife crime in different national and cultural contexts. The author explores the sociocultural circumstances surrounding international, regional, national and local attempts to address wildlife crime. This chapter aims at contributing complex strategic reflections to transform failures in wildlife crime eradication into mindful strategies which take cultural aspects into consideration to defeat international wildlife crime successfully in the context of green criminology.

Part VII directs attention to mistakes and errors in the medical arena.

Chris P. Subbe and **Paul Barach** reflect on the training of clinicians in both nursing and medicine, to reduce error rates to a negligible level. The authors explain that error rates in many areas of medical treatment have not significantly changed for decades, describing dominant philosophies of error reduction, such as "Safety 1", which focuses on understanding errors, and "Safety 2", which looks for ways to strengthen existing successful methods of working safely. In this chapter, another principle is taken into account, namely, the acceptance of fallibility of individual parts and their application into the medical context. Such acceptance is still rare, but necessary to alter organisational culture and clinical outcomes.

The author **Jan S. Brommundt** also focuses on the error management system in medical contexts, its techniques, its structures and its embeddedness in a broader error management culture. He shows that the system of open error management requires an innovative culture, open hierarchies, multicultural perspectives and the empowerment of personnel traditionally working at the lower levels of hierarchical systems. The author concludes that the views proposed are necessary, efficient and cost-effective and provide a basis for an improved error and failure management within medical systems.

According to **Florian Fischer, Franziska Carow and Hannah Eger**, mistakes, errors and failures often offer opportunities for development when managed openly and constructively. However, the fear of mistakes and failures and the cultural assumptions of defining them as a threat to self-esteem often reduce the ability to manage errors, mistakes and failures optimally. By contrast, an open error culture contributes to safety but also to individual health and well-being. This chapter suggests that a humorous handling of errors, mistakes and failure can contribute to individual health and well-being and can thereby become a health-promoting resource.

Part VIII highlights mistakes, errors in traffic and aviation.

In the aviation industry, the safety system is critically dependent on the reporting of adverse events, and, in the majority of cases, these adverse events emanate from multiple systemic failures of which the final failure is the human operator or the air traffic controller in the case of this chapter written by **Jaco van der Westhuizen, Matita Tshabalala** and **Karel Stanz.** The chapter describes how the aviation industry, through the International Civil Aviation Organisation, subscribes to the notion of a just culture, where staff can report mistakes, errors and failures into a safety management system with the promise of amnesty, provided that gross negligence or sabotage is not present. It further introduces the challenges of dealing with mistakes, errors and failures within the South African context which is multicultural—and, with 11 official languages, is also multilingual. The authors discuss the influence of local cultures and performance-setting criteria on the reporting of errors and on views concerning these errors. The authors reveal the hidden potential of learnings regarding errors, failures and mistakes through a group engagement process to manage errors, failures and mistakes professionally.

The following chapter written by **Jan U. Hagen** also deals with the aviation context, explaining how multiple aircraft accidents result from a lack of error communication. The chapter shows that, even though cultural differences have been cited as contributing factors to aircraft accidents, many accidents happen owing to the different hierarchical status of first and second officers and the reluctance of the latter to speak up during critical situations. This is why, three decades ago, crew resource management was developed in the air industry, to achieve open, factual error communication and thereby ensure the safe operation of flights. Today, crew resource management is a mandatory part of flight crew training in civilian and military flight operation worldwide. Since its introduction, accident rates have greatly diminished, but the human factor still remains the main cause of accidents. The chapter provides insight into fatal errors in aviation and focuses on the leadership behaviour involved to increase aviation safety.

Vaclav Linkov and **Petr Zámečník** present a particularly interesting study regarding the impact of cultural differences on driving behaviours. The authors report on drivers from particular cultural backgrounds driving in foreign environments and making mistakes induced by foreign cultural backgrounds in the current traffic contexts. Since people in a variety of countries are used to driving with varying levels of aggressiveness, are used to seeing traffic signs that are positioned in different ways and have been familiar with other traffic signs specific only to their country, mistakes happen easily. Recommendations are provided on how to use these mistakes to inspire governments to change policies regarding traffic rules and improve infrastructure so that foreign drivers more easily adapt to the new environment.

The parts and chapters of this book aim at providing new perspectives on mistakes, errors and failure from different cultural, professional and disciplinary perspectives and across these contexts. We wish the readers of this book new individual, cultural and positive insights into the topic of mistakes, errors and failures.

References

Ackroyd, S. (2007). Organizational Failure. In G. Ritzer, *The Blackwell Encyclopedia of Sociology* (pp. 3306–3307). Oxford, UK: BLACKWELL PUBLISHING.

Amara, N. (2019). Correcting Students' Errors: Theory and Practice. Retrieved from http://www.educationalresearch.info/index.php/er/article/view/26

Amini, A., & Mortazavi, S. (2013). The impact of the broadcasting mistake management culture in a healthy organization on the quality of the personnel work life. Journal of clinical and diagnostic research : JCDR, 7(3), 507–12.

APA Dictionary of Psychology. (2019). Retrieved from https://dictionary.apa.org/error

Arciniega, G. M., Anderson, T. C., Tovar-Blank, Z. G., & Tracey, T. J. G. (2008). Toward a fuller conception of Machismo: Development of a traditional Machismo and Caballerismo Scale. *Journal of Counseling Psychology*, 19–33.

Backert, W. (2004), Kulturen des Scheiterns. Gesellschaftliche Bewertungsprozesse im internationalen Vergleich, in: M. Junge und G. Lechner (Hrsg.), *Scheitern. Aspekte eines sozialen Phänomens*, S. 63–77. Wiesbaden: VS Verlag für Sozialwissenschaften

Bauer, J. (2008). Learning from errors at work. Studies on nurses' engagement in error-related learning activities - Publikationsserver der Universität Regensburg. Retrieved from https://epub.uni-regensburg.de/10748/

Bell, B.S. & Kozlowski, S.W.J. (2002). A typology of virtual teams: Implications for effective leadership. Group & Organization Management, 27(1), 14–49.

Bormann, K. (2012). *Risk Perception and Cultural Differences of Latinos across Residential, Commercial, and Heavy Civil Construction.*. Fort Collins, Colorado: Master Thesis. Colorado State University Fort Collins, Colorado.

Bormann, K., Clevenger, C., Lopez del Puerto, C., & Gilkey, D. (2013). Risk Perception and Cultural Differences of Latinos across Residential, Commercial, and Heavy Civil Construction. In *49th ASC Annual International Conference Proceedings.*. Fort Collins, Colorado: Associated Schools of Construction.

Bornstein, M., & Cote, L. (2001). Mother-infant interaction and acculturation: I. Behavioural comparisons in Japanese American and South American families. *International Journal Of Behavioral Development*, *25*(6), 549–563. doi: https://doi.org/10.1080/01650250042000546

Braun, H. (n.d.). *Scheitern als persönliche Erfahrung und öffentliches Ereignis.* [online] Web. tuomi-media.de. Available at: http://web.tuomi-media.de/dno2/Dateien/NO111-4.pdf [Accessed 3 Jan. 2019].

Brodbeck, F., Frese, M., Akerblom, S., Audia, G., & Bakacsi, G. (2010). Cultural variation of leadership prototypes across 22 European countries. Retrieved 30 November 2019, from https://doi.org/10.1348/096317900166859

Brommundt, J. (2018). Empowerment. In J. Hangen, *How Could This Happen?: Managing Errors in Organizations* (pp. 161–172). Cham: Springer International.

Brüggemann, U. (2009). Modellierung der Alltagsorganisation : ein psychologisch basiertes Agentenmodell zur Erzeugung der Verkehrsnachfrage - Deutsche Digitale Bibliothek. Retrieved from https://www.deutsche-digitale-bibliothek.de/item/GDESBPZZ3JFBEMQ5HECCWWQHU4E4GGFO

Brunette, M. J. (2004). Construction safety research in the United States: targeting the Hispanic workforce. *Injury Prevention, 10*(4), 244–248.

Camras, L. A., Oster, H., Campos, J. J., Miyake, K., & Bradshaw, D. (1997). Japanese and American infants' responses to arm restraint. In P. Ekman & E. L. Rosenberg (Eds.), *Series in affective science. What the face reveals: Basic and applied studies of spontaneous expression using the Facial Action Coding System (FACS)* (pp. 289–301). New York, NY, US: Oxford University Press. (Reprinted from "Developmental Psychology," 28, 1992, pp. 578–583)

Camras LA, Oster H, Campos J, Campos R, Ujiie T, Miyake K, Wang L, Meng Z. Production of emotional facial expressions in European American, Japanese, and Chinese infants. *Developmental Psychology*. 1998;34:616–628.

Camras, LA, Meng, Z, Ujiie, T, Dharamsi, S, Miyake, K, Oster, H, Wang, L, Cruz, J, Murdoch, A, Campos, J. Observing emotion in infants: Facial expression, body behavior, and rater judgments of responses to an expectancy-violating event. *Emotion*. 2002;2:179–193.

Canales, A. R., Arbelaez, M., Vasquez, E., Aveiga, F., Strong, K., Walters, R., et al. (2009). Exploring Training Needs and Development of Construction Language Courses for American Supervisors and Hispanic Craft Workers. [Article]. *Journal of Construction Engineering & Management, 135*(5), 387–396

Cannon, M. D. & Edmondson, A. C. 2005. Failing to learn and learning to fail (intelligently): How great organizations put failure to work to innovate and improve. Long Range Planning, 38(3): 299–319.

Carroll, J. (2018). Understanding Safety Management Through Strategic Design, Political and Cultural Approaches. In J. Hangen, *How Could This Happen?: Managing Errors in Organizations* (pp. 27–44). Cham: Springer International.

Dahlin, K. B., Chuang, Y. T., & Roulet, T. J. (2018). Opportunity, Motivation, and Ability to learn from failures and errors: Review, synthesis, and ways to move forward. Academy of Management Annals, 12(1), 252–277. doi: https://doi.org/10.5465/annals.2016.0049

De Castella, K., Byrne, D., & Covington, M. (n.d.) APA PsycNET Login. Retrieved from http://psycnet.apa.org/psycarticles/2013-14500-001.pdf
Dörner, D. (1989). Die Logik des Mißlingens. Reinbek: Rowohlt Verlag
Edmondson, A. C. (1996). Learning from mistakes is easier said than done: Group and organizational influences on the detection and correction of human error. *Journal of Applied Behavioral Science, 32*, 5–28.
Edmondson, A. (2004). Learning from Mistakes is Easier Said than Done. *The Journal Of Applied Behavioral Science*, *40*(1), 66–90. doi: https://doi.org/10.1177/0021886304263849
Edmondson, A. & Verdin, P. (2018). The Strategic Imperativ of Psychological Safety and Organizational Error Management. In: J. Hangen, ed., *How Could This Happen?: Managing Errors in Organizations*. Cham: Springer International, pp. 81–104.
Elder, N. C. (2004) The Identification of Medical Errors by Family Physicians During Outpatient Visits. The Annals of Family Medicine 2 (2):125–129
Elder, N., Pallerla, H., & Regan, S. (2006). What do family physicians consider an error? A comparison of definitions and physician perception. BMC Family Practice, 7(1). doi: https://doi.org/10.1186/1471-2296-7-73
Fogel A, Toda S, Kawai M. Mother-infant face-to-face interaction in Japan and the United States: A laboratory comparison using 3-month old infants. *Developmental Psychology*. 1988;24:398–406.
Frese, M. (1993). Fehler bei der Arbeit mit dem Computer: Empirische Ergebnisse und Fehlermanagement. Software-Marketing, 93–105. doi: https://doi.org/10.1007/978-3-322-87509-9_5
Frese, M., & Keith, N. (2015). Action Errors, Error Management, and Learning in Organizations. *Annual Review Of Psychology*, *66*(1), 661–687. doi: https://doi.org/10.1146/annurev-psych-010814-015205
Gartmeier, M. (2009). Fehlerfreundlichkeit im Arbeitskontext: Positive Einstellungen gegenüber Fehlern und negatives Wissen als Ressourcen professionellen Handelns. Regensburg: Dissertation an der Philosophischen Fakultät II der Universität Regensburg.
Giolito, V. and Verdin, P. (2018). Executive Perspectives on Strategic Error Management. In: J. Hangen, ed., *How Could This Happen?: Managing Errors in Organizations*. Cham: Springer International, pp. 59–80.
Glendon, A., Clarke, S., & McKenna, E. (2006). *Human Safety and Risk Management* (2nd ed.). Boca Raton: C R C Press LLC.
Goodman, P., Ramanujam, R., Carroll, J., Edmondson, A., Hofmann, D., & Sutcliffe, K. (2011). Organizational errors: Directions for future research. Retrieved from https://doi.org/10.1016/j.riob.2011.09.003
Grote, G. (2018). Errors and Learning for Safety : Creating Uncertainty As an Underlying Mechanism. In J. Hangen, *How Could This Happen?: Managing Errors in Organizations* (pp. 27–44). Cham: Springer International.
Grout, J. (2006). Mistake proofing: changing designs to reduce error. Quality And Safety In Health Care, 15(suppl_1), i44-i49. doi: https://doi.org/10.1136/qshc.2005.016030
Gruber, H. (1999). Erfahrung als Grundlage kompetenten Handelns. Verlag Hans Huber: Bern.
Hagen, J. (2018). How Could This Happen?. Cham: Springer International Publishing.
Harteis C, Bauer J, Heid H (2006) Der Umgang mit Fehlern als Merkmal betrieblicher Fehlerkultur und Voraussetzung für Professional Learning. Schweizerische Zeitschrift für Bildungswissenschaften 28:111–129
Harteis, C., Bauer, J. & Gruber, H. (2008). The culture of learning from mistakes: How employees handle mistakes in everyday work. *International Journal for Educational Re-search, 47*, 223–231.
Heid, H. (1999). Autorität – über die Verwandlung von Fehlern in Verfehlungen. In W. Althof (Hrsg.), *Fehlerwelten. Vom Fehlermachen und Lernen aus Fehlern* (pp. 129–136). Opladen: Leske + Budrich.

Helmreich, R.L. (2000). Culture and error in space: Implications from analog environments. Aviation, Space, and Environmental Medicine, 71(9–11), 133–139.

Helmreich, R. L., & Merritt, A. C. (1998). Culture at work in aviation and medicine: National. Organizational and Professional Influences, Aldershot

Helmreich, R., & Davies, J. (2004). Culture, threat, and error: lessons from aviation. *Canadian Journal Of Anesthesia/Journal Canadien D'anesthésie*, *51*(S1), R1-R4. doi: https://doi.org/10.1007/bf03018331

Helmreich, R.L., Wilhelm, J.A., Klinect, J.R., & Merritt, A.C. (2000). Culture, error and Crew Resource Management. In E. Salas, C.A. Bowers, & E. Edens (Eds.), Applying resource management in organizations: A guide for professionals. Hillsdale, NJ: Erlbaum.

Hofmann, D. A., & Frese, M. (Eds.). (2011). *The organizational frontiers series (SIOP). Errors in organizations.* New York, NY, US: Routledge/Taylor & Francis Group.

Hofstede, G. (1980). Culture's consequences: International differences in work-related values. Beverly Hills, CA: Sage.

Hofstede, G. (1991). Cultures and organizations: Software of the mind. Maidenhead, U.K.: McGraw-Hill.

James, C. (1998). Errors in language learning and use. London: Longman.

Kahnemann, D. (2013). *Thinking, fast and slow (Reprint).* New York: Farrar Straus Giroux.

Kiassat, A. (2013). System Performance Analysis Considering Human-related Factors. Toronto: Dissertation at the University of Toronto.

Kistler, C. E., Walter, L. C., Mitchell, C. M., & Sloane, P. D. (2010). Patient perceptions of mistakes in ambulatory care. Archives of internal medicine, 170(16), 1480–7.

Kitayama S, Markus HR. Yin and Yang of the Japanese self: The cultural psychology of personality coherence. In: Cervone D, Shoda Y, editors. *The coherence of personality: Social- cognitive bases of consistency, variability, and organization.* New York, NY: Guilford Press; 1999. pp. 242–302.

Kitayama S, Markus HR, Matsumoto H, Norasakkunkit V. Individual and collective processes in the construction of the self: Self-enhancement in the United States and self-criticism in Japan. *Journal of Personality and Social Psychology*. 1997;72:1245–1267.

Klement, P. (2018). Error Management in the German Armed Forces' Military Aviation. In J. Hangen, *How Could This Happen?: Managing Errors in Organizations* (pp. 27–44). Cham: Springer International.

Kohn LT (1999), Corrigan JM, Donaldson MS (eds). To Err Is Human. Building a safer health system. Washington, DC: Institute of Medicine, Committee on Quality of Health Care in America 1999

Kohn, L., Corrigan, J., & Donaldson, M. (1999). To Err is Human: Building a Safer Health System. Washington, DC: National Academy Press.

Kryeziu, M. (2015). *Learning from Errors*. Holzkirchen, Germany and Iliria College, Pristina, Kosovo: Felix–Verlag.

Lei, Z. (2018). Fast, Slow and Pause. In: J. Hagen, ed., *How Could This Happen?: Managing Errors in Organizations*. Cham: Springer International, pp. 1–26.

Lei, Z., Naveh, E., & Novikov, Z. (2016). Errors in Organizations: An Integrative Review via Level of Analysis, Temporal Dynamism, and Priority Lenses. Journal of Management, 42(5),

Lewis, M., Takai-Kawakami, K., Kawakami, K., & Sullivan, M. (2009). Cultural differences in emotional responses to success and failure. *International Journal Of Behavioral Development*, *34*(1), 53–61. doi: https://doi.org/10.1177/0165025409348559

Li Y, Johnson K, Cohen A, Williams M, Knowles E, Chen Z. 2012. Fundamental(ist) attribution error: Protestants are dispositionally focused. *J. Pers. Soc. Psychol.* 102:281–90

Lingard, L, Espin, S, Whyte, S, Reghr, G., Baker, G. R., Reznick, R. Bohnen,J. Orser, B., Doran, D., and Grober, E. Communication failures in the operating room: an observational classification of recurrent types and effects. *BMJ Quality & Safety* 2004;**13:**330–334.

Löber, N. (2010). Konstruktive Fehlerkultur in Krankenhaus und Praxis. *Rheinisches Ärzteblatt Forum*, (8), 20–21.

Löber, N. (2012). *Fehler und Fehlerkultur im Krankenhaus*. Wiesbaden: Gabler Verlag / Springer Fachmedien Wiesbaden GmbH.

Love, P.E.D., Edwards, D.J., Irani, Z. & Walker, D.H.T. (2009). Pathogens: The anato-my of omission errors in construction and resource engineering project. IEEE Transactions on Engineering Management, 56(3), 425–435.

Luthans, F. (2002a). Positive organizational behavior: Developing and managing psychological strengths. *Academy of Management Executive, 16*(1), 57–72.

Luthans, F. (2002b). The need for and meaning of positive organizational behavior. Journal of Organizational Behavior, 23, 695–706.

Luthans, F., & Youssef, C. M. (2007). Emerging positive organizational behavior. *Journal of Management, 33*, 321–349

Markus HR, Kitayama S. The cultural construction of self and emotion: Implications for social behavior. In: Kitayama S, Markus HR, editors. *Emotion and culture: Empirical studies of mutual influence*. Washington, D.C: American Psychological Association; 1994. pp. 89–130.

Martin, A.J. (2012). Fear of failure in learning. In N.M. Seel (Ed.). Encyclopedia of the Sciences of Learning. New York: Springer.

Martin, A. J., & Marsh, H. (2003). Fear of failure: friend or foe. Australian Psychologist, 38(1), 31–38.

Mayer, C-H (2020). Failures in Wildlife Crime Eradication and Strategies Forward. In E. Vanderheiden & C-H. Mayer, Mistakes, Errors and Failures across Cultures: Navigating Potentials. Cham: Springer International.

Mayer, C.-H., Vanderheiden, E., & Oosthuizen, R. (2019). Transforming shame, guilt and anxiety through a salutogenic PP1.0 and PP2.0 counselling framework. *Counselling Psychology Quarterly*, 1–17. doi: https://doi.org/10.1080/09515070.2019.1609421

Medizinischer Dienst des Spitzenverbandes Bund der Krankenkassen e.V. (MDS). (2018). Behandlungsfehler-Begutachtung der MDK-Gemeinschaft. Jahresstatistik 2017. Retrieved from https://www.mds-ev.de/fileadmin/dokumente/Pressemitteilungen/2018/2018_06_05/Jahresstatistik_BHF_begutachtung_2017.pdf

Menzel, N. N., & Gutierrez, A. P. (2010). Latino worker perceptions of construction risks. *American Journal of Industrial Medicine, 53*(2), 179–187.

Meurier, C. E., Vincent, C. A. & Parmar, D. G. (1997). Learning from errors in nursing practice. *Journal of Advanced Nursing, 26*, 111–119.

Minsky, M. (1997). Negative expertise. In P. J. Feltovich, K. M. Ford & R. R. Hoffman (Eds.), Expertise in Context: Human and Machine (pp. 515–521). Cambridge: AAAI/MIT Press.

Miyake, K., & Kosuke, Y. (1995). Self-conscious emotions, child rearing, and child psychopathology in Japanese culture. Retrieved 30 November 2019, from https://psycnet.apa.org/record/1995-97661-019

Mohamed, S. (2002). Safety Climate in Construction Site Environments. [Article]. *Journal of Construction Engineering & Management, 128*(5), 375.

Morgenroth, O., & Schaller, J. (2010). Misserfolg und Scheitern aus psychologischer Sicht. In H. Pechlaner, Misserfolg und Scheitern aus psychologischer Sicht. Berlin: Schmidt.

Mu, Y., Kitayama, S., Han, S., & Gelfand, M. (2015). How culture gets embrained: Cultural differences in event-related potentials of social norm violations. *Proceedings Of The National Academy Of Sciences, 112*(50), 15348–15353. doi: https://doi.org/10.1073/pnas.1509839112

Nassaji, H. (2018). Errors Versus Mistakes.Teaching Grammar. Retrieved 30 November 2019, from https://doi.org/10.1002/9781118784235.eelt0059

O'Connor, P.J., Sperl-Hillen, J.M.,Johnson, P.E., Rush, W.A., Biltz, G. (2005). Clinical inertia and outpatient Medical Errors, in: Agency for Healthcare Research and Quality (eds.) Advances in Patient Safety - From Research to lmplementation, *AHRQ Publication* No' 05OO2], Volume 2, Rockville, S. 293–308.

Oser, F. & Spychiger, M. (2005). Lernen ist schmerzhaft. Zur Theorie des negativen Wissens und zur Praxis der Fehlerkultur. Weinheim: Beltz.

Parviainen, J. & Eriksson, M. (2006). Negative knowledge, expertise and organisations. International Journal of Management Concepts and Philosophy, 2, 140–153.

Pitta, D., Fung, H., & Isberg, S. (1999). Ethical issues across cultures: managing the differing perspectives of China and the USA. *Journal Of Consumer Marketing*, *16*(3), 240–256. doi: https://doi.org/10.1108/07363769910271487

Ramanujam, R. (2003). The effects of Dsicontinous change on latent errors in organizations: the moderating role of risk. *Academy of Management Journal*, 46(5), pp. 608–617.

Rasmussen, J. (1982). Human errors. A taxonomy for describing human malfunction in industrial installations. *Journal Of Occupational Accidents*, *4*(2–4), 311–333. doi: https://doi.org/10.1016/0376-6349(82)90041-4

Rasmussen, J. (1997). Risk management in a dynamic society: A modeling problem. *Safety Science*, 27: 183–213.

Reason, J. T. (1990). Human error. Cambridge: Cambridge University Press.

Reason, J. T. (1995). Understanding adverse events: Human factors. *Quality in Health Care, 4*, 80–89.

Reason, J. T. (2005). Safety in the operating theatre—Part 2: human error and organisational failure. *Q. Saf. Health Care* 14:56–60

Roese, N.J.; Vohs KD. 2012. Hindsight bias. *Perspect. Psychol. Sci.* 7:411–26

Rogers, E., Griffin, E., Carnie, W., Melucci, J., & Weber, R. J. (2017). A Just Culture Approach to Managing Medication Errors. Hospital pharmacy, 52(4), 308–315.

Roxburgh, C. (2003). *Hidden flaws in strategy*. [online] McKinsey & Company. Available at: https://www.mckinsey.com/business-functions/strategy-and-corporate-finance/our-insights/hidden-flaws-in-strategy?cid=other-eml-cls-mkq-mck-oth-1704&hlkid=cd2223b723fd41e89836ed5506f376f2&hctky=9693957&hdpid=5c23fe09-d7a0-4dea-80da-8d6f0964846e [Accessed 21 Apr. 2019].

Russo, J. and Schoemaker, P. (1989). *Decision traps*. New York: Simon & Schuster.

Ruttenberg, M. L. (2004). *Spanish-Speaking Construction Workers Discuss Their Safety Needs and Experiences*. Silver Spring: The Center to Protect Workers' Rights.

Schrappe, M. (2015). Qualität 2030. Retrieved from https://www.gesundheitsstadt-belin.de/fileadmin/user_upload/Downloads/Schrappe_Qualitaet_2030_165x240_Download.pdf

Seligman, M.E.P., & Csikszentimihalyi, M. (2000). Positive psychology: an introduction. *American Psychologist*, 55, 5–14.

Senders, J. W. & Moray, N. P. (1991). Human error. Cause, prediction, and reduction. Hillsdale: Lawrence Erlbaum Associate.

Slovic, P. (1987) Perception of risk. Science 236 (4799):280–285

Spychiger, M., Kuster, R., & Oser, F. (2006). Dimensionen von Fehlerkultur in der Schule und deren Messung: Der Schülerfragebogen zur Fehlerkultur im Unterricht für Schülerinnen und Schüler der Mittel- und Oberstufe [Dimensions of mistake culture in school: The measurement "The students' inquiry on mistake culture in the classroom", for grades 4–9]. *Schweizerische Zeitschrift für Bildung- swissenschaften, 28,* 87–110.

van Dyck, C., Frese, M., Baer, M., & Sonnentag, S. (2005). Organizational Error Management Culture and Its Impact on Performance: A Two-Study Replication. *Journal Of Applied Psychology*, *90*(6), 1228–1240. doi: https://doi.org/10.1037/0021-9010.90.6.1228

van Rooij, A. (2015) Sisyphus in business: Success, failure and the different types of failure. Business History, 57(2), 203–223.

Vazquez, R. F., Stalnaker, C Keith. (2004). Latino Workers in the Construction Industry Overcoming the language barrier improves safety. *Professional Safety*.

Von Weizsäcker, C. & von Weizsäcker, E. U. (1984). Fehlerfreundlichkeit. In K. Kornwachs (Eds.), Offenheit – Zeitlichkeit – Komplexität. Zur Theorie der offenen Systeme (pp. 168–201). Frankfurt: Campus.

Von Weizsäcker, E. U. & von Weizsäcker, C. (1998). Information, evolution and "error-friendliness". Biological Cybernetics, 79, 501–506.

Williams Jr, Q., Ochsner, M., Marshall, E., Kimmel, L., & Martino, C. (2010). The impact of a peer-led participatory health and safety training program for Latino day laborers in construction. *Journal of Safety Research, 41*(3), 253–261.

Wong, P.T.P. (2011). Positive psychology 2.0: Towards a balanced interactive model of the good life. *Canadian Psychology*, 52(2), 69–81. Retrieved from http://www.drpaulwong.com/positive-psychology-2-0-towards-a-balanced-interactive-model-of-the-good-life/

Wursten, H. & Lanzer, F. (2013). The EU: The Third Great European Cultural Contribution to the World. White paper.

Zander, L., Kreutzmann, M., & Wolter, I. (2014). Constructive handling of mistakes in the classroom: The conjoint power of collaborative networks and self-efficacy beliefs. *Zeitschrift Für Erziehungswissenschaft, 17*(S5), 205–223. doi: https://doi.org/10.1007/s11618-014-0558-6

Zapf, D., Frese, M. & Brodbeck, F.C. (1999). Fehler und Fehlermanagement. In C.Graf Hoyos und D. Frey (Hrsg). Arbeits- und Organisationspsychologie. pp 398–411.Weinheim: Beltz, Psychologische Verlags Union.

Zimolong, B. (1990). Fehler und Zuverlässigkeit. In: C. Graf Hoyos & B. Zimolong (Eds.), Ingenieurpsychologie. Göttingen: Hogrefe. (pp. 303–345).

Zimolong, B. & Trimpop, R. (1993). Managing human reliability in advanced manufacturing Systems. In G. Salvendy & W. Karwowski (Eds.), Human factors in advanced manufacturing systems (Chapter 15). New York: John Wiley & Sons.

Elisabeth Vanderheiden is a pedagogue, theologian, intercultural mediator, managing director of the Catholic Adult Education Rhineland-Palatinate and the president of the Catholic Adult Education of Germany. Her publishing focuses on the context of basic education for adults, in particular on trainings for teachers and trainers in adult education, as well as vocational and civic education. She edited books on intercultural opening processes and intercultural mediation. Her latest publications focused on shame as resource as well as mistakes, errors and failure and their hidden potentials in the context of culture and positive psychology. She also works as an independent researcher. In a current project, she investigates life crises and their individual coping strategies from different cultural viewpoints. A topic that has also aroused her research interest is humour and how it appears in different cultural perspectives and from various scientific disciplines. She lives in Germany and Florida.

Claude-Hélène Mayer (Dr. habil., PhD, PhD) is a professor in Industrial and Organisational Psychology at the Department of Industrial Psychology and People Management at the University of Johannesburg; an adjunct professor at the European University Viadrina in Frankfurt (Oder), Germany; and a senior research associate at Rhodes University, Grahamstown, South Africa. She holds a PhD in Psychology (University of Pretoria, South Africa), a PhD in Management (Rhodes University, South Africa), a Doctorate (Georg-August University, Germany) in Political Sciences (sociocultural anthropology and intercultural didactics), and a Habilitation (European University Viadrina, Germany) in Psychology with focus on work, organisational and cultural psychology. She has published several monographs, text collections, accredited journal articles and special issues on transcultural mental health and well-being, sense of coherence, shame, transcultural conflict management and mediation, women in leadership in culturally diverse work contexts, constellation work, coaching and psychobiography.

Part I
Individual and Cultural Perspectives on Mistakes, Errors and Failure

Chapter 2
"Ever Tried. Ever Failed. No Matter. Try Again. Fail Again. Fail Better". Life Crisis and Failure as a Resource

Elisabeth Vanderheiden

Abstract Life crises can occur for many reasons, such as the death of a loved one, serious illness or disability, the end of a relationship, divorce, unemployment or even the impact of natural or political disasters. Life crises are often experienced by the affected individual as an expression of personal failure, wrong decision-making or consequences of personal misconduct. These can lead to serious mental health issues including anxiety and depression, to somatic complaints such as heart problems or to post-traumatic stress disorder, multiple addictions or suicide.

However, as demonstrated in several studies in the context of positive psychology, such an event also holds the potential to be a resource. The intention of this chapter is to take a closer look at the particular relationships between life crises and their perception as mistakes or failure. What can trigger such events? Which effects are detectable? How exactly can the perception of error or failure be described in this context? What factors could influence an appropriate assessment, and what differences have been examined in this regard in different cultural contexts? These are all questions addressed in the chapter, which also investigates which factors are relevant for a successful post-stressful event adjustment and post-traumatic growth.

Keywords Mistakes · Errors · Failure · Life crisis · Critical life events · Perception as mistakes or failures · Culture · Failure as resource

---

Samuel Beckett

E. Vanderheiden (✉)
Catholic Adult Education of Germany, Römerberg, Germany
e-mail: ev@keb-rheinland-pfalz.de

E. Vanderheiden, C.-H. Mayer (eds.), *Mistakes, Errors and Failures across Cultures*, https://doi.org/10.1007/978-3-030-35574-6_2

2.1 Introduction

Life crises caused by the death of a loved one, serious illness or disability, the breakup of a relationship, a divorce, the loss of workplace or unemployment—or the impact of natural or political disasters like war, genocide, flight from a country or structural suppression—are often experienced by the affected person as an expression of failure, the result of individual poor decision-making or the consequence of personal misconduct. These experiences can lead to serious mental health disturbances such as constant rumination, anxiety, pessimism or depression (f.e. Silver and Teasdale 2005; Velten et al. 2014), to somatic complaints such as heart problems (f. e. Lee et al. 2014) and tension headaches, to post-traumatic stress disorder, to multiple addictions (f. e. Li et al. 2016; Low et al. 2012; Marwaha 2019) and even to suicide (f. e. Jaiswal et al. 2016; Tang et al. 2015).

In the course of this chapter, the terms *critical life events* and *life crisis* are examined in more detail. Their effects on mental and physical health are discussed and linked to the first and second waves of positive psychology (Positive psychology 2019) and to research findings on failure from various cultural perspectives. In addition, the chapter draws on the interim results of an ongoing international study which the author is currently conducting on life crises, their effects, evaluations by those affected and the coping strategies they consider relevant. Four cases in differing cultural contexts are presented and discussed in terms of the actors' assessments of their own life crises, possible failure experiences and perspectives as well as coping strategies. Finally, future research needs are identified.

2.2 Definition of Life Crisis

It is astonishing how inconsistent the definitions of life crisis and critical life events are and how often they are used synonymously. In the following, the most important definitions are presented, and the terms are distinguished from each other in order to provide a clear conceptual basis for the following case studies. *The APA Dictionary of Psychology* (2019) defines a life crisis as:

> a period of distress and major adjustment associated with a significant life experience, such as divorce or death of a family member. In studies relating health to life crises, individuals experiencing recent major stress-producing experiences are more likely than others to show significant alterations in mental and physical health status.

Life crises can have serious and widespread consequences. From a medical perspective, Kossow (2019, 2) points out that a crisis means the loss of mental and physical equilibrium, which limits the repertoire of personal options for action. This can lead to the identity and independence of the personality being threatened by feelings of fear, panic, helplessness and joylessness.

Life crisis researchers Filipp and Aymanns (2018) name further potential consequences from a stress theory point of view (Table 2.1).

Table 2.1 Potential consequences of life crises according to Filipp and Aymanns (Source: Vanderheiden based on Filipp and Aymanns 2018)

Potential consequences of life crises
They are primarily perceived by those affected as a threat to their physical and psychological integrity (Filipp and Aymanns 2018, 38).
They are often accompanied by a loss of resources, such as a loss of income, an impairment of self-esteem and a reduction in performance (Filipp and Aymanns 2018, 42).
They describe specific characteristics of critical life events, which are usually the preliminary stage of a life crisis and can accumulate in it (Filipp and Aymanns 2018, 58).
They damage the person–environment fit.
Since they usually occur completely unexpectedly, the experiences associated with them are perceived intensively.
They have a high affective content.
In general they are beyond the influence of the person concerned.
There is a lack of predictability, and the surprise content of the event and its experience are typical.
They often lead to a shock of the self and world view and also influence the self-esteem reference.
They have a high target relevance because they cross plans and constrict or close areas of action.
They have a high degree of efficiency, even beyond the primary event context, which is also reflected in their high system reference.

Life crises can be triggered by emotionally intense shocks and transitions in one's life which place high demands on one's ability to adapt (Kossow 2019, 2). The linguistic roots of the word "crisis" are found in the Greek *krisis* (κρίσις) which means divorce, dispute or decision after a dispute (Filipp and Aymanns 2018, 27). Etymologically it is derived from the Greek *krīnein* (κρίνειν), which means to divorce, separate, select, decide, judge or accuse (DWDS, Digitales Wörterbuch der deutschen Sprache 2019; Filipp and Aymanns 2018, 27). This linguistic derivation refers to a decisive characteristic of life crises, namely, that they are frequently connected with a snowballing event, experienced as an interruption of the usual feeling and everyday experience of trust (see also Maddi 2006; Reif et al. 2018). A life crisis is often caused by one or more critical life events. From a psychological perspective, Filipp and Aymanns (2018, 27) confirm that many people experience critical life events as complete disruptions of their everyday lives, putting their beliefs to the test and questioning what they have previously considered safe, good and right up to that point. Critical life events can have a dramatic or traumatic character or can be assumed to be existential threats that exceed the resilience of the people affected, that convey the experience of helplessness and powerlessness or that lead to a profound loss of action orientation and thus—as a consequence—to a life crisis (Filipp and Aymanns 2018, 27).

The Finnish Association for Mental Health (2018) explains that life crises can be experienced as shock or trauma:

> caused by a sudden, unexpected and intense incident. The event produces a significant emotional shock that temporarily overwhelms the individual. Traumatic crisis is a reaction to an event which threatens the essential aspects of life.

People often perceive life crises as turning points in their lives. Overall, people confronted with critical life events tend to experience them as situations of unlimited duration in which they become more or less suddenly aware that the familiar relationship between them and their environment no longer exists and that this imbalance cannot be quickly corrected by a simple intervention. The confrontation with a critical life event can potentially lead to a life crisis if all attempts to reorganise the person's environmental adaptation seem to fail, and even the negative effects occurring cannot be regulated (Filipp and Aymanns 2018, 28).

2.3 Impact of Life Crisis on Health

Stressful life events can have a huge impact on health and well-being. This has been the subject of scientific investigations since the 1990s. For example, Geyer (1999, 2000) was able to demonstrate that stressful life-changing events can be relevant to the development and outbreak a great variety of diseases. Factors such as unemployment and experiences of loss can pose a potential risk. In most cases, it is not possible to establish direct causality for a single, specific disease; rather, critical life events and life crises are regarded as risk factors in the sense of triggering or maintaining conditions for diseases (Filipp and Aymanns 2018, 82; Dohrenwend 2006). In recent decades, researchers studying life events have devoted themselves to this topic—not only investigating the implications that critical life events or life crises have for health but also identifying special resilience or vulnerability factors in different parts of the population. The manifestations of life crises are quite varied. Headaches and chest pains, breathing difficulties, back pain, sleep disturbances as well as diseases of the gastrointestinal tract are named (Filipp and Aymanns 2018, 83–85). Some exemplary studies are presented later in the chapter.

In a large cardiological meta-analysis, Richardson and her colleagues (Richardson et al. 2012) were able to demonstrate that there is an obvious correlation between high perceived stress and a moderately increased risk of coronary heart disease. The studies considered took place between 1970 and 1990. Follow-up periods ranged from 36 to 255 months with an average of 165.9 months of follow-up (or 13.8 years). Two studies were carried out in Sweden and one study each in Scotland, Australia, Denmark and Japan. Two studies considered only men and in one study only women. It was revealed that work-related stress and conflicts in couple relationships in particular could have an influence on the occurrence of heart disease (Richardson et al. 2012).

Another international meta-study by Kivimäki et al. (2012) also confirmed the link between high work demands and heart attacks. In their meta-analysis, the authors examined the relationship between work expectations and heart attacks and were able to show a significant correlation. They had chosen 13 European cohort studies (1985–2006) of men and women without coronary heart disease as the basis for their studies, which were in progress at the time of the baseline assessment. They realised that there is a link between occupational stress and coronary heart disease in terms of gender, age group, socio-economic strata and region, depending on socio-economic status, lifestyle and conventional risk factors. The risk that can be attributed to the population for the workload was 3–4% (Kivimäki et al. 2012, 1).

Another recent study (Giannakopoulos et al. 2017) showed that psychological and physical stress caused by, for example, loss of a loved one, a quarrel with the neighbour, an infection or a fall, can be triggers for Takotsubo cardiomyopathy, the so-called broken heart syndrome. Why and exactly how Takotsubo cardiomyopathy develops has not yet been clarified. However, the study showed that it occurs most frequently in postmenopausal women and can be triggered both by emotionally stressful events and by acute physical complaints. The study was also able to confirm that for men, infections or accidents of any kind that put strain the body are often the triggers for Takotsubo cardiomyopathy.

Many studies have dealt with depression as a consequence of critical life events and life crises (f. e. Bulmash et al. 2009; Brown and Harris 1978). Already in the 1970s, Brown and Harris (1978) discovered in studies that severely threatening events such as loss experiences can trigger depressive episodes. Vulnerability factors in this context are a lack of social support and previous experiences of loss, because they have a certain influence on individual coping possibilities, perceived own competences and self-esteem (Brown and Harris 1978). Later studies confirm this finding. Risch et al. (2009) examined the interaction between the serotonin transporter gene and stressful life events in depression in a meta-analysis based on both published data and individual original data (14 studies). It was found that the number of stressful life events is significantly associated with depression. Similarly, comparable results were found in the gender-specific meta-analysis of data at the individual level (Parakh 2011). The results varied depending on socio-economic conditions. For example, Mezuk and his colleagues (2010) were able to show that socially disadvantaged groups in the USA have an increased risk of becoming depressed in the future. McLaughlin et al. (2009) found that individuals who were victims of sexualised violence in their childhood, or who were neglected and grew up with violence, have an increased risk of depression, post-traumatic stress disorder and anxiety disorder.

In addition to the gender factor, socio-economic conditions, individual traumatic experiences and age can also be potential risk factors in connection with life crises.

In another meta-study based on 25 studies, Kraaij et al. (2002) investigated the influence of life events on depression in older people. They defined life events after traumatic events from the *DSM IV* (*Diagnostic and Statistical Manual of Mental Disorders IV*).

These included violence, disease and natural disasters. Added to this were factors such as separation, loss experiences and financial problems. Although Kraaij and colleagues have found a link between risk factors and the occurrence of depression, these results can only be generalised to a limited extent because some factors have been studied more than others. However, they identified "daily hassles" such as delays, the search for the car keys or small arguments in the family as also being relevant for older people.

In this context, Kossow (2019, 2 translated by Vanderheiden) points to an important aspect, namely, the perception of the crisis and the experience of the available resources:

> The crisis is the climax of a challenging development. A crisis is normally experienced by those who are otherwise healthy, as part to life. However, it limits the flexibility of personal options for action and destabilises the respective psychosocial system. A considerable imbalance is experienced between the (subjectively perceived) significance of the problem and the coping options available to the individual concerned. This leads to a loss of personal balance and may lead to immense feelings of anxiety.

Kossow's (2019) comments suggest that not every life crisis leads to a serious illness or to people judging their lives as failed. There are a number of additional aspects that need to be taken into account; these are dealt with in the following section.

2.4 Impacts of Stressful or Critical Life Events on Perception as Mistakes or Failures

It is thanks to positive psychology in particular (Seligman and Csikszentimihalyi 2000; Mayer and Krause 2011, 2013; see also Oosthuizen's chapter in this book) that since then, the focus of psychological studies has shifted more strongly to what promotes and maintains people's health and well-being. The lens in relation to life crises is therefore less focused on the negative consequences than on the associated opportunities and potential for growth and change—even though the so-called second wave of positive psychology, initiated mainly by Wong (2011), pleads for a stronger understanding of the "dark" side of life experiences for the interpretation of our being and meaning and as an integral part of our well-being (Lomas and Ivtzan 2016; Mayer et al. 2019). In the sense of Antonovsky's (1979) concept of salutogenesis, which has shaped positive psychology to a large extent, the "sense of coherence" is of particular relevance. It consists of three components:

- Comprehensibility
- Meaningfulness
- Manageability.

Wong (1998) underlines the special importance of focusing on meaning, especially when it comes to understanding and coping with events with extremely negative connotations. Mayer et al. (2019, 8) point out that:

> This is the case since negatively experienced emotions can make an individual feel extremely vulnerable in their inherent condition of being alive … If this vulnerability can be embraced by the individual, then something new can be developed and created such as a new perspective, a value or worth and strength. This highlights that truly positive emotions are based on the transformation of negative emotions through comprehensibility, manageability and meaningfulness. Based on these SOC [sense of coherence] components, a positive self-worth and self-concept can be developed which is not based on denial and suppression of shame, guilt and anxiety, but on focusing on overcoming these negative emotions.

Table 2.2 Relevant factors for failure assessment according to Morgenroth and Schaller (Source: Vanderheiden based on Morgenroth and Schaller 2010)

1	Objectives are often not clearly and specifically defined (there are, for example, a variety of potentially relevant criteria for assessing the achievement of objectives, hierarchies of objectives may be affected, or a particular objective may be assessed as a failure, while, at the same time, another related objective is regarded as a success).
2	In most cases there are no objective standards for the evaluation of results of action which justify such a judgement (the same event is evaluated completely differently by two individuals; criterion contamination can also play a role, because the criterion applied for the evaluation is influenced by other factors which lie outside the individual's evaluation or influence).
3	Judgements are bound to a concrete judgement context (such as in the case of the actor–observer difference known from attribution research (Fincham and Hewston 2002)) and are also strongly dependent on the interpretation and on how the information available to the person concerned at this point is interpreted and contextualised: this is called framing (Tversky and Kahneman 1981; Wehling 2018).
4	Failure judgements are also placed in a cultural context and depend, among other things, on the social consequences of failure that are assumed or foreseeable in the respective cultural context (Backert 2004).
5	The negative assessment of a crisis could be linked to people's fear (see also Oosthuizen's in this book) that, because they are in a personal crisis and may be perceived as psychologically conspicuous, they might have to fear stigmatisation.
6	A potential negative assessment as failure is associated with the danger of losing hope and the danger that a new beginning cannot emerge from failure (Morgenroth and Schaller 2010, 9).

As emphasised by Morgenroth and Schaller (2010, 2), in developmental psychology and clinical psychology, the terms *crisis* and *critical life event* are preferred to speaking of failure. However, both are understood here in the broader sense that they not only concern situations in which a targeted goal is missed but also events such as a separation or the sudden death of one's partner. It is assumed that critical life events and life crises influence the development of an individual (Morgenroth and Schaller 2010, 2).

Morgenroth and Schaller (2010, 3) refer to important factors that determine whether one considers oneself as having failed (Table 2.2).

In the following section of this chapter, selected case studies are used to illustrate how people perceive life crises, how they are related to failures and which strategies have proven successful in coping with these crises.

2.5 Case Studies

The following case examples are taken from an ongoing study the author is currently conducting on the subject of life crises. In an online questionnaire (English or German) made available on the Internet (Vanderheiden 2019), the participants are asked to define what they understand by a life crisis, how they evaluate it and which coping strategies they have experienced as successful. At the time of writing, 27 persons have answered the questionnaire (16 persons in German, 9 in English). The invitation to complete the questionnaire is made via private and professional international networks and according to the snowball principle. Because the study is ongoing, no final research results are presented yet, but exemplary case studies are featured.

The age range is from 11 to 81 years, with 18 female and 7 male participants. The participants come from or live in Germany, South Africa, Iran, Vietnam, India, Mexico, Lebanon, Turkey, Afghanistan, Australia, the USA and Canada.

Fifteen questions on the questionnaire relate to biographical data. The remaining 23 questions ask what the persons concerned understand as a life crisis, what theirs consisted of, which metaphor they associated it with, which factors have they experienced as conducive or hindering to overcoming it, what consequences this crisis has had for them, which aspects were relevant for them in coping with it (e.g. faith, love, humour, educational offers, digital resources) and any further comments they wished to add. A qualitative content analysis for inductive categorisation was chosen as the approach (Kuiper 2012). Mayring (2016, 37) explains the core idea of qualitative thinking:

> Here, qualitative thinking contrasts with the concept of rules …; it assumes that people do not function quasi automatically according to laws, but that at most[,] regularities in their thinking, feeling and acting can be determined. Such regularities are not purely automatic processes, but are also caused by man himself: Deviations are thereby permitted ("no rule without exception"). Rules are always also "bound" to situational, socio-historical contexts.

With 27 questionnaire responses received to date, only a relatively narrow database is currently available, so generalisability or representativeness cannot be assured. However, according to Mayring (2010, 23, 2001), this survey could serve as a pilot study for further research. Mayring (2010) notes that qualitative projects usually adapt the instruments (e.g. redesign interview guidelines) to suit the specific subject and the related question. This is normally done in a pilot study. Wherever new instruments have been developed, they should at least be tested on a small sample. This was realised for the present study in February 2019.

2.5.1 Case Study 1: Divorce and Job Loss as Catalyst for a Life Crisis

> Tom is 55, a white US-American IT specialist who holds an MBA degree. He is homosexual and has spent 24 years in a relationship with a man from Sweden; for some years they were also married. After 23 years of living in Sweden, Tom's homesickness became overwhelming, and, in consultation with his spouse, he accepted a job offer in his home country from the international company he worked for. A short time later, his spouse revealed to him that he had a relationship with someone else and wanted the separation. Tom's proactive attempts to save the marriage failed because his partner lacked the interest to encourage continuation. This triggered a severe life crisis for Tom, which was exacerbated by the fact that his job was lost in a worldwide wave of job cuts and he became unemployed. He himself described his state with the following metaphor: "I fall and fall and fall and fall and fall

> ever deeper". Significant strategies for him in this crisis were conversations and fellowship with friends and family but above all his faith. It was also important to him to keep his house in order, to rebuild and beautify it and to pay attention to his figure and appearance, not to let himself go. He began a long-distance learning course for further professional qualifications and dealt intensively with questions of personality development. Online dating platforms are an important strategy for him. Even though he has not yet found a new permanent partner, as a very attractive man, he receives much positive feedback. He chooses a very pragmatic approach, which he considers typically American, to the management of this crisis, "to move forward", "to take one step after the other", "not to make too big plans but to formulate goals, to check them, to adjust and to redefine them if necessary". Above all, in this context, he wants to "look with gratitude at what one has, not to look at what is no longer available". It is also important to him to keep as many options open as possible. Meanwhile, he is once again successful in his professional life, more successful than ever. He perceives the "failure" of the marriage as failure to the extent that he wonders whether he should have noticed possible signs of failure earlier. He wonders if he could have done more, also because he still remembers his partner as an ideal partner and misses him. But he does not regard his life as failed simply because the relationship has failed; the assessment refers to marriage as a failed singular event. In retrospect, Tom evaluates this life crisis—while perceiving the ambivalence—not as a failure experience but as a positive opportunity for personal growth and development: "I believe life crises are important for the development of the self and others. They weigh heavily if dependent others such as children are involved and one carries the responsibility for them as well through the crisis. For me, feelings associated with this life crisis are fear, frustration, sadness, depression, but also developing happiness and relief when I found a way out of the life crisis."

Tom regards his marriage as an experience of failure, but does not interpret his whole life as failed. Rather, in response to an unfortunate "upheaval or turning point" (Filipp and Aymanns 2018, 43) in his life, the following coping strategies have essentially been developed and realised. These are faith, pragmatic handling of pending problems, a close relationship with old friends and family, ensuring control and experience of self-efficacy (Bandura 2019) in relation to his own living environment and body, constructive use of digital resources (online dating platforms, digitally based postgraduate studies) and professional training activities/education (Krause 2018).

Research has also dealt intensively with these phenomena: Divorces are experienced by many affected people as very traumatic. Often, however, the people concerned succeed in developing coping strategies and, in retrospect, no longer see this event as a failure but as an opportunity for growth and further development. Whether this succeeds depends on a variety of factors and their interdependencies. In a study, Graff-Reed (2004) evaluated 140 participants' questionnaires that collected demographic variables as well as assessed stress, perceived social support, coping styles, divorce adjustment and post-traumatic psychological growth. Gender, educational attainment, emotional stability, consistency with the custody decision and perceived social support proved to be relevant factors in this study. The way stress was assessed and the coping style available to the person also had an impact on the judgement, as did the number of years since divorce and divorce-related counselling services were provided, which mitigated the impact of the estimated stress on divorce adjustment. A new relationship also mitigated the effect of assessed stress on post-traumatic growth. Women reported a higher level of perceived social support than men and also a higher level of post-traumatic growth after divorce. These findings were confirmed by a meta-analysis in 2007. Here, Kramrei et al. (2007) studied the role of social relationships in the adaptation of adults after divorce. Twenty-one studies were analysed and compared in relation to "specific relationships" (personal contact with a particular person, such as a friend) and "network relationships" (as part of a group, such as a support group or church fellowship). The study examined to what extent positive adaptations to mismatches and other components of postdivorce adaptation (well-being, effects, psychopathology and physiological symptoms) can be identified. The results showed that social relationships during the postdivorce period are associated with a higher degree of positive adjustment and a lower degree of mismatch. Network relationships are particularly important for promoting positive adaptation, while specific relationships are particularly important for buffering against misadaptation.

In the meantime, a number of empirical studies (see Mayer 2011, 2012; Plante 2012) have shown that there is a connection between well-being and faith or spirituality. Empirical research has shown that faith has many physical and psychological benefits. This may be related to a more pronounced sense of coherence (Mayer 2011, 2012; Mayer et al. 2019). This topic is dealt with in more detail in the following case.

2.5.2 Case Study 2: Health Restrictions as a Trigger for a Life Crisis

Clara is 52 years old, a Dutch citizen who lives in Germany, married to a German. She worked as a salesgirl but had to quit when her husband changed jobs. Fifteen years ago, they moved from the big city of Berlin to a small town in a region with a very weak infrastructure. She first worked in a supermarket. But she soon had to give up this job owing to her health: working at the cashier with coins caused allergies; she could not stand for long because of her extreme obesity, and could not bend down to fill shelves. Her lung functions are severely restricted by chronic asthma but also by the fact that she has been smoking since she was 11 years old. Meanwhile she needs oxygen on a permanent basis. At the age of 45, she declared herself no longer able to work. This led to massive financial losses, as she was too young to receive a state pension, and she decided not to go through any procedures to receive state compensation, such as a disability pension. Retraining is out of the question for her; she thinks she is too old to learn anything new and says, "my life is over anyway". She has barely left the house since then, has put on weight and needs a walker. In addition, she experiences incontinence and other medical difficulties and has become a "professional patient". All her thoughts revolve around this topic, but she does not believe her state of health can be improved. In retrospect, she considers her life to have largely failed. "When you're so seriously ill, that's a very serious limitation. Often there were times when I didn't want to live at all. But sometimes it's better again. But there were also times when I tried to kill myself, especially when I was young. There was an abortion, it was very difficult for me. For a very long time."

She has dyslexia, which she considers an essential element of this failure. In her youth, she also chose to follow the wrong role models; in so doing, she believes that she blocked many possibilities for herself. Two critical life events are still significant. In the course of her first partnership, she was exposed to massive violence but knew how to hide it. Even in the close family circle, nothing was known about it as long as the relationship lasted. Second, in the subsequent relationship, she had an abortion at the age of 18. For her as a believing Catholic, this created a great moral dilemma. Several suicide attempts followed. Her strategy for coping with this life crises is now to withdraw almost exclusively into her private life and concentrate on her relationship with her husband. With the exception of very sporadic short visits every year or two, there is only telephone contact with her family and a single friend whom she visits once every few months. Even though she has often had to struggle with her past and her circumstances, she has now come to terms with them and accepts the status quo. This leads to the fact that, because she feels safe and loved in her relationship with her husband, she nevertheless comes to a positive assessment of her life. According to that, Clara formulates the final evaluation of these life crises more openly: "I don't know; I'm just glad I'm still alive and have my husband."

Clara has already been confronted with several serious life crises and evaluates her life in a certain way as having failed; however, she does not finally fall into complete resignation and hopelessness, in spite of some suicide attempts in earlier years. Her "reinforcement strategies" are essentially to focus on the couple relationship, withdraw into private life and overcome unattainable goals and false hopes by discarding them.

Serious crises caused by massive illnesses have been well investigated, especially at the individual level (Primono et al.1990; Rowland 1990; Badr and Acitelli 2005; Filipp and Aymanns 2018, 250). Researchers have been able to demonstrate, for example, the positive effects of a supportive partner for an individual coping with illness, through practical support and mutual affection. However, there are significantly fewer studies dealing with the effects of chronic illness on the couple relationship (see Karrasch and Reichert 2011; Berg and Upchurch 2007).

Kossow (2019, 2), among others, makes it very clear that (severely) ill people can have a significantly different response to a critical life experience compared to other people; he refers to factors such as context, gender and educational differences. Whether this applies to the case study cannot be determined conclusively and unambiguously, but Clara's statements show that she has a poor estimate of her own self-efficacy. According to Morgenthaler and Schaller (2010, 8), personal expectation of self-efficacy is a very relevant characteristic that has a major influence on the demands placed on one's own performance, in terms of being confident of achieving a goal through one's own actions. This is very important in connection with the individual response to failure; research results (e.g. Schwarzer and Schulz 2003; Schwarzer 1993) show that self-motivated persons set themselves ambitious goals, make more intensive efforts to achieve goals and show more stamina in pursuing goals.

Morgenthaler and Schaller (2010, 8) point to another consideration which seems relevant in this case study, namely, that an important aspect of the process of failure can be the maturing of an insight that a desired goal can no longer be achieved. Especially in the case of sick persons, after months or even years, this can lead them to recognise the limits of their own problem-solving attempts and allow them to enlist professional help. This is clearly so with Clara, since she has the perception that she has little to no influence on her overall health conditions, which she accepts as a given. She compensates for the resulting limitation of her range of movement and social life by concentrating on an extraordinarily positive evaluation of her partnership. At the same time, she does not quarrel with her fate and adapts her goals and visions of the future to the supposedly or actually unchangeable circumstances.

2.5.3 Case Study 3: Migration and Perceived Educational Deficits as Factors Triggering a Life Crisis

Lin is 45 years old, was born in Vietnam and lives as a German citizen in Germany today. At the age of 18, she left her homeland alone after graduating from high school and first went to Czechoslovakia, where she worked in various factories. There she met her husband, who also comes from Vietnam. Together they managed to migrate to West Germany. In the meantime they have two adult children who are studying and performing well. Lin earned her living in West Germany as a cleaning woman, a job she deeply rejected: "I find my work as a cleaner humiliating and shameful. I have completely different talents, but here in Germany I can't realise them in a profession without training. But you have to hold out and stay strong for the children." Since her school degree was not recognised in Germany and she had no further formal vocational training, this situation repeatedly triggers crises for her because it stands in stark contradiction to her self-image and her life goals, in which education plays a very important role. Without an academic degree in accordance with her self-image—which would have been possible if the political circumstances in her home country had been different and she had not been forced to migrate—she considers this a failure.

She uses an important strategy in dealing with these crises. She has been involved in the Vietnamese community for many years and has set up a cultural centre for children and young people of Vietnamese origin, where Vietnamese language, writing and culture are taught. "I—and my husband—have tried very hard to build something here. I have visited many German courses, I have attended sewing classes. I have set up courses here for the Vietnamese community. I teach children and young people in Vietnamese language and writing, but also in dance, music and culture. I even develop the teaching materials and the curriculum myself and we have made the most of this crisis. My children are now studying or getting a good education. We even bought a house." Her activities in the Vietnamese community are supported ideologically, politically and financially by German local politicians, and she has a very good reputation far beyond the Vietnamese community. She loves to sing, has a beautiful voice and also performs in public, e.g. at Vietnamese New Year celebrations, and regularly posts vocal contributions from herself on her own Facebook, and she also posts to a Vietnamese Facebook page.

She says that Buddhism, to which she and her family originally belonged, left too many questions open. Therefore, they converted to the Catholic faith as a family 15 years ago and are very active in the Vietnamese Catholic community in Germany. She has been able to give up her unloved cleaning job almost completely because she has learned, in many courses, how to sew, and in the meantime she owns a small tailoring business. Asked about her assessment of the life crisis, she replies: "I am a thoughtful person. I am very interested in understanding things and making connections. It is important to me to also incorporate perspectives that are shaped by my Vietnamese culture. Thinking about this crisis is very important. Those are the roots, yesterday shapes our now and our tomorrow. We must pause, again and again, and think about it and draw conclusions."

Even though Lin could not fulfil her major life dream of completing vocational training or studies and being able to work in a qualified profession, and even though she regards this as a failure experience, she has developed several coping strategies which, retrospectively and as a whole, make what she has experienced and suffered seem meaningful and worthwhile. Her sacrifices and efforts give meaning to the failure and to the resulting living conditions. She emphasises that positive consequences grow from this situation. A better future for her children is her highest life goal, to which she subordinates personal needs for self-realisation. As a partial consequence of her voluntary engagement in the Vietnamese community, not only in her place of residence but also far beyond, she experiences herself as a talented woman with creative power, influence and respected status. Her main strategies are construction of meaning from this presumed failure, construction of positive consequences (better future for her children), faith, experience of self-efficacy and respect in a culturally significant community, creativity in the form of artistic activity (public singing performances in her mother tongue) and trust in education.

Under the particular circumstances for survivors of National Socialist concentration camps and the massive crisis experiences associated with them, Viktor Frankl has described the special significance of the search for or construction of meaning in connection with crises, when he states:

> There is no situation in life that is really meaningless. This is due to the fact that the seemingly negative sides of human existence, especially the tragic triad of suffering, guilt and death, can be combined, even in something positive, into one achievement if they are met only with the right attitude. (Frankl cited in Lukas 2009, 23, translated by Vanderheiden)

and

> The will to create meaning is man's primary motivational force. (Frankl cited in Biller and de Lourdes Stiegeler 2008, 192, translated by Vanderheiden)

The psychologist and meaning researcher Schnell (2016) has been able to demonstrate in various studies the major significance of the determining meaning in life and describes it as an important aspect of self-transcendence, self-realisation, sense of life structure as well as being part of the feeling of togetherness and well-being. All four categories (Schnell 2016, 18) can be easily identified in Lin's case. In self-transcendence, according to Schnell (2016), spirituality, explicit religiousness (see also Ellison et al. 2011; Good et al. 2014), self-awareness, social commitment and generativity are closely connected. This can be observed in Lin's situation, in the way she intensively deals with questions of her own religiousness, but she also connects them with questions of her cultural identity as a person with Vietnamese background and roots who now lives in Germany and has found her home there. At the same time, she combines this with commitment and dedication to the Vietnamese language and culture, which she passes on to Vietnamese children and young people through language and writing classes. She also teaches Vietnamese dance and music and organises the annual Vietnamese New Year festival with hundreds of visitors, attended by German politicians. In connection with the life sense category of self-realisation, Schnell (2016) refers to challenges, individualism, achievement, knowledge or creativity as relevant dimensions. Lin can live and experience those dimensions in these contexts. The (3) sense of a life structure is connected with tradition, practicality or morality. Here, too, Lin's honorary and artistic commitment offers the opportunity to practise this third dimension, for instance, by regularly collecting donations for charity projects in Vietnam at events organised by the Vietnamese community. The (4) sense of togetherness and well-being, involving community, fun, love, caring and awareness, is also reflected in Lin's life. Lin's commitment to and support for the Vietnamese community is very important; she is a key person in this community. She is requested nationally for event facilitation and singing performances, is appreciated and enjoyed and is a highly accepted part of the community and a relevant institution there.

From all of these experiences in her "other life", she is able to reframe her assumed failure, her failure to study, her work as a cleaning woman and, from her perspective, her inappropriate social status in German society—and give it a meaning. Other aspects that are more frequently encountered in connection with the construction of meaning are *benefit-finding* or *positive reappraisal* and *reframing* (Filipp and Aymanns 2018, 201) in the sense that the individuals can subsequently gain something positive from the crises through their own interpretation or can retrospectively see it with completely different eyes.

For Lin, music has a special meaning, particularly as a crisis management strategy and compensation tool. This is examined in more detail below. Lin not only sings in a private context but is also invited to make public appearances. Through her Facebook account, she can share these experiences with her community, her family in Vietnam and her German friends.

For migrant women, the special significance of listening to and making music from their country of origin has been investigated in a recent study among Korean women in Germany. Lee (2017) examined whether identification with the traditional music of their country of origin stabilises for these women in the host country and whether taking part in home country-orientated music groups can have positive effects on the lives of migrant women in a foreign country. In general, this raises the question of what influence home music can exert on identity formation and integration. In her study, Lee (2017) paid particular attention to women in stress and crisis situations, as the women interviewed were not only migrants but also mothers of children with disabilities ($n = 6$). She found that singing songs in one's native language can brighten one's mood, give strength, reduce stress and evoke beautiful memories of childhood (Lee 2017, 241). Such music is experienced by those affected, as a stabilisation of their identity and as a strengthening of their inner balance. Most respondents stated that their mental resilience was strengthened by listening to traditional music from their home country, according to their specific biographical experiences during their migration processes (Lee 2017, 243). This created comfort, security, encouragement and the feeling of connectedness and strengthened an inner force (Lee 2017, 251). The interviewees explicitly describe making music by themselves and listening to music as a resource that they use to cope with certain situations and crises in life (Lee 2017, 252).

2.5.4 *Case Study 4: Flight, Migration and Loss of Loved Ones as Causative Factors for a Life Crisis*

Amir is 19 years old. At the age of 16, he set off with his parents from Afghanistan to Germany. In Turkey he lost his parents and then he went alone to Germany, all the way on foot. He learned German, finished secondary school and started a vocational training in media design and film-making. He describes the loss of his parents on the flight to Germany as a great life crisis. In Turkey, the flight almost failed and he almost gave up. But he was motivated by the fact that his father always said "never give up". He says he feels obliged to succeed; it gives him strength and so everything makes sense. "My father has always encouraged me never to give up. I want him to be proud of me. I try to do the right thing and behave well." He is also interested in digital resources because they enable him to stay in touch with friends and relatives, even in Afghanistan. For example, he owns a YouTube channel and actively uses Messenger services to stay in touch. As part of his training, he made a short film about his flight experiences and his new life in Germany which was also broadcast on local television and for which he was awarded a prize. Even though he experienced his life crisis as very stressful and challenging, he does not evaluate himself as a failure but as positive in the end. "It was very difficult and hard, but positive. I now have a new home and am building a new life. That's what my parents wanted for me."

Amir experienced leaving home and especially the loss of his parents as a severe life crisis. Because he lost his parents in this way, it is very important to him to exclude failure from every situation, because to fail would be to take away the meaning of the losses. This is why he can never and will never give up. Amir's main strategies are construction of meaning from this presumed failure, construction of positive consequences (better life in Germany), constructive use of digital resources (Messenger services, YouTube channel, digital learning resources), professional training activities, creativity in the form of artistic activity (film production) and concentration on further education (Kobe 1999).

At present, massive refugee and migration movements are taking place worldwide. In 2014 alone, 60 million people around the world were fleeing their countries (Brown et al. 2017). These major flight and migration movements in the face of man-made or natural disasters often lead to enormous crisis experiences, which also attract increasing attention in research, particularly with regard to the consequences for the children and young people affected. In addition to the study by Brown et al., Lindert and her colleagues (Lindert et al. 2009) have also conducted a meta-study, stating that anxiety, depression and post-traumatic stress disorder are the most important psychopathological symptoms in refugees.

The psychologist Jan Ilhan Kizilhan (2013) stresses the special importance of the narrative approach of biographical and identity work, especially when working with this target group. He understands narration as a culture-sensitive coping strategy in the sense of salutogenesis (Antonovsky 1987), which must be understood as culturally bound and contributing to an integrated identity (see also McAndrew et al. 1998; Patton 2019; Schock et al. 2016; Tweed et al. 2004; Young et al. 2018). Ilhan Kizilhan (2013, 126) makes the following observations:

The basis of this approach is the power of narration and healing given by culture and socialisation, especially in collective cultures, which today have a stronger reliance on it in their

> everyday lives than, for example, Western cultures. Due to the differences in socialisation, culture and handling of memories, the aspect of memory performance and stress processing must also be taken into account in the narration of people from other cultures. In oriental-patriarchal societies, for example, memories are not individually linked to a specific event, but are always reminiscent of connections with the collective, i.e. with ancestors, family, tribal structures, etc. Thus, understanding, manageability and the meaningfulness of individual events are seen in connection with collective events and a sense of coherence is developed from both dimensions (individual and collective).

This can be found in Amir's case, for whom it was important to share his narrative and choose a film as medium, thus combining his need to give meaning to what he experienced and share this with others using the new professional and creative skills he is currently acquiring through his vocational training as a media designer and film-maker.

Although Amir plans his future in Germany, he finds it important not to lose the connections to his country of origin. He thus constructs a kind of "patchwork identity" (Mayer 2007, 5). Mayer points out that this can be a central resource, especially for people with a flight or migration history:

> People with an awareness of their multiple identities and their multiple aspects of identity can open a new and diverse access to social strata and people of different cultural backgrounds. (Mayer 2007, 6)

Such extensions of cultural identities can be used not only to construct affiliations to intercultural identities and to create feelings of belonging (Mayer 2007, 7) but also to establish coherence (Mayer 2007, 8) and to actively increase the number of resources available (Mayer 2007, 12).

2.6 Discussion

How people can cope with these life crises depends on many factors. Kossow (2019, 3) points out that the cultural, historical, social and individual contexts in which the life crisis occurs play a role but that gender-specific differences can also be demonstrated, as well as connections to the educational level and state of health of the person concerned. The table below provides an overview of the cases presented in this chapter, indicating the diversity of views, judgements of life crises and failure experiences and the diversity of coping strategies (Table 2.3).

What all cases have in common is that, in retrospect, the affected person ultimately assesses the failure experience in connection with the life crisis presented as more positive overall, albeit in different ways. This is shown in the table below (Table 2.4).

In positive and developmental psychology research, numerous studies confirm that many, though not all, people can succeed in seeing failure experiences as opportunities for reorientation, personal growth and further development. The various factors which have an influence here have been discussed intensively in this chapter.

Table 2.3 Overview of cases, actual or assumed failure experiences and coping strategies (Source: Vanderheiden 2019)

Case	Life crises/assumed failures	Strategies
Tom	Divorce	Faith
		Pragmatic handling of pending problems
		Close relationship with old friends and family
		Ensuring control and experience of self-efficacy in relation to own living environment and body
		Constructive use of digital resources (online dating platforms, digitally based postgraduate studies)
		Professional training activities/education
Clara	Abortion	Focus on the couple relationship
	Suicide attempts	Withdrawal into private life
	Dissatisfaction with own biography	Discarding unattainable goals and false hopes
	Multiple diseases	
Lin	No formal educational qualifications or corresponding professional position	Construction of meaning in this presumed failure
		Construction of positive consequences (better future for her children)
		Faith
		Experience of self-efficacy and respect in a culturally significant community
		Creativity in the form of artistic activity (singing for self and others in her mother tongue)
		Education
Amir	Flight from Afghanistan to Germany and loss of parents in this way	Construction of meaning in this presumed failure
		Construction of positive consequences (better life in Germany)
		Constructive use of digital resources (Messenger services, YouTube channel, digital learning resources)
		Professional training activities
		Creativity in the form of artistic activity (film production)
		Education

2.7 Conclusion

Whether people perceive a life crisis as a failure or as the result of wrong decisions depends crucially on their individual assessment of the events. Of course, resources also play a role, but the question of whether people can perceive resources, make use of them or expand their corresponding repertoire seems to be decisively influenced by their attitude to the events. The selected cases described here have confirmed results of other studies, particularly in the field of positive psychology. For example, the perception and evaluation of a life crisis depends decisively on whether

Table 2.4 Retrospective evaluation of the failure experience in relation to the individual cases (Source: Vanderheiden 2019)

As necessary in the sense of a better future for the descendants	Lin
As a chance for a new life in security and freedom	Lin, Amir
As an occasion for gratitude for the past	Tom, Lin, Amir, Clara
As an opportunity to focus on the couple relationship and gratitude for the remaining resources	Clara
As a chance for a new career start	Tom, Amir
As an opportunity to live one's own cultural values and share them with others	Lin, Amir
As a chance to lead a meaningful life	Tom, Lin, Amir
As a new chance to look at the positive in one's past and present life	Tom, Lin, Amir
As having brought about an important strengthening in faith	Tom, Lin

it is regarded as manageable or understandable and whether those affected are capable of giving meaning to what has been happening.

The cases presented in this chapter also demonstrate that cultural backgrounds can play a specific role in the emergence of life crises, for example, in Amir's case, whose crisis was triggered by the living conditions, flight and loss of parents. Culture (Chang and Baard 2012; Dinges and Joos 1988) can also influence the coping strategies used, as indicated by Tom's case and his reference to "American pragmatism".

2.8 Need for Future Research

From the abovementioned descriptions, it can be seen that many good studies on critical life events and their coping strategies are already available. However, far fewer are to be found specifically dealing with life crises. There is still much research to be done in this field, especially with regard to whether and to what extent life crises are understood and treated by those affected as failure experiences, or in connection with wrong decisions or misconduct.

Particular attention should be paid to cultural contexts, considering that they are only taken into account in a few studies, although they can have far-reaching consequences for the coexistence of people, for their interactions and also for therapy and counselling. In view of the worldwide migration movements—for example, in connection with globalisation, human or natural disasters—such crises are potentially increasing and must therefore be reflected in corresponding culturally sensitive research projects.

An exciting future research task could be to address the question of faith in coping with life crises from a multireligious perspective. The role played by emotions such as pride, guilt, shame, humility and love in triggering and overcoming life crises has not yet been sufficiently explored, especially from various cultural perspectives.

Only a few studies have paid attention to the role education offers in handling and overcoming life crises, especially not under diversity aspects. Particular attention could also be given to the role of digital services in managing such crises from the point of view of stakeholders. Since this is a relatively new phenomenon that is developing rapidly, there are hardly any research results on the topic.

Acknowledgement I would like to express my gratitude to my colleague and friend Claude-Hélène Mayer. Her presence, her patience and her professional advice have inspired me throughout the process of editing this book and writing this chapter.

References

Antonovsky, A. (1979). Health, stress and coping. San Francisco: Jossey-Bass.

Antonovsky, A. (1987). Unraveling the mystery of health. How people manage stress and stay well. San Francisco: Jossey-Bass.

APA Dictionary of Psychology. (2019). Retrieved from https://dictionary.apa.org/life-crisis

Backert, W. (2004), Kulturen des Scheiterns. Gesellschaftliche Bewertungsprozesse im internationalen Vergleich, in: M. Junge und G. Lechner (Hrsg.), Scheitern. Aspekte eines sozialen Phänomens, S. 63–77. Wiesbaden: VS Verlag für Sozialwissenschaften

Badr, H., & Acitelli, L. (2005). Dyadic Adjustment in Chronic Illness: Does Relationship Talk Matter?. Journal Of Family Psychology, 19(3), 465–469. doi: https://doi.org/10.1037/0893-3200.19.3.465

Bandura, A. (2019). Self-efficacy defined. Retrieved from https://www.uky.edu/~eushe2/Bandura/BanEncy.html

Berg, C., & Upchurch, R. (2007). A developmental-contextual model of couples coping with chronic illness across the adult life span. *Psychological Bulletin, 133*(6), 920–954. doi: https://doi.org/10.1037/0033-2909.133.6.920

Biller, K., & de Lourdes Stiegeler, M. (2008). *Wörterbuch der Logotherapie und Existenzanalyse von Viktor E. Frankl. Sachbegriffe, Metaphern, Fremdwörter.*. Wien: Böhlau.

Brown GW, Harris T (1978) Social origins of depression: a study of psychiatric disorders in women. Tavistock, London

Brown, R., Witt, A., Fegert, J., Keller, F., Rassenhofer, M., & Plener, P. (2017). Psychosocial interventions for children and adolescents after man-made and natural disasters: a meta-analysis and systematic review. *Psychological Medicine, 47*(11), 1893–1905. doi: 10.1017/s0033291717000496

Bulmash, E., Harkness, K., Stewart, J., & Bagby, R. (2009). Personality, stressful life events, and treatment response in major depression. Journal Of Consulting And Clinical Psychology, 77(6), 1067–1077. doi: https://doi.org/10.1037/a0017149

Chang, C., & Baard, S. (2012). Stresserleben bei der Arbeit im Kulturvergleich. Handbuch Stress Und Kultur, 293–313. doi: https://doi.org/10.1007/978-3-531-93449-5_18

Dinges, N., & Joos, S. (1988). Stress, Coping and Health: Models of Interaction for Indian and Native Populations. American Indian And Alaska Native Mental Health Research, 8–64. doi: https://doi.org/10.5820/aian.mono01.1988.8

Dohrenwend, B. (2006). Inventorying stressful life events as risk factors for psychopathology: Toward resolution of the problem of intracategory variability. Psychological Bulletin, 132(3), 477–495. doi: https://doi.org/10.1037/0033-2909.132.3.477

DWDS – Digitales Wörterbuch der deutschen Sprache. (2019). Retrieved from https://www.dwds.de/wb/Krise
Ellison, C., Bradshaw, M., Kuyel, N., & Marcum, J. (2011). Attachment to God, Stressful Life Events, and Changes in Psychological Distress. Review Of Religious Research, 53(4), 493–511. doi: https://doi.org/10.1007/s13644-011-0023-4
Filipp, S., & Aymanns, P. (2018). Kritische Lebensereignisse Und Lebenskrisen (2nd ed.). Stuttgart: Kohlhammer Verlag.
Fincham, F. & Hewstone, M. (2002). Attributionstheorie und -forschung – Von den Grundlagen zur Anwendung. W. Stroebe, K. Jonas & M. Hewstone (eds), Sozialpsychologie,. Eine Einführung. p. 215–263. Berlin, Heidelberg: Springer
Geyer, S. (1999). Macht Unglück krank? Weinheim; München: Juventa Verlag.
Geyer, S. (2000). The role of social and psychosocial factors in the development and course of cancer. Wiener Klinische Wochenschrift, 112, 986–944.
Giannakopoulos, K., El-Battrawy, I., Schramm, K., Ansari, U., Hoffmann, U., Borggrefe, M., & Akin, I. (2017). Comparison and Outcome Analysis of Patients with Takotsubo Cardiomyopathy Triggered by Emotional Stress or Physical Stress. *Frontiers In Psychology, 8*. doi: https://doi.org/10.3389/fpsyg.2017.00527
Good, M., Inzlicht, M., & Larson, M. (2014). God will forgive: reflecting on God's love decreases neurophysiological responses to errors. Social Cognitive And Affective Neuroscience, 10(3), 357–363. doi: https://doi.org/10.1093/scan/nsu096
Graff-Reed, R. (2004). Positive effects of stressful life events. Oxford, Ohio: Miami University.
Ilhan Kizilhan, J. (2013). Salutogene Narration zur Biographie- und Identitätsarbeit in der Beratung und Psychotherapie bei Menschen mit Migrationshintergrund. *Praxis Klinische Verhaltensmedizin Und Rehabilitation*, (92), 120–130.
Jaiswal, S., Faye, A., Gore, S., Shah, H., & Kamath, R. (2016). Stressful life events, hopelessness, and suicidal intent in patients admitted with attempted suicide in a tertiary care general hospital. Journal Of Postgraduate Medicine, 62(2), 102. doi: https://doi.org/10.4103/0022-3859.180556
Karrasch, R.-M., & Reichert, M. (2011). Auswirkungen der Pflege eines Partners auf Partnerschaft und Sexualität. *Zeitschrift für Familienforschung*, *23*(1), 102–116. https://nbn-resolving.org/urn:nbn:de:0168-ssoar-376478
Kivimäki, M., Nyberg, S., Batty, G., Fransson, E., Heikkilä, K., & Alfredsson, L. et al. (2012). Job strain as a risk factor for coronary heart disease: a collaborative meta-analysis of individual participant data. *The Lancet*, *380*(9852), 1491–1497. doi: https://doi.org/10.1016/s0140-6736(12)60994-5
Kobe, L. (1999). Stress, stress utilization, and creativity. Masterthesis. Omaha: University o f Nebraska.
Kossow, K. (2019). Der kranke Mensch: Überfordert in Krisensituationen Klaus-Dieter Kossow - PDF. Retrieved from http://docplayer.org/25252179-Der-kranke-mensch-ueberfordert-in-krisensituationen-klaus-dieter-kossow.html
Kraaij, V., Arensman, E., & Spinhoven, P. (2002). Negative Life Events and Depression in Elderly Persons: A Meta-Analysis. The Journals Of Gerontology Series B: Psychological Sciences And Social Sciences, 57(1), P87-P94. doi: 10.1093/geronb/57.1.p87
Kramrei, E., Coit, C., Martin, S., Fogo, W., & Mahoney, A. (2007). Post-Divorce Adjustment and Social Relationships. *Journal Of Divorce & Remarriage*, *46*(3–4), 145–166. doi: https://doi.org/10.1300/j087v46n03_09
Krause, N. (2018). Assessing the relationships among stress, god-mediated control, and psychological distress/well-being: Does the level of education matter?. The Journal Of Social Psychology, 159(1), 2–14. doi: https://doi.org/10.1080/00224545.2018.1431604
Kuiper, N. (2012). Humor and Resiliency: Towards a Process Model of Coping and Growth. Europe'S Journal Of Psychology, 8(3), 475–491. doi: https://doi.org/10.5964/ejop.v8i3.464
Lee, M. (2017). Musik als Ressource der Lebensbewältigung von Migrantinnen aus Südkorea mit Kindern mit und ohne Behinderung in Deutschland. Dissertation an der Fakultät

Rehabilitationswissenschaften der Technischen Universität Dortmund. Retrieved from https://doi.org/10.17877/DE290R-18842

Lee, J., Kim, H., Kang, J., & Suh, I. (2014). Association between stressful life events and resting heart rate. BMC Psychology, 2(1). doi: https://doi.org/10.1186/s40359-014-0029-0

Li, H., Zou, Y., Wang, J., & Yang, X. (2016). Role of Stressful Life Events, Avoidant Coping Styles, and Neuroticism in Online Game Addiction among College Students: A Moderated Mediation Model. Frontiers In Psychology, 7. doi: https://doi.org/10.3389/fpsyg.2016.01794

Lindert, J., Ehrenstein, O., Priebe, S., Mielck, A., & Brähler, E. (2009). Depression and anxiety in labor migrants and refugees – A systematic review and meta-analysis. *Social Science & Medicine*, *69*(2), 246–257. doi: https://doi.org/10.1016/j.socscimed.2009.04.032

Lomas, T., & Ivtzan, I. (2016). Second wave positive psychology: Exploring the positive-negative dialectics of well-being. Journal of Happiness Studies, 17(4), 1753–1768.

Low, N., Dugas, E., O'Loughlin, E., Rodriguez, D., Contreras, G., Chaiton, M., & O'Loughlin, J. (2012). Common stressful life events and difficulties are associated with mental health symptoms and substance use in young adolescents. BMC Psychiatry, 12(1). doi: https://doi.org/10.1186/1471-244x-12-116

Lukas, E. (2009). *Den ersten Schritt tun*. Freiburg: Kösel-Verlag.

Maddi, S. (2006). Hardiness: The courage to grow from stresses. The Journal Of Positive Psychology, 1(3), 160–168. doi: https://doi.org/10.1080/17439760600619609

Marwaha S (2019) Presumptive stressful life events among addicts and non-addicts; a comparative analysis. Retrieved from http://www.allresearchjournal.com/vol1issue1/PartA/pdf/51.1.pdf

Mayer, C.-H. (2007): Ressourcen interkultureller Identitäten. Krause, C., Lehmann, N., Lorenz, F. & Petzold, T.D. (eds.) (2007): *verbunden gesunden - Zugehörigkeitsgefühl und Salutogenese*. Heckenbeck/Bad Gandersheim: Verlag Gesunde Entwicklung, p. 251–262.

Mayer, C.-H. (2011). *The meaning of sense of coherence in transcultural management*. Münster: Waxmann.

Mayer, C.-H. (2012). Der Einfluss von Kultur und Spiritualität auf die Gesundheit. Der Mensch, *Zeitschrift Für Salutogenese und Anthropologische Medizin*. Ausgabe Kultur und Gesundheit., (44(1), 5–21.

Mayer, C.-H., & Krause, C. (2011). Promoting mental health and salutogenesis in transcultural organizational and work contexts. International Review Of Psychiatry, 23(6), 495–500. doi: https://doi.org/10.3109/09540261.2011.636549

Mayer, C.-H., & Krause, C. (2013). Salutogenese in Beratung und Psychotherapie. Klinische Verhaltensmedizin und Rehabilitation, 26(2), 91–178.

Mayer, C.-H., Vanderheiden, E., & Oosthuizen, R. (2019). Transforming shame, guilt and anxiety through a salutogenic PP1.0 and PP2.0 counselling framework. *Counselling Psychology Quarterly*, 1–17. doi: https://doi.org/10.1080/09515070.2019.1609421

Mayring, P. (2001). Kombination und Integration qualitativer und quantitativer Analyse. Retrieved from http://www.qualitative-research.net/index.php/fqs/rt/printerFriendly/967/2110

Mayring, P. (2010). *Qualitative Inhaltsanalyse*. Weinheim: Beltz Verlag.

Mayring, P. (2016). *Einführung in die qualitative Sozialforschung*. Weinheim Basel: Beltz.

McAndrew, F., Akande, A., Turner, S., & Sharma, Y. (1998). A Cross-Cultural Ranking of Stressful Life Events in Germany, India, South Africa, and the United States. Journal Of Cross-Cultural Psychology, 29(6), 717–727. doi: https://doi.org/10.1177/0022022198296003

McLaughlin, K., Conron, K., Koenen, K., & Gilman, S. (2009). Childhood adversity, adult stressful life events, and risk of past-year psychiatric disorder: a test of the stress sensitization hypothesis in a population-based sample of adults. *Psychological Medicine*, *40*(10), 1647–1658. doi: https://doi.org/10.1017/s0033291709992121

Mezuk, B., Rafferty, J., Kershaw, K., Hudson, D., Abdou, C., & Lee, H. et al. (2010). Reconsidering the Role of Social Disadvantage in Physical and Mental Health: Stressful Life Events, Health Behaviors, Race, and Depression. *American Journal Of Epidemiology*, *172*(11), 1238–1249. doi: https://doi.org/10.1093/aje/kwq283

Morgenroth, O., & Schaller, J. (2010). Misserfolg und Scheitern aus psychologischer Sicht. In H. Pechlaner, Misserfolg und Scheitern aus psychologischer Sicht. Berlin: Schmidt.

Parakh, P. (2011). Gender issues in life event research in India: A critical appraisal of the presumptive stressful life events scale. Asian Journal Of Psychiatry, 4(1), 19–21. doi: https://doi.org/10.1016/j.ajp.2011.01.001

Patton, D. (2019). Perspective Taking, Cultural Stress, and the Individual: From the Inside Out. Retrieved from https://www.arl.army.mil/arlreports/2014/technical-report.cfm?id=7074

Plante, T. G. (Ed.). (2012). *Religion, spirituality, and positive psychology: Understanding the psychological fruits of faith*. Santa Barbara, CA, US: Praeger/ABC-CLIO.

Positive psychology. (2019). Retrieved from http://www.positivedisintegration.com/positivepsychology.htm

Primono, J., Yates, B.C., & Woods, N. (1990). Social support for women during chronic illness: The relationship among sources and types of adjustment. Research in Nursing and Health, 13, 153–161.

Reif, J., Spieß, E., & Stadler, P. (2018). Effektiver Umgang mit Stress: Gesundheitsmanagement im Beruf. Heidelberg: Springer.

Richardson, S., Shaffer, J., Falzon, L., Krupka, D., Davidson, K., & Edmondson, D. (2012). Meta-Analysis of Perceived Stress and Its Association With Incident Coronary Heart Disease. *The American Journal Of Cardiology*, *110*(12), 1711–1716. doi: https://doi.org/10.1016/j.amjcard.2012.08.004

Risch, N., Herrell, R., Lehner, T., Liang, K., Eaves, L., & Hoh, J. et al. (2009). Interaction Between the Serotonin Transporter Gene (5-HTTLPR), Stressful Life Events, and Risk of Depression. *JAMA*, *301*(23), 2462. doi: https://doi.org/10.1001/jama.2009.878

Rowland, J.H. (1990). Interpersonal resources: Social support. In J.C. Holland & J. H. Rowland (Eds.), Handbook of psychooncology (pp. 58–71). New York: Oxford University Press.

Schnell, T. (2016). Psychologie des Lebenssinns. Berlin - Heidelberg: Springer-Verlag.

Schock, K., Böttche, M., Rosner, R., Wenk-Ansohn, M., & Knaevelsrud, C. (2016). Impact of new traumatic or stressful life events on pre-existing PTSD in traumatized refugees: results of a longitudinal study. European Journal Of Psychotraumatology, 7(1), 32106. doi: 10.3402/ejpt.v7.32106

Schwarzer, R. (1993), Stress, Angst und Handlungsregulation, Stuttgart: Kohlhammer

Schwarzer, R., & Schulz, U. (2003). Stressful Life Events. Handbook Of Psychology. Wiley Online Library. Retrieved 1 December 2019, from https://doi.org/10.1002/0471264385.wei0902

Seligman, M. E. P., & Csikszentimihalyi, M. (2000). Positive psychology: An introduction. American Psychologist, 55, 5–14.

Silver, E., & Teasdale, B. (2005). Mental Disorder and Violence: An Examination of Stressful Life Events and Impaired Social Support. Social Problems, 52(1), 62–78. doi: https://doi.org/10.1525/sp.2005.52.1.62

Tang, F., Xue, F., & Qin, P. (2015). The interplay of stressful life events and coping skills on risk for suicidal behavior among youth students in contemporary China: a large scale cross-sectional study. BMC Psychiatry, 15(1). doi: https://doi.org/10.1186/s12888-015-0575-x

The Finnish Association for Mental Health. (2018). Traumatic crises. Retrieved from https://www.mielenterveysseura.fi/en/home/mental-health/crises/traumatic-crises

Tversky, A. & Kahneman, D. (1981), The framing of decisions and the psychology of choice, Science, 211, pp. 1124–1131

Tweed, R., White, K., & Lehman, D. (2004). Culture, Stress, and Coping. Journal Of Cross-Cultural Psychology, 35(6), 652–668. doi: https://doi.org/10.1177/0022022104270109

Vanderheiden, E. (2019). Study Life Crisis. Online Questionnaire. Retrieved from https://crisis.jimdosite.com

Velten, J., Lavallee, K., Scholten, S., Meyer, A., Zhang, X., Schneider, S., & Margraf, J. (2014). Lifestyle choices and mental health: a representative population survey. BMC Psychology, 2(1). doi: https://doi.org/10.1186/s40359-014-0055-y

Wehling, E. (2018). *Politisches Framing*. Berlin: Ullstein.

Wong, P. T. P. (1998). Implicit theories of meaningful life and the development of the Personal Meaning Profile (PMP). In P. T. P. Wong & P. Fry (Eds.), The human quest for meaning: A handbook of psychological research and clinical applications (pp. 111–140). Mahwah, NJ: Erlbaum.

Wong, P. T. P. (2011) Positive psychology 2.0: Towards a balanced interactive model of the good life.. Canadian Psychology/Psychologie canadienne 52 (2):69–81

Young, C., Craig, J., Clapham, K., Williams, S., & Williamson, A. (2018). Stressful life events and resilience among carers of Aboriginal children in urban New South Wales: cross-sectional findings from the Study of Environment on Aboriginal Resilience and Child Health (SEARCH). BMJ Open, 8(6), e021687. doi: https://doi.org/10.1136/bmjopen-2018-021687

Elisabeth Vanderheiden is a pedagogue, theologian, intercultural mediator, managing director of the Catholic Adult Education Rhineland-Palatinate and the president of the Catholic Adult Education of Germany. Her publishing focus centres on in the context of basic education for adults, in particular on trainings for teachers and trainers in adult education, as well as vocational, and civic education, edited books on intercultural opening processes and intercultural mediation. Her latest publications—together Claude-Hélène Mayer—focused on shame as resource as well as mistakes, errors and failure and their hidden potentials in the context of culture and positive psychology. She also works as an independent researcher. In a current project, she investigates life crises and their individual coping strategies from different cultural viewpoints. A topic that has also aroused her research interest is humour and how it appears in different cultural perspectives and from various scientific disciplines. She lives in Germany and Florida.

Chapter 3
Communication About Communication in Love Letters: Addressing and Avoiding Failures, Mistakes, and Errors in Written Communication

Paul C. Rosenblatt

Abstract How do people build a relationship when communicating via love letters? Communicative failures, mistakes, and errors can occur in any relationship. Written communication is more at risk of failures, mistakes, and errors than face-to-face communication because it lacks the nonverbal information of face-to-face interaction and the opportunity available in face-to-face interaction for immediate clarifying exchanges about potential or actual failures, mistakes, and errors. What goes on in love letter exchanges to shelter the couple relationship from the challenges inherent in communicating, particularly in written communicating?

Thematic analysis was carried out with ten sets of published love letters from diverse eras (the 1820s to the 1940s).

Some lovers wrote about the potential of written communication for failures, mistakes, and errors. Some asked for clarity about what was said in a previous letter, particularly early in their relationship when they were still getting to know one another as people and correspondents. Most correspondents raised concerns about the meaning of gaps in communication, and most provided explanations when they were responsible for gaps. Most letter writers assumed brevity could be a problem for the other and offered explanations for brevity. In sum, the key strategy for addressing and avoiding potential or actual failures, mistakes, and errors inherent in exchanging love letters was communication about communication.

Keywords Couples · Interpersonal communication · Love letters · Misunderstandings · Written communication · Mistakes · Error · Failure

P. C. Rosenblatt (✉)
Department of Family Social Science, University of Minnesota, St. Paul, MN, USA
e-mail: prosenbl@umn.edu

E. Vanderheiden, C.-H. Mayer (eds.), *Mistakes, Errors and Failures across Cultures*, https://doi.org/10.1007/978-3-030-35574-6_3

3.1 Introduction

How do two people building a relationship via love letters avoid or address communicative failures, mistakes, and errors? The stakes are high in love letter exchanges, because with a positive and escalating relationship there is likely to be considerable vulnerability and hope for the future for both parties. With stakes so high, the need to avoid or address communication failures, mistakes, and errors is particularly great. What goes on in love letter exchanges to shelter the couple relationship from the failures, mistakes, and errors inherent in written communication?

When a couple communicates by letter, the only tool they have to avoid or address failures, mistakes, or errors in their communication is their letter writing. That means an important part of sustaining a relationship built on written communication may well be communication about communication. In the process of communicating about communication, the two correspondents can avoid, overcome, or correct potential or actual failures, mistakes, and errors. But do couples address relationship issues in love letter exchanges through communication about communication? Is communication about communication present and substantial in love letter exchanges? The research reported here investigated communication about communication in love letters.

According to communication theorists and researchers, any interpersonal communication is at risk of failure, mistakes, and errors (e.g., Bavelas et al. 1990; Grant 2007; Robinson 2006; Sillars et al. 2004; Weeks and Gambescia 2016). So of course there are risks in love letter exchanges of failures, mistakes, or errors. Those risks have not been systematically examined in research on love letters. In this report about love letters using qualitative research, I consider a communicative failure to have occurred or to be at risk of occurring if either correspondent considers that a falling short, deficiency, or lack of success has occurred or may have occurred in the correspondence. I consider a communicative mistake to have occurred or to be at risk of occurring if either correspondent believes a misunderstanding or miscommunication has occurred or may have occurred. Similarly, I consider a communicative error to have occurred or to be at risk of occurring if either correspondent believes that there has been or may have been a communicative inaccuracy, departure from what is right or proper, or falsehood in the correspondence. Although many collections of love letters have been published or are available to researchers in public archives, there has not been research on a sample of love letter collections exploring how love letter writers address or avoid potential or actual communicative failures, mistakes, and errors.

The literature on electronic communication indicates that written communication is more challenging than face-to-face communication in part because written communication lacks the nonverbal supplementary information (such as facial expressions and voice intonation) of face-to-face communication to address or avoid failures, errors, and mistakes (e.g., Hertlein and Ancheta 2014; Juhasz and Bradford 2016; Murray and Campbell 2015; Paldam 2018). In addition, written communication with the inevitable time passage that comes with communicating by snail mail (unlike face-to-face communication and electronic communication between two parties who are both online and providing immediate responses to one another) lacks the capacity for immediate clarifying exchanges to address actual or apparent communicative failures, mistakes, or errors (e.g., Hertlein and Ancheta 2014; Juhasz and Bradford 2016).

Communication about communication has been understood since the early days of theorizing about problems in couple and family relationships to be a key to avoiding and addressing problems, including those arising from communicative failures, mistakes, and errors (Rosenblatt 1994, pp. 162–169; Watzlawick et al. 1967, ch. 2; Wilmot 1980). Communication about communication may be called "metacommunication." Whether through nonverbal behavior or through words said or written along with a communication, we may metacommunicate (communicate about our communication). When engaging in written communication, and thus lacking the capacity to metacommunicate nonverbally, people must use their written words to "metacommunicate." Thus, it seemed reasonable to explore communication about communication as an approach love letter writers might take to address or avoid potential or actual communicative failures, mistakes, or errors.

3.2 Research Methods

3.2.1 Sample

The sample of love letter collections was drawn from the University of Minnesota Library, which according to Wikipedia ("List of the largest libraries in the United States," accessed April 12, 2019) is one of the top 25 research libraries in North America. The university's online catalog lists more than 1400 books of or about love letters. I sifted through the books in the order presented by the catalog (which began with books in which the first words of the title are "love letters"). The criteria for a love letter collection to be included in the sample were love letters exchanged by a heterosexual couple who initially were not married to each other and eventually married, a total of at least 30 premarital letters, letters written in or translated into English, and letters from both parties. I put no limitations on the cultural background of the letter writers. My sample consisted of the first ten books of love letters found that fit the criteria.

The research analysis focused on the letters up to the time a couple married. The ten love letter collections are listed in the references for this chapter, with each book marked with an asterisk (∗). For the love letters of Woodrow Wilson and Edith Bolling Galt, I used three sources, Link et al. (1980a, b), and Tribble (1981), because Tribble's footnotes covered useful matters that the Link et al. footnotes did not, but the Link et al. books included more of the couple's correspondence.

The cases included a letter collection translated from German (Albert Einstein and Mileva Marić) and one translated from Russian (Anton Chekhov and Olga Knipper). Fourteen of the 20 letter writers were from the United States, 2 from Russia, and 1 each from Great Britain, Germany, the Austro-Hungarian Empire, and Australia. The letters were written as early as the 1820s and as recently as the 1940s.

Some sets of letters were brief (not much more than 30 letters); others were extensive (over 1000 letters). I did not want to weigh the large letter collections more than the smaller ones in analyzing the data, so I created equal-sized samples of letters from each collection. Because I wanted to sample across the trajectory of the couple relationship, I chose the first ten, middle ten, and last ten letters before the couple married. I considered the middle ten letters to be those written half way between the date of the first letter in the collection and that of the last letter before marriage, with the first five of the middle ten being immediately before the midpoint date and the next five being immediately after the midpoint date. With the Sandburg-Steichen letters (Sandburg 1987), I respected the editor's opinion that the first Sandburg-Steichen letters were not love letters and chose as the first love letter the one the editor said was the one that marked the beginning of the love relationship.

3.2.2 Research Analysis Methodology

I photocopied the first middle and final ten letters before marriage in each letter collection and then read and reread every letter identifying each instance of what seemed to be communication about communication—for example, asking for clarification of something the other had written or commenting on the limitations of communicating through writing. The next step was to carry out a thematic analysis (Braun and Clarke 2006) of the letter passages that seemed to involve communication about communication. The analysis was open to whatever the letter writers had to say that could be taken as communication about communication, but it was also informed by theoretical works on communication about communication in couples and families (e.g., Rosenblatt 1994, pp. 162–169; Watzlawick et al. 1967, ch. 2; Wilmot 1980) concerning the circumstances that would be likely to create a need for communication about communication (e.g., failures to communicate, misunderstandings, and communications that hurt the other's feelings). Categories were generated that were descriptive and linked closely to the words the letter writers used. The Findings section of this chapter offers illustrations of the themes, and that enables readers to check on the fit between the data and the themes that were generated in the analysis.

The presentation of the findings, driven as it was by what the letter writers had to say that seemed to be communication about communication, is descriptive, but it also is interpretative in that without any possibility of my communicating with the letter writers I have to rely on my interpretations of what they wrote. The interpretations are informed by the letter writers offering contexts for what they have written and interacting with one another about what they have written. But still, there are interpretative stretches in the analysis, perhaps particularly in the analysis of letter writers thanking one another for writing.

3.2.3 *Study Limitations*

Participants in love letter exchanges need a reasonable amount of literacy and a functioning postal system or other means of conveying written communications (Ahearn 2000). Love letter writing is facilitated by social or physical contexts that keep couples apart—for example, norms that make it difficult or inappropriate for couples to see each other face-to-face (Ahearn 2000), norms that make arranged marriage relatively unlikely (Ahearn 2000), and occupational, family, or transportation barriers that keep the partners apart.

Another limitation is that because one partner wrote more letters than the other or one partner's letters were more likely to be saved, in some couples, one partner's writings provide more of the data about the issues researched.

Love letters are saturated with cultural rules, understandings, and practices (Janning 2018; Lyons 1999, 2013). That means in studying love letters one must be sensitive to the cultural contexts, values, and meanings that shape and limit the letters. Consider, for example, cultural standards about gender roles, the importance of marriage, and what one must say one feels about a potential partner in order to be attractive to that person. Furthermore, across eras and countries, writers of love letters have had the potential to use etiquette books and books on writing letters to shape what they chose to write in a love letter (e.g., Lyons 1999; Lystra 1989, pp. 13–14). That means that one limitation of research on love letters is that it may not be so much about human psychology as about what the cultural rules were for the letter writers. That also means that it is possible to mistake the requirements of letter writing etiquette for communications about concrete realities. Love letters, particularly those from diverse eras and cultures, confront the researcher with many interpretative challenges (Bergs 2014). It is not simply that there may be words and phrases that have meanings that elude one, but also there are cultural codes about what to write, and these codes may reveal and hide what people feel and mean. Perhaps the ten letter sets used in this research, spanning more than a century and located in a diversity of countries, allow for assertions that are not hopelessly culture bound and limited by culture. But perhaps all ten sets of letters represent a single love letter writing culture or a group of very similar love letter writing cultures, and that makes it possible that what I take to be communication about communication to address or avoid potential or actual failures, mistakes, and errors is often only an expression of cultural etiquette. Perhaps, for example, in the culture of the letter writers, the proper lover always apologizes for something. That means it can be risky to take the apologies in the letters on face. What I take as communication about communication may actually be an expression of a cultural code for epistolary politeness.

Another limitation of this research is that it is impossible to know how representative the ten letter collections are of all love letters, many of which are unpublished. One reason to be concerned about the representativeness of published letter collections, including those in the sample for this chapter, is that often at least one of the partners was famous or became famous. We can assume that the fame was a key reason why the letters were edited and published. For a researcher like me, having a letter collection in print makes the collection much easier to research. There are no problems, for example, with travel to archives or reading handwriting. But a limitation of working with published letter collections that so often involve letters by someone who was famous is that we then have less confidence about what goes on in love letters of couples in which neither partner is famous. Might fame or budding fame alter love letter writing? Perhaps whatever might make for fame, for example, ambition, outstanding verbal skills, and strong willingness to take risks, makes for unusual communication about communication in love letters.

This study was done only with love letters in heterosexual relationships and only with letters of couples who eventually married. One cannot assume that communication issues and strategies are the same for other relationships.

3.3 Findings

Findings of the analysis of the selected love letters will be described in the following by presenting these findings within nine constructed categories.

3.3.1 Writing Is Harder than Talking

Some letter writers complained that writing felt forced or unnatural and that speaking would be easier and would lead to better understanding. With writing it was harder to say all that was in their heart. There is, for example, this from Edith Bolling Galt to Woodrow Wilson about the frustrations and limitations of written as opposed to face-to-face communication, May 4, 1915:

> I wish you were here so I could talk to you—for then I know you would understand, and a written word is so cold, so capable of conveying more or less than we can express in speech. (Tribble 1981, pp. 8–9)

Mirroring that viewpoint Wilson wrote to Galt, August 5, 1915:

> This hand is so hard to manage when there's a pen it in and the pen lags so far behind the thoughts that run eagerly out to seek my Darling. It's a poor, slow substitute at best for the conversations with my sweet One that have filled the past weeks with joy and comfort. (Link et al. 1980a, p. 101)

Similarly, Alice Freeman wrote to George Herbert Palmer, February 27, 1887, how communication by letter was harder, especially during a relationship crisis they were having, than communicating face to face:

> Of all times in our joint history this is the one when we need to see each other, and talk frankly together. It is quite impossible to say on paper all I want to say. (Palmer and Palmer 1940, p. 118)

Another example of communication about the difficulty of written communication is this from Zelda Sayre to F. Scott Fitzgerald, March 1919:

> Maybe you won't understand this, but sometimes when I miss you most, it's hardest to write—and you always know when I make myself—Just the ache of it all—and I can't tell you. If we were together, you'd feel how strong it is. (Bryer and Barks 2002, p. 15)

Thus, for some writers, spoken communication was at times, if not always, easier, richer, and more accurate than written communication. In a sense statements about the challenges of written communication were warnings of and apologies for the inadequacy of written communication and for the potential in written communication for failure, mistakes, or errors.

3.3.2 Correcting Misunderstanding

There seemed to be more potential or actual misunderstandings (communicative mistakes) early in the relationship, or at least more writing about such misunderstanding, before the two correspondents had ideas as clear as they eventually did about how to communicate to and understand one another. To illustrate, here is something Sally McDowell wrote on September 12, 1854, early in her relationship with John Miller:

> My dear Sir, We are both in fault as to the style of our letters. I have found yours somewhat ambiguous and obscure; and mine, I know now, must have been as indeed you clearly intimate they were, in some parts, utterly unintelligible to you. The mistake has arisen from the fact that we, with limited personal acquaintance, have each presupposed such a knowledge upon the past of the other, of our character, principles, and opinions, as have led us to think the generalities and mere allusions we have used amply sufficient upon a subject which, in truth, demanded the most explicit and unequivocal language. To remedy this error, to some extent, I pray you bear with a very plain recital of my views upon the case at issue between us. (Buckley 2000, p. 8)

Similarly, there was insecurity in Wilson's early letters to Galt about whether he was being understood. For example, on May 5, 1915, he wrote:

> Forgive all errors in what I have said,— read it with your heart, as I know you can, and will, and know that whatever happens, you will have the companionship, the gratitude, the loyalty and the devoted, romantic love of Your devoted friend, Woodrow Wilson. What would I not give for words that would really make you see and feel what is in my heart! You could not shrink! How much of my life has gone into this note you will never know, unless, some day—. (Tribble 1981, p. 13)

However, misunderstandings were not limited to early correspondence. Some arose later in correspondence, particularly when new and difficult situations arose. For example, there was this in a letter of Palmer to Freeman, February 25, 1887:

> Forgive me darling, that I let a phrase slip into my letter which must have wounded you and seemed distrustful....I was thinking how little difference it could make to me what people might say—to me so rich a man possessing you—and I must have spoken this out in some way that implied that I had no such feeling. That would be cruel. I know you love me as genuinely as I you, though I can never see that you have the same cause for exultation. I did not mean to hint a deficiency. (Palmer and Palmer 1940, pp. 115–116)

3.3.3 Correspondence Gaps

In eight of the ten letter collections, at least one partner expressed concern at some time about a gap (potential or actual communicative failure) in the correspondence from the partner—for example, this from Carl Sandburg to Lillian Steichen, May 6, 1908:

> [Your] letters had been plopping in to me, two every 24 hours. Suddenly, I draw blanks, zeros, for all 48 hours. At 5 o'clock this afternoon I hadn't heard from you since last Saturday night--Sunday, Monday & Tuesday, unaccounted for! (Sandburg 1987, p. 180)

Similarly there was this from Chekhov to Knipper, June 16, 1899:

> What is happening? Where are you? You seem quite determined not to give us any news, so that we've been reduced to idle speculation—perhaps you've forgotten us, or have married someone in the Caucasus. If so, who is he? Will you give up the theatre? The writer has been forgotten, how awful, how cruel, how heartless! (Benedetti 1996, p. 6)

Then there was this from Eugene Petersen to Marian Smith, March 12, 1944:

> Thought that you had forgotten about me when I didn't hear from you for about a week. (Petersen 1998, p. 4)

Lyons (2013, pp. 57–58), commenting about the writing culture of ordinary people, said that gaps and delays are common in letter exchanges and may upset a correspondent whose expectations are violated by the failure to receive a letter. In fact, a gap in written communication can imply a breakdown of an implicit social contract about communicating regularly (Lyons 1999, 2013, p. 57; Teo 2005). In all ten letter collections, at least one letter writer at some point anticipated that their partner in the exchange might be upset about a correspondence gap and so explained to their partner why they had not written for a while. They thus addressed the apparent contradiction between their expressions of great love for the partner and their not having written recently. There were three common explanations letter writers offered for a gap in communication.

3.3.4 Too Busy

In nine of the ten collections, at least one partner wrote that there was a delay in sending at least one letter because she or he had been too busy with work, visitors, caring for a sick family member, classes, or other matters. For example, Edward Dickinson wrote to Emily Norcross, February 1, 1827:

> I have intended to write two or three times before, but my business, which you know, must always be first attended to, has prevented. I have been unusually occupied for the last two or three weeks. (Pollak 1988, p. 88)

Similarly, Freeman wrote to Palmer, January 25, 1887:

> I have been too busy to get a word on paper! (Palmer and Palmer 1940, p. 102)

3.3.5 Postal Problems

In four couples, at least one gap in communication was attributed to problems with the postal service, including the postal schedule changing, the partner forgetting to stamp a letter, and the mails being slow.

3.3.6 Too Tired

In three letter collections, a lover explained a gap in communicating by saying she or he had been too tired to write. For example, Agnes Miller wrote to Olaf Stapledon, April 23, 1916:

> I meant to begin writing to you when we first came up 3 days ago, but we have been out picknicking each day & in the evening when we get in we always have to turn to & light our fire & get a meal & wash up & then Daddy reads aloud or we are too tried & are ready for bed. (Crossley 1987, p. 141)

3.3.7 Other Explanations of Correspondence Gaps

There were ten other explanations for a gap in communication offered in some love letter collection. All of them assure the partner that the gap did not indicate a decline in love for the partner. The ten explanations include feeling that it was a mistake to write because doing so would expose the couple relationship to others in a situation where exposure would be embarrassing or create family or community difficulty, being in a situation where one could not write or mail a letter, being in a bad mood, concern about boring the other, and having nothing to say. The ten other explanations also included delaying writing until one had acquired a specific piece of information that was important to give the other, not writing because the partner hurt the writer's feelings, not being bored (the partner had told her not to write until she was bored), being distracted by the beauty of vacation surroundings, and having torn up a letter without sending it because the writer felt that it was a mistake to send that letter as drafted.

3.3.8 Thanks for Writing

Perhaps because letter exchange was so much the vehicle of the relationship and because gaps in communication could be worrisome, there were instances in all ten letter collections of thanks given to the partner for writing the letter most recently received. In some collections, thanks were offered in quite a few letters. Thanking the partner may reflect the anxiety inherent in gaps in communication (fear of communicative failure), and it is a way of acknowledging that since the relationship is a corresponding one, the letters are crucial to the relationship. Thanking the partner also may be a way to encourage the partner to continue writing, and, if thanks were offered about specific things written, thanks could be understood as encouraging the continuation of writing like that.

Some expressions of thanks were very simple, something like, "Thank you for your letter." However, thanks often involved expressions of love and intensely worded gratitude. This was particularly so when the partner had sent an especially loving expression of affection and commitment. For example, Wilson wrote to Galt, May 5, 1915:

> That wonderful note…[was] the most moving and altogether beautiful note I ever read, whose possession makes me rich; and I must thank you for that before I try to sleep--thank you from the bottom of a heart that your words touch as if they knew every key of it. I am proud beyond words that you should have thought of me in such terms and put the thoughts into such exquisite, comprehending words. (Tribble 1981, p. 11)

Then there was this from Miller to McDowell, September 24, 1855:

> How could you send me such a letter altogether unannounced? Why it's the sweetest & dearest I ever received. Do you know it is about the first full disclosure of passionate affection for me that you have ever made. I feel as if I had inherited a kingdom. Darling Sally, I love you ever since I broke the seal with an entirely new devotion. I will live for you. A woman that endows me with so much passion shall be my warmly cherished & highest pleasure in life...I think you have been concealing from me & keeping back a sort of devotion which God approves & which he intended should be planted in all married relations…. Oh, I love that letter so! I have read it over & over this morning. (Buckley 2000, p. 398)

3.3.9 Why This Letter Is So Brief

No letter receiver complained about a letter being unusually brief, but 13 of the 20 letter writers (in 9 of the 10 letter collections) assumed that sending an unusually brief letter would be a communicative error (departure from what is right or proper) or communicative failure. Perhaps the underlying logic was that there is an inconsistency between saying "I love you very much" and writing only a little bit. The explanations for letters that were unusually brief often paralleled explanations for a gap in correspondence, with being too busy the most frequent explanation. However, there were explanations that were not offered for communication delays but were offered for letters being unusually brief, including that the letter had to be brief because the mail was about to be picked up and that the writer was on a train or in a horse-drawn coach and the shaking of the vehicle made for many writing errors.

3.4 Discussion

Potential or actual communicative failures, mistakes, or errors were addressed in all ten love letter collections. Some love letter writers expressed concern that written communication was harder than communicating face to face. They wrote of the potential of communication via letters for communicative failures, mistakes, and errors, which fits what the communication literature reviewed for this chapter suggested would be a risk. Some love letters corrected misunderstandings, particularly early in a couple's correspondence, which addresses potential or actual communicative mistakes and fits the relationship literature cited at the beginning of the chapter about the value of communication about communication. In another area of communication about communication, in most of the ten love letter collections, there were instances of correspondence addressing the potential or actual communicative failures inherent in correspondence gaps. In all ten letter collections, there were instances of one letter writer thanking the other for writing, and among the ways that could be understood is that the thanking arises from anxiety about the possibility of failure to maintain correspondence. In all but one of the ten letter collections, there were instances of explaining why and apologizing for a letter being brief, which can be taken as addressing the possibility that the other would think it is a communicative error (a departure from what is right or proper) or a communicative failure (a falling short or deficiency) for a letter to be too brief.

3.5 Conclusion

In response to the questions raised at the beginning of this chapter that were driven by theoretical work on communication in general and communication in couples and families in particular, communication about communication was present and seemed important in the ten love letter collections. Communication about communication seemed to have an important role in overcoming, minimizing, or avoiding communicative failures, mistakes, and errors arising from letters being the vehicle of communication. The findings reported here link to the theory and research literature cited at the beginning of this chapter by indicating that in the ten love letter collections, there were challenges from communicating in writing that the literature on communication would lead one to expect, and these challenges were addressed, as might be expected from the literature on communication in couple and family systems, by communication about communication. That all ten of the couples eventually married is an indication that they successfully addressed or avoided communicative failures, mistakes, and errors. This chapter thus helps to fill a gap in the literature on love letters and links that literature with the literature on failures, mistakes, and errors, with the literature on communication, and with the literature on premarital relationships.

3.6 Directions for Future Research

The research reported here offers ideas for research on love communications that are conveyed via text message and e-mail. Although letter writing is still important in some modern relationships, for example, between deployed members of the US military and their spouses (Carter and Renshaw 2016), modern life offers an array of ways to communicate electronically (Hertlein 2012; Janning 2018). Some approaches approximate face-to-face communication with visual and audio information in real time and thus are less likely to face the failures, mistakes, and errors love letter writers face. However, some romantic relationships make use of written electronic communications such as e-mail and text messaging, which risk the failures, mistakes, and errors the love letter writers encountered (Hertlein and Ancheta 2014) as well as the attributional challenges of gaps in the correspondence, which, as this chapter suggests, are problems present in love letters. Arguably there can be as much need for communication about communication with some modes of electronic written communication as there is for messages written on paper. Perhaps there is even need for more. Modern messages are often relatively brief (Bergs 2014), and that brevity may increase the likelihood of failures, mistakes, and errors in communicating because there is less redundancy in a communication and less context to clarify message meanings. That potential for failures, mistakes, and errors arguably makes it more necessary for frequent communication about communication. Are such communications frequent and useful? That is a potential topic for research.

A social information processing theory perspective (Walther 2015; Walther et al. 2015) suggests that if there is substantial redundancy in a couple's love letter exchanges, the redundancy might promote greater clarity and strength of messages. Even if there is less informational redundancy in a typical written communication than there is in a face-to-face exchange (because there is no nonverbal or nonlexical information and because people may often say less to each other when they write than when they speak), there might be considerable redundancy across communicative exchanges, with rather the same things said in many letters. Related to that, there may be more requests from a partner for repetition in written communication than in spoken communication. The frequent expression of thanks discussed in this chapter may, for example, be understood as the encouragement of redundancy. So one direction for future research built on the research reported here is to investigate redundancy in love letters—how much is there, how much is there in love letters versus face-to-face romantic interactions, and do love letters with frequent thanks for previous letters have a higher level of redundancy?

The sense that failures, mistakes, and errors are challenges in love letter exchanges offers an alternative perspective on explanations given for delaying writing or writing too little. Many of the explanations letter writers offered can be interpreted to mean that writers chose not to write when they were more likely to make errors or to be less clear in communicating. Consider, for example, explanations such as not writing when tired (when one's error rate would be greater), when too busy (hence, possibly more errors because of being rushed and distracted), or when riding in a jouncing vehicle (which would increase one's error rate through slips of the pen).

If communication about communication facilitates the development of a couple relationship in which love letters play a major part, one might expect that future research would show that couples who were exchanging love letters and who broke up might have had a lower level of communication about communication, and that lack, leading to unresolved communicative failures, mistakes, and errors, may explain their breaking up.

3.7 Practical Implications

Lovers, whether communicating electronically or writing paper letters, might benefit from instructions online or in print about the value of communication about communication (metacommunication) and about how to do it. The research reported here suggests that communication about communication can be a valuable way for addressing or avoiding communicative failures, mistakes, and errors.

References[1]

Ahearn, L. M. (2000). True traces: Love letters and social transformation in Nepal. In D. Barton & N. Hall (Eds.), *Letter writing as a social practice* (pp. 199–207). Philadelphia: John Benjamins.

Bavelas, J. B., Black, A., Chovil, N., & Mullett, J. (1990). *Equivocal communication*. Thousand Oaks, CA: Sage.

[1] References marked with an asterisk (∗) were the data sources for this report.

∗Benedetti, J. (1996). Dear writer, dear actress: *The love letters of Anton Chekhov and Olga Knipper*. Hopewell, NJ: Ecco Press.

Bergs, A. T. (2014). Investigating love letters across time: Semiotic, sociolinguistic and cognitive problems and perspectives. In E. L. Wyss (Ed.), *Communication of love: Mediatized intimacy from lover letters to SMS, Interdisciplinary and historical studies* (pp. 165–180). Bielefeld, Germany: Transcript Verlag.

Braun, V., & Clarke, V. (2006). Using thematic analysis in psychology. *Qualitative Research in Psychology*, 3(2), 77–100. doi: https://doi.org/10.1191/1478088706qp063oa

∗Bryer, J. R., & Barks, C. W. (2002). *Dear Scott, Dearest Zelda: The love letters of F. Scott and Zelda Fitzgerald*. New York: St. Martin's Press.

∗Buckley, T. E. (Ed.) (2000). *"If you love that lady don't marry her": The courtship letters of Sally McDowell and John Miller 1854–1856*. Columbia, MO: University of Missouri Press.

Carter SP Renshaw KD (2016). Spousal communication during military deployment: A review. J Fam Issues, 37: 2309–2332 https://doi.org/10.1177/0192513X14567956

∗Crossley, R. (1987). *Talking across the world: The love letters of Olaf Stapledon and Agnes Miller, 1913–1919*. Hanover, NH: University Press of New England.

∗Einstein, A., & Marić, M. (1992). *Albert Einstein & Mileva Marić: The love letters*. J. Renn & R. Schulmann (Eds.), S. Smith (translator). Princeton, NJ: Princeton University Press.

Grant, C. B. (2007). *Uncertainty and communication: New theoretical investigations*. New York: Palgrave Macmillan.

Hertlein, K. M. (2012). Digital dwelling: Technology in couple and family relationships. *Family Relations*, 61, 373–387. doi: https://doi.org/10.1111/j.1741-3729.2012.00702.x

Hertlein, K. M., & Ancheta, K. (2014). Advantages and disadvantages of technology in relationships: Findings from an open-ended survey. *The Qualitative Report*, 19 (11), 1–14.

Janning, M. (2018). *Love letters: Saving romance in the digital age*. New York: Routledge.

Juhasz, A. & Bradford, K. (2016). Mobile phone use in romantic relationships. *Marriage & Family Review*. 52, 707–721. doi: https://doi.org/10.1080/01494929.2016.1157123

∗Link, A. S., Hirst, D. W., Little, J. E., & Gordon, D. (1980a). *The papers of Woodrow Wilson, vol. 34, July 21 – September 30, 1915*. Princeton, NJ: Princeton University Press.

∗Link, A. S., Hirst, D. W., Little, J. E., & Gordon, D. (1980b). *The papers of Woodrow Wilson, vol. 35, October, 1915 – January 27, 1916*. Princeton, NJ: Princeton University Press.

Lyons, M. (1999). Love letters and writing practices: On écritures intimes in the nineteenth century. *Journal of Family History*, 24, 232–239. doi:10.1177%2F036319909902400206

Lyons, M. (2013). *The writing culture of ordinary people in Europe, c. 1860–1920*. Cambridge, UK: Cambridge University Press.

Lystra, K. (1989). *Searching the heart: Women, men, and romantic love in nineteenth-century America*. New York: Oxford University Press.

Murray, C. E. & Campbell, E. C. (2015). The pleasures and perils of technology in intimate relationships. *Journal of Couple & Relationship Therapy*, 14, 116–140. doi: https://doi.org/10.1080/15332691.2014.953651

Paldam, C. S. (2018). Overcoming absence: From love letters to Skype. In A. Malinowska & M. Gratzke (Eds.), *The materiality of love: Essays on affection and cultural practice* (pp. 68–84). New York: Routledge

∗Palmer, A. F. & Palmer, G. H. (1940). *An academic courtship: Letters of Alice Freeman and George Herbert Palmer, 1886–1887*. Cambridge, MA: Harvard University Press.

∗Petersen, E. T. (Ed.) (1998). *Chance for love: The World War II letters of Marian Elizabeth Smith and Lt. Eugene T. Petersen, USMCR*. East Lansing: Michigan State University Press.

∗Pollak, V. R. (Ed.) (1988). *A poet's parents: The courtship letters of Emily Norcross and Edward Dickinson*. Chapel Hill: University of North Carolina Press.

Robinson, J. D. (2006). Managing trouble responsibility and relationships during conversational repair. *Communication Monographs*, 73(2), 137–161. doi: https://doi.org/10.1080/03637750600581206

Rosenblatt, P. C. (1994). *Metaphors of family systems theory*. New York: Guilford.

*Sandburg, M. (Ed.) (1987). *The poet and the dream girl: The love letters of Lilian Steichen & Carl Sandburg*. Urbana: University of Illinois Press.
Sillars, A., Canary, D. J., & Tafoya, M. (2004). Communication, conflict, and the quality of family relationships. In A. L. Vangelisti (Ed.), *The Routledge handbook of family communication* (pp. 413–446). Mahwah, NJ: Routledge.
Teo, H-M. (2005). Love writes: Gender and romantic love in Australian love letters, 1860–1960. *Australian Feminist Studies*, 20 (#48). doi: https://doi.org/10.1080/08164640500280282
*Tribble, E. (Ed.), (1981). *A president in love: The courtship letters of Woodrow Wilson and Edith Bolling Galt.* Boston: Houghton Mifflin.
Walther, J. B. (2015). Social information processing theory: Impressions and relationship development online. In D. O. Braithwaite & P. Schrodt (Eds.), *Engaging theories in interpersonal communication: Multiple perspectives, 2nd ed.* (pp. 417–428). Thousand Oaks, CA: Sage.
Walther, J. B., Van Der Heide, B., Ramirez, A. Jr., Burgoon, J. K., & Peña, J. (2015). Interpersonal and hyperpersonal dimensions of computer-mediated communication. In S. S. Sundar (Ed.), *The handbook of the psychology of communication technology* (pp. 3–22). Chichester, UK: Wiley.
Watzlawick, P., Beavin, J. H., & Jackson, D. D. (1967). *Pragmatics of human communication.* New York: Norton.
Weeks, G. R. & Gambescia, N. (2016). Expanding levels of communication. In G. R. Weeks, S. T. Fife, & C. M. Peterson (Eds.), *Techniques for the couple therapist: Essential interventions from the experts* (pp. 47–50). New York: Routledge.
Wilmot, W. W. (1980). Metacommunication: A re-examination and extension. In D. Nimmo (Ed.), *Communication Yearbook*, 4, 61–69. New Brunswick, NJ: Transaction Books.

Paul C. Rosenblatt (PhD) has a PhD in Psychology and is Professor Emeritus of Family Social Science at the University of Minnesota. He has published 14 books and roughly 200 journal articles and chapters in edited books. Much of his work has focused on the social psychology, anthropology, and sociology of people's closest relationships and what the personal and relationship impacts are of the ending of a close relationship. His work on couples includes studies of how the death of a child affects the parent couple's marital relationship, knowing and not knowing in couple relationships, and the challenges of such mundane factors in everyday couple life as couple bed sharing. Relevant to mistakes, errors, and failures, Rosenblatt's work includes explorations of shared obliviousness in family systems, the mistakes would-be helpers might make in supporting grieving people, how fatal accidents play out in families, and the ways that oppressive societal systems may create failings in family relationships. His chapter for this volume is based on analysis of personal documents (love letters). His previous research includes a number of studies using personal documents such as autobiographies, memoirs, and diaries.

Chapter 4
Steely Dan's Donald Fagen: A Case of Mistaken Self-Identity, Corrected by Self-Reformulation

James L. Kelley

Abstract Throughout Donald Fagen's life, he used the concept of bohemianism to position himself vis-à-vis his family, peers, and the mainstream culture as a whole. A psychobiographical examination of the subject with an object relations emphasis found that Fagen used his role as a successful musician to confer on himself a sense of legitimacy and to distance himself from the strictures of conventional, "bourgeois" existence. However, by the end of the first phase of his band Steely Dan's recording career, Fagen found himself in a musical, romantic, and social dead end, his bohemianism's promise of self-contained aesthetic completion being revealed as a mistaking of the ideal for the real. This chapter shows that Fagen recovered meaning in life, and thus a multilayered positivity, through psychotherapy, which led to the singer's reentry into the worlds of music, family, and friendship by tempering the perfectionism and isolationism concealed within his bohemian self-image. Ironically, Fagen's reality principle gained in strength as he loosened his grip on his mistaken self-identification as a bohemian; Fagen's self-reformulation late in life allowed him to turn a category error about the artist's role in modernity into a positive adaptation to a society that requires an adult to play multiple, often contradictory, roles.

Keywords Mistakes · Errors · Failures · Bohemianism · Donald Fagen · Object relations · Positive psychology · Psychobiography

J. L. Kelley (✉)
Independent researcher, Norman, OK, USA

E. Vanderheiden, C.-H. Mayer (eds.), *Mistakes, Errors and Failures across Cultures*, https://doi.org/10.1007/978-3-030-35574-6_4

4.1 Introduction

Positive psychology is concerned with how human beings achieve vitality and generativity through internal and interpersonal development (Gable and Haidt 2005). However, one limitation of much positive psychology research has been its overemphasis on traits and on affect polarity, with a concomitant de-emphasis on subjective evidence such as life narratives and therapeutic disclosures (Moneta 2013). Psychobiography centers on the strategies and therapies creative individuals utilize to correct mistaken self- and other-directed judgments, errors that often lead to internal and interpersonal conflicts (Mayer 2017: 26–27); thus, the psychological study of life histories can serve as an idiographic corrective to the more common, nomothetic version of positive psychology (Jørgensen and Nafstad 2005). The present study seeks to apply insights from positive psychology to the life of Donald Fagen (1948–), lead singer of the innovative musical group Steely Dan.

From his youth until middle age, Donald Fagen's fundamental error was his utilization of a version of bohemianism that was too self-directed to position himself vis-à-vis the culture at large as a means to personal and artistic authenticity. Fagen carried on a tradition—which many trace back to 1830s France (Gluck 2000; Seigel 1986)—that viewed the artist as a special being whose unique capacity to embody the social bond depended, paradoxically, on her existential distance from the more materialistic and egoistic societal mainstream (Graña 1964; Kelley 2018, October). Beginning in late adulthood and continuing into old age, Fagen has undertaken a self-reformulation by broadening his concept of bohemianism, thus correcting his mistaken self-identity. Specifically, Fagen became more other-directed in his vocational and familial projects, cogenerating and co-directing a rarified intersubjective space within which family, friends, and collaborators could abide without being infected with the perceived crassness and materialism of non-bohemian society.

During his childhood years, Fagen sought escape from the TV culture of Cold War suburbia (McNulty 2013, 18 October) by embracing the existential sensibility that pervades jazz and Beat literature (Dinerstein 2013). By the time he entered Bard College at the age of 18, Fagen was already an accomplished keyboardist, but the alienation he felt, especially toward the opposite sex, was assuaged only once he found his place among like-minded college students (Fagen 2013a: 72–85). In 1967, Fagen met Walter Becker, and together they formed the musical group Steely Dan (Sweet 2015: 12, 52–66). Fagen and Becker were totally dedicated to writing and recording music for the band from 1972 to 1980; Fagen in these years became a "workaholic" (Pollock 2012/2018: 257) who had little investment in any life outside of recording studios. It seems the self-ascribed beatnik had to go through a personal life-crisis to psychically appropriate the consequences of his fundamental error, that of identifying artistic authenticity with social isolation.

Once Steely Dan stopped recording in 1980, Fagen fell into a writer's block that brought on bouts of depression and panic attacks (Choban 2017, 7 December). At this crossroads, Fagen turned to a psychotherapist and took responsibility for his situation by involving himself in a series of committed romantic relationships and also by writing a series of magazine articles about his early life (Hoskyns 2018: xvi). Both occupations indicated that Fagen was seeking meaning in life beyond the narrow confines of a purist hipster ideal that needed to be updated for the "me decade." In the latest phase of Fagen's life, he has pursued generativity through a return to recording and touring with Steely Dan. Indeed, Fagen's affirmation of the value of art and life has survived the September 3, 2017, death of Walter Becker, his writing partner and archetypal Beat muse (Rolling Stone 2017, November 15).

4.2 Theoretical Background

This study links bohemianism's core binary "bohemian-bourgeois" to various analogues in post-Freudian psychoanalytic theory in order to demonstrate their relevance to both generative and destructive acts in the life of Donald Fagen. The appropriateness of using the aesthetic theory of bohemianism in concert with the psychological theory of psychoanalysis is indicated by Donald Fagen's self-applying bohemian terms like "Beat" (Sweet 2015: 168) and "hipster" (Fagen 2013a) and by his undergoing psychotherapy in the 1980s (Gill 1995) to avoid what we might call the ego's primal mistake: an "attempted flight" from the self-world interchange that amounts to a "turning away from the way things are" (Freud 1926/1950: 48–49).

4.2.1 Bohemianism

It has been said that modernity emerged when the self was first recognized as a distinct problem with its own contours and nuances (Baumeister 1987). If this is the case, then Paris in the 1830s and 1840s may be where the modern subject emerged (or at least it is a paradigmatic example of its emergence). In the years that followed, 1789, the French Revolutionaries did away with many intermediate groupings such as estates and guilds, membership in which had afforded the individual a ready-made position in the society. Once the restored Bourbon monarch Charles X was ousted in 1830, many Frenchmen wondered exactly what kinds of social limits could and should be legitimated in the new France (Seigel 1986: 9–10). The question was twofold: First, what are the characteristics that define this new subject, radically free from the chains of the Old Regime? Second, what will bind these newly liberated subjects together as a society?

One group held that the new subject par excellence was the artist, the person whose very life embodied each and every walk of life, since ideally the artist can create every possible character and can express every possible thought (De Botton 2004: 270; Kierkegaard 1843/2009: 15, 23). Indeed, the artist's relatively authentic self-relation was the key to understanding how society should be patterned (Berlin 1991: 228). But the French government established in 1830 has been called, not the

"Aesthetic" Monarchy, but rather the "bourgeois," since public life was dominated by the economic concerns of middle-class businessmen and professionals. To use two terms that came to the fore during this period, the new bourgeois subject was seen by many as bereft of any "association" (Strube 2017, November: 199) or "sentiment" (Banfield 2007) not tainted by her own desires for power and mammon.

The bohemian theory of the subject was a reformist, rather than a revolutionary, critique of the July Monarchy mainstream. According to the bohemian view, the artist's power of recapitulating the societal whole through her exquisite life is the sole means of reversing the bourgeois descent into an egoism whose only value is economic productivity. Indeed, from the standpoint of bohemianism, every particular bourgeois desire could be both derived from and related to the artist's all-encompassing and untarnished (because self-produced and self-authored) desire (Schmitt 1925/1986: 14–17). From one point of view, the bohemian notion of subjectivity avoids the error of solipsistic aestheticism, with its lack of both social responsibility and internal coherence, by insisting on the democratic identification of the quantitative (the will of the bohemian minority) with the qualitative (the will of the people as a whole) (Schmitt 1921/2014).

Though the term *bohémien* had been used from the fifteenth century to refer to the gypsies who were encountered in France, it was not until the 1830s that "bohemian" began to be appropriated by Romantic artists to designate their uniquely aesthetic mode of living (Brown 1985: 21, 27). By mid-century, this notion of the bohemian artist was common parlance, and *bohémien* became a buzzword somewhat akin to today's "hippy" or "beatnik" (Rorabaugh 2015: 8). For our purposes, we will simplify the complex history of bohemianism by reducing it to an aesthetic that hinges on the opposition "bohemian versus bourgeois." In order to illustrate this dichotomy in a manner that underscores its relevance to positive psychology, we will offer a few words about the bohemian's self-image as illuminator of the supposedly benighted bourgeois.

The bohemian sees herself as relating *symmetrically* to other bohemians, with whom she shares a similar life-orientation, but *asymmetrically* to the bourgeois—the ordinary nonartist—whose lack of sociocultural sensitivity evinces her need of the bohemian's guidance. On the one hand, the bohemian has a mission to improve society by making it more bohemian; on the other hand, the bohemian's only responsibility is to live out her aesthetic to the full and so to be a perfect beacon for the bourgeois. Thus, bohemian revolutionary activism can be seen to conceal a gradualist-quietist duality. That is, the bohemian must work on the material provided by bourgeois society to bring out supposedly deeper bonds of sympathy and authenticity latent therein. However, this reformist aim hidden within bohemianism's utopian trappings often morphs into solipsistic reverie and fey cynicism. After all, life is already transmuted into art in the artist's mind through the latter's power of imaginative production; if the wider world refuses to follow suit, then one can merely fall back on one's infinitely productive inner life. The present study seeks to show this reformist-quietist tension at work in the life of Donald Fagen, who often struggled *through* his art to find connection to the world *outside* his art.

The question may now arise: Is there a historically continuous connection between bohemianism and the outsider stance of Donald Fagen, or are we dealing with a superficial analogue or likeness? Intellectual historians have noted that the bohemianism of 1830s France survived in the dandyism of the fin-de-siecle, the refined primitivism of early twentieth-century literary Modernism, the existentialism of the 1940s, and the Beat Generation of the 1950s (Wilson 2003). Sartre's novel *La nausée* (1938), a favorite of Fagen's, ends with the central character finding in the outsider culture associated with jazz the inspiration to continue living (McBride 2012). And, of course, Steely Dan was named after a fearsome sexual aid from beat writer William S. Burroughs' novel *Naked Lunch* (1959). Says Fagen's collaborator, Walter Becker, of Burroughs: "He wasn't *just* a bohemian joker; he had points to make" (Martin 2003, June 6/2018: 237, emphasis added).

The final word on the aptness of our aestheticist frame comes from Donald Fagen himself, who has not only discussed his life and art as being thoroughly "Beat," "existential," and "hipster," but who describes his creative process in words that reflect our proposed bohemian-bourgeois structure: "...I think [our songwriting is] a way of viewing the actual world through our eyes. (...) I think...we're synthesising what we see" (Watts 1976/2018: 86). Fagen has even named Igor Stravinsky, that most bohemian of the twentieth-century composers, as one of his strongest influences (Regen 2013, January: 16, 18). In fact, Stravinsky and his collaborator Sergei Diaghilev are indirectly conjured forth in the Steely Dan song *Here at the Western World* (Steely Dan 1978: track 10), set at the Venice Lido, where the *Le Sacre du printemps* creators are known to have sallied forth in the company of Coco Chanel (Ross 2008), who helped create the *faux-luxe* postwar fashion culture which also presaged Fagen's ambivalently slick aesthetic (Sweet 2015: 168–169; Fagen 2013a: 15–151). Chanel made her fateful plunge from the cloistered milieu of culture and history into the bohemian world of art-as-life by walking out of her hotel and onto the celebrity-peopled Lido beach (Saikia 2011: 91). In any case, *Here at the Western World's* line "knock twice, rap with your cane" certainly brings to mind Diaghilev, who rarely appeared in public without a top hat and walking stick (Russian Ballet History 2010) and whose vision for a new kind of primitivist ballet seems to be inextricably linked to the notorious beach that Fagen sang about in the line: "Down at the Lido they welcome you with sausage and beer."

4.2.2 Post-Freudian Psychoanalytic Theory

Melanie Klein's famous dichotomy "paranoid-schizoid position versus depressive position" can be understood in terms of the creative individual's lifelong struggle to achieve reciprocity with significant others without losing a sense of her core self, the latter being the source of agential authenticity and personal continuity/integrity (Klein 1935). The depressive position sees a tempering of the errant absolutism of the paranoid-schizoid layer in that the latter's splitting of the Other (and the self) into perfect nourisher, on the one hand, and perfect inhibitor, on the other, is displaced by a sense that the Other is a creative agent that mirrors the freedom and integrity of the self but also that both self and Other are fallible nurturers who inevitably frustrate and injure (Klein 1940, 1946). The injuries, however, can be repaired through ongoing positive ministrations in the here and now. Many perhaps miss the truly positive content of Klien's therapy; for her, theory must be completed by reparative acts that paradoxically affirm the inviolability of the creative self through acknowledging that reciprocity can only be maintained by crossing the line and making the self vulnerable to the Other's aggression (Klein 1937). For Klein, it could be said mistakes are necessary materials upon which we build closer approximations to truth through reparation.

For D.W. Winnicott, the depressive position is achieved once the individual is able to experience inner reality as necessarily "parallel to the objective" world outside (Winnicott 1941: 153). However, there is a core part of the self, comprising its decisionist depth, that is, incommunicable; this core self is the only survival of the absolute thinking of the paranoid-schizoid layer: there must be a self to decide, to process information about the environment, and to relate to other agents whose selves are equally inviolable (Tuber 2008: 33).

This is the central Kleinian-Winnicottian precept about the self: The individual is, at each life stage, in danger of losing the personal quality of her experience by being unable to bridge the gulf between inner processes and interpersonal or environmental reality (Mitchell and Black 1995: 124). An expanded notion of creativity sees at the self's core an artist who must create reparative analogues between, on the inside, the creative processes that spring from inner life, and, on the outside, the Other-generated realities that the creative self tends to mistakenly interpret as threats to the self but which must be transmuted into positivity through an ongoing "negotiat[ion of] intersubjective experience" (Bollas 1987: 13; cf. Klein 1937; Winnicott 1991: 69). Our choice of Kleinian object relations as a lens through which to view Donald Fagen's life is based upon the singer's development from an original Other-object repression (an id-centered infantilism) to his eventual turn to reparation of his primal ego error through therapy and social openness (a reality-mediated maturity) (Freud 1920, 1923).

4.3 Methodology

The present work is a single case study that uses object relations theory and psychobiography to uncover the motivational complexities that have accompanied the subject's interpersonal relations over the course of his life. Positive psychology will be utilized to gain insight into the subject's attempts to retain a sense of vitality toward work, colleagues, family, and society as a whole. It is becoming more apparent that individuals make narrative sense of their lives by dovetailing complex self-orientations, such as irony or nostalgia, with thought domains and semantic fields of concern to their personal development (Sedikides, et al. 2015; Zhou et al. 2009). This being the case, positive psychology is useful in exploring how subjects orient themselves to apparent failures, errors, and humiliations from their past that continue to loom in their present self-image (cf. the other chapters in this volume). The subject of this study, Donald Fagen, took a stance toward the world based upon what we have termed primal ego error. He spent his later adulthood re-evaluating his use of this mistaken idea that the self can become authentic through art alone. For data, this study uses Donald Fagen's recordings, published writings, and interviews, along with both interviews and writings of important persons in Fagen's life as well as secondary sources relevant to Fagen's motivations and life choices. This selection of material was evaluated using the author's idiosyncratic dovetailing of object relations psychobiographical theory contextualized through a history of ideas focus.

4.4 Findings

4.4.1 Childhood and Adolescence (1948–1967)

Donald Jay Fagen was born on January 10, 1948, in Passaic, New Jersey. His father, Joseph "Jerry" Fagen, was an accountant; his mother, Elinor Fagen, née Rosenberg, took care of Donald and his younger sister Susan, who was born in 1954 (Sweet 2015: 7). Two influences seem to have been formative of Fagen's child psyche: The first, which we may associate more with Fagen's father Jerry, was the family's move to Kendall Park, a planned community in New Jersey, in 1958; the second was Fagen's relationship with mother Elinor, an interaction that was fraught with tension but which also held within it Fagen's aesthetic path of escape from the "identity confusion" (Erikson 1968: 197) that accompanied life under his parents' roof.

The Fagen family's move to Kendall Park was traumatic for 10-year-old Donald, who would thereafter consider himself a "prisoner," deprived as he had become of Passaic's racial diversity and comparative cultural richness, not to mention the relatives who were left behind in the city (Goodman 2006, April 13). What scene greeted the young boy as the family car pulled up to their new home? It was a caricature of a neighborhood, or so Fagen recalls: The "housing development...was very isolated, it was built on farmland. It had just been built so there were these big mounds of dirt still on every corner..." (Fagen 2013b, November 29). Kendall Park's yards of overturned sod and "little twigs instead of trees" (Sweet 2015: 8) that had to be held up by metal wires (Fagen 2013b, November 29) suggested more a Gothic graveyard than a welcoming community to the young Fagen, who "expected coffins to come out of the ground, just like in...that movie Poltergeist" (Fagen 2013a, November 29).

Though he blamed both of his parents for the move, Donald may have put more of the onus on his accountant father, who "actually worked for the guy who built [the houses]" at the Kendall Park development (Sweet 2015: 8). The real presence in the Fagen household, though, was its matriarch, Elinor Fagen. Though Jerry seemed to have no sensitivity to music or art (Fagen 2013a: 73), Elinor was, in Donald's words:

> a fine swing singer who from the age of five through her teen years worked with a trio in a hotel in the Catskills.... Her career as 'Ellen Ross' came to an end at sixteen when stage fright prevented her from walking up to the microphone on Major Bowes Amateur Hour.... After that, she performed only...while she was at her housewifely chores, waking the kids up, vacuuming, cooking and cleaning (Fagen 2013a: 1).

Donald's vocal style was thus a development of his mother's peculiar manner of phrasing, which he heard constantly from his earliest days: "I can't ever remember when there was silence around the house," Donald recalls (Sweet 2015: 7). However, with Elinor's gift of music came a liability: she passed her nervousness, which could take the form of panic attacks and stage fright, to Donald, whose later obsession with doing scores or even hundreds of takes helped to extend already interminable recording schedules and whose predisposition to performance anxiety contributed to an absence from the stage between 1974 and 1995. This "double-bind" (Bateson et al. 1956) aspect of Donald's relationship with his mother reflects what Edith Jacobson describes as a mother's contribution to her infant's "development of functional ego activity" by, among other nurturing activities, "sing[ing] to him" (Jacobson 1965: 37; as cited in Bollas 1987: 13). Such motherly serenading provides a sense of the outside world's reality both by stimulating the child to act and by shaping the contour of any of the child's possible acts by calling them forth according to the parent's idiosyncratic, personal style.

By the time Donald reached his early teens, he used the musical sensibility derived from his mother to distance himself somewhat from his stultifying domestic milieu. He gave up on the rock and roll and R&B records he had been listening to and turned into a "jazz snob" (Sweet 2015: 8). Being one of the only Jews in his high school class (Rzepka 2001, 28 February) surely contributed further to his growing sense of alienation, as did his feeling of inadequacy vis-à-vis the opposite sex. Later on, though, when Fagen entered Bard College, he realized that a return to soul, blues, and folk rock would be necessary, in the interests of "relevance and authenticity," along with a concern for where "the most desirable girls were gathering" (Fagen 2013a: 19). In both of these moves, we see Fagen's bohemianism, his dual concern to remain, in Winnicott's words, "isolated" without being "insulated" (Winnicott 1965: 187) from mainstream culture. In other words, Fagen sought out a nuanced position in relation to various musical genres so as to preserve, on the one hand, his connection to the "beatster" or "hipster" alternative culture, but, on the other hand, a more diffused association with humanity at large.

4.4.2 Early Strivings to Early Dan (1967–1977)

At Bard College in 1967, Fagen met Walter Becker (1950–2017), and the duo immediately began writing songs together (Kim 2017, 3 September). Becker was, for the more reticent and detached Fagen, something of a beatnik muse. Becker had lived through a traumatic childhood, having been told his absent mother was dead when, as he later found out, she was alive and well and living in the United Kingdom (Sweet 2015: 110). As if one parental trauma was not enough, before Becker reached adulthood, his father had a heart attack and later died (Raidió Teilifís Éireann 2017, 23 September). Becker's disordered beginnings give us insight into Donald's attraction to him: Fagen wished to gain distance from his conventional upbringing and Becker's very mode of being seemed an exile from normality. Against Fagen-the studied cultivator of the bohemian-one could certainly contrast the more authentic Becker, the latter having his beatness forced upon him by adverse circumstances. Together, Fagen and Becker straddled all the classic bohemian binaries: Whereas Donald was especially attuned to notes on a musical staff, Becker was more logocentric, a bender of words and phrases (Watts 1976/2018: 68). Fagen was jazz; Becker was blues. Fagen viewed the comfort of his *faux-luxe* suburban upbringing with a wistful irony; Becker's alienation from the mainstream was more profound, his sardonicism more layered, filmic, and surrealistic, the better to conceal his inner orphan (Palmer 1982, 20 October; Himes 2017, 5 September).

The songs that the pair began to compose reflected their bohemian concern to both dramatize and work through their ambivalence toward their early experience of straight culture and the various escape routes that hip culture seemed to present. An early trio of Becker-Fagen compositions uses the metaphors of a foxhole, a well, and a cave to represent the protagonists' object relations, their inner representations of significant others who stand in for society's values. The narrator of *Fire in the Hole* (Steely Dan 1973: side B, track 2) is undergoing a mental breakdown, and he uses the trope of a pot of liquid "boiling over," leaving "nothing left to burn" to express his overwhelming mental arrest. His crisis has been caused by the straight world's insistence, which the narrator hears as a superego-installed "woman's voice" that he "serve and not...speak." Pressure from the conflicting motives of compliance and resentment dries up the narrator's vital moisture, leaving the foxhole-interred speaker "wish[ing] someone would open up the door." *Gullywater*'s (Steely Dan 2017) narrator likens the mind of a jealous lover to a desiccated well that yields only mud. The second verse speaks of a dog enclosed in a room who seems to be smiling as he is given a new leash, which the lyric sardonically dubs a "lifeline." The room is the human mind and the dog represents the ease with which humans ensnare themselves, ironically, through the only means they have of finding freedom: their mental apparatus. In *Stone Piano* (Steely Dan 1969–1971/2002: track 4), the narrator is torn between the reality of his life as a clerk in a "ten-cent store" and his fantasies of being outside of society as an "outlaw" or "samurai." He finds a bohemian third option by listening to the song of his internal objects, which, like the automated sounds of a player piano, both are and are not subject to his conscious control. Contact with the unconscious ground of thought is maintained through this mineral instrument, but the metaphor is given a darker turn by the lyrics about being "Calvary bound." Is this strange keyboard also a tomb? Once again, we find in Fagen the bohemian who stands on the fence between two degrees of alienation from the mainstream, one mild and optimistic, another extreme and antisocial.

4.4.3 Apex to Nadir (1977–1993)

The apex of Steely Dan's recording career may have been their 1977 release *Aja*, the first of their 1970s albums to sell over a million units (Breithaupt 2011: 68). By this time, Fagen and Becker had perfected their approach to writing and recording, and though their use of expensive hired musicians and studio equipment made the price tag for *Aja* higher than any of their previous albums, the end seemed to justify the means, both artistically and fiscally (Sweet 2015: 161).

However, once Fagen and Becker reconvened to begin recording *Aja*'s follow-up, which was to be titled *Gaucho* (Steely Dan 2000), cracks in the facade began to show. First, there were technical issues. The elaborate and detailed process of recording now had to be measured not in months, but in years, involving scores of musicians and teams of engineers and assistants. They "worked on one song for so long and listened back to it so many times that they actually wore the oxide off the [analog reel-to-reel] tape" (Sweet 2015: 137). To further complicate matters, Fagen and Becker gave their engineer Roger Nichols a large sum of money to build an 8-bit computer that became a forerunner of the drum machine (InfoWorld 1984, April 30). Those involved in the tortuous sessions recall Nichols typing digital code into his computer for hours on end, all in order to create subtle deviations in the timing of the drum beats that would give the mechanized sounds a quasi-human feel (liner notes to Steely Dan 2000). Then came a true recording disaster: in December 1979 an inexperienced recording engineer accidentally erased three-fourths of a nearly completed track called *The Second Arrangement*, which upset Fagen and Becker so much that they decided against rerecording it, even though it was one of the best songs they had written for the album (Aaron 2012, 29 April). One month later, Becker's girlfriend Karen Stanley died of a drug overdose in the New York apartment she shared with the goatee-sporting guitarist (Smith 1994, 27 January). Lastly, Becker, whose addiction to various drugs was causing him to become uncharacteristically undependable (Sweet 2015: 189), was hit by a taxicab while crossing a New York City street, breaking both of his legs and causing him to miss much of the album's mixing (Pareles 2017, 3 September).

At the beginning of summer 1981, Fagen announced that Steely Dan had officially disbanded (Palmer 1981, 17 June). Walter Becker moved to Maui, replaced drugs with health food, and got into a relationship with his yoga instructor, who quickly became his first wife (Gill 1995). Fagen released his first solo album, *The Nightfly* (1982), but soon found himself unable to finish any songs, though he composed on the piano for hours each day (Smith 1993, 20 May). Long after his recovery, Fagen revealed that his writer's block was a result of depression and paranoia over the failure of his life to live up to idealizations he first formed in childhood. "I think I was a very childlike person," Fagen admitted. "I was very idealistic as a child about certain things, about the kind of life I'd have and the kind of relationship I'd have, and when these things didn't work out…it was very disappointing to me"

(Cromelin 1991, 3 November). This mistaken perfectionism, in Fagen's later appraisal, not only caused his post-*Nightfly* malaise but also precipitated two breakups: that between Fagen and Becker and that between Fagen and his most important 1980s love interest, novelist Marcelle Clements. It seems that Fagen's bohemian ideal of a quasi-utopian life could not be easily detached from the prefabricated Kendall Park homestead where it began nor could it be divorced from the voice of his mother, whose songs offered an unstable mixture of security and exoticism. In an unguarded moment, Fagen likened his tendency to hole up in recording studios to the womb-like qualities of his childhood home: "[Recording studios] remind me of my parents' house; wall-to-wall carpets, bland colours, Swedish furniture. I find them very comforting" (Sweet 2015: 232). Here we see the bohemian ambivalence toward the *faux-luxe*, the affordable domestic "luxury": The desire is for an authenticity that retreats teasingly from the plush surfaces of walls and furniture whose velvet sheen speaks the language of European sophistication but with a Woolworth accent.

In any case, Fagen began seeing a New York City psychotherapist who helped him to recognize that the same perfectionism that led him to withdraw into music was impairing his relationships with friends, family, and romantic partners. It appears that Fagen turned to therapy in desperation over his breakup with writer Marcelle Clements, a situation that was doubtless exacerbated by his lack of musical direction. Around 1983, Fagen composed *On the Dunes* (Fagen 1993, track 7), a song that summed up his hitting rock bottom in the wake of *The Nightfly*. The song's narrator becomes despondent, even suicidal when his romantic partner breaks off their relationship: "When you spoke, you must have known it was a kind of homicide." Like the rooted-to-the-spot figure in C.D. Friedrich's *Der Wanderer über dem Nebelmeer* (c. 1818), or like the hapless protagonist of Kobo Abē's *Woman of the Dunes* (1964), Fagen's narrator finds himself trapped in a landscape whose dynamism contrasts with his own relative immobility. To be on the dunes is to be betwixt and between, neither on the more level beach face nor on the firmer ground further inland. The man of the dunes sees the inexorable pulse of nature, of time, in the swells that flow in from the immense sea, but they only mirror his own inner sterility as they break against the shore, their force dissipated. He sees couples living a picturesque life of "pretty boats, sweeping along the shore," an ideal that in his case has proven to be a mistake, since it is unattainable in the real world. Indeed, he cannot rid himself of the vision of "pretty women, with their lovers by their side," living out the happy life from which he is exiled. Hence, the song's lyrics offer a vivid picture of a "defense against internal bad objects" (Pataki 2014: 423), wherein omnipotence and a sense of tying off all loose ends are purchased at the price of self-objectification and a "sense of lifelessness" (Ogden 2002: 773). Also, Fagen's repeating of the adjective "pretty" brings to mind the last cynical line of Hemingway's fictionalized chronicle of Parisian Bohemia, *The Sun Also Rises* (1926), wherein an emasculated Jake Barnes, in response to his lover's suggestion that the past could have been different, answers "Isn't it pretty to think so?"

4.4.4 Dan Mark II (1993–)

With the release of his second solo album, *Kamakiriad* (1993), the former Steely Dan frontman began to conceptualize his primal ego error in his art, and thus he began the slow process of object reparation. The album's appearance marked the healing of the two most important relationship areas in Fagen's life: Walker Becker produced the album and thus restored to Fagen the aesthetic relationship that the *Gaucho* debacle had severed; on the romantic front, Fagen had found the love of his life in singer-songwriter Libby Titus (née Jurist, b. 1947), who, like Becker, co-wrote a song on the new album. By 1989, Fagen was living with Titus and her two teenage children, and he was soon coaxed onstage by his new partner at an informal club show she produced (Sweet 2015: 251–252). This led to Fagen reuniting with Becker onstage at further Titus-organized shows, the end result being, in the wake of *Kamakiriad*'s release, a reformed Steely Dan touring again for the first time in close to two decades.

Before Walter Becker fell ill and died in the fall of 2017, the reformed Dan had recorded two albums and completed numerous sold-out world tours. Not all was sweetness and light during these years, however. Becker admitted his stamina for endless recording sessions was diminished, leading him to focus more on his family and other nonmusic interests, a fact that led Fagen to record a pair of solo albums without Becker's presence. On the Fagen home front, an ominous blip occurred on January 4, 2016, when Donald spent a night in a NYC jail after "shoving" his spouse Libby (Blistein 2016, 5 January). In the face of all difficulties, though, Fagen has remained passionately devoted to his wife, and despite the loss of his lifelong writing partner, he continues, even to the time of this writing, to keep his music alive through steady touring. Overall, our examination of Donald Fagen has offered glimpses of how transformation of errors into emotional growth and fulfillment can be achieved in the life of a creative individual caught in the pressure-filled arena of the modern capitalist marketplace.

4.5 Conclusions and Recommendations for Further Research

Throughout his life, Donald Fagen utilized the concept of bohemianism to shield his core self from the conventional lifestyle and culture that surrounded him in postwar America. Beat poets and jazz musicians lived within the bourgeois world but were not of it, and the budding muso embraced their stance as both a self-definition and a criterion for communion with other outsiders. However, planted within Fagen's bohemianism was a seed of potential discord: If it is true that community is purchased through aesthetic authenticity, there is a danger of replacing real-life interaction with an all-encompassing focus on the creative act. Obsession with creating the perfect Steely Dan track was the salient manifestation of Fagen's primal ego error; this Other-object repression led to the implosion of Fagen's primary creative relationship when Walter Becker left for Hawaii in the early 1980s. His failures to sustain both his creative verve and his romantic life led to Fagen's near breakdown by 1983. This situation forced Fagen to reach out beyond his comfort zone; he underwent psychotherapy and entered a relationship with an extrovert in Libby Titus, who pushed him back onto the stage and back into a less restrictive social space.

Overall, this study suggests that positive psychology as it is usually conceived is unable, on its own, to render a full-bodied understanding of the self. Object relations theory, coupled with a history of ideas approach, has yielded unexpected insights into the motivations and life strategies that allowed Fagen to survive and even thrive in a society that often seemed to him devoid of value, aesthetic, or otherwise. The psychology of error and failure has been contextualized through our analytical narration of a popular musician's life, and we have made tangible how cultural and ideological beliefs interact with traumatic and generative life events. Donald Fagen initially viewed his achievement of a bohemian self-image as an idealistic overcoming of the childhood alienation from family, peers, and society; however, through various psychological, interpersonal, and professional setbacks, the singer came to see his Beat self-object (Kohut 1971) as a dead end that had to be completed by more open-ended, interactive relationships that provided a more sure grounding for his reality principle (Freud 1926/1950) and which, at the same time, punctured the isolation booth that, so we have contended in this chapter, Fagen had constructed out of his own Cold War version of bohemianism.

On the psychobiography front, more research could result in a fuller picture of the other half of Steely Dan, Walter Becker, whose psyche formation and later life experiences differed from Donald Fagen's in that, as we have been suggesting, Becker embodied avant-garde bohemianism to a much greater degree than did Fagen. Analysis of Becker's ambivalent embrace of quasi-New Age healthy living in Maui and his efforts to become a father and husband could give us more insights into positive psychology as it intersects with addiction and family dynamics. In terms of the psychology of mistakes and errors, this chapter could serve as a springboard for further forays into the interface between creativity and social/familial expectations. A promising theme in this line of research would be the developing artist's overriding perception that she is betraying or failing expectations even as she is carving out her own psychosocial space. We expect that a concept of errors/mistakes, if it is to be serviceable in studies of creative lives, will need further elaboration in the context either of Klein's notion of reparation (Klein 1937/1975) or of any number of similar corrective theories that attend to the aesthetic personality, such as those of Winnicott and Milner (Glover 2009).

References

Aaron, S. V. (2012, 29 April). The second arrangement (1979, unreleased). *Something Else*. Retrieved 10 September 2019, from http://somethingelsereviews.com/2012/04/29/steely-dan-sunday-the-second-arrangement-1979-unreleased/.

Abē, K. (1964). *The woman in the dunes*. New York: Alfred A. Knopf.

Banfield, M. (2007). From sentiment to sentimentality: A nineteenth-century lexicographical search. *19: Interdisciplinary Studies in the Long Nineteenth Century,* 4. DOI: https://doi.org/10.16995/ntn.459.

Bateson, G., Jackson, D.D., Haley, J. & Weakland, J. (1956). Toward a theory of schizophrenia. *Behav. Sci.*, 1(4): 251–254.

Baumeister, R. F. (1987). How the self became a problem: A psychological review of historical research. *J. of Personality and Soc. Psych.*, 52(1): 163–176.

Berlin, I. (1991). *The crooked timber of humanity: Chapters in the history of ideas*. New York: Alfred A. Knopf.

Blistein, J. (2016, 5 January). Steely Dan's Donald Fagen arrested for domestic assault. Retrieved 10 September 2019, from https://www.rollingstone.com/music/music-news/steely-dans-donald-fagen-arrested-for-domestic-assault-50634/.

Bollas, C. (1987). *The shadow of the object: Psychoanalysis of the unthought known*. New York: Columbia University Press.

Breithaupt, D. (2011). *Aja*. New York and London: Continuum.

Brown, M. R. (1985). *Gypsies and other Bohemians: The myth of the artist in nineteenth-century France*. Ann Arbor, MI: UMI Research Press.

Burroughs, W. S. (1959). *Naked lunch*. New York: Grove Press.

Choban, M. (2017, 7 December). Turn that heartbeat over again: Donald Fagen flies solo. *Oregon Artswatch*. Retrieved 10 September 2019, from http://www.orartswatch.org/turn-that-heartbeat-over-again-donald-fagen-flies-solo/.

Cromelin, R. (1991, 3 November). Return of the nightfly: Steely Dan co-creator Donald Fagen resurfaces after nearly a decade of silence, with new works and a new outlook on life. *Los Angeles Times*. Retrieved 10 September 2019, from http://articles.latimes.com/1991-11-03/entertainment/ca-1778_1_steely-dan.

De Botton, A. (2004). *Status anxiety*. New York: Pantheon Books.

Dinerstein, J. (2013). The mask of cool in postwar jazz and film noir. In U. Haselstein, et al. (Eds.), *The cultural career of coolness: Discourses and practices of affect control in European antiquity, the United States, and Japan* (pp. 109–126). Plymouth, U.K.: Lexington Books.

Erikson, E. (1968). *Identity: Youth and crisis*. New York and London: Norton.

Fagen, D. (1982). *The nightfly* [LP record album]. Warner Brothers Records.

Fagen, D. (1993). *Kamakiriad* [audio CD]. Reprise Records.

Fagen, D. (2013a). *Eminent hipsters*. New York: Viking.

Fagen, D. (2013b, 29 November). Donald Fagen on being a professional hipster (D. Dye, Interviewer) [Audio file]. Retrieved 10 September 2019, from https://www.npr.org/artists/15120953/donald-fagen.

Freud, S. (1920). *Beyond the pleasure principle*. S.E., 18: 1–64.

Freud, S. (1923). *The ego and the id*. S.E., 19: 1–66.

Freud, S. (1926/1950). *The question of lay analysis: An introduction to psychoanalysis*. New York: Norton. (Work originally appeared in 1926)

Friedrich, C. D. (c. 1818). *Der Wanderer über dem Nebelmeer* [Oil on canvas]. Hamburger Kunsthalle, Hamburg, Germany.

Gable, S. L. & Haidt, J. (2005). What (and why) is positive psychology? *Rev. of Gen. Psych.*, 9(2): 103–110.

Gill, A. (1995). The return of Steely Dan. *Mojo*. Retrieved 10 September 2019, from https://steelydan.com/mojo.html.

Glover, N. (2009). *Psychoanalytic aesthetics: An introduction to the British School*. London: Karnac.

Gluck, M. (2000). Theorizing the cultural roots of the bohemian artist. *Modernism/Modernity*, 7(3): 351–378.

Goodman, C. (2006, 13 April). A long-awaited third solo album finds Donald Fagen exploring the romantic edge. Retrieved 10 September 2019, from http://www.montereycountyweekly.com/news/local_news/a-long-awaited-third-solo-album-finds-donald-fagen-exploring/article_fbaa70cf-8379-5448-b75f-a285aadbab82.html.

Graña, C. (1964). *Bohemian versus bourgeois: French society and the French man of letters in the nineteenth century*. New York: Basic Books.

Hemingway, E. (1926). *The sun also rises*. Charles Scribner & Sons.

Himes, G. (2017, 5 September). Walter Becker was the Larry David of Steely Dan: An appreciation. *Paste*. Retrieved 10 September 2019, from https://www.pastemagazine.com/articles/2017/09/walter-becker-steely-dan.html.

Hoskyns, B. (2018). A squonk's tears: Steely Dan at forty-five. In B. Hoskyns (ed.), *Major dudes: A Steely Dan companion* (pp. xiii-xxiv). New York: Overlook Press.

InfoWorld. (1984, 30 April). Wendel: The amazing drum machine. *InfoWorld*, 6(18): 24.

Jacobson, E. (1965). *The self and the object world*. London: Hogarth.

Jørgensen, I. S. & Nafstad, H. E. (2005). Positive psychology: Historical, philosophical, and epistemological perspectives. *Tisddkrift for Norsk Psyckologforening*, 42: 885–896.

Kelley, J. (2018). Jim Jones and Romantic socialism. *The Jonestown Report*, 20. Retrieved 10 September 2019, from https://jonestown.sdsu.edu/?page_id=80804.

Kierkegaard, S. (1843/2009). Repetition: An experiment in experimental psychology. In Søren Kierkegaard, *Repetition and Philosophical Crumbs* (pp. 1–81). Oxford and New York: Oxford University Press. (Work originally appeared in 1843)

Kim, M. (2017, 3 September). Steely Dan's Donald Fagen pens tribute to Walter Becker. *Pitchfork*. Retrieved 10 September 2019, from https://pitchfork.com/news/steely-dans-donald-fagen-pens-tribute-to-walter-becker/.

Klein, M. (1935). A contribution to the psychogenesis of manic-depressive states. *Int. J. Psycho-Anal.*, 16: 145–174.

Klein, M. (1937/1975). Love, guilt and reparation. In *Love, guilt and reparation and other works, 1921–1945* (pp. 306–343). London: Hogarth. (Work originally appeared in 1937)

Klein, M. (1940). Mourning and its relation to manic-depressive states. *Int. J. Psycho-Anal.*, 21: 125–153.

Klein, M. (1946). Notes on some schizoid mechanisms. *Int. J. Psycho-Anal.*, 27: 99–110.

Kohut, H. (1971). *The analysis of the self: A systematic approach to the psychoanalytic treatment of narcissistic personality disorders*. Chicago: University of Chicago Press.

Martin, G. (2003, 6 June/2018). A droll double act. In B. Hoskyns (ed.), *Major dudes: A Steely Dan companion* (pp. 235–240). New York: Overlook Press. (Work originally appeared in *Independent*, 6 June, 2003)

Mayer, C.-H. (2017). *The life and creative work of Paulo Coelho: A psychobiography from a positive psychology perspective*. Cham, Switzerland: Springer.

McBride, W. (2012). Existentialism as a cultural movement. In S. Crowell (ed.), *The Cambridge companion to existentialism* (pp. 50–69). New York: Cambridge University Press.

McNulty, B. (2013, 18 October). Eminent Hipsters by Donald Fagen, review. The Telegraph. Retrieved 10 September 2019, from https://www.telegraph.co.uk/culture/books/artsandentertainmentbooksreview/10382567/Eminent-Hipsters-by-Donald-Fagen-review.html.

Mitchell, S. A. & Black M. J. (1995). *Freud and beyond: A history of modern psychoanalytic thought*. New York: Basic Books.

Moneta, G. B. (2013). *Positive psychology: A critical introduction*. Basingstoke, U.K.: Palgrave Macmillan.

Ogden, T. H. (2002). A new reading of the origins of object-relations theory. *Int. J. Psychoanal.*, 83: 767–782.

Palmer, R. (1981, 17 June). The pop life: Steely Dan duo going it alone. *New York Times*, p. 25.

Palmer, R. (1982, October 20). The pop life: Donald Fagen returns to 50's roots. *New York Times*, p. 24.
Pareles, J. (2017, 3 September). Walter Becker, guitarist, songwriter and founder of Steely Dan, died at 67. *New York Times*. Retrieved 10 September 2019, from https://www.nytimes.com/2017/09/03/arts/music/walter-becker-dead-steely-dan.html.
Pataki, T. (2014). Fairbairn and parititive conceptions of mind. In: D. Scharff & G. Clarke (Eds.), *Fairbairn and the object relations tradition* (pp. 417–430). London: Karnac.
Pollock, B. (2012/2018). Donald Fagen. In B. Hoskyns (ed.), *Major dudes: A Steely Dan companion* (pp. 255–259). New York: Overlook Press. (Work originally appeared in *Songfact*, 7 November, 2012)
Raidió Teilifís Éireann. (2017, 23 September). Walter Becker wrongly believed his mother had died. Retrieved 10 September 2019, from https://www.rte.ie/entertainment/2017/0923/907002-walter-beckers-troubled-childhood-recalled/.
Regen, J. (2013, January). Donald Fagen: Inside the process. *Keyboard*, 39(1): 14–20.
Rolling Stone (2017, 15 November). Walter Becker's widow details Steely Dan co-founder's swift illness, death. Retrieved 10 September 2019, from https://www.rollingstone.com/music/music-news/walter-beckers-widow-details-steely-dan-co-founders-swift-illness-death-120254/.
Rorabaugh, W. J. (2015). *American hippies*. New York: Cambridge University Press.
Ross, A. (2008). *The rest is noise*. London: Fourth Estate.
Russian Ballet History (2010). Diaghilev's Ballets Russes, 1909–1929. Retrieved 10 September 2019, from http://www.russianballethistory.com/sergediaghilevfounder.htm.
Rzepka, S. (2001, 28 February). Bringing up Steely Dan. *Cleveland Jewish News*. Retrieved 10 September 2019, from https://www.clevelandjewishnews.com/archives/bringing-up-steely-dan/article_75f7e03b-bd4e-51bb-9337-81d6a526b2d1.html.
Saikia, R. (2011). *The Venice Lido: A Blue Guide travel monograph*. Taunton, Somerset, U.K.: Somerset Books.
Sartre, J.-P. (1938). *La nausée*. Paris: Gallimard.
Schmitt, C. (1921/2014). *Dictatorship: From the origin of the modern concept of sovereignty to proletarian class struggle*. Cambridge: Polity. (Work originally appeared in 1921)
Schmitt, C. (1925/1986). *Political Romanticism*. Cambridge and London: MIT Press. (Work originally appeared in 1925)
Sedikides, C., Wildschut, T., Routledge, C., Arndt, J., Hepper, E. G., & Zhou, X. (2015). To nostalgize: Mixing memory with affect and desire. *Adv. Exp. Soc. Psy.*, 51: 189–273.
Seigel, J. E. (1986). *Bohemian Paris: Culture, politics, and the boundaries of bourgeois life, 1830–1930*. New York: Viking.
Smith, G. (1993, 20 May). From nought to 40 in 11 years.... *UK Independent*. Retrieved 10 September 2019, from https://www.independent.co.uk/arts-entertainment/music/interview-from-nought-to-40-in-11-years-donald-fagen-has-been-away-a-long-time-desperately-avoiding-2323998.html.
Smith, G. (1994, 27 January). A big hello from Hawaii.... *UK Independent*. Retrieved 10 September 2019, from https://www.independent.co.uk/incoming/pop-a-big-hello-from-hawaii-seeking-to-recover-after-steely-dan-walter-becker-hid-out-on-an-island-1402869.html.
Steely Dan (recording artist). (1969–1971/2002). *Android warehouse* [audio CD]. Delta Music. (Work originally recorded 1969–1971)
Steely Dan (recording artist). (1973). *Can't by a thrill* [LP record album]. ABC Records.
Steely Dan (recording artist). (1978). *Greatest Hits* [audio CD]. MCA.
Steely Dan (recording artist). (2000). Gaucho [audio CD reissue of original 1980 recording].
Steely Dan (recording artist). (2017). Gullywater [audio file]. Retrieved 10 September 2019, from https://www.youtube.com/watch?v=yeoOq1mlRsU. (Work originally recorded ca. 1972)
Strube, J. (2017, November). Socialism and esotericism in July Monarchy France. *Hist. Rel.*, 57: 197–221.
Sweet, B. (2015). *Steely Dan: Reelin' in the years*. 2nd ed. London: Omnibus.
Tuber, S. (2008). *Attachment, play, and authenticity: A Winnicott primer*. Lanham: Jason Aronson.

Watts, M. (1976/2018). Art for art's sake. In B. Hoskyns (ed.), *Major dudes: A Steely Dan companion* (pp. 66–99). New York: Overlook Press. (Work originally appeared in *Melody Maker*, 19 June 1976)

Wilson, E. (2003). *Bohemians: The glamorous outcasts*. London: I.B. Tauris.

Winnicott, D. W. (1941). The observation of infants in a set situation. *Int. J. Psycho-Anal.*, 22: 2

Winnicott, D. W. (1965). Communicating and not communicating leading to a study of certain opposites. In *The maturational processes and the facilitating environment: Studies in the theory of emotional development* (pp. 179–192). London: Hogarth Press and the Institute of Psycho-Analysis.

Winnicott, D. W. (1991). *Playing and reality*. Hove & New York: Brunner-Routledge.

Zhou, X., Vohs, K. D., & Baumeister, R. F. (2009). The symbolic power of money: Reminders of money alter social distress and physical pain. *Psy. Sci.*, 20: 700–706.

James L. Kelley after receiving his education at three American universities, settled into a life of researching and writing about, among other things, the fascinating lives of creative people. His first two books are *A Realism of Glory: Lectures on Christology in the Works of Protopresbyter John Romanides* (Rollinsford, NH: Orthodox Research Institute), published in 2009, and *Anatomyzing Divinity: Studies in Science, Esotericism and Political Theology* (Walterville, OR: TrineDay), published in 2011. His third book, *Orthodoxy, History, and Esotericism: New Studies* (Dewdney, B.C.: Synaxis Press, 2016), is a history of esoteric influences on Western religious culture.

Part II
Mistakes, Errors and Failure in Society

Chapter 5
Mistakes, Errors, and Failures in the Cultural Context of Aging

Sofia von Humboldt

Abstract The increase of longevity of and within the older global population itself is incrementing the proportion of older adults. Looking at the worldwide diversity in population aging implies that this concept is seen through different cultural presuppositions.

Although an incidence on the role of culture in aging is not novel, different cultural interactions strengthen the pertinence of exploring mistakes, errors, and failures in the cultural context of aging well.

Diverse aging perceptions in different cultures influence the use of that information to build accurate culturally sensitive measures. Moreover, an appropriate response to distortions and conventions in communication with cross-cultural older adults in policy interventions and an awareness of possible drawbacks in the interpretation of the outcomes point out relevant innate challenges when working cross-culturally in old age. Cultural concerns concerning the communicative style, emotional states, awareness of the intervention format, and the local hierarchy of values (e.g., socially desirable viewpoints) may invalidate research and policy interventions among older populations. The present chapter discusses mistakes, errors, and failures in the cultural context of research, policy, and interventions in old age. The chapter will conclude with a discussion of future suggestions for research and policy interventions.

Keywords Mistakes · Errors · Failures · Interventions · Mistakes · Policy · Older adults · Research

5.1 Introduction

Old age has been defined in various manners, in different circumstances, and for a range of social groups. In most cases, it can be characterized either by purpose, by chronology, or by cultural standards. Someone is considered culturally old when they seem old by society standards and are looked upon as old according to physical

S. von Humboldt (✉)
William James Research Center, ISPA – Instituto Universitário, Almada, Portugal

E. Vanderheiden, C.-H. Mayer (eds.), *Mistakes, Errors and Failures across Cultures*, https://doi.org/10.1007/978-3-030-35574-6_5

or lifestyle particularities commonly related to old age, though not necessarily regarding their abilities or self-evaluation about being old (Botelho and Thane 2001; Stavenuiter and Bijsterveld 2000). Indeed, gerontologists initially focused on culture as one of the principles in the sociocultural process of aging (Perkinson and Solimeo 2013).

Current cross-cultural studies of aging and well-being have considered cultural divergence in different settings (e.g., Hilton et al. 2012; Lewis 2011; von Humboldt et al. 2013c). Indeed, research has highlighted cultural differences, in particular comparing non-Western to Western cultures (Iwamasa and Iwasaki 2011; von Humboldt and Leal 2014). Considerable variation was found in studies comparing American and Japanese perceptions of successful aging, for instance, in terms of health, longevity, genes, life satisfaction, loneliness, friends and family, and choices making (Iwamasa and Iwasaki 2011; von Humboldt and Leal 2014).

Cultural definitions are generally implicit, that is, they are not often explicitly pointed out by older adults, and, as a consequence, they are less likely to be disclosed in quantitative data. Indeed, cultural definitions are incorporated in cultural practices, which are commonly implicit and standardized. Nevertheless, they may provide the cultural framework for understanding the context of aging (Hilton et al. 2012).

Furthermore, the validity of aging measures may be questioned, namely, when researchers are performing comparisons across cultures. Interestingly, there are as yet insufficient cross-culture comparisons regarding aging (von Humboldt and Leal 2014).

Different cultural interactions strengthen the pertinence of exploring errors, mistakes, and failures in gerontological literature. For instance, triad evaluation has been adopted to interpret recreation and work in a Thai hill tribe older population. Free listing has also been adopted to characterize cultural diversity in distinct settings in the United States and Mexico (Schrauf and Sanchez 2008).

The older population (aged 85 or over) is expected to triple in the next 30 years. Additionally, as dementia is a common condition at age 85 (Jaul and Barron 2017) and the probability of losing the ability to think clearly increases, further difficulties in obtaining data may culminate in potential mistakes and intervention failures among the oldest-old (Wild et al. 2012).

This chapter is dedicated to mistakes, errors, and failures in cultural context of aging and is divided in the following sections: Sects. 5.2, 5.3, and 5.4

5.2 Mistakes and Errors in Gerontological Research

A cultural understanding and definition of aging is crucial. Nevertheless, measuring aging inside one culture and across different cultures has been an enduring challenge with potential errors and mistakes.

Indeed, research in gerontological literature is frequently prone to bias. Assessing different aspects of aging may be sensitive to various measurement error and bias in replies, such as general bias in response, answering in a socially approved way (social desirability bias), refraining from the use of extreme reply categories (central tendency bias), and not responding to the content of an element (acquiescence bias). Indeed, there are measurement errors and mistakes that can affect the quality of data (von Humboldt 2016).

5.2.1 General Bias in Response

An origin of general bias is innate to semantics; participants interpret words in a distinct way, and different understandings may exist (Veenhoven 1996). In addition, there is a debate about whether responses to questions concerning aging may actually be measuring other phenomena. One issue is that participants may have no opinion about their perspectives on aging. While we may suspect that questions about aging are well understood, responses may be false. For example, older adults who are satisfied with their lives may tend to respond that they are well overall (von Humboldt 2016).

Mistakes and errors may also be due to interview variation, such as the characteristics of the interviewer, sequence of questions, and diversification of the place where the interview is conducted (Sperlinger et al. 2004). Additionally, different means of interview administration, such as face-to-face interviews, via phone, or online, or whether participants can read the available answers may influence their response. In the situation where participants are unable to see the response options, answering imposes a memory load. As participants vary in their ability to manage such load, this increases the probability of bias and errors in the analysis (Patton 2002).

5.2.2 Social Desirability Bias

A common concern in gerontological research is whether interviewees provide specific replies in order to influence the interviewer and contribute to errors and mistakes, frequently with the goal of building a particular kind of culturally desired message. In fact, social desirability is the predisposition to reply to questions in a socially acceptable way (Li et al. 2013). Social desirability bias entails a significant problem in gerontological research with self-report measures and hinders the comprehension of individual tendencies and differences (Li et al. 2013).

Additionally, social desirability may have an effect on potential errors and mistakes and on the result validity. Hence, methods such as the application of forced-choice elements and use of proxies to provide answers may be used to prevent or decrease social desirability bias (Li et al. 2013).

5.2.3 *Acquiescence Bias*

Acquiescence is the predisposition to choose the higher or agreement replies (e.g., "yes," "true," or "agree") rather than the lower or disagreement replies (e.g., "no," "false," or "disagree"), regardless of content. Acquiescence bias may have an effect on any question where choices involve confirmation of an element, may be widely problematic in agree-disagree questions, and may become a significant source of errors and mistakes in gerontological literature (Martin et al. 2011).

Participants may choose answers to satisfy or impress individuals who appear more informed or with higher social status, such as researchers (Vannette and Krosnick 2014). These biased answers have a deep effect on the individual's genuine outlook of the construct being assessed by a gerontological measure and lead to relevant errors and mistakes. Around 15–20% of participants, on average, seem to exhibit acquiescence across studies (Krosnick et al. 2011). Acquiescence is more common with participants who privilege motivation and when an element needs substantial cognitive work to be answered accurately. Therefore, acquiescence bias may illustrate a major obstacle for researchers (Vannette and Krosnick 2014; Saris et al. 2010). Research legitimacy can be jeopardized by acquiescence bias, as it increases the probability of errors and mistakes concerning relationships between variables (Podsakoff et al. 2003). Furthermore, research has proposed that acquiescence bias is linked to the mental effort required to fully evaluate the validity of an affirmation and is related to some characteristics, such as restricted cognitive and verbal skills (Vannette and Krosnick 2014).

Rather than discard "agree/disagree," "true/ false," and "yes/no" answer styles, researchers have developed methods for minimizing acquiescence bias (Vannette and Krosnick 2014). One solution is to show elements with a specific set of construct responses. In short, if a question aims to assess the personal meaning of a problem to a participant, it is desirable to ask the participant, "What is the importance of this matter to you? Extremely important, very important, moderately important, unimportant, or anything important?", rather than asking whether they "agree" or "disagree" with a statement like: "This question is important to me." This approach tends to eliminate pressure toward an affirmative response (Vannette and Krosnick 2014).

The set of answers has several implications for research using quantitative tools. First, systematic population disparities in responses may promote misreading the questionnaire data and therefore errors and mistakes. Moreover, data from older adults reveal a greater acquiescent predisposition compared to younger individuals (Moum 1988). This is also true for psychiatric patients, who also have high acquiescent responses (Stones 1977). The abovementioned problems have not yet been appropriately addressed, even in procedures that include equivalent shares of positive and negative elements, since biased responses scores are predicted to be distributed closest to the numerical center of the scale and away from the ends of the distribution, which may lead to major errors and mistakes in the results.

5.2.4 Central Tendency Bias

Central tendency bias indicates that individuals may show an inclination for middle range (or midpoint) replies (e.g., 3–5 on 7-point scales) and refrain from extreme replies (e.g., "1" or "7" on 7-point scales). The mentioned midrange may be understood by participants as an ampler category compared to other values on the scale. Participants may also give identical, midpoint replies or ratings for multiple elements, rather than show solid points of view regarding the question subject matter. This may lead to subsequent errors and mistakes in the analysis of the results. Contrary to this central tendency bias, some participants may decide to choose the extreme values in their replies. Furthermore, some people are drawn to particular values, such as a popular numbers, like "7" (Sperlinger et al. 2004).

Taking into account the obstacles intrinsic to using open-ended narrative data, researchers often consider the alternative of using clear-cut numbers: "I'd give myself a five." Actually, numbers virtually code themselves. Nevertheless, what they mean and what they appear to say is not necessarily the same for each participant. For example, there is a significant emphasis in East-Asian philosophy on the middle, which may imply general constraint. For instance, respondents may refrain from assessing themselves with a six as it may seem arrogant or because they still have unfulfilled objectives, even though they perceive their lives as very good. In Western areas, for instance, in Ireland, where stoicism is often positively perceived, respondents may assess themselves with high ratings. Indeed, answers to questionnaires in the context of aging may be affected by the cultural context (von Humboldt 2016).

Refraining from extreme responses undermines data significance as it approaches the means of the group. To avoid this bias, a possible solution is to have fewer questions. This has proven to decrease the central tendency bias in results. An alternative solution is to modify the order of questions, making them seem more interesting to respondents. Considering that data should be as appropriate as accurate, the central tendency bias implies misunderstanding the genuine perspective of the participant on the subject and ultimately leads to significant errors and mistakes (Sperlinger et al. 2004).

Elaborating plans and policies based on the present conditions among older adults, given the lack of research on upcoming cultural changes, may lead to significant mistakes. More research on aging should be designed to be directly translatable into future intervention strategies in the lives of older people or recommendations for local or general policies (Kunkel and Morgan 2015).

5.3 Failures in Interventions, Policies, and Methods Among Older Populations

During the most recent decades, numerous researchers have studied culturally diverse meanings. Considerable transcultural differences have the potential to affect the underlying causes of aging; hence addressing them in interventions is relevant for preventing failures (Diener and Suh 2000). Moreover, in Western and non-Western backgrounds, there is evidence of cultural disparities in aging style, with significant implications for aging policies and preventing potential failures (Danyuthasilpe et al. 2009). When not taken into account, different cultural perspectives may contribute to failures in policy and intervention format and design. Most of methodologies were designed and certified for use with older groups of people in developed countries of North American and European continents (von Humboldt and Leal 2014). Hence, their relevance for older segments in other regions, such as East Asia, or in other developing countries is fairly arguable (Draper 2007; von Humboldt and Leal 2014). In this section, we will discuss culturally diverse meanings in interventions, transcultural differences in policies, and format challenges for interventions and policies.

5.3.1 Culturally Diverse Meanings in Interventions

An issue that may lead to failure in interventions is the question of which cultural contexts should be included, especially when minorities and other ethnic groups are encompassed in interventions. Up to date, there is a lack of information in the literature about this relevant issue (Potter and Hepburn 2005; Humboldt 2016). Adapting interventions to a different cultural context is much more complex than simply translating the elements into another language. In fact, participants reply to questions by using their specific cultural knowledge. When cultural sensitivity is not considered, the results of interventions and polices may be seriously compromised, and failures may occur.

From a transcultural perspective, there are culturally common notions of self and relationships. Therefore, older individuals in diverse cultures may classify diverse events and their involvement in relationships as relevant in the context of aging (Diener and Suh 2000). For example, the literature proposes that, in Western cultures, positivity and negativity are commonly perceived as contrasting. In relation to this, Ji and his colleagues (2001) presented diagrams demonstrating linear or nonlinear preference by American and Chinese participants and invited them to choose the diagram that best illustrated their lifetime progression of well-being. American participants often selected a linear diagram. On the contrary, Chinese participants frequently selected a nonlinear diagram. In fact, research has confirmed that meaning and experience differ culturally, thus influencing policy planning and interventions (Diener and Suh 2000; Uchida et al. 2004).

Moreover, in Western countries, personal goals are often prioritized as a function of the group's goals, while in interdependent cultural contexts, such as non-Western contexts, the person is connected to others and part of a comprehensive social unit, where the group takes precedence over personal needs (Markus and Kitayama 1991). In fact, in Western countries, personal self-fulfillment is culturally valued. Negative feelings and characteristics of the self are therefore seen as restricting happiness and successful aging. In a study of Portuguese older adults, social support, health and well-being, and stability and security were the main dimensions to represent feeling adjusted to aging (von Humboldt et al. 2013a). On the contrary, in Eastern cultures, social harmony and the balance between individuals in a relationship are dominant.

In addition, different studies have evaluated transcultural perspectives upon negative and positive emotions. For example, Americans perceive positive and negative emotions as bipolar extremes; in contrast, Asians seem to perceive the same emotions as coexisting. In addition, Kitayama et al. (2000) proposed that people in individualistic and independent cultures may be motivated to make the most of pleasant emotions and restrain unpleasant emotions; on the contrary, old people in interdependent cultures may be attracted to maintaining a balance between positivity and negativity (Uchida and Kitayama 2009: von Humboldt et al. 2013a, c; von Humboldt and Leal 2014).

Similarly, there are relations between East Asian perception of social harmony and specific Asian elements (e.g., religious elements). What is perceived as positive individually is often likely to result in collective complications (Suh 2002). For example, there is a strong recognition that a negative outcome can be related to personal achievements, appealing to the jealousy of other individuals (Suh 2002).

Likewise, a circumstance valued as negative individually is often perceived as a source for specific positive social outcomes. For example, an individual failure may become an opportunity to obtain social approval from others (Kan et al. 2009; von Humboldt and Leal 2014). The above examples illustrate the need to include the cultural context in policies and interventions in order to avoid failures.

5.3.2 *Transcultural Differences in Policies*

Aging policies are diverse, often harmonized with the context of Western countries, while frequently absent in developing countries.

Western countries, for example, in Europe, have implemented policies promoting active aging over the past two decades. Great importance has been given to a prolonged working life and opportunity for stressful employment in old age (Walker and Maltby 2012). In addition, organizations such as the European Commission, World Health Organization, and United Nations have been supporting active aging. The lack of economic support in old age is likely to lead to more older workers, which can be considered a disadvantage to well-being and health in advanced adulthood (Lloyd et al. 2013). In fact, stability and a good financial situation were some of the categories most often reported by older Germans as contributing to adjustment to aging (von Humboldt et al. 2012). Given the relevance of active aging to cultural and national diversity across Europe, there are wide disparities across Europe, both in style and in standards, which may culminate in failures when adopting generic policies (Walker 2002). Indeed, policies for active aging should consider cultural diversity, in addition to respecting national and international neutrality, human rights, and laws, for preventing failures (Bowling 2009).

In Europe, active aging is widely emphasized, while in the United States, the emphasis is on successful aging (Boudiny 2013). Indeed, the interests of key stakeholders: policy makers, citizens, nongovernmental organizations, and business interests, should be taken in account, in order to promote successful aging (Walker and Foster 2013).

From a different perspective, the literature has stressed policies that promote good aging among non-Western older adults while at the same time criticizing an individualistic, active, and successful aging as an consumerist Westernized style, and not considering individual experiences from non-Western older adults (Liang and Luo 2012). Transcultural government policies can prevent failures by comprising the needs of other ethnic groups and minorities, such as older African and Eastern individuals (Liang and Luo 2012; von Humboldt and Leal 2014).

5.3.3 Format Challenges for Interventions and Policies

The most frequent approach to obtain information is by inquiring older adults, using two methodologies. One employs open-ended qualitative studies to generate categories based on the perspective of older people. The other adopts psychometric approaches, which require forced-choice items, and multivariate evaluation to indicate different aspects of aging and to achieve a final variable score (von Humboldt et al. 2013b).

The value of data in the cultural context of aging is affected by the conditions under which data were obtained and by the methods applied. Indeed, considering that most of the studies in the area of cultural aging are cross-national, these studies fail as they do not provide an adequate analysis of causality and cannot provide a direct estimate of age changes for accurate interventions. Current interventions and policies would benefit from additional experimental control of variables, while age changes can only be accurately determined by longitudinal studies. In fact, experimental controls and a temporal relationship between data sets are relevant when examining data collection methods for aging and when making interventions with older adults (von Humboldt and Leal 2015). Experimental studies are essential for testing hypotheses, while controls in experimental studies, particularly when containing qualitative interviews or assessments, test the extent to which causal relationships between variables are valid. In-depth interviews are relevant for examining the multidimensional context of aging and necessary for planning adequate interventions (Potter and Hepburn 2005). Considering that aging is essentially interactional, the differentiation of correlates and follow-up effects can be demanding and subject to failure. Therefore, there is also a need to deal with research to validate the stability of aging, to allow causal assumptions between correlates and components, and to prevent failures in cultural interventions with older adults (von Humboldt 2016).

Furthermore, insufficient recruitment is one of the main reasons for the failure of studies and interventions and can contribute to reduce statistical power and hinder the production of meaningful results (Buckwalter 2009; Tarlow and Mahoney 2000). Obstacles encountered in recruiting older people include mistrust and transportation obstacles (Gonzalez et al. 2007; Shearer et al. 2010); caregiver burden, medical concerns, and indifference (Saunders et al. 2003); sensory and cognitive limitations (Mody et al. 2008); and frail health (Shearer et al. 2010). The design of the intervention may represent additional obstacles to recruitment, if there are excessive restrictions on eligibility, which limit the ability to generate a desirable sample size for statistical power and to adequately represent the intended population (Yancey et al. 2006). Uybico et al. (2007) reported some additional barriers to recruiting minorities, which may lead to failures: security concerns, lack of access to medical care, lack of confidentiality, scheduling conflicts, lack of knowledge, and linguistic/cultural differences. Among African Americans, these barriers were categorized into three main areas: (a) historical context associated with prior unethical research, (b) lack of access to and use of health care, and (c) researcher bias, including the researcher's personal values, sense of fairness, and subsequent decisions about study design and participant inclusion (Dennis and Neese 2000). Additionally, difficulty in recruiting can be related both to the unique culture of each group and to researcher's inability to understand community dynamics and establish positive relationships with community members and leaders (Stahl and Vasquez 2004). As an example, among some minority populations in the United States, especially Latino noncitizens, there is fear that sharing information may lead to deportation (Eakin et al. 2006; Levkoff and Sanchez 2003). Insufficient or inadequate recruitment of a target number of participants is a significant source of failure in interventions with older underrepresented cultural groups (Peterson et al. 2004). Indeed, all parties should be treated as representative for an adequate older population intervention, and also to guarantee greater willingness to participate in further interventions and less failures (Mody et al. 2008).

The ability to compare aging interventions across countries may also be compromised due to failures in dealing with language differences, rather than genuine differences in interventions and policies. This issue has been assessed in multilingual countries, such as Belgium, Canada, and Switzerland, where interventions and policies must be applied in different regions with different languages (Veenhoven 1993). These authors showed that translation problems are not a major constraint in comparing variables in different societies. Comparing responses of bilingual older adults who responded to a study in English or Mandarin, Diener and his colleagues (1995) observed very similar mean scores in both languages and a correspondence in associations of both scales with other variables. Therefore, previous results on language variation have ensured limited failures in this area.

Cultural aspects regarding conversation style, emotion states, recognition of the interview setup, and the prioritization of values (e.g., socially desirable perspectives) may also discredit the acquired data and lead to analysis failures (von Humboldt et al. 2013a, b, c).

Furthermore, interventions may fail because data are simply not easily obtainable outside Western countries and are often not comparable between developing and developed countries. Hence, considering that researchers may intend to compare older groups across cultures, there are increased challenges to validity and reliability (von Humboldt et al. 2013a, b, c).

A final aspect is the appropriate use of technology. Even when older adults show a positive attitude toward using new technologies (Vaportzis et al. 2017), many still have difficulties using them, which may lead to failures in interventions (Wild et al. 2012).

5.4 Concluding Remarks and Future Perspectives

During the most recent decades, numerous researchers have studied culturally diverse meanings in old age. Cultural definitions are incorporated in types of cultural habits, which are commonly implicit. These provide the cultural framework for a given generation. Research and policy interventions require accurate definitions of the cultural understanding and involvement of older individuals and an adequate perception of how this cultural knowledge affects the theories and methods developed to assess aging. Studies confirm that the meaning of aging differs with cultural situations, influencing planning and interventions. For example, in Western countries, personal self-fulfillment is culturally valued, while in non-Western contexts, greater value is given to how a person is connected to others, where the group takes precedence over personal needs.

Inherent mistakes and errors may emerge when assessing aging issues within one culture and across different cultures. Aging assessment may be prone to specific measurement mistakes and biases in replies, namely, general bias in response, answering in a socially approved way (social desirability bias), refraining from the use of extreme answers classes (central tendency bias), and complying with declarations as given, that is, not responding to the content of an element (acquiescence bias).

Moreover, developing tailored formats for interventions and policies for older populations has been a challenge when considering transcultural disparities and different cultural aspects of aging. Until now, most designed interventions and policies have been constructed and validated for older groups in developed countries, in particular from North America and Europe, often excluding the interests of other older groups in developing countries.

Finally, some good practices that may prevent future mistakes, errors in research, and failures in formats, interventions, and policies will be discussed below.

Data on aging has been mostly based upon cross-sectional quantitative studies (von Humboldt et al. 2013a, b, c). Despite its general applicability, this approach has innate restrictions and offers various possible occasions for failure. Indeed, experimental studies are essential for testing hypotheses. Multi-assessment studies are necessary to achieve a higher validity in our assessments across cultures and to prevent errors and mistakes in research and the failures in policies and interventions with old populations. Additionally, we emphasize the need for good-quality psychometric data, supported by appropriate, valid, and reliable single-item and multi-item methods in the gerontological literature, which ultimately will help researchers and social and health professionals to better assess and diagnose errors and mistakes and promote a deeper understanding of cultural perspectives on aging and old age.

Gerontologists should further invest in developing culturally sensitive measures and should consider differences in language and communication with older participants. In fact, additional culturally adapted studies are supposed to bring aging forward, considering that older individuals are sources of culture, skill, and knowledge.

Moreover, old minorities and groups may impose the present social security and social security systems to be culturally decisive and assure that procedures are coherent with resources capable of meeting the care needs of older adults. More and more specialized research, policies, and interventions, which are more culturally appropriate, to serve challenges and prevent errors, mistakes, and failures in the cultural context of aging are suggested. A "one size fits all" method is just not be suitable.

Aging policies should consider cultural diversity, in addition to respecting national and international neutrality, human rights, and laws. Additionally, policies and interventions should consider partnerships between older participants, researchers, governments, families and institutions, and other interested parties, to tackle challenges in old age and to prevent errors, mistakes, and failures.

Finally, policies and interventions that include the involvement of older people may significantly contribute to exploring specific issues. Additionally they should include relevant topics, such as the relationship between body appearance and aging well; spirituality; intimacy and sexuality, family and non-family networks, and resulting policies to support them; aging in place; minority interests, refugees, and migration issues; and the relationship between work, efficiency, and retirement.

Different cultural dimensions are relevant for a better understanding of the process of aging. Therefore, researchers should consider the significance of cultural variation, with less focus on ethnic backgrounds and more focus on equitable backgrounds for aging all over the globe.

In brief, there are many variations to the experience of aging. Many of these worldwide cultural changes regarding aging are dynamically decided by older adults. Without a doubt, it's necessary to understand how to deal with them, as they will influence how professionals deal with mistakes, errors, and failures and the way future policy, research, and practice will be conducted.

References

Botelho, L., & Thane, P. (2001). *Women and ageing in British society since 1500*. London: Longmans. doi: https://doi.org/10.4324/9781315839868

Boudiny, K. (2013). Active ageing: From empty rhetoric to effective policy tool. *Ageing and Society*, 33, 1077–1098. doi: https://doi.org/10.1017/S0144686X1200030X

Bowling, B. (2009). Transnational policing: The globalization thesis, a typology and a research agenda. *Policing: A Journal of Policy and Practice*, 3(2), 149–160. doi: https://doi.org/10.1093/police/pap001

Buckwalter, K. C. (2009). Recruitment of older adults: An ongoing challenge. *Research in gerontological nursing*, 2(4), 265–266. doi: https://doi.org/10.3928/19404921-20090816-01

Danyuthasilpe, C., Amnatsatsue, K., Tanasugarn, C., & Kerdmongkol, P. (2009). Ways of healthy aging: A case study of elderly people in a northern Thai village. *Health Promotion International*, 24, 394–403. doi: https://doi.org/10.1093/heapro/dap038

Dennis, B. P., & Neese, J. B. (2000). Recruitment and retention of African American elders into community-based research: lessons learned. *Archives of Psychiatric Nursing*, 14(1), 3–11. doi: https://doi.org/10.1016/S0883-9417(00)80003-5

Diener, E., & Suh, E. M. (2000). Measuring subjective well-being to compare the quality of life of cultures. In E. Diener & E. M. Suh (Eds.), *Culture and subjective well-being* (pp. 3–12). Cambridge, MA: The MIT Press. doi: https://doi.org/10.7551/mitpress/2242.003.0004

Diener, E., Suh, E. M., Smith, H., & Shao, L. (1995). National differences in reported subjective well-being: Why do they occur? *Social Indicators Research*, 38, 247–280. doi: https://doi.org/10.1007/BF01078966

Draper, P. (2007). Conducting cross-cultural research in teams and the search for the "culture proof" variable. *Menopause*, 14, 680–687. doi: https://doi.org/10.1097/gme.0b013e3180986289

Eakin, E. G., Bull, S. S., Riley, K., Reeves, M. M., Gutierrez, S., & McLaughlin, P. (2006). Recruitment and retention of Latinos in a primary care-based physical activity and diet trial: The Resources for Health study. *Health education research*, 22(3), 361–371. doi: https://doi.org/10.1093/her/cy1095

Gonzalez, E. W., Gardner, E. M., & Murasko, D. (2007). Recruitment and retention of older adults in influenza immunization study. *Journal of Cultural Diversity*, 14(2), 81.

Hilton, J. M., Gonzales, C. A., Saleh, M., Maitoza, R., & Anngela-Cole, L. (2012). Perceptions of successful aging among older Latinos, in cross-cultural context. *Journal of Cross-Cultural Gerontology*, 27, 183–199. doi: https://doi.org/10.1007/s10823-012-9171-4

Iwamasa, G. Y., & Iwasaki, M. (2011). A new multidimensional model of successful aging: Perceptions of Japanese American older adults. *Journal of Cross-Cultural Gerontology*, 26, 261–278. doi: https://doi.org/10.1007/s10823-011-9147-9

Jaul, E., & Barron, J. (2017). Age-Related Diseases and Clinical and Public Health Implications for the 85 Years Old and Over Population. *Frontiers in public health*, 5, 335. doi: https://doi.org/10.3389/fpubh.2017.00335

Ji, L., Nisbett, R. E., & Su, Y. (2001). Culture, change, and prediction. *Psychological Science*, 12, 450–456. doi: https://doi.org/10.1111/1467-9280.00384

Kan, C., Karasawa, M., & Kitayama, S. (2009). Minimalist in style: Self, identify, and well-being in Japan. *Self and Identity*, 8(2), 300–317. doi: https://doi.org/10.1080/15298860802505244

Kitayama, S., Markus, H. R., & Kurokawa, M. (2000). Culture, emotion, and well-being: Good feelings in Japan and the United States. *Cognition and Emotion*, 14, 93–124. doi: https://doi.org/10.1080/026999300379003.

Krosnick, J. A., Villar, A., & MacInnis, B. (2011). *Do introductory sentences cause acquiescence response bias in survey questions?* Stanford, CA: Woods Institute for the Environment.

Kunkel, S. R., & Morgan, L. A. (2015). *Aging, society, and the life course*. Springer Publishing Company. doi: https://doi.org/10.1891/9780826121738

Levkoff, S., & Sanchez, H. (2003). Lessons learned about minority recruitment and retention from the Centers on Minority Aging and Health Promotion. *The Gerontologist*, 43(1), 18-26. doi: https://doi.org/10.1093/geront/43.1.18

Lewis, J. P. (2011). Successful aging through the eyes of Alaska Native elders. What it means to be an elder in Bristol Bay, AK. *The Gerontologist*, 51, 540–549. doi: https://doi.org/10.1093/geront/gnr006

Li, A., Bagger, J., & Friske, W. (2013). Social desirability in the selection process: New insights from a novel context. *Asia Pacific Journal of Human Resources*, 51(1), 45. doi: org/10.1111/j.1744-7941.2012.00032.x

Liang, J., & Luo, B. (2012). Toward a discourse shift in social gerontology: From successful aging to harmonious aging. *Journal of Aging Studies*, 26, 327–334. doi: https://doi.org/10.1016/j.jaging.2012.03.001

Lloyd, L., Tanner, D., Milne, A., Ray, M., Richards, S., Sullivan, M., … Phillips, J. (2013). Look after yourself: Active ageing, individual responsibility and the decline of social work with older people in the UK. *European Journal of Social Work*. Advance online publication. doi: https://doi.org/10.1080/13691457.2013.829805

Markus, H. R., & Kitayama, S. (1991). Culture and the self: Implications for cognition, emotion, and motivation. *Psychological Review*, 98, 224–253. doi: https://doi.org/10.1037/0033-295X.98.2.224

Martin, W. C., Engelland, B. T., & Collier, J. E. (2011). Assessing the impact of acquiescence response bias on marketing data. *Marketing Management Journal*, 21(1), 31–46.

Mody, L., Miller, D. K., McGloin, J. M., Freeman, M., Marcantonio, E. R., Magaziner, J., & Studenski, S. (2008). Recruitment and Retention of Older Adults in Aging Research: (See editorial comments by Dr. Stephanie Studenski, pp 2351–2352). *Journal of the American Geriatrics Society*, 56(12), 2340–2348. doi: https://doi.org/10.1111/j.1532-5415.2008.02015.x

Moum, T. (1988). Yea-saying and mood-of-the-day effects in self-reported quality of life. *Social Indicators Research*, 20, 117–139. doi: https://doi.org/10.1007/BF00302458.

Patton, M. Q. (2002). *Qualitative research and evaluation methods*. Thousand Oaks, CA: Sage.

Perkinson, M. A., & Solimeo, S. M. (2013). Aging in cultural context and as narrative process: Conceptual foundations of the anthropology of aging as reflected in the works of Margaret Phelan, E. A., Anderson, L. A., Lacroix, A. Z., & Larson, E. B. (2004). Older adults' views of "successful aging": How do they compare with researchers' definitions? *Journal of the American Geriatrics Society*, 52, 211–216. doi: https://doi.org/10.1111/j.1532-5415.2004.52056.x

Peterson, E. D., Alexander, K. P., Malenka, D. J., Hannan, E. L., O'conner, G. T., McCallister, B. D., … & American Heart Association Chronic CAD Working Group. (2004). Multicenter experience in revascularization of very elderly patients. *American heart journal*, 148(3), 486–492. doi: https://doi.org/10.1016/j.ahj.2004.03.039

Podsakoff, P. M., MacKenzie, S. B., Lee, J., & Podsakoff, N. P. (2003). Common method biases in behavioral research: A critical review of the literature and recommended remedies. *Journal of Applied Psychology*, 88, 879–903. doi: https://doi.org/10.1037/0021-9010.88.5.879

Potter, J., & Hepburn, A. (2005). Qualitative interviews in psychology: Problems and possibilities. *Qualitative Research in Psychology*, 2, 281–307. doi: https://doi.org/10.1177/1461445607075348

Saris, W. E., Revilla, M., & Krosnick, J. A. (2010). Comparing questions with agree/disagree response options to questions with item-specific response options. *Survey Research Methods*, 4, 61–79.

Saunders, S. D., Greaney, M. L., Lees, F. D., & Clark, P. G. (2003). Achieving recruitment goals through community partnerships: The SENIOR Project. *Family & Community Health*, 26(3), 194–202. doi: 10.1097/00003727-200307000-00004

Schrauf, R. W., & Sanchez, J. (2008). Using freelisting to identify, assess, and characterize age differences in shared cultural dimensions. *The Journals of Gerontology Series B: Psychological Sciences and Social Sciences*, 63B, 385–392. doi: https://doi.org/10.1093/geronb/63.6.s385

Shearer, N. B. C., Fleury, J. D., & Belyea, M. (2010). An innovative approach to recruiting homebound older adults. *Research in gerontological nursing*, 3(1), 11–18. doi: https://doi.org/10.3928/19404921-20091029-01

Sperlinger, D., Clare, L., Bradbury, N., & Culverwell, A. (2004). *Measuring psychosocial treatment outcomes with older people*. Leicester, UK: The British Psychological Society.

Stahl, S. M., & Vasquez, L. (2004). Approaches to improving recruitment and retention of minority elders participating in research. *Journal of Aging and Health*, 16(5_suppl), 9S–17S. doi: https://doi.org/10.1177/0898264304268146

Stavenuiter, M., & Bijsterveld, K. (2000). Images and self-images of elderly women in the past. *Journal of Family History*, 25(2), 179–247.

Stones, M. J. (1977). A further study of response set and the Eysenck Personality Inventory (EPI). *Journal of Clinical Psychology*, 33(1), 147–150. doi: https://doi.org/10.1002/1097-4679(197701)33:1+<147::aid-jclp2270330130>3.0.co;2-z

Suh, E. M. (2002). Culture, identity consistency, and subjective well-being. Journal of Personality and Social Psychology, 83, 1378–1391.

Tarlow, B. A., & Mahoney, D. F. (2000). The cost of recruiting Alzheimer's disease caregivers for research. *Journal of Aging and Health*, 12(4), 490–510. doi: https://doi.org/10.1177/089826430001200403

Uchida, Y., & Kitayama, S. (2009). Happiness and unhappiness in East and West: Themes and variations. *Emotion*, 9, 441–456. doi: https://doi.org/10.1037/a0015634

Uchida, Y., Norasakkunkit, V., & Kitayama, S. (2004). Cultural constructions of happiness: Theory and empirical evidence. *Journal of Happiness Studies*, 5(3), 223–239. doi: https://doi.org/10.1007/s10902-004-8785-9

UyBico, S. J., Pavel, S., & Gross, C. P. (2007). Recruiting vulnerable populations into research: a systematic review of recruitment interventions. *Journal of general internal medicine*, 22(6), 852–863. doi: https://doi.org/10.1007/s11606-007-0126-3

Vannette, D. L., & Krosnick, J. A. (2014). Answering questions. A comparison of survey satisficing and mindlessness. In A. Le, C. T. Ngnoumen, & E. J. Langer (Eds.), *The Wiley Blackwell handbook of mindfulness* (Vol. I, pp. 312–327). New York: Wiley.

Vaportzis, E., Giatsi Clausen, M., & Gow, A. J. (2017). Older adults perceptions of technology and barriers to interacting with tablet computers: A focus group study. *Frontiers in psychology*, 8, 1687. doi: https://doi.org/10.3389/fpsyg.2017.01687

Veenhoven, R. (1993). *Happiness in nations: Subjective appreciation of life in 56 nations 1946–1992*. Rotterdam, The Netherlands: Erasmus University Rotterdam.

Veenhoven, R. (1996). Developments in satisfaction research. Social Indicators Research, 37, 1–46. doi: https://doi.org/10.1007/BF00300268

von Humboldt, S. (2016). *Conceptual and methodological issues on the adjustment to aging: Perspectives on aging well*. New York, NY: Springer. doi: https://doi.org/10.1007/978-94-017-7576-2

von Humboldt, S., & Leal, I. (2014). Adjustment to aging in old adulthood: A systematic review. *International Journal of Gerontology*, 8(5), 108–113.doi: https://doi.org/10.1016/j.ijge.2014.03.003

von Humboldt, S., & Leal, I. (2015). The old and the oldest old: Do they have different perspectives n adjustment to aging? *International Journal of Gerontology*, 9(3), 156–160. doi: https://doi.org/10.1016/j.ijge.2015.04.002

von Humboldt, S., Leal, I., & Pimenta, F. (2012). Assessing subjective age and adjustment to aging in a Portuguese and German older population: A comparative multiple correspondence analysis. *International Journal of Psychological Studies*, 4(2), 141–153. doi: https://doi.org/10.5539/ijps.v4n2p141

von Humboldt, S., Leal, I., & Pimenta, F. (2013a). Analyzing adjustment to aging and subjective age from Angolan and Portuguese community-dwelling older adults' perspectives. *International Journal of Gerontology*, 27(4), 209–215. doi: https://doi.org/10.1016/j.ijge.2013.05.001

von Humboldt, S., Leal, I., Pimenta, F., & Maroco, J. (2013b). Assessing adjustment to aging: A validation study for the Adjustment to Aging Scale (AtAS). *Social Indicators Research*, 119 (1), 455–472. doi: https://doi.org/10.1007/s11205-013-0482-9

von Humboldt, S., Leal, I., Pimenta, F., & Niculescu, G. (2013c). In the eyes of older adults: Self Reported age and adjustment in African and European older adults. *Health SA Gesondheid*, 18 (1), 712–722. doi: https://doi.org/10.4102/hsag.v18i1.712

Walker, A. (2002). A strategy for active ageing. *International Social Security Review*, 55, 121–139. doi: https://doi.org/10.1111/1468-246X.00118

Walker, A., & Foster, L. (2013). Active ageing: Rhetoric, theory and practice. In R. Ervic & T. Skogedal Linden (Eds.), *The making of aging policy: Theory and practice in Europe* (pp. 27–53). Cheltenham, UK: Edward Elgar. doi: https://doi.org/10.4337/9781781952481.00009

Walker, A., & Maltby, T. (2012). Active Ageing: A strategic policy solution to demographic ageing in the European Union. *International Journal of Social Welfare*, 17, 117–130. doi: https://doi.org/10.1111/j.1468-2397.2012.00871.x.

Wild, K. V., Mattek, N. C., Maxwell, S. A., Dodge, H. H., Jimison, H. B., & Kaye, J. A. (2012). Computer-related self-efficacy and anxiety in older adults with and without mild cognitive impairment. *Alzheimer's & Dementia*, 8(6), 544–552. doi: https://doi.org/10.1016/j.jalz.2011.12.008

Yancey, A. K., Ortega, A. N., & Kumanyika, S. K. (2006). Effective recruitment and retention of minority research participants. *Annual Review of Public Health*, 27, 1–28. doi: https://doi.org/10.1146/annurev.publhealth.27.021405.102113

Sofia von Humboldt (Dr.) is a clinical and health psychologist with a long-standing experience with older adults. Her current research interests include sexual well-being, adjustment to aging, well-being, mental health, and cross-cultural studies with older populations. Dr. von Humboldt is Associate Professor and Principal Investigator in William James Center for Research at ISPA-Instituto Universitário. Deeply committed to working with older adults, she has written papers, chapters, and books on the multidimensional and cross-cultural approach to sexual well-being and health and mental in old age.

Chapter 6
Doing the Unconventional, Doing 'Dirty' Work: The Stigmatization of Sexuality Work and Unforeseen Encounters with Love

Aliraza Javaid

Abstract We are storytellers to our own lives. When we do sexuality research, which Irvine (2014) calls 'dirty' work, we are in the midst of creating a story. In this book chapter, I provide a snapshot of my story in respect of doing sexuality research. I have encountered numerous pitfalls, dilemmas and problems when doing such 'dirty' work, but here I only tell a few by drawing on the qualitatively derived research method tool known as autoethnography. It is a method that requires the writer to use hindsight in order to resurrect not only memories of pain, torture, and stigma but also of liberation and freedom. I mainly refer to the dark memories in this book chapter to raise awareness of them for other like-minded queer writers. I argue that it is possible to write from both our heads and hearts, rather than solely from the former because we are pressured from institutions to sustain sheer 'objectivity' when that may not always be possible to do given that human values always enter at the beginning and the end of research. Human values are present when we interview participants. In sexuality work, the process of interviewing participants is a creative space. Interviews, whether online or offline, are spaces where subjectivities are actively created and where emotions are involved and formed.

Keywords Mistakes · Errors · Failure · Sexuality research · Male sexuality

6.1 Introduction

We are storytellers to our own lives. When we do sexuality research, which Irvine (2014) calls 'dirty' work, we are in the midst of creating a story. In this book chapter, I provide a snapshot of my story in respect of doing sexuality research. I have

A. Javaid (✉)
University of East London, London, UK
e-mail: ajavaid@uel.ac.uk

E. Vanderheiden, C.-H. Mayer (eds.), *Mistakes, Errors and Failures across Cultures*, https://doi.org/10.1007/978-3-030-35574-6_6

encountered numerous pitfalls, dilemmas and problems when doing such 'dirty' work, but here I only tell a few by drawing on the qualitatively derived research method tool known as autoethnography. It is a method that requires the writer to use hindsight in order to resurrect not only memories of pain, torture and stigma but also of liberation and freedom. I mainly refer to the dark memories in this book chapter to raise awareness of them for other like-minded queer writers. When doing autoethnography, I am almost reliving those memories of pain. However, it is a useful capsule for making research as transparent as possible since the writer's emotions and human lived experience ultimately shape the research experience, rather than ignoring that they do not exist (Ellis et al. 2011). By writing this autoethnography of my torments of doing sexuality work, I would be alleviating 'the past that had a hold on me, that kept me from the present. I wanted not to forget the past but to break its hold. This death in writing [is] to be liberatory' (hooks, 1989 [2015], p. 261). The evocative stories that I soon tell in autoethnographic, rich detail are done so in the hope that I can be free, free from the shackles of torment and pain that have kept me trapped in the past, holding me from my present. Autoethnography, then, can set us free. Like bell hooks (1989 [2015]), I had become attached to the wounds and sorrows of such memories that emerged during my involvement in sexuality work. Glorious vines were wrapped around my mouth until now where I can share my story as a way of cutting through these vines of silences.

To share my stories, along with the struggles that I encountered during the course of my academic trajectory, autoethnography offers remedies to heal those wounds of pain. While university institutional prisms implicitly tell us that we must sustain 'secrets' in order to prevent university reputational damage, we are sacrificing our integrity and authenticity as queer writers (Ahmed 2017). There has been a legacy of queer writers challenging the status quo of heterosexuality and gender norms, fighting for gay rights during the Gay Liberation Front times (see Weeks 2018), yet now we as queer writers are becoming silenced again and discouraged by the academic community from speaking about our personal and intimate experiences of doing sexuality work (Javaid 2019a; in press). This is because, as Hammond and Kingston (2014) argue, those who study sexuality may face discrimination since sexuality research induces strong scepticism from strangers and non-strangers. When queer writers as willful writers name a problem, they themselves are seen as 'the problem' (Ahmed 2017). Coming from a strict Muslim family who strongly perpetuated stubborn inequalities and oppression, despite my resisting them with love and faith (Javaid 2019c), I always had the unmoving habit of always letting something 'slip' that should not be known according to the strict confines of the family institution and similarly of university institutions. I do not want to be a traitor to one's own 'academic home', the teller of secrets in doing sexuality work, but a queer writer is one of bravery and is able to tell the truth of one's own life as I had experienced it. I intend not to tell on people, but to transform my stories into knowledge and theory (Javaid 2019a; in press). My stories of struggle soon follow below, with the assistance of Ken Plummer's (1995) idea of 'sexual stories'. For him, queer and sexuality writers form part of the procedure of producing sexual stories so are part of the development of formulating sexual knowledge and theory. Sexual stories stem from one's own everyday life, so 'personal narratives…are socially embedded in the daily practices of everyday life' (Plummer 1995, p. 15).

The main argument in this piece is that stigma is associated with sexuality research and might be perceived as a form of 'failure, error and mistake.' At various points, I will largely be drawing on the notion of 'failure' to indicate that the researcher's professional role is potentially compromised and he or she has momentarily failed to stick to the researcher script/role or that the participants failed to stick to the participant script/role. In both instances, a deviation occurs. In the case of a researcher momentarily deviating from their researcher role/script, stigma can be reproduced, and I show how throughout this piece. I also highlight the implications of their stigma.

6.2 Contouring 'Dirty' Work

In this section, I detail some background literature relating to autoethnography and sexuality work in which other writers express their own experiences of conducting sexuality research and highlighting their experiences of 'failing' to stick to the researcher role/script and/or the participants 'failing' to adhere to the participant role/script. Providing some context will 'set the scene' for my own sexual stories and for my own experiences of 'failing' to adhere to the researcher role/script. These sexuality writers have bravely spoke about their experiences of 'doing' sexuality research even though others may see them as, according to Attwood (2010), crude and casting suspicion against such writers. They have risked their professional reputation in the hope that their stories can shed light on the pitfalls, dilemmas and problems of doing 'dirty' work. Attwood (2010) illustrates that although:

> in late modern societies we are 'incited' to speak about sex, tensions and silences still persist and some types of speech and speakers are strongly discouraged. (p. 178)

Huysamen (2018, p. 1) establishes that:

> As researchers, our sexualities, both self-identified and those assumed by our participants, are always relevant to the research process.

She carried out interviews with 43 South African men about paying for sex. The men were all identified as clients of women sex workers. She critically reflects on her relationship with the men during the interviews, showing how the men 'failed' to adhere to the participant role/script in a professional manner. She was positioned in what Connell (1987) calls 'emphasised femininity'[1] as a passive and subordinate listener, 'titillating' her male participants' ego and facilitating their control during the interviews. She writes that she did not contest or resist her male participants' racist or sexist gestures and comments, facilitating 'the production of these problematic discourses during interviews' (p. 3). Some could argue that this is a 'mistake' because she implicitly reinforced gender inequality, but remaining silent does

[1] 'Emphasised femininity' refers to the maintenance and reproduction of traditional gender roles. Connell (1987) argues that the concept is relationally constructed to hegemonic masculinity, 'performed especially to men' (p. 188).

ensure that the participants remain engaged and that the researcher is then able to collect the required data. The researcher can, then, given that she remained powerless during the research, reclaim back her power and voice by having collected the data and then being able to publish her story. Huysamen (2018) herself felt that her subordination and powerlessness were sustaining gender inequality and male dominance, both at the discursive and material levels, discursive because of the sexist and racist comments that the South African men made and material because of the bodily gestures the men made and because of the researcher's social position in the interviews as lacking symbolic and cultural power in relation to the men, unquestioningly listening to the men and encouraging them to talk and not challenging male supremacy. The gender order remained strongly in tact. However, power is fluid and dynamic: on the one hand, the female writer is subordinate and powerless during the course of her interviews; on the other hand, by the very fact that the South African men are objects of her study, she ultimately had control over the data comprising the men. They offered her the 'gift' of data that she could exploit whenever and however she chooses. The men's voices and stories were in her hands. They were *her* research 'objects', props in a play that she could choose to manipulate in whichever way she chooses. By remaining silent and not challenging gender inequality during the interviews, she performs an illusion of competence. The men found the interviews with her to be erotic, arousing and a 'turn on'. We see here, then, that the researcher can become sexualized and objectified as the participants 'failed' to follow the participant script/role. For example, one of her male participants states, 'I'll probably have to go rub-off [masturbate] after this [interview]' (Dan, 37). Huysamen (2018) writes:

> [W]hen I ask Dan why he would not have been willing to be interviewed by a male researcher, Dan likens my listening to his sexual stories to other erotic acts (like massages) that a woman might offer him. In this moment, rather than just being the interviewer, I become a woman with whom he could potentially have a sexual encounter. (p. 8)

For some writers, the interview process can be one where the participant constructs it as a potential erotic encounter rather than a professional setting. Almost all of her male respondents had asked her whether she had ever sold sex, whether she would consider it, or suggested that she ought to sell sex. Consequently, being stigmatized in this way and being 'sexualised by my participants was threatening to me because it had the potential to make me feel like a "whore"' (Huysamen 2018, p. 10). Researchers can become sexual objects or sexual conquests during their sexuality research. This view is echoed in other sexuality works. Hammond and Kingston (2014) argue that they both, as female sex work researchers, experienced the 'whore stigma'[2] for being associated with the sexuality research of sex work. They indicate their experiences of being seen as 'kinky' or 'up for it' because of the type of sexual activity that their research was associated with. For instance, the

[2] Sex workers often face the 'whore stigma', too, so this form of stigma transposed itself onto the female sex work researchers.

second author, Sarah Kingston, describes one of her experiences in which she was 'hit on' by one of her male participants who was a male senior police officer after an interview she conducted with him[3]:

> Yeah was cool to meet one so chilled and open minded – don't let the gay thing put u off if you fancy a bit of casual sex (just don't tell the bf! [Boyfriend]) Defo give me a shout though I'll settle for coffee x. (Hammond and Kingston 2014, p. 335)

Kingston was seen as 'sexually liberal' for doing sexuality research on prostitution; the presumption that prostitutes invariably have casual sex with multiple strangers and always 'consent' to sex momentarily became transposed onto Kingston. For sexuality writers, then, sexual overtures can be frequent. Huff (1997, p. 117) also experienced sexual overtures, getting 'attention [that] consisted of unwanted romantic overtures, such as touching, hugging, poking and comments such as "hey hot lips"'. From her male respondents, Grenz (2005) also gained unwanted sexual overtures that consisted of the men wanting to masturbate over her, wanting to reveal their penises to her and requesting that she wear a short skirt. All these sexuality writers experienced sexual harassment, sexual talk and sexual objectification from their participants who 'failed' to obey the participant role/script. The researchers were assumed to be sexually available. Kevin Walby (2010), a male queer writer, argues that participants may not always see you as a professional sexuality researcher but rather as someone who is sexualized:

> As much as the researcher positions as a sociologist, the respondent may position the researcher as a sex object. My body as a researcher…is part of this milieu of sexualisation…Gestures interpreted as non-sexual may be taken in another direction. For instance, I purposefully wore business attire for the interviews…the intention was to seem professional and asexual, my appearance could have been interpreted otherwise. Some of these men clearly wanted to turn the interview into more of a touching encounter. During interviews, I was often propositioned to receive sexual favours. (p. 650)

Doing sexuality research on male sex work, Walby (2010) conducted interviews with 30 male-for-male Internet escorts in Montréal, Ottawa, Toronto (Canada), Houston and New York (USA) and London (England). He became sexualized during the interviews, with many of the respondents asking him, 'Are you gay?' at the start of the interviews. Walby's (2010) response to the 'Are you gay' question was, 'I have slept with all kinds of people' (p. 647). Walby (2010) felt that his 'respondents wanted our meeting to become a touching encounter' (p. 641). For example, one of his respondents declared that, 'Oh and by the way…you are a sexy man!' (p. 649) and another respondent offering Kevin a session of S&M (sadism and masochism: the practice of using pain as a sexual stimulant):

> Kevin: Do you think you could walk me through, because not everyone does this kind of service, like a typical S&M scene?
> Ricky (Toronto): I could show you.

[3] Sarah Kingston's sexuality research included the exploration of community attitudes regarding men who buy sex. She conducted interviews with business employees, residents, the police, and local authority officials in a large northern city (see Kingston 2014).

Kevin: You could show me …
Ricky (Toronto): A simple S&M scene? Those words don't go together.
Kevin: OK, yeah, not a typical S&M scene, but what exactly does the work of that consist of?

From this dialogue, the researcher becomes sexualized. In male sex work, there is a great inclusion of sexualizing and being sexualized (Javaid 2019d; Walby 2010). Ricky, the male sex worker, momentarily broke away from the respondent role with his response of 'I could show you'. He 'failed' to conform to the expectations of a participant. It could be argued that a 'failure' occurred here whereby ethical boundaries between researcher and participant were clearly not drawn from the outset or, if they were, then, the participant deviated from those boundaries. There can be slippage between being 'professional' and 'unprofessional', the two are muddy waters. A 'failure' manifested in that the respondent failed to adhere to the participant script/role of professionalism. For example, Kevin Walby writes that, when Ricky said this to him, it 'came along with an impassioned glare from across the table. He had the curl of a smile forming in the corner of his mouth' (p. 650). He wanted a sexual interaction, attempting to transform the interview into an erotic casual encounter, parting ways from the researcher-respondent interaction script. Over the phone, another respondent said to Walby (2010, p. 652), 'I can give you head after we talk, you can fuck me if you want' as a way of transforming the research into a site of eroticism and sexualization.

In addition, Walby would hug the male sex workers after the interviews as a way of saying goodbye. Again, this might be seen as 'failing' to stick to the researcher script/role because it could be seen as crossing the line of becoming too immersed and 'too' friendly with your participants. Objectivity is now potentially contaminated, but one could argue that this instance is simply a characterization of 'being human' given that human values always enter in the beginning and the end of research. Hugging, for some people, could be viewed as a 'failure' or 'mistake' because the sex workers would see this as a sign that the researcher wanted more, wanted something more intimate and sexual, when the true intention was to just say goodbye. As a consequence, the role of the 'professional' researcher becomes compromised. In Toronto, one sex worker walked Walby to his hotel after they hugged; the escort asked for more hugs at each red light they waited at. Walby had to discuss that he was not in a position to have sexual and erotic relations with participants when the sex worker suggested it would be good if he accompanied Walby to his room. Here, the professional researcher attempts to rectify his potential 'failure' by drawing strict boundaries between researcher and participant. On other occasions after the interviews, some sex workers asked Walby to come back to their house to 'hear more, first hand'. This construction of gay culture can be defined by only one strand of gay culture, that is, sexual promiscuity amongst gay men. Whilst I am not claiming that all gay men engage in fleeting, casual sex, some gay men can exploit the interview setting as a way to configure sexual and erotic relations. Reflecting on his history and methodological journey, Ken Plummer experienced moments when his respondents 'went for him':

> In one of the interviews a curious, tall, bearded Eastern Orthodox priest in full mufti came in – and you have to remember I was 21 and not entirely ugly – and he just went for me! There were a whole series of interviews that were very risky...this particular man pursued me for several months and he was nice enough but he didn't want the same thing that I wanted [a romantic relationship]...*there was also one time when I thought I was falling in love with the person I was interviewing* and had to restrain myself so it also happened the other way round! (Morris 2018, pp. 341–342; emphasis mine)

Here, we can see that Plummer talks candidly about his falling in love with one of his participants who he interviewed. Falling in love is unexpected and cannot be determined during fieldwork given that love is socially and culturally constructed (Javaid 2018a). Plummer goes on to say that his participants 'had little regard for me (because sometimes they were pursuing me quite dangerously)' (Morris 2018, p. 347). This intimate experience in the fieldwork could be seen by some as a perceived 'failure' for getting too close to a participant or becoming too immersed into the fieldwork. Boundaries were arguably not drawn, and ethical procedures were not strict during the time Plummer was researching. However, this might be a *perceived* rather than an actual 'mistake' because human emotions cannot necessarily be controlled and compartmentalized. Further, it is more likely that the respondent deviated, and so creating a 'failure' from his participant role/script. Plummer elucidates that, at a time when he was interviewing gay men, they were dangerously pursuing him for an erotic encounter. He suggests they lacked care and dignity for him solely in the pursuit for sex with him. The researcher, again, becomes constructed as a sexual object with which to be used to gratify one's sexual interests[4]. Rather than thinking that Plummer ought to have taken precautionary measures when going into the field, we should instead consider social and cultural contexts or the field as being a place of unpredictability that an ethics board cannot in any way determine. The field is not only a place of exploration but also a place of danger and risk.

According to Altork (1995)[5], she cannot imagine doing fieldwork without involving her emotions, feelings and sensual input. Researching fire fighters, Altork (1995) was seduced and 'turned on' by their demeanour:

> Even as I struggled to analyze their 'fire language', and to situate it as a language of power and appropriation, I felt myself to be seduced by it, and felt privileged to be privy to it as a temporary 'insider', an experience both uncomfortable and intriguing. (p. 114)

---

[4] Ken Plummer highlights that although the interview setting can be dangerous and highly eroticized, it can also be a space for liberation. For instance, some people were coming out in his interviews, and they were, for the very first time, articulating what it means to be gay for them. Thus, his interviews were changing some people's lives. What he and his gay men respondents embodied were the 'outsider' and 'deviant' status of being gay; the interviews were spaces for their marginalized voices to speak and to be heard.

[5] Altork (1995) provides an interesting account of her subjectivities when she involves herself with masculine and sturdy fire fighters. She sarcastically critiques objectivity on the grounds that it weakens a writer's work and their sense of self for humans are not devoid from human values and emotions. In addition, we use our bodies together with our minds and hearts to understand something, resulting in objectivity becoming impracticable or impossible (Altork 1995).

When she locked eyes with one fire fighter who agreed to be interviewed by her, she felt an adrenaline rush of what felt like the feelings of love, arguing that 'intense encounters with people in the field can have, at times, a seductive quality to them' (p. 115). A romantic and sexual relationship can emerge from the fieldwork between the researcher and participant, although my view is that this should not be viewed as a 'failure, mistake or error'. Instead, we should think through the ways in which our professional and personal lives can slip into one another, how they can create implications for others, and us, and how we can be best prepared to address such ramifications. Altork goes on to reflect on a past conversation she had with a fellow anthropologist who flirted with one of her informants. The fellow anthropologist said to Altork that, 'We never actually had intercourse, but it certainly got intense there for a while!' (p. 120). The fellow anthropologist believed that her work would be discredited or seen as 'failing' to be proper work if anyone were to find out she had developed a sexual interest in an informant, and hence being seen as a 'failed' researcher who got too immersed into the field, got too attached to a participant, and making the 'mistake' of losing sight of the aims of the research and the role as a 'professional' researcher. Objectivity could be lost and this could be viewed as a perceived 'failure'. Sexual relations can and do physically happen in the field, though. Malinowski (1989) met a woman in the fieldwork who he engaged in a meaningful relationship with and who would later become his wife. Again, their role as a 'professional' and 'objective' researcher can become questioned and viewed as a perceived 'mistake, error or failure' for becoming too immersed into the field. During his early fieldwork in Morocco, Rabinow (1977) also experienced a sexual encounter. He describes how he made love to a woman from another village, confessing that, 'I had never before had this kind of sensual interaction in Morocco' (1977, p. 65). Frank (2015) establishes that having some sort of romantic or sexual relationship with a respondent can, indeed, help develop rapport and can gently ease one into the community that is being researched. This can help address the issue of a perceived 'failure, mistake or error' about becoming too immersed into the field and losing sight of a researcher's professional objective role. However, sex in fieldwork can be dangerous, as Moreno (1995) details in her book chapter in which she discusses her experience of being raped in the field.

6.3 Stigma and Queer Work

There is wide agreement amongst some scholars that sexuality work is often stigmatizing and unconventional, deviating from 'normal' and more acceptable research (e.g. Attwood 2010; Hammond and Kingston 2014; Irvine 2014; Javaid 2018b). Here, I introduce the works of Erving Goffman to help shed light on the stigma of sexuality research and how that stigma often spreads onto queer writers doing queer work, making it seem that queer writers inherently 'fail' to abide by the professional researcher role/script.

Goffman (1968) discusses stigma as a relational entity that is situationally constructed in relation to others, whereby one occupies a role that becomes relationally stigmatized. Stigma is contextually bound; it is not an inherited entity but rather actively negotiated through social relations. Goffman (1968) writes that stigma is 'an attribute that is deeply discrediting...[including] a relationship between attribute and stereotype' (pp. 13–14). With regard to the queer writer, then, he lacks a particular attribute of heterosexuality, and so he is cast as an outsider, a deviant, someone who is devalued with a 'spoiled identity'[6]. For Goffman (1968), a homosexual is classified as not a 'real' man, and so one could infer that he may be constructed as not a 'real' researcher as he deviates from the normalization of heterosexuality so is potentially positioned as undesirable or as someone who is deemed unimportant. He 'fails' to occupy a 'real' researcher role. Goffman (1968) makes a distinction between two types of stigma: first, the discredited stigma, which is stigma that can be seen and is visible, so one's own gender or ethnicity, and second, the discreditable stigma, which is stigma that is concealed until shown otherwise, so this relates to information control whereby certain strands of information has the potentiality of inducing stigma. For instance, one might confess their homosexuality to family members and strangers and, subsequently, acquire a sexual stigma to mark him as somehow 'different' and unequal to the rest of the heterosexual population (Plummer 1975). To know whether a type of information can be stigmatizing is reliant upon the relationship between the storyteller and the person who is at the receiving end of this (potentially stigmatizing) information.

A queer writer doing sexuality research is, it could be argued, 'a blemished person, ritually polluted, to be avoided, especially in public places' (Goffman 1968: ii). A 'spoiled identity' is often projected onto me as a queer writer, and my research often becomes stigmatized, separated into a distinct category that is labelled as dangerous and risky. Thus, when queer writers reveal their involvement with sexuality research, they may encounter a discreditable stigma. Scott (2013) argues that:

> Discreditable stigmas are in some ways more dramaturgically stressful to manage in everyday life, insofar as the actor must work at keeping their attribute secret, and remain constantly vigilant about the threat of discovery. (p. 208)

However, to get ethical approval from an ethics board, sexuality writers have to confess their involvement with sexuality research, risking their encounter with discreditable stigma. Irvine (2014) found that Institutional Review Boards (IRBs) see sexuality research as too risky since they deem the researcher to be 'vulnerable', yet they play a significant but largely unnoticed role in the marginalization of sexuality research. Arguably, constructing queer writers as 'vulnerable' may be a substitute for a discreditable stigma. A female sociologist researching individuals who identify as 'kinky' declares that an IRB did not give her approval to enter a participant's home for this would be 'unsafe' (Irvine 2014). IRBs reproduce what Ken Plummer (1975) calls sexual stigma. They can discourage sexuality research, halt its development or

[6] Goffman (1968) develops the notion of 'spoiled identity' to indicate an identity that creates a person to experience stigma.

completely stop it from taking place. As a result, Irvine (2014) found that many queer writers simply divorce themselves from conducting sexuality work. Queer writers become 'doubly stigmatized' both for being a homosexual and for engaging with 'dirty' work, and so we must be somehow impure, deviant or alien or somehow 'failing' to conduct 'acceptable' work. These assumptions can manifest 'into normative expectations…making certain assumptions as to what the individual[s] before us ought to be' (Goffman 1968, p. 12), resulting in strangers and non-strangers not wanting to 'live within the world of one's stigmatized connexion' (Goffman 1968, p. 43). We often become estranged or cast as discredited 'outsiders', as 'failures'.

There are mechanisms to deal with stigmatizing information or to address a discredited character. Goffman (1968) writes about strategies that can be used to hide conduct and to conceal 'truths' of us in social contexts. For Goffman (1968), the key is not to manage tension through social relations but to manage information: 'to display or not to display; to tell or not to tell…to lie or not to lie' (p. 57). As queer writers, we can 'pass' as normal and of equal citizen by managing 'undisclosed discreditable information about the self' (Goffman 1968, p. 58). For example, during romantic dates or when I am on a night out and speaking with strangers, I do not reveal my sexuality research because I fear it would induce discreditable stigma and could result in feelings of embarrassment for the 'failed' performer if he is suspected to be lying about his occupation. I fear the consequences of revealing my work to others given that stigma is powerful. It can hurt us, it can pain us, and it can be difficult to handle once we relationally become stigmatized. Dating partners will no longer want to date us. Family members would no longer want to become associated with our stigma. Withdrawing from conversations about my line of work is hard work and tiresome but necessary to emotionally and, sometimes, to physically protect myself. Instead, when strangers and non-strangers would ask about my occupation, I would declare, 'I am a Dr'. Although it is never my intention to mislead others, as some people assume that I am a medical Dr as opposed to an academic Dr, it offers me an avenue to 'pass' as acceptable and 'normal'. I am in control of how I present myself to others at particular contexts, times and places, forming a particular 'presentation of self' (Goffman 1959) that creates an illusion of competence. It enables me to make conversations work without a discreditable stigma emerging. The irony of all this is that, although I may define myself as a queer writer and scholar, I start to question 'who am I?' in the midst of putting on and taking off masks.

6.4 The Research Project

There is a particular research project that I draw upon in the next section that is based on rich, autoethnograpahic descriptions. The project is entitled *Masculinities, Sexualities and Love* (Javaid 2018a). It sought to examine the ways in which love is socially and culturally constructed, questioning what is love? Why does love hurt so much when a significant other leaves us? Why does love matter to us? Is love even relevant in current society for gay and bisexual men or has sexual promiscuity taken over? These questions, and more, have fascinated us when we experience emotion, pain or heartbreak. This project sought to problematize the notion of love. It paid close attention to the ways in which love intersects with men, masculinities and sexualities. It draws on empirical data gained from interviewing/speaking with 23 gay and bisexual men to understand how they construct and re-construct love. Thus, the men's subjective experiences of love and loneliness were considered in this project. I had informal conversations with these men via Grindr, Tinder and POF (Plenty of Fish), which are popular apps that men often use to seek casual, 'no strings attached' sex; infrequently, men also use these apps to seek dates/relationships. Access was straightforward. Prior to the research commencing, I already had Grindr, Tinder and POF profiles. I continued to use these profiles when getting access to the men, reaching out to them and having unstructured and open-ended conversations with them. I had identified as gay, which I still continue to identify as, which made it easier for the men to connect with me. The conversations lasted, approximately, anywhere from 1 h to 5 h during 2016–2017 in England. The unstructured interviews with the men generated some interesting data, though some data were not useful since sometimes some of the men steered the conversations to sex. They wanted to have sex with me. Many sexual proposals were offered, which I declined, as I solely wanted to gain an understanding of their constructions and views about love. To help overcome this challenge of 'distraction', I employed covert research. To understand more about the methods and methodology of the project, see Javaid (2018a). In the next section, I detail some of my personal and intimate experiences with some of the men who I interviewed for this project, using authoethongraphy so using hindsight to resurrect my memories and experiences with the men.

6.5 Doing the Unconventional: Falling in Love

6.5.1 Biography

I identify as a male gender and sexuality theorist and have conducted sexuality research for about a decade. I am a British Muslim/Pakistani who does queer research. For the Muslim community to which I belong, this is difficult to accept; so I am often estranged or cast as an 'outsider' because I deviate from the radical perspective of Islam. I strongly sustain a liberal perspective of Islam. There is an expectation of me to get married to a woman and to sustain heteronormativity in the household. My identity, as a gay Muslim single, fuels tensions in the Muslim community. I am constructed as deviant. Rahman (2014), too, draws attention to the suspicions that are often cast upon us as gay South Asians/Muslims since there is seemingly an incompatibility between the paradigm of Islam and embodying a queer identity. The former is constructed as non-Western, whereas the latter is seen solely as a Westernized phenomenon and that the two are simply antithetical

(Rahman 2014). When the two coincide, an explosion of violence, abuse and exclusion is encountered. I still identify as Muslim, Pakistani and queer, nevertheless. I do believe in the divine other from a very *liberal* viewpoint – I pray on a daily basis to strengthen my emotional and spiritual connection, repairing my broken soul and heart with faith and love. A radical stance on Islam sustains an evil outlook on life, 'killing' love, beauty, and faith whereas a more liberal stance counteracts evil. I was born in 1989 in Wales (Newport). I am a sociologist and a criminologist by training, and my doctorate thesis explored male rape, masculinities and sexualities (see Javaid 2018b), looking at the ways in which male rape is socially and culturally constructed, and a number of publications have emerged from this project (e.g. see Javaid 2017, 2018c). I also write around violence (e.g. Javaid 2019b). I identify as middle class and a professional, working as an academic at a university in London. I live alone in the West Midlands, UK, as a single person. For Lahad (2017, p. 118), the single is stigmatized, whereby others view him/her as 'the lonely spinster without anyone to go out with'. I embody this stigmatized, single identity in my everyday life, having been single for over 7 years at the time of writing this. I am very often alone and single in my daily life, attending bars on my own, going to the cinema as a single, eating alone and walking alone, all of which reinforce my single identity in my social life. Lahad (2017) argues that the performance as a single person can lead to the risk of stigma, embarrassment and shame occurring under the close observation of others. For a long time, I have struggled to contest my single identity and to become 'unsingle' in order to defeat the stigmatized category of singlehood that I am positioned in. In the fieldwork, however, it was a space of hope, of possibilities, with which to address the stigma of my gay Muslim single identity because it offered intimacy and love. In this section, I detail the manners in which I momentarily deviated from my professional researcher role/script and how it brought about stigma. I 'failed' to adhere to a 'professional' researcher role/script on some occasions due to the ideology of love and because of my faith.

6.5.2 *Perils in Sexuality Research: Encounters with Love*

6.5.2.1 Case Study 1: Chris

I am on a long bus journey to Teesside, which typically takes 1 hour or so to reach my destination. The travel to work often gives me substantial time to peacefully reflect. I sit at the near front of the bus to do this, catching glimpses of the sunlight outside the grimy bus windows. This double deck bus is not so full; many seats are unoccupied. I can breathe and relax in this silence, preparing for my class to teach. The silence in the bus seems to comfort me, but it is painfully silent; boredom soon creeps in. Nobody else on the bus is talking to each other. I sit silent, and then suddenly one of my participants messages me through POF. I light up, and, all of a sudden, butterflies erupt in my stomach. How can this be? Surely, I should not be feeling in this way as a 'professional' researcher? I am supposed to be 'objective'. However, us humans have no control over how we feel; our emotions are uncontrollable. On POF, I used my profile to recruit some of my respondents, including Chris who messages me during my being on this bus. He was so handsome, attractive and good-looking, with his muscular toned white body and pale white skin. At the time of his inclusion in the covert research, he is 27 years old, white, British born and a Geordie and works as an engineer; he is away a lot for work. He is roughly of 5′7 height. He identifies as pansexual and currently had a girlfriend during the time of the research. He is not out of the closet as pansexual; people know him as straight. He may not know this, but I had seen him out on nights out some years ago prior to the research-taking place; I longed for him then, too. Now, he is speaking to me, interested in *me*. It was like my dreams were coming true, but should they come true when I am including him in my research? Whilst on the bus, he continues to message me flirtatious and sexual messages: 'I think I'd like to be penetrated, I'd like to ride you I think so I'm in control of it [my penis] inside me, I want to make you cum!…As you're entering me for the first time I'd like to guide it in so I'm controlling how it feels!' I feel my butterflies flattering their wings, and I smile on the quite bus. I am blushing, like the old teenage boy that I was who had his first crush on his handsome geography teacher.

The boundaries are now blurred between the 'value free' researcher and 'respectful participant'. I could not just disclose my research to him now, having come so far into it. The covertness would be jeopardized, so what do I respond to Chris? I flirt back. I 'failed' to stick to the professional researcher role/script; objectivity was compromised. He made me feel good, making me feel like I am the only person in the world. My naivety took over as a single, hopelessly romantic person. He knew how to say the right words. I suggested to him, 'I want you inside me' to 'make love to me'. The double-deck bus is still active, and I am nowhere near my destination yet. Chris messages me some more. He talks about love, making me think, 'Could he be the one?'. He says: 'Love is something that builds between two people when they genuinely like each other and each other's company!…Big thing for me, I want someone who I connect with and can trust. [T]hat doesn't come overnight you know'. Love is, according to him, something that gets actively created. Jamieson (2011) calls this notion 'practices of intimacy' that allow, produce and maintain a subjective sense of closeness and being attuned and special to one another. I figured, as he is practising emotion and telling me all his secrets and desires, he is making the conscious effort to build love between him and I: he is 'doing' love. I continue to naively think, 'I found the one' and that 'I am may no longer be single, finally'. Oh, how terribly wrong I was.

> I'm not really attracted to guys I'm more pansexual, attracted to personality. I've only ever been [in] a relationship with women, I fancy women but I'd love to have a guy on the side like a secret life. Sex is about enjoyment, excitement, the feeling of pleasure. Secret life may be a bit of a harsh terminology, I meant to explore my sexuality, I don't want my life broadcast I'd like to be discreet oh and I haven't had sex with men…I'll never be a boyfriend, I might class myself as a lover but not a boyfriend! (Chris, 27)

Now, my hopes and dreams that were erect on the bus crumbled as fast as the wheels on the bus were turning. I gathered, 'He just wants sex'. He makes it clear to me that I would just be a bit of 'fun', nothing serious, especially when he has a girlfriend. The sunlight outside the window of the bus suddenly seems to be fading, I crawl back into the seat of the bus and deeply reflect: 'How could he cheat on his girlfriend?' I thought. I'll never be anything more to him in a romantic sense. He is not 'out'; therefore, only discreet sexual activity can take place between him and I Chris says to me: 'I think there's a lot of straight guys who have bi sexual thoughts, me for one;) [emoticon via POF message] [sic] although I want to act on mine!' (Chris, 27). I look at his pictures non-stop, flicking through them while the wheels on the bus go round and round. Although we did not have sex, and although I did not even kiss or hold him, the thoughts were there where I imagine his muscular body on mine, where I imagine his soft lips on mine and where I move my hands into his light brown hair whilst he is on top of me. As Altork (1995) writes, 'protecting oneself from being "touched" by the field, might be unnessary [sic] in certain circumstances' (p. 121). I did, however, 'protect' myself, as I did not meet with him to have sex with him but only chose to not do so for my not getting hurt and emotionally involved given that he has a girlfriend. Still, I 'failed' to sustain objectivity and to draw boundaries between the participant and myself. I 'failed' to take on the professional role of a researcher. I knew I would be nothing more than just sex. The feelings I had for him made me momentarily believe that I was 'in love'. For queer writers, the feeling of being 'in love' can be encountered at any stage of the research, although this is not specific to queer authors. We cannot know with any certainty when/if this falling in love will occur.

After my research was completed, and I included him in my book (see Javaid 2018a), many months had passed until I saw him again in the flesh. On my own, I was out on the gay scene in the North East region. He was with a group of friends, including his girlfriend. On the noisy dance floor, with loud pop music playing, from Lady Gaga to Britney Spears, we locked eyes together whilst my close proximity to him. It felt like the whole bar had stopped for a minute or two; both of our souls were reuniting. The feelings of love came rushing back to me for a few moments. His eyes were deep as the ocean; I felt like I was sinking in love, again, with no way of swimming out of his eyes. No words were shared between him and I. His eyes sparkled with desire as he continues to stare at me. I wondered, 'What could he be thinking? Does he remember me?' My heart tells me he does. Next to him, his very tall and plump female friend, with short flamboyant black hair, interrupts our souls reconnecting. She acts as a vessel for his words and states to me: 'He has told me everything about you and him. He's just a bit unsure about his sexuality'. Quickly, she becomes concerned given that his girlfriend is only five steps away, concerned that I might tell her that her boyfriend had been cheating on her with me as the other 'side chick'. Although I would never tell on him, not only because it was not my place to tell her but also because I still cared for him, his tall friend rapidly collects her friends together to announce that, 'We are leaving. Onto the next bar'. They left. I never did see him again ever since (either online or offline). His words leave an imprint on my memory of what could have been. As they left, my 'spoiled identity' (Goffman 1968) was reproduced because their leaving me acted as a catalyst for reinforcing the notion that the gay Muslim single is stigmatized as the 'other' for falling in love with the forbidden (Javaid 2019c).

6.5.2.2 Case Study 2: Kieran

Kieran is 24 years old at the time of speaking with him. He identifies as bisexual, saying that, 'I'm bisexual. I thought my parents knew, but then I brought my previous two exs home and then they thought not haha [sic]'. He had the look of a slim, toned, 'straight-acting' model. He was beautiful, with golden tanned complexion. He was roughly of 5′10 height. His dark, blonde hair made him stand out. As an aircraft engineer, he tells me that he is often away from his home. He is always 'on the go'. Whilst based in the East Midlands, UK, he travels frequently with his friends either within the UK or abroad. Because of his hectic lifestyle, it can sometimes get in the way of sustaining a romantic relationship: 'My career gets in the way', he says. From all the men I spoke with for the project, Kieran was the one I connected with the most. He opened up to me in a way that a patient opens up to their counselor. He had told me his secrets that propelled me to deeply connect with him, resulting in my 'failing' to adhere to the professional researcher role/script on some occasions.

For example, on one particular ordinary evening at my family home, I was laying back on my parent's gold two-seater sofa. I am relaxing on there, wearing my pyjamas. My mother who is now estranged from me occupies the three-seater sofa across me. The room was silent; my mother reading her magazine while I am navigating on my silver MacBook. Suddenly, Kieran messages me on Tinder. My eyes light up as I flick through his handsome pictures. In every picture, he is clothed, making me wonder what is behind such clothes. He wants to see me; he wants to be with me. This feeling that I feel is all too familiar—could it be the feelings of love? Again, I question my objective researcher role, as I 'should' be treating him solely as an emotionless research participant and treating myself as a heartless researcher, devoid from human values. I am 'failing' to follow my script.

In fact, the reality is we are both humans with human feelings and values. Walby (2010) argues that the researcher stopping himself/herself from being 'touched' by the field may be unnecessary because, in some cases, it might be necessary to get close to one's respondents. This is true in order to develop rapport and a trusting relationship. I felt that I got very close to Kieran; he opened up to me. Had I not developed a close relationship with him, I believe I would not have gotten rich, detailed data. Kieran wants to see me urgently when he messages me while I am on the sofa. My heart beats at an unusual rate, and, in a panicky state, I think, 'What do I do?' He says:

> [M]y house does get a bit lonely…The only real way to get to know someone is in person. Give it 2 months, I could be talking shit…people can talk shit over text and act all different in person. Only real way to know someone is in person. My thinking anyway…I've never met anybody that I've met on here [Tinder] that I don't get bored of. If I don't meet someone soon, it's like nah boring. I hate texing. I think its [sic] boring and fake. Ive [sic] met people before that and they have been different to what they made out to be on text. And I really do get bored of texting haha. I need to meet someone like nearly straight away…otherwise for me it's like talking to a wall. Nothing may ever happen and it's pointless. Like I don't even want to just have sex or anything straight away, I just need to meet someone properly rather than texting…it's just not natural to talk to someone you haven't met. When you meet

someone for the first time on a night out, what is the [difference] if you don't get on; you go separate ways. With chatting on the phone, after one phone call, I'd be like, "right lets meet up." It's just more natural to meet someone in person. I'm not a modern day guy. (Kieran, 24)

He puts pressure on me to meet him as soon as possible. I look to my mother, but she does not suspect anything. She continues to read her magazine. I reach out for my can of coke, tasting the fizziness to dilute the butterfly feeling in my stomach; the butterflies are flattering their wings like no tomorrow: my stomach hurts. Why am I worrying so much? He wants to meet, fine; but I feel I am not ready to meet him. Although he claims he does not want sex on the first meet, I silently thought to myself, 'What would we do? What would I talk to him about? Could I continue to keep my research covert when/if I meet with him?' These questions, and more, rushed to my head like the speed of light. I am 'failing' to address this interaction as a professional researcher: I do not know what to do. Kieran gets annoyed that I prolong to meet him when I say, 'It's too soon to meet'. I do indicate that 'I want to meet', but when I am ready. I also confessed my liking him. I 'failed' to sustain an objective and professional barrier between myself and the participant; the wall came down and I let him in. I made the 'mistake' of becoming too immersed into the field. Nonetheless, Oakley (1981) establishes that some personal, mutual disclosure should be a necessity in qualitative research. Both Kieran and I have now disclosed personal disclosures as a way of building rapport and eradicating any power imbalances during our conversations. We talk some more. He 'touches' me through his words, disclosing what Ken Plummer (1995) calls 'sexual stories'. For instance, he tells me an intimate story, which is a 'practice of intimacy' (Jamieson 2011) as it gets me closer to him because it creates and sustains a subjective sense of closeness and being attuned and special with one another. He gets emotionally and spiritually closer to me by telling me about his deceased ex, Beth:

I had a girlfriend, love of my life, childhood sweet heart. I'd just turned 18. My ex girlfriend died. She was also a close family friend. Was meant to go funeral with my best pal dale. He text saying we should go together, as when she got bullied out of school, it was only us left that were her friend. He never showed. I had to go with my girlfriend, who ironically enough was in the friendship group that bullied Beth out of school. After that day of losing [both] Beth and Dale (like haven't spoken to Dale since, and it's been 6 years), I don't know why he never replied, I saw him in town like 6 months later, confronted him and he said, "Don't run this up again and walked off". After losing them, I was just angry and upset, blamed it all on my girlfriend, saying "[You] bullied her out of school, or her friendship group did and she just watched and didn't help, yet she had the right to come to her funeral and pretend to care and cry. I said things I shouldn't have [said] and lost 3 close people…Horrific. Never got over it…Ever since my first love, I keep a guard up. And I've not managed to love anyone since then. As soon as it gets to nearly that point, I end things. Guess I'm scared of love again. Too painful when it ends…I don't know how I'll get over it…I feel like a dick but I can't help it…I find out it's me getting scared. I had a bad experience that's left me broke to say the least. I let no one in…I hope I get over it, I keep telling myself I am, then am clearly not…and now I'm scared to love…Real life is hard and isn't as easy as words are. I go to [Beth's] house every Christmas and knock on the door and her mum still breaks down in tears and holds me for 5 minutes. It's heartbreaking…I just don't take well to letting people in now because its heartbreaking when they leave. And the less you let in, the less you feel when they go. Shit way of thinking, but I cant [sic] help it. Not good really…I'm pretty sure I am slightly depressed and socially isolate myself at times,

> and pretty sure I have a lot of anxiety going on but, what can you do? In fact, that's the first time I've ever admitted that, so, weird feeling haha...I doubt I'll ever truly be happy again, well I know I won't because I've got this OCD self consciousness that every morning and afternoon and night, [including] random points of the day when I'm not busy, and it just says 'Beth'. It's been 6 bloody years. Surely I could go a day without thinking about her.

As mentioned, Kieran has told me 'sexual stories' that he has not told anyone ever before. He trusted me. He confined in me, which strengthened the feeling of closeness and being attuned and special with one another. He suggests to me that he cannot love someone ever again, including me. Tears start to form in my eyes. Again, I 'failed' to stick to the researcher script/role to sustain objectivity; instead, I became emotional, and my human values entered the field, whereby I became emotional. I showed human feelings and emotions and the boundaries between 'professional researcher' and 'being human' became blurred. As we had reached the threshold that propels Kieran to block out 'almost lovers', he had ended things with me and eventually deleted me on Tinder. Those butterflies that kept fluttering their wings could no longer flap their wings. They died. Not only had they died, but also my dreams and hopes with him had deceased. Whilst I had his stories kept on file to document in my book, my stigmatized single identity was reinforced. Kieran will never 'love again', he implies, resulting in my 'waiting for the one' and being positioned in a stigmatized category as the gay Muslim single. I miss him.

6.6 Conclusion

Sexuality research is controversial and risky. It opens up countless possibilities for 'failures'. Drawing upon my own personal experiences of conducting what Irvine (2014) aptly calls 'dirty work', I shed light on my different (sometimes presumed) 'failures' when doing sexuality work. I located my experiences in their cultural and social contexts, delving into hindsight to resurrect those memories of pain and loneliness when doing sexuality work, with the assistance of autoethnography. In this chapter, I exposed my vulnerabilities with regard to doing sexuality work and what this could mean for other queer and sexuality writers. I provided honest examples of such 'failures'. The raw examples that I offered detailed some of the implications that I encountered when doing 'risky' and stigmatizing research, providing an individual and personal reflective account to elucidate and make sense of such 'failures'. These experiences of mine are likely to resonate with other like-minded queer writers' similar incidents. The raw experiences that I provide include falling in love with respondents, which meant that I momentarily 'failed' to adhere to the professional researcher role/script to sustain sheer objectivity. I used autoethnography to speak about my subjective and personal experiences that elucidated how I 'failed' to draw strict boundaries between researcher and participant. As Altork (1995, p. 120) argues, 'all relationships and events with which we are involved in the field change us in subtle ways and affect the way we perceive, and write about, the field'. By talking about my own experiences and feelings of love in the field, I am able to offer a more transparent and honest account of my research and the processes by which I reached my conclusions in my work. I argue that it is possible to write from both our heads and hearts, rather than solely from the former because we are pressured from institutions to sustain sheer 'objectivity' (also known as institutional 'evil') when that may not always be possible to do given that human values always enter at the beginning and the end of research. Human values are present when we interview participants. I argue that, in sexuality work, the process of interviewing participants is a creative space. Interviews, whether online or offline, are spaces where subjectivities are actively created. Plummer (1995) argues that interviews are best conceived as performative collaborations since both the researcher and the respondent have the capacity to shape the encounter. Emotions and feelings are created during interviews with participants.

As bell hooks (1989 [2015]) profoundly reminds us:

> The longing to tell one's story and the process of telling is symbolically a gesture of longing to recover the past in such a way that one experiences both a sense of reunion and a sense of release. (p. 265)

For me, by using hindsight to relive the memories that I share in this book chapter, I momentarily recaptured the feelings of love. I resurrected those feelings and emotions. It had been so long. The need to remember and temporarily hold onto that feeling of love and what it taught me has been all the more important. It has allowed me to emotionally protect myself in the future when doing further queer work with human participants and to try to stick to the 'professional' researcher role/script as best that I could so that I do not get emotionally hurt. Reflecting on my history, past experiences and biography allowed me to see love from a dissimilar perspective, notably from a liberal Islamic perspective with the use of my unmoving faith, to use this perspective/knowledge for self-growth and transformation in a productive way. It reproduces love, a love that is unbreakable by evil. Writing saved me; it rescued that young, naïve and hopelessly romantic queer writer from being uncared for. Using hindsight formed part of therapy through words. These words I shared healed my broken heart, making it whole again to making it possible to truly love myself first and to not let 'evil' hinder self-love.

References

Ahmed, S. (2017) *Living a Feminist Life*. Durham and London: Duke University Press.

Altork, K. (1995) "Walking the Fire Line: The Erotic Dimension of the Fieldwork Experience," in Kulick, Don, and Margaret Willson (eds.). *Taboo: Sex, Identity, and Erotic Subjectivity in Anthropological Fieldwork*. London: Routledge. Pp. 107–139.

Attwood, F. (2010) 'Dirty work: Researching women and sexual representation'. In: Ryan-Flood, R., and Gill, R. (eds.) *Secrecy and Silence in the Research Process*. London: Routledge, pp. 177–187.

Connell, R. (1987) *Gender and Power: Society, the Person and Sexual Politics*. Cambridge: Polity.

Ellis, C., Adams, T. E., & Bochner, A. P. (2011) 'Autoethnography: An overview'. *Forum Qualitative Sozialforschung/ Forum: Qualitative Social Research*, 12(1), 10. http:// nbnresolving.de/ urn:nbn:de:0114- fqs1101108

Frank, K. (2015) 'Observational Methods in Sexuality Research'. In: DeLamater, J., and Plante, R. F. (eds.). *Handbook of the Sociology of Sexualities*. Switzerland: Springer. Pp. 123–146.

Goffman, E (1959) *The Presentation of Self in Everyday Life*. New York: Anchor Books.

Goffman, E. (1968) *Stigma: Notes on the Management of Spoiled Identity*. Harmondsworth: Penguin Books.

Grenz, S. (2005) 'Intersection of sex and power in research on prostitution: A female researcher interviewing male heterosexual clients'. *Signs: Journal of Women and Culture in Society*, 30(4): 2091–2113.

Hammond, N., and Kingston, S. (2014) 'Experiencing stigma as sex work researchers in professional and personal lives'. *Sexualities*, 17(3): 329–347.

hooks, b. (1989 [2015]) *Talking Back, Thinking Feminist, Thinking Black*. New York and London: Routledge.

Huff, J. (1997) 'The sexual harassment of researchers by research subjects: Lessons from the field'. In: Schwartz, M. (ed.) *Researching Sexual Violence against Women: Methodological and Personal Perspectives*. London: SAGE, pp. 115–128.

Huysamen, M. (2018) 'Reflecting on the interview as an erotic encounter'. *Sexualities* [Advance Online Publication].

Irvine, J. M. (2014) "Is sexuality research 'dirty work'? Institutionalized stigma in the production of sexual knowledge". *Sexualities*, 17(5–6): 632–656.

Jamieson, L. (2011) "Intimacy as a Concept: Explaining Social Change in the Context of Globalisation or Another Form of Ethnocentricism?" *Sociological Research Online*, 16(4): 15.

Javaid, A. (2017) 'The invisible, the alien and the marginal: Social and cultural constructions of male rape in voluntary agencies'. *International Review of Victimology*, 25(1): 107–123.

Javaid, A. (2018a) *Masculinities, Sexualities and Love*. London: Routledge.

Javaid, A. (2018b) *Male Rape, Masculinities, and Sexualities: Understanding, Policing, and Overcoming Male Sexual Victimisation*. Hampshire: Palgrave.

Javaid, A. (2018c) 'The Unheard Victims: Gender, Policing and Sexual Violence'. *Policing and Society*.

Javaid, A. (2019a, in press) Reconciling an Irreconcilable Past: Sexuality, Autoethnography, and Reflecting on the Stigmatisation of the 'Unspoken'. Sexualities.

Javaid, A. (2019b) *Violences in Everyday Life: Power, Gender and Sexuality*. London: Zed Books.

Javaid, A. (2019c) The Haunting of Shame: Autoethnography and the Multivalent Stigma of Being Queer, Muslim, and Single. Symbolic Interaction.

Javaid, A. (2019d) 'Sex and the City: Male Sex Work and the Negotiation of Stigma and Masculinities'. In M. Boskovic (Ed.) Globalization and Its Impact on Violence Against Vulnerable Groups (pp. 95–121). Hershey, PA: IGI Global.

Kingston, S. (2014) *Prostitution in the Community: Attitudes, Action and Resistance*. London: Routledge.

Lahad, K. (2017) *A Table for One: A Critical Reading of Singlehood, Gender and Time*. Manchester: Manchester University Press.

Malinowski, B. (1989) *A Diary in the Strict Sense of the Term*. Stanford: Stanford University Press.

Moreno, E. (1995) 'Rape in the field: Reflections from a survivor'. In: Kulick, D., and Wilson, M. (eds.) *Taboo: Sex, Identity, and Erotic Subjectivity in Anthropological Fieldwork*. London: Routledge, pp. 166–189.

Morris, C. (2018) 'An Interview with Ken Plummer'. In: *Researching Sex and Sexualities* (eds.). Morris, C., Boyce, P., Cornwall, A., Frith, H., Harvey, L., Huang, Y. London: Zed Books. Pp. 339–358.

Oakley, A. (1981) 'Interviewing women: A contradiction in terms.' In: Roberts H (ed.) *Doing Feminist Research*. London: Routledge, pp. 50–61.

Plummer, K. (1975) *Sexual stigma: An interactionist account*. London: Routledge & Kegan Paul.

Plummer, K. (1995) *Telling Sexual Stories: Power, Change and Social Worlds*. London: Routledge.
Rabinow, P. (1977) *Reflections on Fieldwork in Morocco*. Berkeley, California: University of California Press.
Rahman, M. (2014) *Homosexualities, Muslim cultures and modernity*. London: Palgrave.
Scott, S. (2013) 'Performing the blush: a dramaturgical perspective from sociology'. In: Crozier, W Ray and de Jong, Peter J (eds.) *The psychological significance of the blush*. Cambridge University Press, Cambridge. Pp. 203–221.
Walby, K. (2010) 'Interviews as encounters: Issues of sexuality and reflexivity when men interview men about commercial same sex relations'. *Qualitative Research*, 10(6): 639–657.
Weeks, J. (2018) *Sex, Politics and Society: The Regulation of Sexuality Since 1800* (4th edition). Abingdon: Routledge.

Aliraza Javaid (Dr.) has a BSc (Hons) Criminology, an MSc Clinical Criminology and an MRes Social Sciences and has completed his PhD in Sociology and Social Policy. His research interests are gender, sexualities, masculinities, police and policing, sexual violence, the sociology of 'evil' and the sociology of love. His first sole-authored book, which is entitled *Male Rape, Masculinities, and Sexualities: Understanding, Policing, and Overcoming Male Sexual Victimisation*, has been published by Palgrave (2018). His second sole-authored book, entitled *Masculinities, Sexualities, and Love*, is published by Routledge (2018). His other publications around his research interests can be found here: https://alirazajavaid.wordpress.com/publications-2/

From a sexuality research perspective, Aliraza Javaid opens up about possibilities for mistakes, errors and failures. Drawing upon his personal experiences of conducting what Janie M. Irvine aptly calls 'dirty work', he sheds light on his different (sometimes presumed) mistakes, errors and failures when doing sexuality work. He locates these in their cultural and social contexts, delving into hindsight to resurrect memories of pain and loneliness when doing such work, with the assistance of research diary extracts. In his chapter, Javaid exposes researchers' vulnerabilities with regard to doing sexuality work and what this could mean for other and potential sexuality writers. He provides examples of his own work and opens it up for further discussion about how to deal with 'risky' research constructively.

Chapter 7
Qualities of Communication Failures in Hierarchical Relationships: A Theoretical Model for Conflict Prevention

Maike Baumann

Abstract Many social relationships people engage in are hierarchically structured, such as boss–employee, doctor/therapist–patient or teacher–pupil. Reasons to assign a leading role to one party in an interpersonal relationship can include advanced knowledge or expertise, seniority, agreement and ownership or control of resources. Differences in hierarchical status lead to particular expectations of and specific responsibilities assigned to the involved parties. The expectations include qualities of interaction, responsibilities, the other's value system and, consequently, the other's behaviour as well as assumptions concerning the other party's expectations (i.e. expectations of second and third order). During communication the different agents often assume divergent appraisals and expectations as obvious and do not share these presuppositions explicitly. In addition, cognitive biases can be expected to systematically influence the social behaviour of all parties involved without the interacting people being fully aware of them. As a consequence, communication failures and different qualities of conflict can be expected to (re)occur frequently in hierarchical social relationships. In this chapter a model of communication failures in hierarchical relationships within Western cultures is proposed. This model can be useful for teaching purposes to prevent conflict in, for instance, medical or educational contexts. In addition, the proposed model helps in analysing existing conflict dynamics and repeatedly occurring conflicts with the goal of enabling the development of understanding and a change of behaviour. The model uses insights from a systemic approach on human communication, research on cognitive biases as well as motivational psychology and research on the interrelation of emotions, stress and coping behaviour.

Keywords Mistakes · Errors · Failure · Communication failures · Cognitive biases · Hierarchical relationships · Expectations · Attribution theory

M. Baumann (✉)
Institut für Lebensgestaltung-Ethik-Religionskunde, University of Potsdam, Potsdam, Germany
e-mail: mbaumann@uni-potsdam.de

E. Vanderheiden, C.-H. Mayer (eds.), *Mistakes, Errors and Failures across Cultures*, https://doi.org/10.1007/978-3-030-35574-6_7

7.1 Introduction

In this chapter, a model of communication failures in hierarchical social relationships within Western cultures is proposed. I will first introduce my understanding of communication and communication failures and from that infer the motivation for the development of the model. I will then briefly discuss the basic theoretical background of the model with regard to the interrelation of emotions, stress and coping behaviour in contexts of social relating. Finally I will present the actual model and point out practical applications as well as its limits.

The model has a strong theoretical motivation. Besides it is based on a series of semi-structured expert interviews. These interviews showed strong indications that conflicts between people in certain hierarchical social relationships have a high likeliness to develop characteristic emotional and behavioural qualities. The special type of conflict that is being modelled seems to repeatedly occur in distinct hierarchical social relations and may be understood as consequences to communication failures.

The experts for the interviews were chosen based on their professional abilities and experiences, and the interviews were conducted via telephone over the course of 1 week. The answers were recorded in written form, and the data was anonymized, which all experts were aware of in advance. The experts did not receive any compensation for their participation. All experts held a professional qualification in methods of conflict resolution. Their average number of years in practice was 18.3 with a range of 6–36 years of experience. The main fields of practice were the medical sector and business mediation in companies ranging from small local companies to international companies. All experts had a German background.

7.2 Theoretical Background

7.2.1 Communication and Communication Failures

The concept of communication is a highly complex one, and in trying to reach a general definition, a very diverse range of approaches may be found. For an overview on the different lines of discussion, see, for example, Griffin (2012) or Shepherd et al. (2006). Adopting a systemic view upon communication, it may be understood as a series of interpersonal feedback loops as each person within this certain context of interpersonal exchange is affected by the behaviour of each other person (cf. Watzlawick et al. 2011). Speech may be understood as one possible behavioural option within the context of interpersonal communication. Besides any interpersonal communication "is largely influenced by, and in turn influences, the context in which their interaction takes place" (Watzlawick et al. 2011, p. 18). So the phenomenon of communication may be understood as "the observable vehicle of manifestations of relationships" within certain interactional contexts (cf. Watzlawick et al. 2011).

Accepting these assumptions, any communication at any time is always a complex systemic happening and should take contextual as well as inter- and intrapersonal factors such as social relations and emotional reactions into account. Thus understanding communication as an intentional process of relating (Condit 2006), I understand communication failures as unintended relational outcomes.

So if any communication is entered with the intent to influence a certain social relationship according to the acting person's relational goals, experiences of conflict due to diverging goals, misunderstandings, situational factors or else may be expected to occur on a regular basis.

7.2.2 *Appraisal, Stress, Emotion and Failing Communication*

Experiences made are constantly being appraised by the experiencer, and due to the appraisal, certain emotional and emotivational reactions are elicited. The process of appraisal is a rapid, at least two-stage process, resulting in a certain emotional state, creating a certain action readiness. Frijda and Scherer (2009) proposed a description of the entanglement of appraisal and emotion when describing the four major functions of emotions. They are cited in short by Scherer and Moors (2019, p. 721) describing a framework for an emotion episode as follows:

> (a) The appraisal of events that happen to us in terms of their relevance and consequences for our needs, plans, and values (elicitation of an emotion episode); (b) the preparation of action appropriate for dealing with or adapting to these events both mentally, in the form of states of action readiness or action tendencies, and physically, in the form of physiological responses; (c) the integration of information acquired from these two steps into a central representation that allows monitoring and regulation of the potential responses; and (d) often, although not always the categorization and communication of the emotion episode to other people.

For an overview on the interconnection of human appraisal and emotions, see also Scherer et al. (2001) and Scherer and Moors (2019).

Unintended relational outcomes might come expected or unexpected to the communicating agents. To fall short of reaching intended relational outcomes has a high probability of eliciting certain rather negative qualities of emotional reactions, such as anger and the experience of frustration and stress (Lazarus 2001; Roseman 2001). The exact quality of the emotional experience is mediated by the degree of expectancy (Roseman 2001) and the individual socialization-dependent evaluation for that particular relational experience elicited by the communication. Unexpected outcomes elicit a state of surprise, followed by a general orientation reaction and reach a final emotional valence only after a second situational appraisal by the communicator (cf. Meyer et al. 1997; Reisenzein and Meyer 2009), with a tendency to an initial slightly negative emotional state (Noordewier and Breugelmans 2013).

Unintended but expected outcomes on the other hand might elicit a whole range of different emotional reactions. It may be concluded that, independent from the communicators expectancies, the quality of the final emotional state following a communication failure depends on the individual evaluation of the entire situation, including social information internalized during the interacting parties socialization.

According to Lazarus' revised model of stress and coping (Lazarus 2001), emotions depend on relational meanings of person–environment relationships and the personal significance assigned. In his model, person and environment variables, including personal goals, get appraised in a two-step process by the acting person, resulting finally in a discrete emotional state. During the first stage of appraisal, the relational meaning assigned may cause psychological stress and coping behaviour, resulting in a second appraisal, finally causing a discrete emotional stage. Psychological stress, resulting in coping behaviour, is defined by Lazarus and Folkman (1984) as "constantly changing cognitive and behavioral efforts to manage specific external and/or internal demands that are appraised as taxing or exceeding the resources of the person" (p. 141).

7.2.2.1 The Culture-Dependent Nature of Emotions

Emotions and their display in communication underlie cultural and thereby socializational restrictions, so-called feeling rules and display rules (Hochschildt 1983). In consequence a model of communication failures that includes the communicator´s emotional reactions and behavioural impulses will be confined by these culture-bound emotional feeling- and display rules (for a comparison on individualistic and collectivistic cultures' feeling rules, see Eid and Diener 2009).

So the emotional valence and the exact discrete emotion that evolves in consequence to a communication failure may be expected to be influenced by the communicator's socialization. In turn the feeling rules will limit the possible range of imaginable appraisals.

Any model on communication failures, considering certain qualities of emotional and consecutively behavioural reactions, is automatically a culture-bound model and is dependent on the cultural frame of reference that was chosen for data acquisition. As the database for the model proposed is concerned purely with experts from an individualistic Western culture (Germany), referring to the great majority of cases to conflict parties from individualistic Western cultures (Europe and the USA), the scope of the model is bound to that particular cultural frame of reference, although the basic modelling assumptions might be used to adapt the model to different cultural frames of reference on a corresponding database.

7.2.3 Hierarchical Social Relationships

A very common context where communication failures arise on a regular basis is social contexts where one agent is in need of the help of another agent. Such contexts put the helping agent in a more powerful position than the person in search for help. Such relationships may be characterised as "intense, non-reciprocal relationships involving inherent power-imbalances" (Silver 1999). To name just a few, such helping relations may be found, for example, in juridical contexts, in pedagogical contexts or in medical contexts. In addition such contexts often concern complex matters where highly relevant values such as life and death or freedom are at stake. Also such helping relations often require a long period of repeated interaction and communication, leaving plenty options for unintended relational outcomes.

The high frequency of communicative failures, for example, in medical contexts is mirrored in institutionalized clinical ethics committees. According to empirical data, the majority of cases clinical ethics committees in different Western cultures are confronted with are concerned with patients or patient's relatives who are feeling troubled by treatment decisions or the behaviour of members of the clinical staff.

Another group of cases are concerned with medical staff seeking advice from clinical ethics committees in cases where patients seem to act in a self-harming and irrational way or are showing non-compliant and reactant behaviour (cf. Seifart et al. 2016; Breslin et al. 2005). Both types of conflict may be understood to arise from unintended relational outcomes, such as feeling neglected by the other agent, interpreting the other agent's behaviour as threat or perceiving the other agent as incompetent or lazy in respect to the joint goal, instead of the expected cooperative and helpful experience. So in order to analyse communication failures, such hierarchical social helping contexts seem to be a good choice. A subsequent in-depth literature search on models of communication failures in such hierarchical social contexts did not produce any comprehensive model.

In order to gather a database, highly experienced professional conflict facilitators were interviewed, and a series of seven qualitative semi-structured expert interviews was conducted. These showed strong indications that conflicts between people in hierarchical social relationships have a high likeliness to develop characteristic emotional and behavioural qualities.

7.2.3.1 Characteristics of the Major–Minor Relationship

While hierarchical human relations and social dependency dynamics are ubiquitous in everyday life and clearly form an interesting and active field of research, I will restrict myself in the following to the particular type of helping relationships indicated above. To underline the imbalance of power within these relationships, I name such relationships "major–minor relationships". Thereby I am following the tradition in drama, being a context playing with motive of imbalances of social power, to describe the more powerful, leading character as major and the following character as minor. The major–minor relationships in social contexts which I am taking into focus always include a minor actively choosing a major to assist him and to collaborate with him to reach a predefined goal of the minor.

In major–minor relationships, it is typically agreed upon that the major receives some sort of compensation for his efforts. The compensation can be made by the minor himself and/or by a third party (insurance, government, relatives, etc.) and can be of different qualities (e.g. money, work, favours, assistance, gratitude, etc.).

The relationship ends or loses its particular status as a major–minor relationship (a) in case of final success or final failure concerning the minor's goal, (b) when one of the agents actively cancels the agreement or (c) in case of death of one of the agents (note that the definition of success and failure concerning the minor's goal may differ depending on the major's or the minor's point of view). Major–minor relationships can be found in many different areas of society. Consider the following examples for illustration: healthcare professional–patient, lawyer–client, architect–client, coach–coachee, teacher–student, social worker–client, financial advisor–investor, etc.; but also social relations such as volunteer–displaced person or priest–faithful can be understood as major–minor relationships. Major–minor relationships often underlie at least partly legal constraints concerning rights and duties of both agents as well as definitions concerning the scope of the major's expertise.

In summary, major–minor relationships are typically initiated by the minor finding himself unable to satisfy a relevant need by his own efforts and seeking assistance of the major. The major is expected to possess a special expertise enabling him to assist the minor to satisfy the need in question. The major actively rejects or accepts the assignment. In case the major accepts the assignment, he implicitly agrees to help the minor regarding his need and in consequence takes on a part of the responsibility to reach this goal (or at least what the major understands the minor's goal should be). Hence this agreement implies a certain degree of goal-related cooperation. Understanding cooperative situations as possible conflict situations, I apply the basic principle from conflict research that the relevance a party assigns to the outcome of a conflict for himself has predictive value to that agent's conflict behaviour. Integrating this basic idea of dual concern models of conflict (cf. Hall 1969; Pruitt and Rubin 1986) and Tuomelas analysis of cooperation as joint action (2010), as well as research on reciprocity and the impact of the fairness norm on human cooperation and interaction (cf. De Cremer and Tyler 2007), different interactional outcomes may be expected when two parties are working by agreement on the same goal and possibly assign different degrees of relevance to the joint goal. Each party may assign high or low relevance to the joint goal such that a 2 × 2 matrix can visualize the possible goal-directed interactional outcomes as illustrated in Table 7.1.

Major–minor relationships easily develop characteristics of parentalistic relationships (e.g. Strauss 1987) as in many cases the major takes over at least part of the responsibility for certain aspects of the minor's current situation in life. Parentalistic tendencies of major's are no necessary part of major-minor relationships and stand in opposition to the fundamental freedom rights of any human being. The frequent occurence of parentalistic tendencies of major's in major-minor relationships is rightfully followed by continuous legislation processes to restrict such behavioural tendencies of major's (cf. patient's rights legislation, legislation concerning informed consent, etc.) thus illustrating a quality of an unintended relational outcome in major-minor relationships occurring so often that it's increasingly regulated by law.

Table 7.1 The goal-orientation/cooperation-matrix: when two parties are assigned to work together on the same goal, the quality of cooperation to be expected is understood as dependent upon each party's subjectively assigned relevance of the goal itself (authors own construction)

Self	assigns low/no relevance to goal	**A** no cooparation no goal directed behaviour possibly no social interaction with each other feelings of shame/guilt possible in case of violation of personal values or of 3rd party's interests due to own lack of action joint goal assignment followed by joint inactivity creates social bond	**B** no cooperation, no goal-oriented behaviour of Self / goal-oriented behaviour of Other Self possibly feels socially stressed by Other (due to active pressing behaviour and/or experiences shame/guilt) and avoids contact Fairness norm might lead to reactive goal related inactivity by Other Estrangement/social distance CONFLICT
	assigns high relevance to goal	**C** no cooperation, Goal-oriented behaviour by Self / no goal-oriented behaviour by Other Self might execute pressure on Other to perform Self might feel morally superior to Other and proud of own performance Fairness norm might lead to reactive goal-related inactivity by Self Estrangement/social distance CONFLICT	**D** direct and/or indirect cooperation both parties invest in goal as much as they are able to social differences may be put aside for duration of task fulfillment collective and shared proudness of successes possibly team performance is experienced as more effective and satisfying than single performance team experience builds up trust, confidence and social cohesion

In case of a newly established major–minor relationship, both interacting parties may expect that the relationship will be characterized by a cooperative quality as illustrated in Table 7.1, field D, as both parties may expect the other to assign high relevance to the joint goal as the goal itself is a defining criteria of the relationship they entered in: A preexisting goal orientation of the minor was his reason to seek out the major's assistance in the first place, and the major actively agreed to cooperate.

The exact procedure and frequency a specific cooperation takes are sometimes legally predefined (e.g. in psychotherapy or school) and sometimes defined privately by the two agents (e.g. at an architect's office). In case the exact definition of the minor's goal is not discussed explicitly and fixed in a precise contract, conflicts are very likely to occur quickly. Also important to note is the fact that during the process of goal approach, the interpretation of the goal and also the commitment to the goal might change on each side (major/minor) compared to the time when the cooperation was decided upon.

7.2.4 Theoretical Background in Attribution Theory and Cognitive Biases

The model proposed below assumes several additional variables that are expected to influence the quality of the agents' cooperational experience of the major–minor relationship.

These variables are seen as determinants to both parties' qualitative overall evaluation of the other agent's behaviour, their respective emotional reactions to this evaluation and the following impulses to react to each other while cooperating on behalf of the minor's predefined goal. The determinants are chosen with regard to research on (a) goal-directed behaviour indicating the relevance of expected success or failure for goal-directed behaviour and (b) attribution theory predicting certain social interactive consequences depending on the attributed wilfulness of action of a social partner. On the influences of sociolinguistic discourse studies on conflict communication and pragmatic failure, I unfortunately cannot elaborate on in the scope of this chapter.

Ad a) Goal attainment processes are highly complex and underlie several internal and external factors. For a summary see Locke and Latham (2002) and Monzani et al. (2015). For the modelling purpose, I focus on the concept of goal expectancy as the assigned probability of goal achievement or the individual's evaluation whether the desired state can be reached through action (cf. Liberman and Förster 2008). In cases of high levels of expectancy, individuals actively invest effort in their goal and show high goal commitment. On the opposite, with a low expectancy of success, people tend to abandon their goal and disengage (Carver and Scheier 1998; Wortman and Brehm 1975).

Ad b) The human ability to detect intentionality can be proven in infancy already (i.a. Woodward 1999), and, depending on the assigned intentionality of an observed behaviour, different modes of explanation are ascribed (Malle 1999). "Events perceived to be unintentional are explained by causes that mechanically brought about the event; those perceived to be intentional are typically explained by the agent's reasons for acting" (Malle et al. 2007, p. 492). In goal related major–minor interactions, I assume both agents to perceive the other's actions as (intrinsically or extrinsically) motivated and therefore to be intentional. I thus expect the interacting agents to assume reasons as causes for each other's actions, specifically the reasons of acting out of their own free will or of acting due to external stimuli. The so-called actor–observer asymmetry (Jones and Nisbett 1971) is a well-established bias hypothesis in social psychology. It states that people tend to explain their own behaviour with situational causes and other people's behaviour with internal causes. This leads to people tending to underestimate situational influences on other people's behaviour (Gilbert and Malone 1995; Jones and Nisbett 1971; Malle et al. 2006). In the case of interpersonal conflict, I therefore assume the interacting agents to apply this bias in their attributions of the cause of another person's actions.

To briefly sum up, the necessary determinants identified to model and predict major–minor relationships are:

- Basic precondition for entering the particular hierarchical social interactive relationship at all
- Agreement of both agents to intentionally cooperate on behalf of minor's goal (related to minors needs/personal values)
- Agreement that minor will compensate major's investment (payment, work, etc.)

Relevant conditions during their cooperative process:

- Probability of success/failure of reaching the goal, individually assigned by each party
- Perceived wilfulness of the other agent's actions on behalf of the predefined joint goal (intrinsically/extrinsically motivated)
- Fairness norm (internal evaluation of the other party's effort to reach the joint goal as low investment/high investment)

7.2.5 Coping in Hierarchical Relationships

All goal pursuits can fail, and all cooperative relationships can lose their cooperative quality. As communication failures within a cooperative relationship is what the model focusses on and such failures imply the experience of stress, majors and minors are expected to show coping behaviour (see Sect. 2.2). Following Folkman and Lazarus (1990), the behavioural reaction to stress can be targeted on different aspects of the stressing experience. Reactions can be directed (a) at the emotional experience, (b) at the problem itself or (c) at the evaluative perspective taken.

In the particular dyadic constellation explored here, i.e. major–minor relationships, the problem-oriented behavioural reaction to stress can concern different aspects of the situation, depending on the aspect in focus of the agent. Possible aspects facing the agents willing to cope in a problem-oriented fashion within this type of dyadic relation could be (a) goal-related, (b) related to the other agent's behaviour or (c) related to external factors that are assumed to influence the other agent.

Possible starting points for emotional coping may be to offer assistance to the other agent for interpersonal emotional regulation or to aim for self-caring behaviour and intrapersonal emotional regulation. A third option, namely, the option to cope with the situation by re-evaluation of the situation, in principle also exists. Mediation itself can be understood as one type of evaluative coping as it is a highly structured procedure aiming to reach a re-evaluation/reframing of a conflict situation in a stuck state. In a further step, this re-evaluation can then be helpful for all participants in the conflict to generate new interactive behavioural options. Even though I understand such an evaluative coping in a structured form as the prime option to solve a stressful interpersonal conflict experience, I will not explore such behavioural impulses further within the model below, because the model is supposed to describe qualities of stuck state experiences.

Table 7.2 Different types of dyadic coping in major–minor relationship (authors own construction)

Coping style	Behavioural examples		
Emotional coping	Interpersonal emotional regulation (ECO)		Caring, comforting
	Intrapersonal emotional regulation/self-care (ECS)		Withdrawal, relaxing, distraction, let oneself be comforted
Problem-oriented coping	Goal-oriented coping (PCG)	+	Work extra hard, invest more resources
		–	Reduce own investment in goal
	Coping behaviour oriented to the other agent's goal-related behaviour (PCO)	+	Explain, motivate, install incentives
		–	Execute behaviour control, reprimand other agent, terminate contract
	Coping behaviour oriented to external factors (PCE)	+	Call third party in to execute control/force, reinforce third party, install distractors
		–	Tell third party off, reduce distractors
Evaluative coping	Re-evaluation/reframing (EvC)		Find new and stress-reducing interpretations on levels of emotion, other, self, external factors, definition of goal, evaluation of outcome, etc.

For an overview of the different coping options in the dyadic constellation of a major–minor relationship, different to re-evaluative coping strategies, see Table 7.2.

Coping behaviour as part of the individual's emotional regulatory processes and as part of the possible behavioural options in social relationships also should be expected to underlie at least partly culture-bound socializational factors. The actual behavioural examples given in Table 7.2 have also been derived from a Western cultural frame of reference and should be reviewed before applying the model to different cultural contexts.

7.3 A Model of the Qualities of Communication Failures in Major–Minor Relationships

As presented in Sect. 2.3.1, in the ideal case, a major–minor relationship forms when both parties see a good chance for an interaction of type D (compare Table 7.1) before agreeing on a collaboration. I will therefore assume in the following that this is indeed the case in all major–minor relationships.

In order to actually predict the possible interactional qualities in major–minor relationships, including different conflict experiences, I suggest to put the three conditions identified in Sect. 2.4 as variables in relation to each other. We can then identify eight different interactional qualities, as shown in Figs. 7.1 and 7.2. Note that Figs. 7.1 and 7.2 essentially represent similar information but differ with respect to the point of view taken, i.e. the minor's and major's interpretative perspectives of the other agent's qualitative influence on the cooperational experience. Figure 7.1

presents the major's view on the minor's goal-related behaviour, while Fig. 7.2 shows the minor's view on the major's goal-related behaviour.

The first variable included is the influence of the expected overall success/failure: Each of the interacting agents is to be expected to have a private opinion on whether the whole project is more likely to succeed or more likely to fail in the end, compared to a private standard of success. Very often neither this first appraisal nor the private standard of success is communicated openly between major and minor prior to the process of collaboration. It is well-known from coping research that in steps of secondary appraisal, the attributed likeliness of success of an action is essential for the actual selection of an action, and I assume this to be highly relevant in major–minor relationships as well. The influence of the expected overall success/failure is represented at the very bottom of the model in Figs. 7.1 and 7.2.

The second necessary variable is the appraisal of the other agent's behaviour as either low-investing or as high-investing goal-oriented behaviour. Again, the appraisal process is generally kept private and follows individual standards which usually are not communicated openly to each other. This second variable, indicating the appraisal of the other's quality of investment in the joint goal, can be found at the very top of the model in Figs. 7.1 and 7.2.

The third variable included in the model is the locus of behavioural control one agent attributes to the other agent. The other agent's actions can be interpreted either as wilful actions (intrinsic motivation) or as externally motivated actions (extrinsic motivation). The variable representing the motivational quality of the other's actions is located on the left of the model in Figs. 7.1 and 7.2.

On the right-hand side of the model, I include reading information for the different lettering (bold, italics, capitals) within the central panels of the model.

The qualitatively distinct emotional reactions deduced in the central panels of the model together with the evaluative judgements are derived partially from the expert interviews mentioned in the introduction, are in line with my own professional experience and are theoretically based on current research on emotions in conflict. Distinct emotional involvement is generally understood as an inevitable part of social conflict experiences (for an overview on emotions in conflict communication, compare Jones 2000; Jones and Bodtker 2001; Bodtker and Jameson 2001 and Jones 2006).

Comparing the minor's and the major's evaluations and points of view concerning each other's behaviour, we can qualitatively model the communicative failures named by the experts in conflict mediation who were interviewed previously as noted in the introduction.

Note that the assumption made above, that the interacting agents generally tend to keep their attributions, appraisals and opinions on each other's behaviour to themselves, is in line with the vicious circle of conflict communication described by Schulz von Thun (2008) as well as with the systemic concept on expectations of second and third order (cf. von Schlippe and Schweitzer 2012, p. 116) as a cause of conflict and communicative failures. From a developmental point of view, keeping emotionally arousing information to oneself is actually a behaviour to be generally expected from late childhood on, as the acquisition of sufficient strategies for emo-

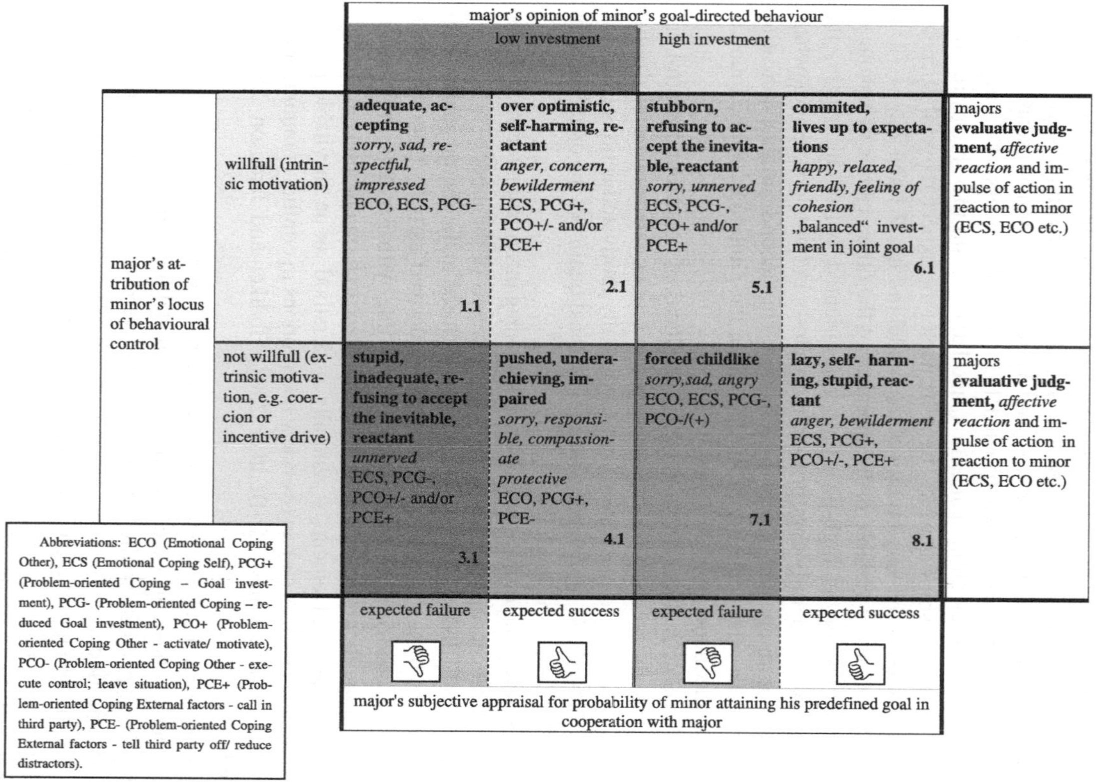

Fig. 7.1 Possible qualities of major–minor interactions from the major's point of view. The major's expectations, attributions and appraisals are based upon the major's private standards, the major's experience and the major's interpretation of the behaviour of the minor. For details on the dyadic coping strategies (ECS, ECO, etc.), see Table 7.2. (Authors own construction)

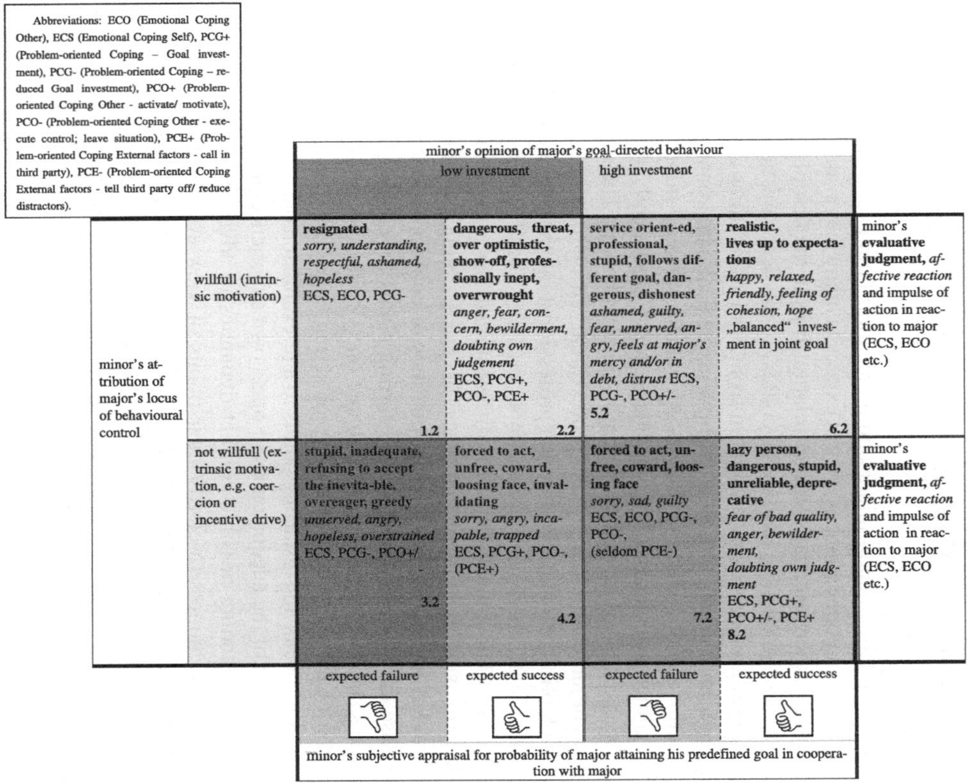

Fig. 7.2 Possible qualities of major–minor interactions from the minor's point of view. The minor's expectations, attributions and appraisals are based upon the minor's private standards, the minor's experience and the minor's interpretation of the behaviour of the major. For details on the dyadic coping strategies (ECS, ECO, etc.), see Table 7.2. (Authors own construction)

tional regulations is an important developmental task during middle childhood. From that age onwards, true information on one's emotional state is mostly kept private, except in situations of reciprocal emotional exchange with close friends and family members and in exceptional emotionally overwhelming situations (cf. von Salisch 2002).

7.4 Applications and Conclusion

Although this model of major–minor communication failures is culture-bound, it has a broad scope of application, as we can expect as many major–minor communications failures as there are major–minor relationships in the first place. The model was primarily developed to be used in the context of medical care, notably to facilitate conflict resolution processes brought in front of medical ethics committees. By analysing such high conflicting relationships in medical care contexts, it became obvious that this specific kind of relationship, namely, a major–minor relation, can be found in numerous contexts of human interaction. Consequently, the scope of the model has been extended to include all major–minor relations. The model can then be used in communication training in a professional setting for all occupations that leads to the adoption of a major position in professional interaction (attorneys, managers, medical staff, therapists, counsellors, teachers, social workers, architects, consultants, etc.). The knowledge of the different qualities of communication failures can help to avoid them in the first place. In case of conflict, the model can also further an understanding of the different qualities of conflict experiences and it is possible to use the model components as starting points for conflict resolution: To lay open one's standard of perfection, to name one's goal expectations, to disclose one's opinion of the other agent's quality of action or to question one's locus of behavioural control can all be starting points to a re-evaluation of situational factors, of expectations and of the adequateness of one's own experience of communicative failure. By understanding possible conflict dynamics in advance, the model also enables majors and minors to clarify their points of view even before entering a cooperation and thereby to reduce possible nuclei of communication failures. The model can therefore be seen as having as its purpose such diverse aspects as conflict prevention, conflict resolution, self-reflection as well as mentoring, supervision and professional conflict resolution processes like mediation.

References

Bodtker, A. M. & Jameson, J. K. (2001). Emotion In Conflict Formation and its Transformation: Application to Organizational Conflict Management. *The International Journal of Conflict Management*, 12(3), 259–275 doi.org/10.1108/eb022858

Breslin, J. M., MacRae, S. K., Bell, J. & Singer, P. A. (2005). Top 10 health care ethics challenges facing the public: views of Toronto bioethicists. *BMC Medical Ethics*. 6 (5), 5–8. doi.org/10.1186/1472-6939-6-5

Carver, C.S. & Scheier M.F. (1998). *On the self-regulation of behaviour.* Cambridge University Press, New York, NY, US.

Condit, C.M. (2006). Communication as Relationality. In G.J. Shepherd, J. St. John & T. Striphas (Eds.) *Communication as…Perspectives on Theory* (pp. 3–12). Sage Publications, Inc.: Thousand Oaks, London, New Delhi.

De Cremer, D. & Tyler, T.R. (2007). The Effects of Trust in Authority and Procedural Fairness on Cooperation. *Journal of Applied Psychology*, 92 (3), 639–649. doi.org/10.1037/0021-9010.92.3.639

Eid M. & Diener E. (2009). Norms for Experiencing Emotions in Different Cultures: Inter- and Intranational Differences. In: Diener E. (eds) *Culture and Well-Being. Social Indicators Research Series,* vol 38. Springer, Dordrecht doi.org/10.1007/978-90-481-2352-0_9

Folkman S. & Lazarus, R. S. (1990). Coping and Emotion. In Nancy L. Stein, Bennett Leventhal, Thomas R. Trabasso (Eds.), *Psychological and Biological Approaches To Emotion* (pp. 313–333). Hillsdale, NJ: Erlbaum.

Frijda N. & Scherer K.R. (2009). Emotion definitions (psychological perspectives). In D Sander, KR Scherer (Eds.), *Oxford Companion to Emotion and the Affective Sciences* (pp. 200–202). Oxford, UK: Oxford Univ. Press.

Gilbert, D.T. & Malone, P.S. (1995). The correspondence bias. *Psychological Bulletin*, 117, 21–38.

Griffin, E.M. (2012). A first look at Communication Theory (8th ed.). McGraw-Hill: New York.

Hall J. (1969). *Conflict Management survey: A survey of one's characteristic reaction to and handling of conflict between himself and others.* Conroe, TX: Teleometrics.

Hochschild, A. R. (1983). The managed heart: Commercialization of human feeling. Berkeley, CA: University of California Press.

Jones, T. S. (2000). Emotional communication in conflict: Essence and impact. In W. Eadie & P. Nelson (Eds.), *The language of conflict and resolution* (pp. 81–104). Thousand Oaks, CA: Sage.

Jones, T. S. (2006). Emotion in mediation: Implications, applications, opportunities and challenges. In M. Herrmann (Ed.), *Handbook of mediation*, (pp. 277–306). Oxford: Blackwell Publishers.

Jones, T. S. & Bodtker, A. M. (2001). Mediating with Heart in Mind: Addressing Emotion in Mediation Practice. *Negotiation Journal,* 17(3), 217–244. doi.org/10.1023/A:1013283710190

Jones, E. E., & Nisbett, R. E. (1971). *The actor and the observer: Divergent perceptions of the causes of behaviour.* Morristown, NJ: General Learning Press.

Lazarus, R. S. (2001). Relational Meaning and Discrete Emotions. In K.R. Scherer, A. Schorr & T. Johnstone (Eds.), *Appraisal Processes in Emotion, Theory, Methods, Research* (pp. 37–67). New York: Oxford University Press.

Lazarus, R. S., & Folkman, S. (1984). *Stress, appraisal, and coping.* New York: Springer.

Liberman, N. & Förster, J. (2008). Expectancy, value and psychological distance: A new look at goal gradients. *Social Cognition,* 26, 515–533.

Locke, E.A. & Latham, G.P. (2002). Building a Practically Useful Theory of Goal Setting and Task Motivation. A 35-Year Odyssey. American Psychologist, 57(9), 705–717 doi.org/10.1037//0003-066X.57.9.705

Malle, B. F. (1999). How people explain behaviour: A new theoretical framework. *Personality and Social Psychology Review*, 3, 21–43.

Malle, B.F. (2006). The Actor–Observer Asymmetry in Attribution: A (Surprising) Meta-Analysis. *Psychological Bulletin,* 132 (6), 895–919. doi.org/10.1037/0033-2909.132.6.895

Malle, B.F., Knobe, J.M. & Nelson, S.E. (2007). Actor–observer asymmetries in explanations of behaviour: New answers to an old question. *Journal of Personality and Social Psychology*, 93 (4), 491. doi.org/10.1037/0022-3514.93.4.491.supp

Meyer, W. U., Reisenzein, R., & Schützwohl, A. (1997). Towards a process analysis of emotions: The case of surprise. *Motivation and Emotion,* 21, 251–274.

Monzani, D., Steca, P., Greco, A., D'Addario, M., Pancani, L. & Cappelletti, E. (2015). Effective pursuit of personal goals: The fostering effect of dispositional optimism on goal commitment and goal progress, *Personality and Individual Differences*, 82, 203–214, doi.org/10.1016/j.paid.2015.03.019.

Noordewier, M.K. & Breugelmans, S.M. (2013). On the valence of surprise, *Cognition and Emotion*, 27 (7), 1326–1334. doi.org/10.1080/02699931.2013.777660
Pruitt, D.G. & Rubin, J.Z. (1986). *Social Conflict: Escalation, Stalemate ana Settlement.* New York: Random House.
Reisenzein, R., & Meyer, W. U. (2009). Surprise. In D. Sander, & K. R. Scherer (Eds.), Oxford companion to the affective sciences (pp. 386–387). Oxford: Oxford University Press.
Roseman, I. (2001). A Model of Appraisal in the Emotion System. In K.R. Scherer, A. Schorr & T. Johnstone (Eds.), *Appraisal Processes in Emotion, Theory, Methods, Research* (pp. 68–91). New York: Oxford University Press.
Scherer, K. R. & Moors, A. (2019). The Emotion Process: Event Appraisal and Component Differentiation. *Annual Review of Psychology*, 70 (1), 719–745. doi.org/10.1146/annurev-psych-122216-011854
Scherer, K. R., Schorr, A. & Johnstone, T. (Eds.). (2001). *Appraisal Processes in Emotion, Theory, Methods, Research* (pp. 37–67). New York: Oxford University Press.
Schulz von Thun, F. (2008). *Miteinander reden: 1–3* (Sonderauflage). Reinbek bei Hamburg: Rowohlt.
Seifart, C., Simon, A. & Schmidt, K. W. (2016). Ambulante Ethikberatung in Deutschland – eine Landkarte bestehender Konzepte und Strukturen. Ungekürzter Beitrag, der auf einer Umfrage zur ambulanten Ethikberatung im Rahmen einer deutschlandweiten Tagung „Ambulante Ethikberatung in Deutschland – aktueller Stand und künftige Entwicklung" im Oktober 2016 basiert. https://www.laekh.de/images/Hessisches_Aerzteblatt/2018/04_2018/Langversion_Amb_Ethiberatung_Seifart.pdf (Abruf am 20.05.2018).
Shepherd, G. J, St. John, J. & Striphas, T. (Eds.). (2006). Communication as…Perspectives on Theory. Sage Publications, Inc.: Thousand Oaks, London, New Delhi.
Silver, M. A. (1999). Love, Hate, and Other Emotional Interference in the Lawyer/Client Relationship. *6 Clinical L. Rev.* 259, 259–313.
Strauss, M. (1987). Toward a Revised Model of Attorney-Client Relationship: The Argument for Autonomy, *N.C. L. Rev.* 65 (2), 315–349. http://scholarship.law.unc.edu/nclr/vol65/iss2/3
Tuomela, R. (2010). Cooperation as Joint Action. *Analyse und Kritik* 2,65–86. Stuttgart: Lucius & Lucius.
von Salisch, M. (Hrsg.). (2002). Emotionale Kompetenz entwickeln. Grundlagen in Kindheit und Jugend. Stuttgart: Kohlhammer.
von Schlippe, A. & Schweitzer, J. (2012). Lehrbuch der systemischen Therapie und Beratung I. Vandenhoeck & Ruprecht: Göttingen.
Watzlawick, P., Bavelas, J.B., Jackson, D.D. (2011). Pragmatics of Human Communication: A Study of Interactional Patterns. WW Norton & Co: New York, London.
Woodward, A. L. (1999). Infants' ability to distinguish between purposeful and non-purposeful behaviors. *Infant Behavior and Development*, 22,145–160.
Wortman, C.B. & Brehm J.W. (1975). Response to uncontrollable outcomes: An integration to reactance theory and the learned helplessness model. In: L. Berkowitz (Ed.), *Advances in experimental social psychology, Vol. 8*, Academic Press, New York, 277–336.

Maike Baumann is a scientific associate at the University of Potsdam, Germany. She holds a diploma in psychology with specializations in clinical psychology/work and organizational psychology and is currently working as a behavioral therapist, coach and trainer. Beforehand she studied linguistics and philosophy with a special focus on the philosophy of religion (University of Potsdam, Germany). Extra-occupationally she is doing a doctorate on the topic of cultural influences on social scripts at the European University Viadrina, Germany. Additionally she is internationally certified as a mediator with a special expertise in business mediation. Until now she has published various articles and monographies on schematherapy, forgiveness, psychology of self, positive psychology and diverse topics in the field of work and organizational psychology.

Chapter 8
On Being "Outside the Box" or Being "Inside": Intercultural Communication, Relationship-Building and Identity Ascription Failures

Claude-Hélène Mayer and Lolo Jacques Mayer

Abstract In this chapter, the authors present an ethnographic case study which refers to the experience of failure in intercultural communication and relationship-building for members of different cultural and racial groups within a specifically selected public space in South Africa. The authors focus on concepts of erroneous identity ascriptions, intersectionalities and power which respond to the question "Who am I?" in a specific socio-cultural context. The aim of the chapter is to explore ascribed identities and their erroneous potential on a micro-level of intercultural interaction observed in a public municipal swimming pool. The consequences of failure in intercultural communication, relationship-building and ascribed erroneous identity intersectionalities are reflected. The research methodology used is an ethnographic description of observations and narrations of experiences within the specific cultural context, using a qualitative case study approach. Findings show that failed intercultural communication and ascribing identities in intercultural contexts can lead to erroneous assumptions about "the other", interwoven in conscious and unconscious discourses of race, power and accessibility to resources—which contribute to the failure of employee–client relationship-building in intercultural public spaces. Conclusions are drawn, and the discussion explores how to transform failure and errors in the described context. Recommendations for future research and peaceful intercultural practice in public spaces in multicultural societies are presented.

C.-H. Mayer (✉)
Department of Industrial Psychology and People Management, University of Johannesburg, Johannesburg, South Africa

Institut für Therapeutische Kommunikation und Sprachgebrauch, Europa Universität Viadrina, Frankfurt (Oder), Germany

L. J. Mayer
Courtney College International, Pretoria, South Africa

E. Vanderheiden, C.-H. Mayer (eds.), *Mistakes, Errors and Failures across Cultures*, https://doi.org/10.1007/978-3-030-35574-6_8

Keywords Mistakes · Errors · Failure · Intersectionalities · (Ascribing/ascribed) Identity · Power · Cultural belonging · Intercultural public spaces · South Africa

8.1 Introduction

Many research studies have pointed out that in a dynamic and rapidly changing, globalised work environment, flexible identity creations have increased in importance (Mayer and Flotman 2017). To create identity and to respond to the question "Who am I?" in changing contexts, it appears that reflection and critical new discourses within and transecting cultural contexts is needed (Cruz and Sonn 2014; Mayer 2015), not the least of which includes the recovering of critical, intercultural self-reflexivity (Bhabha 2015).

In this chapter, an ethnographic case study which takes place in a South African organisational public space is presented, and ethnographic observations with regard to identity creation in a post-apartheid public municipal space are described. Identity is thereby viewed, according to Ting-Toomey (2017), as multifaceted, including cultural, ethnical, spiritual, religious, social, class, gender, age, sexual orientation, professional, family and relational roles and markers, as well as personal images based on a mutual meaning-construction level. It is further assumed that individuals create their identities through socio-cultural learning, interactions and lifelong experiences and that identity tensions are experienced when crossing cultural boundaries (Ting-Toomey 2017).

The aim of this chapter is to explore intersectionalities of identity markers of a black, gifted, adopted young South African–German boy in a specific South African context. The intersectional perspective implies the assumption that intersecting social identities and relations such as race, gender and sexual orientation are interwoven in complex ways and that they are influenced by and influence systems of oppression, domination and discrimination (Weber and Parra-Medina 2003). Additionally, the intersectional perspective emphasises that identity markers, as described above, are to be viewed, understood and analysed as combined categories, since all the different identity markers are experienced simultaneously within the individual person (West and Fenstermarker 1996). Research on intersectionalities of race and gender has, for example, pointed out in the South African context that black women aim at creating new individualised intersecting identities, while in practice often previous categories influenced by apartheid concepts and concepts of inferiority and feelings of racial oppression are still valid (Mayer 2017). Oostendorp and Jones (2015) note that in South African workplaces, tense, ambivalent and contradictory identities are created which relate more to racial group membership and belonging than to individualised characteristics. This shows that racial and gender group belonging has not yet been transformed in the workplaces and that more research is needed in post-apartheid South Africa to improve the understanding of the interplay of intersectionalities in the contemporary society (Nkomo 2015; Mayer

2017). Experiences observed on the micro-level, which are connected to macro- and meso-level experiences within the South African municipal organisational context and society, are described in this book chapter.

The authors present the case of selected experiences of a mother and her son made in a predominantly middle-class South African suburb in one of the largest cities in the country. Thereby, the authors mainly describe the micro-level interpersonal communication between a young boy and his mother in interpersonal contact with the professional deputy manager of a municipal swimming pool. After introducing the setting, the context and the entry situation, the authors describe observations made from two perspectives: from a white, female, middle-aged, middle-class German viewpoint of the adoptive mother of the boy and from a black, male, adolescent, middle-class German–South African perspective, that of the adoptee.

Further, the authors analyse the observations made with reference to intersectionalities such as nationality, age, gender, giftedness, adoptive mother–son relationship, bilingualism and biculturalism, religion, social class and belonging to majority or minority groups within a specific societal context. The authors show how these observations affect identity creation, belonging, marginalisation and exclusion—and thereby power, referring to the recent literature on culture, intersectionalities and power (see Syed 2008; Syed and Özbilgin 2009; Mahadevan and Mayer 2017). The micro-level experiences in the organisational context of the municipal swimming pool as a service provider for the community, the clients and the observer are reflected within the broader organisational management context (meso-level) and the societal context (macro-level). These micro-level experiences take place in an intercultural setting.

Culture is here defined as "the coordination of meaning and action within a bounded group" (Bennett 2017). Interculture refers to the space in which members of the culturally bounded groups meet to create new meaning and action in the in-between of their cultural groups. The central concepts of failure and error are defined in the following paragraphs.

Failure in intercultural communication and in building trustful relationships is defined as a person not having succeeded in a particular communicative and relationship-building activity (modelled after Lingard et al. 2004). Failure, therefore, refers in this chapter to a lack of success in communicating and/or in building relationships. Failure in intercultural communication situations combined with erroneous ascriptions of identity classification can easily lead to a failure in building trustful intercultural employee–client relationships.

Errors are defined in this chapter as "mistakes" and can occur for different reasons, such as a result of ignorance, a personal decision or preference, a habit, forgetfulness, lack of awareness or similar psychological issues (defined in reference to Love et al. 2009). With regard to the concepts of error and identity, "erroneous identity ascriptions" are ascriptions of identity which contain references to identity markers or identity parts which do not agree with the self-descriptions of an individual and are therefore perceived as mistaken. That does not mean that these ascriptions are false in an objective way but rather that they do not fit the socio-cultural construction of "the other person" involved in the communicative interaction.

Based on the described ethnographic observations, the authors respond to the question of how to define intersectional identities within this specific racial and power-related construction of identity and power based on clashing intersectionalities. The experiences presented are discussed and explained in terms of how intersecting socio-cultural identities and relations are interwoven systems, relating to race, gender, age and religion (West and Fenstermaker 1996; Wells et al. 2015; Mayer 2017). The authors also discuss their findings in the light of systems of oppression, domination and discrimination (McCall 2005; Weber and Parra-Medina 2003; Mayer and Flotman 2017), as well as power and power inequalities.

The contribution of this chapter lies in the in-depth, rich descriptions and interpretations of intersectionalities at play in a particular cultural context to provide the reader with new insights into categorical complexity (McCall 2005; Kerner 2012) and into the failure of intercultural communication and relationship-building involved. The chapter concludes by highlighting how erroneous ascriptions and failure of relationship-building can be used to turn the experiences into personal growth and self-development.

8.2 Erroneous Identity Ascriptions, Power and Failure of Intercultural Relationships

Identity discourses are manifold, interdisciplinary and intercultural (Bamberg et al. 2011; Mayer 2008), and identity constructions in post-modern globalised societies have become highly complex and relevant in a world that consists of hybridity and multiplicity (Frost and Regher 2013; Jeldtoft and Nielsen 2014; Sveningsson and Alvesson 2003).

Identities are created through thoughts, perceptions, social and intra-psychological processes and ascriptions of self and others in interpersonal communication processes and interactions (Mayer and Flotman 2017). Identity constructions are created and re-created across the life span of an individual and are built on intrapersonal and interpersonal negotiations around the question of "Who am I?" by self and others (Mayer 2015). It follows that identity is always socio-culturally constructed and contextually embedded (Coté and Levine 2015) and individuals may use different self-concepts of identity ascriptions derived from multifold memberships of different groups (Stets and Burke 2000). Sandhu and Higgins (2016) emphasise that identity ascriptions can only be comprehended fully when the context—particularly in post-colonial settings—is taken into account. In post-colonial contexts, identity ascriptions are built on labels of class, ethnicity, language and gender and can be countered with concepts of hybridity (Bhabha 2015). Referring to Said's (1978) West and East construction of "self and other" (the West as the self, the East as the other), the self and the other can be regarded as similar in terms of Western–African relationships where the identity of "the West" (as self) was often reshaped by constructing the boundary of "the African" (the other). Post-colonial identity constructions and constructs of power are often connected to power relations and racial classifications, and this is particularly true for South African post-colonial, post-apartheid contexts (Mayer 2005).

Vargas and Kingsbury (2016) emphasise that racial identity ascriptions are often used in a reductionist way, although racial identity is a complex, multidimensional concept. This concept also needs social, cultural and contextual definitions of identity, to understand perceptions of race and membership in particular racial groups (van Heelsum and Koomen 2016). Debebe and Reinert (2014) point out that an approach to multiple identities and the ascriptions of "our whole selves" can support the understanding of self and others, particularly when it comes to professional identities and leadership roles. Mayer and Louw (2013) further highlight that particularly in management and organisations, identity topics become core issues of employee–leader and employee–client relationships, referring to discourses on diversity and standardisation (Frost and Regher 2013).

Particularly in intercultural and/or interracial interactions, false or erroneous identity ascriptions and declarations of forms of "otherness" combined with specific power ascriptions can lead to irritation, misunderstanding and conflicts (Ting-Toomey 2017). To transform "otherness" and erroneous identity ascriptions, Radford (2016) defines individuals who facilitate bridging differences between members of diverse cultural groups as "transversal enablers" (see Wise 2009). They usually contribute positively to intercultural communication scenarios and heighten the understanding across cultural divides.

Identity ascriptions in intercultural communication can either contribute to and affirm the identities individuals would like others to recognise in them, or else they contrast with self-identity ascriptions. Affirmative and successful negotiation of identity constructions might lead to the construction of mutually acceptable identities and requires a type of "competent facework" which includes the use of competent communicative strategies which neither threaten the identity of "the other" nor deconstruct "face" (Cumpach and Imahori 2005). Identity ascriptions that are considered false or erroneous might lead to constraints in relationship-building across cultural boundaries and can affect self-definitions and the negotiating of identities in intercultural communication situations.

These ascriptions might also explain intercultural communication failures and help to avoid them, since intercultural communication failures usually create impediments to trust and relationship-building (Elo et al. 2015). Further, intercultural communication failures can relate to false or erroneous identity ascriptions which are experienced as discriminating or stereotypic and even as failures of minority rights, diversification attempts and inclusiveness in certain group membership or on the macro-level of society.

8.3 Methodology

The authors use a single case study design (Yin 2009) with an ethnographic, narrative approach to present, reflect, interpret and discuss the impact of the above-mentioned intersectionalities (McCall 2005) critically with regard to identity and power in the defined context. The case study is based on the social constructivist research paradigm (Berger and Luckmann 1966) and assumes that culture is a learned social dimension in which meaning and sense-making are created and negotiated.

Through description and analysis of the ethnographic, personal experiences of two individuals in a specific socio-cultural context, this ethnography aims to understand specified life experiences from contextual and cultural perspectives through personal narratives (Berry 2007; Ellis et al. 2010). The narratives draw on significant, remembered moments in life (Denzin 1989) and open possibilities of identity development (Wood 2009) and learning through the experience of errors and failure.

Analysis of data uses the five-step model of Terre Blanche et al. (2006). The case description provides readers with references to intersectional identities and emic, in-depth perspectives, referring to selected cultural frames (Chang 2007; Denshire and Lee 2013). It then leads to the redefinition of error and failure towards personal growth, identity-building intersectionalities and the building of trusting relationships across employee–client intercultural relationships.

Data was collected from the author's participative observation at the swimming pool, as well as from interviews with the researched. One of the researchers had visited the pool on a daily basis for years, while the other researcher's pool visits were more sporadic. However, both researchers were well known to the staff members.

8.4 Case Presentation

In the following, the case setting is described. This provides contextual information to understand the intersectionalities of cultural and power frames of analysis and interpretation, with regard to erroneous ascriptions of identity and failure of relationship-building.

K is a 10-year-old boy of black African origin[1] and German and South African citizenship. He grew up bilingual, speaking English and German, and has lived in both Germany and South Africa for several years. K was adopted shortly after his birth in South Africa and since then grew up in a predominantly white German fam-

[1] Black South African racial categorisations in South Africa include individuals with African, Coloured (mixed race) and Indian origin (SA Department of Labour 1998). Members of these groups are defined as members of "previously disadvantaged groups" owing to racial discrimination and segregation during apartheid and are currently empowered through structural and institutional legal actions, for example, "Black Economic Empowerment" and "Affirmative Action".

ily, with an older sister and one younger brother. K, as a highly gifted learner, has already skipped three school classes during his school career. He is aware of his intellectual abilities. He does not enjoy social contact and prefers solitude and reading. K's adoptive mother, B, is a middle-aged white German woman who has lived in various African countries for over 13 years. She has worked as a professor at different universities in Germany and South Africa. K and B speak English as their language of communication and share an interest in theoretical discourses and reflections.

8.4.1 Setting

This case is anchored in post-apartheid South African society, which officially turned from an authoritative state of oppression and discrimination pre-1994 to a pluralistic, democratic society thereafter. Organisations have become key players in transforming the society—which had been built on racial separation, racial discrimination and oppression (Cloete et al. 2015)—into a multicultural society which is based on equality and human rights.

In post-apartheid South Africa, governmental and municipal organisations such as the swimming pool service-provider in this study are classified as designated employers (SA Department of Labour 1998) and are legally bound to ensure diversity and inclusion in annual employment equity plans (Council on Higher Education [CHE] 2015) which outline policies and practices to diversify demographics and facilitate inclusivity (Cloete et al. 2006). Accordingly, the staff members running the pool are exclusively of African origin.

However, according to the opinion of black members who took part in the study, transformation has scarcely taken place in South African organisations. They believe that white male employees stay in the positions of leadership, while black employees are workers, lacking education and career development opportunities (Mayer and Barnard 2015). This impression creates frustration, depression and anger within the society. A criticism levelled at organisations is that the focus is mainly based on changing "racial numbers" in Affirmative Action (AA) and Employment Equity (EE), instead of addressing issues of "de-racialization, de-colonialization, de-gendering and de-mascularization" (Badat 2016, p. 80). Therefore, it is necessary that discourses on transformation, race and gender open up to address the underlying issues and emotions (Du Toit 2000).

8.4.2 Organisational Context and Interactions

The micro-level interactions described in this chapter took place over a period of 5 years in the context of a municipal swimming pool which is open to the public, as well as to the national swim clubs which train for international competitions and even for Olympia. The pool is located in the university area of one of the largest cities in the South Africa. The suburb is fairly multicultural and accommodates South African citizens from all cultural and racial backgrounds. The swimming pool is run by two black African male staff members and two assistants. The cleaning personnel are two black African women.

The pool itself is used during the week by predominantly white South African male and female clients of all ages. Usually, these swimmers train seriously for competitions, and one can even observe a prior Olympic swimmer training younger achieving swimmers. At the weekends and during the summer holidays, the pool is also used by black African clients (mainly children, adolescents and families) who use the pool primarily to "cool down", to learn how to swim or for social gatherings, sometimes even for baptisms. Occasionally the police force trains the predominantly black African police members in the pool area. The same is true for a South African Airways company which trains flight attendants and service personnel in life-saving and swimming.

Observing the swimming pool facilities, it is clear that the pool was once a very modern, well-equipped training facility for high-level swimmers. During apartheid it was exclusively used by white swimmers. During the past years, the pool has become run-down; many parts of the pool area are broken or out-of-order, the heater does not usually work in winter owing to missing parts or unpaid electricity bills, the management frequently runs out of chlorine, and the hygienic situation is sometimes dubious. However, since no alternative pool exists nearby for training, clients continue to use this pool as a training facility and pay privately for heater repairs or missing chemicals, to enable themselves and their trainees to continue using the pool.

Since there is a significant lack of resources (electricity and chemicals) available, it seems as if the power has been moved away from the personnel and the municipality to the privately paying swimming community who buy spare parts for maintenance. By providing private funds, the swimming clientele has gained in influence and has a say in the management of the pool (e.g. in terms of booking of swimming lanes and cleanliness). Accordingly, the management team of the pool experiences a lack of influence and ability to manage the pool, owing to the lack of resources from top management. The power of running the pool has shifted (at least covertly) back to the "white swimming community", while the black management appears to be representing the post-apartheid state striving for equality and distributed power in terms of employment on the surface of the organisation and society.

8.4.3 Individual Interactions at the Pool

The described family members swim in the pool very often, most of the year on a daily basis. The presence of K in the pool, as a boy of black African descent, instantly caught the attention of the staff members and has become a major long-term intercultural encounter. The development of this encounter can be divided into three stages over 5 years, which are described below, and which include a shift of identity ascription and construction through intersectionalities which was clearly interrelated with a shift in power, and boundary shift of exclusion ("being outside the box") and inclusion ("being inside the box"). The ascriptions of identity have been experienced by K and B as "failures in intercultural communication", "errors of identity ascriptions" and "failure to manage employee–client relationships successfully".

8.5 A Question of Belonging and the Failure of Erroneous Identity Ascriptions

During B and K's first visits to the pool, the staff members observed the "strange couple" closely, since they did not seem to understand how the two—a black boy and a white woman—could belong together. At the entrance, the mother was repeatedly asked by the different male African staff members: "Do you pay for him?" "Are you here together?" "Does he belong to you?" The staff were obviously surprised by the interracial relationship.

The question about payment implicitly included the staff members' assumption that "the woman invited the boy swimming; she probably doesn't even know him well but wanted to do him a favour or teach swimming". The staff member questioning the payment reduced the relationship of the woman and boy to the idea that it was built on a financial dependence only, a favour or an invitation owing to economic resource or ability (swimming ability) inequalities, and it implied an ascribed difference of power and resources which was connected to the intersectionality of race, age, ascribed social strata and competence (swimming).

The staff members' questioning of the belonging and the "being together" was based on difference in diversity markers which obviously could not be bridged in the mind through a more open understanding of existing relationships across racial groups. The idea of two individuals belonging together or of being "transversal enablers" (Radford 2016; Wise 2009) was far-fetched.

The "difference in thought" expressed a mindset of segregation and "inner apartheid", a presumed segregation (Mayer 2005). K, who perceived himself as part of the family, felt irritated by the constant and continuing questioning of his space within the family and his belonging. He began to ignore the questions of the black male staff members by withdrawing from greeting or interacting with them in any way.

It was still during the first year that the female cleaning personnel approached the mother, B, to ask whether K "could not even speak Zulu". B explained that K spoke German instead of an African language since he was a German citizen and had lived in Germany for some time. One of the female cleaners showed an expression of surprise, as if it was impossible that K—with his physical features—could learn German, and she said: "This is not possible. And why does he not speak Zulu?" The mother replied that K did not want to learn an African language which created even more upheaval.

This interaction shows how physical, racial features were ascribed to the ability to learn or even to speak a certain language and how the intersections of race and language in terms of mother tongue were interconnected intersections in the mind of the female staff member. K felt that he was perceived as being "outside the box" since he could not fit the expectations of being a black South African boy from the perception of the black staff members, while he felt that he could not blend in with "being German" since he was "usually not perceived as German" based on his physical appearance. The errors of ascriptions of socio-cultural belonging, race and language created a slight identity crisis and sense of resignation for K and resulted in a non-trusting interpersonal relationship, a kind of failed relationship from the perspective of K and B with regard to the pool personnel.

This socio-cultural ascription implied an "outside the box" phenomenon in terms of either racial belonging or language ability and created a feeling of disturbance in K which increased when staff members started to talk to K in their mother tongues, their African languages. K perceived this as arrogance and ignorance, since they knew he did not speak any African languages, and as an affront, particularly since they spoke English to his mother and did not expect her to speak any of the African languages (since she was white). B's racial appearance put her into a space of accepted inability to understand or speak an African language, and nobody questioned her missing abilities. This was acceptable to the staff members, because the mother could stay "inside the box of being white, speaking a white language", while K had crossed the boundaries through his intersecting identities and was assumed to be "outside the box", because he was "white inside and black outside". The failure of intercultural communication experienced by K and B (asking curiously private questions, questioning the relationship, the identity and the belonging of K and his language abilities) was experienced as "erroneous" and as a failure to build a professional, trustful employee–client relationship in a public setting beyond racial, social and language ascriptions. On the one hand, the error was mainly perceived as being based in the inability of staff members to develop a differentiated and intersecting image of an individual identity without using pre-assumed racial, apartheid-related categories. On the other hand, the hybridity inside the family was viewed as a challenge for the socio-cultural environment, particularly since it was combined with failure to comply with the values and social norms of the public utility.

8.6 Intercultural Communication: The Failure of Relationship-Building

During years 2–4 at the pool, K did not enjoy interaction with the pool's staff members since he felt unaccepted in terms of his intersectional identities. He refused to hold small talk with them, and he constantly refused to greet them. This caused considerable disruption for the black male staff members, and they showed their irritation openly: "Eh, wena, this boy! He is in a bad mood, this guy. He does not even greet. He has to greet people". K kept on ignoring them, explaining that he does not want to have to do anything with them. K's behaviour could be interpreted as a protective measure to keep his intersecting identities intact which would not fit the socio-cultural expectations and racial ascriptions of the staff members. However, the staff members interpreted his behaviour as "ill-behaved, rude and impossible", while his mother struggled to keep the social values and norms intact ("a boy has to greet elders and respect them"), as they were expected by the staff members. While B explained to K constantly that it was important that he kept the social norm and greeted the staff members to show them respect, she was constantly asked by the staff members to comment on K's behaviour: "He must learn to greet people. As a boy you have to respect the adults and other people".

K's space of predefined socio-cultural norms was established ("children greet adults, children respect adults and greeting is a norm to show respect"), and the mother was expected to teach the boy the appropriate behaviour. While she overtly agreed with the statement and responded: "Yes, it is important to greet and respect each other", she felt an intrapersonal attitude of solidarity with her son. She, however, understood that his behaviour of "not greeting" strengthened his position of "being outside the box", outside the norm and not being part of their community (and traditional value set) of a black African male boy. By refusing to greet the staff members—who held the key to the entrance to the pool and thereby to the communities of white swimmers—K rejected fitting into the role as "a boy of their culture" and the expected, culturally normed behaviour. He had retracted into a position of complete resistance.

While the male staff members continued to emphasise that the mother should "teach him", B continued to agree with them on the surface and felt unable to change the son's attitude: an experience of failure as a mother. Not being able to recognise any improvement in behaviour in K over the years, the female cleaning personnel started to show solidarity with the mother and commented gently: "He is just a child. He will change when he grows up. You must teach him and pray for him, and he will be all right".

Because the female staff members interpreted the situation of being "out of the hands of the mother"—and therefore being, in a sense, uncontrollable—they started to put K's fate into the hands of God. They highlighted that "being a mother to this boy is not easy" while implying that the background of coming from two different racial, cultural and family backgrounds would make it almost impossible for the mother to bring him up in an "acceptable manner". They implied that K would behave adequately if he had grown up in a black African community. A new space of power "outside the pool area boundaries" was created through the involvement of prayer and God, beyond human communication, interaction and influence to overcome, in their terms, the failure of interracial family bonds.

K and B both felt unaccepted in their roles as mother and son, as well as in their holistic, multiple identities which were obviously not fitting with the racial and cultural categorisations of the staff members. They further interpreted the staff members' behaviour as jealousy of K's gained status of being "outside the box", of being part of African and European cultural contexts and at the same time of "being within", of being in a "power position" by being part of the community of (mainly white) swimmers in the pool area on a daily basis and thereby part of a community with "access to a potentially better life".

By including God in this intercultural communication situation, the staff members opened a new field of power, gave up responsibility for the communication failure and K's behaviour and released themselves, as well as B, from the duty and responsibility to change "the unpleasant situation, the misbehaviour".

8.7 Access and Exclusion: Failure in Reframing New Boxes

In year 5, the staff members had to maintain the pool during normal business hours when K and B were swimming. The deputy manager (DM) of the pool approached K while swimming, to "make space and swim in a different lane". According to K, the DM spoke in "broken English" and "was not clear about his instructions". Therefore, K decided to get into an argument with him, telling him that he was not giving clear instructions and therefore K would not change lanes.

K, who was in the water, and the DM who was standing at the shallow end of the pool's edge argued loudly with each other. K seemed unimpressed by the DM's threats, nor by his mother's attempts to convince him to listen to the staff member for the sake of peace. The DM complained: "He is disrespectful and he does not listen and he disturbs our work". The mother apologised for the misconduct and they left the pool. K pointed out that the DM "cannot speak English well, cannot give precise instructions and is just the DM". With this statement, K drew a clear boundary between the DM and himself, highlighting the DM's incompetence in failing to "speak the same language and giving clear and precise instructions without accent". K criticised the DM's professional skills (his language competency) and his ability to conduct his work tasks professionally. Therefore, K, based on his position as being "outside the box in any way", did not accept the DM's instructions, considering him as "unskilled, unable to do his job and not on the same wavelength". By not taking any instructions, K changed the roles and placed the DM "outside the box of his professional tasks", not accepting his professional role, reframing the categories of the DM's identity from a professional to a non-professional without a say, without power. K changed the roles in that he was now the one "placing the other outside the box of professionalism", thereby degrading and excluding the DM while implicitly highlighting his own "higher social status, higher educational standard and language competency" and his "arguing skills". From the staff members' perspectives, this type of behaviour from a boy towards an adult was rude, shameful and unacceptable.

On the next occasion that B and K visited the pool—this time with K's siblings on a weekend when the pool users were of various racial origins—K was not allowed to enter the pool area owing to his previous misconduct. The DM said, "He is a very arrogant boy and he does not listen. He does not obey the rules and instructions and therefore he is not allowed in the pool area. The family can go in, but not him".

The DM had created a split between the family and K by using his power to control the entry (or non-entry) of clients to the pool. B said that she would not accept the splitting of the family and that she could not watch the siblings inside while watching K outside in the parking lot. Further, she said that she would not accept a racial divide of the family and that this racial split would "look strange" in the view of other pool guests. The DM then personally offered to "look after him" in the parking area (leaving his professional role as a DM), while the family could enjoy their swim. This split situation resulted in a limited access of K into the pool (who had gained the offer of a new male child-carer, almost as of an older brother or even a father) and a reframing of "insiders and outsiders" to the pool. The DM established himself as the guardian and child-carer (a black male father figure) of K outside of the pool area, establishing a new constellation of relationships between himself and K, almost like a family relationship. Thereby, K automatically became a member of the new constellation of in-groups who were now taking responsibility for him, splitting him off from his European family. K felt "awkward about this offer" since he would not accept the DM as a "person to look after me".

The reframing of the intercultural relationship by limiting access and entry to the pool showed power and authority on a new (family) level. The offer to become the guardian of K outside the pool area showed a redefinition of relationship and an attempt to redefine roles and positions within the relationship constellation. K was placed "inside the box of black male staff members", creating a new relationship line based on gender: a type of "father–son guardian relationship" through the display of power and authority from the male DM who aimed at establishing his authoritative role via this new family relationship offer, rather than through being a professional DM at a public pool. At the same time, at a deeper level, the DM possibly came closer to the European family through his establishment as "a black father". However, K and the family did not accept the shift in power and relationship and interpreted the situation as an unprofessional attempt to reconstruct power relations through a misconducted, failed employee–client interaction.

While the family interpreted the entire situation as a failure in employee–client interaction terms, the pool staff members discussed the situation as one in which authority would have to be re-established by the pool area professionals, due to the fact that the mother could not manage to control K or teach him respectful behaviour and communication skills. This was interpreted as a failure of an interracial mother–son relationship and an erroneous way of educating and bringing up children. This failure was interpreted as based on the differences of racial belonging of the mother and the child, and thereby as an expression of a necessary failure of interracial family relationships. The identity of the family members was reduced to their ascribed racial identities, to specific behavioural values and norms and specific role ascriptions in terms of their behaviour as adults, children, professionals and family members. Accordingly, power was ascribed based on race, professional and family roles, age, language and ascribed, one-dimensional racial belonging and membership.

8.8 Conclusions

The findings show that failed intercultural communication leads to failed relationship-building through the repeated ascription of identity markers which do not fit with the self-ascriptions of the communication partner. Within the described intercultural context, identity ascriptions refer strongly to conscious and unconscious discourses of race, power and accessibility to resources according to racial divides which were established during apartheid. Racial identity ascriptions therefore play a predominant role in the intercultural interaction and dominate all other potential identity markers which only seem to exist in relation to the racial concept of identity. The predominance of racial concepts interwoven with assumptions and ascriptions of class and social standing, professionalism, age and gender roles, the concept of family and family roles and finally religious and spiritual identity markers (prayer and God) contribute to the mutual failure of employee–client relationship-building in this public space.

Unsuccessful intercultural communication situations lead to experiences of mutual disrespect but also to feelings of marginalisation and exclusion. They represent, to a certain degree on the micro-level, the meso- and macro-level experiences within South African organisations and society which reconstruct discourses of apartheid in contemporary identity contexts. Findings also show that the concept of creating multiple identities as described by Debebe and Reinert (2014) is scarcely applied at all in the described situation, nor does the establishment of "transversal enablers" (Wise 2009) happen in the intercultural communication scenario to deconstruct one-dimensional, racial ascriptions. Ascriptions rather seem to segregate and "threaten the other" and mismatch the self-ascriptions, thereby creating a loss of face (Cumpach and Imahori 2005).

In the case study described, the questioning of belonging and identity markers beyond racial divides, the identity ascriptions which were viewed as erroneous, the mutual critical attitudes towards racial group membership and ability to use a language resulted in a mutual trustless interpersonal employee–client relationship. The failure in the intercultural communication through choice of topic, experienced curiosity and entrance in the "private life" of the clients led further into escalating the conflict potential on the one hand, while the inability of the family members to adjust to the social values and norms of the staff members posed a challenge to order in the public utility. During the failed intercultural communication on both sides, the individuals involved experienced themselves as having failed within their roles, for example, as a son (K), as a mother (B), as a professional (DM) and as a group member on either one side or the other (K). Therefore, all the individuals involved had the experience of a way being "outside the box, not being inside".

Power in various forms and connected to different identity parts was used in the situation: power based on racial group membership, professional identity, family roles, age (adulthood-childhood), social-cultural belonging, social standard and language abilities.

Finally, the question arises how failure and erroneous ascriptions could be transformed into successful intercultural communication, relationship-building across cultural and racial divides and successful identity constructions which contribute to respectful and enhance intercultural relations which contribute to individual growth and well-being.

8.9 Transforming Failure in Intercultural Communication and Relationship-Building Through Erroneous Identity Ascriptions

Transforming errors in identity ascriptions and failure in intercultural communication scenarios to build up trustful intercultural relationships can happen when particular techniques are mindfully applied. These techniques are discussed here.

Individuals in intercultural communication situations need to display a reflexive approach to the situation with regard to the context, their personal involvements and their group memberships. This requires a deeper understanding of intersectional identity parts and their contextual development. This deeper understanding can be gained through an increased self-reflection practice, through meta-communicative strategies with individuals of different socio-cultural group memberships, and open communication about the experiences. Individuals could learn communication techniques such as active listening, reframing and the use of metaphors, as well as gain deeper cultural insights through intercultural competences to increase the understanding of self and others. Professional managers should be trained in communication techniques and intercultural competences by municipal authorities and organisations. Managerial trainings could be of significant use here.

Additionally, work with specific psychological or therapeutic techniques, such as "shadow work", could further help to dissolve the categorisation of "self and others" and thereby focus on similarities and differences of members of the same groups and/or others. For example, working with the personal "shadow" refers to the individual looking at his or her own personal, unconscious mistakes, errors and failures which that individual would usually refrain from taking into account. Jung (1917, p. 103) defines the shadow as "the negative side of the personality, the sum of all those unpleasant qualities we like to hide, together with the insufficiently developed functions and the contents of the personal unconscious". It is assumed that every person carries a shadow, and the less it is embodied in the individual's conscious life, the denser it is. If individuals take their "shadow" into account consciously and work with it constructively, they do not need to project it onto another person, onto "the other". This means that individuals might reduce their projection of negative qualities or stereotypes onto the potential "other" and act and behave more freely to see the self in the other and the other inside the self.

In this context of working with the "shadow", power relations need to be questioned, power concepts with regard to the different situations could be analysed and ideas on how to transform power relations could be developed by the individual or within the intercultural communication situation. If topics of failure and errors cannot be addressed directly, they could be addressed through third party intervention and, for example, negotiation, mediation or facilitation across cultural groups. In the case of the swimming pool communication failure, a third party, for example, a municipal officer or the swimming pool manager, could be called in to negotiate and mediate between the DM and the clientele.

Finally, each individual living in the globalised, hybrid world should become aware of their own identity markers and of developing individual, flexible strategies to reflect on intercultural communication situations to transform experiences of failure in intercultural communication, loss of face and experienced disrespect into a constructive learning experience. Only then will power relations be reframed and equalised through mindful interaction, a human approach to intercultural communication, and multiple identity construction incorporating one's whole self.

8.10 Recommendations

Recommendations for future research in the field of failure in intercultural communication, relationship-building and erroneous identity constructions should combine qualitative and quantitative methodological approaches. Research not only should focus on ethnographic observations and interview narrations but should also take a broader variety of research methods into account. Particularly future research should focus on strategies to transform failure and errors in the intercultural context and look at culture-specific and culture-general approaches to manage, cope with and transform these interactions into individual growth and learning experiences.

In terms of intercultural practice, individuals living and working in intercultural, hybrid (post-colonial) contexts should be trained specifically in intercultural awareness in intercultural communication, power and relationship-building. Organisations, particularly in post-colonial contexts, need to provide their employees with methods and techniques to learn how to conduct intercultural employee–client interrelationships in a constructive, culturally aware and positive way. Organisations should be prepared to create an organisational culture which is open to address failure and errors and deal with them proactively across hierarchical levels. Workshops could eventually train the employees in intercultural communication and relationship-building, professional identity-building and constructive client interaction.

References

Badat, S. (2016). Deciphering the meanings and explaining the South African Higher Education Student Protests of 2015–16. *Pax Academica*, 1&2, 71–106.

Bamberg, M., De Fina, A., & Schiffrin, D. (2011). *Discourse and identity construction*. Washington, DC: APA Press.

Bennett, M. (2017). Definition of culture. Personal email communication. 30 April 2017.

Berger, P.L., & Luckmann, T. (1966). *The social construction of reality*. London: Penguin Books.

Berry, K. (2007). Embracing the catastrophe: Gay body seeks acceptance. *Qualitative Inquiry*, 13(2), 259–281.

Bhabha, H.K. (2015), Foreword. In P. Werbner & T. Modood. (Eds.), *Debating cultural hybridity. Multicultural identities and the politics of anti-racism*. London: Zed Books.

Chang, H. (2007). Autoethnography: raising cultural consciousness of self and others. In G. Walford (Ed.), *Methodological Developments in Ethnography. Studies in Educational Ethnography*, Vol. 12. (pp. 207–221). London: Emerald Group.

Cloete, N., Maassen, P., Fehnel, R., Moja, T., Gibbon, T., & Perold, H. (2006). *Transformation in Higher Education. Global Pressures and Local Realities*. Dordrecht, The Netherlands: Springer.

Cloete, N., Bunting, I., & Maassen, P. (2015). Research Universities in Africa: An Empirical Overview of Eight Flagship Universities. In N. Cloete, P. Maassen, & T. Bailey (Eds.), *Knowledge Production and Contradictory Functions in African Higher Education* (pp. 18–31). Cape Town: African Minds.

Coté, J.E., & Levine, C.G. (2015). *Identity formation, agency, and culture: A social psychological synthesis*. Mahwah, NJ: Lawrence Erlbaum Associates.

Council on Higher Education [CHE]. (2015). *Annual report 2014/2015*. http://www.che.ac.za/sites/default/files/publications/CHE%20Annual%20Report%20of%20the%20Council%20on%20Higher%20Education.pdf.

Cruz, M.R., & Sonn, C.C. (2014). (De)colonizing culture in community psychology: reflections from critical social science. *American Journal of Community Psychology*, 47(1–2), 203–214.

Cumpach, W.R., & Imahori, T. (2005). Identity management theory: facework in intercultural relationships. In W. Gudykunst (Ed.), *Theorizing about Intercultural Communication* (pp. 195–210). Thousand Oaks, CA: Sage.

Debebe, G., & Reinert, K.A. (2014). Leading with our whole selves: a multiple identity approach to leadership development. Handbook of race-ethnicity and gender in psychology. In M. Miville & A. Ferguson (Eds.), *Handbook of Race-Ethnicity and Gender in Psychology* (pp. 271–293). New York: Springer.

Denshire, S., and Lee, A. (2013). Conceptualizing autoethnography as assemblage: Accounts of occupational therapy practice, *International Journal of Qualitative Methods*, 12, 221–236.

Denzin, N. K. (1989). *Interpretive biography*. Newbury Park, CA: Sage.

Department of Labour. (1998). Employment Equity Act, No. 55 of 1998. http://www.labour.gov.za.

Du Toit, A. (2000). Critic and citizen: the intellectual, transformation and academic freedom, *Pretexts: Literary and Cultural Studies*, 9(1), 91–104.

Ellis, C., Adams, T.E., & Bochner, A.P. (2010). Autoethnography: An Overview, *Forum: Qualitative Social Research*, 12(1), Art. 10. http://nbn-resolving.de/urn:nbn:de:0114-fqs1101108.

Elo, M., Benjowski, C., & Nummela, N. (2015). Intercultural competences and interaction schemes—four forces regulating dyadic encounters in international business. *Industrial Marketing Management*, 48, 38–49.

Frost, H.D., & Regehr, G. (2013). "I am a Doctor": Negotiating the discourses of standardization and diversity in professional identity construction. *Academic Medicine*, 88(10), 1–8.
Jeldtoft, N., & Nielsen, J.S. (2014). *Methods and contexts in the study of Muslim Minorities. Visible and Invisible Muslims*. London: Routledge.
Jung, C.G. (1917). The psychology of the unconscious. In *Collected Works of C.G. Jung, Volume 7: Two Essays in Analytical Psychology*. UK: Routledge & Kegan Paul.
Kerner, I. (2012). Questions of intersectionality: Reflections on the current debate in German gender studies. *European Journal of Women's Studies*, 19(2), 203–218.
Lingard, L, Espin, S., Whyte, S., Regehr, G., Baker, G.R., Reznick, R., Bohnen, J., Orser, B., Doran, D. & Grober, E. (2004). Communication failures in the operating room: an observational classification of recurrent types and effects, *BMJ Quality & Safety*, 13(5), 321. doi: https://doi.org/10.1136/qhc.13.5.321.
Love, P.E.D., Edwards, D.J., Irani, Z. & Walker, D.H.T. (2009). Pathogens: The anatomy of omission errors in construction and resource engineering project. *IEEE Transactions on Engineering Management*, 56(3), 425–435.
Mahadevan, J., & Mayer, C.-H. (Eds.) (2017). *Muslim Minorities, Workplace Diversity and Reflexive HRM*. London & New York: Routledge, Taylor & Francis Group.
Mayer, C.-H. (2005). *Mauern aus Glas*. Münster: Waxmann.
Mayer, C.-H. (2008). *Managing conflict across cultures, values and identities. A case study in the South African automotive industry*. PhD thesis. Rhodes University, South Africa. Reihe Wirtschaftswissenschaften, Band 20. Marburg: Tectum Verlag.
Mayer, C.-H. (2015). Travelling inner landscapes: A longitudinal study on intercultural identity development. *Equality, Diversity and Inclusion: An International Journal*, 34(4), 272–292.
Mayer, C.-H. (2017). A 'Derailed' Agenda?: Black Women's Voices on Workplace Transformation. *Journal of International Women's Studies*, 18(4), 144–163. http://vc.bridgew.edu/jiws/vol18/iss4/11.
Mayer, C.-H., & Barnard, A. (2015). Balancing the scales of gender and culture in contemporary South Africa. In S. Safdar & N. Kosakowska-Berezecka (Eds.), *The Psychology of Gender and Culture* (pp. 327–352). New York: Springer.
Mayer, C.-H., & Flotman, A.-P. (2017). Constructing identity. Implications for reflexive HRM. Chapter 4. In J. Mahadevan & C.-H. Mayer (Eds.), *Muslim Minorities, Workplace Diversity and Reflexive HRM*. (pp. 61–76). London & New York: Routledge, Taylor & Francis Group.
Mayer, C-H. & Louw, L. (2013). "Who are you?" – Constructing managerial identities in post-Apartheid South Africa. *Management Revue*, 24(4), 289–308.
McCall, L. (2005). The complexity of intersectionality. *SIGNS*, 30(3), 1771–1800.
Nkomo, S.M. (2015). Challenges for Management and Business Education in a "Developmental" State: The Case of South Africa. *Academy of Management Learning and Education*, 14(2), 242–258.
Oostendorp, M., & Jones, T. (2015). Tensions, ambivalence, and contradiction: a small story analysis of discursive identity construction in the South African workplace. *Text & Talk*, 35(1) 25–47.
Radford, D. (2016). 'Everyday otherness' – intercultural and everyday multiculturalism in a South Australian rural town. *Journal of Ethnic and Migration Studies*, 42(13), 2128–2145.
Said, E. (1978). *Orientalism*. New York: Pantheon.
Sandhu, P. & Higgins, C. (2016). Identity in post-colonial contexts. In Preece, S. (Ed.), *The Routledge handbook of Language and Identity* (pp. 179–194). London: Routledge.
Stets, J. E., & Burke, P. J. (2000). Identity Theory and Social Identity Theory. *Social Psychology Quarterly*, 63(3), 224–237.
Sveningsson, S. & Alvesson, M. (2003). Managing managerial identities: organizational fragmentation, discourse and identity struggle. *Human Relations* 56(10), 1163–1193.
Syed, J. (2008). Employment prospects for skilled migrants: A relational perspective. *Human Resource Management Review*, 18(1), 28–45.

Syed, J., & Özbilgin, M. (2009). A relational framework for international transfer of diversity management practices. *International Journal of Human Resource Management*, 20(12), 2435–2453.

Terre Blanche, M., Durrheim, K., & Kelly, K. (2006). First steps in qualitative data analysis. In M. Terre Blanche, K. Durrheim, & D. Painter (Eds.), *Research in practice. Applied methods for the social sciences* (pp. 321–344). Cape Town, South Africa: University of Cape Town Press.

Ting-Toomey, S. (2017). Identity negotiation theory. *Encyclopedia of Intercultural Communication*. Wiley Online Library. https://doi.org/10.1002/9781118783665.ieicc0039.

Van Heelsum, A., & Koomen, M. (2016). Ascription and identity. Differences between first- and second generation Moroccans in the way ascription influences religious, national and ethnic group identification. *Journal of Ethnic and Migration Studies*, 42(2), 277–291.

Vargas, N. & Kingsbury, J. (2016). Racial identity contestation: Mapping and measuring racial boundaries. *Sociology Compass*, 10(8). https://doi.org/10.1111/soc4.12395.

Weber, L., & Parra-Medina, D. (2003). Intersectionality and women's health: Charting a path to eliminating health disparities. *Advances in Gender Research*, 7, 181–230.

Wells, C.C., Gill, R., & McDonald, J. (2015). "Us foreigners": intersectionality in a scientific organization, *Equality, Diversity and Inclusion: An International Journal*, 34(6), 539–553.

West, C., & Fenstermaker, S. (1996). Doing difference. In E.N. Chow, D. Wilkinson, & M. B. Zinn (Eds.), *Race, class, & gender: Common bonds, different voices* (pp. 357–384). Thousand Oaks, California: Sage.

Wise, A. (2009). Everyday Multiculturalism: Transversal Crossings and Working Class Cosmopolitans. In A. Wise, & S. Velayutham (Eds.), *Everyday Multiculturalism* (pp. 21–45). Basingstoke: Palgrave Macmillan. doi: https://doi.org/10.1057/9780230244474_2.

Wood, J.T. (2009). *Gendered lives: Communication, gender, and culture*. Boston: Wadsworth.

Yin, R.K. (2009). Case study research: Design and methods. (2nd edition). London, UK: Sage.

Claude-Hélène Mayer (Dr. habil., PhD, PhD) is a Professor in Industrial and Organisational Psychology at the Department of Industrial Psychology and People Management at the University of Johannesburg, an Adjunct Professor at the European University Viadrina in Frankfurt (Oder), Germany, and a Senior Research Associate at Rhodes University, Grahamstown, South Africa. She holds a PhD in Psychology (University of Pretoria, South Africa), a PhD in Management (Rhodes University, South Africa), a Doctorate (Georg-August University, Germany) in Political Sciences (socio-cultural anthropology and intercultural didactics) and a Habilitation (European University Viadrina, Germany) in Psychology with focus on work, organizational and cultural psychology. She has published several monographs, text collections, accredited journal articles and special issues on transcultural mental health and well-being, sense of coherence, shame, transcultural conflict management and mediation, women in leadership in culturally diverse work contexts, constellation work, coaching and psychobiography.

Lolo Jacques Mayer is an aspiring young author and public speaker. He has started his career as an author for children's books and holds talks on contemporary socio-cultural topics at international conferences. His research interests are race, culture and identity.

Chapter 9
Mistakes and Demise: Mikhail Gorbachev and the Dissolution of the Soviet Union

Klas-Göran Karlsson and Bo Petersson

Abstract This chapter focuses on the final stage of the history of the Soviet Union, from 1985 to 1991, when the last Communist Party and Soviet state leader Mikhail Gorbachev tried to reform his country by making economic life more effective, widen the scope of political participation, open up history and culture for debate, and introduce a new, peaceful thinking in international affairs. Gorbachev wanted to save the Soviet system but ended up destroying it. His initially successful strategy of taking a middle-of-the-road position to gain support worked well during the first years of reform, but the mid-position became successively narrower until it finally dissolved. Gorbachev's increasingly desperate attempts to negotiate a new and revised union treaty led in 1991 to the failed August Coup which, in turn, dealt the final death blow to the Soviet Union. By way of conclusion, political mistakes are often difficult to distinguish from failures caused by structural problems. As is illustrated by the case of Gorbachev and the Soviet Union, this is particularly salient in societies in which statist power and cultural patterns have traditionally played decisive roles in historical developments.

Keywords Mistakes · Errors · Failure · Dissolution · Gorbachev · Reform · Soviet Union

9.1 Introduction

In the end of 1991, the Soviet Union collapsed and disappeared from the map of the world, to be replaced by 15 successor states with the Russian Federation as the primary heir. Simultaneously, the Cold War came to a definite end. The rules of

K.-G. Karlsson (✉)
Lund University, Lund, Sweden
e-mail: klas-goran.karlsson@hist.lu.se

B. Petersson
Malmö University, Malmö, Sweden
e-mail: bo.petersson@mau.se

E. Vanderheiden, C.-H. Mayer (eds.), *Mistakes, Errors and Failures across Cultures*, https://doi.org/10.1007/978-3-030-35574-6_9

international politics changed dramatically when one of the two main Cold War contenders ceased to exist. No doubt, failures and miscalculations, the theme of this book, played its part in the process. The leader of the Soviet Union at the time, Mikhail Gorbachev, had not intended his state to dissolve, nor could he have anticipated the revolutionizing chain of events. When he in the preceding years had initiated a series of governance reforms, his intention had been to save the Union. Instead he ended up bringing about its demise. How could this happen? This is the main theme around which our chapter is woven.

It is well-known in history as well as in political science that a middle-of-the-road position may be a safe and inclusive stance when events proceed smoothly, but in a tougher political climate, polarization tends to occur, and the middle strip of the road may vanish ever so quickly (Fleisher and Bond 2004; Handlin 2017). Through history, the dilemma to find a middle way between political and ideological extremes, between revolutionaries and autocratic conservatives, has been recurrent for Russian and Soviet actors with liberal-democratic or reform communist ideas. Tsarist as well as Soviet politicians with ambitions to change state and society in Russia with gradual measures have constantly needed to take this predicament into account. Gorbachev had to handle this dilemma too, with for him devastating results.

9.2 Scholarly Interpretations

Among scholars, there is no consensus on how to explain the fall of the Soviet Union. There are experts who analyze its demise mainly from an external perspective. Most popular is probably the idea that the Soviet Union, normally always prepared to standing up against the United States' arms buildup, succumbed to imperial overstretch (Kennedy 1988) and failed to compete in the Cold War global arms race accelerated by the American President Ronald Reagan to defeat the "evil empire." Igor' Klyamkin, a Soviet commentator, wrote in 1990 that a change of politics was necessary since "we would in the future be incapable of solving our defense problems at the expense of social programs and other sectors of the economy" (Klyamkin, quoted from Dunlop 1993).

However, most commentators are inclined to look for the causes of the Soviet collapse in internal factors and processes. According to such interpretations, the Soviet system was doomed to failure from the outset (Malia 1994), due to several aspects: a planned economy that could neither be developed nor improved, although the Soviet Union had most natural resources in the world; a political system that was impossible to reform, other than within the framework of the single allowed party; a communist ideology that was never permitted to be tested against and legitimized by social reality; an opposition that was always met with violence, repression, or silence; and an imperial structure that had to be upheld. There is some correspondence between this interpretation and totalitarianism theory (Friedrich and Brzezinski 1965), which rests upon the idea that there are certain immutable basic elements, such as repression, censorship, and propaganda, that keep up the totalitarian society. When sheer repression ends, some other forms of social control will need to replace it to maintain stability in society, and here social scientists would tend to suggest legitimacy as the prime candidate (Weber 1978; Holmes 1997). However, legitimacy was evidently in short supply in the Soviet Union of the 1980s and early 1990s.

To avoid crude determinism, it is necessary to pose questions such as: Given this predestination, then why did the Communist Soviet Union last nearly three quarters of a century? Surely, totalitarian control ended roughly with Stalin, and yet the Union endured for almost another 40 years. What, finally, caused its collapse? The latter question allows for a much larger scope for individual and collective agents, such as the nationalist popular fronts in the Soviet republics, and their intentions and motives. Explanations that put forward individual agents and their ideas, albeit in confrontation with social structures and cultural inheritance, can hardly avoid turning their attention to Mikhail Gorbachev. That is also the route that we endeavor to take in this chapter.

9.3 Gorbachev's Reform Agenda

On 11 March 1985, Mikhail Sergeyevich Gorbachev, 54 years old and a young politician according to Soviet appointment standards since the Brezhnev era, was unanimously elected General Secretary of the Communist Party of the Soviet Union (CPSU) by the highest party organ, the Politburo. To be sure, he was not without contenders, but both Viktor Grishin, aged 71, and Grigorii Romanov, 62, backed out and fell in line behind Gorbachev, who had the full support of influential older politicians such as the long-term foreign minister Andrei Gromyko (Taubman 2017). With Gorbachev, a new generation that had not worked in Stalin's industrialization drive, participated in the purges, or fought in the Great Patriotic War against Nazi Germany, took power. Instead, they had their formative political experiences during Khrushchev's destalinization and reform years.

Gorbachev was also the first Soviet leader since Lenin's generation to have a formal university education. After attending Moscow State University, where Gorbachev studied law and became full member of the Communist Party in 1952, the new leader started climbing the party ladder and served as party leader in his region of birth Stavropol between 1969 and 1978. In this period, he rose through the ranks and entered the CPSU Central Committee. In 1978 he was appointed Moscow-based party secretary responsible for agricultural affairs (which hitherto had been considered a dead-end mission), and 2 years later, he was made a full member of the Politburo.

Soon after taking over the highest power position as General Secretary, Gorbachev demonstrated an ambition to change the Soviet Union with peaceful and gradual means. Revolutionary, violent change was not an option for him. He realized that the country needed a new course of reforms to revitalize a stagnant command economy and to liberalize political life, but what this really meant and how far change should reach was not clear to him. The problem of Soviet modernization was obvious: Was it even possible to carry out economic and political reforms without radically changing the authoritarian political system, the party, and the structures of the planned economy?

Already in the first period after his appointment, Gorbachev stated that people did not like to live "in the old way" anymore and called for an acceleration, uskorenie, and a restructuring, perestroika, of the economy. To achieve this general goal, he called for increased labor discipline, higher productivity, and an end to corruption. Long years of erosion of meaning in Soviet political discourse made it initially difficult to see the novelty of Gorbachev's ideas, and several elements were reminiscent of Nikita Khrushchev's reform efforts a little more than two decades earlier (Schroder 1990). However, when Gorbachev introduced his first concrete reform, an anti-alcohol campaign, it was certainly a radical move, aiming at improving discipline, health, and work efficiency, but it did not make him very popular in Soviet society or among his associates. In the Soviet republic of Georgia, e.g., the anti-alcohol campaign included the actual destruction of vineyards and was received as an attempt to strike a lethal blow at Georgian wine-based culture and way of living (White 1996). Besides, the Soviet state lost large incomes with the restrictions of sales of alcohol. All in all, the General Secretary's campaign, in popular parlance transforming him to mineral'nyi sekretar' (mineral water secretary, to be compared with general'nyi sekretar', for general secretary), was his first major political failure.

These early, after all rather cautious, initiatives, presented in a 5-h speech at the 27th Party Congress in February 1986, answered to Gorbachev's belief in the Communist Soviet Union and to his ambition to make the economy more efficient and competitive by attacking inertia and apathy in party and society. This was not primarily intended to introduce qualitatively new policies but to implement the old ones in a better and more efficient way. The initiatives were clearly inspired by some of his first scholarly advisors, such as the economist-sociologist Tatyana Zaslavskaya, who blamed economic stagnation on "the human factor," on a situation in which people had "no reason to work well, do not want to work well, and do not know how to work well" (quoted from Taubman 2017; 187).

During 1987, Gorbachev' modernization strategy assumed a more clear and elaborate form, introduced as it was by an extremely hardworking politician with an entirely new, open, and popularly accessible leadership style, with a new political self-confidence, and probably with a new understanding that the first reforms would not be effective enough for a successful Soviet modernization drive. The overall perestroika idea had fallen into three main parts in a package of reforms that was introduced gradually, both in the Soviet Union and into the international lexicon. In January, Gorbachev called for demokratizatsiya, that is, a democratization of the authoritarian political system by ensuring more power to ordinary people and "guaranteeing that past mistakes will not be repeated" (Gorbachev 1987). In July, he introduced various economic reforms in terms of perestroika. In November, on the 70th anniversary of the October Revolution, he delivered a candid speech in which he condemned Stalin's crimes against his own population, thereby triggering a politics of openness, glasnost', that Soviet politicians had not experienced since Khrushchev's secret speech in 1956.

While perestroika did not bring about immediate economic progress, but, due to glitches such as unwieldy procedures of quality control and transportation problems, rather led to shortages of consumer goods from 1988 onwards, the glasnost reform was a tremendous success, at least as measured by cultural and historical openness. Journalists, writers, theater producers, and other intellectuals revealed aspects of Soviet history that so far had been debated seldom or not at all, such as Stalin's long-term terror against his own population. However, as a policy meant to strengthen Soviet society, the success was less evident and definite. Rather it set processes in motion that struck at the very foundations of the political system.

From the outset, Gorbachev had probably not intended glasnost' to be total transparency, but an openness which would facilitate the implementation of the reform package as a whole. Increasingly, however, glasnost' became a way to try to increase the legitimacy of government in the Soviet Union. Gorbachev realized that the Stalin-time repression and crimes were gross liabilities for the regime. Therefore, he advocated going back to what he perceived as the uncontested ideological roots of the Soviet Union, to Lenin as the founding father of the Soviet state. Lenin's legacy, the argument went, had subsequently been squandered and corrupted by Stalin and the oppressive regime that he led. However, the fundamentally critical debates did not stop at Stalin. They went further back in time, and revelations about atrocities being committed already under Lenin during and after the Bolshevik coup and the civil war found their way to the public debate, serving to erode legitimacy rather than resurrecting it. With hindsight, Gorbachev's underestimation of the processes unleashed by glasnost', and his belief in the regime's ability to keep them within restricted bounds was one of his gravest strategic mistakes. Once the genie has been let out of the bottle, there was simply no way of forcing it back in.

9.4 The Reform Pace Quickens

Perestroika, economic change, was still considered the main reform for Gorbachev, even if he introduced a second, more broadly reformist, and decidedly altogether more far-reaching stage in 1987, starting from the idea that the different reform packages must reciprocally influence and strengthen each other. Historian Geoffrey Hosking notes the importance of Gorbachev's change from a moderate perestroika Mark One, generally in line with Soviet experiences, to a more radical perestroika Mark Two of the year 1987, "which soon led him into uncharted territories, awakening suspicion and resentment among some of those who had helped him to come to power" (Hosking 1991).

As already hinted at, and as noted in several of the best biographies written about Gorbachev, the reform ideas were not entirely his own (Brown 1996; White 1990). In a political generation shift, he soon assembled a team of new leaders around him and promoted them to Politburo members. The liberal internationalist Aleksandr

Yakovlev, once an exchange student at Columbia University in New York, former Soviet Ambassador to Canada, Politburo member, and the acting head of the Department of Propaganda at the Central Committee, was a key person behind the party leader's reform program. In 1983, Gorbachev spent a week in Canada, where he and Yakovlev became friends (Taubman 2017, pp. 182–186). It is probable that Yakovlev, together with the newly appointed foreign minister Eduard Shevardnadze, was involved in Gorbachev's reorientation in the international arena with major elements such as the drastic reduction of the arms race, the successive release of the East European satellite states, the revocation of the Brezhnev doctrine, and ultimately the termination of the Cold War. No doubt, this new foreign policy, called new thinking or novoe myshlenie, might have had idealistic traits, but it was also a way of reducing the costs of military competition with the United States. The idea that domestic needs should dictate Soviet foreign policy, and not the other way around, was surely a new feature in Soviet politics.

Yakovlev is also considered to be the main architect behind glasnost', which no doubt corresponds well with Zaslavskaya's idea of the importance of the "human factor": Only informed, educated, and motivated people acting in a society more open than the traditional Soviet one and with means of making their own decisions based on verified information can constructively contribute to true economic development. The need for a democratization of political life can be motivated from a similar idea that increased political participation would have a beneficial effect on the engagement for economic reform work.

However, the political recipe that Gorbachev offered to the Soviet people was not a transition to democracy but rather a half measure. In one major political reform, voters were given the opportunity to choose among several candidates for parliamentary bodies at different levels of the state structure but without abolishing the leading role of the Communist Party in the political process. However, in this way, a group of old, anti-reformist, and unpopular communists could at least be made to step down.

Moreover, the power of the party institutions and the bureaucracy was reduced in favor of the Soviet state structures. In February 1990, while keeping on to the position of Party General Secretary, Gorbachev created for himself the new, formal position as President of the Soviet Union (Robinson 1992). It seemed at the time as if the move was undertaken by Gorbachev to try to guarantee him continued key political influence, should the power of the Communist Party erode and prove to be insufficient as a basis. An erosion of the power of the CPSU would certainly take place soon enough, but the occupancy of the formal position as president of the Soviet Union eventually did little to protect Gorbachev from falling from grace.

9.5 The Cross-Pressure Increases

Not surprisingly, Gorbachev's reform packages provoked different reactions among different Soviet camps. Whereas he during the first years of reform could successfully balance out the different camps against each other, the strategy eventually backfired as the opposing groups increasingly attacked him, the leader of the middle ground, instead of their adversaries on the other side of the spectrum. Polarization increased, Gorbachev's mid-strip shrank, and the once so successful strategy turned out to be another fateful mistake.

Among groups of zapadniki, Western-minded liberal reformists in political and cultural circles, Gorbachev's politics meant a badly needed modernization, and a closer association of the Soviet Union to Western and European institutions and values, necessary for the invigoration of politics and society. These groups appreciated the ambition to democratize the political system and played an important role in the rapid implementation of the openness policies in mass media and cultural life. While some in this group gradually became supporters of a further radicalization of the reform activity, aiming at a democratic Soviet Union, others successively realized that Gorbachev's ideas carried a revolutionary appeal that they could not share.

Not only democrats saw Gorbachev's reforms as a hope for a systemic change. The new openness had also allowed scope for nationalist ambitions in the Soviet republics. Everywhere, historical and ecological complaints were lodged against Soviet rule (Nove 1989; Davies 1989). The criticism took different forms in different parts of the Soviet Union. While in south Caucasian Armenia and Azerbaijan violent ethnic conflicts exploded in February 1988 and developed relatively independently of the Kremlin, so-called popular fronts in the Baltic republics, initially created in the summer of 1988 to support Gorbachev, soon levelled sharp criticism against Moscow and called for sovereignty, understood as exit from the Union and the proclamation of independent Baltic states. This development seemed to be unexpected by Gorbachev, who appeared to have problems understanding the power of nationalism and did not find a formula for how to placate the popular fronts (Plokhy 2015). Recurrent declarations of sovereignty from the Soviet republics in 1990 underscored the acuteness of the situation. When even the largest Soviet republic, the Russian Federative Republic (Russia), demonstrated its intention to deviate from the Soviet course by issuing its declaration of sovereignty, the Soviet Union's days were numbered. In the end, "Gorbachev became "a fireman rushing from one conflagration to the next" (Suny 1998).

On the conservative, not to say reactionary, end of the spectrum, the newspaper Sovetskaia Rossiia printed on 13 March 1988 a letter from a chemistry teacher, Nina Andreyeva, titled "I cannot betray my principles." In an aggressive tone, she attacked all those "who have brought us to believe that our country's past was a long chain of mistakes and crimes" (Andreyeva 1988). The publication of the letter, and its replication in several other newspapers, was the start of an attack on Gorbachev's reforms, probably initiated by more powerful persons than Andreyeva, and a signal from conservative forces that the reform work must be brought to a close, lest it threaten the entire Soviet system. For this group, not only what they considered as far-reaching reforms as such but also Gorbachev's adventurous international politics, his friendly advances toward the capitalist and purportedly aggressive West, and his lack of support for the communist regimes in the Eastern European satellite states were mortal threats to the Soviet system. In particular, Gorbachev's decision that the satellites were free to chart their own courses, independently of the Soviet Union, aroused the anger of many conservatives, who regarded external strength and internal consolidation as two sides of the same coin.

9.6 The Conservative Turn

Feeling the pressure from all sides, Gorbachev chose in the winter of 1990–1991 to try to align himself with the conservatives. There were many signs that he had started to retreat from his initial liberal reform-mindedness, apparently in order to preserve the Union from disintegration. In January 1991, special Soviet troops were sent to Riga and Vilnius to quell manifestations of opposition. Tens of lives were lost during the violence that followed, and disillusionment grew among reformists at home and Gorbachev's supporters abroad. It has never been proven that Gorbachev had ordered the action (Lasas 2007), but at the time, it was frequently interpreted that way.

Gorbachev's conservative turn was borne out beyond doubt by his choice of new associates. In several cases he replaced reform-minded persons in his closest political environment with conservatives. Thus, the liberal minister of the interior, Vadim Bakatin, was replaced with Boris Pugo, former leader of Latvia's Communist Party and a convinced supporter of a preserved Communist Soviet Union. The communist apparatchik Gennadii Yanayev was appointed to the new post of vice-president of the Soviet Union. Both Pugo and Yanayev were later to become members of the putschist group that acted to remove Gorbachev from office in August 1991. So did Anatolii Lukyanov, whom Gorbachev had made chairman of the new Soviet parliament in 1989, and Valerii Boldin, a key aide who had become his chief of staff. However, as was soon be shown, these moves did not placate the conservatives; rather they became more active in their measures behind the stage. The conservatives had certainly been alarmed by Gorbachev's reformist political agenda already long before, but new developments related to the president's policies, in particular the growth and increased strength of nationalist movements in the Soviet republics, increased their uneasiness and preparedness to take more radical measures to stop what they saw as unfolding.

While Gorbachev's conservative turn was deemed insufficient by the hard-liners, many of his hitherto loyal liberal followers took it badly. Close associates such as the reform architect Yakovlev started to abandon him as they believed that he was no longer true to their ideals. Several others of his reformist collaborators, such as the foreign minister Eduard Shevardnadze, distanced themselves from his politics – Shevardnadze resigned in December 1990 – and Gorbachev's former ally Boris

Yeltsin left the Communist Party and engaged himself fully in Russian politics. He soon reached the prominent position of spokesman for a democratic, anti-Communist Russian Federative Republic and was popularly elected as Russia's first President in the spring of 1991. Thereby, he emerged as an outspoken adversary of the continued existence of the Soviet Union and the main rival of Gorbachev.

As a third party, the international community put additional pressure on Gorbachev, often with the best of intentions. As an extremely popular politician in the West, who not only wanted to change his own country from within but had also liberated Eastern Europe from Communist rule and brought the Cold War to a peaceful end, Gorbachev was awarded the Nobel Peace Prize in 1990. The award was not well received by Soviet conservatives, who saw it as another surrender of Soviet, anti-Western values. Conversely, democratic and nationalist radicals regarded the award as a promise for the future but wanted the president to pursue his reform program at higher speed. The mid-strip where Gorbachev was maneuvering grew ever smaller.

9.7 The August Coup Attempt

Throughout 1991, Gorbachev continued to look for solutions that may have been a miracle cure 5 years earlier but were now hopelessly outdated. He was working relentlessly for negotiating a new union treaty, replacing the one that had formed the legal basis of the Soviet Union since 1922, and providing a greater amount of autonomy for the constituent republics. Six of the republics – Estonia, Latvia, Lithuania, Georgia, Armenia, and Moldavia – refused to participate in the negotiation process, but the other nine went on, finally hammering out a draft treaty in the summer of 1991.

The negotiations for achieving a new draft treaty illustrated Gorbachev's dilemma and his miscalculations. The six republics that refused to take part in the process insisted that the draft treaty was obsolete and not far-reaching enough, whereas several of the remaining, including the Russian Federative Republic under the energetic leadership of Boris Yeltsin, shared much of that criticism. They simply wanted bigger concessions. On the other hand, the hardliners within the Communist Party and the security apparatus held that the draft treaty went way too far and risked selling out the Soviet Union altogether. They also believed that the fact that several republics had been allowed to refrain from participating could inspire others to defect. This was one of the major reasons for the coup attempt that would soon follow: to stop the implementation process in its tracks and to salvage the old Union.

The attempt itself was carried out in August 1991 by a junta of reactionary and hardline Communist politicians and apparatchiki – the gang of eight – who had the conservative ambition to save the state from disintegration. The group thus included Gorbachev's recent top appointees during his conservative turn: Pugo, Yanayev, Lukyanov, and Boldin. With hindsight, these appointments can certainly be regarded as miscalculations from the president's side. It is indeed a mistake to engage co-workers who conspire to dethrone you. However, they were also evidence of the increasingly polarized political situation in the late Soviet state and society, with Gorbachev caught between, on the one hand, radicals with democratic or nationalist agendas, and on the other, conservative Communists who were prepared to preserve the Soviet Union whatever the cost might be.

The coup attempt was a frontal attack against the reform-minded Gorbachev, whom the coup ringleaders had confined to house arrest at his dacha in the Crimea. By proclaiming a state of emergency, they hoped to be able to restore Soviet order, based on a reborn Communist Party and recovered state authorities. Instead, the unsuccessful and aborted coup, in Russian Avgustskii putsch, accelerated the process of demise of the Soviet state and ended a dictatorship that had lasted since the first Communist coup d'état by Lenin and his Bolsheviks in November 1917. Weaknesses and poor preparations from the putschists' side, lack of the anticipated support from groups within the military and security police, and a determined resistance led by the democratically elected president of the Russian Federative Republic Boris Yeltsin sealed the Soviet Union's fate. At the height of his charisma at the time, Yeltsin emerged as the true leader of Moscow and Russia, whereas Gorbachev paled into insignificance. When the Soviet president was liberated from his Crimean confinement and brought back to Moscow by air, he had completely lost his political momentum to Yeltsin.

Whereas in the face of the theme of the book, several things could be said about the mistakes of the coup ringleaders, as they accelerated the demise of the Union by their badly performed coup attempt, this is a side story to our narrative. However, even as the coup was defeated, Gorbachev went on tirelessly, and in vain, to bring about a new union treaty and did not realize that its time had passed altogether. Even in the fall of 1991, there was a new string of meetings, and new drafts were proposed (Russell 1996). However, finally, the leaders of the Russian, Ukrainian, and Belorussian republics gathered in Belovezha, in today's Belarus, and signed on December 8, 1991, the Treaty of the Commonwealth of Independent States (Shushkevich 2013). The Russian president, Boris Yeltsin, was dominating the meeting, and Gorbachev was not even invited to attend. In consequence with the formation of the Commonwealth of Independent States, the three leaders declared the Soviet Union null and void. Gorbachev was still the formal president of the Union, but the state did not exist de facto anymore, and by the end of that year, it had ceased to exist altogether as a legal entity.

9.8 The Burden of the Past

Modernization had been a principal political goal for many Russian tsars and Soviet leaders at least since Peter the Great's era in the years around 1700. Confronted with Western ideas, states, and societies in military campaigns or peaceful interaction, reform-minded tsars such as Aleksandr I och Aleksandr II and their councilors recognized that Russia was backward and must change to be able to compete with the more modern societies and states in the Baltic area, in Europe, and in the world. For

Lenin, the establishment of Soviet power must go together with economic modernization, symbolically expressed as electrification. Consequently, after military defeats, modernist technical, economic, and military projects were started up, including the establishment of various educational institutions. Nevertheless, the ambitions to modernize often ended halfway, as an unbalanced and limping process. When modernization became threatening to the political stability and their own power positions, the Russian and Soviet rulers retracted. Many of them ended up as staunch defenders of the established order, which meant that all reform ideas were drawn back.

Furthermore, and consequentially, Russia and the Soviet Union were wanting in the categories and institutions that had forced the pace of Western modernization: the bourgeoisie, an independent educational system, a free press, and a civil society. All the time, the process in Russia had a top-down character, while bottom-up initiatives were absent or, if they occasionally occurred, were actively opposed by the state or passively resisted by broader, uneducated, and alienated strata of the population. The goal of the Russian and Soviet modernization was to satisfy the needs and demands of the state, not of individuals or collectives within that state. Thus, the Soviet Union could for long successfully compete with the West when strictly industrial and military developments were on the agenda, but the production of consumer goods for the citizens was considered of secondary importance and lagged. When the development of the "human factor" was on the table, efforts von oben were weak and indecisive. Democracy was never an alternative that was seriously contemplated. Cultural discourse always geared into eligible patriotic or Communist tracks and was strictly controlled from above.

Initially, Mikhail Gorbachev's reform plans followed this political-turned-cultural pattern. Perestroika, economic reform, was presented as the main goal of the modernization, while democratization and openness were intended as additional reforms to support and strengthen the economic acceleration. But Gorbachev was probably aware – or had been informed – of the basic Russian/Soviet cultural predicament: economic modernization without activation of the human factor does not lead to positive results or can even end in a conservative backlash. It is more doubtful whether he was aware of the other side of the coin: that an economic modernization that gives too much space to the same human factor, to democratization and openness, might endanger the entire system, especially in a country in which there had never been a liberal, reformist middle way between, on the one hand, autocratic and one-party rule and, on the other, radical revolutionary change.

A lingering question is why Gorbachev did not follow the example of his predecessors and suppressed unintended political consequences of the reform work. The most convincing answer is probably that he did not want to use large-scale repressive means. He had excluded violence from the beginning of his tenure. Another answer is that he at least to some extent had followed the historical path by taking a more conservative attitude in the final years of the Soviet Union, expressed increasing doubts in a transformation that had slipped out of his hands, and even accepted, or at least had not protested, when internal special forces were dispatched to Riga and Vilnius in early 1991 to quell the independence process in the Baltic republics.

A third explanation is that new circumstances and phenomena had rendered a repetition of the historical pattern impossible. It has been argued that a middle class, a broad reformist elite, and a civil society had finally come into existence in the Soviet Union, radically changing the rules of the game of Russian and Soviet politics and political culture (Keep 1996; English 2000). For the first time in Russian and Soviet history, the one-sidedly top-down modernization pattern was defied, with revolutionary consequences that Gorbachev had not expected or intended. With this interpretation, the political and cultural tradition that Russian and Soviet rulers had adjusted to and relied on for centuries was no longer applicable for Gorbachev in his effort to change and preserve the Soviet society and state.

9.9 The Mistakes and Failures

Political mistakes are often difficult to distinguish from failures caused by structural problems and inflexibilities. The actual policies may have been based on prudence, sober evaluations, and good judgements all along and indeed been flawless in their individual components, but still they emerge as failures since they are implemented in contexts that are intransigent and unyielding. In the end, Gorbachev was fighting windmills. No doubt he did so bravely, astutely, and for all the good reasons, but eventually he still came across as the epitome of failure, simply because he tried to reform that which could not be reformed.

The general structural dilemma is particularly salient in societies in which statist power and cultural patterns have played decisive roles in the historical development, traditionally leaving a limited scope for individual initiatives, especially those questioning and threatening the stability of the system. Russian and Soviet historical development eloquently proves this point. In fact, most of the problems that Gorbachev faced and that led to the dissolution of the Soviet Union must be analyzed in terms of his encounters and clashes with the old political and cultural structures (Tompson 1993). Whether those problems were due to what should be called mistakes or mismanagement is not clear, since Gorbachev in so many ways was caught in structures with a high degree of resistance and durability. He had to challenge the system, but it struck back at him and his reform work, which gave rise to a variety of unintended consequences. His perestroika reform package hardly ever had a chance of being successfully implemented given the hegemony of the institutions, principles, and procedures of the planned economy and the only permitted party, but Gorbachev cannot be blamed for having had the courage to try.

However, there are certainly several mistakes, tactical as well as strategic, that must be attributed to Gorbachev. He did not demonstrate a fingerspitzgefühl in his selection of aides and associates, but rather appointed some who would turn out to be his implacable opponents. The consequences of his modernization program were not always reflected. The anti-alcohol campaign that he initiated, an early effort to master problems of discipline in the Soviet work force, was a mistake that not only affected the strained Soviet economy negatively but also hurt his popularity in wider circles. Possibly, it installed hesitance at his continuous reform work.

What is more, some of the later reforms were obviously not sufficiently prepared. The democratization and openness policies implied that the old rulers should be held responsible for mistakes and failures in the past. Gorbachev gravely underestimated the severe criticism directed toward the Communist Party and the Soviet state from large groups of citizens, a criticism that he, as the highest political leader, could not dissociate himself from.

It has often been argued that the internal stability of Russia is dependent on an aggressive foreign and imperial policy, based on assertiveness, fear, and presence in the conquered territories. External aggression promotes internal consolidation (Hutcheson and Petersson 2016). The fact that Gorbachev permitted the Eastern European states to follow their own paths and abandon communist rule and their dependence on the Soviet Union, that he thus refrained from curbing the revolutions that transformed Eastern Europe, and that he did not use political or military force to counter the liberalization movements in the Soviet republics, was from this perspective serious mistakes. From an ethical perspective, however, it is of course praiseworthy that Gorbachev did not use the force of arms against his opponents but rather held on to the peaceful principles that he had laid down from the beginning.

All in all, to walk a reformist, third-way road between the extremes of autocracy and revolution, between conservative standstill and radical transformation, without slipping back into one of them, proved to be too difficult for Gorbachev. As a representative of the Soviet system, he wanted a gradual reform process that could change mentalities and structures, and his great accomplishment was that he was capable of starting the reform process and eliminate some of the obstacles that he met on this way, especially those represented by the conservative defenders of an unreformed Communist Soviet Union. However, he let the reform work get out of hand so that he faced a revolutionary process that not only destroyed or incapacitated the old structures, but also many of the new modernizing structures that were created at his own initiative, and finally swept away the Soviet society and state altogether.

Democratization and glasnost' triggered a revolution of expectations of another life and society that Gorbachev could not cope with, live up to, and satisfy. Ronald Grigor Suny has caught Gorbachev's predicament well when he notes that he "wanted to be both Martin Luther and the pope, both revolutionary reformer and defender of the existing power structure" (Suny 1998, 457). He tried to play both these roles, or rather combine the two, by initiating radical reforms in order to preserve the Soviet Union. With the benefit of hindsight, this was his most fateful mistake.

9.10 Epilogue

So, how will then Gorbachev go down in history – as a hero, as a tragic person, or perhaps as both? Perspectives may of course vary depending on the political inclinations of the beholder, but regardless of the outcome, there is a rather sad epilogue to the Gorbachev story. In 1996 regular presidential elections were held in the Russian Federation. This was a time when post-Soviet Russia seemed to be in endless crisis. The economy was in free fall, the dependence on the United States and the other leading Western powers was monumental, Russia's international influence was receding into insignificance, and domestically Chechnya was rebelling, trying to fight its way to independence, risking provoking a row of falling dominoes if successful. At the same time, there was a profound crisis of leadership. The incumbent president, the once so charismatic and energetic Boris Yeltsin, was ailing and suffered from ill health and an excessive consumption of alcohol. According to the initial polls, he was about to be defeated by other top contenders, such as the leader of the Communist Party of the Russian Federation, Gennadii Ziuganov, and was not even deemed likely to make it to the final round between the two top performers of the first round. This was the situation when Gorbachev decided to run for the presidency.

The campaign leading up to the election turned out to be something quite different from what Gorbachev had probably anticipated. Maybe he had envisioned a de Gaullian return of sorts, where the people would greet him with open arms as he offered to take the lead of the country again in its hour of need. Nothing of the kind took place. At campaign meetings he was heckled, spat at, and, according to his own statement, subjected to an assassination attempt (Russian Election Watch 1996). When the voters' verdict was passed on the contestants, Gorbachev gained around 0.5% of the vote, which ranked him 7 out of 11 candidates (Colton 2009). Yeltsin, for his part, with no so little help from his oligarch friends in the media, surged miraculously to a win against Ziuganov in the second round. The tragic twist to the story about Gorbachev was not that he was utterly defeated in the election but that he ran in the first place, not realizing that his time as a top politician had passed. As the General Secretary of the CPSU, he had made it a habit of referring to himself in the third person, and now his capacity to self-aware reflection seemed to have abandoned him completely.

References

Andreyeva N (1988) Ne mogu postupat'sia printsipami. Sovetskaya Rossiia, March 13
Brown A (1996) The Gorbachev factor. Oxford University Press, Oxford/New York
Colton TJ (2009) Transitional citizens: voters and what influences them in the new Russia. Harvard University Press, Cambridge, MA, p 234
Davies RW (1989) Soviet history in the Gorbachev revolution. Macmillan, Houndmills
Dunlop JB (1993) The rise of Russia and the fall of the Soviet Union. Princeton University Press, Princeton, p 4
English RD (2000) Russia and the idea of the West: Gorbachev, intellectuals and the end of the Cold War. Columbia University Press, New York
Fleisher R, Bond JR (2004) The shrinking middle in the US congress. Br J Polit Sci 34:429–451
Friedrich CJ, Brzezinski ZK (1965) Totalitarian dictatorship and autocracy. Harvard University Press, Cambridge, MA

Gorbachev M (1987) Perestroika – Krovnoe delo naroda. Rech' XVIII s'ezde professional'nykh soiuzov SSSR 25 fevralia 1987 goda. In: Gorbachev M (ed) Izbrannye rechi i stat'i. Tom 4. Izdatel'stvo Politicheskoi literatury, Moskva, p 431

Handlin S (2017) State crisis in fragile democracies: polarization and political regimes in South America. Cambridge University Press, Cambridge

Holmes L (1997) Post-communism: an introduction. Duke University Press, Durham

Hosking G (1991) The awakening of the Soviet Union. Harvard University Press, Cambridge, MA, p 141

Hutcheson DS, Petersson B (2016) Shortcut to legitimacy: popularity in Putin's Russia. Eur Asia Stud 68(7):1107–1126

Keep J (1996) Last of the empires: a history of the Soviet Union 1945–1991. Oxford University Press, Oxford/New York

Kennedy P (1988) The rise and fall of the great powers: economic change and military conflict from 1500 to 2000. Random House, New York

Lasas A (2007) Bloody Sunday: what did Gorbachev know about the January 1991 events in Vilnius and Riga? Journal of Baltic Studies 38:179–194. https://doi.org/10.1080/01629770701345099

Malia M (1994) The Soviet tragedy: a history of socialism in Russia, 1917–1991. The Free Press, New York

Nove A (1989) Glasnost' in action. Cultural renaissance in Russia. Unwin Hyman, Boston

Plokhy S (2015) The last empire: the final days of the Soviet Union. Oneworld, London, pp 33–46

Robinson N (1992) Gorbachev and the place of the party in Soviet reform, 1985–91. Sov Stud 44:423–443

Russell J (1996) Improbable unions: the draft union treaties in the USSR, 1990–1991. Rev Cent East Eur Law 22:389–416

Russian Election Watch (1996, May 15) Retrieved 10 September 2019, from https://web.archive.org/web/20000127204701/http://ksgnotes1.harvard.edu/BCSIA/Library.nsf/pubs/RE21

Schroder GE (1990) Economic reform of socialism: the soviet record. Ann Am Acad Pol Soc Sci 507(1):35–43. https://doi.org/10.1177/0002716290507001004

Shushkevich S (2013) The end of the Soviet Union: Stanislau Shushkevich's eyewitness account. Demokratizatsiya 21(3):315–338. Retrieved from https://search-proquest-com.proxy.mau.se/docview/1551181114?accountid=12249

Suny RG (1998) The Soviet experiment: Russia, the USSR, and the successor states. Oxford University Press, New York/Oxford, p 475

Taubman W (2017) Gorbachev: his life and times. Norton, New York/London, pp 205–208

Tompson WJ (1993) Khrushchev and Gorbachev as reformers: a comparison. Br J Polit Sci 23(1):77–105

Weber M (1978) Economy and society: an outline of interpretive sociology, vol 1. University of California Press, Berkeley

White S (1990) Gorbachev in power. Cambridge University Press, Cambridge, p 193

White S (1996) Russia goes dry: alcohol, state and society. Cambridge University Press, Cambridge, p 68

Klas-Göran Karlsson is Professor of History at Lund University, Sweden. Within contemporary international history, he has written extensively within three fields: Soviet and Russian studies, especially history of historiography, migration and nationality problems; genocide studies; and European uses of history. At present, he conducts a larger research project, focusing on the historical lessons of Communism and Nazism. Karlsson's latest publications in English are (ed.) *Perspectives on the Entangled History of Communism and Nazism* (Lexington 2015), "Making Sense of Lessons of the Past: Theoretical Perspectives on Historical Learning," in Holger Thünemann et al. (eds), Begriffene Geschichte – Geschichte begreifen. Jörn Rüsen zu Ehren (Peter Lang 2016), "Lessons at the limits: on learning Holocaust history in historical culture," in Andy Pearce (ed.), *Remembering the Holocaust in Educational Settings* (Routledge 2018), and "Putin's history. Aspects of Russian historical culture in the twentyfirst century," in Kari Aga Myklebost and Stian Bones (eds.), In the North, the East and the West Meet (Orkana Academisk 2019).

Bo Petersson is Professor of Political Science at Malmö University, Sweden, where he is also Advisor to the Vice Chancellor on Research and Doctoral Studies and Director of the research platform Russia and the Caucasus Regional Research (RUCARR). His special areas of interest include nationalism, legitimacy, authoritarianism, norm diffusion, and political developments in Russia and the former Soviet Union. His most recent publications include Bo Petersson and Karina Vamling (eds): *The Sochi Predicament: Contexts, Characteristics and Challenges of the Olympic Winter Games in 2014* (Cambridge Scholars, 2013); Hans-Åke Persson, Bo Petersson & Cecilie Stokholm Banke (eds.): *Playing Second Fiddle? Contending Visions of Europe's Future Development* (Universus Academic Press, 2015); and articles in the journals of *Demokratizatsiya, East European Politics, Europe-Asia Studies*; *International Journal of Cultural Studies, Sport in Society, and Problems of Post-Communism.*

Part III
Mistakes, Errors and Failure in Organisations

Chapter 10
Practical Examples of Handling Mistakes at Work in Different Cultures

Fernando Lanzer Pereira de Souza

Abstract A useful way of analyzing how mistakes are handled in organizations across different cultures is offered by looking at them through the prism of Huib Wursten's Mental Images, a framework that takes Hofstede's four classic value-dimensions and combines them into six different styles of organizational culture. In addition to that, Japanese organizations provide a seventh and different style.

In each of these styles, culture influences (A) what is regarded as a mistake and (B) how mistakes and errors are handled in terms of (1) attributing responsibilities, (2) assigning guilt, (3) using shame as a form of punishment and as a way to atone for guilt, (4) making corrections, and (5) taking measures that will avoid the repetition of similar mistakes in the future.

These seven business culture styles (Contest, Well-Oiled Machine, Network, Social Pyramid, Traditional Family, Solar System, and Japanese) are described in terms of how they differ in the way that they identify and deal with mistakes. Several practical examples taken from real-life situations are described in detail.

Organizations must increase their awareness of how culture influences the kind of mistakes that are made in each institution, in order to avoid their occurrence and recurrence. Special attention is required to identify blind spots in organizational culture, which elude detection. Institutions that operate in different geographies and employ multinational teams need to become aware of how different national cultures have impact on their way of working, so that they may become more effective and efficient in each operating environment.

Keywords Contest · Mistakes · Error · Failure · Individualism · Japan · Network · Organizational culture · Performance orientation · Power distance · Social pyramid · Solar system · Traditional family · Uncertainty avoidance · Well-oiled machine

F. Lanzer Pereira de Souza (✉)
LCO Partners BV, Amstelveen, The Netherlands

E. Vanderheiden, C.-H. Mayer (eds.), *Mistakes, Errors and Failures across Cultures*, https://doi.org/10.1007/978-3-030-35574-6_10

10.1 Introduction

The aim of this chapter is to provide a series of examples as to how a conceptual model can be used in practice, relating it to work situations in international organizations. The focus is on explaining how the use of this model can help executives and professionals better understand how mistakes are perceived and handled in different cultural environments, in practical terms.

The basic underlying logic of the seven basic "types" (or "styles") of culture is briefly explained and then linked to how managers most often behave when handling mistakes at work. The explanations and examples are based on my own extensive experience working across cultures since 1976 and on the extensive descriptions provided by Hofstede and his associates in (2); Hofstede et al. (2002); Hofstede (2003a, b).

Wursten (Wursten and Lanzer 2013) has described a framework of cultural "Mental Images" based on Hofstede's previous work (Hofstede 2003a, b) that may be extremely useful for looking at different cultures by grouping them into clusters according to similar patterns in their value-dimension scores. These Mental Images are known as *Contest*, *Network*, *Well-Oiled Machine*, *Social Pyramid*, *Traditional Family*, and *Solar System* cultures. It should be noted that the culture of Japan stands separately from these six types of culture, with a pattern of its own (regarding value-dimension scores). For a detailed description of the Mental Images, please see Wursten and Lanzer (2013) and Lanzer (2018). For an explanation of Hofstede's model of value-dimensions, please see Hofstede (2003a, b) and Lanzer (2017).

Contest cultures have a low Power Distance (PDI) score, a high Individualism (IDV) score, a low Uncertainty Avoidance (UAI) score, and a high Performance Orientation (PER) score.

Well-Oiled Machine (WOM) cultures also have low PDI and high PER. What differentiates them from Contest cultures is that they score much higher in UAI. IDV is not a differentiating factor for WOM cultures.

Network cultures have also low PDI and high IDV, but the differentiating factor is low PER. UAI is not a differentiating factor for Network cultures.

Social Pyramid cultures score high in PDI, by contrast with the previous three types. They have low IDV and high UAI. PER is not a differentiating factor for them.

Traditional Family cultures are also high in PDI and low on IDV. They differentiate from Social Pyramid cultures because they are low in UAI, by comparison. Once again, PER is not a differentiating factor for them.

Solar System cultures are unique due to the fact that they are high in PDI, IDV, and UAI. PER is also not a differentiating factor for them.

Japan is different from all the previous combinations because it is high in PDI, PER, and UAI while low in IDV. It is the only culture among the 100 that have been researched by Hofstede and his associates that has this combination. The other six categories have at least four different national cultures sharing a category.

Table 10.1 Wursten's model of culture styles

	Power distance (PDI)	High individualism (IDV)	Performance orientation (PER)	Uncertainty avoidance (UAI)
Contest	Low	High	High	Low
LOW	Low	ND[a]	High	High
Network	Low	High	Low	ND
Pyramid	High	Low	ND	High
Family	High	Low	ND	Low
Solar system	High	High	ND	High
Japan	High	Low	High	High

[a]*ND* not a differentiating factor

In Table 10.1 you can see a summary of how the four dimensions combine differently for each culture type.

In my experience as an executive working for international organizations for 28 years, and as a management consultant to multinational companies and nongovernment organizations for 16 years, I have often used this model (as early as in 1993) as a tool to help novice audiences understand culture differences, and apply these concepts in the solution of people management and communication issues, notably when working across cultures (Lanzer 2012, 2015, 2017, 2018; Lanzer and Chandansingh 2016; Lanzer and Pereira de Souza 2015, 2016; Lanzer et al. 2014). Since the focus of this section of the book is more on practice than on academic research, let me begin by clarifying what I mean when I use the term "mistake" in my practice and in the scope of this chapter.

What is a mistake? It is an action that yields an unwanted outcome. In other words, an action, decision, or judgment that produces an unwanted or unintentional result. These are simple and straightforward definitions, but in real-life situations, there are people looking at what has happened and making the judgment calls to decide if they are looking at a mistake (unwanted result) or not.

Such judgment calls are affected by the observer's cultural values; and these values will heavily influence how the situation is perceived and assessed, plus any actions decided upon for correction and prevention of future repetition.

Using Wursten's framework is convenient because it reduces the complexity of analyzing how mistakes are handled across more than 100 different cultures that have been subject to research thus far, to looking at seven different patterns emerging from that analysis. Like any typology or classification of phenomena into a set of styles, it does not aim to preclude deeper analysis of specific situations as warranted, looking at each occurrence's unique characteristics. Therefore, the framework should be used responsibly and with due moderation.

10.2 If at First You Don't Succeed

My experience has shown that in Contest cultures, the emphasis is placed on striving, confronting, and competing for achievements that will bring rewards and social recognition. Children are taught at a very early age that they should behave competitively. They are taught that life is a competition with winners and losers; if you make a mistake, it might be costly; however, you can always try again.

Everyone deserves a second chance; and this means that there is a succession of competitions. The show must go on; and in this case, the show is the plethora of competitions that are seen everywhere, all the time.

Contest organizational culture styles are most often found in Anglo-Saxon cultures; they are typical of the United States, the United Kingdom, Australia, and Canada.

In Contest organizations, competition is fierce. Yes, there are winners and losers. Winners are hailed extravagantly and losers despised. But victory is not permanent, and neither is defeat. The competition never stops, so both winners and losers must live to fight another day.

Mistakes are often treated quite harshly, even dramatically, and that might seem to outsiders as a draconian approach. However, there is always the assumption that this is not definitive. Punishment, however harsh, shall be followed by a second chance, and even a third one, for the worst scenario would be that those who made mistakes were to be completely abandoned. Rather, the underlying assumption is that even though they may be thrown overboard, they could still be invited back onto the boat again. Or more often than not, the thinking is that they will climb aboard another boat, since there are so many of them moving around at all times. In any case, people will live to compete again, feeding the continuation of the Contest process.

Contest organizational cultures focus on results and "the bottom line": when all is said and done, what is the net outcome? This is key to defining, in a way that is perceived as fair and just, who is winning or losing the competition. Measurement is therefore considered to be quite important.

If a mistake affects the final desired results, it will be treated very seriously. If the impact is small, the mistake might be easily overlooked. The key issues are: Did the mistake affect the results? and How quickly can the competition continue?

This means that managers do not dwell very long on mistakes; the competition needs to continue as quickly as possible. Organizations foster an attitude of optimism and looking forward to the next Contest round. Such a positive attitude feeds the continuation of the Contest. Critical thinking is often regarded as pessimistic. It is discouraged, for it might lead to people losing the motivation to continue competing.

Dismissing people is a frequent happening at Contest culture organizations, and it happens swiftly. One day you are hailed as a hero and suddenly you make a mistake and you are fired. The firing, or dismissal, is immediate and can seem even brutal, because it all happens so fast. People are asked to pack up their personal belongings in a box and leave the premises within the same day, if not at the very instant. You can see it often in American movies and TV: people walking out of their workplaces carrying a box as if they were refugees fleeing from a war zone.

Cruel as it may seem, the culture assumes that jobs are comparatively abundant and easy to find. Firing happens fast, but hiring is also a speedy process. The labor markets in Contest cultures are quite dynamic.

The overriding concept is that competitions are constant and abundant. For that to continue happening, the culture needs people who are constantly motivated to continue competing.

The worst that can happen is when people in these cultures decide to stop competing. This is the exact opposite of what the culture needs in order to continue nourishing its values. Therefore, organizations will do their utmost to encourage people to never give up.

When people make a mistake, what organizations want to hear from them is (a) acknowledgment, (b) apology, and (c) asking for another chance, to stay in the competition and to keep trying.

When these three conditions are met, organizations can display some mercy and generosity. People will be praised for taking responsibility and being honest (acknowledgment); they will also be praised for showing regret and expressing that they feel sorry (apology); and they will be praised especially for showing that they are ready and willing to return to the competition and try again.

The concept of accountability in organizations is a cornerstone of Contest cultures. The term, by the way, is difficult (if not impossible) to translate into languages other than English. Determining accountability is key to identifying who made a mistake and to determining winners and losers; in other cultures, this may not be as important as it is in Contest.

On the other hand, perfection is not as important in Contest cultures as it is by contrast, for instance, in Well-Oiled Machine cultures or in Japanese organizations. In Contest cultures, there is a certain tolerance for making mistakes, especially if they have little impact on results. Keeping the competition going is more important than putting most of your energy in avoiding mistakes.

This notion supports many company programs aiming to foster innovation, such as Sony Corporation's "Fail Fast" program (Kelly and Li 2011) in the early 2000s. The program encouraged product developers to take more risks in early stages of development, leaving perfectionism aside, abandoning ideas that were not working (rather than insisting on them), and shifting to start something new. It was supported by Howard Stringer, later appointed CEO, and a host of Contest culture consultants who championed the acceptance of mistakes as necessary occurrences in the path to innovation. However, their approach clashed with the company's Japanese culture of avoiding uncertainty and seeking perfection.

Paul Arden (2003) advocated that ambition is more important than being satisfied with mediocre performance. The issue here is that in Contest cultures, there is a certain tolerance for mistakes when they are considered a by-product of seeking innovation. The ambition in Contest cultures is to excel in breakthrough innovations, even if mistakes are made along the journey. The ambition in Japanese-styled organizations is to avoid mistakes even at the cost of innovation breakthroughs, which is why these organizations support incremental innovation programs more than seeking breakthroughs.

Part of the Contest culture mentality is to think in a short-term perspective, with an eye on quarterly results and stock markets. This is consistent with the notion that mistakes can happen, and going for the next round in the competition is more important. You should aim for the short term, knowing that there will be other rounds and other chances to continue competing.

Another supporting concept for Contest cultures is the notion that corrections can be made quickly. Thinking in the short term allows for frequent follow-ups and frequent corrections of mistakes. The idea is that this also supports flexibility and rapidly adapting to change.

The avoidance of the repetition of mistakes is not as important as getting back into action (Peters and Waterman 2015). Having "a bias for action" is considered in Contest cultures to be one of the keys for obtaining excellence.

This was evident also in the handling of the global financial crisis in 2008, when Contest culture advocates in the United States and United Kingdom pressed the American Federal Reserve Bank and the European Central Bank for quick short-term corrective actions, while Well-Oiled Machine culture advocates in Germany and Switzerland stressed the need for reviewing existing structures and processes in order to avoid the repetition of similar problems in the future. These differences in culture perspectives affect not only microeconomic management issues within organizations but also macroeconomic issues in terms of public policies.

As a consequence of mistakes, guilt has greater weight than shame when it comes to Contest cultures. These cultures are more individualistic (rather than collectivistic), and therefore feelings of guilt (failing in regard to your own standards) tend to be stronger than feelings of shame (failing in the eyes of your reference group).

10.3 Was the Mistake Caused by a Faulty Process?

The emphasis in Well-Oiled Machine (WOM) organizational cultures is more on process rather than on results. Certainly results are important in these cultures, but the typical response to a mistake is: What went wrong with the process and caused this mistake to happen? Was the process faulty by design, or was execution the problem? How can we fix the process (or structure, or procedure) in order to make the process "fool-proof," thereby avoiding the mistake ever repeating itself?

These organizational cultures are more typically found in countries with Germanic national cultures: that is to say, Germany, Austria, and Switzerland. Still, they may be found in other parts of the world, with less frequency.

WOM cultures operate on the premise that the most important thing is for the organization to have an overall order superseding everything. Organizations need planning, structures, regulations, policies, and procedures that will allow work to be done smoothly. If everyone does their job according to the rules, tasks will be carried out efficiently according to plan. When something goes wrong and/or a mistake happens, the first question is generally: Was there something wrong with the plan? How can we correct the plan?

The assumption is that people in general have a natural desire to perform well and avoid mistakes. If a mistake does happen, then surely the plan (or structure, process, etc.) must be at fault and needs to be corrected.

Individual accountability is also enforced, with a strong link to discipline. If an individual strays away from the established process and makes a mistake, it becomes very difficult to justify that deviation from an established norm. Such deviations can be punished very strictly, but the person is not regarded as "a loser" as is the case in Contest cultures. Rather, the social punishment is the loss of credibility. A person who shows lack of discipline is considered unworthy for promotions or displays of recognition in organizations.

Firing does not happen as easily as it does in Contest cultures; it is actually quite rare. The notion of an overall order includes keeping everyone on board and avoiding exclusion by severance. WOM cultures are also quite egalitarian and that also means that everyone is entitled to a second chance. However, the criteria for judging people vis-à-vis their mistakes are different. If the person who made the mistake was following established norms, blame is shifted to the faulty norms, plans, or structures, and the person is exonerated from blame. Such a person deserves many new chances, since he/she is absolved. If lack of discipline is detected, then blame falls squarely on the person.

As in other individualistic cultures, guilt is more important than shame. This means that regardless of the pain involved in losing credibility in the eyes of others, having failed to satisfy your own highly demanding standards is a stronger punishing factor.

The strong respect for norms means that exceptions are not accepted. While in other culture exceptions can almost become the rule, in WOM cultures they are almost nonexistent. All of this can sometimes stifle creativity and innovation, but it does not preclude them. There needs to be a set time and place for creativity and an established procedure. As long as those boundaries are respected, innovation may flourish. And if mistakes happen within those innovation-seeking boundaries, they are not regarded as such.

Avoiding mistakes in any other environment is a priority. The motivation is not to avoid negative impact on results but to avoid upsetting the overall order. This is achieved through detailed planning and organizing and disciplined execution and also by relying on experts.

Expertise is highly valued in WOM cultures. Experts are more highly revered than people in positions of authority or people who are top performers. However, experts need to cope with the fact that this recognition comes with a price: they are expected to never make mistakes. If people who make mistakes are despised, then people who were regarded as experts and make mistakes are strongly despised. Their expert status may be immediately lost, and they might lose the credibility they had accumulated over years of study and hard work.

Correcting mistakes is important, but in WOM cultures, corrections are supposed to be done carefully, not necessarily in a hurry, to avoid making things worse. Rather than "a bias for action," WOM culture organizations have "a bias for thinking twice before jumping." A badly made correction can do more damage than the initial mistake, so treading carefully is crucial. As previously stated, the priority is placed on correcting the faulty process, more than quickly fixing something that might happen again unless the process is verified.

10.4 Never Exclude Anyone

Network organizational cultures are typical of the Scandinavian countries and of the Netherlands. These organizations are more egalitarian than most and tend toward decentralized decision-making structures. They are characterized by frequent discussions without reverence to hierarchy and by reaching decisions through consensus.

The main distinction between Network cultures and the previously described Contest and WOM cultures is that the latter two put greater emphasis on performance, compared to the former. Network cultures show significant care for people issues, work-life balance, and quality of life, more than the other two organizational culture types.

This creates room for mistakes to happen (because there is less emphasis on performing to the highest possible standards), and it strongly influences how mistakes are handled.

Network cultures have a certain reputation for tolerance. This refers not only to social behaviors, but it also applies to assessing performance and to deciding on what is regarded (or not) as a mistake, to begin with.

Performance levels regarded as unacceptable in Contest and WOM cultures may be tolerated in Network organizations; mistakes are often regarded as "not material enough to be regarded as such." For instance, if a sales clerk often takes longer than the standard to make a gift-wrapped package, and the end product turns out to be usually rather sloppy, these might constitute reason enough for dismissal in Contest cultures. In Network cultures, there is less pressure on speed and lower standards for gift-wrapping. Therefore, a mediocre performer might continue to underperform without sanction for quite a while.

In Network organizational cultures, missing a deadline is also not regarded as a major problem, compared to Contest and WOM. If delivery is late by a day or two, this is often considered acceptable. This is simply because Network culture organizations tend to consider that people should not be required to make significant personal sacrifices in order to deliver according to client expectations. This does not mean to say that Network organizations have poor standards; it is simply that they do not enforce those standards with 100% rigor. They tend to leave a little bit of room for tolerance and for accommodating exceptions.

By contrast with WOM cultures, Network organizations expect people to assess any given situation and make a personal judgment call on how to handle it, following procedures automatically or deciding to make exceptions to the rules. In Network cultures, people are expected to make exceptions, as long as they can justify them. Justifications are often based on humanitarian reasons, rather than to obtain better results or out of respect for authority figures.

There is also a lot of sympathy for "underdogs." This means that, when personal accountability for a mistake is to be ascertained, the culture influences people to be merciful and lenient toward those who are perceived to be less fortunate. If someone is regarded as "a social case," that means that such a person somehow deserves support from everyone in society, including their peers, supervisors, and direct reports. In practice, all of this means that it is very rare for people to get severely punished or even fired for making mistakes, even if they make them rather often. Frequently managers cite protective labor legislation as being an obstacle to severance of underperformers; but the actual fact is that culture values play a more influential role in the process.

Network cultures are also individualistic, so once again guilt plays a stronger role than shame as a negative feeling. This is even stronger in Network cultures because whenever people are publicly exposed to shame, people around them tend to quickly side with the person being shamed, feeling sorry for them. When someone is publicly put to shame in Network cultures, everyone around them feels the pain; therefore, such situations are better avoided.

Corrections of mistakes can be made quickly and on the spot, due to the usually decentralized decision structure. However, the speed of decisions to correct may also be affected by the need to seek consensus among stakeholders. If the situation falls clearly within the mandate of an individual, the decision can be made quickly. However, if it involves different stakeholders, it will be necessary to consult all of them, perhaps slowing down the process. If a quick decision is absolutely necessary, subsequent endorsement of that decision should be requested, humbly, explaining why the consultation was not possible earlier. Such a posteriori endorsements should never be taken for granted, for failing to consult stakeholders a priori is something not easily forgiven.

Avoiding the repetition of mistakes is not as important as it is in WOM cultures. Rather, in Network organizational cultures, there is a bigger concern on learning from the mistake. If the person who made the mistake has learned from it, possibly painfully, then it is considered that it is highly likely that this person will never make the same mistake again. Therefore, it is better to keep the person on that same job; this should ensure that the mistake would not happen again.

10.5 My Friends Can Make Mistakes

Social Pyramid organizational cultures have relationships and respect for hierarchy as their main distinctive characteristics. The underlying assumptions are that (a) power distribution is uneven in organizations; (b) you should assert the power of your position to those below you, while respecting the authority of those in positions above you; and (c) having friends in high places will do wonders to help you climb up the hierarchical structure.

The Social Pyramid organizational culture is quite typical of Latin America and Africa; it is also found often in Portugal, Greece, and in many countries of Eastern Europe, including Russia. There is a Brazilian popular expression that nicely summarizes the typical attitude toward mistakes found in these organizations: *aos amigos, tudo; aos demais, os rigores da lei* (to my friends, everything; to all others, the rigors of the law).

This means that when mistakes are made, the way they are handled depends significantly on the relationships involved, more than the actual facts. If the person who made the mistake is regarded as a loyal friend, people will be tolerant and lenient toward what has happened. If, however, there is no significant relationship in place between the people involved, those deciding about how to handle it will be much more strict and rigorous.

Power structures also have a huge influence in these organizations. Therefore, a mistake is whatever your boss considers it to be a mistake. Never mind if you achieved the results expected; never mind if you strictly followed the procedures. Your boss's opinion counts more than anything else. Regardless of discipline and getting results, your boss might think you made a mistake if (a) your actions implied a lack of respect for the boss's position; or (b) your actions might be interpreted as lacking in loyalty (to the boss, to the company, or to your reference group).

Since power holders are seen to have absolute power, fear of that perceived power leads people to often hide mistakes from their superiors. A basic challenge for senior management is to identify problems at the beginning, before they grow into a bigger issue. Often they are only made aware of mistakes when it is too late or when they have turned into bigger problems that are much more difficult to handle.

In such relationship-oriented cultures, shame carries much more weight than feelings of guilt. "Saving face" is of paramount importance in such environments; and when someone makes a mistake, their primary concern is how that will affect their image vis-à-vis their reference group and their superiors. Discipline toward compliance is not regarded as crucial. Being caught by your friends or your boss when making a mistake is much more important.

Paraphrasing the Zen Buddhist riddle: if someone makes a mistake in the middle of the forest and nobody sees it, is it still a mistake (in a Social Pyramid culture)? Actually, it depends on whether the mistake will be identified later and traced back to the person responsible. There might be better dividends to obtain by confessing to your boss and friends, thereby showing honesty and courage, rather than risking being found out later. The key mechanism is still: "what will others think" (shame), rather than "what do I think about myself" (guilt).

When determining whether a mistake has been made and how to handle it, observers within a Social Pyramid culture will typically ask: who were the people involved? If they were authority figures or celebrities, mistakes are likely to be easily downplayed and perhaps forgiven. If, on the contrary, the people involved are on the lower levels of the social hierarchy, there is a higher probability that they might be treated harshly. If they happen to be friends with the power holders, that will also affect how things are handled.

Conflicts can quickly turn personal, causing emotions to flare. This is perceived as a serious threat to group identity. Because of this, conflicts within the same group are avoided, in order to maintain harmony. Dissenting opinions within groups are suppressed. Conflicts do occur between different groups, rather than between individuals in the same group. The implication for handling mistakes is that typically opinions will be framed as "the people in production" versus "the people in sales," rather than between two different engineers within the production department, for instance.

In any case, since decisions are usually centralized at the top, it will be up to those power holders to decide on how to handle most mistakes, and their decisions are less likely to be challenged. Therefore, one way of avoiding conflict is to quickly escalate, delegating upward. The boss will decide, so we don't have to fight.

Family relatives of power holders enjoy privileged status in these cultures and often get away with making frequent mistakes without any consequence to their standings.

If one such privileged individual is found to be making mistakes rather frequently, this creates an embarrassment for the organization, since it exposes the fact that performance is actually secondary. To avoid that embarrassment, key players will often go out of their way to protect the boss from losing face. They might surround the mistake-prone relative with safeguarding mechanisms to help that person's performance. For instance, the boss's son might be given a "safe" job where his incompetence will have little impact or will not be evident; or he might be assigned to work with a very competent assistant who will do all the work and allow the boss's son to get the credit.

These mechanisms will also be used to avoid the repetition of mistakes. If a mistake has involved a key figure losing face, the primary concern tends to be: "how can we avoid the losing face to happen again," more than "how can we avoid the mistake happening again." Relationships and hierarchy will always be at the center of people's concerns.

10.6 Is This a Mistake or an Error?

Solar System organizational cultures are a bit more complicated to read by outside observers, because they show certain characteristics that create contradicting pressures. In such cultures, there is significant respect for hierarchy, similar to the Social Pyramid cultures; but there is also significant value placed on individual responsibility, freedom of expression, and direct communication, similar to what is observed in Contest, Network, and Well-Oiled Machine cultures.

This creates a tension between respecting the boss and speaking up to occasionally challenge her/him. Solar System cultures also show significant concern for avoiding uncertainty, something that only increases the stakes regarding the tension between Power Distance and Individualism.

The implications for handling mistakes are very interesting. Determining what is regarded as a mistake or not is not as straightforward as in egalitarian organizational cultures (Contest, Network, and WOM); it is affected by the respect for hierarchy. Therefore, people do ask: "who was involved?" And if the reply is that a figure of authority was involved, this might mean greater tolerance and also a concern for "saving face," similar to what happens in Social Pyramid cultures.

However, relationships and group loyalty play a lesser role; and high Individualism means that there is some support for expressing dissenting opinions and applying rules and criteria regardless of hierarchy. Typically, discussions ensue (also supported by Individualism). In such discussions, people walk a fine line between communicating openly while respecting hierarchy and avoiding loss of face by superior officers.

In retrospect we can say that in egalitarian and individualistic cultures such as Contest, Network, and WOM, discussions about mistakes focus on "what" and "how": What happened? How did it happen? How can we fix it? What needs to be done? How can we avoid it happening again?

By contrast, in collectivistic and hierarchical cultures such as the Social Pyramid style, discussions about mistakes emphasize the "who": Who did this? Who else was involved? Who will decide what to do? Who will be affected by the fix we implement? Who will decide on avoiding repetition? Who will be in charge of implementing corrective and preventive measures?

In Solar System cultures, we see a combination of the two approaches. "What" and "how" are important from an individualistic perspective; but "who" is emphasized from a hierarchical perspective.

The outcome might be decided by resorting to an overriding conceptual framework and making the discussion more about theories, concepts, and principles, rather than about whether or not the boss is right. The underlying principle is to avoid personal confrontation, shifting the focus of discussion to a theoretical debate. Questions often asked include: Is this an error or a mistake? What are the criteria for differentiating these two? Do we have a detailed policy describing what to do in cases like this one? Often there are, indeed, very detailed policies in Solar System organizations, to avoid the uncertainty of having to decide on a case-by-case basis.

Solar System organizational cultures were thus named because what often happens is a reinterpretation of policies and strategies at each level of the organization. The top boss (or top team) is "the sun" in the Solar System, around which the planets (direct reports) move in orbit. Each planet, however, has its own satellites. Directives emanating from the top boss are thus often reinterpreted by the middle managers, resulting in movements that might be seen as contradicting the seniormost directives. These reinterpretations are supported by Individualism; and middle managers demand respect from their immediate reports (consistent with the high Power Distance).

The overall outcome is that there are constant discussions across different levels of authority, challenging authority (but not too much). Superior officers need to assert their authority frequently, but also leaving some room for individual freedom to be expressed. These discussions often take the form of elaborate power games and diplomatic conversations, carefully treading the fine line between respecting hierarchy and allowing room for Individualism.

Solar System organizational cultures are more frequently found in France, Belgium, Italy, and Spain; but they may also be found in Poland and in Argentina.

High Individualism means that guilt plays a stronger role than shame; but there is also concern for saving face to preserve hierarchical status (less than to preserve relationships and group harmony). One might say that the importance of guilt and shame vis-à-vis making mistakes come out even, depending very much on the specific situations.

Corrections are made rather quickly, though sometimes the respect for hierarchy will lead people to escalate unnecessarily. At other times, decisions might be made at lower levels, asserting "planet" authority. Abundant documented policies are usually the guidelines for escalating or not.

To prevent repetitions of mistakes, Solar System organizations turn to robust conceptual thinking as a foundation for policies and procedures. Discussions can be quite heated (supported by Individualism) at the beginning, when supporting theories are being debated. Once a concept is agreed upon, things can move more quickly toward detailing and implementation. However, we must remain aware of the fact that preventive policies will still be subject to interpretation, in practice. Constant supervision may be required to ensure alignment is still there after a while.

10.7 Contingency Rules

In so-called Traditional Family organizational culture styles, hierarchy and relationships are very important, often even more than in Social Pyramid styles, with which they share many similarities. The main differentiating factor, according to Wursten (2017), is Uncertainty Avoidance: it is higher in Social Pyramid cultures and lower in Traditional Family styles.

The Family style is typical of most Asian cultures (Thailand and Pakistan are exceptions where the Social Pyramid style is often prevalent). In summary, the difference is that in Family styles, there is less formality and structure. Often there is no organization chart in the classic sense of the term, but rather a somewhat fuzzy set of reporting lines that were never clearly documented or communicated. Everybody knows who their direct boss and direct reports are; everything else is not necessarily clear. Even the CEO's authority may not be clear-cut. Informal power relations, especially in family-owned companies, often override formal mandates. An uncle who is not even part of the company might be making all the important decisions and relaying them informally through relatives inside, bypassing top management.

Written policies, when they exist at all, are often vague and broad guidelines, lacking in detail. This means that decisions are taken by the (often informal) power holders, based on their relationships more than anything else.

Since these power holders are perceived to have absolute power, mistakes are often hidden from them, from fear of harsh punishment or dismissal. The only factor acting as an incentive to reveal mistakes is that it may show loyalty to your superiors, especially if someone else gets the blame. But if blowing the whistle (a very popular expression in Contest cultures) means exposing some power holders, what usually happens in practice is that people prefer not to run the risk of retaliation; therefore, they choose to remain silent. Anonymous whistle blowing sometimes works as a mistake-identifying mechanism, but the challenge is convincing people that they can truly remain anonymous and safe from retribution.

When mistakes do come to the attention of decision-makers, their task is to examine every situation carefully according to its specific contingencies. The process is similar to what has been described for the Social Pyramid organizational culture style, but in Traditional Family organizations, it is even more fluid and relativistic, because of enhanced informality. This is also linked to what Michael Harris Bond has identified (Bond 2015) as a distinct value-dimension, which Hofstede later incorporated as a "fifth dimension" in his own framework.

This fifth dimension measures the degree in which a culture adopts a flexible, long-term-oriented, and relativistic stance when complying to norms, versus a more disciplined, short-term-oriented, and normative stance. Although this dimension was not part of Wursten's original work, it has been found that the Asian cultures that were classified as Traditional Family styles all score high on this dimension as well, meaning that they value flexibility and a contingency-based approach when handling mistakes.

Every mistake is then assessed and corrected looking primarily at who was involved, what were the circumstances, who shall decide on correction, and what could be the consequences (impacting whom) of corrective action. Existing norms, contracts, and previous commitments play a secondary role. Each situation stands on its own to be assessed. Decisions on correction and prevention will be made bearing in mind who is involved at present and will be involved in a possible recurrence. Hierarchy plays a central role in assessing who will be affected by decisions.

Since Uncertainty Avoidance is lower than in Social Pyramid cultures, this means that there is a greater tendency to accept risk. This aspect also influences the attitude of leaving norms and contract commitments aside, assessing each situation without a bias toward precedents or even existing regulations.

Shame and saving face are much more important than individual feelings of guilt. In the end, it is all about what others (especially authority figures) will think of me, rather than assessing my behavior against my own standards.

10.8 Avoiding Mistakes Through Rituals

Japan (and the typical Japanese organizational culture) does not fit in under the criteria that Huib Wursten defined when creating the six styles we've seen so far.

Japanese organizations have respect for hierarchy, but not as high as can be observed in Social Pyramid, Solar System, and Traditional Family organizational culture styles. They have a rather unique bottom-up, level-by-level consensus-seeking decision-making process, through which decisions rise slowly to be eventually decided upon by senior management. Yes, there is greater respect for hierarchy than in egalitarian cultures, but there is room for each level to influence decisions (collectively, not individually). Collectivism and valuing relationships are high; this, in itself, is not a differentiating factor. Making decisions in this circular, bottom-up way is unique (Hoffman 2015).

Performance Orientation (Hofstede's "Masculinism" dimension) is the highest measured by research. Japanese organizations are known for demanding utmost dedication from its members and breeding workaholics, even more than Contest and WOM cultures.

Furthering the case for Japanese-style uniqueness is the equally high Uncertainty Avoidance, a very evident aspect of Japanese organizations. This is typified by avoiding risk and adopting rituals as a path to ensuring consistency.

It is interesting to note that in Japanese cultures, there is a rather high flexibility and relativism. What this means in practice is that there is an apparent contradiction between avoiding uncertainty and treasuring performance (and striving for short-term results) in assessing situations and a pull toward contingency attitudes taking into account the long-term perspective, relationships, and hierarchy. Situations must be assessed on a case-by-case basis, like in Traditional Family organizational cultures (asking the "who" questions); but the need to avoid uncertainty and achieve results brings in the observance of rituals to attain a certain balance between these forces.

The implications for identifying and handling mistakes are many.

The value placed on excellent performance and on avoiding risk translates into the adoption of ambitious and highly detailed quality standards. Japanese organizations have enjoyed a global "best-practice" reputation for quality since the 1980s. Quality Circles and Total Quality programs spread from Japan and were imitated all over the world. However, in many organizations, such programs failed. They usually were not as successful as their originators in Japan, and more often than not "Japanese culture" was named as the crucial differentiating factor.

Japanese-style organizations (they do exist outside of Japan) treat their approach to quality as a series of rituals. These rituals allow the identification of mistakes early on, before they become larger problems.

However, as we've seen in the example of Toyota in the United States (Alvarez 2016), the need to save face can come in and, at a senior level, allow for behaviors that result in trying to hide mistakes from regulators and from public view. Quality rituals were followed at the operational levels; but at senior levels, managers decided to shun their own standards and take a contingency approach. After a while, they could not maintain that approach any longer and were forced to recant and apologize. The Toyota brand suffered considerable damage, and it took years to regain trust in the eyes of the American public.

When such mistakes happen in Japanese organizations, public shame serves to atone for guilt. Executives apologize in public, following a ritual that is closely watched to ascertain how deep and low will said executives bow (the deeper the bow, the more profound the apology).

Corrective and preventive actions will follow the quality rituals previously described (Karatsu 1988): proposals will be created through a bottom-up, level-by-level consensus approach, until decisions are made by senior management. This means that decisions can take much longer than, for instance, in Contest organizational cultures, but implementation is usually smoother, quicker, and with the benefit of more employee engagement, due to the great amount of participation at middle and lower levels.

10.9 Conclusion

When it comes to identifying and handling mistakes across cultures, the challenges for international organizations are many. They start and finish with understanding their own organizational cultures at Head Office; they go on to adapting their practices according to the cultures under which they operate in different countries, taking stock of how those local cultures affect the identification, correction, and prevention of mistake recurrence. Adapting practices, by the way, does not mean that organizations must let go of their corporate standards. What it does mean is that the path to meeting those standards may be different according to each environment.

The process ends, as culture awareness increases, with becoming aware of an organizational culture's "blind spots." Since cultural values affect everything we do, including our perception of reality, organizations much learn how to identify their own culture bias, which is likely, at first, to prevent them from seeing certain issues in their own culture and also in the culture of others.

For instance, in Network cultures, people may readily identify culture differences regarding hierarchy; but they often overlook the importance of having a bias toward quality of life and caring in detriment of striving for high performance. In Contest cultures, their bias for action makes it more difficult to give situation analysis enough time before jumping to conclusions. Respect for hierarchy in Social Pyramid, Solar System, and Traditional Family cultures can sometimes lead to underrating contributions from young talent sitting in the lower levels of their structure. Well-Oiled Machine cultures tend to overlook the importance of constant supervision to ensure compliance, because they tend to think that everyone will have the strict self-discipline that they enjoy at Head Office. And Japanese organizations tend to miss the fact that in many cultures, most people may value their families more than they value their jobs.

I recommend that managers and professionals begin by seeking to understand their own national and organizational cultures, to become aware of how their personal culture bias might shape their perception, especially when looking at certain situations in a culture that is different from their own. Management effectiveness can increase significantly when managers understand their own culture values and also those of their stakeholders from different cultures.

In terms of handling mistakes, understanding the underlying logic of each culture style will help managers to understand why people approach mistakes differently and use diverse arguments for prevention, identification, and correction of mistakes. This will help them make more effective and efficient decisions when planning, when designing policies and procedures, and when troubleshooting critical incidents concerning mistake-handling.

Understanding your own culture bias may also help you communicate more effectively and clarify your own arguments when discussing mistakes across cultures. Effective communication may be enhanced by increasing your ability to stand in your stakeholder's shoes and also by allowing you to clarify your own point of view to others. As a result, I expect that managers will become more effective in handling mistakes whatever the culture environment they operate in.

References

Alvarez Villacis, D. (2016). The Toyota Recall Crisis Case Study. White paper at www.academia.edu.

Arden, P. (2003). It's Not How Good You Are, Its How Good You Want to Be: The World's Best Selling Book [Ebook]. London: Phaidon Press.

Bond, M. (2015). The Oxford handbook of Chinese psychology. New York: Oxford University Press.

Hoffman, M. (2015). In the Land of the Kami: A Journey Into the Hearts of Japan. College Station: VIRTUALBOOKWORM.COM PUB.

Hofstede, G. (2003a). Culture's Consequences: Comparing Values, Behaviors, Institutions and Organizations Across Nations. Thousand Oaks, Calif.: SAGE.

Hofstede, G. (2003b). Culture's consequences. Thousand Oaks, Calif.: Sage Publications.

Hofstede, G., Hofstede, G., & Pedersen, P. (2002). Exploring Culture: Exercises, Stories and Synthetic Cultures. Boston: Intercultural Press.

Karatsu, H. (1988). Wisdom of Japan: Managing for Total Quality Control. London: Productivity Press.

Kelly, T., & Li, K. (2011). SPECIAL REPORT-Sony stumbles: Did Stringer's makeover fail?. Retrieved from https://www.reuters.com/article/sony-stumbles/special-report-sony-stumbles-did-stringers-makeover-fail-idUSN2220673820110523

Lanzer, F. (2012). Take Off Your Glasses. North Charleston: Create Space.

Lanzer, F. (2nd edition 2015). The Meaning Tree. North Charleston: Create Space.

Lanzer, F. (2017). Leading Across Cultures in Practice. North Charleston: Create Space.

Lanzer F (2018) Organizational culture and climate: understanding, maintaining and changing. Create Space, North Charleston

Lanzer, F. & Chandansingh, R. (2016). Trust Me. North Charleston: Create Space.
Lanzer, Fernando & Pereira de Souza, J. (2015) - Era Uma Vez… Mas Não Erra de North Charleston: Create Space. Lanzer, F. (2018). Organizational Culture and Climate: Understanding, Maintaining and Changing. North Charleston: Create Space.
Lanzer, Fernando & Pereira de Souza, J. (2016). Para Entender A Cultura Brasileira. North Charleston: Create Space.
Lanzer, F.; Wursten, H., & Fadrhonc, T. (2014). Managing Across Cultures – White paper published at www.academia.edu.
Peters, T., & Waterman, R. (2015). In search of excellence. London: Profile Books.
Wursten, H. (2017). Mental Images Mental images of culture: a perspective to understand misunderstandings in politics, business, religion and… to make some sense of the challenges in today's confusing world, White paper published at www.academia.edu
Wursten, H. & Lanzer, F. (2013). The EU: The Third Great European Cultural Contribution to the World. White paper.

Fernando Lanzer Pereira de Souza is Dutch, born in Brazil, living in the Netherlands since 2003. He enjoyed a career alternating between consultancy services and positions as a Human Resources Executive in international companies. A former member of the ITIM International network up to 2016, he has been a guest lecturer at business schools in Europe and in Brazil.

Fernando is also a former chair of the Supervisory Group of AIESEC International. He currently sits on the Board of Trustees of the International School of Amsterdam (ISA).

He is the author of the books *Take Off Your Glasses* (2012), *The Meaning Tree* (2015), *Bedtime Stories For Corporate Executives* (2015), *Trust Me* (with Reynold Chandansingh, 2016), *Leading Across Cultures in Practice* (2017), and *Organizational Climate and Culture* (2018), in addition to many published articles.

He holds a B.A. in Clinical, Educational, and Organizational Psychology, from PUCRGS, Porto Alegre, Brazil.

Chapter 11
A Systems Psychodynamic Perspective on Conflict and Failure at Work

Claude-Hélène Mayer

Abstract This chapter provides an in-depth insight into ethnographic experiences of conflict and failure in a South African work context. The conflict is analysed and interpreted from systems psychodynamic theory perspectives, to provide new and differentiated ideas on the in-depth complexity of conflict experiences in a specific cultural context. The purpose of this chapter is to offer insight into an intra- and inter-psychological conflict experience from an ethnographic perspective, in the South African post-apartheid work context. An ethnographic research methodology, which is anchored in the research paradigm of Dilthey's modern hermeneutics and a natural research approach, is used. This chapter presents a single case study of an intrapersonal and interpersonal conflict in a selected South African workplace. This conflict escalated over 4 years, remained unresolved and was therefore experienced as a failure from the perspective of the participant of the research study. The aim of this chapter is to provide insights into conflict experiences which arose between two individuals of different cultural origins at work and their underlying system psychodynamic impacts of the experienced failure. The research methods used include: interviews, field notes, contextual descriptions and interpretations based on the theoretical framework of systems psychodynamics. Recommendations for future theory and practice to overcome intercultural conflict and experiences of failure at work are offered.

Keywords Mistakes · Errors · Failure · Organisational ethnography · Failure · Intercultural work conflict · Systems psychodynamic · Cultural embeddedness · Interpretative hermeneutics

---

C.-H. Mayer (✉)
Department of Industrial Psychology and People Management, University of Johannesburg, Johannesburg, South Africa

Institut für Therapeutische Kommunikation und Sprachgebrauch, Europa Universität Viadrina, Frankfurt (Oder), Germany
e-mail: claudemayer@gmx.net

E. Vanderheiden, C.-H. Mayer (eds.), *Mistakes, Errors and Failures across Cultures*, https://doi.org/10.1007/978-3-030-35574-6_11

11.1 Introduction

From Western perspectives, the African continent is often associated with violence, war and unresolved conflicts (Janzen 2016). Western perspectives on conflict and failure and their resolution in African countries and work contexts have been discussed critically with regard to power relations, inequality and ideology—and a call for different perspectives on conflict and its management has evolved (Mayer and Louw 2012; Nader and Grande 2002).

The management of conflict and failure in African contexts is an issue that has been well-researched from various disciplinary perspectives, such as management (Mayer and Louw 2012), psychology (Van Niekerk 2013) or cultural anthropology (Vigh 2008), and is often described in Western, etic terms (Mayer 2005). This, however, leads to the presentation of conflict in African contexts through Westernised worldviews and does not necessarily lead to differentiated, heterogeneous and culture-specific insights into emic concepts of conflict and its management (Mayer 2005, 2008; Mayer and Louw 2012). This might lead to stereotypic views, culturalisation and generalisation when defining and understanding conflict and its management within a certain cultural context (Lin 2010).

Culture is characterised by hybridisation and inner complexity and can be defined, according to Bennett (2017), as "the coordination of meaning and action within a bounded group". This allows for a broad and general understanding of the cultural concept which yields, on an individual level, the culture of worldview while including the idea of the individual being part of a group with boundaries. According to Berry (1989), emic approaches provide culture-specific insights and detailed, fairly non-stereotypic information.

Mahadevan and Mayer (2017) find that because of increasing sociocultural diversity within organisations and societies, new and context-specific approaches and insights are needed to understand and revise power relations and conflict. Mayer (2008) emphasises that conflict needs an emic understanding from the inside of the self and the sociocultural context. Syed (2008) highlights that specific contours of cultural diversity in societies, as well as in the workplace, need to be taken into account and context-specific research is needed to deal with diversity and cultural phenomena on an intersecting level (Syed 2008; Syed and Özbilgin 2009). This is specifically true for reoccurring conflictual communication situations in specific cultural contexts and for individuals of different cultural origins acting within these (organisational) contexts (Mayer and May 2018). Accordingly, conflict is defined as being part of sociocultural interaction (Mayer and Louw 2012) in which the interaction is experienced from different points of views and interest, which might lead to clashes (Mayer 2006). Failure to manage conflict often leads to distrust and diminished relationship building (Elo et al. 2015) but may also be seen as a resource to develop and grow individually.

Micro-level ethnographic investigation can shed new light on conflict as a terrain of context, action and meaning (Vigh 2008; Beek and Göpfert 2012), calling for ethnographic, reflexive case study research on conflict in work contexts in sub-Saharan Africa to develop increasingly differentiated knowledge and understanding of conflict from a systemic perspective. In-depth knowledge is created when different layers of systems are taken into account, and the creation of meaning of conflict experiences unfolds at different systemic levels to develop a differentiated and reflexive knowledge, questioning implicit power relations (Mahadevan and Mayer 2017). These different levels can be explored by applying systems psychodynamic theory to ethnographic descriptions, thereby addressing individual and group level perspectives in an in-depth, systemic manner (Schruijer and Curseu 2014). Systems psychosocial dynamic approaches are used in this research to explore a single-case communication situation in South Africa between two colleagues of different cultural origins. This exploration of new perspectives can foster in-depth insights, individual development and personal growth (Vikkelso 2012).

11.2 Purpose and Aim

The aim of this chapter is to present a single-case conflict, experienced by one individual and presented as an ethnographic description which is analysed and interpreted through the lens of systems psychodynamics theories. The purpose is to present an in-depth insight into a selected example of culturally embedded conflict and provide the reader with a new and differentiated understanding of an interpersonal and intrapersonal conflict while taking power relations and conscious and unconscious systems psychodynamics on individual and group level into account.

11.2.1 Systems Psychodynamics and Group Relations

The systems psychodynamics theory provides theoretical approaches based on psychoanalytic patterns of interpretation which attempt to understand the experiences, processes, feelings and behaviour of groups by including the analysis and interpretation of conscious and unconscious processes and structures (Miller 1993; Cilliers et al. 2012; Steyn and Cilliers 2016).

Systems need to deal with emotions and uncertainties. In case the system is not able to contain these emotions or thoughts, individuals within the system become "containers" and are thereby unconsciously absorbed into the system (Motsoaledi and Cillers 2012). If the emotions run high, they might be projected onto an object within the system to contain the unbearable (Motsoaledi and Cillers 2012). Anxiety is often motivating unconscious and conscious dynamics within systems, impacting on behaviour, emotions and thoughts (Klein 2005; Shongwe 2014), thereby defending against powerlessness and paralysis and anxiety itself (Sievers 2009). When emotions are not addressed, defence mechanisms occur, such as splitting, projection, idealisation, rationalisation, simplification and denial (Blackman 2004; Stapley 1996, 2006), which can lead to conflict.

Splitting describes a dynamic in which individuals fail to see the self and others as a unit or as a cohesive whole individual owing to unconscious anxieties (Klein 1988). Splitting leads to an all-or-nothing thinking, and individuals might split off unwanted feelings, thoughts or experiences which are unappreciated or which they reject (Cilliers and Smit 2006). In this thinking, the whole cannot be integrated. This splitting applies to the dynamic of inclusion and exclusion (Cilliers and Smit 2006) and can occur in subgroups and along boundaries, such as national belonging, age, work abilities or other perceived differences, such as race or gender (Shemla et al. 2014). In this case, the system splits up parts which are not attainable and projects them onto "the other". The other contains the unwanted or even idealised parts, until the system grows in strength and is able to retrieve what belongs to itself and with what it can now deal with (Cilliers and Smit 2006).

This defence mechanism of projection refers to projecting undesirable feelings, thoughts, experiences, attitudes or parts—which are unconsciously inherent in the system—onto a system's object. The person projecting cannot cope with a certain part and therefore projects it onto another object in the system, thereby imagining that this part belongs to the other, not to the self (Huffington et al. 2004; Cilliers and May 2010). Since life experiences are usually a product of previous experiences which have been gained during childhood (Fraher 2004) or in previous important relationships, they impact on contemporary experiences by being projected onto contemporary situations (Klein 1997).

Based on the projections, the projector's unwanted parts enter the psychological system of the other, and the recipient starts identifying with the projections, creating a process of projective identification (Cilliers and Smit 2006). The recipient claims ownership of the projected parts, and the projector believes that the projections are part of the recipient, while the receiver's behaviour changes in accordance with the needs of the projector (Campbell and Huffington 2008). Strong emotions and high anxiety levels might stimulate communication of needs through projective identification (Bion 1961; Klein 1997; Myburg 2009; Van Tonder 2012).

The defence mechanism of introjection describes a dynamic in which the individual needs an object to identify with and to internalise and contain projections (Klein 1997; Fraher 2004). Thereby, the individual internally replicates behaviours, attributes or other fragments of the environment or surrounding world (Cilliers 2012). During this process, the individual takes experiences from the outside world into the self while being unaware of the whole system (Cilliers et al. 2012). Through introjection (in terms of internalisation), experiences from the past, such as those with the family of origin, are transferred into the present and unconsciously impact on the current behaviour of the individual (Stapley 2006).

Rationalisation and intellectualisation provide the individual with intellectual explanations for systems psychodynamic mechanisms, for example, splitting or projection, and for their behaviour (Cilliers 2005; Cilliers and May 2010). Another defence mechanism is idealisation, in which individuals relate to an object within the system by idealising it, for example, an imagined caring parental figure (Cilliers 2017). The idealisation is often based on idealised (symbolic) interactions or on idealised imagined figures. Simplification is also a defence mechanism, working with concepts which are reduced in complexity and understanding, based on a simplified image of the world, the phenomenon or the system (Cilliers and Terblanche 2010).

Finally, denial is defined as an act of disowning the unaccepted parts of the self, an experience or behaviour, by applying the idea that this part no longer exists. By using this defence mechanism, the part remains part of the system's unconsciousness and of the self. Therefore, denial is usually only a temporary solution since it reoccurs within the system (Stapley 1996).

11.2.2 Conflict and Systems Psychodynamics

From a systems psychodynamic perspective, conflict can be seen as a macro-systemic competition of status, power and privilege that evokes certain behaviour and dynamics on individual and interpersonal levels (Cilliers 2012). It is used as a powerful defence against group dynamics which result from uncertainty and anxiety (Myburg 2009). The conflict might manifest on individual levels or between levels and might turn into the experience of failure. When conflict manifests intrapersonally, it is usually expressed through conflicting feeling or ideas. When conflict occurs interpersonally, it might be expressed in arguments or misunderstandings (Cilliers and Koortzen 2005). Conflict can occur in individuals or subgroups on behalf of the larger systems which the individuals and subsystems are part of (Rice 1951). They might also reflect the larger system.

Further, the individual who contains the emotions within a system is often associated with being a symbolic parent through containment and is therefore experienced as a protective force (Kaplan and Lipinsky-Kella 2015; Shongwe 2014). When the defence mechanisms to deal with anxieties and insecurities within a system are intense, it is possible that containment of feelings can become a real challenge which then might lead to conflictual situations (Aram et al. 2015; Armstrong and Rustin 2015). When power modes change, for example, in terms of gender modes, conflict might occur, and containers for emotions and certain group dynamics, anxieties and uncertainties could change (Kinnear 2014; Shongwe 2014). This could lead to conflict, the experience of chaos, limited resources or other challenges (Meyer and Boninelli 2007) and might be associated unconsciously with conflicts anchored earlier in life (Krantz 2001).

Conflict might be based in identity challenges, identity confusion or reconstruction (identity-based conflict), or it could be anchored in interests (Cilliers and Terblanche 2010). Interest-based conflict is founded in the unconscious need for recognition, dignity, safety and control (Cilliers and Terblanche 2010). Conflict, however, might also occur as the result of confusion around roles and authorities (Cilliers and Koortzen 2005; Cytrynbaum and Noumair 2004; Naik 2014), blurred or undefined boundaries and boundary management (Cilliers and Terblanche 2010) or transference and countertransference in symbolic relationships which are reconstructed from earlier life experiences. Within systems, conscious and unconscious psychological boundaries are usually created between conflicting individuals and/or subsystems (Kets De Vries 2007). Conflict and bullying often circle around questions of containment and the definition of boundaries in combination with the search for recognition (White 2004). Bound to the issue of boundaries are questions of defining formal and informal authority, as well as self-authority (Cilliers and Koortzen 2005; Naik 2014; Stapley 2008) which might lead to conflicts within systems (Stapley 2006).

11.2.3 Research Methodology

This study uses an ethnographic research approach (Ellis 2007) anchored within the research paradigm of Dilthey's (2002) modern hermeneutics. In this approach, the past experiences of a single individual are remembered and reviewed from a present perspective (Abrahhao 2012) while viewing and interpreting the personal and subjective experience of the self within the social and cultural context (Reed-Danahay 2001). The research uses the subjective perspective in the findings and thereby provides in-depth and rich, differentiated insights (Doloriert and Sambrook 2012).

The study uses multiple ethnographic research methods which were applied over a longitudinal period, such as interviews, field notes, diary writing and observation. Field notes in an organisational context were taken by the researcher. Field notes and diaries were written, and personal documentation and information was used to reconstruct the described situation through the "reconstructive memory" (Adams et al. 2017). Interviews were conducted with the individual and colleagues in the work context. The situation described was chosen from various conflict experiences observed owing to its varied in-depth layers and multifold, complex systemic context. Data types were analysed through content analysis and interpreted and reconstructed by referring to Terre Blanche, Durrheim and Painter's (Terre Blanche et al. 2006) qualitative analysis model.

This ethnographic approach is based on qualitative research criteria, including confirmability, credibility, transferability and dependability (Lincoln and Guba 1985). The descriptions are based on the openness of the individual as well as on managing the complexity of the experiences from an in-depth perspective. Ethical considerations are important in this ethnographical research due to the fact that narrations on self and others carry a moral responsibility (Richardson 1990) and ethical implications. In this research, internal confidentiality was provided, and anonymity of people involved was assured (Ellis 2007).

The findings are not provided to produce generalisable insights but rather to relate to in-depth knowledge and experiences which might create new and complex, context-specific insights and understanding, to build a base for future research on conflict and its management.

11.2.4 Findings and Discussion

A single-case situation is presented here, which was experienced as conflictual by a selected individual during 4 years of working at a higher education institution in South Africa. The researcher presents the situation described by a single individual, through the use of the above-mentioned research methods.

The conflict occurred at a university in post-apartheid South Africa at which the researched person worked for several years. During that time, South Africa found itself in uncertain and challenging times, with a decreasing economy and increasing brain drain, violence and corrupt elites as well as governmental scandals. At the same time, universities were challenged financially, as well as by student protests on campuses throughout the country, with movements like #FeesMustFall (a student movement fighting for the possibility to study without paying fees). Sometimes the campuses were closed for days due to violent protests, and security measures were increasing, as was the competition of academics in search of funds. Consequently several academics left the institution and the country, in search of more peaceful and stable societies to live in, while the actions of black economic empowerment (BEE) and affirmative action (AA) policies increased, promoting employees from "previously disadvantaged groups" (namely, "Black", including African, Coloured and Indian employees). The conflict described occurred during these contextual challenges and uncertainties. The researched person had just begun working in the institution. She is of German descent and had lived in the country for many years and had worked in different positions in higher education institutions.

Excerpts of interviews are presented with regard to the conflict and failure experienced by the researched person (Y). These excerpts were all recorded in 2016 when Y looked back at her past 4 years having worked at the institution. In the following, two selected conflict narrations will be analysed and discussed, based on systems psychodynamic theory.

> When I came to work this morning, I met X, one of my African junior colleagues, in the car park. He usually asks me how I am and when I will be returning to Germany. Since I started working in the department, four years ago, I have had a lot of short interactions with him. The first day I met him in 2012 he told me he loved Germany—such a "rich, developed and safe country"—and that he was looking for a German girlfriend. I just nodded and did not react verbally. This happened several times over the first two years until I told him that I was married. Since then there were hardly any interactions between us. If we talk, he asks me how Germany is and I respond that "Germany is fine, as far as I know." However, I always wonder why he only talks with me about my national origin. (At work, February 2016)

11.2.4.1 The Love for Germany and a German Girlfriend

The collegial relationship between X and Y started with the statement that X loved Germany and that he attempted to find a German girlfriend. He restated this several times during the first year of the work relationship, which left Y questioning why he would say something like that and feeling irritated and confused about it. These feelings were completely contrary to her thoughts, her rationalisations and her intellectualisations of the situation (Cilliers 2005; Cilliers and May 2010). Y rationalised that she should see this statement as a friendly act of connecting with her, of an expression of appreciation of her origin, as an act of small talk and an attempt to create contact. She thereby intellectualised the situation and the statement.

Focusing on this communication from a systems psychodynamic perspective, the statement was a defence mechanism using splitting (Klein 1988; Cilliers and Smit 2006), in terms of nationality and gender. It created X as a South African citizen (internal) and Y as a German (external). This dynamic can be interpreted as an indication of uncertainty on how to approach her as a foreign national, as an outsider, in X's department, country and nation. It indicates that X did not integrate Y into his systems (national, organisational, self) but rather saw her as an external, as a representative of the European (White) culture within his system. In the case of seeing her as a White representative, his rejection might have been a projection of his anger connected to Whites having been the "perpetrators" as colonialists during apartheid, a projection which carries strong historical content.

In Y's understanding, X had reproduced the split regarding possibly historically motivated in-group/out-group experiences unconsciously, perhaps based on fear and anger from previous experiences, recreating exclusion (Cilliers and Smit 2006) through the defence mechanism of idealisation regarding national belonging and gender (Shemla et al. 2014), highlighting: "I always wanted a German girlfriend".

As a female professor, Y felt reduced by this gendered statement that associated her with a "girlfriend" rather than with a professional colleague. She felt as if she had not been taken seriously, interpreting this association as a denial of her professional identity as a woman. She was aware of being involved in a deep-rooted conflict which is reduced to nationhood, culture and gender and interpreted it as if the organisational and societal system could not yet deal with the diversity represented. The system seemed to use her instead for simplifications and idealisations, as defence mechanisms—according to systems psychodynamic concepts (Cilliers and Smit 2006)—to overcome anxiety, uncertainty and anger in establishing how to deal with "the intruder" and the "new diversity" in the internationalising and globalising workplace. This seemed to Y to be a mirroring of the macro level of society which, at this time, also dealt with the uncertainty of how to construct a respectful inner diversity in the country and how to best handle global and international influences, competition and cooperation.

Realising the complexity of this situation, Y felt X's anger and his irritation at being pressured to deal with intercultural and interracial diversity within the department. He therefore projected his feelings onto Y, wrapped into the idealisation of being German. Y felt that he could not contain his (and the system's) anger and anxieties within this interpersonal, intercultural communication.

At the same time, Y encountered a projective identification, believing that the feelings of irritation, confusion and uncertainty were her own feelings. She experienced herself, and her methods of building work relationships, as a failure. Based on this assumption, she increasingly felt guilty, ashamed and irritated. These feelings were strongly connected to the idea that her feelings were hers in the first place, while she was not able to comprehend why she would feel so strongly about her colleague's statements on German girlfriends. Y, therefore, went into a mode of avoidance and denial of the colleague (Stapley 1996), not actively seeking communication with this colleague but rather withdrawing unconsciously: "I never visited him in the office or made contact with him in departmental meetings. I just stayed away and went on with my work".

She believed that particularly the "German-ness" of her origin became an important image for X and that this was wrong; she felt like an "object based on nationhood, not like a professional colleague". In some of the conversations between X and Y, X associated "being German" with being "rich, technologically advanced, powerful and with ranging in the league of a global player". The German-ness therefore might have been unconsciously a symbolic figure (Cilliers 2017) for X, showing "advancement and a positive, higher status and a bright future".

X was also aware of Germany's past and war history which, Y believed, also made him associate German-ness with perpetuation and takeover. Therefore, X's projection onto Y of being an "intruder" in his department and society might have been unconsciously associated with the history of Germany and Whites in South Africa, according to Y's interpretation.

Through the idealisation and wishing for a German girlfriend, X showed, according to Y's interpretation, the idea of "including and integrating the perpetrator into his perspective, while striving to accept the White presence and reconcile with the history of white dominance in his country". Y even assumed that the wish for a German girlfriend included the wish for "increased power, dominance, supremacy and advancement within himself and in his work context".

As a German female who had grown up in post-World War II with numerous narrations of war, loss and trauma of the world wars, Y was very aware of topics regarding perpetuation, power, territory, authority and leadership, as well as connected feelings, such as anxiety, fear, shame, guilt and anger. Based on experiences of collective guilt in terms of her German origin, Y could not easily accept X's idealisation of Germany and his reductions of defining an ideal girlfriend based on nationality. Y was very critical of Germany and its past and felt very irritated by X's idealisation of her country of origin. She could not contain his idealisation owing to her own critical views on German nationality.

Further, she felt that X's statement about German girlfriends was "out of context", reducing the colleagues to gender roles and their relationship to gendered images. The conflict consequently began to assume the dimension of an identity-based conflict, including role confusion and reconstruction (Cilliers and Terblanche 2010). Y felt "disrespected in terms of the professional identity and reduced to gendered images, and as a potential German girlfriend". She believed that X's unconscious need to be in control of "his" department as a male South African lecturer was undermined by her presence "as a foreign professor". She imagined that "he feels inferior and even questions his own professional ability on a professional level, therefore denying my professional identity and reducing my role to my gender identity" which might have impacted on the loss of professional boundaries (Cilliers and Koortzen 2005; Cytrynbaum and Noumair 2004; Naik 2014).

Y only established a "clear boundary when I clarified my status of being married". This direct statement enabled X to realise that he had overstepped a professional boundary. Y narrates: "From this moment on he never talked about German girlfriends again". She was surprised that she had to set this clear boundary, that he had not consciously recognised it before and that she had to "provide him with private information to stop him intruding my boundaries". His overstepping of boundaries might, however, be a counterreaction of X experiencing Y (as representative of the collective of European/Whites) having overstepped his (African) boundaries constantly in historical and even contemporary perspective. This interaction therefore may have carried aspects of projection and projective introjection.

Although policies such as AA and BEE were in place, Y interpreted X's behaviour as if he had viewed her employment, "although untenured, as a threat and competition and unaligned with BEE, increasing his uncertainties about the future management regarding cultural diversity and AA within the institution". She felt that the societal South African conflict of the redefinition of interracial and intercultural relationships, with all its insecurities and anxieties, was transferred from the macro level of society into the organisational subsystem and the interpersonal system's level (see Rice 1951).

Besides this unconscious transfer of macro-level dynamics into the work context, X's question: "How is Germany?" over a period of 4 years made Y feel as if "a part of my South African life and identity was ignored and denied … denying my being in South Africa and my inclusion as a colleague into the department". Her personal, professional and South African identity was reduced to a German national identity. She felt that the complexity of her identity had been denied and simplified (Cilliers and Terblanche 2010).

She rationalised that this question about Germany was an act of "small talk" and that "he just wants to be nice and friendly". No matter which rationalisation she found for his behaviour, however, she did not feel comfortable with it. Y also felt "irritation since I felt excluded as a foreigner". She experienced their communication as a projected exclusion.

A split had not only occurred on the interpersonal and projected level but had also deepened on the intrapersonal level. Y started to experience "a split inside of me" (projective introjection), since she felt "more at home in South Africa than in Germany and I idealised my life in this country over the life I had left behind many years ago". This situation contributed for her to reflect on cultural and social idealisations and denial.

Further, she said she was not prepared to contain "X's anger of the past", and she highlighted that she was not willing to take on the role of a symbolic parent nor as a protective force within the system as Kaplan and Lipinsky-Kella (2015) and Shongwe (2014) previously highlighted. Y felt that she was experienced as an element that unconsciously increased X's feelings of anxiety, anger and uncertainty. The situation therefore became challenging and in the end manifested as an open conflict (Aram et al. 2015; Armstrong and Rustin 2015) which both X and Y seemed to experience as a failure.

A few months later, Y responded in an interview as follows:

> Today I met X at the car park when I arrived at work. I was quite surprised that he drives a German car. He asked me how Germany is (as usual) and when I will be returning to Germany—which was a new slant to our conversation! I told him that I'm planning to visit Germany, but I'm not sure when to leave for good since I enjoyed the work and the life here. He then asked if I had not watched the news and if I was not aware what was happening in the country? I asked him what he meant and he responded: "Did you not see that terrorism is now starting in South Africa?"
>
> I knew that he referred to the arrest of two brothers who had planned to bomb a shopping centre, but who had been caught by the intelligence during the planning process. It had been on the news last night."Oh", I said, a bit surprised about this statement which went far beyond our usual talk and I agree that this was unsettling.
>
> He looked at me and said: "And this all happens because of you and your country where you are coming from. You people from Europe—you brought terrorism here!"
>
> The statement and the aggression with which X stated his views left me in surprise, shock and confusion. I responded: "I'm not sure what you mean exactly, and I think it's a bit difficult to just refer to all European countries and connect my origin to this incident."
>
> He turned around and left the conversation.
>
> When I sat in my office, several arguments occurred to me why what he said was wrong, and why his behaviour was just inadequate. I wondered what had triggered this conversation. (At work, February 2016)

11.2.4.2 Terrorism

In response to media reports and the news, X seemed to be overwhelmed by anxiety regarding a new wave of crime, terrorism and external influence of power within South Africa. This was, according to Y, shown by "his reference to Europe and Germany as sources of terrorism in South Africa, linking this accusation to me personally when he said, 'you people from Europe'". X's growing levels of anxiety, powerlessness and paralysis, as explained by Sievers (2009), motivated new levels of defence mechanisms of generalisation and simplification, creating new layers of defence mechanisms (see Blackman 2004, and Stapley 1996, 2006). These new layers are analysed in the following paragraphs.

X first questioned Y's awareness of the political and social events happening in the country, showing his incredulity that she "was [still] in the country". Y interpreted this as an identity attack and as an expression of X's wish for her to leave, highlighting the new wave of insecurity, violence and terrorism as motivators. When Y responded by agreeing that the situation was "unsettling", thereby connecting to the thread of the conversation, aiming to show empathy, concern and solidarity, "I was directly attacked as a representative of Europeans who had brought terrorism into South Africa".

Y felt paralysed and confused, and reacted by rationalising this simplification, expressing her inability to comprehend his message, and used defence and denial as a defence mechanism. She was "overwhelmed by X's accusation and aggression" and by the entire responsibility which she felt obliged to contain for the past. Through rationalising the statement, identifying the problem of simplification and using intellectual analysis, Y used defence mechanisms to defend herself against containing the anger, violence and aggression she experienced from X. She responded by criticising his simplification and rejecting the direct responsibility for terrorism in South Africa. At the same time, she realised that she felt collective guilt, anxiety, collective responsibility and shame for "parts of the German history and for the impact and consequences of European settlement in Africa". However, she was very clear about the fact that she "refused to take on responsibility for Islamist terrorism in South Africa".

Y felt an intrapersonal split through X's projection of "collective guilt, shame and responsibility of Whites in general" which showed her own denial of her origin and the intra-psychological unwillingness to take collective responsibility of the actions taken in the past in her country of origin and in Europe. Apart from refusing to contain these collective responsibilities, Y rationalised and intellectualised the situation with her colleague at work. She rationalised that "colonialism, imperialism and apartheid have caused terrorist attacks in South Africa during the past, and anti-apartheid fighters have often been classified as 'terrorists' by the apartheid government". Therefore, Y believed that the terroristic attacks stood in a relationship with the contextual past rather than with European settlement.

Y interpreted X's accusation as: "X split the world repeatedly into Europeans or Germans as perpetrators, and South Africans as victims". This simplified, split worldview into "good and bad" caused irritation and denial in Y as well as in X, who denied the complexity of the situation owing to overwhelming feelings of anxiety, anger and irritation anchored in the past. The experienced denial perceived by Y on both sides led her into feelings of incapability and failure to build up a "normal work relationship with X".

During the past years, Y had increasingly witnessed a change in her colleagues' perceptions of Europe which "seemed to dissolve the idealised image of Europe as a 'haven for safety and security'". In X's accusation, this often idealised image of a "safe" Europe had also been deconstructed and changed into a "terrorist" Europe. This change from idealisation to devaluation was no longer holding a possibility of projection of safety and peacefulness, nor was the idealised image of the potential German girlfriend. The interpretation of Y was that the image of the ideal German girlfriend had changed into the projection and image of a supporter of terrorism. The defence mechanism of X splitting the world into "perpetrators and victims" might have helped him to deal with his collective and individual fear and anger within the context of changing global and local power dynamics.

The communication process of Y and X seems to be connected to anxiety and anger with regard to clashing African and Western perspectives within the specifically described context, referring to unresolved conflict (Janzen 2016). Different sociocultural and systems psychodynamic perspectives are reflected and are based on cultural intrapersonal, interpersonal and intercultural perceptions, interconnecting macro-, meso- and micro-level experiences within an interpersonal conflict situation.

11.3 Conclusions

The aim of this chapter was to provide insight into a culturally embedded conflict experienced in the South African context, interpreted and discussed from a systems psychodynamic perspective, using an ethnographic single-case study approach, analysing an interpersonal conflict at work between two colleagues of different genders, cultures of origin and backgrounds.

During the entire conflict process, splitting, denial and rationalisation as systems psychodynamic elements were present. While X mainly used splitting, denial and projections, Y found herself in denial, rationalisation and intellectualisation. Underlying feelings of anxiety, anger and uncertainty on macro-, meso- and micro levels fuelled both intrapersonal and interpersonal conflict and led to engagement with systems psychodynamic mechanisms within the intercultural communication and conflict process.

The conflict represents layers of societal macro-level changes in post-apartheid South Africa, changes in perceptions of South Africa and Germany/Europe on macro levels and the impact of globalising influences and increase in international diversity in the workplace. These processes are reflected in the micro-level communication and contain feelings, thoughts and behaviours on different system levels to redefine power relations and equalise inequalities across system layers.

As Mahadevan and Mayer (2017) contend, in-depth analysis of conflict at the micro level is needed, since it entails new, in-depth and emic worldviews and shifts in perceptions of culture, power and identity. Analysis of shifts at this level can lead to changes in context-specific perceptions and power relations at work, based on a more diverse, differentiated and contextual understanding of sociocultural realities and their implications for power. This interpretation strengthens the argument of Syed (2008), and Syed and Özbilgin (2009), that further in-depth research is necessary to explore diversity and cultural phenomena and provide new information on intersecting communication levels of individuals holding different cultural perspectives. This can lead to a conscious understanding and a shift in cultural power relations through empathetic and mindful communication, in which individuals are aware of the underlying sociocultural and psychological phenomena in systems.

The findings show that simplified concepts and categorisations of African and Western contexts, and the power relations ascribed to them in the past, are now being challenged locally and globally. New dimensions of intrapersonal and interpersonal communication levels are being negotiated and created. The conflict situation described in this chapter represents the interlinkages of intrapersonal and interpersonal conflict on various levels. The difficulty of resolving this conflict situation on a micro level leads to feelings of failure to build a functioning and harmonious intercultural work relationship between two colleagues of different origin.

This example of conflict shows that defence mechanisms are used when systems psychodynamics are overwhelming on different system levels and cannot be contained owing to the experience of overwhelming emotions such as anxiety, anger and uncertainty. High levels of anxiety and insecurity which are not contained or dealt with on a conscious, integrative level, and which are not taken on in terms of ownership and collective or individual responsibility, lead to splitting, projection, introjected projection, simplification, rationalisation and denial. The feelings appear to be disowned at different levels. They are not contained by governments (at the macro level) nor by departmental/organisational leadership (meso level) nor by individuals at the micro level. These feelings are consequently projected onto an element in the system, in this case Y, who seems—in the constellation of work relationships—to be a container for free-floating emotions in the context of diversity, change and power management. However, since the emotions could not be contained, the dynamics were experienced as personal failure on micro levels.

11.4 Recommendations for Future Research and Practice

Future research needs to explore conflict and the experience of failure in specific cultural contexts and across cultures from systems psychodynamic perspectives. The analysis of individual, intrapersonal and interpersonal levels of conflict can support a deeper understanding of conflict across system levels and thereby contribute to create awareness, mindfulness and a deeper comprehensibility of unconscious intercultural conflict dynamics within organisations. Based on a deeper understanding of the dynamics, defence mechanisms can be identified and consciously addressed on a practical level. Employees in organisations should become aware and mindful of the complex interactions and relationships of the systems psychodynamics which might lead to conflict and the experience of personal failure within individuals of diverse backgrounds in organisations.

References

Abrahhao, M.H.M.B. (2012). Autobiographical research: Memory, time and narratives in the first person. *European Journal for Research on the Education and Learning of Adults,* 3(1), 29–41.

Adams, T.E., Ellis, C., & Holman Jones, S. (2017). *Autoethnography. The Internaitonal Encyclopedia of Communication Research Methods.* London, UK: Wiley & Sons, Inc. http://onlinelibrary.wiley.com/doi/10.1002/9781118901731.iecrm0011/full.

Aram, E., Baxter, R., & Nutkevitch, A. (2015). *Begirate IV: Exploring the impact and relevance of group relations work within and beyond its network.* London: Karnac.

Armstrong, D., & Rustin, M. (2015). *Social defences against anxiety: explorations in a paradigm.* London: Karnac.

Beek, J., & Göpfert, M. (2012). Police violence in West Africa: Perpetrators' and ethnographers' dilemmas. *Ethnography,* 14(4), 477–500.

Bennett, M. (2017). *Culture.* Defined in an email communication on 30 April 2017.

Berry, J.W. (1989). Imposed etics-emics-derived etics: the operationalization of a compelling idea. *International Journal of Psychology,* 24(2), 721–35.

Bion, W.R. (1961). *Experiences in groups,* London, UK: Routledge.

Blackman, J.S. (2004). *101 Defences. How the mind shields itself.* New York, NJ: Brunner-Routledge

Campbell, D., & Huffington, C. (2008). *Organisations connected. A handbook of systemic consultation.* London: Karnac.

Cilliers, F. (2005). Executive coaching experiences. A systems psychodynamic perspective. *South African Journal of Industrial Psychology,* 31(3), 23–30.

Cilliers, F. (2012). A systems psychodynamic description of organisational bullying experiences. *South African Journal of Industrial Psychology,* 38(2). https://doi.org/10.4102/sajip.v38i2.994.

Cilliers, F. (2017) The systems psychodynamic role identity of academic research supervisors. South African Journal of Higher Education 31 (1), 29–49

Cilliers, F., & Koortzen, P. (2005). Working with conflict in teams – the CIBART model. *HR Future,* October, 51–52.

Cilliers, F., & May, M. (2010). The popularisation of Positive Psychology as a defence against behavioural complexity in research and organisations. *South African Journal of Industrial Psychology/SA Tydskrif vir Bedryfsielkunde,* 36(2). doi: https://doi.org/10.4102/sajip.v36i2.917.

Cilliers, F., & Smit, B. (2006). A systems psychodynamic interpretation of South African diversity dynamics: a comparative study. *South African Journal of Labour Relations,* 30(2), 5–18.

Cilliers, F., & Terblanche, L. (2010). The systems psychodynamic leadership coaching experiences of nursing managers. *Health SA Gesondheid,* 15(1). https://doi.org/10.4102/hsag.v15i1.457.

Cilliers, F., Greyvenstein, H., & Africa, S. (2012). The impact of silo mentality on team identity: An organisational case study, *SA Journal of Industrial Psychology,* 1–9. doi:https://doi.org/10.4102/sajip.v38i2.993.

Cytrynbaum, S., & Noumair, D.A. (2004). Group dynamics, organisational irrationality, and social complexity: Group relations reader 3. Jupiter, FL: A. K. Rice Institute.

Dilthey, W. (2002). The formation of the historical world in the human sciences. In R.A. Makkreel & F. Rodi (Eds.), Wilhelm Dilthey selected works (vol. 3). Princeton, NJ: Princeton University Press.

Doloriert, C. & Sambrook, S. (2012), "Organisational autoethnography", Journal of Organizational Ethnography, Vol. 1 Iss: 1 pp. 83–95.

Ellis, C. (2007). Telling secrets, revealing lives: Relational ethics in research with intimate others, *Qualitative Inquiry,* 13(3), 3–29.

Elo, M., Benjowski, C., & Nummela, N. (2015). Intercultural competences and interaction schemes – four forces regulating dyadic encounters in international business. *Industrial Marketing Management,* 48, 38–49.

Fraher, A.L. (2004). Systems psychodynamics: the formative years of an interdisciplinary field at the Tavistock Institute. *History of Psychology,* 7(1), 65–84. https://doi.org/10.1037/1093-4510.7.1.65.

Huffington, C., Armstrong, D., Halton, W., Hoyle, L., & Pooley, I. (2004). *Working below the surface: The emotional life of contemporary organizations.* London: Karnac.

Janzen, J.M. (2016). The anthropology of violence: context, consequences, conflict resolution, healing, and peace building in Central and Southern Africa. *Journal of Public Health Policy,* 37(1), 122–132.

Kaplan, O., & Lipinsky-Kella, K. (2015). Virtual Teams and Group Relations in the WEB 2.0 Era: Insights from an MBA Experiential Distance-learning Course, p. 21–33. In: Aram, E.,

Nutkevitch, A., and Baxter, R. (Eds.). Exploring the Impact and Relevance of Group Relations Work within and beyond its Network. London: Karnac Books.

Kets De Vries, M.F.R. (2007). *Coach and couch*. London: Palgrave.

Kinnear, L. (2014). *A critical analysis of the emerging models of power amongst South African women business leaders*. Unpublished doctoral thesis, University of KwaZulu-Natal, Durban, South Africa.

Klein, M. (1988). *Envy and gratitude and other works 1946–1963*. London: Hogarth.

Klein, M. (1997). *Envy and gratitude and other works 1946–1963*. London: Vintage.

Klein, L. (2005). *Working across the gap. The practice of social science in organisations*. London: Karnac.

Krantz, J. (2001). Dilemmas of organizational change. A systems psychodynamic perspective. In L. Gould, M. Stapley, M. Stein (Eds.), *The Systems Psychodynamics of Organizations: Integrating the Group Relations Approach, Psychoanalytic, and Open Systems Perspectives*. New York, NY: Karnac Books.

Lin, C. (2010). Studying Chinese culture and conflict: a research agenda. *International Journal of Conflict Management*, 21(1), 70–93. https://doi.org/10.1108/10444061011016632.

Lincoln, Y.S., & Guba, E.G. (1985). *Naturalistic Inquiry*. Newbury Park, CA: Sage Publications.

Mahadevan, J. & Mayer, C.-H. (2017). Muslim Minorities, Workplace Diversity and Reflexive HRM. London and New York: Routledge Taylor & Francis Group.

Mayer, C.-H. (2005). *Artificial Walls. South African Narratives on Conflict, Difference and Identity. An Exploratory Study in Post-Apartheid South Africa*. Stuttgart: Ibidem Verlag.

Mayer, C.-H. (2006). *Trainingshandbuch interkulturelle Mediation und Konfliktlösung*. Münster: Waxmann.

Mayer, C.-H. (2008). *Managing conflict across cultures, values and identities. A case study in the South African automotive industry*. Marburg, Germany: Tectum Verlag.

Mayer, C.-H., & Louw, L. (2012). Editorial. Managing cross-cultural conflicts in organizations. *International Journals of Cross Cultural Management*, 12(1), 3–8.

Mayer, C.-H., & May, M. (2018). Of being a container through role definitions: Voices from women leaders in organizational ethnography. *Journal of Organizational Ethnography*, 7(3), 373–387. doi: https://doi.org/10.1108/JOE-10-2017-0052.

Meyer, T.N.A., & Boninelli, I. (2007). *Conversations in leadership. South African perspectives*. Randburg, South Africa: Knowres.

Miller, E.J. (1993). *From dependency to autonomy: Studies in organization and change*. London: Free Association.

Motsoaledi, L., & Cillers, F. (2012). Executive coaching in diversity from the systems psychodynamic perspective. *South African Journal of Industrial Psychology/SA Tydskrif vir Bedryfsielkunde* 38(2). https://doi.org/10.4102/sajip.v38i2.988.

Myburg, H. (2009). *The experience of organisational development consultants working in the systems psychodynamic stance*. Doctoral dissertation, University of South Africa, Pretoria, South Africa. http://uir.unisa.ac.za/handle/10500/1473.

Nader, L., & Grande, E. (2002). Current illusions and delusions about conflict management – in Africa and elsewhere. *Law & Social Inquiry*, 27(3), 573–591.

Naik, B. (2014). *The systems psychodynamics underlying the work-family interface amongst managerial women in the public sector*. Doctoral dissertation, University of South Africa, Pretoria, South Africa.

Reed-Danahay, D. (2001). 'This is your home now!': conceptualizing location and dislocation in a dementia unit. Qualitative Research. https://doi.org/10.1177/146879410100100103.

Rice, A.K. (1951). The use of unrecognized cultural mechanisms in an expanding machine shop. *Human Relations*, 4, 143–160.

Richardson, L. (1990). Narrative and Sociology. *Journal of Contemporary Ethnography*, 19(1), 116 –135.

Schruijer, S.G.L., & Curseu, P.L. (2014). Looking at the gap between psychological and psychodynamic perspectives on group dynamics historically. *Journal of Organizational Change Management*, 27(2), 232–245.

Shemla, M. Meyer, B., Greer, L., Jehn, K.A. (2014), A review of perceived diversity in teams: Does how members perceive their team's composition affect team processes and outcomes? Journal of Organizational Behaviour, https://doi.org/10.1002/job.1957

Shongwe, M. (2014). *Systems psychodynamic experiences of professionals in acting positions in a South African organisation*. Doctoral dissertation, University of South Africa, Pretoria, South Africa. http://uir.unisa.ac.za/handle/10500/14616.

Sievers, B. (2009). *Psychoanalytic studies of organizations: Contributions from the International Society for the Psychoanalytic Study of Organizations*. London: Karnac.

Stapley, L.F. (1996). *The personality of the organisation. A psycho-dynamic explanation of culture and change*. London: Free Association.

Stapley, L. (2006). *Individuals, groups, and organizations beneath the surface: An introduction*. London: Karnac Books.

Steyn, M., & Cilliers, F. (2016). The systems psychodynamic experiences of organisational transformation amongst support staff. *SA Journal of Industrial Psychology/SA Tydskrif vir Bedryfsielkunde,* 42(1). https://doi.org/10.4102/sajip.v42i1.1367.

Syed, J. (2008) 'Employment prospects for skilled migrants: a relational perspective', Human Resource Management Review 18(1): 28–45.

Syed, J. and Özbilgin, M. (2009) 'A relational framework for international transfer of diversity management practices', International Journal of Human Resource Management 20(12): 2435–2453.

Terre Blanche, M., Durrheim, K., & Kelly, K. (2006). First steps in qualitative data analysis. In M. Terre Blanche, K. Durrheim, & D. Painter (Eds.), *Research in practice. Applied methods for the social sciences*. (pp. 321–344). Cape Town, South Africa: University of Cape Town Press.

Van Niekerk, A.M.M. (2013). *An ethnographic exploration of intrapersonal, interpersonal and intra-group conflict management interventions in an institution of higher education*. Doctorate of literature and philosophy. University of South Africa, Pretoria, South Africa. http://uir.unisa.ac.za/bitstream/handle/10500/9365/thesis_van%20niekerk_amm.pdf?sequence=1.

Van Tonder, V. (2012). *Group-as-a-whole as a context for studying individual behaviour : A group diagnostic intervention*, 38(2). https://doi.org/10.4102/sajip.v38i2.1011.

Vigh, H. (2008). Crisis and chronicity: anthropological perspectives on continuous conflict and decline. *Journal of Anthropology,* 73(1), 5–24.

Vikkelso, S. (2012). The fragility of a robust therapeutic technique: the case of BionÄs experience group. *Theory and Psychology,* 22, 213–233.

White, S. (2004). A psychodynamic perspective of workplace bullying: containment, boundaries and a futile search for recognition. *British Journal of Guidance & Counselling,* 32(3), 269–280.

Claude-Hélène Mayer (Dr. habil., PhD, PhD) is a Professor in Industrial and Organisational Psychology at the Department of Industrial Psychology and People Management at the University of Johannesburg, an Adjunct Professor at the European University Viadrina in Frankfurt (Oder), Germany, and a Senior Research Associate at Rhodes University, Grahamstown, South Africa. She holds a PhD in Psychology (University of Pretoria, South Africa), a PhD in Management (Rhodes University, South Africa), a Doctorate (Georg-August University, Germany) in Political Sciences (sociocultural anthropology and intercultural didactics) and a Habilitation (European University Viadrina, Germany) in Psychology with focus on work, organizational and cultural psychology. She has published several monographs, text collections, accredited journal articles and special issues on transcultural mental health and well-being, sense of coherence, shame, transcultural conflict management and mediation, women in leadership in culturally diverse work contexts, constellation work, coaching and psychobiography.

Chapter 12
Resilience to Emotional Distress in Response to Failure, Error or Mistakes: A Positive Psychology Review

Rudolf M. Oosthuizen

Abstract Perceptions of failure have been implicated in a range of psychological disorders, and even a single experience of failure can heighten anxiety and depression. However, not all individuals experience significant emotional distress following failure, indicating the presence of resilience (Johnson J, Wood AM, Cogn Ther Res, 2015). This chapter synthesised studies investigating resilience factors to emotional distress resulting from the experience of failure in organisational settings. For the definition of resilience, the Bi-Dimensional Framework for resilience research (Johnson J, Resilience: the bi-dimensional framework. In Wood AM, Johnson J (eds) Positive clinical psychology. Wiley, Chichester, 2016; Johnson J, Wood AM, Gooding P, Taylor PJ, Tarrier N et al, Clin Psychol Rev 31:563–591, 2011b; Johnson J, Jones C, Lin A, Wood S, Heinze K, Jackson C, Psychiatry Res 220:217–225, 2014) is used, which suggests that resilience factors are those which buffer the impact of risk factors, and outlines criteria a variable should meet in order to be considered as conferring resilience. This chapter introduces the impact of failure experiences and conceptualises resilience-based approaches (Bonanno GA, Am Psychol 59:20–28, 2004; Masten AS, Am Psychol 56:227–238, 2001; Masten AS, Powell JL, A resilience framework for research, policy, and practice. In: Luthar SS (ed) Resilience and vulnerability: adaptation in the context of childhood adversities. Cambridge University, New York, pp 1–25, 2003). The Bi-Dimensional Framework of resilience research is deliberated. This chapter concludes by discussing the implications for psychological resilience-building interventions in response to failure, error or mistakes for individuals and teams in organisations.

Keywords Mistakes · Errors · Failure · Attributional style · Perfectionism · Resilience · Self-esteem · Stress

R. M. Oosthuizen (✉)
Department of Industrial and Organisational Psychology, School of Management Sciences, College of Economic and Management Sciences, Pretoria, South Africa
e-mail: oosthrm@unisa.ac.za

E. Vanderheiden, C.-H. Mayer (eds.), *Mistakes, Errors and Failures across Cultures*, https://doi.org/10.1007/978-3-030-35574-6_12

12.1 Introduction

Jean-Paul Sartre (2010) stated, "All men are afraid of failure. Who is not afraid is not normal; this has nothing to do with courage". Like Sartre, reflections on fear have been a common denominator of many other social thinkers. Indeed, fear is a universal component of human emotion, essential for the survival of the species; its absence would mean failure to react to potentially life-threatening situations. There are many phobogenic factors – causers of fear – in the contemporary workplace. Smart Technology, Artificial Intelligence, Robotics, Algorithms and constant transformations of management systems have increased the pressures to excel and achieve better productivity, intensifying the demands of professional life (Cunha 2006). In most cases, this situation is perceived by organisational researchers as something harmful, able to compromise the psychological and even physical integrity of employees, negatively influencing organisational functioning (Suarez 1993; Applebaum et al. 1998). However, some see a positive side to fear of failure, identifying it as a useful management tool when properly used. Dejours (1992), for example, observed that fear of failure may promote productivity and is often used by managers to do so (De Souza and Tomei 2016).

Given that failure and failure-related distress have been implicated in the development of a range of mental health disorders (Bulik et al. 1990; Johnson et al. 2008a, b; Reinherz et al. 1999), a fuller and more detailed understanding of resilience in relation to failure could have important implications for psychological interventions. This knowledge could be particularly important for employees and groups likely to experience significant failure events in their occupations, for example, health professionals, most of whom will be involved in patient safety failure and clinical errors during their career (Johnson et al. 2017; Sirriyeh et al. 2010).

12.2 Theoretical Background of the Impact of Failure Experiences in Organisations

This section conceptualises fear and fear in the workplace as theoretical underpinning of the impact of failure experiences. It also focuses on fear of failure and how to recover from failure, error or mistakes in organisations.

12.2.1 Fear

According to the Cambridge Dictionary (Cambridge University Press 2008), fear is defined as:

> An unpleasant emotion or thought that you have when you are frightened or worried by something dangerous, painful, or bad that is happening or might happen.

The definition indicates that "fear" is a feeling, an emotion. Emotions are complex phenomena and have been the subject of analysis by researchers in various fields of knowledge. Emotions have an individual nature because they involve an evaluation, by the individual, of a situation experienced (Frijda 2000). However, according to Seymor (1980), emotions can be considered a socially constructed syndrome, based on the individual's perceptions of a specific situation (De Souza and Tomei 2016).

To understand how individuals react to a specific emotion, like fear, it is necessary to focus on different fields such as psychology, social psychology and even physiology. Mira y López (1972) defines fear as a series of successive phenomena of paralysis or cessation of the vital course that occurs in living things, from the simplest organism to the most complex, when subjected to sudden or disproportionate situational changes. Mira y López (1972) cites three forms of fear, instinctive, rational and imaginary, and divides its evolution in human beings into four phases. *Instinctive fear* is the most primitive kind of fear, which is characterised by the lowering of the vital metabolism in face of a direct and immediate potentially harmful situation. It is a reactive fear, perceived a posteriori, "When it reaches the cortical centres, the wave of stimulus has already determined various reflexes and inhibitions at the medullar and sub-cortical levels" (De Souza and Tomei 2016).

Rational fear is a "prophylactic" fear. The reaction to threatening situations is conditioned by prior experiences and is rationally based. It is a fear that is comprehensible, even by those who do not feel it directly. Thus, the phobogenic pattern can be transmitted, as it is logical. The individual may not fear something initially, but when the individual becomes aware of the damage that can be caused by the object, subject or situation, the individual starts to feel afraid. Finally, *imaginary fear* is considered as the most torturous. The reason is that the harmful events that would be the starting point of this type of phobia never in fact constituted a cause of organic fear itself. The individual, through a fluid and precariously structured network of associations, becomes afraid, making imaginary fear unjustified and incomprehensible (De Souza and Tomei 2016).

According to Mira y López (1972), the feeling of fear in individuals evolved in four phases. From an evolutionary perspective, he states that fear has its origin as a simple cellular reaction to stimuli, which in its last phase turned into a creative process derived from random musings. In the *first phase*, environmental changes are the trigger to a progressive decrease of vital activities. These stimuli caused by fear can result in temporary or even permanent shutdowns, only seen in extremely simple organisms, without a structured nervous system. In the *second phase*, phobic impulses inhibit the prompt response of the higher nerve centre, leaving the employee static, suspended and distressed (De Souza and Tomei 2016).

The *third phase* is marked by a first reaction of the individual intending to escape the situation that is causing the fear. However, Mira y López (1972) affirms that it is also at this stage that the fear becomes associative, which is considered a "double-edged sword". By trying to escape from the situation of fear, the individual "suffers not only for the real and absolute event but also for the signs from now on associated to it". "At every scare, a hundred new fears are created", as a result of the new references, related to the phobic agents. The *fourth phase* is the one in which imaginary fear happens. Emerging from random and fantastic assumptions, relying on the imagination as an ally, the phobic impulses become diverse and somehow inconsistent. Mira y López (1972) draws attention to the paradox established in this evolutionary phase of fear. The more unrealistic and less attached to the reality a fear is, the harder it is to rationally fight against it (De Souza and Tomei 2016).

12.2.2 Fear in the Workplace

Some theoretical studies have examined fear in the organisational environment. A dialectic perspective is delineated by Koury (2002), according to whom fear, as a social construct, is one of the main structural pieces of the group experience. Fundamental for sociability processes and working as an instrument for order and disorder, fear plays a role as a social organiser in its everyday action. De Souza and Tomei (2016) state that individuals are faced with a social reality, feel fear about their adaptation and permanence, internalise the existing rules and perpetuate them.

Suarėz (1993) advocates the idea that when managed through constructive actions, fear can become a motivating agent. The possibility of transforming fear to something useful is only a matter of proper organisation. Regarding the expectations of employees, an efficient action would be to have clear and objective rules. Employees should be aware of their rights, duties and roles in the organisation. Concerning communication, it is important to establish mechanisms for constant feedback, ensuring that employees correctly understand the information received. However, the negative effects of fear and the fact that its extinction in the workplace is impossible should be acknowledged. For Kohn (1986), fear is a stimulator of competition that generates anxiety among those who experience it. It is harmful in companies, not only individually but socially as well, because it undermines the relations of trust and unleashes a series of inappropriate behaviours (De Souza and Tomei 2016).

By losing pleasure in their professional activity, employees become limited: they are content to remain in a comfort zone and avoid errors, instead of striving for the best performance possible. In the organisational context, the majority of fears are associated with a hierarchical position, authority, power and social and individual psychological factors. Applebaum et al. (1998) analysed the use of positive reinforcement and punishment. The more fear a punishment generates, the more efficient it will be, due to the influence on the resulting behavioural patterns. Fear is a reason for individuals to avoid certain behaviour (De Souza and Tomei 2016).

12.2.3 Fear of Failure

The first academic articles related to the fear of failure construct were behavioural theories such as those by Murray (1938). Listing 20 basic human needs, the item "infavoidance" was included, a term coined by him to define individuals' need to avoid humiliation by concealing failings. According to Lewis (1992), the effects of feelings of shame are extremely painful to people, incisively impairing their perception of themselves. The sensation of negative exposure among peers causes feelings of disparagement, belittlement and imminent abandonment (Andrews 1995; De Souza and Tomei 2016).

The unidimensional perspective of the fear of failure is demonstrated by the academic production on the feeling of shame resulting from a frustrated attempt to do something (Elliot and Thrash 2004). However, some studies take a multidimensional approach of the fear of failure. Birney et al. (1969) started from the premise that individuals perceive consequences of failure negatively. Therefore, a model was proposed that decomposes fear of failure into three dimensions: decreased self-estimates of ability, non-ego punishments and social devaluation. David Conroy (2002), based on the work of Birney et al. (1969) and with the intention of postulating an instrument to measure the fear of failure, hierarchically disaggregated the concept into five dimensions as indicated in Table 12.1.

Fear of failure, in general, is related to the negative physical and mental consequences of failure. However, it is worthwhile enumerating other "symptoms" of the fear of failure (Conroy 2002), already observed scientifically. According to Elliot and Church (2003), the fear of failure causes the appearance of a defensive/pessimistic stance and limits individuals' abilities. High levels of anxiety (Elliot and McGregor 1999), diffuse attention and discomfort, a tendency to avoid challenges and stress when relating to other people (Conroy et al. 2009) are some other indicators of the occurrence of this emotion (De Souza and Tomei 2016). Failure is one of life's most common traumas, yet people's responses to it vary widely. Some bounce back after a brief period of malaise; others descend into depression and a paralysing fear of the future (Seligman 2011).

Table 12.1 Five dimensions of fear of failure (Conroy 2002)

Dimension	Description
Shame and embarrassment	The individual feels ashamed and embarrassed after the failure.
Devaluing self-esteem	The individual's self-esteem is diminished as a consequence of the failure.
Uncertainty about the future	The future becomes more uncertain after the failure.
Loss of interest by important others	People who are important to the individual lose interest in him or her because of the failure.
Upsetting important others	People who are important to the individual suffer negative consequences of the failure and become upset.

A large body of research (McCarty et al. 2008; Reinherz et al. 1999) suggests that experiencing failure has marked emotional and psychological consequences across a range of individuals and settings. Longitudinal studies indicate that academic failure in adolescents increases risk for clinical depression in adulthood, and in those who are depressed, perceived failure has been associated with suicide attempts (Bulik et al. 1990). Even a single experience of failure in nonclinical groups can have significant emotional sequelae. In healthcare professionals, involvement in medical errors or patient safety failures is reported to result in feelings of shame, depression and anxiety, which can then increase the risk of further errors (Johnson et al. 2017; Sirriyeh et al. 2010; West et al. 2009).

However, not all individuals experience significant emotional distress in response to failure, and several psychological models highlight the role of psychological responses to failure in the development of failure-related distress and emotional disorder. For example, cognitive models of suicide have emphasised the role of situation appraisals, suggesting that suicidal thoughts occur when individuals appraise their circumstances in terms of failure (termed "defeat") and entrapment (Johnson et al. 2008a; Williams 1997). Yet such models have been criticised for their acceptance of an overly negative, disorder-based approach to understanding mental health (Johnson and Wood 2015). By focusing on the development of mental health problems rather than mental wellbeing, it has been suggested that such approaches fail to identify and capitalise on natural coping mechanisms (Johnson and Wood 2015). As such, they may be missing potential points for psychological interventions to target and develop (Johnson et al. 2017).

12.2.4 How to Recover from Failure, Error or Mistakes

The following example illustrates how to recover from failure, error or mistakes by means of resilience. Douglas and Walter, two University of Pennsylvania MBA graduates, were laid off by their Wall Street companies 18 months ago. Both went into a tailspin: they were sad, listless, indecisive and anxious about the future. For Douglas, the mood was transient. After 2 weeks he told himself, "It is not you; it is the economy going through a bad patch. I am good at what I do, and there will be a market for my skills". He updated his résumé and sent it to a dozen New York firms, all of which rejected him. He then tried six companies in his Ohio hometown and eventually landed a position. Walter, by contrast, spiralled into hopelessness: "I got fired because I cannot perform under pressure", he thought. "I am not cut out for finance. The economy will take years to recover". Even as the market improved, he did not look for another job; he ended up moving back in with his parents. Douglas and Walter (actually composites based on interviewees) stand at opposite ends of the continuum of reactions to failure. The Douglases of the world bounce back after a brief period of malaise; within a year they have grown because of the experience (Seligman 2011).

The Walters go from sadness to depression to a paralysing fear of the future. Yet failure is a nearly inevitable part of work; and along with dashed romance, it is one of life's most common traumas. People like Walter are almost certain to find their careers stymied, and companies full of such employees are doomed in hard times. It is people like Douglas who rise to the top and whom organisations must recruit and retain in order to succeed. But how can you tell who is a Walter and who is a Douglas? And can Walters become Douglases? Can resilience be measured and taught? Seligman (2011) worked with colleagues from around the world to develop a programme for teaching resilience (Seligman 2011).

It was tested in an organisation of 1.1 million people where trauma is more common and more severe than in any corporate setting: the US Army. Its members may struggle with depression and post-traumatic stress disorder (PTSD), but thousands of them also experience post-traumatic growth. Their goal is to employ resilience training to reduce the number of those who struggle and increase the number of those who grow. Seligman (2011) believe that business people can draw lessons from this approach of resilience, particularly in times of failure and stagnation. Working with both individual employees and managers, it is possible to create "Douglases" who can turn their most difficult experiences into catalysts for improved performance (Seligman 2011). Bardoel et al. (2014) propose that one of the theoretical approaches to resilience applied in the workplace is based on positive psychology and positive organisational behaviour. Positive psychology is conceptualised in the following section.

12.3 Positive Psychology

Organisational and management literatures (Peterson and Seligman 2003) have begun to consider the potential benefits of incorporating positive psychological principles to enhance the corporate experience. Although organisations are stereotypically concerned with maximising the financial bottom line, the best companies also seek to enhance employees' experiences of work. Unfortunately such positive organisational practices were put aside in favour of techniques that focused directly on the bottom line, often neglecting the worker. With the re-emergence of positive psychology, such a focus on the employee experience has come to the forefront. Wang (2011) recognises the business world's increasing attention to positivity in the workplace, for example, the US Army, which recently adopted a technique for increasing soldiers' resilience (Cornum et al. 2011; Mills et al. 2013).

Some research (Steele et al. 2012) has begun to highlight the importance of employee strengths and positive states on a broader level as they relate to individual- and organisational-level outcomes. Theoretical support (Fredrickson 2001) suggests that positive emotions expand thought processes (e.g. creativity and brainstorming), thereby building resources, and that the process is cyclical such that exercising some aspects of positive psychology in the workplace in turn enhances the frequency with which one is likely to experience other positive psychology facets also. This is in line with the emotional contagion perspective (Hatfield et al. 1994), which suggests that something as simple as managers displaying positive emotions is likely to promote positivity not only in themselves but also among their subordinates (Johnson 2009). The same applies to teams, whereby one positive experience between two team members can multiply such that other team members soon share similar positive experiences (Walter and Bruch 2008). The various constructs and domains within the workplace function interrelatedly, thereby enhancing the potential power of each construct (Mills et al. 2013). Thus, in positive psychology, resilience is described as a response where an individual adapts positively to exposure to a subjectively significant threat, risk or difficulty, without losing the ability to function normally (Bardoel et al. 2014; Bonanno 2004; Meintjes and Hofmeyr 2018). Resilience is explained in detail in the next section.

12.4 Resilience

In recent years, researchers (Bakker and Demerouti 2007) have focused on resilience – a psychological resource capacity, generally defined as the capability of an individual to withstand hardship and, while facing adversity, continue to lead a functional and healthy life (Turner 2001). Luthans (2002) defines resilience as the positive psychological capacity to rebound, "to bounce back" from adversity, uncertainty, conflict, failure or even positive change, progress and increased responsibility. Brooks and Goldstein (2004) assert that a resilient perspective is helpful in every aspect of ordinary living as it provides the strength to undertake routine challenges and sudden problems. Crisis or adversity for an employee can be any problem at a personal level related to work or family. It may be a non-congenial environment or an unsupportive manager. Similarly, a female worker may face problems such as sexual harassment, glass ceiling and lack of family support (Moran 1994), which she might be unable to express. These seemingly small but significant problems not only affect the efficiency of the worker but also change the attitude of the employee towards the company (Paul et al. 2016).

Resilience is being explored in the context of the working population as it relates to how employees deal with the challenges of the business world (Badran and Kafafy 2008; Caverley 2005). However, in an organisational context, it still remains an emerging concept (Luthans and Youssef 2004). Also, the majority of the research on resilience has been conducted with a younger and treatment-seeking population (Campbell-Sills et al. 2006). The application of positive psychology at the workplace as positive organisational behaviour (POB) (Youssef and Luthans 2007) has encouraged studies on resilience in an organisational context (Paul et al. 2016).

12.4.1 Conceptualisation of Resilience

There are several definitions for the term "resilience", which widen the scope of its meaning. A large number of studies have also considered different facets of resilience (personal resilience, trait resilience, psychological resilience, emotional resilience, career resilience and ego resilience) in individual and organisational contexts (Block and Block 1980; Block and Kremen 1996; Bolton 2004; Dulewicz et al. 2003; King 1997; Waugh et al. 2008). In general, authors agree that resilience is a capacity that reflects in behaviour, deals with change and relates to overcoming some unwanted situation (Paul and Garg 2012; Paul et al. 2016). Furthermore, resilience is defined as the capability to bounce back from adversity and failure – and even eustressful events such as new responsibilities (Luthans 2002); resilience is an important adaptive capacity. Yet, resilience goes beyond simply recovering from adversity, including the capacity to improve past one's previous state by harnessing the positive power of the setback by recognising and internalising lessons learned (Luthans et al. 2006). When individuals learn from failure, they develop skill repertoires enabling them to more effectively deal with future adversities – a crucial skill in employees, particularly during turbulent economic times, during which organisations often experience unforeseen hindrances preventing expected progress.

Resilience has been linked to various outcomes vital to organisational success, including effective leadership (Harland et al. 2005), successful coping with stress (Zunz 1998) and flourishing under hardship (Ryff and Singer 2003). Caza and Milton (2012) emphasised the importance of social support in enhancing resilience at the employee level, although resilience is best enhanced by cultivating it at three distinct levels: individual, group and organisational. The possibility also exist of enhancing organisational-level resilience by hiring for resilience in the selection process, but doing so would be an "impoverished viewpoint" that fails to consider the developmental possibilities of resilience interventions (Mills et al. 2013).

Additional strategies proposed to enhance resilience include those identified by Masten and Reed (2002), who proposed a three-pronged intervention utilising asset-focused tactics (e.g. modifying job characteristics, knowledge- and skill-based training and establishing mentoring relationships that allow for assistance when the need arises) and risk-focused tactics (e.g. mitigating challenging situations by eliminating performance detractors), as well as a focus on processes such as self-awareness and self-regulation to develop coping mechanisms. Of particular importance is approach-based coping (vs. avoidance-based coping), wherein the individual deals with a problem immediately and directly. Similar to the asset- and risk-focused aspects of resilience, this process aspect can be developed on an individual level as well as on a broader, organisational level, such as via strategic planning initiatives (Luthans and Youssef 2004). Sutcliffe and Vogus (2003) identified strategies to enhance resilience at the individual, group and organisational levels.

All were couched in enhancing employee competence and efficacy by increasing access to and effective use of resources (both tangible and intangible [e.g. social]), fostering a learning orientation aimed at continual training and flexible growth. Employee experiences are also structured to allow them to make autonomous decisions that are likely to lead to successes and/or successful recovery from mistakes. In essence, providing employees with personal as well as external resources with which to be flexible and adaptable, and therefore the skills to successfully improvise in the face of uncertainty, may serve to foster employee resilience (Sutcliffe and Vogus 2003). Meyer (1982) found that employee resilience was positively associated with efficacy and negatively associated with organisational rigidity that inherently stifled learning. Orzech et al. (2009) further found that fostering mindfulness can enhance resilience, a link likely to apply at the employee level given that mindfulness enhances the ability to identify and thoughtfully attend to potential threats (Mills et al. 2013).

Wagnild and Young (2009) named five essential characteristics that constituted resilience: (1) meaningfulness of life or the realisation that life has a purpose and the recognition that there is something for which to live; (2) perseverance or the act of persistence despite adversity or discouragement; (3) self-reliance or belief in oneself with a clear understanding of own capabilities and limitations; (4) equanimity or balanced perspective of life and experiences which might be viewed as sitting loose and taking what comes, thus moderating extreme responses to adversity; and (5) existential aloneness or the realisation that each person is unique and that while some experiences can be shared, others must be faced alone. Zautra et al. (2010) asserted that the personal characteristics which led to healthy outcomes after a stressful situation determined the resilience processes (Paul et al. 2016).

Recent applications of resilience in occupational literature focus on occupations associated with a high risk for experiencing acute stress and trauma, such as police officers and fire fighters (Freedman 2004; Peres et al. 2011; Vanhove et al. 2015). However, Vanhove et al. (2015) propose that resilience may also be of significance in an employment context where stress can accumulate over time because of influences such as work overload, work relationships, lack of resources and support, emotional and physical exhaustion and work-life conflict. Johnson et al. (2005) identify teachers, ambulance workers, customer and social service workers, call centre staff and prison officers as examples of jobs where the above-mentioned influences and accumulated stress can have a negative effect on employee wellbeing and organisational functioning (Vanhove et al. 2015). Although no reference is made to sales employees, the nature of sales positions suggests that the sales environment can also be viewed as an employment context where resilience is of significance. Krush et al. (2013) support this view with the observation that resilience enables positive responses towards adversity while simultaneously inhibiting negative responses. Resilience in the workplace is also defined as the "positive psychological capacity to 'bounce back' from adversity, uncertainty, conflict, failure, or even positive change, progress and increased responsibility" (Kotzé and Nel 2013; Luthans 2002). Thus, a key component of resilience is whether an individual demonstrates simultaneous growth and positive change following a stressful event. Although some definitions refer to positive change, most simply require successful adaptation to adversity (Bande et al. 2015; Meintjes and Hofmeyr 2018).

12.4.2 Resilience-Based Approaches

Resilience-based approaches have the potential to highlight skills and tendencies that individuals can develop to maintain psychological health, leading to a more positively oriented approach to wellbeing. However, this body of literature has suffered from two main limitations (Johnson et al. 2017).

First, there has been a lack of clarity concerning the criteria for identifying a "resilient" outcome. The common definition of resilience as factors which reduce negative outcomes in the face of adversity would suggest that resilience variables are those which moderate or attenuate the association between risk factors and negative outcomes. In contrast, many studies of resilience have used a correlational approach. These studies have assumed that resilience variables are those which are "positive" and have investigated whether high levels of a proposed resilience variable (e.g. high perceived social support) are directly associated with lower levels of a negative outcome (e.g. suicidal thoughts). However (Johnson and Wood 2015; Johnson et al. 2011b), every negative variable exists on a continuum with its positive inverse. Returning to the above example, using this approach, it could just as easily be suggested that low perceived social support is a risk factor for suicidal thoughts (Johnson et al. 2017).

Second, a common approach is to propose a concept of resilience, to develop a questionnaire to measure it and to investigate the association of this variable in relation to various outcome variables in different populations. This approach does not enable the proposed resilience variable itself to evolve in order to accommodate new research findings. Indeed key questions regarding the nature of resilience remain, which may be linked to the limitations of this approach. These questions are whether factors which confer resilience vary depending on the outcome under consideration (e.g. whether resilience to general mental wellbeing is similar to resilience to negative behavioural outcomes such as suicidality) and whether factors which confer resilience vary according to the risk factor/adversity individuals are facing (Johnson et al. 2017).

12.5 The Bi-dimensional Framework (BDF) for Resilience Research

The Bi-Dimensional Framework (BDF) for investigating resilience (Johnson 2016; Johnson et al. 2011b, 2014) addresses these criticisms of the field of resilience research and enables the development of evidence-based concepts of resilience. The BDF outlines clear criteria that a variable should meet in order to be considered as conferring resilience. In line with definitions of resilience, it indicates that resilience factors are those which interact with (or statistically moderate) the likelihood that risk will lead to negative outcomes. Individuals who are low on resilience will show increasing evidence of negative outcomes with increasing risk, but high resilience individuals will maintain low levels of a given negative outcome, despite risk exposure (see Fig. 12.1) (Johnson et al. 2017).

As such, it purports that any investigation of resilience should include three variables, (1) the risk factor, (2) the resilience factor and (3) the outcome variable, and studies directly investigating associations between a predictor variable and an outcome are insufficient to establish a resilience effect. In line with the observations that all variables lie on a continuum from positive to negative, the BDF indicates that all factors can be viewed as "bipolar" and whether they are framed in positive or negative terms is essentially arbitrary (see Fig. 12.2). As such, unlike previous resilience approaches, the emphasis of the BDF is not upon identifying "positive" factors which are inversely linked with negative outcomes but upon identifying psychological factors which can alter the impact of risk (Johnson et al. 2017).

A particular strength of the framework is that it offers a way to aggregate and review existing studies based on (1) a particular outcome of interest (e.g. emotional/behavioural outcome), (2) whether a risk factor has been included and (3) whether a psychological factor has been examined as a moderator of a risk factor. Although

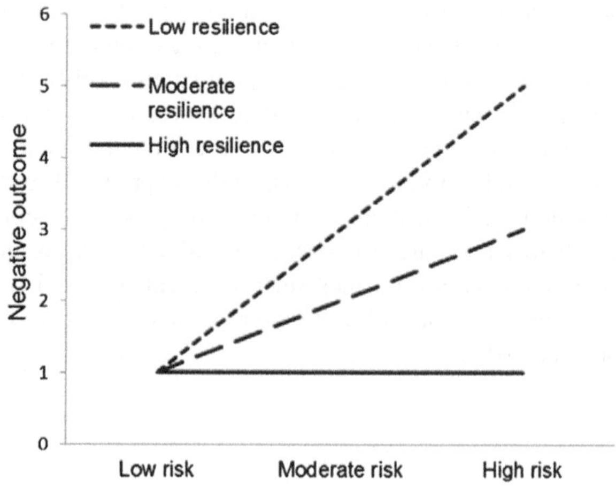

Fig. 12.1 Hypothetical resilience interaction (Johnson et al. 2017)

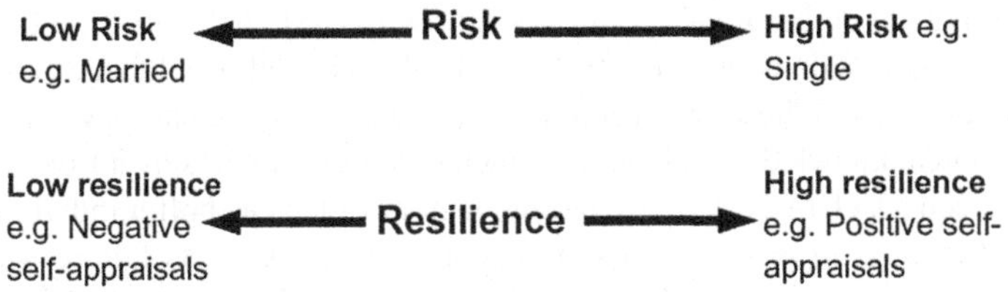

Fig. 12.2 Risk and resilience as separate bipolar dimensions (Johnson et al. 2017)

there have been very few studies which have explicitly aimed to investigate resilience to failure, by using the framework, it is possible to define failure experiences as the risk variable of interest, measures of emotional distress as the outcome variable and psychological factors as the potential resilience variable and to use these terms to search the literature. This approach offers a systematic route to identifying factors which confer resilience to emotional distress/dysfunction in response failure. Given the centrality of emotional distress to most mental health disorders, results from this review could have broad relevance to psychological interventions (Johnson et al. 2017).

12.6 Implications for Psychological Resilience-Building Interventions in Response to Failure, Error or Mistakes

The concept of building resilience has been an implicit aspect of psychological interventions. Resilience-building interventions on individual, group and organisational level will be described in the following sections.

12.6.1 Resilience-Building Interventions on Individual Level

12.6.1.1 Cognitive Behaviour Therapy

On the individual level, cognitive behaviour therapy (CBT) aims to help clients develop skills and techniques for managing low mood and stress which they can put into practice in daily life when the need arises (Beck 1976; Tarrier and Johnson 2015). Although the focus of the therapy may be on alleviating the client's current distress, an underlying assumption has been that these skills will be a source of resilience for the client after therapy has ceased. Recent years have seen a growing focus on this element of interventions, with therapeutic approaches being developed or refined specifically to prevent subsequent relapses (Williams et al. 2014). There has also been increasing interest in resilience-focused interventions in populations which are not currently experiencing psychological disorder, but may be at heightened risk (Johnson et al. 2017).

These include children and young adults (Dray et al. 2014; Lynch et al. 2004), military families (Saltzman et al. 2011) and healthcare staff (Goldhagen et al. 2015; Mealer et al. 2014). These interventions have been designed and developed on the basis of clinical knowledge and factors which predict symptoms over time. However, there has been a lack of evidence regarding factors which can buffer individuals from emotional distress in response to subsequent stressors, such as failure, which is a strong and consistent trigger of emotional distress (Bulik et al. 1990; Johnson et al. 2011a; McCarty et al. 2008; Reinherz et al. 1999). By identifying factors that these psychological interventions can target in order to reduce risk of emotional distress in response to subsequent failure experiences, results from the review provide an evidence base for these interventions to draw on. These results are supported by the experimental and longitudinal design of most of the studies, which provide evidence that the proposed resilience variables may have a causational impact on subsequent mood. In particular, resilience-building interventions should aim to increase levels of self-esteem, develop a more positive attributional style and reduce levels of perfectionism (particularly socially prescribed perfectionism) (Johnson et al. 2017).

12.6.1.2 Master Resilience Training (MRT)

Master Resilience Training (MRT) can be seen as management training for teaching individuals how to embrace resilience and then pass on the knowledge. The content of MRT is divided into three parts – building mental toughness, building signature strengths and building strong relationships. Individuals receive training in the three parts in plenary lectures and breakout sessions that include role playing, work sheets and small group discussion (Seligman 2011).

12.6.1.2.1 Building Mental Toughness

This segment of MRT starts with Albert Ellis's ABCD model: C (emotional consequences) stem not directly from A (adversity) but from B (one's beliefs about adversity). The individual works through a series of A's (e.g. falling out of a 3-mile run) and learns to separate B's, heat-of-the-moment thoughts about the situation ("I'm a failure"), from C's, the emotions generated by those thoughts (such as feeling down for the rest of the day and thus performing poorly in the next training exercise). They then learn D, how to quickly and effectively dispel unrealistic beliefs about adversity. The next focus will be thinking traps, such as overgeneralising or judging a person's worth or ability on the basis of a single action (Seligman 2011).

"Icebergs" are also discussed, which are deeply held beliefs such as "Asking for help is a sign of weakness", and individuals are taught a technique for identifying and eliminating those that cause out-of-kilter emotional reactions: Does the iceberg remain meaningful? Is it accurate in the given situation? Is it overly rigid? Is it useful? Finally, individuals are trained how to minimise catastrophic thinking by considering worst-case, best-case and most likely outcomes. For example, an individual receives a negative performance evaluation from his supervisor. He thinks, "I won't be recommended for promotion, and I don't have what it takes to stay in the organisation". That's the worst case. Now, let's put it in perspective. What's the best case? "The negative report was a mistake". And what's the most likely case? "I will receive a corrective action plan from my counsellor, and I will follow it. I'll be frustrated, and my supervisor will be disappointed" (Seligman 2011).

12.6.1.2.2 Building Signature Strengths

The second part of the training begins with Peterson's Values in Action signature strengths survey, which is taken online and produces a ranked list of the test taker's top 24 character strengths. Small groups discuss the following questions: What did you learn about yourself from the survey? Which strengths have you developed through your career? How do your strengths contribute to you reaching your goals? What are the shadow sides of your strengths, and how can you minimise them? The individuals are divided into teams and told to solve a problem using the team members' character strength profiles. Finally, the individuals write their own "strengths in challenges" stories (Seligman 2011).

12.6.1.2.3 Building Strong Relationships

The third part of MRT focuses on practical tools for positive communication. Individuals who respond actively and constructively (as opposed to passively and destructively) to someone who is sharing a positive experience, love and friendship increase. The individuals complete a work sheet about how they typically respond and identify factors that may get in the way of active and constructive responses (such as being tired or overly focused on themselves). Individuals are also trained in effective praise and assertive communication, distinguishing it from passive or aggressive communication. What are the language, voice tone, body language and pace of each of the three styles, and what messages do they convey? Enhancing mental toughness, highlighting and honing strengths and fostering strong relationships are core competencies for any successful individual.

Leadership development programmes often touch on these skills, but the MRT programme brings them together in systematic form to ensure that even in the face of terrible failures, individuals flourish rather than flounder. Managers can change the culture of their organisations to focus on the positive instead of the negative and, in doing so, turn pessimistic, helpless Walters into optimistic, can-do Douglases (Seligman 2011).

12.6.2 Resilience-Building Interventions on Group Level

In addition to clinical groups, resilience-based interventions could have important implications for groups who may not currently suffer from mental health difficulties, but who are regularly confronted with failure as part of their training or work. One such group are healthcare professionals, who may undertake ongoing training and assessment alongside their practice and who may also be involved in medical errors (Sirriyeh et al. 2010). Research suggests that involvement in medical errors can cause significant emotional distress and that experiencing distress can then increase the risk of involvement in subsequent errors (Hall et al. 2016; Sirriyeh et al. 2010; West et al. 2009). In this group, resilience-based interventions could enable the development of psychological resources which may both reduce emotional distress in response to failure and errors and improve patient safety (Johnson et al. 2017).

12.6.3 Resilience-Building Interventions on Organisational Level

Persevering in the face of failures, error or mistakes is critical for organisations getting ahead. It has the power to take organisations farther than IQ, education or experience alone. It's applicable across all roles and all lines of business in every industry around the world. And yet, organisations do not spend nearly enough time developing resilience in their workforce. Resilience is a skill that needs to be learned and practised in organisations. Seligman (2011) studied resiliency to understand why some organisations rebound after a failure and why others fall into a state of learned helplessness. He and his team created the Penn Resiliency Program. They train businesses in resiliency and reduce the number of those who struggle in adversity and increase the number of organisations who grow (Philip 2017).

Corporate leaders must first help organisations build mental toughness. This requires recognising that employees' response to failure is based solely on their own beliefs about what it means to fail. If employees believe failure means not getting something right on the first try, they will stop trying. Being mentally tough means organisations know that this moment is temporary, and employees have the emotional sophistication to shake off negative thoughts and try again. Next, employees need to learn to recognise their unique strengths and how they make a positive contribution to the project or the organisation. This helps to give employees the confidence to innovate and push forward, even after temporary setbacks. The last step is about changing the way of communication in organisations and responding to employees. Responding in an active and constructive way versus a passive or dismissive way will contribute to employees becoming more resilient. For example, consider the manager that merely says, "Good work", in a performance review versus the manager that praises specific achievements, their value and a worker's personal growth. Employees of the second type of manager will rebound much quicker from a failure, error or mistakes because they have an active and engaged relationship and experience their value (Philip 2017).

Studies have shown that resilient organisations are "happier" and have a higher lifespan. In the workplace, resilient people experience less stress and are able to grow in their careers from what they have learned from their challenges or setbacks. They take less time off, are more productive and can adapt more quickly to change. The rapidly expanding global market is transforming the way we work and confronting organisations with an unprecedented pace of change. Change can be a force of good, pushing individuals to learn and develop and driving organisations to evolve and grow. It can also become overwhelming for employees and businesses, if they are ill prepared. Leaders need to focus on equipping their employees with the resilience and the mental agility to adapt and thrive in this ever-changing world. Organisations need to be "happy places", productive and successful and deliver incredible value to their customers and the people they work for. Their success is not guaranteed and their failures, errors and mistakes do not need to define their destiny. It is their optimism and resilience that will help organisations to respond positively to challenging situations and the opportunity to dream big and push forward. Leaders must contribute to creating resilient employees who can steer through change, pressure, uncertainty and ambiguity and have the coping strategies to manage stress, overcome setbacks and continue to innovate (Philip 2017).

12.7 Chapter Summary

This chapter focused on investigating resilience factors to emotional distress resulting from the experience of failure in organisational settings. In this chapter the parameters for the study of resilience in the workplace were set. The impact of failure experiences was described and resilience-based approaches conceptualised. The Bi-Dimensional Framework of resilience research was deliberated. This chapter concluded by discussing the implications for psychological resilience-building interventions in response to failure, error or mistakes for individuals, groups and organisations. As determinants of the demonstration of resilience in employees are uncovered, practitioners and researchers will have a better understanding of the most important attributes to select for and develop in order to maximise employees' capacity for resilience.

References

Andrews, B. (1995). Bodily shame as a mediator between abusive experiences and depression. *Journal of Abnormal Psychology, 104*(2), 277–285.

Applebaum, S.H., Bregman, M. & Moroz, P. (1998). Fear as a strategy: effects and impact within the organization. *Journal of European Industrial Training, Vol. 22*(3), 113–127.

Badran, M. A., & Kafafy, J. H. (2008). The effect of job redesign on job satisfaction, resilience, commitment and flexibility: The case of an Egyptian public sector bank. *International Journal of Business Research, 8*(3), 27–41.

Bakker, A. B., & Demerouti, E. (2007). The job demands-resources model: State of the art. *Journal of Managerial Psychology, 22*(3), 309–328.

Bande, B., Fernández-Ferrín, P., Varela, J. A., & Jaramillo, F. (2015). *Industrial marketing management emotions and salesperson propensity to leave: The effects of emotional intelligence and resilience*. Industrial Marketing Management, 44, 142–153. https://doi.org/10.1016/j.indmarman.2014.10.011.

Bardoel, E. A., Pettit, T. M., De Cieri, H., & McMillan, L. (2014). Employee resilience: An emerging challenge for HRM. *Asia Pacific Journal of Human Resources, 52*(3), 279–297. https://doi.org/10.1111/1744-7941.12033.

Beck, A. T. (1976). *Cognitive therapy and the emotional disorders*. Oxford, England: International Universities Press.

Birney, R.C., Burdick, H., & Teevan, R.C. (1969). *Fear of Failure*. Van Nostrand, New York, NY.

Block, J. H., & Block, J. (1980). *The role of ego-control and ego-resiliency in the origination of behavior*. In W. A. Collings (Ed.), The Minnesota symposia on child psychology (Vol. 13, pp. 39–101). Hillsdale, NJ: Erlbaum.

Block, J., & Kremen, A. M. (1996). IQ and ego-resiliency: Conceptual and empirical connections and separateness. *Journal of Personality and Social Psychology, 70*(2), 349–361.

Bolton, D. (2004). Change, coping and context in the resilient organisation. *Mt Eliza Business Review, 7*(1), 57–66.

Bonanno, G. A. (2004). Loss, trauma, and human resilience: Have We underestimated the human capacity to thrive after aversive events? *American Psychologist, 59*, 20–28.

Brooks, R., & Goldstein, S. (2004). *The power of resilience*. New York: McGraw-Hill.

Bulik, C. M., Carpenter, L. L., Kupfer, D. J., & Frank, E. (1990). Features associated with suicide attempts in recurrent major depression. *Journal of Affective Disorders, 18*, 29–37.

Cambridge University Press. (2008). *Cambridge online dictionary, Cambridge Dictionary online*. Retrieved at April 23, 2008, from the website temoa: Open Educational Resources (OER) Portal at http://temoa.tec.mx/node/324.

Campbell-Sills, L., Cohan, S. L., & Stein, M. B. (2006). Relationship of resilience to personality, coping, and psychiatric symptoms in young adults. *Behaviour research and therapy, 44*(4), 585–599.

Caverley, N. (2005). Civil service resilience and coping. International Journal of Public Sector Management, 18(5), 410–413.

Caza, B. B., & Milton, L. P. (2012). *Resilience at work: Building capability in the face of adversity*. In K. S. Cameron & G. M. Spreitzer (Eds.), The Oxford handbook of positive organizational scholarship (pp. 895–908). New York, NY: Oxford University Press.

Conroy, D.E. (2002). Multidimensional fear of failure measurement: the Performance Failure Appraisal Inventory. *Journal of Applied Sport Psychology, 14*(2), 76–90.

Conroy, D.E., Elliot, A.J., & Pincus, A.L. (2009). The expression of achievement motives in interpersonal problems. *Journal of Personality, 77*(2), 495–526.

Cornum, R., Matthews, M. D., & Seligman, M. E. (2011). Comprehensive soldier fitness: building resilience in a challenging institutional context. *American Psychologist, 66*(1), 4.

Cunha, E.G. (2006). *A Gestão do Medo como Instrumento de Coerção nas Organizações Públicas*. UFRGS, Porto Alegre, RS.

De Souza, D.O.S., & Tomei, P.A. (2016) Fear of failure in the workplace among Brazilian employees. *Academia Revista Latinoamericana de Administración, 29*(4), 407–418, https://doi.org/10.1108/ARLA-11-2015-0299.
Dejours, C. (1992). *A loucura do trabalho: estudo de psicopatologia do trabalho*. Cortez – Oboré, São Paulo.
Dray, J., Bowman, J., Freund, M., Campbell, E., Wolfenden, L., Hodder, R. K., & Wiggers, J. (2014). Improving adolescent mental health and resilience through a resilience based intervention in schools: Study protocol for a randomised controlled trial. *Trials, 15*, 1.
Dulewicz, V., Higgs, M. J., & Slaski, M. (2003). Emotional intelligence: Construct and concurrent validity. *Journal of Managerial Psychology, 18*(5), 405–420.
Elliot, A.J., & Church, M.A. (2003). A motivational analysis of defensive pessimism and self-handicapping. *Journal of Personality, 71*(3), 369–396.
Elliot, A. J., & McGregor, H. A. (1999). Test anxiety and the hierarchical model of approach and avoidance achievement motivation. Journal of Personality and social Psychology, 76(4), 628.
Elliot, A.J., & Thrash, T.M. (2004). The intergenerational transmission of fear of failure. *Personality and Social Psychology Bulletin, 30*(8), 957–971.
Fredrickson, B. L. (2001). The role of positive emotions in positive psychology: The broaden-and-build theory of positive emotions. *American Psychologist, 56*, 218–226.
Freedman, T. G. (2004). Voices of 9/11 first responders: Patterns of collective resilience. *Clinical Social Work Journal, 32*(4), 377–393. https://doi.org/10.1007/s10615-004-0538-z.
Frijda, N.H. (2000). *Psychologists point of view*. In Lewis, M. and Haviland-Jones, J. (Eds), Handbook of Emotions, Tue Guilford Press, New York, NY, 68–87.
Goldhagen, B. E., Kingsolver, K., Stinnett, S. S., & Rosdahl, J. A. (2015). Stress and burnout in residents: *Impact of mindfulness-based resilience training. Advances in Medical Education and Practice, 6*, 525.
Hall, L. H., Johnson, J., Watt, I., Tsipa, A., & O'Connor, D. B. (2016). Healthcare staff wellbeing, burnout, and patient safety: A systematic review. *PloS One, 11*, e0159015.
Harland, L., Harrison, W., Jones, J. R., & Reiter-Palmon, R. (2005). Leadership behaviors and subordinate resilience. *Journal of Leadership & Organizational Studies, 11*(2), 2–14.
Hatfield, E., Cacioppo, J. T., & Rapson, R. (1994). *Emotional contagion*. New York, NY: Cambridge University Press.
Johnson, S. (2009). Do you feel what I feel? Mood contagion and leadership outcomes. *Leadership Quarterly, 20*, 814–827.
Johnson, J. (2016). *Resilience: The bi-dimensional framework*. In A. M. Wood, & J. Johnson (Eds.), Positive clinical psychology. Chichester: Wiley.
Johnson, J., & Wood, A. M. (2015). Integrating positive and clinical psychology: Viewing human functioning as continua from positive to negative can benefit clinical assessment, interventions and understandings of resilience. *Cognitive Therapy and Research.*
Johnson, S., Cooper, C., Cartwright, S., Donald, I., Taylor, P., & Millet, C. (2005). The experience of work-related stress across occupations. *Journal of Managerial Psychology, 20*(2), 178–187. https://doi.org/10.1108/02683940510579803.
Johnson, J., Gooding, P., & Tarrier, N. (2008a). Suicide risk in schizophrenia: Explanatory models and clinical implications, the Schematic Appraisal Model of Suicide (SAMS). *Psychology and Psychotherapy: Theory, Research and Practice, 81*, 55–77.
Johnson, J., Tarrier, N., & Gooding, P. (2008b). An investigation of aspects of the cry of pain model of suicide risk: The role of defeat in impairing memory. *Behaviour Research and Therapy, 46*, 968–975.
Johnson, J., Gooding, P. A., Wood, A.M., Taylor, P. J., & Tarrier, N. (2011a). Trait reappraisal amplifies subjective defeat, sadness, and negative affect in response to failure versus success in nonclinical and psychosis populations. *Journal of Abnormal Psychology, 120*, 922–934.
Johnson, J., Wood, A. M., Gooding, P., Taylor, P. J., & Tarrier, N. (2011b). Resilience to suicidality: The buffering hypothesis. *Clinical Psychology Review, 31*, 563–591.

Johnson, J., Jones, C., Lin, A., Wood, S., Heinze, K., & Jackson, C. (2014). Shame amplifies the association between stressful life events and paranoia amongst young adults using mental health services: Implications for understanding risk and psychological resilience. *Psychiatry Research, 220*, 217–225

Johnson, J., Panagioti, M., Bass, J., Ramsey, L., & Harrison, R (2017). Resilience to emotional distress in response to failure, error or mistakes: A systematic review. *Clinical Psychology Review 52*, 19–42, https://doi.org/10.1016/j.cpr.2016.11.007.

King, A. S. (1997). The crescendo effect in career motivation. *Career Development International, 2*(6), 293–301.

Kohn, A. (1986). *No Contest: The Case against Competition*. Houghton Mifflin, Boston, MA.

Kotzé, M., & Nel, P. (2013). Psychometric properties of the adult resilience indicator. *SA Journal of Industrial Psychology, 39*(2), 1–11. https://doi.org/10.4102/sajip.v39i2.1132

Koury, M.G.P. (2002). Medo e sociabilidade. Revista de antropologia experimental, 1(2), 194–207.

Krush, M. T., Agnihotri, R. A. J., Trainor, K. J., & Krishnakumar, S. (2013). The salesperson's ability to bounce back: Examining the moderating role of resiliency on forms of intrarole job conflict and job attitudes, behaviors and performance. *Marketing Management Journal, 23*(1), 42–56.

Lewis, M. (1992). Shame: The Exposed Self. Free Press. New York, NY.

Luthans, F. (2002). The need for and meaning of positive organizational behavior. *Journal of Organizational Behavior, 23*, 695–706. https://doi.org/10.1002/job.165

Luthans, F., & Youssef, C. M. (2004). *Human, social, and now positive psychological capital management: Investing in people for competitive advantage*.

Luthans, F., Avey, J. B., Avolio, B. J., Norman, S. M., & Combs, G. M. (2006). Psychological capital development: toward a micro-intervention. Journal of Organizational Behavior: *The International Journal of Industrial, Occupational and Organizational Psychology and Behavior, 27*(3), 387–393.

Lynch, K. B., Geller, S. R., & Schmidt, M. G. (2004). Multi-year evaluation of the effectiveness of a resilience-based prevention program for young children. *Journal of Primary Prevention, 24*, 335–353.

Masten, A. S. (2001). Ordinary magic: Resilience processes in development. *American Psychologist, 56*, 227–238.

Masten, A. S., & Powell, J. L. (2003). *A resilience framework for research, policy, and practice*. In S. S. Luthar (Ed.), Resilience and vulnerability: Adaptation in the context of childhood adversities (pp. 1–25). New York, US: Cambridge University, US.

Masten, A. S., & Reed, M. J. (2002). *Resilience in development*. In C. Snyder & S. Lopez (Eds.), Handbook of positive psychology (pp. 74–88). New York, NY: Oxford University Press.

McCarty, C. A., Mason, W. A., Kosterman, R., Hawkins, J. D., Lengua, L. J., & McCauley, E. (2008). Adolescent school failure predicts later depression among girls. *Journal of Adolescent Health, 43*, 180–187.

Mealer, M., Conrad, D., Evans, J., Jooste, K., Solyntjes, J., Rothbaum, B., & Moss, M. (2014). Feasibility and acceptability of a resilience training program for intensive care unit nurses. *American Journal of Critical Care, 23*, e97–e105.

Meintjes, A., & Hofmeyr, K. (2018). The impact of resilience and perceived organisational support on employee engagement in a competitive sales environment. *SA Journal of Human Resource Management/SA Tydskrif vir Menslikehulpbronbestuur, 16*(0), a953. https://doi.org/10.4102/sajhrm.v16i0.953.

Meyer, A. D. (1982). Adapting to environmental jolts. *Administrative science quarterly*, 515–537.

Mills, M.J., Fleck, C.R., & Kozikowski, A. (2013) Positive psychology at work: A conceptual review, state-of-practice assessment, and a look ahead. *The Journal of Positive Psychology, 8*(2), 153–164, DOI: https://doi.org/10.1080/17439760.2013.776622.

Mira y López, E. (1972). *Quatro Gigantes da Alma*. José Olympio, Rio de Janeiro.

Moran, K. (1994). *Harassment in the workplace*. Physiotherapy, 80(4), 239–243.

Murray, H. (1938). *Explorations in Personality*. Oxford University Press, New York, NY.

Orzech, K. M., Shapiro, S. L., Brown, K., & McKay, M. (2009). Intensive mindfulness training-related changes in cognitive and emotional experience. *Journal of Positive Psychology, 4*, 212–222.

Paul, H., & Garg, P. (2012). Mutualistic perspective of individual resilience and organizational commitment: A path analysis model. *International Journal of Management and Behavioural Sciences, 1,* 107–119.

Paul, H., Bamel, U.K., & Garg, P. (2016). Employee Resilience and OCB: Mediating Effects of Organizational Commitment. *VIKALPA The Journal for Decision Makers 41*(4) 308–324, DOI: https://doi.org/10.1177/0256090916672765.

Peres, J. F. P., Foerster, B., Santana, L. G., Fereira, M. D., Nasello, A. G., Savoia, M., & Lederman, H. (2011). Police officers under attack: *Resilience implications of an fMRI study. Journal of Psychiatric Research, 45*(6), 727–734. https://doi.org/10.1016/j.jpsychires.2010.11.004.

Peterson, C., & Seligman, M. E. P. (2003). *Positive organizational studies: Thirteen lessons from positive psychology*. In K. S. Cameron, J. E. Dutton, & R. E. Quinn (Eds.), Positive organizational scholarship: Foundations of a new discipline (pp. 14–27). San Francisco, CA: Berrett-Koehler.

Philip, E. (2017). *Resilience: The Opportunity To Dream Big And Push Forward. Leaders need to teach workers resilience to navigate change*. HCM Sales, Marketing & Alliance Excellence Essentials: HR.com, Inc.

Reinherz, H. Z., Giaconia, R.M., Hauf, A.M. C., Wasserman, M. S., & Silverman, A. B. (1999). Major depression in the transition to adulthood: *Risks and impairments. Journal of Abnormal Psychology, 108*, 500.

Ryff, C. D., & Singer, B. (2003). Flourishing under fire: Resilience as a prototype of challenged thriving. *Flourishing: Positive psychology and the life well-lived,* 15–36.

Saltzman, W. R., Lester, P., Beardslee, W. R., Layne, C. M., Woodward, K., & Nash, W. P. (2011). Mechanisms of risk and resilience inmilitary families: Theoretical and empirical basis of a family-focused resilience enhancement program. *Clinical Child and Family Psychology Review, 14*, 213–230.

Sartre, J.P. (2010). Esboço para uma teoria das emoções. Coleção L & Pocket Plus, Porto Alegre.

Seligman, M.E.P. (2011). Failure Recover from It Building Resilience. *Harvard Business Review*, April, 100–106.

Seymor, E. (1980). Personality: Basic Issues and Current Research, Prentice-Hall. Englewood Cliffs, NJ.

Sirriyeh, R., Lawton, R., Gardner, P., & Armitage, G. (2010). Coping with medical error: A systematic review of papers to assess the effects of involvement in medical errors on healthcare professionals' psychological well-being. *Quality & Safety in Health Care, 19*, 1–8.

Steele, J. P., Rupayana, D., Mills, M. J., Smith, M. R., Wefald, A. J., & Downey, R. G. (2012). Relative importance and practical utility of positive worker states. *Journal of Psychology: Interdisciplinary and Applied, 146*, 617–650.

Suaréz, J.G. (1993). *Managing Fear in the Workplace*. (TQLO Publication No. 93-01), Office of the Under Secretary of the Navy, Total Quality Leadership Office, Washington, DC.

Sutcliffe, K. M., & Vogus, T. J. (2003). *Organizing for resilience*. In K. S. Cameron, J. E. Dutton, & R. E. Quinn (Eds.), Positive organizational scholarship: Foundations of a new discipline (pp. 94–110). San Francisco, CA: Berrett-Koehler.

Tarrier, N., & Johnson, J. (Eds.). (2015). *Case formulation in cognitive behaviour therapy: challenging and complex cases*. Hove: Routledge.

Turner, S. G. (2001). Resilience and social work practice: Three case studies. Families in Society: *The Journal of Contemporary Human Services, 82*(5), 441–448.

Vanhove, A. J., Herian, M. N., Perez, A. L. U., Harms, P. D., & Lester, P. B. (2015). Can resilience be developed at work? A meta-analytic review of resilience-building programme effectiveness. *Journal of Occupational and Organizational Psychology, 89*, 1–30. https://doi.org/10.1111/joop.12123.

Wagnild G., & Young, H. (2009). *The resilience scale user's guide for the US English version of the resilience scale and the 14-item resilience scale* (RS-14). Worden, MT: The Resilience Center.
Walter, F., & Bruch, H. (2008). The positive group affect spiral: A dynamic model of the emergence of positive affective similarity in work groups. *Journal of Organizational Behavior, 29*, 239–261.
Wang, S. (2011). Is happiness overrated? *The Wall Street Journal, 60*, D1–D6.
Waugh, C. E., Fredrickson B. L., & Taylor, S. F. (2008). Adapting to life's slings and arrows: Individual differences in resilience when recovering from an anticipated threat. *Journal of Research in Personality, 42*(4), 1031–1046.
West, C. P., Tan, A. D., Habermann, T. M., Sloan, J. A., & Shanafelt, T. D. (2009). Association of resident fatigue and distress with perceivedmedical errors. *JAMA, 302*, 1294–1300.
Williams, J. M. G. (1997). *Cry of pain*. London: Penguin.
Williams, J. M. G., Crane, C., Barnhofer, T., Brennan, K., Duggan, D. S., Fennell, M. J., Von Rohr, I. R. (2014). Mindfulness-based cognitive therapy for preventing relapse in recurrent depression: A randomized dismantling trial. *Journal of Consulting and Clinical Psychology, 82*, 275.
Youssef, C. M., & Luthans, F. (2007). Positive organizational behavior in the workplace: The impact of hope, optimism, and resilience. Journal of Management, 33(5), 774–800.
Zautra, A. J., Hall, J. S., & Murray, K. E. (2010). Resilience: *A new definition of health for people and communities*. In J. W. Reich, A. J. Zautra, & J. S. Hall (Eds), Handbook of adult resilience. New York, NY: The Guilford Press.
Zunz, O. (1998). *Why the American century*?. University of Chicago Press.

Rudolf M. Oosthuizen (DLitt et Phil) received a BA degree (Cum Laude) from the University of Pretoria in 1992 and obtained a BA (Honours) in Psychology at the same university in 1993. In 1999, he received an MA degree in Industrial and Personnel Psychology from the Potchefstroom University for Christian Higher Education. In 1999, he registered as Industrial Psychologist with the Health Professions Council of South Africa. In 2005, he completed a DLitt et Phil in Industrial and Organisational Psychology at the University of South Africa (Unisa). Currently Rudolf Oosthuizen is an Associate Professor in the Department of Industrial and Organisational Psychology at the University of South Africa. Rudolf is the Manager for the MComIOP programme, and he is responsible for the lecturing of honours subjects and the supervision of master's and doctoral students. He has presented conference papers at national and international conferences and published articles in accredited scientific journals. His fields of interests are (1) career psychology, career development and management from an individual and organisational perspective in the twenty-first-century world of work; (2) positive psychology, with the focus on salutogenesis, sense of coherence, locus of control, self-efficacy, the hardy personality and learned resourcefulness; and (3) employment relations and the improvement of the quality of employment relations in organisations and in society in general.

Chapter 13
Errors and Failures in European Banking: A Cultural Perspective

Alessandro Carretta, Paola Schwizer, and Lucrezia Fattobene

Abstract Misconduct is still widespread in banking. It often leads to economic and reputational losses and negatively affects trust in the economic and financial systems. Misconduct is mainly a result of errors in policies and procedures, of mistakes or malpractices in individual behaviours and of failure in management and control systems. Elaborating on the new theory of risk culture in banking, we develop a general framework of errors and failures in banking, on the basis of existing literature and taking into account the empirical evidence that is currently available. Particularly, we focus our attention on the influence of national cultures, the role of the organizational environment, errors and management practices and the impact on reputational risk role of banking regulators and supervisors in the handling of errors and mistakes. Our work helps demonstrate that culture is the main driver of organizational and individual behaviours and consequently of errors, mistakes and failures in bank management. Moreover, in a "sound" risk culture environment, the ability to manage errors must be in the toolkit of bankers and banking supervisors, enhancing cultural capital while preserving stability and efficiency of the whole financial system.

Keywords Mistake · Error · Failure · Risk culture · Banking · Conduct risk · Reputational risk · Risk management

A. Carretta
Department of Management and Law, University of Rome Tor Vergata , Rome, Italy
e-mail: carretta@uniroma2.it

P. Schwizer
Department of Economics and Management, University of Parma, Parma, Italy
e-mail: paola.schwizer@unipr.it

L. Fattobene (✉)
School of Economics, LUM Jean Monnet University, Bari, Italy
e-mail: fattobene@lum.it

E. Vanderheiden, C.-H. Mayer (eds.), *Mistakes, Errors and Failures across Cultures*, https://doi.org/10.1007/978-3-030-35574-6_13

13.1 Introduction

The banking system is one of the most heavily regulated sectors of the economy. Rules are aimed at enhancing consumer protection against risks linked to market failures as asymmetric information and at maintaining financial stability, considered to be a public good in light of the need for an efficient payment system and an effective resource allocation to the real economy and the potentially systemic consequences of a bank distress (Quintyn and Taylor 2004; Heimler 2006). Nevertheless, the continuous introduction of new regulations, which occurred at an ever-increasing pace following the 2008–2009 global financial crisis, seems not to be able to erase misconducts and misbehaviours from bank practices. These often translate into heavy fines and reputational costs, also because of the intensifying pervasiveness of supervision on financial institutions. All this makes it more difficult to restore the public trust in banking – seriously eroded by the crisis – which is a crucial asset for the effectiveness of the financial system and for society as a whole. Misconduct is mainly a result of errors in policies and procedures, of mistakes or malpractices in individual behaviours and of failure in management and control systems. It is now widely recognized that this phenomenon depends on a weak corporate culture in bank management, which has yet not incorporated the values of integrity, honesty and sound risk management and control, making in many cases compliance with laws and regulations to be a pure formal, "tick-the-box" exercise. So culture, and particularly a sound risk culture, must be seen as a fundamental, and mostly important, component of an effective corporate and internal governance system, and it has to be properly implemented, widespread and continuously monitored throughout the organization, in order to ensure effective decision-making and good professional conduct, beyond pure compliance, to the benefit of all stakeholders involved. Notwithstanding the efforts of regulators and supervisors in trying to include organizations' behaviours and corporate values into their scope, and those of senior managers, engaging in changes and improvements of their practices, still "bank conduct and culture are at the center of a slow, uphill battle for trust" (Group of Thirty 2018, xi).

Leveraging on the importance of a sound corporate and risk culture, our contribution provides a general framework of errors and failures in banking. We elaborate on the existing literature and take into account the empirical evidence, data and case studies that are currently available.

Our thesis is that only a cultural perspective on errors and failures can help banks prevent and manage misconduct and misbehaviours, thus reducing operational and reputational losses.

We built our framework on ten statements, and we conclude that misconduct is favoured by macroeconomic, market, organizational and individual factors, relating to both the demand and the supply of financial services. In managing conduct risk, it is of utmost importance to consider the context within organizations in which actors – who can never be considered as atomized and undersocialized agents – interpret and apply procedures and models, because no context-free individual's decision exists, acknowledging that risk culture is partly a by-product of national attitudes and believes.

However, culture, and its effects on conduct risk, can and must be measured and managed, starting with an increase in awareness on its root causes, developing adequate indicators and metrics for behaviours and social dynamics and enhancing a "healthy" error management culture. A deep understanding and an effective management of the determinants of human decision-making require a multidisciplinary approach, which integrates psychology, cognitive neuroscience, evolutionary biology and ecology with the experience and the knowledge from the economic and financial domains.

So ultimately, our work helps demonstrate that culture is the main driver of organizational and individual behaviours and consequently of errors, mistakes and failures in bank management. Moreover, in a "sound" risk culture environment, the ability to manage errors must be in the toolkit of bankers and banking supervisors. This would enhance cultural capital while preserving stability and efficiency of the whole financial system.

13.2 Conduct Risk Plays a Central Role in the Current Debate on Financial Systems Stability and Efficiency

Conduct-related scandals have seriously weakened the financial systems conferring a crucial role to *conduct risk* in the current debate among academics, financial institutions and authorities. Far from being a new issue – concern on this risk dates to the Banking Act of 1933 – misconduct episodes in the past 50 years have seriously exposed financial institutions to severe economic and financial damages (Fig. 13.1). Even if a master definition of conduct risk is not yet available, it has been acknowledged as a new risk category (FSB 2015) and broadly defined as "the current or prospective risk of losses to an institution arising from inappropriate supply of financial services including cases of wilful or negligent misconduct" (EBA 2016). The emerged awareness of the importance of considering conduct risk – inside the wider concept of risk culture (RC) – as a variable to manage in order to create value rather than a fixed value to blindly accept (Carretta and Schwizer 2017a) is leading banking regulators to shift their focus from compliance to organizations' behaviours (Gond et al. 2014). Worldwide, authorities, sharing the view that prevention is better than cure, have all been active in enhancing conduct in the banking industry, with the goal to preserve confidence in financial markets. The alertness toward conduct risk exhibited by regulators and supervisors is also shown by firms operating in the financial industry, as emerged from the last Report on Culture and Conduct Risk (English et al. 2018).

In 2018, despite supervisory focus, financial firms' efforts and regulatory interventions, the number and the volume of cases regarding conduct risk increased (EBA 2018), generating broad classes of costs that encompass sanctions (including fines and financial penalties), redress costs and legal expenses (Resti 2017). Negative externalities associated with conduct risk manifestation extend beyond the subject who misbehaves and impact the whole organization. Misconduct costs can introduce frictions and raise the cost of intermediation, damaging firm's reputation; deflecting managers' attention from the core business activity; affecting the workforce composition; eroding firms' capital (FSB 2017); creating uncertainty about the business model, solvency and profitability of banks (ESRB 2015); absorbing financial resources through fines and penalties (Chaly et al. 2017); and thus depleting the loss-absorbing capacity of financial firms (FSB 2017). Furthermore, misconduct risk generates the opportunity cost of not investing in profitable activities and the negative stock market reaction associated with negative investor sentiment. While reducing the flow of financial services, these costs spill over to consumers, firms and other financial institutions, eliciting a negative public perception which endangers banks capital resilience and the whole financial system's stability and efficiency. Finally, rising during period of crisis, misconduct losses have a procyclical impact on the financial sector (ESRB 2015).

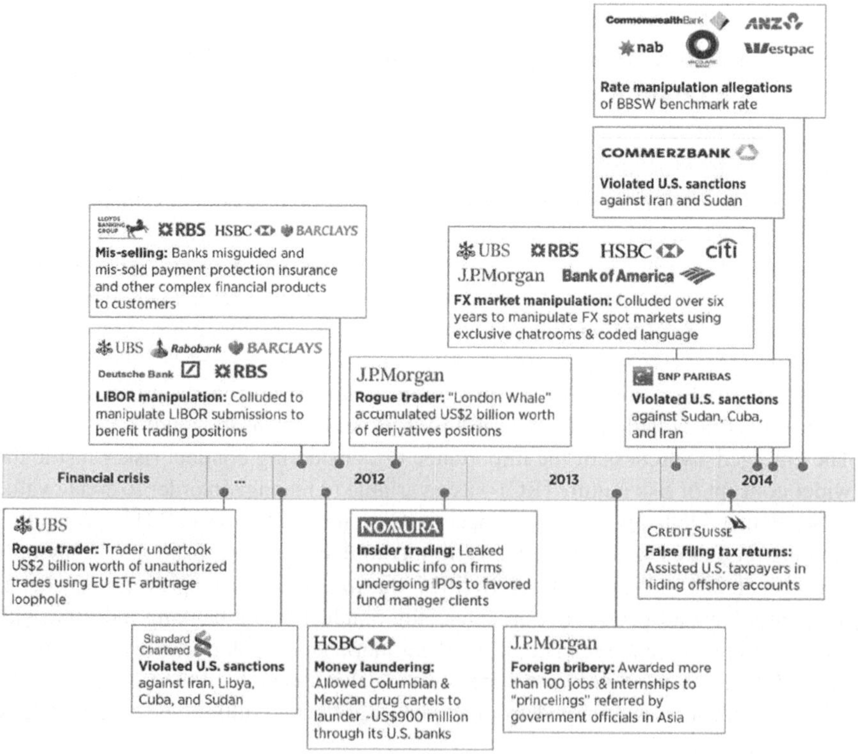

Fig. 13.1 Example of conduct scandals since the financial crisis. (Source: Group of Thirty 2018) Note: *AML* anti-money laundering, *BBSW* Bank Bill Swap Rate, *ETF* exchange-traded fund, *EU* European Union, *FX* foreign exchange, *IPO* initial public offering, *LIBOR* London Inter-bank Offered Rate

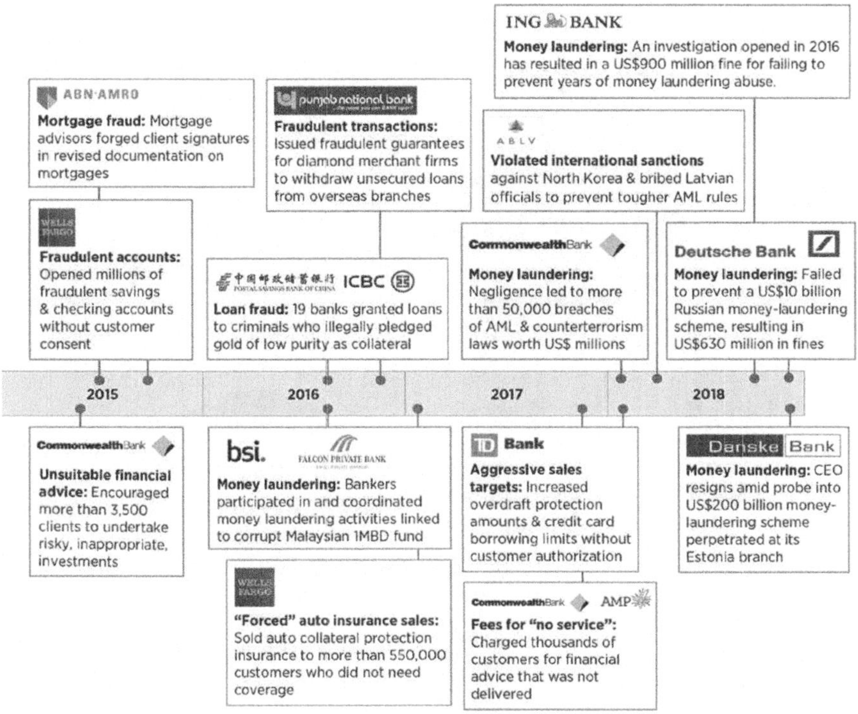

Fig. 13.1 (continued)

13.3 At the Root of Misconduct, There Are Errors and Inadequacies in Individual and Organization Behaviours, as well as in Policies, Practices and Management Procedures

If a unique definition of conduct risk is not available nor desirable, neither is the taxonomy of the key drivers of misconduct. The FCA (2013) identifies several elements at the root of conduct risk, grouping them as (1) *inherent factors* (information problems, inadequate financial capabilities and biases and heuristics), (2) *structures and behaviours* (conflict of interests, culture and incentives and ineffective competition) and (3) *environmental factors* (economic and market trends, technological developments and regulatory and policy changes). A high-level taxonomy surrounding misconduct risk is also presented by the FSB (2017) who identifies different classes of activities and risk types: (1) *business disruption and damage to assets*; (2) *execution, delivery and process management*; (3) *internal fraud*; (4) *employment practices and workplace safety*; and finally (5) *clients, products and business practices* (Fig. 13.2). ESRB (2015) provides a non-exhaustive list of misconduct types, categorizing them in (1) *mis-selling of financial products to retail customers*, (2) *mis-selling of financial products to professional clients*, (3) *violation of national and international rules and*

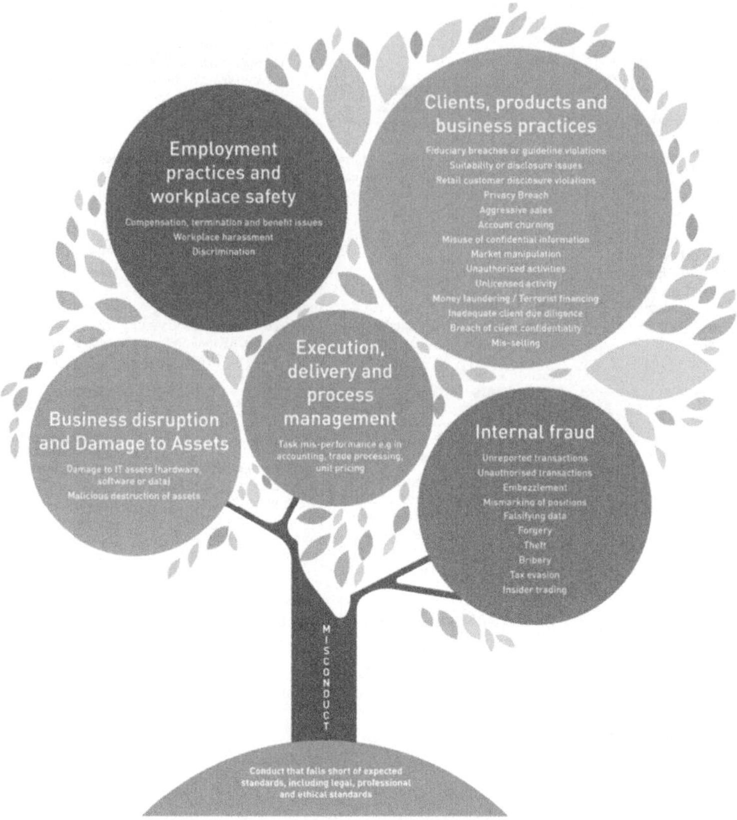

Fig. 13.2 FSB's high-level taxonomy of activities and risk types surrounding misconduct risk. (Source: FSB 2017)

regulations and (4) *manipulation of financial markets.* Interestingly, in the quest to categorize the drivers of misconduct, it is possible to recognize them in two out of three components of RC identified by Di Antonio (2017), i.e. (1) *customer risk*, which falls in the ethical/competitive domain and includes mis-selling of financial products, lack of transparency and conflict of interest, and (2) *compliance risk*, concerning the legal domain and comprising market manipulation, rigging of market benchmarks, tax evasion, money laundering and fraud.

13.4 Errors' Comprehension and Management Framework Is Represented by Risk Culture

According to the system approach, opposite to the person approach, since humans are fallible, mistakes occur also in the most efficient and profitable organizations. While changing the inherent human nature is not possible, changing the conditions in which individuals behave is feasible: system defences represent one way to prevent failures. Nevertheless, the different defences which are placed in sequence can have weaknesses – as active failures (e.g. procedural violations) or latent conditions (e.g. unreliable indicators) – and when those manifest simultaneously across the different layers, failures occur. This concept is better conveyed through the "Swiss cheese" metaphor, according to which barriers are the slice of cheese and weaknesses the holes in the slices which could line up in a trajectory that permits the accident to occur (Reason 2000). In this perspective, an effective and efficient system of internal controls in the banking sector helps to pursue a safe and sound risk management and to reduce the probability that adverse events occur originating bank failures. The internal control system in the banking sector posits "three lines of defence", i.e. three independent lines of control functions, i.e. one that owns and manages risks, one that oversees risks and one that provides independent assurance; senior management and governing bodies complete the scheme ensuring that this model permeates the whole organization. Figure 13.3 presents an application of the Swiss cheese metaphor to banking failures, highlighting how errors might be considered the results of the simultaneous manifestation of weaknesses across the three lines of defence and regulators and supervisors' behaviour. In particular, second- and third-line independent controls are extremely important to detect errors which manifest in the underneath layer of defence and whose repetition can be avoided only if properly analysed, likely suggesting improving internal policies. Disregarding their usefulness, internal controls in banks are often perceived as a burden, an unjustified expense, a complication of organizational structure or even an area which creates the risk of administrative sanctions (Schwizer 2016), while the recent financial crisis and

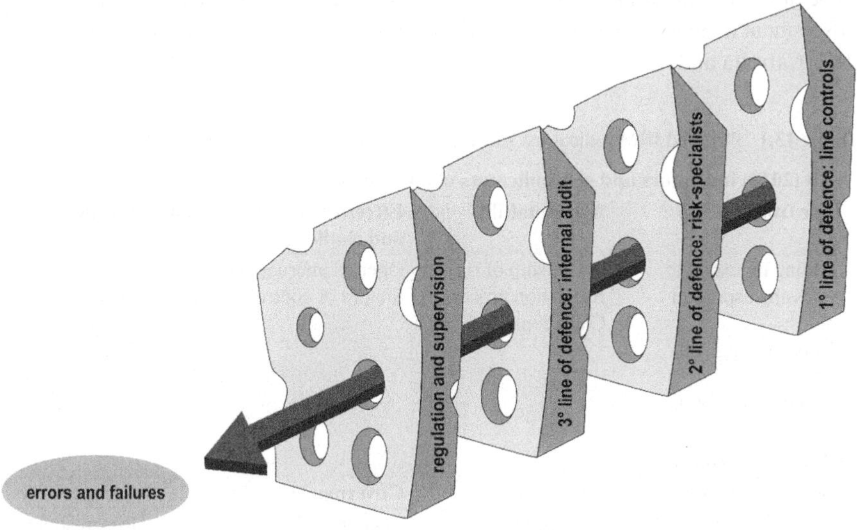

Fig. 13.3 In the banking sector, errors and failures occur when there is a simultaneous manifestation of weaknesses in different layers of protections: in the three lines of defence of the control systems and in regulators and supervisors' actions

the widespread losses in the financial sectors have raised the importance of a sound system of internal governance to help the company reach its strategic targets. In the last two decades, the recurrent failures in the financial industry have driven many regulatory interventions which led to an evolution of banking culture from a "culture of control", to a "culture of compliance", to finally acknowledging the importance of a sound RC as the element essential to avoid the holes in the slices of cheese to enlarge or to align across the different layers. We argue that the transformation from hazard to errors occurs when a bank is affected by an unsound RC, which drives the three lines of defence to be simultaneously violated, and supervisors and regulators do not impede the errors to manifest. This might happen, for instance, when "formal" controls rather than "real" ones are implemented, through the dominance of the form over the substance or when there is no overlapping between espoused and practiced values within the company. Assessing RC is an intricate task, but complexity should not lead the debate to be limited to pure speculative exercises: recently, the FSB (2014), the Institute of Risk Management (IRM 2012) and national professional associations (AIIA 2015) have proposed specific indicators of RC, as summarized below (Table 13.1). Starting from the FSB's categories, AIIA (2015) has identified 51 specific qualitative elements, the control objectives (COs), out of which 16 are considered "key" objectives and represent a specific target through which control effectiveness can be assessed; they are a preferential tool to assess soft evidence, which is difficult to capture through quantitative approaches. To support the qualitative analysis realized through COs, a useful tool is that of the risk culture indicators (RCIs), i.e. metrics that synthetize the probability that the combination between the potential occurrence of an event and the consequences deriving therefrom exceeds the organization's risk appetite. Indicators are not exhaustive, do not represent a checklist or an end-point and should not be considered separately, but rather a collective assessment is more appropriate to build awareness of the level of health of institutions' RC (Carretta and Schwizer 2017b).

Table 13.1 FSB and IRM indicators, sub-indicators and aspects of (a sound) RC

FSB (2014) indicators and sub-indicators of a sound RC			
Tone from the top	**Accountability**	**Effective communication and challenge**	**Incentives**
Leading by example Assessing espoused values Understanding and awareness Learning from past experience	Ownership of risk Escalation process Clear consequences	Open to alternate views Stature of control function	Remuneration Succession planning Talent development
IRM (2012) aspects of RC			
Tone from the top	**Decisions**	**Governance**	**Competency**
Risk leadership Dealing with bad news	Informed risk decisions Reward	Accountability Transparency	Risk resources Risk skills

Source: Authors' re-elaboration from FSB (2014) and IRM (2012)

13.5 National Cultures Influence Organizations' Error Perception and Reaction to It

The multi-faceted and complex relationship between national culture (NC) and failures in the banking sector can be explored focusing on management practices, including the error management process. According to Hofstede's influential schema, country's citizens share core values and practices developed through religion, education, political and economic systems, which influence the way they see the world and, thus, think and behave. He classified this "collective programming of the mind" that shapes organizational culture and behaviour, through six dimensions as collectivism/individualism, power distance, uncertainty avoidance (UA), masculinity/femininity, long-term orientation and indulgence (Hofstede 1983, 2001). In an error management perspective, a large distance between superiors and subordinates, as in high power distance organizations, is considered to negatively impact on error communication and planning, since superiors are seen as unquestionable authorities and tend to discourage active participation, while subordinates accept indications in an uncritical way (Hofstede 1991) and are not motivated to detect errors except if it is not their specific job (Slater and Narver 1995). Moreover, since in these strong hierarchies superiors are particularly interested in their reputation, there is a higher tendency to blame subordinates for mistakes, rather than the system. Error prevention is higher in collectivistic cultures where individuals put more effort in avoiding failures, compared with individualistic organizations where, conversely, members aim to reach personal successful outcomes and might be distracted from implementing error avoidance strategies. In addition, while collectivistic-oriented organizations focus on self-criticism, individualistic ones focus on self-enhancement, and this affects the likelihood of error detection. Another Hofstede's cultural dimension linked to error management is UA: in fact, high-UA cultures rely on routines and designed strategies, and this enhances their perception of control of the environment, reducing, in turn, the monitoring and the responsiveness in recognizing errors. At the same time, since in high-UA organizations errors are perceived as a manifestation of inadequate preparation, there is a stronger inclination to blame rather than reporting (defensive attributions) (Hofstede 2001). Moreover, errors are usually unexpected and perceived as very dangerous, so when they occur, people have highly negative attitudes (Hofstede 1991). Finally, since high-UA organizations usually adopt formal communication, which requires more time than informal one, and promote a restriction of information flow, response to errors can be slower and less effective than in low-UA organizations. On the other hand, high-UA culture attaches attention and devotes deep analysis to error situation increasing the degree of error prevention.

Despite the increasing standardization that follows globalization, management and accounting practices across national systems may be different: even if a McDonald's burger can taste the same everywhere, McDonald management procedures are not the same across different countries. Newman and Nollen (1996) analyse work units in 18 countries and observe that when management practices had a better fit with

NC, the work units reported higher financial performance than when the fit was not as good, leading them to suggest managers that "when in Rome, do as the Romans do". Focusing on the banking sector in the pre-financial crisis period, Kanagaretnam et al. (2011) report banks' tendency to manage earnings to just meet or beat the prior year's earnings when they have high levels of individualism and masculinity and are low in the UA cultural dimension. They also find that individualism and power distance are positively related to and UA is negatively related to banks' income-smoothing behaviour. Notwithstanding the influence of NC on practices and errors, it is important to mention that nowadays citizens are frequently and in large number moving from one country to another for educational, employment or personal reasons, taking with themselves their "programming of the mind", likely reshaping the culture landscape through the cultural interpenetration, contamination, pluralism, hybridization and the deterritorialization dynamics (Craig and Douglas 2006). Therefore, studies on the role of NC in affecting behaviours should not fail in considering the inherently dynamic nature of culture.

13.6 Errors Do Not Depend Only on the People Who Make or Allow Them but also on the Cultural and Organizational Contexts Where They Occur

Financial scandals are usually tied to the business culture in which bank employees are embedded, considered to tolerate dishonest behaviours. When studying unethical behaviour in business, a pervasive theory is the "bad apple" one, according to which it suffices to identify and remove the bad actor within a company to make it safe: a naïve vision that fails to consider that individuals' behaviour is the product of the context where they operate (Treviño and Brown 2004). Gonin et al. (2012) broaden this view, suggesting that at the origin of misbehaviour is not a "bad apple" neither a "bad barrel" while rather a "bad larder"! The authors point out the importance of considering the context within organizations in which actors – who can never be considered as atomized and undersocialized agents – interpret and apply models and that no context-free individual's decision exists. In the same way, while inspecting rogue trading scandals, Gilligan (2011) suggests taking into account the normative and structural drivers that may contribute to disasters, addressing to the "bad luck", "bad apple", "bad tree" and "bad orchard" problem (see Box 13.1). If moral behaviour is not an inherent trait of personality, it does not display cross-situational stability (Magnusson and Stattin 1981) and depends on the context. It is thus important to build a sound organizational culture which reduces the probability that generally honest people at home behave dishonestly when at the workplace. Congruently, a positive work environment does not involve a "culture of fear", which can be either the fear of the boss, of not achieving targets and of reprisal when reporting others' unethical behaviour. As shown by social psychologist Milgram's experiments (1961, 1963) on the obedience to authority, also ordinary individuals could be induced by a legitimate authority to behave with cruelty and against their own values.

Attempting to assess if banking culture has a causal effect on dishonesty, Cohn et al. (2014) conduct a laboratory experiment involving bank employees and observe that when their professional identity is rendered salient, a proportion of them becomes dishonest. The shift in behaviour observed does not occur for employees from other industries or students, allowing the authors to state that it is an effect specific to the business culture of the banking industry. Interestingly, an experimental approach applied to study the influence on dishonest behaviour of modern communication technologies (Cohn et al. 2018) revealed that human interaction is crucial to mitigating dishonest attitudes and that individuals cheat significantly more when they interact with a machine rather than a person. The evidence of the effects played by human interaction in reducing fraudulent behaviour might be particularly interesting for the fintech industry, suggesting the idea that fully renouncing to the human component for robo-advisors might undermine the creation of an environment which promotes a healthy/sound culture.

Clear implications for managers, regulators and supervisors trying to prompt honesty thus include to control environmental pressures and reward and incentive systems. A large body of literature documents how incentives and compensation measures are a powerful corporate governance mechanism to align individual and organizational goals and enhance firms' performance (Condly et al. 2003) but also that they play a pivotal role in originating misconduct, as "whenever there is misconduct, there are almost always issues with incentive design" (Group of Thirty 2018). Compared with manufacturing firms, unproper designed incentives are very dangerous for banks because their higher leverage makes them vulnerable to risk-shifting agency problems and since depositors are the main claimholders, incentives that aim at aligning top management merely with equity holders, without adequately considering debtholders, are not efficient (John and Qian 2003). The large misuse of financial incentives is leading banks to rethink their remuneration schemes and to integrate cultural and behavioural metrics into performance scorecards, so that not only the "what" but also the "how" of an employee's work is assessed and better incentives for appropriate conduct are provided (Group of Thirty 2018; FSB 2018).

At the same time, besides acting on the offer-side, interventions should also fill gaps on the demand-side by improving banking customers' financial literacy and numeracy. In fact, at the root of the misconduct risk, there are both environmental factors (e.g. rising pressure on business model adjustment after the crisis) and structures and behaviours (e.g. conflicts of interest) but also inherent factors, including clients' limited financial capabilities which exacerbate market failures as information asymmetries.

Box 13.1: Rogue Trading

Joseph Jett, Nick Leeson, Toshihide Iguchi, Yosuo Hamanaka, John Rusnak, Kweku Adoboli and Jérôme Kerviel are only some of the names of rogue traders. Among the most reverberating cases, there is the one of Kerviel, a trader in the arbitrageur department at the Société Générale who exploited his knowledge on audit procedures learnt in the previous 5 years he worked for auditing trading positions within the bank, to avoid and fool risk controls and manipulate the bank's software taking unauthorized positions on stock futures for 50 billion euros. The trader's misconduct was not discovered on time, despite the 17 inspections in the years 2006–2007 of the Bank of France, the two letters of inquiry from Eurex, the 74 alerts about anomalies in trading activity and the emails that Kerviel's boss received about the unusual purchase of 6,000 forward contracts in a time interval of only 2 h (Brochet 2010). The trader declared that his superiors at the bank turned a blind eye and that he would not have been able to execute the trades without others knowing.

13.7 Inside an Organization, There Might Be Different Risk Cultures Which Underlie Widely Differing Errors Philosophy

Organizational culture is not a monolithic phenomenon: inside an organization, different cultures shared by a significant group of individuals can develop, originating "subcultures". Organization-specific subcultures may emerge from membership to various groups within the firm as department, business units, workgroups and teams, and thus they are likely to emerge in large and complex organizations such as financial institutions. As revealed through anecdotal evidence, in the large bank Citicorp, three different conflicting subcultures coexisted with respect to risk: consumer banking, investment banking and institutional banking cultures (Rogers 1993). The first is based on standardization of products and procedures; the investment banking culture is anti-bureaucracy, focused on short-term and based on speed and flexibility; the institutional culture attaches importance to standardization of products and procedures while caring on long-term relationships with customers. Also Ware and Robinson (2011) identify three subcultures in investment banks, the "tribes" (investment, operations and distribution), which differ in their peripheral values. Clearly, the coexistence of different cultures and social capital within the same organization gives rise to different attitudes and behaviours, representing the keystone to interpret specific cases of failures in the banking sectors. When the accounting department is close to a culture of number while the R&D department to innovation and creativity or when traders focus on short-term results for bonuses, meticulously measure market risk and rely on virtual relationships whereas salesmen work on long-term personal relationships and risk taking is not at the centre of their activity, organizational climate can be very complex. When the complex organizational climate is not properly managed, differences between groups might translate into conflicts within a fragmentated company's culture (Di Antonio 2017), and, as delineated by Lewis (1989) and Smith (2011), a department may prevail over the other imposing his culture and causing failures.

Recently, the meteoric rise of fintech is leading numerous changes and affecting RC at interorganizational level, by transforming banks' business focus, customer interaction, core competencies, vertical integration level, service portfolio, automation and IT architecture (Alt et al. 2018). Machine and algorithms certainly allow to reduce biases which influence decision outcomes, but a major drawback is that when they work incorrectly – and this happen since we are still far from eliminating human fallibility in artificial intelligence – they can be detrimental for the organization, and also negatively affect the environment, as revealed by the Dow Jones Flash Crash described in Box 13.2. The increasing banks' reliance on technology and automation in their processes and workflows poses new challenges and the need to be vigilant on the unintended and unexpected consequences. If on the one hand machine learning applications can create value operating in a more effective and efficient way and correctly using data and analytics, then on the other hand they can be associated with misconduct behaviours that originate from cyber risk (i.e. loss of data, phishing, malware), model risk (i.e. errors in the algorithm) or technology risk (i.e. problems with hardware), as when customer service chatbots do not work properly or when loan approval algorithms contain biases or bugs (Group of Thirty 2018). At the same time, algorithmic decision-making introduces new complexities, and determining who or what is responsible when technology fails (the bank, the technology itself, the developer, the product manager or the owner?) has important legal and economic implications.

Box 13.2: The Flash Crash: A Window into the Potential Consequences of Algorithmic Finance

On May 6, 2010, the prices of many US-based equity products experienced dramatic fluctuations in prices; nearly 3 million dollars of market capitalization vanished and quickly recovered. This systemic intraday event which consisted of severe price fluctuations of both broad-market indexes and individual securities, in different phases, was named as "Flash Crash", and since then, the expression is used to indicate "an extremely rapid decline in the price of one or more commodities or securities, typically one caused by automated trading" (Oxford Dictionary).

One of the important lessons learned from this event is that "the interaction between automated execution programs and algorithmic trading strategies can quickly erode liquidity and result in disorderly markets" (CFTC-SEC 2010). That day began with negative sentiment due to political and economic news concerning the debt crisis in Europe; according to the Commodity Futures Trading Commission (CFTC) and the Securities and Exchange Commission (SEC), the subsequent rapid drop in market prices was triggered by a large

(continued)

Box 13.2 (continued)

fundamental trader who executed a sizeable sell order through a Sell Algorithm that only targeted trading volume, and neither price nor time, executing the sell program in only 20 min. This pressure on the market was initially absorbed by high-frequency traders, other intermediaries and fundamental buyers in the future market and cross-market arbitrageurs (CFTC-SEC 2010); but even if the orders were not yet absorbed by the market, the Sell Algorithm reacted to the increased volume, increasing, in turn, the feeding rate of the orders in the market, thus originating a liquidity crisis.

13.8 Do Errors and Inadequacies Affect Banks' Reputation?

Since banks' business entirely relies on depositors, creditors and marketplace's confidence, the concept of corporate reputation is extremely relevant, especially after the last financial crisis which has seriously undermined trust in the banking sector. A bank's positive reputation can increase survivorship and profitability by signalling to potential competitors the existence of entry barriers and reducing the cost to preserve relationships with stakeholders (Dinc 2000), whereas disclosure of fraudulent activities, or errors and inadequacies in conducting the business practices, may cause higher costs of financial funding, fines and penalties, rating downgrading, loss of present and future customers and difficulties in hiring valuable employees and in finding business partners.

Regulators identify reputational risk as a risk that occurs following another risk (primary risk), and thus it tends to be considered as a consequential risk. According to the Basel Committee on Banking Supervision, the main primary risk is represented by the operational risk, since its manifestation severely affects banks' reputation. Empirical studies report severe reputational losses in the case of operational losses associated with internal frauds (De Fontnouvelle and Perry 2005; Gillet et al. 2010) and that "trading and sales" and "payment and settlement" are the two business lines mostly associated with considerable reputational damage (Fiordelisi et al. 2012). The same authors (2013) empirically study the determinants of reputational risk in the banking sector and identify the following six factors: bank riskiness, profitability, level of intangible assets, capitalization, size, the entity of the operational loss and the business units that suffered the operational losses. Recently, the inadequate robustness and spread of RC within the financial institution, which gives rise to misconduct, has been identified as one of the possible sources at the origin of the reputational risk. Gabbi et al. (2017) conduct two cases studies on the Monte dei Paschi di Siena (MPS) and Banca Carige Italian credit institutions, who suffered severe sanctions by authorities because of their unhealthy RC. The authors observe that beyond the negative net impact on capitalization represented by the sanctions, of approximately 5 million euros for MPS and 1.9 million euros for Banca Carige, the reputational damages in the 6 days surrounding the announcement reached about 225 and 5.5 million euros, respectively. Overall, these findings suggest that overlooking the importance of a sound RC, and the possible sources of errors and inadequacies while conducting banking activities, can be detrimental and trigger reputational damages which extends beyond the operational losses associated with the primary risk manifestation.

13.9 Control Authorities Make Mistakes Too

"[T]he staff found no evidence of fraud". With this sentence, on November 21, 2007, the SEC closes the investigation opened on January 24, 2006, in response to the financial analyst Harry Markopolos' memorandum (dated November 7, 2005)[1] through which he provides evidence that Madoff is running a Ponzi scheme, which later actually resulted to be the world's largest one. If the SEC would have acted, it could have saved the victims' billion dollars of investments, avoiding one of the most famous examples of authorities' mistake. Two possible explanations – both uncomfortable – are proposed to explain how it was possible that the most important market regulatory agency did not see this fraud, disregarding the memorandum: the first concerns a deficit in competence and training of SEC's lawyer regulators and the second is structural corruption (Rhee 2009), and the most plausible explanation seems to be the first one; lawyers did not understand, even if illustrated in the memorandum, the basic working of markets and technical features of transactions in a very complex environment, as the financial one. Lack of skill, training and knowledge might drive authorities' errors and mistakes in financial markets. Slowness in taking actions could also exacerbate the negative consequences associated with frauds and scandals, as revealed in the HSBC money laundering case, when the Office of the Comptroller of the Currency (OCC) surely failed in taking prompt actions (Box 13.3).

Box 13.3: HSBC Money Laundering and the Regulatory Failures of the OCC

One of the largest scandals in the banking sector concerns the HSBC's money laundering case occurred in 2012, which cost the bank a fine of $1.92 billion for the activities of its US affiliate HBUS. The Permanent Subcommittee on Investigations (PSI) conducted a case study investigation on the bank (USA Homeland Security 2012), observing that HSBC facilitated money laundering while exposing the USA to the risks of drug smuggling and terrorism.

(continued)

[1] Please see: "The World's Largest Hedge Fund Is a Fraud" Letter from Harry Markopolos to SEC, available at http://online.wsj.com/documents/Madoff_SECdocs_20081217.pdf

Box 13.3 (continued)

This case study points out serious deficiencies in regulation and supervision. In fact, the OCC started raising concerns regarding HBUS and their anti-money laundering (AML) actions in 2002, but it did not issue any supervisory letter outlining concerns and AML weaknesses until 2010 (Naheem 2016). In the report, the PSI dedicates a whole section to outline the major regulatory failures of this case, which "did not happen overnight", while it accumulated over time also because some of the problems relating to AML were not solved due to OCC's ineffective oversight efforts. In fact, OCC failed to classify as legal violations some of the 83 "Matter Requiring Attention" within a 5-year period. One of the biggest OCC's mistakes was not considering AML issues when assigning bank's management rating while only taking them into account during the assignment of the bank's consumer compliance rating: national banks, therefore, did not suffer a rating downgrade and did not increase the deposit insurance for incurring heightened risk. Moreover, as highlighted in the report executive summary, additional OCC failures include "the practice of conducting narrowly focused AML examinations of specific banking units without also assessing HBUS' overall AML program; the OCC's reluctance, despite mounting AML deficiencies, to make timely use of formal and informal enforcement actions to compel improvements in HBUS' AML program; and the practice by some OCC examiners to issue Supervisory Letters that sometimes muted AML examination criticisms or weakened recommendations for AML reforms at HBUS" (p. 9).

Authorities' mistakes can also manifest through wrong regulatory interventions, which, instead of help to reach specific goals, foster unintended consequences. For instance, to tackle systemic risk as emerged from the mid-1970s' crisis, the Basel Committee on Banking and Supervision promoted the Capital Accord, to increase the stability of the international banking system and to diminish existing sources of competitive inequality amongst international banks. In spite of positive effects, a limited differentiation of credit risk, a static measure of default risk, lack of recognition of term structure of credit risk, a simplified calculation of potential counterparty risk and lack of recognition of portfolio diversification effects represent all severe weaknesses of Basel I, which undermined financial stability leading to Basel II that involuntarily became an even more pernicious agreement. After the financial crisis, exacerbated by these regulatory oversights and mistakes, the new framework of Basel III was implemented, but the monitoring of the effects of the regulatory reforms poses new challenges, highlighting possible unintended negative implications, which include capital and liquidity requirements, policy measures for G-SIFIs, reforms of the OTC derivative market and structural reform initiatives (BIS 2014). Poor risk management practices were only one root cause of the crisis; the raw corporate governance of banks points out to a deeper problem in financial institutions, i.e. a poor culture of risk (Carretta and Bianchi 2016). Therefore, to pursue a stable and sound banking union, regulators and supervisors have started to focus on *cultural capital* in addition to capital requirements, acknowledging that a *cultural ratio* might be even more important than a capital one and that the fact that culture is hard to measure should not discourage from taking it into account (Carretta 2015) since it is a relevant factor in financial failures, errors and misguiding (Carretta and Bianchi 2016). Finally, also the harmonization of supervisory styles plays a central role in ensuring the stability of the banking system. As empirically observed by Carretta et al. (2015) who focused on EU-15 banks, the culture of banking supervisory authority, proxied by applying Hofstede et al. (2010)'s framework, is focused on bank soundness. A supervisory culture oriented to collectivism and to avoid uncertainty increases the banks' distance to default, while a power distance-oriented supervision culture decreases it.

13.10 Errors' Management Requires a Multidisciplinary Approach

Errors are not easy to define (Senders and Moray 1991), and understanding their root and classifying them are quite hard tasks which encompasse different disciplines. A first distinction when studying individual's mistakes is based on intentionality. In fact, while some errors are the result of a conscious improper behaviour, even if influenced by the cultural and organizational context, others are associated with the inherent fallacies of human decision-making. Our decision-making process occurs through systematic simplifications, i.e. heuristics or rule of thumbs, which sometimes drive suboptimal decision outcomes. Decision-making biases are quite pervasive and persistent, but interestingly they are also systematic, thus predictable and avoidable. It is from this standpoint that the Behavioural Insights Team (or the Nudge Unit) proposes some lessons from behavioural sciences to reduce frauds, errors and debts, through different steps; the team has already launched some trials to apply these insights in practices, gaining positive results in reducing misconducts. Recently, also neuroeconomics is proven to be helpful in shedding light on the automatic and unconscious processes which underlie biases in economic and financial decision-making (Ceravolo et al. 2019; Fattobene and Ceravolo 2018).

Technology developments could help to reduce individuals' biases, limiting human discretion in decisions. For instance, the introduction of the stop-loss clause during financial negotiations helps traders to reduce their desire to "get even" and their risk-seeking behaviour while losing. High-frequency trading and quantitative asset management could help to overcome human limitations in computing, by selling and buying shares in fractions of a second, while the use of computer algorithms to trade stocks could eliminate the incidence of different factors which affect "rational" decision-making, as stress, arousal, anxiety, excitement, attachment to portfolio, etc. Anyway, it is important to underline that behind technology inventions and artificial intelligence, there is always a human mind, and therefore while some errors inherent in decision-making can be minimized, attempts to fully eliminate any form of errors in human behaviours will be in vain.

13.11 Good Error Management Practices Could Represent an Efficient and Effective Management Tool

Christopher Columbus wanted to discover a direct route to India sailing West, but his error made him accidentally arrive in the Americas: errors can have either negative consequences or positive ones, as learning, innovation and increased resilience. According to the theoretical framework of Van Dyck et al. (2005), common practices in the error management culture enhance firm performance (goal achievement, survivability, return on assets) through mediators that work simultaneously on decreasing/increasing negative/positive error consequences, via control of these consequences or through learning, initiative and innovation. These common practices include communicating about errors, sharing error knowledge, helping in error situation, quick error detection and damage control, analysing errors, coordinating error handling and effective error handling. *Communicating about errors* is probably the most important practice, since it promotes all the others: communication allows to create common knowledge and provides the basis for getting help from others; moreover, it facilitates the quick detection of the error that, in turns, helps in managing the negative consequences of it, also through a coordinated and effective intervention. Shared knowledge on different error situations allows secondary errors prevention, which is one of the mediators to firms' success. *Analysing errors* is also a very important practice since errors disclose very important information about companies' practices providing the basis for the identification of error-prone system design. Lower-level errors, as those related to absent-mindedness, in fact, may originate from a systematic source, which can therefore be corrected: for instance, writing down incorrect orders, whether in a restaurant or during financial negotiations, could result from very similar names of the menu items and could easily be put right by changing those names (Zhao and Olivera 2006).

A good error management culture is related to favourable organizational outcomes: in an environment where employees are not expected to be punished for their errors, even when occurred while attempting to act proactively, they will show personal initiative and experimentation (Frese and Fay 2001), positively affecting firms' performance.

An important supplemental control tool within organizations is the whistleblowing practice (Zhuang et al. 2005): it was because of this practice that, for instance, it emerged the case of the money laundering scandal at Danske Bank which involved 200 billion euros in suspicious payments realized through Danske's Estonian branch between the years 2007 and 2015. Given their crucial role in the fight against financial and economic crimes, whistle-blowers are protected by the law and should be immune from repercussions; however, they do not always feel safeguarded by the organization, as revealed by the episode at Barclays, where the bank's chief executive Jes Staley was fined £1.1 million by British regulators after he tried to identify the employee who criticized another employee of the bank by sending letters.

Research that investigates error management culture is still in its beginning especially in the banking sectors where the numerous scandals and mistakes clearly address for the need to adopt an error management approach in order to understand how to prevent errors and how to manage their consequences, minimizing the negative and promoting the positive ones.

References

Alt, R., Beck, R., Smits, M.T. (2018). FinTech and the transformation of the financial industry. *Electron Markets,* 28(3), 235–243.

Associazione Italiana Internal Auditors (AIIA) (2015). Risk Culture. December.

Bank for International Settlements (BIS) (2014). Impact and implementation challenges of the Basel framework for emerging market, developing and small economies. Prepared by the Basel Consultative Group, November.

Brochet, F. (2010). Société Générale (A): The Jérôme Kerviel Affair, Harvard Business School, Case Study, 23rd April.

Carretta, A. (2015, February 6). Serve a poco iniettare capitale nella banca se questa non ha un'adeguata cultura del rischio. *Milano Finanza,* p. 16.

Carretta, A., & Bianchi, N. (2016). Risk Culture in Financial Institutions, regulators and supervisors. In A. Carretta and M. Sargiacomo (Ed.), *Doing Banking in Italy: Governance, Risk Accounting and Auditing issues* (pp. 167–195). London: McGraw-Hill Education.

Carretta, A., & Schwizer, P. (2017a). Risk Culture. In A. Carretta, F. Fiordelisi and P. Schwizer (Ed.), *Risk culture in Banking* (pp. 11–30). London: Palgrave Macmillan.

Carretta, A., & Schwizer, P. (2017b). Risk Culture in the Regulation and Supervision Framework. In A. Carretta, F. Fiordelisi and P. Schwizer (Ed.), *Risk culture in Banking* (pp. 73–96). London: Palgrave Macmillan.

Carretta, A., Farina, V., Fiordelisi, F., Schwizer, P., Stentella Lopes, F. S. (2015). Don't Stand So Close to Me: The role of supervisory style in banking stability. *Journal of Banking & Finance,* 52(1), 180–188.

Ceravolo, M.G., Farina, V., Fattobene, L., Leonelli, L., Raggetti GM. (2019). Presentational format and financial consumers' behaviour: an eye-tracking study. *International Journal of Bank Marketing,* 37(3), 821–837.

Chaly, S., Hennessy, J., Menand, L., Stiroh, K., Tracy, J. (2017). Misconduct Risk, Culture, and Supervision. Federal Reserve Bank of New York.

Cohn, A., Fehr, E., Marechal, M. A. (2014). Business Culture and Dishonesty in the Banking Industry. *Nature,* 516, (7529), 86–89.

Cohn, A., Gesche, T., Marechal, M. A. (2018). Honesty in the Digital Age. University of Zurich, Department of Economics, Working Paper No. 280.

Commodity Futures Trading Commission (CFTC)- Securities & Exchange Commission (SEC) (2010). Findings regarding the market events of May 6, 2010. September, 30.

Condly, S. J., Clark, R. E., Stolovitch, H. D. (2003). The Effects of Incentives on Workplace Performance: A Meta-analytic Review of Research Studies 1. *Performance Improvement Quarterly,* 16(3), 46–63.

Craig, C. S., Douglas, S. P. (2006). Beyond national culture: implications of cultural dynamics for consumer research. *International Marketing Review,* 23(3), 322–342.

De Fontnouvelle, P., Perry, J. (2005). Measuring Reputational Risk: The Market Reaction to Operational Loss Announcements. Federal Reserve Bank of Boston Working Paper.

Di Antonio, M. (2017). Risk Culture in Different Bank Businesses. In A. Carretta, F. Fiordelisi and P. Schwizer (Ed.), *Risk culture in Banking* (pp. 31–71). London: Palgrave Macmillan.

Dinc, S. (2000). Bank Reputation, Bank Commitment, and the Effects of Competition in Credit Markets. *Review of Financial Studies,* 13(3), 781–812.

English, S., Hammond, S., Kovas, A., Parry, H. (2018). Culture and Conduct Risk 2018: Benchmarking 5 years of implementation. Thomson Reuters.

European Banking Authority (EBA) (2016) EU-wide Stress Test: Methodological Note, February 2016

European Systemic Risk Board (ESRB) (2015) Report on misconduct risk in the banking sector June 2015

European Banking Authority (EBA) (2018). Risk Assessment Report, December 2018.

Fattobene, L., & Ceravolo, M.G. (2018). Neurofinance: new frontiers and further perspectives. In GM. Raggetti, M.G. Ceravolo, and L. Fattobene (Ed.), *Neuroeconomics: theory, applications, and perspectives* (pp. 187–202). Milano: EGEA Bocconi University Press

Financial Conduct Authority (FCA) (2013) FCA Risk Outlook 2013

Financial stability board (FSB) (2015, November 6) Measure to reduce misconduct risk

Financial Stability Board(FSB) (2014). Guidance on Supervisory Interaction with Financial Institutions on Risk Culture. A Framework for Assessing Risk Culture. 7 April 2014.

Financial Stability Board (FSB) (2017). Stocktake of efforts to strengthen governance frameworks to mitigate misconduct risks. 23 May 2017.

Financial Stability Board (FSB) (2018). Strengthening Governance Frameworks to Mitigate Misconduct Risk: A Toolkit for Firms and Supervisors. 20 Aprile 2018.

Fiordelisi, F., Soana, M. G, Schwizer, P. (2012). Reputational losses and operational risk in banking. The European Journal of Finance, 20(2), pages 105–124

Fiordelisi, F., Soana, M. G, Schwizer, P. (2013). The Determinants of Reputational Risk in the Banking Sector. *Journal of Banking and Finance,* 37(5), 1359–1371

Frese, M., & Fay, D. (2001). Personal Initiative (PI): An Active Performance Concept for Work in the 21st Century. In B. M. Staw, and R. M. Sutton (Ed.), *Research in Organizational Behavior* (pp. 133–187). Amsterdam: Elsevier Science.

Gabbi, G., Pianorsi, M., Soana M.G. (2017). The Impact of Risk Culture on Bank Reputation. In A. Carretta, F. Fiordelisi and P. Schwizer (Ed.), *Risk culture in Banking* (pp. 177–194). London: Palgrave Macmillan.

Gillet, R., Hubner, G., Plunus, S. (2010). Operational Risk and Reputation in the Financial Industry. *Journal of Banking and Finance,* 34(1), 224–235.

Gilligan, G. (2011). Jérôme Kerviel the 'Rogue Trader' of Société Générale: Bad Luck, Bad Apple, Bad Tree or Bad Orchard?. *The Company Lawyer,* 32(12), 355–362.

Gond, J-P., Spicer, A., Patel, K., Fleming, P., Mosonyi, S., Benoit, C. and Parker, S. (2014). A Report on the Culture of British Retail Banking. London, UK: New City Agenda and Cass Business School.

Gonin, M., Palazzo, G., Hoffrage, U. (2012). Neither bad apple nor bad barrel: how the societal context impacts unethical behavior in organizations. *Business Ethics European Review,* 21(1), 31–46.

Group of Thirty (2018). Banking Conduct and Culture: A Permanent Mindset Change, pp. 1–62.

Heimler, A. (2006). Competition Policy, Antitrust Enforcement and Banking: Some Recent Developments, OECD - Inter-American Development Bank, Fourth Meeting of The Latin American Competition Forum (San Salvador, 11th and 12th July 2006)

Hofstede, G. (1983). The Cultural Relativity of Organizational Practices and Theories. *Journal of International Business Studies,* 14(2), 75–89.

Hofstede (1991) Culture and organizations: Software of the mind. McGraw Hill, Berkshire

Hofstede, G. (2001). *Culture's consequences: Comparing values, behaviors, institutions, and organizations across nations.* Thousand Oaks, CA: Sage Publications.

Hofstede, G., Hofstede, G. J., & Minkov, M. (2010). *Cultures and organizations: Software of the mind.* Revised and Expanded 3rd Edition. New York: McGraw-Hill.

Institute of Risk Management (IRM) (2012). Risk Culture Under the Microscope. Guidance for Boards, London.

John, K., Qian, Y. (2003). Incentive Features in CEO Compensation in the Banking Industry. *Economic Policy Review,* 9(1), 109–121.

Kanagaretnam, K., Lim, C. Y., Lobo, G. J. (2011). Effects of national culture on earnings quality of banks. *Journal of International Business Studies,* 42(6), 853–874.

Lewis, M. (1989). *Liar's Poker.* New York: W. W. Norton & Company.

Magnusson, D., Stattin, H. (1981). Stability of cross-situational patterns of behaviour. *Journal of Research in Personality,* 15(4), 488–496.

Milgram, S. (1961). *Dynamics of obedience.* Washington: National Science Foundation.

Milgram, S. (1963). Behavioral study of obedience. *The Journal of Abnormal and Social Psychology,* 67(4), 371–378.

Naheem, M. A. (2016). Risk of money laundering in the US: HSBC case study. *Journal of Money Laundering Control*, 19(3), 225–237.

Newman, K. L., Nollen, S. D. (1996). Culture and Congruence: The Fit Between Management Practices and National Culture. *Journal of International Business Studies,* 27(4), 753–779.

Quintyn, M., Taylor, M.W. (2004). Should Financial Sector Regulators Be Independent?. International Monetary Fund, March 8.

Reason, J. (2000). Human error: models and management. *British Medical Journal,* 320, 768–770.

Resti, A. (2017). Fines for misconduct in the banking sector: what is the situation in the EU?. Scrutiny paper on the Single Supervisory Mechanism provided at the request of the Economic and Monetary Affairs Committee. European Parliament PE 587. 400.

Rhee, R. J. (2009). *The Madoff Scandal, Market Regulatory Failure, and the Business Education of Lawyers.* Gainesville, FL: University of Florida.

Rogers, D. (1993). *The Future of American Banking. Managing for Change.* New York: McGraw-Hill.

Schwizer, P. (2016). Internal controls: tools and processes. In A. Carretta and M. Sargiacomo (Ed.), *Doing Banking in Italy: Governance, Risk Accounting and Auditing issues* (pp. 79–109). London: McGraw-Hill Education.

Senders, J. W., & Moray, N. P. (1991). *Human error: Case, prediction, and reduction.* Hillsdale, NJ: Erlbaum.

Slater, S.F., Narver, J.C. (1995). Market Orientation and the Learning Organization. Journal of Marketing, 59(3), 63–74.

Smith, G. (2011). *Why I left Godman Sachs.* A Wall Street Story. New York: Grand Central Publishing.

Treviño, L. K., Brown, M. E. (2004). Managing to be ethical: Debunking five business ethics myths. *Academy of Management Perspectives,* 18(2), 69–81.

USA Homeland Security (2012). HSBC exposed US financial system to money laundering, drug, terrorist financing risks from permanent subcommittee on investigations: US Senate.

Van Dyck, C., Frese, M., Baer, M., Sonnentag, S. (2005). Organizational Error Management Culture and Its Impact on Performance: A Two-Study Replication. *Journal of Applied Psychology,* 90(6), 1228–1240.

Ware J., Robinson, K. (2011). Investment Tribes: Understanding the Subcultures in Asset Management Firms. Focus Consulting Group Inc.

Zhao, B., Olivera, F. (2006). Error reporting in organizations. *The Academy of Management Review,* 31(4), 1012–1030.

Zhuang, J., Thomas, S., Miller, D. L. (2005). Examining Culture's Effect on Whistle-Blowing and Peer Reporting. *Business & Society,* 44(4), 462–486.

Alessandro Carretta is Full Professor in Economics and Management of Financial Intermediation and former Director of the PhD Program in Banking and Finance at University of Rome Tor Vergata (Italy). He has been teaching Banking and Finance for more than 35 years, being formerly at the Universities of Urbino, Lecce and Milan Bocconi. He is a Fellow at Bocconi School of Management. His main research interests relate to banking management, focusing on regulation and control, corporate governance and culture and organizational change in banks. He has published widely, having produced more than 150 books and articles in academic journals. He is the past President of the Italian Academy of Management (AIDEA) and is a member of the committees and boards of journals, research bodies and financial and academic institutions.

Paola Schwizer is Full Professor in Financial Markets and Institutions at University of Parma (Italy) and Professor at SDA Bocconi School of Management. Previously, she has been a researcher at Bocconi University and Associate Professor in other Italian universities. She is board member in several Italian financial and non-financial listed companies. Since 2007 she is a member of Editorial Board of the Journal of Management and Governance. She has extensive experience in training on corporate governance, risk management and internal control systems, in Central Banks, private banks and non-banks listed companies. She is an author or co-author of several publications on banking strategies and organization, corporate governance, regulation and competition in the financial system.

Lucrezia Fattobene is Assistant Professor in Financial Markets and Institutions at LUM Jean Monnet University (Bari, Italy). She was Research Fellow at Polytechnic University of Marche (Ancona) and University of Rome Tor Vergata (Rome). Before earning a PhD in Management from the University of Rome Tor Vergata in 2016, she was a visiting research scholar at the Rotterdam School of Management, Erasmus University. Her main research interests are in the fields of Corporate Governance, Neuroeconomics and Behavioural Finance.

Chapter 14
Turning Bicultural Critical Incidents into Inclusive Bicultural Identities and Organizations in US Subsidiaries in Japan

Clifford H. Clarke and Naomi Takashiro

Abstract In the context of US managers of subsidiaries in Japan, there have been numerous mistaken perceptions, errors in judgment, and failures of execution (MEF) observed in critical incidents (CI) between Japanese and Americans that resulted in financial losses from decreased productivity for the companies and damaged careers of individual managers of both cultures due to communication breakdowns in task performance.

Our purposes were to demonstrate a pathway for avoiding this result and to challenge researchers, consultants, and organizations to engage together in achieving the goals of transforming individual identity and of developing bicultural organizations.

Methods employed were a qualitative phenomenological ethnographic research approach of observation, interview, analysis, and resolution formation by paired teams of Japanese and US researchers and facilitators in navigating MEF-provoked employee CIs.

Results showed that employees in these processes were enabled (a) to reduce MEF frequency, (b) to increase productive time-on-tasks, (c) to increase satisfaction with bicultural partners, (d) to increase confidence in evolving bicultural identities, and (e) to increase commitment to working in a bicultural organization. The benefits for organizations were reductions in costs and increased productivity.

Practical implications from this study were that inclusive bicultural identity and the development of bicultural organizations were achieved by this exceptional integration of researchers and practitioners. It serves as a model for other researchers, practitioners, and organizations with common goals.

Limitations were the inadequate number of bicultural CIs to illustrate the multiplicity of learning outcomes of this CI technique (CIT). Nine other CIs were

C. H. Clarke (Retired) (✉)
Affiliated Graduate Faculty, University of Hawai'i, Mānoa, Hawaii

N. Takashiro
Department of Global Tourism, Kyoto University of Foreign Studies, Ukyō-ku, Kyoto, Japan

E. Vanderheiden, C.-H. Mayer (eds.), *Mistakes, Errors and Failures across Cultures*, https://doi.org/10.1007/978-3-030-35574-6_14

not included due to space limitations. Some limitation on expanding researcher' roles were the result of a few client commitments of resources.

Our originality in this study was that integration of researcher and consultant roles in long-term embedded positions in bicultural business contexts uniquely demonstrated how research and development through focused exploration of work-stopping MEF-caused CIs created bicultural workforces and transforming bicultural identities among Japanese and US managers.

Keywords Mistakes · Errors · Failures · Intercultural management development · Japan-US business · Bicultural identity development · Critical incident technique

14.1 Introduction

There are often mistaken perceptions, errors in judgment, and failures of execution that occur in communications between Japanese and American managers, their leaders at headquarters, and their local workforce in their country of assignment. These can result in damaged individual careers and financial losses from decreased productivity in the organizations. The causes and consequences of such MEF (Mistakes, Errors, and Failures) were investigated by our intercultural specialists in multiple roles within bicultural organizations on 2- to 3-year assignments. They were on-site at the client's subsidiary as embedded participant-observers engaged in qualitative phenomenological ethnographic methods of research. Their roles evolved throughout assignments to include consulting, training, coaching, facilitating, and counseling in order to contribute to goals of transforming individuals and developing a bicultural organization. As researchers and facilitators, their focus was on MEF-provoked Critical Incidents (CI).

The experiential data for this study was drawn from earlier intercultural organizational development or culture change (ODCC) projects of Clarke Consulting Group (CCG) (Clarke 2008, 2017) and Clarke and Takashiro (2019). Sixteen long-term projects extending over 20 years all included CCC teams that had examined the organizational cultures of clients' headquarters and Japanese subsidiary operations. The leadership of each client organization in Japan and the USA welcomed these research teams in nearly all on-site operations, except in performance reviews. These bicultural teams had on-going access to observe, analyze, interpret, and facilitate resolutions to countless critical incidents (CI) that occurred in on-going intercultural workplace interactions. They engaged in data gathering and in navigating through each CI with a modified CIT (CI Technique) process. They were trained in a semi-structured interviewing technique, in role modeling intercultural competencies, and a culture-interactive process for analyzing the results collaboratively with clients. A consequential increase of the clients' intercultural competencies contributed to the reduction of intercultural MEF-caused CI, transformations of individuals' identities, and development of managers for their bicultural organizations.

14.2 Theoretical Foundations, Concepts, and Models

This is not intended to be a traditional literature review but rather a review of the theories, concepts, and models that have given us guidance and assurance that our designs and methods would be effective. It is our desire to adequately demonstrate and celebrate the value of weaving theoretical knowledge into the practice of transforming individual and team performance in bicultural organizations. These interdisciplinary foundations informed our process of selecting, interpreting, and navigating through each CI provoked by MEF. These applied resources are divided into five segments below. The selection criterion was that they contributed to our understanding of bicultural workplaces from multicultural including Japanese perspectives.

14.2.1 Respect, Trust, and Transformative Identity Development in Bicultural Businesses

Respect and trust are essential elements of partnerships within bicultural organizations as well as for those who are contracted to work with them, especially when dealing with individuals' mistakes, errors, and failures. Trifiletti and Capozza's (2011) study found that status differentiation impacted trust differently. We used status equalization methods learned from Cohen (1994, 1995), which resulted in the increasing equalization of status desired. Motivations were strengthened by building mutual respect, interdependency of tasks in boxed jobs, and shared organizational goals.

Kowner (2002) found that barriers to trust result from Americans choosing familiar informal language used in a Japanese workplace primarily from higher-level managers to lower-level employees. We found such linguistic barriers often create mistaken interpretations, feelings of embarrassment or loss of face, and even disrespect and distrust (see CI 4.1 below). In another of our CIs, a Japanese who was very impressed with his American peer's technical skill yelled above the machine noise, "I can't believe [it]" ("shinjirarenai"). The American threw down his tool, ran into the cafeteria, and told his fellow Americans "that SOB [an expletive] just called me a liar." It was a simple mistaken interpretation. The Japanese actually thought the American was fantastic!

Nishishiba and Richie's (2000) insightful study of comparative trust concepts found that Japanese give organizational commitment high value, while Americans choose personal integrity as a core value in judging trustworthiness. This creates miscommunication about trustworthiness at every turn because Japanese who often speak to their American bosses in "tatemae" (public) style designed to maintain harmony and save face (see 2.5) are often judged as lacking integrity, (see CI 4.3). Yuki et al. (2005) found that Japanese expected trust to be based on the likelihood of "sharing direct or indirect interpersonal links," whereas Americans tended to trust people primarily based on "shared category memberships."

Williams (2007) discussed the difficulties of trusting across organizational boundaries due to an inherent perception of threat from those outside one's group. She focused on emotional management of perceived threats as a key to understanding the development and maintenance of trust. Of her three categories of threat, (a) opportunism of the other, (b) neglect of one's interest, and (c) identity damage, the latter is of primary importance in developing bicultural teams and organizations. It is especially important to focus any identity development work on both cultural groups, i.e. in one CI our Japanese refused to accept learning English until we assured them that the Americans were also learning Japanese. This resulted in a positive competitive spirit between groups and was the first step toward expanding identities.

Markus and Kitayama (1991) studied the differences between self-construal as independent or as interdependent and found that:

> Each of these divergent construals should have a set of specific consequences for cognition, emotion, and motivation….(p. 224)

For Japanese self-construals conceive of being inextricably linked to others in a social circle, as one whose felt emotions are those of others in part and one whose motivation is other-directed rather than self-directed. Such would be the self-construal of an interdependent identity. Researchers also found that:

> individual-level factors (i.e., self construals and values) are better predictors of low- and high-context communication styles across cultures than cultural individualism-collectivism. (Gudykundst et al. (1996) p. 510)

These studies elucidate the identity threats felt by participants in bicultural organizations, and this is why "transformation" is so critical a concept in developing new bicultural identities.

Four concepts that we have discussed in understanding identity development through the analysis of CI are (a) the "single potent link" of Gulker and Monteith's (2013) research that we found group members experienced with their boxed-job partners in which interdependence was required for personal and company goal achievement, the "split identification" theory of Gutierrez et al. (2010) wherein managers were supportive of (b) maintaining their self-identities as well as (c) developing their new "reference group" identity (Hyman 1960), and (d) Morizuma's (2011) multifaceted cultural identity theory. Each of these four processes of evolving cultural identities was enabled by a transforming commitment to a bicultural partner's joint performance and a bicultural organization's goals that required a development and an expansion of their identities in cognitive, affective, and behavioral ways. The ultimate result was a strong esprit de corps with pride in their bicultural teamwork and new bicultural organization.

14.2.2 Learning from Mistakes, Errors, and Failures in Bicultural Organizations

Our purpose in using the Critical Incident Technique (CIT) for this study was to learn from negative MEF but in other settings we have used CIT to learn from positive MEFs, i.e., in an investigation of a company' stop performer profiles (Clarke 2017). Many researchers influenced our approach to learning from MEF from a variety of orientations. Bandura (1988) discussed how developing competencies through mastery modeling, strengthening self-efficacy, and increasing self-motivation were processes that contributed to performance improvement.

Yamazaki (2005) studied the impact of Kolb's (1984) learning styles in Japan. His findings utilized Hall's (1976) high-low context culture constructs to find:

> Those with high-context culture [such as Japan] tend to learn through the abilities of CE [concrete experience], whereas those with low-context culture [such as the U.S.], tend to learn through those of AC [abstract conceptualization]. (p. 525)

Yamazaki and Kayes' (2007) more recent study of Japanese expatriates' learning styles compared to Americans, both working in Japanese subsidiaries in the USA, found that "…Japanese managers are more concrete and reflective, whereas American managers are more abstract and active" (p. 1380). We found the same in our bicultural projects.

Organizations' culture and climate have been found to determine why failures are hidden or exposed and thereby decrease or enhance productivity. This key element is determined by whether revealed MEF evoke an attitude of "let's tackle this together and learn from it" or with an attitude of "let's find and blame the one who's at fault." The role of value congruence has been important in organizational culture and climate studies (Gronewold et al. 2013). If management authentically acts upon their espoused values, and individuals are committed to the same values, then the organization's effectiveness will be high (Malbasic et al. 2018). Both of these findings suggest authenticity and alignment of values influence productivity and effectiveness in organizations.

Mezirow (2003) suggests:

> transformative learning is learning that transforms problematic frames of reference – sets of fixed assumptions and expectations (habits of mind, meaning perspectives, mindsets) – to make them more inclusive, discriminating, open, reflective, and emotionally able to change. (p. 58)

But Mezirow says it is "deceptive to speak of culture as an influence on rationality and logic" (Mezirow 2004, p. 70). However, Eastern and Western cultural distinctions that influence our respective understandings about transformative learning require mutual respect in order to grow beyond such natural ethnocentric perspectives. Ruben and Kealey (1979) suggested that we personalize rather than universalize our knowledge in order to facilitate intercultural communication. They also found mutual respect aided effectiveness.

14.2.3 Critical Incident Techniques (CIT) for MEF Analysis in Bicultural Organizations

Flanagan (1954) described critical incidents (CI) as a phenomenon from which the causes of success and failure can be learned. We applied it as a dialogical interviewing assessment method to investigate participants' assumptions, expectations, behavior, interpretations, and attitudes about a specific event. CITs have been widely adapted and refined by assessment researchers. Clarke and Lipp (1998a, b) utilized CI to explore the reasons for MEF in Japanese US subsidiaries. Clarke (2017) also gathered participant positive CIs to collaboratively develop standards for managerial functions in a US client's bicultural organization development project in Japan.

Edvardsson and Roos (2001) developed a framework for evaluating the degree of criticality as perceived by customers in the service industry, but it was dependent upon the quality of their memories and delayed judgment processes. Also instrumental in the CIT are qualitative interviewing skills. Rubin and Rubin (2012) focused on in-depth interviewing techniques and the art of hearing the interviewee. We found such techniques to be particularly necessary across different languages and cultures where reading between the lines, spiraling, appropriate turn taking (Clarke and Kanatani 1979), and intercultural communication competencies (Ruben and Kealey 1979), including deep appreciation for both cultures, are critical.

14.2.4 Intercultural Communication Competency Applied in Bicultural Organizations

Competencies such as *meta-cognitive* (mindfulness) (see Petherick in this book), Broome's (2009) *meta-affective* (empathy), *meta-behavioral* (universal or alternative behaviors), and Thomas's (2006) *cultural intelligence* (CQ) have inspired researchers to investigate deeper and wider horizons in order to understand and transfer the generalizable characteristics, attitudes, and behaviors to others who live in multicultural environments. From decades ago Barnlund's (1976) components of interpersonal meaning, IpM = *f*(Perception Orientation–PO) + (System of Values–SV) + (Communication Style–CS have influenced training designs and course curricula. Each of these three integrated elements provided guidance to interacting participants developing shared interpersonal meanings.

Other insights from intercultural scholars have influenced our thinking, professional engagements, and personal relationships. These are Barnlund's public and private self in Japan (1989), Hall's (1987) hidden dimensions, Mendenhall et al. (2009) global competencies for Japanese management, Thomas and Toyne's (1995), Yamazaki and Kayes's (2004) exploration of Japanese expatriates in the USA, and West et al. (2017) focus on biculturalism in multicultural work contexts. Most recently Moore-Jones (2018) reviewed the extant literature on intercultural competency and intercultural intelligence and provided a valuable summary of the earlier decades of research in the field.

Ruben and Kealey (1979) and Hawes and Kealey's (1981) studies of seven intercultural competencies have provided the core behavioral foundation for our project work. These skills are:

(a) Displaying empathy.
(b) Demonstrating respect.
(c) Exhibiting behavioral flexibility.
(d) Expressing a personal orientation to knowledge (particularistic, rather than universalistic).
(e) Displaying a posture of interaction (curiosity, rather than judgmental).
(f) Managing interactions with mutual reciprocity.
(g) Demonstrating a tolerance for ambiguity.
We have added:
(h) Persevering with patience. (Both are essential in working with Eastern cultures.)

14.2.5 *Japanese and US Cultural Analysis Models and Materials*

The core foundations of our cultural value models used in analyzing and navigating through bicultural CI data were found in the value systems from Eastern and Western religions and philosophies (applied in Clarke 1992). The associated communication styles model Clarke and Yoshikawa developed from a literature review of Japanese and US literature has been widely utilized but never published. *(Clarke will send pdf forms of these models by email if requested.)* American cultural values from a Japanese perspective are often observed as the opposite of Japanese values, i.e., independence, rationality, equality, inclusivity, honesty, and informality, rather than interdependent, intuition, hierarchy, exclusivity, harmony, and formality, among others. An important critical distinction undergirding values was the American assumption of a coherent independent identity and the Japanese assumption of a coherent interdependent identity (Markus and Kitayama 1991). The Japanese consistency is evident in the continual balancing of the "Yin" and "Yang" in constantly changing contexts – "all things exist as inseparable and contradictory opposites" (Cartwright 2018). This context-oriented perspective is supportive of Hall's (1976) observation of high- and low-context cultures, represented in Japan and the USA, respectively.

We interpreted each CI from these Japanese and American cultural perspectives incorporated in Clarke's BMW framework for analyzing respective systems of values and intercultural communication styles of Japanese (Clarke 1992). "BMW" refers to the Confucian "Ba" (place or position), the Buddhist "Ma" (space or time), and Shinto "Wa" (harmony). This framework provides a contrast-culture (Yin – Yang) interpretation of opposites as continua held as assumptions by the American and Japanese workers within each CI. Japan's first constitution written by Prince Shōtoku Taishi in 604 A.D. – the "Seventeen Article Constitution" – reflects the influences of Japan's three philosophy/religions referenced in the principles in the

"BMW" framework. Multiple derivatives grounded on these principles are the concepts and behavioral styles that guide Japanese in their intercultural relations and communications.

Bejinaru (2010) discussed the concept of "Ba," and Nonaka and Konno (1998) applied the role of "Ba" in knowledge creation in organizations. In business relationships it influences which place (context) permits or prohibits certain kinds of communication styles and at the same time the hierarchy of the relationship, either "up" or "down," which further determines what language to use, formal polite ("teineigo"), toward upper status ("keigo"), or informal casual ("futsūgo") Japanese ("Nihongo") (CI 4.2 and CI 4.3).

Pilgrim (1986) and Oosterling (2005) explained the concept of "Ma" as the interval between space, as between objects or among persons, which influences objective and subjective relationships between individuals, i.e., who are either "in or out" ("uchi" – "soto") of their group. This further influences whether one uses public or private ("tatemae" – "honne" communication styles (Barnlund 1989). "Ma" also influences intervals in time, as in conversations and when to be silent to create "Ma" or reflection time. Japanese take 30% longer pauses between expressions than Americans (Clarke and Kanatani 1979), which is one reason why they have difficulty keeping up with and interrupting Americans in conversations.

An outcome of the "Wa" concept of harmony (Wierzbicka 1991; Konishi et al. 2007) was "kata" (form or formal), which structures behavior in a way that saves face and maintains harmony. "Kata" is used in "tatemae" (public and front) style of communication, which can be either formal polite "teineigo" or "keigo" style when communicating with guests and bosses, and in ceremonies and other formalities, i.e., when meeting your fiancée's parents for the first time. Black and Mendenhall (1993) were insightful in demonstrating how these many derivatives could explain the maintenance of these concepts and further discussed the impact of "on" (obligation) and "giri" (duty), especially as they applied them in conflict resolution processes, particularly in hierarchical relationships. Nonaka et al. (2008) discussed how difficult a task managing "Ba, Ma, and Wa" can be in their comparison of Japanese and Anglo-American ways of thinking because there is a Yin and Yang in each of them. This difficulty leads many Japanese women in the USA to comment on how emancipated they feel speaking English without the sensitivities to all of these social relationship factors in Japan.

14.3 Method

14.3.1 Data Criteria for Selection of CI

Utilized bicultural CIs selection criteria were: (a) the CI's criticality, (b) the inclusion of all three MEF, and (c) the cultural richness inherent in the CI. A CI's criticality was measured primarily by the impact on individual and team performance in terms of the length of delays in task performance and diminished employee morale, measured by walkaways, refusal to engage, and obstinacy of opinions. Cultural richness or intercultural complexity was determined by the inclusion of data drawn from both cultural values and communication styles.

14.3.2 Our CI Analysis and Interpretation Process

We analyzed clients' CIs interactively during interviews by:

1. Identifying hidden assumptions and expectations behind MEFs that contributed to critical breakdowns in communication.
2. Identifying the individual and organizational consequences of those CI.
3. Identifying initial causal explanations articulated by both members of the CI.
4. Interpreting those causal factors in a broader intercultural perspective with cultural frameworks of analyses.
5. Identifying the means of resolving the CI utilized by each client's project team.

14.4 Results

14.4.1 Leadership and Managerial Roles: "Yankee Go Home!"

Japanese technical managers in a production plant erroneously judged the nature of American technical managers' roles that resulted in a major CI. Americans found "Yankee go home!!!" in large red letters on a bathroom mirror. The Japanese employees' collective assumption was that US technology trainers were expert "generalists" in the whole production process rather than "specialists" in one specific process station. The historical yell of "Yankee go home" had survived since WWII occupation days. The Americans were observably offended and cursed their colleagues. Production halted for two hours at the plant, while the Japanese top manager explained in Japanese his understanding of "position expertise" and general expertise. Above the noise an American yelled, "Why didn't you just tell us to our face?" After much discussion, the Japanese manager summarized with a convincing explanation, and peace was restored with handshakes all around. Japanese managers acknowledged how much depth about each position they still did not know, i.e. about the troubleshooting phase ahead of start-up production. They learned from their seasoned boss more details about production processes and decided the Americans were still needed. Respect and trust had a chance to be repaired amidst the stressful operations of a new plant start-up.

Summary: A Japanese error in judgment about role functions based on mistaken perceptions of job definitions. The consequences were a lot of hostility and negative destructive accusations that destroyed a year of building respect and trust, due to its fragile bicultural nature. Also a delay of online work of two hours occurred in order to resolve this highly critical CI. Japanese and American plant workers have clear differences of expected scope in their job descriptions based on the traditional Japanese circular promotions vs. the American business experience of promotions up the same departmental ladder. Their interdependent and dependent self-construals manifested themselves in those two patterns of promotions. The Japanese writing on the mirror juxtaposed against the American demand to be told directly reflects differences in communication styles, i.e., the Japanese uses of a co-between and avoidance of direct conflict vs. American speaking the truth directly in a constructive conflict resolution process. One client's Japanese managers refused to be trained in the company's conflict resolution process until we added the word "constructive." These important distinctions of norms of behavior grounded in values and communication styles need to always be discussed in a bicultural workplace before CIs and misunderstandings reach the point of explosion. In this CI case, the bicultural team was fortunate to be led by a more informed, insightful, and skilled Japanese top manager.

14.4.2 Motivating Local Employees: "Reward the Best Salesman as a Team Role Model"

This statement was based on assumptions about independent reward systems and role modeling in the USA. It was a mistaken perception of how local employees can be motivated. This American sales manager said, "I just wanted to reward him by sending him to Europe to receive the reward for best salesman of the year at our global sales meeting." However, at the meeting the manager announced his decision to the team leader in a team meeting, which caused the Japanese top salesman to refuse to go to the annual sales meeting. The befuddled American manager asked him for an explanation, and he kept silent along with everyone else. The "Wa" had been disturbed. During a break in the meeting, he again asked him, "Why"? The Japanese expressed his fear that the team would reject him if he went to Europe to accept the reward personally. The bicultural facilitator helped the Japanese explain his reasoning and used the proverb about "the nail that sticks up gets hammered down." The American manager's assumption was that by singling out one model leader others would be motivated by their normal competitive spirit and desire to emulate him, a natural view from an independent self's worldview. After facilitated discussions the manager, the individual who demonstrated his interdependence, and later with his team, collectively decided by consensus that he could go if he could accept the reward in behalf the team and express his team's gratitude for the award in his acceptance speech. The team together prepared the speech he read at the ceremony. A failure was avoided!

Summary: This was a mistaken perception of the Japanese core value by an American assumption of independency in social relations. It was also an error of judgment presuming the universality of Western motivation theory that was not transferrable to Japan in this case. Assumptions about the principles in motivating employees are not universal but rather are determined by cultural context. The team meeting extended an extra hour because of the private discussion with the salesman. He could not discuss the subject within the team-meeting context due to it not being the right "Ba" for such discussions without preparatory discussions. The risk of face loss for the manager and the salesman would have been unacceptable in that it could violate the principle of "Wa." Additional time was taken for the team to write the award speech in English, which required coaching from the facilitator. Unfortunately the manager did not seek advice on his approach to the meeting beforehand and made an error of judgment on two counts, values of "Wa" and communication "Ba."

14.4.3 Japanese and American Communication Styles: "I can't stand that 'tatemae'!"

A Japanese worker was called into the American manager's office to share what was happening on his slow-moving project. When asked directly to be truthful, the worker withdrew from the conversation in silence and just sat there in "Ma." The Boss said, "Don't give me that 'tatemae' stuff again, I just want your 'honne'" ("private" thoughts or in this case "the truth") because his "tatemae" was mistakenly perceived as a "lie" by his boss. The effort failed, he excused the worker, and the boss turned to the consultant and said, "I can't stand that 'tatemae.' He'll be difficult to promote." What is surprising is that even though the American had been in Japan seven years experiencing boss-subordinate relationships and face-saving "tatemae" communication, he chose to retain his American perception. He consistently made negative erroneous judgments about his employees who would not speak from their "honne" in his office – the wrong "Ba." Instead he persisted in accusing Japanese of lying or secrecy. He perceived the only way to do business was by speaking honestly and truthfully in any context. That was an extreme CI resulting in obstinacy and failure from which the Japanese suffered the consequences in his career.

Summary: Mistaken perceptions about each other's communication styles often result in critical incidents between Japanese and Americans working together in vertical relationships. The Japanese was practicing the "*kata*" he had learned for sustaining "Wa" in public relationships in his interdependent world. The American mistakenly perceive "*tatemae*" as lying instead of as respect for the manager and protecting him from a loss of face in their quest for harmony, which is the Japanese path to integrity. The Japanese may have mistakenly perceived his boss' thirst for openness and directness as risky and aggressive when he was really looking for honesty, which was his path to integrity. Both could learn to respect and trust the other when they realize that they are after the same goal in relationships – integrity – but first they have to demonstrate mutual respect for each other's values and styles.

The Japanese would welcome telling his manager what's really going on and even what is wrong with his business judgments if the environment was changed, i.e., to a bar while sharing drinks after work. The change of "Ba" permits the private face (true feelings) of *honne* to be expressed in a more suitable context. The American would welcome learning about his Japanese way of seeing the world if the Japanese would only explain it. With both taking a step toward the other, their business and relationship may improve. That goal is something to which they could both commit. Together they need to understand each other's intentions by practicing intercultural communication appropriate to each particular context and withhold the judgments that lead to failure.

14.5 Discussion and Implications

14.5.1 Discussion

Investigating MEF-provoked CIs with this method and process offered advantages in researching and facilitating transformative changes in individual self-construals and organizational culture. The long-term on-site processes of investigating CI enabled tracking of transformations in individual and team identities and organizational culture changes.

In this qualitative approach, we assumed an integrated objectivity and subjectivity in team roles enabled broader goals to be served in behalf of the teams and the organizations through more holistic, natural, and supportive environments. It eliminated the concern about memory loss in reports of CI, encouraged a process that reduces uncertainty anxiety, built upon differences to develop shared standards for work performance, created inclusivity through team interdependencies that contributed to respect and trust building, created a common membership in team bicultural identity development through a single potent link in their team partners, and was driven by coherent and authentic corporate values that supported bicultural organization development.

We did not advocate a transformation from one identity to another but rather from two separate identities as team members into a third collaboratively developed bicultural team identity that was multifaceted or a split identity in personal and organizational contexts. It would be flexible, inclusive, and expansive of one's behavioral repertoire, value system, and capability to imagine and incorporate alternative paths to a common goal, i.e., behaviors could be learned for both high- and low-cultures, and self-construals could include independent and interdependent identities dependent on surrounding contexts.

Transformative changes encouraged through the CIT required goal and value alignments, supportive policies that encouraged CI analyses and resolution, interdependency in work tasks, competencies of facilitators, and approval of the time required in multiple CI for breakthroughs to that "ah-ha!" moment. Language and communication style modifications for intercultural contexts were used to prevent the imposition of any external standard of transformative processes. The processes required were respectful, empathetic, and trusting in a way that facilitated achievement of individual, team, and organizational goals.

Researcher-consultant-facilitator capacities enabled the application mastery role modeling of intercultural communication competencies while navigating through each CI. With multiple CIs involving nearly all participants, there were multiple repeat opportunities for continual learning in supportive relationships committed to "kaizen" (incremental improvements toward perfection). Further, equalizing status attributions by raising self-efficacy beliefs with positive feedback and aligning personal and corporate goal systems increased motivation and strengthened commitment to the organization.

We found distinction of learning styles were suggestive of alternative approaches to interviewing participants in CIs, i.e., by reversing the sequencing of the cognitive, affective, and behavioral elements (Yamazaki, 2005). We first asked interviewees to share their hidden assumptions and expectations about the CI, which they had previously thought of as "common sense" but found that they were not universally applicable. What the Japanese and American actually perceived in the CI was usually not the other's intention. Those differences were the causes of the MEFs. Those assumptions and expectations were based on mistaken perceptions that actually led to errors in judgment and failures in execution in some cases. In facilitating collaborative CI analyses with Ruben and Kealey's (1979) competencies, we found efficacy in adding the D.I.E. method of inquiry (three levels of communication, describe, interpret, and evaluate). Generally, dialogue in bicultural CI analyses without facilitation begins with mistaken evaluations, errors in judgments, and negative accusations followed by anger and behavioral disengagement.

This embedded approach further enabled the growth of associates' professional roles to progress from researchers into consultants, trainers, facilitators, coaches, counselors, and collaborative evaluators of outcomes and benefits to an organization. Even the researcher-consultants had transforming experiences in the process of these engagements!

14.5.2 Implications

Our findings indicate that this research method of qualitative culture analysis of intercultural CIs as they occur in multinational workplaces offers practitioners business managers an effective alternative approach to organizational change and transformative individual identity development in a bicultural organization. This embedded method motivates participants to improve their own performance by their own thinking, feelings, and behavioral efforts, including consequentially those of researcher-consultants.

We found that CEOs of large companies and leaders of overseas subsidiaries accepted this approach to transforming their cultural issues into productive bicultural organizations, sometimes due to their own transformative experiences. This model was found to be an effective model for others based on their flexible perceptions, inclusive values, and intercultural competencies. It supported the development of bicultural identities and effective intercultural organizations with such competencies and commitments to continual learning from other cultures. Others could achieve similar results from such collaborations with capable management consultants.

14.6 Limitations

Limitations on organizational learning and replicability through this research process are an organization's policies that undermine learning by expats and only focus on developing local nationals. Limitations on the sustainability of an organization's CIT approach depend on the support for organizational learning through the transfer of these skills from consultant internally to a division of Human Resources perhaps. Transferability to other countries is limited by the availability of trained resources and corporate support.

Limitations placed on our processes were the time required for customization, administrative record keeping, and continual training and sustaining of capable associates, for maximizing communications among our associates scattered around the client organizations and for language barriers among clients' participants, and the time to raise such competencies.

14.7 Conclusion

In addition to the summaries in Sects. 14.4.1, 14.4.2 and 14.4.3, we found that by engaging in intercultural analyses of CIs as they occur enables researchers and practitioners to contribute to creating transformative knowledge through a process that can facilitate transformative changes. Questionnaire-based investigations of participant's perceptions of CIs have revealed multiple issues and produced only partial analyses. Adding a qualitative phenomenological ethnographic approach created greater holistic clarity and enabled transformations simultaneously. This approach required training in multiple skills that may be in short supply. Bicultural teams and organizational support are required for execution and receptive organizations beneath the executives must commit to the time and funding required and practice the corporate values.

This grounded research approach and action-oriented process combined to demonstrate results in (a) the facilitation of the development of knowledge based on cultural insights; (b) changed attitudes toward greater inclusivity based on mutual respect, empathy, and trust; and (c) contributed to intercultural skill development that has changed individual identities and organizational cultures. These results should encourage a broader professional and organizational commitment to these challenges and achieving these goals could bring more clarity and peace in a culturally chaotic world.

Acknowledgments We thank our clients for their commitment to resolving their intercultural organizations' issues, our full-time associates for their compassion and excellence, and our external researchers' inspirational support and for their published articles on our work (in *italics*). These research-consultants were *Dean Barnlund, Harumi Befu, Kline Harrison, Todd Imahori, Mitch Hammer, Judith Martin, Michael Paige, Paul Pedersen, George Renwick, Steven Rhinesmith,* and *Muneo Yoshikawa.* Their roles were described in Clarke (2008). Above all, we thank our God, our families, and Pata-Pata for their sustaining support.

References

Bandura, A. (1988), Organizational applications of socio-cognitive theory. *Australian Journal of Management*. 13, 275–302.

Barnlund, D. C. (1976, July). Multileveled, Multidimensional, Multidirectional, Multi-Coded Intercultural Communication. Paper Presented at the 1st Stanford Institute For Intercultural Communication, Stanford University, Palo Alto, CA.

Barnlund, D.C. (1989) Public and private self in communicating with Japan, *Business Horizons*, March-April. 32–40.

Bejinaru, R. (2010). Knowledge dynamics and the concept of 'BA'. The Annals of "The Stefan cel Mare" University of Suceava, Romania. 10, 339–943.

Black, J. S. & Mendenhall, M. (1993). Resolving conflicts with the Japanese–Mission Impossible? *Sloan Management Review* (Spring). 34(3), 49–59.

Broome, B. J. (2009). Building relational empathy through an interactive design process. In D. D. J. Sandole, S. Byrne, I. Staroste-Sandole, J. Senihi (Eds.), *Handbook of Conflict analysis and resolution* (pp. 184–200). New York: Routledge.

Cartwright, M. (2018). Yin and Yang. Ancient History Encyclopedia. Retrieved from: https://www.ancient.eu/Yin_and_Yang/

Clarke, C. H. (1992). Communicating benefits to a culturally diverse employee population. *Employees Benefits Journal* (March). 17(1), 26–32.

Clarke, C. H. (2008). Practicing the integration of discipline and compassion. *Journal of Intercultural Communication*. 11, 1–21.

Clarke, C. H. (2017). Reflections From History: How Shifting Paradigms Created Intercultural Innovations. *Journal of Intercultural Communication*, 20, 1–26.

Clarke, C. H. & Kanatani, K. (1979). Structure of turn taking. *Language, Education, and Technology*. 12–24. NII Electronic Library Service (in Japanese).

Clarke, C. H. & Lipp, G. D. (1998a). *Danger and Opportunity–Resolving Conflict in U.S. Based Japanese Subsidiaries*. Yarmouth, ME: Intercultural Press.

Clarke, C. H. & Lipp, G. L. (1998b). Conflict resolution for contrasting cultures, *Training & Development*, February. 22–33. Arlington, VA: ASTD Press.

Clarke, C. H. & Takashiro, N. (2019). Transforming shame to collective pride and social equity in bicultural organizations in Japan. In C. H. Mayer & E. Vanderheiden (Eds.), *The Bright Side of Shame*. Switzerland: Springer Nature. (pp. 267–28).

Cohen, E. G. (1994), Restructuring the classroom: Conditions for productive small groups. *Review of Educational Research* (Spring). 64(1), 1–35.

Cohen, E. G. (1995), Producing equal-status interaction in the heterogeneous classroom. *American Educational Research Journal* (Spring). 32(1), 99–120.

Edvardsson, B. & Roos, I. (2001). Critical Incident Techniques: Towards a Framework for Analysing the Criticality of Critical Incidents. *International Journal of Service Industry Management*. 12(3), 251–268.

Flanagan, J. C. (1954). The Critical Incident Technique. *Psychological Bulletin*. 51(4), 327–358.

Gronewold, U., Gold, A., Salterio, S. E. (2013). Reporting Self-Made Errors: The impact of organizational error-management climate and error type. *Journal of Business Ethics*. 117, 189–208.

Gudykundst, W. B., Matsumoto, Y., Ting-Toomey, S., Nishida, T., Kim, K., & Heyman, S. (1996). The influence of cultural individualism-collectivism, self-construals, and individual values on communication styles across cultures. *Human Communication Research*, 22(4), 510–543.

Gulker, J. E. and Monteith, M. J. (2013). Intergroup boundaries and attitudes: the power of a single potent link. *Personality and Social Psychology Bulletin*. 39(7), 943–955.

Gutierrez, B., Howard-Grenville, J., & Scully, M. A. (2010). Split Identification and an unlikely change effort. *Academy of Management Journal*. 53(4), 673–699.

Hall, E. T. (1976). *Beyond Culture*. Garden City, NY: Anchor Press/Doubleday.

Hall, E. T. (1987). *The Hidden Dimension*: Doing Business with the Japanese. Garden City, NY: Anchor Books/Doubleday.

Hawes, F. & Kealey, D. J. (1981). An empirical study of Canadian technical assistance: Adaptation and effectiveness on overseas assignment. *International Journal of Intercultural Relations*. 5(3) 239–258.

Hyman, H. H. (1960). Reflections on Reference Groups. *Oxford Academy's Public Opinion Quarterly*. 24(3), 383–396).

Kolb D. A. (1984). *Experiential learning: Experience as the source of learning and development*. Englewood Cliffs, New Jersey: Prentice Hall.

Konishi, E., Yahiro, M., Ono, M., and Nakajima, N. (2007). Harmony (Wa): The Japanese traditional value and its implications for nursing ethics in Japan. *Japan Association for Bioethics* (September). 17(1), 74–81. NII–Electronic Library Service.

Kowner, R, (2002). Japanese communication in intercultural encounters: the barrier of status-related behavior. *International Journal for Intercultural Relations*. 26, 339–361.

Malbasic, I., Mas-Machuca, and Marimon, F. (2018). Through the decreased values gap to increased organizational effectiveness: The mediating role of organizational commitment. *Journal of Human Values*. 24(2), 1–15.

Markus, H.R. and Kitayama, S. (1991). Culture and the self: implications for cognition, emotion, and motivation. *Psychological Review*. 98(2), 224–253.

Mendenhall, M., Oddou, G. R., Stevens, M. J., Bird, A., Osland, J., Furuya, N. (2009). Developing Global Competencies in Japanese Managers: Research, Process, and Recommendations. *Journal of Strategic Management Studies* (October). 7(2), 57–67.

Mezirow, J. (2003). Transformative Learning as Discourse. *Journal of Transformative Education* (January). 1(1), 58–63.

Mezirow, J. (2004). Forum comment on Sharan Merriman's "The role of cognitive development in Mezirow's transformational learning theory". *Adult Education Quarterly* (November). 55(1), 69–70

Moore-Jones, P.J. (2018), Intercultural Sensitivity, Intercultural Competence & Intercultural Intelligence: A Review of Literature and a Proposition of a Linear Relationship, *Journal of Education and Culture Studies*. 2(2) 75–86.
Morizuma (2011). Constructing multifaceted cultural identity theory: Beyond dichotomization of individualism-collectivism. *China Media Research*. 7(2) 17–25.
Nishishiba, M. & Richie, L. D. (2000), The concept of trustworthiness: A cross-cultural comparison between Japanese and U.S. business people, *Journal of Applied Communication Research*. 28(4) 347–367.
Nonaka, I. & Konno, N. (1998). The Concept of "BA": Building a foundation for knowledge creation. *California Management Review*. 40(3), 40–54.
Nonaka, I., Ray, T., & Umemoto, K. (2008). Japanese knowledge creation in Anglo-American environments. *Prometheus–Critical Studies in Innovation*. 16(4), 421–439.
Oosterling, H. (2005). MA or Sensing Time–Space: Towards a culture of the inner. Internet reprint of lecture, Berlin. Retrieved from: https://www.henkoosterling.nl/pdfs/lect_berlin_ma_2005.pdf.
Pilgrim, R. B. (1986). Intervals ("Ma") in Space and Time–Foundations for a Religio-Aesthetic Paradigm in Japan. *History of Religions* (February). 25(3), 255–277
Ruben, B.D. & Kealey, D.J. (1979). Behavioral assessment of communication competency and the prediction of cross-cultural adaptation. *International Journal of Intercultural Relations*. 3 15–47.
Rubin, H. J. & Rubin, I. S. (2012) (2nd Edition). *Qualitative Interviewing: The Art of Hearing Data*. Thousand Oaks, CA: SAGE.
Thomas, D. C. (2006). Domain and Development of Cultural Intelligence: The Importance of Mindfulness. *International Journal of Intercultural Relations*. 31, 78–99.
Thomas, D. C. & Toyne, B. (1995). Subordinates' responses to cultural adaptation by Japanese expatriate managers. *Journal of Business Research*. 32, 1–10.
Trifiletti, E. & Capozza, D. (2011). Examining group-based trust with the investment game. *Social Behavior and Personality*. 39(3), 405–410.
West, A. L., Zhang, R., Yampolsky, M., Sasaki, J. Y. (2017). More Than The Sum of Its Parts: A Transformative Theory of Biculturalism. *Journal of Cross-Cultural Psychology*. 48(7), 963–990.
Wierzbicka, A. (1991). Japanese Key Words and Core Cultural Values. *Language in Society* (September). 20(3), 333–385.
Williams, M. (2007), Building Genuine Trust Through Interpersonal Emotion Management: A Threat Regulation Model of Trust and Collaboration Across Boundaries. *Academy of Management Review*. 32(2), 595–621.
Yamazaki, Y. (2005), Learning styles and typologies of cultural differences: A theoretical and empirical comparison. *International Journal of Intercultural Relations*. 29, 521–548.
Yamazaki, Y. & Kayes, D. C. (2004). An Experimental Approach to Cross-Cultural Learning: A Review and Integration of Competencies for Successful Expatriate Adaptation. *Academy of Management Learning & Education*. 3(4), 362–379.
Yamazaki, Y. & Kayes, D. C. (2007). Expatriate learning: exploring how Japanese managers adapt in the U.S. *International Journal of Human Resource Management* (August). 18(8), 1373–1395.
Yuki, M., Maddux, W. W., Brewer, M. B., and Takemura, K. (2005). Cross-Cultural Differences in Relationship- and Group-Based Trust. *Personality and Social Psychology Bulletin*. 31, 48–62.

Clifford H. Clarke (Retired) He was raised in Japan through high school by second-generation expatriate parents, whose own parents first moved to Japan in 1898, the year the USA forced the Queen to abdicate her crown in the Kingdom of Hawai'i.

His higher education focused on the goal of becoming an effective "bridge person" by studying world religions and philosophies (B.A.) at Wake Forest University, Asian studies (PGS) at ICU in Tokyo, counseling across cultures (M.Div.) at Duke University, and interdisciplinary studies in the social sciences (ABD) at Stanford University's Graduate School of Education.

His four careers have evolved through 11 years of counseling foreign students at Cornell and Stanford universities, 13 years of teaching intercultural communication at Stanford and the University of Hawaii, 25 years of intercultural business management consulting mostly in U.S. -Japan business relationships, and 6 years of educational program design and evaluation in the State of Hawaii public schools.

Clarke has published 25 papers, chapters, or books in these areas, given 45 presentations at professional societies and universities, and been interviewed by 25 newspapers and magazines in Japan, the USA, and Europe. He also founded three NPOs, including the Stanford Institute for Intercultural Communication (SIIC) and two LLCs, including the Clarke Consulting Group (CCG), and cofounded SIETAR (1971) and SIETAR Japan (1984).

Naomi Takashiro With a PhD in Educational Psychology, she has been teaching English classes as adjunct faculty in the Department of Global Tourism at the Kyoto University of Foreign Studies and its junior college in Kyoto, Japan. Growing up in a low-SES family in Japan, her academic interests are socioeconomic status, inequality, and motivation in education, and she has published several articles in the area. She lived in Hawaii for 20 years and worked in multicultural organizations before coming back to Kyoto 3 years ago. In her spare time, she likes to read, walk, cook, and play with birds. She has been looking for a full-time job at a university. She remains grateful to God for His guidance in writing this paper.

Chapter 15
Error-Culture in Value-Based Organizations: A Christian Perspective

Elmar Nass

Abstract Credible corporate culture in value-based organizations (e.g. in the non-profit sector) exists when the commitment to transparent values corresponds with the living practice. Christian companies must be measured by Christian business ethics. This makes them reliable and distinguishable as an employer and as a provider (e.g. of services) in the market. The Christian image of humans presupposes the defectiveness of men. Lived mistake-culture is therefore an essential indicator for the credible shaping of rules and relationships. I hypothesize that this aspect of Christian corporate culture has not been adequately researched yet. But there are corresponding shortcomings in practice. Closing this gap is an ambitious goal and I want to take a step into this direction.

Therefore, I present a systematic approach to how the Christian image of man is a basis of values, which should determine the mistake-culture. This includes motivation, communication, control in the company, as well as the qualification of executives and also educational measures. The image of people handling their own and the mistakes of others are intensively addressed. I want to systematically link company sociology and leadership ethics with each other, so that a Christian profile (from a Catholic point of view with ecumenical accents) can merge in theory and practice.

First, I introduce the Christian image of man as a cultural value base with its ethical implications. Following, I identify areas of application of the mistake-culture in the company. Finally, I propose some principles of Christian mistake-culture as a normative compass for organizations.

Keywords Mistakes · Errors · Failure · Human dignity · Justice · Mercy · Christian Business ethics · Image of man · Leadership ethics · Defectiveness of man

E. Nass (✉)
Department Ethik und Philosophie, Wilhelm Löhe Hochschule, Fürth, Germany
e-mail: elmar.nass@wlh-fuerth.de

E. Vanderheiden, C.-H. Mayer (eds.), *Mistakes, Errors and Failures across Cultures*, https://doi.org/10.1007/978-3-030-35574-6_15

15.1 Introduction

"Learning from your mistakes". "We all make mistakes"! "To err is human". "Great things never come easily". These and other life wisdoms are like soothing balm after mistakes have been made. This also applies in everyday working life. There is not always such comfort or encouragement under the pressure of time, money, vanity and competition. Occasionally there may also be a need for warnings or sanctions. Mistakes also have a dark side, as in health care: for example, in the American study "To err is human" (see Vanderheiden and Mayer Introduction and Brommundt), conducted by the Institute of Medicine in 2000, it was found that 44,000 to 98,000 deaths in US clinics would have been preventable (cf. Bechtel 2012). So how to deal with mistakes? Is the learning effect the main focus? And what role may play punishment or forgiveness?

It is an essential part of the respective corporate culture in organizations how those affected by mistakes (e.g. those who caused the damage, those who are suffering the effects in the company, superiors, team, etc.) are dealing with or should be dealing with mistakes. It is about the normative evaluation of human mistakes and especially about the evaluation and design of the associated contexts of human interaction between the people who make mistakes and those who are affected by them (through direct or indirect physical, health, material, temporal or psychological consequences or conditioned by roles – e.g. a manager in relation to his employees – within the hierarchy of the organization or the like). Mistakes-culture (ideally and in lived practice) is thus the object of systematic reflection through corporate ethics. The practice should be aiming towards the ideal, which may be publicized in mission statements or guidelines, and should coincide with it as far as possible.

We find some recent ideas of Christian business ethics (cf., e.g. Melé and Cantón 2014; Keppeler 2014; Rohrhirsch 2013). But the idea of a coherent system of Christian business ethics is still pioneering work (cf. Nass and Kreuer 2018). An application of such theory to a corresponding culture of mistake is not yet known to me (cf. Hahn 2009). It cannot be resorted to a generally accepted model here. First and foremost, it is not easy to recapitulate a Christian culture of mistakes for companies. Rather, this requires a creative reflection.

With this goal I do not continue to differentiate between ideal and lived mistakes-culture, I formulate principles into an ideal for credibly established practice instead.[1] In this way I want to propose a normative guideline from a Christian perspective (after a Catholic point of view). Dealing with mistakes in this way has something to do with responsibility, justice, and possibly forgiveness. A concept of "mistakes - forgiveness - new beginnings" is so obvious to us that we hardly think about its Christian origin (cf. Hahn 2009). This underexposed reflection should be made here. The explicitly Christian perspective on this subject is also being demanded by

[1] For a principle-based comparison of ideal and practice, cf. Jaensch et al. (2015) with a view to a diaconal corporate culture. Empirical surveys are required as next steps into practice, which could apply these principles.

representatives of secular philosophy. For example, Charles Taylor recognizes that the Christian faith can offer a much better argumentative foundation for forgiveness, love, and justice than secular theories do. This has two consequences: (1) Christians should express such justifications, and (2) secular people can learn something about their self-understanding and how they interact with each other (cf. Taylor 2007; Kühnlein 2018; Wenzel 2013).

The guideline proposed in this chapter is not simply a Decalogue compiled in laborious diligence from guidelines of Christian organizations, for example, in the health and social services. As far as the mistakes-culture is concerned, there is too little to be found in such sources (cf. Hahn 2009). I develop such reflected theses as thought-provoking impulses on the basis of the Christian image of man, for mission statements and even more for lived practice. I will explain the concept of mistake first and will identify organizations or contexts for which a Christian mistakes-culture is an ideal or a challenge second. I will outline the ethical standards at last and finally present some examples of application in the field of tension between ideal and practice.

15.2 Focus on Mistakes

I define first, which working life situations will be considered as mistakes and which not.[2] Undoubtedly, I am reducing complexity, to help focus on the essential issues.

Mistakes in working life can be of very different character. I propose to differentiate exemplary four types:

1. Objective and technical mistakes: A hospital nurse confuses the medication of a patient.
2. Mistakes of estimation: The supervisory board has appointed a new manager which, although he presents himself splendidly, was already known to other companies as an opportunistic "grasshopper". Soon after his appointment, he turns out to show his real character again with corresponding negative effects for the company.
3. Strategic mistake: An employee of the research institute, which depends on money, sharply criticizes the representative of the potential sponsor at a meeting for his late arrival.
4. Moral mistake: A group leader learns about the death in the closest family of an employee, who is visibly affected by it. The supervisor chooses to ignore this information, shows no empathy and urges to keep working concentrated instead (see Ryan in this book).

[2] Differences are made between mistakes (as wrong behaviour), errors (e.g. in a scientific or mathematical sense) and failure (consequence of mistakes and mistakes). In this article mistakes are the core of reflection.

The first case is clearly identifiable as a mistake. The second to fourth examples enable diverse interpretations which could come to different conclusions. The examples are merely intended to illustrate the different "quality" of mistakes, irrespective of the concrete evaluation. I will simply assume that all four examples can be classified as mistakes. But what connects and what separates technical, estimative, strategic and moral mistakes?

Definition 1
Mistakes have in common that an alternative behaviour would be preferable in each case and those responsible could have known or done it better.

I can identify mistakes clearly under such circumstances. It becomes more difficult, if one of these conditions is not fulfilled, like in the following varied situations:

- A patient absolutely and immediately needs a certain medical compound, which is not available. A substitute substance is taken which does not achieve the full effect. This is objectively considered a mistake, but could not be avoided in the concrete situation, as there was no better alternative.
- If the applicant for the management board position was a blank piece of paper, if he presented himself well, if everything was perfectly examined and if the supervisory board also wanted to offer a chance to younger managers, the nature of the new manager, which later turns out to be negative, could not have been predicted. This situation remains objectively and retrospectively a mistake that could not be foreseen. With the preconditions the members of the supervisory board could not have known better.

I will not discuss such and even more complex constellations, because they challenge us to identify certain situations as mistakes at all. This debate is not part of my comprehensive treatise. I do not wish to continue that reflection any longer, although this might be part of a paper with a different focus. My question therefore should be how should it responsibly be dealt with clearly identified mistakes in working live (see examples 1–4 on the basis of Definition 1). With this simplification, I can now narrow down my definition of mistakes and focus on small, but important, differences (cf. Unger 2009).

Additionally, I can also take into account what certain types of mistakes have or have not in common. A separating factor in my examples is that it must be applied in each case in order to identify the preferred situation. As mentioned in the situations above, this is (1) compliance with the patient's prescribed medication, (2) careful interpretation of existing facts, (3) careful consideration of the benefits and harms of an action and (4) orientation towards a moral idea of the good. From this follows my expanded definition:

Definition 2
The mistakes I am looking at here are clearly violations of objective and prudent reasonableness, wisdom and morality, to which there are preferable alternatives that could and should have been chosen by those responsible.[3]

15.3 Focus on Value-Based Organizations

Errors and mistakes happen wherever people interact and take responsibility. I will focus particularly on organizations for which a credible Christian corporate culture and thus also a mistakes-culture can, should or must be relevant (see also Ryan and Hallay-Witte and Janssen in this book). I think of expressly Christian organizations and agencies first, such as churches (including pastoral care, administration, diplomacy), Diaconia, Caritas and other Christian charities; foundations and associations (such as Christian Scouts, Kolping, etc.); and political associations or their substructures with a Christian claim (Christians in the Socialist Party, etc.). This also applies to all other companies, sponsors and organizations that profess a Christian culture in their mission statement, vision and mission. This can also be for-profit companies led by Christian leaders, with or without a public confession. Furthermore, Christianity always has the claim to have an inviting effect on society (cf. Taylor 2007): as light of the world, as a leaven and in this sense missionary. This mission is not to be understood aggressively (cf. Zerth et al. 2015). Rather, the credible idea and practice of a Christian way of living together (and to this belongs also the handling of mistakes), wanting to set an example from which non-Christian organizations and non-Christians can get orientation. In this sense the profiling of a Christian mistakes-culture is not only part of an internal morality, but also an example of good human cooperation beyond this context. Other organizations without Christian reference can get an orientation or a challenge but with comparable images of man and value priorities. The principles must also be communicable in not expressly Christian contexts, without abandoning my own level of justification (reference to Jesus Christ and the Holy Scripture).

I propose principles of Christian mistake culture, which want to be understood as normative mirrors for various Christian organizational contexts and also as a winning invitation to other value-based cultures (cf. Nass and Kreuer 2018).

[3] Further differentiations could be well justified here. Taking the focus of this contribution into account, I will limit myself to a simplification, which is undoubtedly only exemplary.

15.4 Focus on Moral Mistakes

After the mistake definition and the defined field of application, I now will present relevant aspects of the Christian conception of mankind, the guideline. It will help us to identify from this point of view the mistakes-culture in organizations. I take moral mistakes as our starting point, since those also impair the relationship of man with God in theology and are especially important. One can distinguish between two kinds of moral mistakes. The first kind is based on a free, conscious decision and is therefore a culpable breach. The second type of moral mistakes base on not intended actions (cf. Büschges et al. 1998, pp. 89–92). These consequences (as failure) happen by chance or are based on negligence. The second type of mistake is only morally relevant if they are intrinsically evil (e.g. a so-called *intrinsece malum*) (cf. Demmer 1987). For example, a child runs accidently in front of a truck and dies as a consequence; the killing per se remains a bad act. However, the attentive truck driver could not be morally certified to have made a mistake. Such differentiations in turn have a very high potential for complexity. I therefore concentrate in this article on situations which can intuitively be regarded as moral mistakes from a Christian point of view. Taking this for granted, I can draw conclusions for dealing with different types of mistakes.[4]

15.5 Human Dignity and Limits as a Point of View

On the one hand, human beings are created as God's images as written in the biblical story of creation (*Old Testament*). Thus, humans have a prominent position within creation, which justifies the unique quality of the inviolable dignity of every person. Although human individuals are not equally talented, they are nevertheless equally worthy. The dignity of men should not be measured in terms of qualities such as health, intelligence or age, nor should the dignity of a human being be attributed or denied by political parties, the economy or powerful people. The same dignity is rather a non-negotiable characteristic, which can't be lost through technical or moral mistakes.

On the other hand, humans are different from God, because they are defective and, also seducible to guilt or sin. This is described paradigmatically in the biblical story of Adam and Eve in paradise, through rich images. It phrases clearly, that humans are, in spite of their creation as image of God, different. The degree of this separation is judged differently in the Christian denominations. According to

[4]Even factual, technical and other mistakes should not be assessed just in terms of the act. The consequences are as important as the actual mistake. Examples are as follows: a patient suffers serious damage as a result of a confused medication, and a company has to pay high fines due to incorrect accounting.

Catholic understanding, there remains a remnant of good-being in mankind even after being expelled from paradise. God gives us the ability to distinguish between good and evil. He also provides humans with garments of skins (Gen 3:21f.). As a conclusion people also have an active part in their salvation from God.[5] According to Luther's interpretation, the relationship between humans and God is initially fundamentally shattered. Only through God's grace humans escape their ruin. The redemptive work of Jesus as a second Adam and the theological doctrine of original sin and grace play an essential role for this distinction. I do not want to deepen that thought further. It is important to note that the consequence of God's appearance through Jesus Christ is that every human being is called to discipleship with all their faults and sinfulness. The biographies of the apostles and the first great confessors (such as Saulus becoming Paulus) prove that even faulty human beings are called to discipleship. The nomination can be by God's grace or with the participation of the persons own moral achievements. With the central decision to follow Christ, people do not lose their attribute of sinfulness. Let us remember St. Peter, who denies Jesus three times during the night of Good Friday. Yet St. Peter is the rock on which the foundation of the church was built. So even the closest disciples of Jesus have made mistakes. This is due to the fact that I am never and I will never be the same as God. Such an essential existential of being human explains the special bond between humans and Jesus. He is God and human. And in this very complex symbiosis, he is a human being in everything except that he doesn't sin. The apostle Paul emphasizes this in the Epistle to the Romans a lasting human trait:

> For the good which I have a mind to do, I do not: but the evil which I have no mind to do, that I do. But if I do what I have no mind to do, it is no longer I who do it, but the sin living in me. So, I see a law that, though I have a mind to do good, evil is present in me. In my heart I take pleasure in the law of God, But I see another law in my body, working against the law of my mind, and making me the servant of the law of sin which is in my flesh. (Rom 7:19-23)[6]

So, the sinfulness of mankind remains our dominant characteristic, and seduction is also a possible trait even for saints and apostles. If this dark side of moral mistake is intrinsically attached to us from a Christian point of view, then how much more likely is the seduction to err, to produce factual mistakes or even mistakes of estimation. To err is therefore deeply human. No one can free themselves. On the other hand, no one loses dignity through it.

[5] Cf. Chap. 8 in this article.

[6] Cf. to a Catholic interpretation Anzenbacher (2001), 167, to a Protestant interpretation Frey et al. (1997), 78. Even in the Calvinist or Puritan doctrine of predestination, the occurrence of misconduct is not proof that God has deprived man of their grace. This refers to the predestined, as to all sinners. Cf. Weber (2000), 333.

15.6 Focus on Responsibility

From a Christian point of view, people bear a responsibility that is threefold: It follows the threefold commandment of love (Lk 10:27), given by Jesus. As a moral existence, in accordance with the biblical commandment of love, humans also carry this responsibility (cf. Nass and Kreuer 2018):

- Towards God: It is expressed by understanding life in the light of the Creator God, by being thankful for his gift and by developing freedom as a moral being in this light.
- Towards oneself: It is expressed by the self-awareness to be a creation in the image of God with an unconditional dignity and at the same time by recognizing the undivided dignity of the weak.
- Towards fellow humans: It is expressed by acts of concrete charity on the one hand and by the service for community life out of an affective spirit of social love on the other hand.

It is a moral mistake, if we do not take this threefold responsibility seriously. This does not mean that we lose our dignity. Nevertheless, a conscious, culpable or even negligent violation of it does not remain without consequences for our relationship with God. Taking this responsibility, which also derives from our talents, is – from a Catholic point of view – our active contribution to living accordingly to God's salvific mission.

Example: Threefold Responsible Behaviour in Theory and Practice
It is for example the doctor's responsibility not go to the operating theatre overtired, after working several shifts. At the same time, he has the responsibility to take care for himself and his body, because it is a gift from God. He also has a responsibility towards God, which always mirrors in self-love and charity. Not letting his personal relationship with God die despite work is an important aspect. Man has to take responsibility for his actions before God in the end. If we do not take responsibility in an appropriate way, we do something bad. This will distance us from other people and ourselves and also from God. Such self-caused remoteness from God, however, does not mean a loss of dignity, because we always remain God's image. Through God's grace we are always capable and get his reconciliation. Accordingly, even godless man has full dignity but at the same time the moral duty to change something in his life so that he can overcome the distance. This possibility exists until the moment of death. This means that potential for the good remains the whole life. This empowerment is also part of dignity and goodness, even as a godless man. In a Christian way of living, it is a matter of course to support one another to take one's responsibility and to follow God. Especially Christian leaders need to keep this in mind.

If we do not develop and use our potentials to build a good relationship between other humans and within the church community, then it is a violation of God's mandate. There is a duty to responsibility. In accordance with the principle of "Ultra posse nemo tenetur" (cf. Schockenhoff 2007, 375)[7], however, it must be ensured that the taken responsibility does not exceed one's own talents. Repetitive overstrain and overestimation of one's own self or of others are violations of the responsibility between one's relationship with himself, others or God. If this principle is adhered to, taking responsibility means on the one hand to have the freedom to express oneself and on the other hand to make mistakes. Whoever won't use his talents may not make any mistakes, but also squanders his God-given talents. This is reprehensible from a Christian point of view (Mt: 25,14–30).

Christian life is a risk. Mistakes can therefore also be proof of one's courage. And this deserves recognition. A better life before God is therefore led by one who takes responsibility and makes mistakes. One who assumes no responsibility and makes no mistakes should rethink his attitude. A conscientious doctor is, e.g. called to an operation on short notice and makes a factual mistake without intention. He cannot be put in a moral position, which is worse than the doctor's who would have been on duty but preferred to have a nice afternoon with a cup of coffee.

Every human talent means – from a Christian point of view – great (and also moral) responsibility towards God, ourselves and others. Because other lives and fates may depend on one's actions. The answer to mistakes must be justice and mercy in equal measure.

15.7 Focus on Justice and Mercy

Legal or other sanctions in the sense of justice can produce a learning effect in humans as well as gifted and unexpected mercy and forgiveness. For example, Thomas Aquinas identified transactional justice (in Latin, *iustitia commutativa*) with recourse to Aristotle as a fundamental value. According to this a mistake must have an adequate penalty as a consequence. Taking this into consideration there must be rules (such as laws) to prevent arbitrariness. They are considered fair from a Christian point of view when they correspond to salvific purpose of humans.

[7] The principle can be translated as follows: Nobody should be obliged to do something that he cannot afford with good reason.

Salvation of man through God means in the moment of the last judgment the salvation of man, despite his mistakes.[8] In earthly existence, the free-deciding and thus responsible person should also be empowered by rules to hear the call of God and to say yes to God. There is no safe guarantee for this salvation in the end. It matters how people live here. God takes our freedom and responsibility seriously. Therefore, from the Christian point of view, the final judgment of God will be closely related to man's earthly life. How exactly this judgment looks like remains speculative and can only be approximated in ecclesiastical life. God Himself is the judge with infinite freedom that transcends all human and theological thinking and speculation.[9] God's judgment must and cannot be anticipated on earth. Righteous retaliation or punishment are not simply determined by this. However, they must not go beyond the commandment of the iustitia commutativa (for instance, in the sense of a retaliation or an example set as a deterrent) and must always consider mercy towards the person concerned (cf. Kasper, 2012, 187; Benedict XVI., 2005). Punishment as a response to mistakes is therefore justifiable in Christian terms but must be moderate. God does not deprive his love, even if you make mistakes.[10]

Moral mistakes (such as intrigue, aggression, ambush, false testimony, broken promises, etc.) not only damage the relationship with God but also destroy one's relationship with others and with oneself. Such self-inflicted bondages cannot be overcome alone (cf. Schockenhoff 2007, 365 f.), either the non-sacramental tradition of Luther or the sacramental tradition (Catholic and Orthodox) know about reconciliation. I propose this reconciliation logic for moral mistakes as a systematic orientation for a Christian mistakes-culture and refer especially on the Catholic tradition, which is my focus. I will now sketch it out to relate it to other types of mistakes beyond the narrow theologic context of morality and sacraments. Catholic penance consists of four steps:[11]

[8] "Salvation" in the NT is the epitome of consummation of all human desire for truth and life, freedom and love in God, the creator and finisher of his creature. The eternal salvific will of God gains historical form in his acts of salvation, salvation and liberation. Salvation is therefore not a state of human condition different from God. Rather, salvation in the universal sense is God Himself insofar as He is present in the creaturely self-fulfillment of man as the author and goal of life (cf. Müller 2010, 373). Such deeds mean, for example, forgiveness, mercy, eternal life after death and so on.

[9] Whether hell is empty or not, as it is exactly with the grace of God and the reward for a good life, these are not only dogmatic issues controversial in ecumenical-theological dialogue, which are not discussed further. Cf. for a deepening from a Catholic point of view Müller (2010), pp. 553–568.

[10] Jesus expressly fights serious offences against the Holy Spirit, because they are especially serious. However, the evaluation of the demonic leads us off topic. Cf. for this topic, e.g. Nass (2015).

[11] Cf. Müller (2010): 714 with reference to the Council of Florence in 1439 A.D. My basis is therefore a Catholic perspective. Beyond the catholic sacramentality of penance a comparable logic can also be found in the Protestant tradition by applying the justification idea of the "sola gratia". Cf. Bonhoeffer (2010): pp. 134–136.

1. Repentance: It describes a guilty person's honest feeling of pain about the moral mistake. It also implies the serious intention to do better in the future. [12]
2. Oral confession: The offender stands up openly for the mistake.
3. Forgiveness: In the Sacrament it is the priest who (on behalf of the Church) explicitly pronounces absolution.
4. Penitential work: The penitent is given a penitential task to be performed. In the sense of barter justice, it must not be unreasonably. In the sense of mercy, it may also have a measure which lies below "an eye for an eye and a tooth for a tooth".

These four steps can be detached from the ecclesiastical sacrament in the Catholic tradition. They can also be besides purely moral context – a template for Christian mistakes-culture in organizations.[13] We can derive the following characteristic:

Forgiveness
Honest repentance, standing up for one's own mistakes, a punishment not exceeding the measure of exchange justice as a reaction, an exculpation by superiors or affected persons directed towards the culprit and an associated ticking off of the respective mistake without further postcards[14] are characteristics for forgiveness within the frame of a Christian mistakes-culture.

This logic does not work, if there is no honest repentance or if one's own mistake is attributed to others.[15] In such cases the perpetrator does not lose his dignity, but through a Catholic perspective, he remains reconciled with himself, with God and with those affected by the mistake. For example, Cain is ejected from the community after he murdered his innocent brother Abel. To his snappish question "Am I my brother's keeper?" (Gen 4:9), he is prophesied restlessness (Gen 4:12) (cf. Schockenhoff 2007: 370 f.). Christians nevertheless believe that God can respond to such lack of understanding with mercy and reconciliation. As a principle for a Christian mistakes-culture, the love that transcends peoples' capacity is not helpful, because people are neither equal to God nor angels.[16]

[12] On feelings of guilt, conscience and the inner judgment of man cf. Schockenhoff (2007), pp. 365–372.

[13] Trying to transfer such an ecclesiastical idea of confession as a model for a culture of mistakes in organizations is undoubtedly a pioneering work.

[14] This sustained forgiveness is based on a spirit of mercy that accompanies the commandment of justice. Cf. Kasper (2012), pp. 161–163.

[15] Cf., for example, the descriptions of the Protestant pastor Matthias Storck (2017). His biological father, who was also a pastor, betrayed him to the so called "Staatssicherheit" (Stasi). Storck could not forgive his father as long as he did not admit his guilt.

[16] I have already mentioned this above during the introduction of the Christian image of man in reference to the Epistle to the Romans.

Thomas Aquinas, for example, admitted that all the earth's goods belong to all human beings, because they are a gift from God. People are not completely selfless and also have an egoistic streak. As a result, rules are needed that curb that negative side of humans to avoid greater harm. Thomas justifies from his Christian perspective private ownership as a secondary but necessary natural right. It is a secondary right because it is derived (cf. STh II-II, 66,2 f., Höffner 2011, 212–217, Nass 2013). It is also the same with stubborn people. They may experience mercy from God's judgment. On earth, however, people who interact with narrow individuals must be protected from those ignorance's consequences. They also must be guarded from further mistakes and their consequences as well as from contagious moral decomposition. Luther justifies secular rules with his two-regimental doctrine (cf. Frey 1998). According to him, God's law of love does not yet prevail in this world, because the kingdom of God battles with the empire of evil. Our world is in between this battle. Therefore, we need rules, laws, sanctions and punishments which are not always identical with God's mercy. The result is nearly the same as Thomas'.

15.8 Principles of Christian Mistakes-Culture

I will now systematically record (not only from a Catholic view) on the basis of my remarks on dignity, responsibility, justice and mercy some principles of Christian mistakes-culture. These principles affect those involved in the mistakes or those affected by it with varying intensity.

Untouched dignity: We encounter people who made a mistake as someone with full dignity. The value of the individual won't be reduced through a mistake.

Modesty:We are aware of the fact that we also happen to make mistakes.

Responsibility for each other: We help each other to learn from mistakes. This affects one of the essential responsibilities of man (towards God, themselves and others) in order to reduce or overcome the caused distance from God.

Praise of mistake: Christian life requires taking appropriate responsibility. This increases the risk of mistake. Mistakes can therefore also be an expression of a conscientious Christian life and even deserve positive recognition in this view.

Mercy and forgiveness: Mercy and forgiveness of the superior or of those affected by mistakes presupposes honest repentance, admission and active proof of good will on the part of the causer and should bring about honest forgiveness of the mistakes made and their consequences on the part of those affected by the mistake.

Justice: When there is no insight or where future (moral, physical, health, material, temporal or mental) damages to third parties must be prevented, sanctions and punishments are also permitted or required, but must not exceed the degree of barter justice. This does not damage the dignity of the punished person. [17]

The principles presented here are no more and no less than a guide to Christian mistake-culture. On the one hand, they want to be a concrete orientation for Christian leaders or for leaders in Christian organizations. This is the virtuous side. On the other hand, they also want to be an orientation for corresponding rules in the company, which, for example, set patterns in corporate models (e.g. mission statements) or operationalizations for the appropriate handling of mistakes in the organization. This is the institutional ethical side.

15.9 Conclusion

It can now be stated: The secular invitation of C. Taylor and the lack of a present system of Christian mistake-culture in organizations are essential motivating challenges for this article. They invite us to close the research gap in the framework of ethics and to explicitly argue Christianly. This project will be tackled with this article in a first step.

To this end, the following have been done: (1) Who speaks of mistake-culture must first define transparently what is meant by mistakes. This was done here with the two definitions at the beginning. (2) It is also necessary to identify the context for which such a culture should be investigated. For this purpose, especially Christian and Christian-led organizations were identified. But there is also the claim that this culture can be applied beyond such limits. (3) When speaking of a Christian culture of mistakes, its essential principles must be presented and substantiated. This was done mainly on the basis of the Bible and on the basis of theological thinkers (Thomas Aquinas, Benedict XVI, Christopher Frey, Joseph Höffner, Gerhard Ludwig Müller, Walter Kasper, etc.). The Christian image of man with its good

[17] Thanks to Johanna Karl for linguistic support.

foundation of dignity despite human imperfection and the threefold humane responsibility establish an interplay of justice and forgiveness. This can be found in the ecclesial understanding of penance and reconciliation as a ritual or sacramental institution. Their essence is the model for the principles presented here. They want to be a virtuous and institutional ethical orientation for organizations. These principles of a Christian culture of mistakes are thus proposed as a credible orientation for a Christian corporate culture.

As the following steps in the research on a Christian mistake culture, I see the following: (1) Critical verification of the completeness of the proposed principles, (2) confrontation of the principles with case studies from practice, (3) institution ethical application of the principles and their empirical evaluation and (4) discussion of such principles and their implementation with alternative concepts and mutual enrichment in dialogue in terms of stringency in argumentation and practicality.

References

Anzenbacher, A. (2001): *Einführung in die Ethik*. Düsseldorf: Patmos.

Bechtel, T. (2012): *Aus Fehlern lernen. Qualitätssicherung durch eine ausgeglichene Fehlerkultur*. München: grin.

Benedict XVI. (2005): *Encyclical Letter Deus Caritas est*. Vatican City.

Bonhoeffer, D. (2010): *Ethik* (2nd ed.). Ed. by Tödt, I., Tödt, H. E. (+), Feil, E. & Green, C. Gütersloh: Gütersloher Verlagshaus.

Büschges, G., Abraham, M. & Funk, W. (1998): *Grundzüge der Soziologie* (3rd ed.). München, Wien: Oldenbourg.

Demmer, K. (1987): Erwägungen zum "intrinsece malum". *Gregorianum*, 68 (6/7), 613–637.

Frey, C. (1998): *Die Ethik des Protestantismus von der Reformation bis zur Gegenwart*. Gütersloh: Gütersloher Verlagshaus.

Frey, C., Dabrock, P. & Knauf, S. (1997): *Repetitorium der Ethik für Studierende der Theologie* (3rd ed.). Waltrop: Spenner.

Hahn, H.-J. (2009): Die abendländisch-christlichen Werte als Erfolgsfaktor. *Professorenforum-Journal*, 10, 1, 38–39.

Höffner, J. Kardinal (2011): *Christliche Gesellschaftslehre* (3rd ed.). Erkelenz: Altius.

Jaensch, P., Zirlik, M., Zerth, J & Nass, E. Principal-Agent-Approach meets Christian Spirituality. An interdisciplinary model to implement a virtue-based Enterprise Culture. *Zeitschrift für Marktwirtschaft und Ethik* 2/2015, 40–54

Kasper, W. (2012): *Barmherzigkeit. Grundbegriff des Evangeliums – Schlüssel christlichen Lebens*. Freiburg i.Br.: Herder.

Keppeler, C. (2014): Perspektivische Personalführung. Die katholische Soziallehre als Grundlage für eine zeitgemäße Führungskultur. Marburg: tectum.

Kühnlein, M. (2018): Einführung: Taylors Gegenwart. In: Kühnlein, M. (ed.): *Charles Taylor: Ein säkulares Zeitalter*. Berlin / Boston: De Gruyter, 1–15.

Melé, D. & C. G. Cantón (2014): Human Foundations of Management. Understanding the Homo Humanus. New York: Palgrave.

Müller, G. L. (2010): *Katholische Dogmatik. Für Studium und Praxis der Theologie* (3rd ed.). Freiburg i.Br.: Herder.

Nass, E. (2013): Herkunft und Aktualität der christlichen Eigentumslehre. *Die Neue Ordnung*, 66, 348–361.

Nass, E. (2015): Krieg dem falschen Frieden. *Die Tagespost* 19.12.2015.
Nass, E. (2018): *Handbuch Führungsethik. Teil I: Systematik und maßgebliche Denkrichtungen.* Stuttgart: Kohlhammer.
Nass, E. & Kreuer, E. (2018): Methodology and Applications of Christian Leadership Ethics. *Journal of Values-Based Leadership*, XI (II), 71–88.
Rohrhirsch, F. (2013): Christliche Führung – Anspruch und Wirklichkeit. Führen mit Persönlichkeit und Ethik. Berlin: Springer.
Schockenhoff, E. (2007): *Grundlegung der Ethik. Ein theologischer Entwurf.* Freiburg i. Br.: Herder.
Storck, M. (2017): *Karierte Wolken. Lebensbeschreibungen eines Freigekauften* (4th ed.). Gießen: brendow.
Taylor, C. (2007): *A Secular Age*. Cambridge: Harvard University Press.
Thomas Aquinas (1933–1962): *Deutsche Thomas-Ausgabe.* Ed. by Albertus-Magnus-Akademie Walberberg, Heidelberg, Graz. http://www.corpusthomisticum.org/ 6.1.2019 (STh).
Unger, M. (2009): *Negatives Wissen im Kontext einer positiven Fehlerkultur.* München: grin.
Weber, M. (2000): Religiöse Heilmethodik und Systematisierung der Lebensführung. In: Weber, M.: *Die protestantische Ethik I. Eine Aufsatzsammlung.* Ed. by Winckelmann, J. (9th ed.). Gütersloh: Gütersloher Verlagshaus, 318–357.
Wenzel, K. (2013): Gott in der Stadt. Zu einer Theologie der Säkularität. In: Sievernich, M. (ed.): *Aufbruch in die Urbanität. Theologische Reflexion kirchlichen Handelns in der Stadt.* Freiburg i.Br.: Herder, 330–389.
Zerth, J., Jaensch, P., Zirlik, M. & Nass, E. (2015): Principal-Agent-Approach meets Christian Spirituality. An interdisciplinary model to implement a virtue-based Enterprise Culture. *Zeitschrift für Marktwirtschaft und Ethik,* 3, 40–54.

Elmar Nass (Prof. Dr. Dr.), born 1966, examed banker, ordination priest 1994, vikar in a parish, 7 years human resources department in the church Ordinariate in Aachen (Germany), Doctorates in Theology and in Social Economics. Habilitation in Philosophy. 2013 Professor of Economic and Social Ethics at the Wilhelm Loehe University Fürth. Main Research Areas: Social Market Economy, Social Justice, Communication of Christian Social Ethics, Business Ethics, Leadership Ethics. Recent publications: Manual of Leadership Ethics (2018), Utopia christiana – model for a an attractive church of the future (2019), Manual of Christian Social Ethics (forthcoming). Contributions to the ethics of life, business ethics, currency ethics, technical ethics, ecumenical ethics, etc.

Chapter 16
Institutional Moral Failure: Emotional Intelligence and Practical Reason Serving Justice

Thomas Ryan

Abstract The Catholic Church in Australia emerged as an instance of gross moral failure in the final findings of a *Royal Commission into Institutional Responses to Child Sexual Abuse* of December 2017. The profound damage to thousands of innocent victims has rightly demanded steps to understand and address the causes of this shocking tragedy at the personal, organisational, leadership and cultural levels of the Church. There is an associated imperative of re-evaluating the Church's life, self-understanding and culture, particularly in relation to leaders and religious ministers. This specific case study in moral failure can be approached through the interplay of psychology and moral science. Emotional intelligence and practical reason converge with a common concern for the appreciation of, and response, to values and persons. This can be done, first, by examining culture (here, ecclesial) and how it underpins and shapes attitudes, values, practices and structures. Second, we consider the extent to which moral failure (with error and mistakes) can be seen as cultural constructs and how these three elements can be embodied in social and structural evil. Finally, there is learning from moral failure (with mistakes and errors) in terms of their potential for growth. Such a task can be approached as a four-pronged exercise in emotional intelligence and practical reason serving justice: from human sciences about the valence of shame; from history and the wider community; from victims; and from within the Christian story. Such an approach offers grounds for hope in the task of cultural change.

Keywords Mistake · Error · Failure · Catholic Church · Culture · Emotional intelligence · Justice · Moral · Practical reason · Sexual abuse

T. Ryan (✉)
Hunters Hill, NSW, Australia

University of Notre Dame, Fremantle, WA, Australia

E. Vanderheiden, C.-H. Mayer (eds.), *Mistakes, Errors and Failures across Cultures*, https://doi.org/10.1007/978-3-030-35574-6_16

16.1 Introduction

It is virtually impossible to be unaware of events internationally over the past two decades about sexual abuse in the Catholic Church. The many thousands of perpetrators have been principally clergy and religious. This has been compounded by the reprehensible failures of Church leaders to respond appropriately, even to the point of widespread denial and 'cover-ups'.

The Catholic Church in Australia emerged as an instance of gross moral failure in the Final Report of the Royal Commission into Institutional Responses to Sexual Abuse of December 2017 (henceforth, Final Report). The profound damage to thousands of innocent victims has rightly demanded steps to understand and address the causes of this shocking tragedy at the personal, organisational, leadership and cultural levels of the Church. There is an associated imperative of re-evaluating the Church's life, self-understanding and culture, particularly in relation to leaders and religious ministers.[1]

The above Abstract can serve as a suitable introduction since it distils the key elements and basic structure of this chapter.

16.2 Culture

The moral failure concerning sexual abuse and responses to it by the Catholic Church in Australia was, clearly, 'institutional'. Consequently, strategies to address the past and plan for the future must be institutional in nature. A central issue raised by the Royal Commission was the Church's 'culture' that helped to foster, deny and 'cover-up' the evil with its widespread and profound damage to the innocent. In that sense, the culture contributed to the abuse; hence, a working definition of culture is a helpful guide.

Browning defines culture as 'a set of symbols, stories (myths), and norms for conduct that orient a society or group cognitively, affectively, and behaviorally to the world in which it lives' (Browning 1976, 73). It is captured succinctly by Gerald Arbuckle (2019) – the 'felt meanings' by which we direct our lives, in society or as a faith community. 'Meanings' is used here not just in an intellectual sense. It also connotes a deep emotional attachment. Arbuckle emphasises that:

> through a culture people feel an affective sense of belonging, but also depending on the context other emotions, for example, shame, anger. (Arbuckle 2019, 13)

As we shall see, such emotional responses can occur with sexual abuse, in itself and, most especially, when it is ignored or victims are not taken seriously.

[1] 'Church' in this discussion refers to the Roman Catholic Church, unless otherwise indicated.

Like the air we breathe, we take our culture for granted, whether it be our everyday 'secular' lives or within a religious group, such as a Church. Only when the 'air' supply is cut off (e.g. the traveller's homesickness) or is toxic in some way does culture get our attention. Disruptive events, for instance, can force us to reflect on the beliefs and values we take for granted (e.g. ecclesial). Importantly, such incidents can impel us to address why and how 'professed' beliefs and values are in conflict with the real or operational 'belief and value' system implicit in individual and group behaviour. This is particularly true when resultant actions (or failure to act) damage rather than promote personal and communal well-being and belonging.

The Final Report guides us here. It points to the 'disturbingly similar' pattern of response by Catholic Church authorities to complaints of sexual abuse. The common concern was to avoid public scandal and to maintain the Church's reputation. 'Loyalty' to priests and religious overrode serious attention being given to allegations (Final Report, Executive Summary, 61). The Royal Commission focussed on three closely interrelated factors: theology, governance and culture. Its report captured the linkage between the sacred, power and abuse. Ministers, in the Catholic tradition, work in a context of sacred power (authority) that expresses itself in the sacramental, liturgical and leadership aspects of the Church's life. The concern is not to reject such power but to learn how it can be exercised in a more responsible (and life-giving) manner (Ormerod 2012, 222).

The Final Report pointed out that, theologically, the Church's self-understanding was hierarchical, centred on bishops and priests, autonomous and self-sufficient, with its own system of law. Underlying these was an 'idealisation' of the priesthood and the Catholic Church. Such qualities capture the 'tightly interconnected' elements that can be described as 'clericalism' (68).

Such a theology had systemic repercussions. It meant that matters such as sexual abuse by its members were dealt with internally and in secret. The 'sacredness' of the priest and religious person led to 'exaggerated levels of unregulated power and trust which perpetrators of child sexual abuse were able to exploit' (68). The hierarchical nature of Church organisational structure and governance meant that the power of individual bishops was not subject to 'adequate checks and balances', with insufficient accountability and lack of required transparency (68). The need was highlighted for more accountable and transparent Church governance and, drawing on modern forms in the secular world, for greater participation (lay people) and consultation (Final Report, 69).

The Final Report gave a clear picture (supported by compelling evidence) of grave systemic dysfunction in the Catholic Church. The report, rightly, raised serious questions about the Church's 'operational' culture that led to such widespread damage to innocent children. In other words, how can this form of 'cultural' deformity be viewed in terms of moral failure, structural sin and evil?

16.3 Moral Failure as Construct

Mistakes, errors or failures are part of life. They can result in shame or embarrassment but can also be occasions for learning. Their incidence across cultures will be shaped by the form of cultural arrangements at work, such as predominantly collectivist or individualist. In the former where shame/honour is the dominant framework, modes of address or bodily posture (e.g. the bow in Japan) are foundational in daily and formal relationships. Failures in these areas can have bearing on personal interactions and, for instance, business negotiations in a manner that may not be such a pressing issue in a more individualist-based culture. More broadly, in organisations, such as the Church, certain types of mistakes, errors and failure can have serious consequences for individuals and for the community itself. But they can also trigger new learnings and improvements and, if needed, a shift in the culture.

This brings us to 'moral failure'. What the term means here is not a lapse in decorum or social practice. One sense of the term 'moral failure' is as the equivalent of 'deliberate wrongdoing'. The working assumption of our discussion is that there are certain forms of behaviour that are viewed, across cultures, as gravely damaging to individuals or the group, such as treason, murder, slavery and rape. These capture key moral boundaries that guide human life. Such come under the umbrella of the Universal Declaration of Human Rights to which every adult and child without exception is entitled. Relevant here are the rights of a child to 'develop in a healthy and normal manner' and to be 'protected against neglect, cruelty and exploitation' (Declaration of the Rights of the Child 1959, preamble and principles, 1, 2 and 9). This is our context and brings us to the next consideration.

In this discussion, 'moral failure' has a specific focus. It can refer to deliberate sexual abuse or exploitation of a child (wrongdoing). In that sense, it concerns perpetrators, criminal proceedings and the processes of law. The concern for us is the second sense of 'moral failure', namely, neglect in addressing instances of such harmful, often criminal, activity by denial or cover-up ('culpable error'). This may well be a matter of legal process. For our purposes (as also of the Royal Commission), there still remains the question of moral fault and associated responsibility – concerning both past events and preventative measures in the future.

16.4 Social Sin and Structural Evil

This raises the issue of social sin and structural evil. These are examples of moral failure concerning situations or practices that can involve or promote harm both individually and collectively. They can, at times, be grounded in mistaken or erroneous beliefs made 'in good faith'. In religious terms, the category of deliberate wrongdoing is described as 'sin' – an offence against God. But this can tend to view sin simply as an individual or 'spiritual' matter. Human sinfulness (being prone to evil) is conditioned by the social and cultural world in which we live. As mentioned above, culture is part of the air we breathe. The Church, like our cultural and social world, is the 'backdrop' that shapes our attitudes to situations and the options available in any response that is made (Ormerod 2007, 50). If a culture is deformed in some way (e.g. by racism), it influences individual decisions. 'It is only through the attentiveness to the voice of society's victims that we can begin to recognise the very evil we take for granted' (Ormerod 2007, 52). The sexual abuse issue in relation to the Church's culture is a striking example of this very point.

In an institution involving many persons, moral responsibility is shared, yet, in some ways, diffuse. A category such as 'social sin' tries to recognise the wrongness of a situation 'without exaggerating the personal responsibility of individuals complicit at various levels' (Duffy 1993, 910). Social sin also puts the focus on social relations and power. When this happens, the focus shifts to the victim. Social sin takes embodied form in the structures, policies and practices of any group or culture that privileges those with power. In other words, we are talking about institutionalised injustice (structural evil). Such is the expression of a culture whose 'felt meanings' are either totally deformed or are distorted in some areas. Those warped meanings and values emerge through the policies and accepted practices that influence individual actions.

This was evident in the Catholic Church in its handling of such grave matters as sexual abuse. As an institution, it was, for the most part, blind to the plight of victims. This pointed to a serious defect at the cognitive level in the level of appreciation of something that involved grave harm. Consequently, at the affective level, there was a pattern of not being 'moved' by the victim's situation. There was a resultant lack of, or inadequate response to, the plight of the victim. What emerged was often a reaction of self-preservation and protection of the Church's good name.

In view of this gross moral failure on the Church's part, what is there to learn? Central is the protection of children and those most vulnerable in the future. This will influence the Church at the institutional level of governance (along the lines suggested by the Royal Commission noted above). It will also entail a gradual change in the Church's culture, in the configuration of its 'felt meanings' – our next concern.

16.5 Emotional Intelligence and Practical Reason

These terms, central in our discussion, need to be clarified. Adequate for our purposes is the original definition from Salovey and Mayer of emotional intelligence (EI) as 'the ability to monitor one's own and others' feelings and emotions, to discriminate among them and to use this information to guide one's thinking and actions' (Salovey and Mayer 1990, 189).[2]

[2] In recent times, EI has morphed into other forms, e, g. cultural intelligence (CQ) and social intelligence (SQ).

Allied to such developments is an increasing awareness of the key role of emotions in intrapersonal and interpersonal behaviour (with their psychological and moral implications). This is particularly evident across disciplines such as psychology and moral philosophy (e.g. Narvaez 2014; Helm 2001; Stocker and Hegeman 1996). There is an inherent correlation between EI and positive social outcomes, e.g. healthy social relationships, behaviours and communication, altruism, empathy and the 'personal coherence essential to moral and ethical behaviour' (Keidar and Yagoda 2014, 163).

In a recent review of relevant literature, concerns were raised about the ethical limitations of a range of ECI ('emotional intelligence competency') theories. The authors outline a range of 'competencies' and their components (variable in view of the range of theories). It suffices, given our purposes, to note that the main categories for 'competency' in leadership and management seem to be self-awareness, social awareness, self-management and social skills (Segon and Booth 2015, 791).

These authors propose the inclusion of an ethical management cluster and a number of competencies based on virtue ethics (Segon and Booth 2015, 789). Their concern is not that ECI frameworks are not successful in upholding ethical practice. Rather, these writers consider there is a failure to appeal directly to morality in the various competencies that were surveyed. Their concern is the risk that 'managers and leaders [are] open to potential decision-making and actions that are unethical' (Segon and Booth 2015, 792).

To address this, after weighing up the relative value of utilitarian and duty approaches to ethics, the writers turn to virtue ethics with its emphasis 'on purposiveness that defines human endeavour that transcends the realm of business and defines its place in larger society' (Segon and Booth 2015, 797). Such an approach entails a focus on the conformity between right thinking and desire. Central here is the virtue of practical wisdom (phronesis) that is needed for deliberation and the good judgement that guides choices and actions such that one finds the mean between extremes (Segon and Booth 2015, 796).[3] As noted earlier, emotional intelligence is about how to use our emotions intelligently. But it also concerns how to find intelligence in our emotions – how are they conveyors of truth and value and helpful as wise guides. We consider this matter further.

Drawing on Aristotle's approach to virtue ethics, two forms of knowledge can be distinguished. Theoretical or speculative knowledge (episteme) seeks understanding of the truth whether concerning facts, science or discipline such as mathematics. For instance, we know the London is the capital of the United Kingdom or that two plus two equals four.

Alternatively, there is practical knowledge (or reason, phronesis) that seeks the wise judgement needed about how to act and 'the behaviours to be developed through practice and habit' (Segon and Booth 2015, 798). The object of this form of knowledge is the truth apprehended from the perspective of the 'good', namely, a

[3] Practical wisdom (prudence) is one of the four cardinal virtues in virtue theory, with justice, fortitude and temperance.

value to be pursued and embodied in action. It is an apprehension of a value that is an objective reality (e.g. respect human life, keeping promises) but has a personal significance. In other words, it is best described as 'appreciation'.

We can see practical reason collaborating with emotional intelligence in terms of nurturing personal relationships. Our specific concerns are the damage done to victims from sexual abuse and the associated shame and disgrace on the part of the Church. How can one be discriminating about shame (and humiliation) such that we can use such an emotion to guide future thinking, appraisals, responses and actions? I suggest through the interplay of emotional intelligence and practical reason – which guides later discussion.

So far, we have clarified 'moral failure' through recourse to ideas such as culture, construct, social sin, structural evil, etc. Beginning with the historical context, we now consider the 'hidden potential' of such failure as realised in forms of 'learning' for the Church that concern the past (remedial) and, importantly, the future (preventative).

16.6 Historical Context

For the Church, theological developments since the Second Vatican Council (1962–1965) opened up possibilities built on the autonomy of the secular realm within the divine economy. 'Secular' does not, in itself, connote antireligious. The sacred and secular are not, by definition, in opposition but complement each other and have points of intersection. The secular, symbolised in the city, is the public space for the interaction of the various philosophical and religious traditions within a community. The Church is called to have a dialogical relationship with the wider global community. As noted already, this has taken on a more urgent, if not, imperative quality with the incidence of sexual abuse and its implications for the Church as an institution and its culture.

Further light is thrown on our discussion by Rowan Williams (2000). He suggests that 'we are systematically misled, even corrupted, by a picture of the human agent as divided into an outside and an inside – a "true self", hidden, buried, to be excavated by one or another kind of therapy', whether it be in philosophical or psychological form, as the quest for the 'authentic' self (Williams 2000, 29). Rather, Williams argues that, from the start, personal identity comes into being through human communication and interaction. An unbalanced rhetoric of interiority has serious moral consequences because it suggests that our social or public life is of secondary importance.

Such an insight can be applied analogically (and aptly) to the Church and its self-understanding. This has particular reference to the Church as a sign and instrument of God's presence in the world and its associated holiness. Rather than the Church's self-understanding and holiness being primarily (if not solely) of the interior realm, it must also be viewed as a process. In other words, the Church as a community evolves in its understanding of itself, of its mission and of its moral responsibilities.

This can only occur in a historical setting, hence from a relational and interactive context both vertically (with God) and, importantly, for our purposes, horizontally, namely, in social and public life.

Further, it is recognised that, within the western democratic systems in the past two decades, there is an increasing crisis of trust, an issue addressed by Onora O'Neill's Reith Lectures (O'Neill 2002). The lightning rod for this 'crisis' is primarily around institutions, whether political, governmental or ecclesiastical but also in professions. The erosion of trust in these spheres is often accompanied by a means to replace it, namely, greater transparency. While this may be healthy in some areas, it may also be symptomatic of a wider problem. It is trust that is the glue that holds a community or social group together. Given the context of the discussion here, such a consideration is very relevant to the Church's understanding of, and response to, the sexual abuse issues and the findings of the Royal Commission.

Having clarified the current historical context in which the Church is functioning, we now consider the various modes of learning 'for the sake of justice' prompted by the moral failure under consideration. Justice is another form of the four cardinal virtues, whereby one is disposed to give what is due to others. Determining what is 'due' is set against the overarching notion of justice as right relationships amongst people. The Church, as a historical and human reality, grows in moral wisdom and, specifically, in its appreciation of justice and its scope – a process that embraces both past and future. On that basis, we proceed to the first sphere of the Church's learning, namely, the insights from human sciences into shame.

16.6.1 Learning from Human Sciences About Shame

A task facing the Church is learning from and for healthy relationships and, in particular, through moral emotions and the associated ability to identify and appreciate what is salient in situations and relationships. Given the Church's failure, such an approach involves a readiness to engage with disgrace and the accompanying shame.

Shame can have destructive, even toxic, forms. But this is not always the case. Recent studies in positive psychology and other human sciences have made advances in taking a more constructive approach to shame. Shame, properly engaged, can be transformed and transforming – psychologically and morally. Such a process brings not only a reconnection with one's true self but also for one's vulnerabilities and limitations and those of others. Shame named, embraced and shared leads to greater understanding of both oneself and others, greater empathy and compassion and a heightened appreciation of injustice. In other words, shame can be a positive health resource – personally, culturally and across cultures (Vanderheiden and Mayer 2017).

Shame is a fear of failure to observe an expected standard – of oneself or of others. Rather than a form of conformity, it is argued that, if one participates with others in a life of shared moral practices, then, we need the approval and support of others. To be ashamed over moral failings is essential to being a morally mature person (Calhoun 2004, 129). In the moral failure we are discussing, the Church is being confronted with the question 'have you forgotten what you stand for?' Shame is a prompt to self-examination and to explore various modes of learning which offer specific ways in which practical reason and emotional intelligence are at the service of justice – our next concern.

16.6.2 Learning in the Past: Human Rights

The Universal Declaration of Human Rights (1948) is, historically, relatively recent. This statement is representative of the developmental trajectory across societies globally in the acknowledgement and articulation of human rights. The Church's resistance to human rights' movements must be understood in its historical context and the movements inimical to the Church, particularly in the post-Enlightenment period and in nineteenth-century Europe. In the changing context of the new world and of post-revolutionary Europe, 'freedom' and 'secular' took on less antagonistic meanings. For all that, the historical record clearly indicates how the Church's thinking on, and attitude to, human rights in a more secular context gradually evolved from rejection to discernment, to dialogue and, finally, to proclamation (Cornish 2002).

Looking back, theologian Walter Kasper notes that explicit talk of 'human rights' is peculiar to the modern period but that the associated ideas are as old as Christianity. Rather than the 'image of God' confined to the king or ruler, it was 'democratised' to include every person 'irrespective of race, people, sex, or culture' (Kasper 1990, 49 & 55). Rights can be traced back to the 'dignity' of the human being created in the image and likeness of God (Gen, 1:26) and strengthened by the covenant between God and humankind. On that basis, human dignity is inviolable and inalienable, no matter how much it may be violated by oneself or others. This (and the evolving Hebrew and New Testament ethos) offered a starting point for a secular theory of human rights. It is only in modern times that the legal and political implications of this were systematically elaborated (Hoppe 1994, 455–6).

The Declaration on Religious Freedom (1966) from the Second Vatican Council was emblematic of the shift in Church's own self-understanding, particularly in its stance towards the modern world, shaped by the Enlightenment and post-revolutionary Europe. This applied, most especially, to human and political rights. There was a growing awareness of the Church's need to engage with, and learn from, democratic institutions since there was increased appreciation of how self-government was a mark of social and political maturity. This brings us to the second sphere of learning.

16.6.3 Learning in the Present: Victims

We recall here Ormerod's comment earlier that 'It is only through the attentiveness to the voice of society's victims that we can begin to recognise the very evil we take for granted'. This is made more specific by Pope Francis (2018) in his response to the suffering endured by so many minors due to sexual abuse:

> Crimes that inflict deep wounds of pain and powerlessness, primarily among victims, but also in their family members and in the larger community of believers and non-believers alike…the heart-wrenching pain of these victims, which cries out to heaven, was long ignored, kept quiet or silenced.

The Pope moves on to consider the implications (past and present) of how 'we showed no "care for the little ones: we abandoned them"'. It entails coming to grips with the 'extent and gravity of all that has happened' in a 'comprehensive and communal way'. Acknowledging the truth of all that has happened is 'not enough'. If omission and denial were the pattern in the past, now the task is one of 'solidarity, in the deepest and most challenging sense. As the People of God, we are challenged 'to take on the pain of our brothers and sisters wounded in their flesh and spirit'. This is the groundwork for 'forging present and future history' (Pope Francis 2018, par. 4).

If victims are to lead us about suffering, with any hope of healing and recovery, it demands that victims are heard, taken seriously, understood and acknowledged with responses of regret and repentance. When criminal activity is concerned, the processes of justice need to be invoked. A comprehensive treatment of strategies to achieve these goals (and for establishing structures and procedures needed to protect the innocent and vulnerable) is found in the Final Report of the Royal Commission. These strategies are being diligently applied to the governance structures of the dioceses and Church organisations throughout Australia. Our concern here is to consider the role of restorative justice in the learning process and how it enhances growth in wisdom.

On this matter, there is much to be gained from drawing on legal initiatives such as circle-sentencing and similar trauma healing programmes used amongst Indigenous peoples in Australia and Maori in New Zealand. In collectivist cultures and close communities, to shame an offender can be more effective than retributive sanctions since individuals place great weight on how they are seen by family and friends. When brought face to face with those they have harmed, they can better appreciate the impact of their actions (Probyn 2005, 90–98). Such an approach aligns with Pope Francis' emphasis on solidarity. Listening to victims and the need for retributive justice (and punishment for guilty actions) are paralleled by processes of restorative justice. Here, justice is concerned with identifying harm and how to heal the harm done to relationships. Justice, here, is focussed on restoring right relationships.

In discussing harm and restorative justice, Eli McCarthy draws on the work of Harold Zehr (2002) and points to basic needs involved for three groups – the victims, offenders and community (McCarthy 2016, 71; Zehr 2002, pp. 14–18). As noted above, victims need to be informed about what happened and why it happened, to be able to tell the truth of their own story and to receive 'acknowledgment, empowerment or regaining a sense of control in their lives, and restitution for the harm done' (McCarthy 2016, 71).

Offenders need to take accountability that addresses the harms, 'encourages empathy and responsibility and transforms shame'. A further need of the offender is to be encouraged (a) to experience personal transformation, such as healing for the harms that contributed to their offending behaviour, and (b) opportunities for treatment for addictions and/or other problems, and enhancement of personal competencies. Again, offenders need encouragement and support for integration into the community.

As for the community stakeholders, 'they need attention to their concerns as victims, opportunities to build a sense of community and mutual accountability, and encouragement to take on their obligations for their members, including victims and offenders, and to foster the conditions that promote healthy communities' (McCarthy 2016, 71–2; Zehr 2002, 12–14).

These three groups with their respective needs (victims, offenders and the community) find clear parallels with the situation facing the Church. All are to be embraced within the circle of restorative justice – as indicated earlier.

16.6.4 Learning from the Christian Tradition

Our learning from the Royal Commission, secular world, victims and cultural life will lead, hopefully, to a broader moral horizon, things we feel 'deeply' about and get angry about if they are attacked or undermined. This underlines the 'preventative' aspect of learning from 'moral failure' and its bearing on changes in attitudes and convictions. To 'own' practices and protocols that safeguard and protect innocent children and vulnerable adults, we must, finally, consider what can be learnt from the Christian Tradition and, importantly, about God.

First, we return to the God revealed in the Hebrew story. The prophets often speak of God as 'always faithful', as one who never forgets his people. For God's community, being faithful is to remember; being unfaithful is to forget – who we are (a needed reminder from the Royal Commission). These are the benchmarks against which the God of the Covenant measures fidelity. True worship, then, flowers in mercy and compassion. More importantly, it produces the fruits of justice, particularly in how one treats those most disadvantaged – the widow, the orphan and the stranger. This is not just about mercy. In the Hebrew perspective, it concerns what should be done, the claims of those in need and what we all have a duty to give.

Second, this moral failure of the Church offers another reminder for us, once again, from our Jewish heritage. Holiness primarily denotes God's transcendence and 'otherness' – someone totally beyond us. In the God of our Jewish heritage, the holy and the fostering of what is right and just are closely intertwined. Why? Because the God of Israel is personal. The benchmark of justice (whether divine or human) is 'right relationship' – between God and creation, between humanity and God and between human beings in their dealings with each other. Hence, damage or harm to anyone, especially to the more vulnerable members of society, offends God's holiness. That is why the prophets are so vehement about social justice or, better, social injustice.

One persistent theme in the prophets was God's anger when the Covenant is distorted: when worship was disconnected from its ethical demands – measured by how the most disadvantaged are treated. This is a rupture between holiness and justice and a distortion of what fosters 'right relationships'. These considerations are very relevant here. For whatever reasons, the Catholic tradition may have soft-pedalled such aspects of justice and of God's anger. With recent events, such a consideration cannot be ignored.

This brings us back to the question of holiness and justice. As noted earlier in this chapter, for some time, Catholic morality has tended to be somewhat individualistic, namely, with a focus on 'me and God'. Sin, then, was primarily seen as an offence against God. If that is fixed up by receiving the sacrament of reconciliation, then, all is well in the eyes of God.

These recent events involving such widespread emotional and spiritual damage to myriads of innocent victims highlight the serious inadequacy of such an approach. The Christian moral life is less about me and more about We – recovering our Hebrew roots. Being moral (just) and sharing God's holiness are personal and about fostering and maintaining right relationships with others (and not only with God).

Seen from that perspective, sin is not simply an offence against God as holy. As an evil, more often than not, it entails some form of harm, damage and even injustice. At times, reparation and restoration are imperative. Again, while an action may not be public but private, it still has social repercussions. It can involve a more distorted perception of life (and people) or dispositions to be more self-focussed. Institutional protocols and practices of safeguarding and protection (the 'preventative') are about what really matters to us. It brings to mind the old adage: each of us is our brother and sister's 'keeper'. This brings us back, finally, to the question of culture.

16.7 Cultural Change and Hope

Gerald Arbuckle observes that 'profound cultural change is a messy and painful process. It takes some time for individuals to get their heads and hearts adjusted to the fact that the world has changed, and they must change also' (Arbuckle 2019, 14). Any shift in 'felt' meanings primarily involves the heart and then the head. Structural changes, with policies and protocols for safeguarding and the protection of children and vulnerable adults, need time to become embedded in the life of an institution such as the Church and its members.

Hans Zollner SJ[4] has pinpointed that the task ahead for the Church is about nurturing a culture of trust, a 'heart change', so that 'things come naturally and spontaneously, because you feel it' (Dioceses of Parramatta and Wollongong 2018, 18). This entails destroying structures of sin (or flawed structures) and replacing them with forms of living that are more authentic, life-giving and affectively inclusive. This process of changing the distorted 'felt-meanings' of a Church culture demands the presence of another cardinal virtue, namely, courage (allied with patience). This must be underpinned by faith in the presence of Jesus, the crucified and risen victim. On that foundation, positive engagement with moral failure, and its associated shame and disgrace, can be undertaken with hope.

16.8 Conclusion

We have examined an example of gross moral failure in a religious institution, namely, the Catholic Church in Australia. The profound damage to thousands of victims has serious implications for the culture, structure and governance of the Church. Different ways in which the Church might learn from what has happened were explored.

Central in all this is the quote of Pope Francis cited earlier: 'we showed no care for the little ones; we abandoned them'. Both haunting and poignant in their pain, these words are a salutary (and needed) reminder of the fragility of the human beings in the Church's care. They are also point to the ever-present danger for the Church to become self-serving, most especially, of finding itself morally blind and deaf to the cries for help right in its own back yard. The Pope's words, then, stand as a cameo of a Church called to be a humble servant, a beacon of mercy, but, most importantly, of a loving justice.

References

Arbuckle, G. A. (2019). *Culture and Cover-Up: Refounding the Catholic Church in Trauma.* Maryknoll, N.Y.: Orbis Books.

Browning, D. S, (1976). *The Moral Context of Pastoral Care.* Philadelphia: Westminster Press.

Calhoun, C, (2004). An Apology for Moral Shame. *The Journal of Political Philosophy,* 12(2), 127–146.

Cornish, S. (2002). From Rejection to Proclamation. Retrieved 7 September 2019, from http://www.socialjustice.catholic.org.au/files/Discussion-guides/2002-From_Rejection_to_Proclamation.pdf

Declaration of the Rights of the Child (1959) http://www.cirp.org/library/ethics/UN-declaration/ *Creating a Safe Church from Within: Summary Report.*

[4] President of the Centre for Child Protection at Rome's Pontifical Gregorian University.

'Declaration on Religious Freedom' (Dignitatis Humanae) in Walter M Abbott, S.J. (Ed.), *The Documents of Vatican II* (New York: Guild Press, 1966), 672–700.
Dioceses of Parramatta and Wollongong, Creating a Safe Church from Within: Summary Report (2018). http://www.dow.org.au/news/news-and-media/item/creatinga-safe-church-from-within-summary-report accessed 25.01.2019.
Duffy, S.J. (1993). Sin in Michael Downey (ed)., The New Dictionary of Catholic Spirituality Collegeville, Minn: Liturgical Press/Michael Glazier. 889–901.
Helm, B.W, (2001). Emotional Reason: Deliberation, Motivation and the Nature of Value. New York: Cambridge University Press.
Hoppe, T, (1994). Human Rights in Judith A. Dwyer (ed)., The New Dictionary of Catholic Social Thought. Collegeville, Minn: Liturgical Press/Michael Glazier. 454–470.
Kasper, W, (1990). The Theological Foundation of Human Rights in Human Rights and the Church: Historical and Theological Reflections. Pontifical Council for Justice and Peace, Vatican City, 47–71.
Keidar, D & Yagoda, A, (2014). Emotional Intelligence, Moral, Ethics, Bio-ethics and What is In Between. *Medicine and Law*, 14 (1), 163–205.
McCarthy, E, (2016). Breaking Out: The Expansiveness of Restorative Justice in Laudato Si'. *The Journal of Moral Theology,* 5(2), 66–80.
Narvaez, D, (2014). *Neurobiology and the Development of Human Morality: Evolution, Culture and Wisdom.* New York: W.W. Norton.
O'Neill, O, (2002). *A Question of Trust: The BBC Reith Lectures.* Cambridge University Press.
Ormerod, N, (2007). *Creation, Grace, and Redemption.* Maryknoll, NY: Orbis.
Ormerod, N, (2012). Clergy Sexual Abuse: What Difference did Vatican II Make? In N. Ormerod, O. Rush, D Pascoe, C Johnston & J Hodge (Eds), *Vatican 11: Reception and Implementation in the Australian Church* (pp. 213–224). Mulgrave, Vic: Garratt Publishing.
Pope Francis. (2018). Pope Francis: Letter to the People of God (full text) - Vatican News. Retrieved 7 September 2019, from https://www.vaticannews.va/en/pope/news/2018-08/pope-francis-letter-people-of-god-sexual-abuse.html
Probyn, E, (2005). *Blush: Faces of Shame.* Sydney: University of New South Wales Press.
Royal Commission into Institutional Responses to Child Sexual Abuse. (2017). Final report | Royal Commission into Institutional Responses to Child Sexual Abuse. Retrieved 7 September 2019, from https://www.childabuseroyalcommission.gov.au/final-report
Salovey, P., & Mayer, J. D. (1990). *Emotional intelligence. Imagination, Cognition and Personality,* 9, 185–211.
Segon, M. & Booth. C. (2015). Virtue: The Missing Ethics Element in Emotional Intelligence. *Journal of Business Ethics*, 128, 789–802.
Stocker, M & Hegeman, E. (1996). *Valuing Emotions.* New York: Cambridge University Press.
Vanderheiden, E, and Mayer, C.-H., (2017), (Eds.), *The Value of Shame: Exploring a Health Resource in Cultural Contexts.* Cham: Springer International Publishing.
Williams, R. (2000). 'Interiority and Epiphany: A reading in New Testament ethics'. *Modern Theology,* 13(1), 29–50.
Zehr, H, (2002). The Little Book of Restorative Justice. *Intercourse*, PA: Good Books.

Thomas Ryan is a Marist priest based in Sydney, Australia. He is an Honorary Fellow of the Faculty of Theology and Philosophy of the Australian Catholic University and an Adjunct Associate Professor of the School of Philosophy and Theology of the University of Notre Dame Australia. Apart from chapters in books, he has published numerous articles in theological journals both nationally and internationally.

Chapter 17
Against Forgetting Serious Mistakes, Errors and Failures: The Long Learning Process of the Catholic Church in Germany in Dealing with Sexual Abuse of Minors and Vulnerable Adults

Mary Hallay-Witte and Bettina Janssen

Abstract In 2010 people were shocked about the extent of sexual abuse in the Catholic Church in Germany, how this was concealed and information withheld by church representatives. Victims were not offered help, perpetrators not sentenced and other actions of sexual abuse neglected in favour of the institutions. It seemed a public debate had started in which the Catholic Church put multitude measures in place. However, each diocese and clerical institution still handles the implementation of concepts to prevent sexual abuse with a different consistency and consequence. Up to the present day, victims testify scandalous handling of their cases. Mistakes and omissions made in the past are still being repeated in the present. As a result, perpetrators are not being made accountable, as if there has never been a public debate on clerical sexual abuse in Germany. Church contact persons for intervention and prevention are working isolated. They experience resistance and hostilities. But even if one hopes the debate will ease away, it is a false conclusion to say, this topic will be forgotten. The released findings of the research on *Sexual abuse of minors by catholic priests* outline: The topic of the sexual abuse of minors is still present. Even if one would want this topic to be forgotten: With every new case that appears, the 'dark' present of sexual abuse

---

The article is (slightly modified) published in German in: Remenyi, M. and Schärtl, T. (Editors) (2019). Nicht ausweichen – Theologie angesichts der Missbrauchskrise. Regensburg: Verlag Friedrich Pustet

---

M. Hallay-Witte
Institut für Prävention und Aufarbeitung sexualisierter Gewalt (IPA), Grafschaft-Lantershofen, Germany

B. Janssen (✉)
Business Consultancy, Köln, Germany
e-mail: info@bettina-janssen.de

E. Vanderheiden, C.-H. Mayer (eds.), *Mistakes, Errors and Failures across Cultures*, https://doi.org/10.1007/978-3-030-35574-6_17

will reappear and be discussed by the public. The self-commitment based on the recommendations of the research consortium of the German bishops will be the relevant touchstones for future reappraisal.

Keywords Mistakes · Errors · Failure · Catholic Church in Germany · Institutional failure · Moral failure · Sexual abuse

17.1 Starting Point: One Could Have Known

The 'abuse crisis' is one of the darkest chapters of the universal Roman Catholic Church worldwide. In 2010, this crisis did not suddenly or surprisingly enter public perception in Germany; it has already been made public a long time before. More than three decades earlier, first cases of abuse within the Catholic Church in Canada and the USA had been disclosed already; later in Ireland and Central Europe, further cases also became public. As early as 2002, in connection with the serious allegations against a priest and the co-responsibility of the Bishop of Boston, USA, the first internal church discussion on dealing with cases of sexual abuse began in Germany, although the discussions faded away soon enough again (Hallay-Witte and Janssen 2016, 56).

Those responsible within the church therefore should have been alarmed long before. As in 2010 with the disclosure of cases of sexual abuse, which happened at the Canisius College, a Jesuit school in Berlin, a movement was started through the media. This has been marked with terms such as 'big bang', 'avalanche', 'tsunami' or 'volcano eruption' due to its ferocity (Hallay-Witte and Janssen 2016, 54). The (sub)conscious hope of some, that the public interest soon enough would be forgotten again on account of some innovative measures by the church, was not fulfilled. In 2018, the public discourse developed further dynamics through the publication of the results of the study 'Sexual abuse of minors by Catholic priests, deacons and male religious in the area of the German Bishops Conference' (Dreßing et al. 2018; so-called MHG-Study). The results testify extensive, repetitive mistakes, errors and failures by church leaders in dealing with allegations of sexual abuse, so do other studies (see Unabhängige Kommission zur Aufarbeitung sexuellen Kindesmissbrauchs 2019).

The following description wants to point out the mistakes, errors and failures, which for the past decades are undoubtingly entangled with the atrocious story of the catholic abuse scandal. The aim is to raise awareness and to become sensible, in order to be able to identify signals and risks earlier and to be able to address and counteract them. These are important to be looked at. The reflection and knowledge of possible mistakes, errors and failures can be a vital resource and an incentive to initiate learning processes and enable necessary changes within the culture of an institution.

17.2 Loss of Confidence

With the onset of the abuse scandal in Germany – as in other countries – a downward spiral in confidence in the institution can be observed. With each peak of the periodic crisis in 2002, 2010 and 2018, a new boost with inclining speed can be seen. Although with each peak of public outrage, the willingness of church leaders to implement adopted measures grew even more decisively. However, they soon fell back into old patterns of behaviour as public attention subsided. The seemingly endless counts of criminal offences and border violations by priests, religious and other employees of the Catholic Church are seen as the main cause for the loss of trust and confidence by the faithful. Many priests have abused their ministerial priesthood and the advance of trust granted to them because of their function within the church. However, many people describe their tremendous disappointment about the institutional mishandling of allegations and especially the unwillingness to take on responsibility and to accept the loss of trust, as particularly serious.

Also in politics and business, it can often also be observed that the representatives of respective institutions do not take on any responsibility and draw personal conclusions. Only very few leaders, who have to speak out during a publicly visible crisis, do respond with an admission of guilt and transparency and by actively taking on responsibility (see, e.g. Volkswagen AG, conduct of the Executive Board in the diesel scandal). However, this conduct cannot be justified or legitimized, certainly not with those responsible within the Catholic Church, which raises particular high moral standards for all the faithful. On the contrary, also church leaders must be judged by their own moral standards, especially in the area of sexuality, which the faithful have to apply to. This must also apply to the clergy.

The divergence between these benchmarks and the lived reality within the church enhances the scandal and public outrage ('They don't get it'.). Setting out from such high benchmarks, the fall is particularly deep and fatal (Bintig 2017. Dreßing 2019a). The dynamics of such downward spirals of loss in credibility and trust are accelerated from a certain point on. Once this downward spiral is on its way, it will be more and more difficult to be stopped. This also applies to the establishment of confidence-building measures (Bintig 2017, 190).

With the publication of the MHG-Study in September 2018, it became increasingly clear that the Catholic Church has lost its prerogative of interpretation of Christian action and values for many people. Many believers who felt at home in the Church still have a longing to regain this confidence, but at the same time, they feel sceptical and hopeless. For some, it is already 'five past 12'; for others the church has completely run out of time. The loss of confidence is irreparable (Bintig 2017, 185). They stay away from mass or from parish life or take total distance from church, by leaving and turning away from faith altogether. But if the Christian faith is not actively lived anymore, it cannot be passed on to the next generation. Such a development is significant for the further existence of an institution. It can also endanger its survival (Bintig 2017, 190).

17.3 Specific Risk and Structural Characteristics of the Church

In order to stop a downward spiral initiated by misconduct and abuse, full public responsibility, visible consequences and behavioural changes are required. Standards and guidelines alone will not prevent sexual abuse. It can only happen with an overall institutional attitude and the firm belief of those responsible that things have to change, no matter how difficult and challenging it can be to deal with the issues (Bintig 2017, 190). In addition to standards and procedures, it also needs a common belief and shared values that are anchored by a consistent vision of approval and disapproval of behaviour (Archdiocese of Hamburg 2018, 58).

It requires the acknowledgment 'Yes, there is sexual abuse in our institutions' and engagement in an intensive learning and development process that demands actively taking on responsibility and a change of perspective in many areas. Institutionally, this includes developing and implementing a culture, where the possibility of misconduct/abuse and failures by institutional representatives is not fundamentally excluded but is thought as being a possibility that can happen. In Germany, this is meant by the 'Culture of mindfulness' (German, 'Kultur der Achtsamkeit'). The culture of mindfulness requires a knowledgeable and careful approach to children and adolescents. Equally important is the concentration on dealing with those responsible within the church and individual self-reflection (Hallay-Witte and Janssen 2016, 152).

Beyond that the 'Culture of mindfulness' includes identifying, naming, analysing and decisively drawing necessary conclusions from administrative failure and misconduct. This necessarily requires an atmosphere and a culture of mindfulness within the institution, which enables open, critical and fearless conversations and constructive dealing with mistakes, errors and failures. This also requires professional expertise and a healthy feedback culture (e.g. Archdiocese of Hamburg 2018, 67).

Since the adoption of the FRAMEWORK REGULATION Prevention of sexualized violence against minors and adult charges within the domain of the German Bishops' Conference in 2010, the Catholic Church has been demanding so-called institutional protection concepts for prevention within each amenity. These protection concepts are an interplay of analysis, structural changes, agreements and arrangements, as well as the attitude and culture of an organization. These intend to reduce the institutional risk of becoming the crime scene of sexual, psychological and/or physical violence. In regard to that, the attention must be focused on specific risk and structural characteristics of the Church which promote sexual abuse of minors or make it more difficult to be prevented. In order to do this (fearlessly), all topics have to be brought out into the open. Also the context of a risk analysis (e.g. Archdiocese of Hamburg 2018, 67) needs to be critically questioned. This also includes all corresponding issues of ministerial priesthood, sexual morals, celibacy and the relationship to homosexuality, as well as the admission of women to the ministry of consecration (Dreßing 2019b). In follow-up, the general terms for institutional misconduct are to be addressed on the structural abuse of power, the defence of responsibility and the lack of liability. These mechanisms have been increasingly used to prevent damage to the image of the universal church, to resist structural changes and to protect institutional representatives.

17.3.1 Structural Abuse of Power

The MHG-Study explicitly states that sexual abuse can be facilitated by authoritarian-clerical structures of the Catholic Church (MHG-Study 2018, 14). At the same time, it outlines that sexual abuse is always an abuse of power. Within an organization, such abuse of power is only possible if there are structures which the perpetrator can use to initiate and cover up his actions and which, if the crime is disclosed, do allow him to be fearless about any consequences (MHG-Study 2018, 14). The misconduct that church leaders are accused of is the fact that they not only protected existing structures as well as themselves but also prevented penalties for perpetrators and necessary and painful changes within the church. For example, all this happened in order to prevent financial damage and to prevent loss of credibility, trust and authority, which is at danger through the disclosure of sexual abuse and misconduct.

The attitude of church leaders to protect (accused) perpetrators characterizes the climate within the official church. This not only favours the ongoing abuse of power at various levels of the hierarchal church but also makes the institution prone to the abuse of power (MHG-Study 2018, 14; Hallay-Witte and Janssen 2016, 129).

Structural Violence

The Norwegian peace and conflict researcher Galtung already characterized the concepts of structural and cultural violence in 1975. Structural violence is not directly attributable and in terms of criminal law is difficult to measure. It manifests itself, for example, in unequal power relations and opportunities, in limited participation possibilities or in disadvantages of individuals. It exists when these inequalities are inherently justified within the system. Structural violence in a hierarchy is characterized, according to Galtung, by the fact that a will to social change, which is articulated from the lower hierarchies to higher ranks, is not feasible, because this change is blocked by rule and higher-level measures (Grant-Hayford and Scheyer 2016). Structural violence is anchored in the system. Individuals may be affected by structural violence, but its consequences are difficult to be traced back to direct violence, which is suffered by one or more concrete actors.

17.3.1.1 Cultural Violence

With cultural violence, Galtung marks every characteristic of a culture due to which direct or structural violence can be legitimized. Cultural violence is the social background which enables the justification of acts of violence, so these become possible.

Galtung describes 'structural and cultural violence as the causes of direct violence, by means of violent actors, who revolt against the structures and a culture to legitimize their use of violence' (Galtung 2004). A culture of dominance paired with the feeling, due to certain diversities, to being something special can foster mechanisms of violence such as racism, sexism or homophobia within an institution.

17.3.2 Clericalism

The MHG-Study explicitly identifies 'clericalism' as a cultural cause and a specific structural feature of sexual abuse within the church. Clericalism is defined as a hierarchical-authoritarian system that can lead to an attitude, on the part of the priest, to dominate unconsecrated persons in interactions, because he holds a superior position in office through consecration. Sexual abuse is an extreme outgrowth of this dominance. The study states:

> In the case of church leaders, an authoritarian clerical understanding of office may result in a priest, who has perpetrated sexualised violence, being seen as a threat to his own clerical system, rather than a danger to other children or young people or other potential affected persons. The cover-up of events and the protection of the system can take priority over the ruthless disclosure of such acts. A church raison understood in this way, promotes secrecy, cover-ups and inappropriate reactions such as the [...] transfer or sanctioning practices, which are more likely to protect the institution and the accused and disregard the interests of the persons concerned. (MHG-Study 2018, 13)

17.3.3 Coalitions, Loyalties and Dependencies

Within the Catholic Church, dominance is often consolidated through coalitions, loyalties and dependencies, which reach as far as the Vatican. Personal professional networks, resulting from university times or professional relationships, joint consecration or training years, strengthen the inner cohesion. Fraternal loyalty obliges to the absolute protection of one's own class. 'Old-boy' Networks promote the effect of silent agreements. Such networks of confidents and complicity have a distorted perception and tolerance for confreres who are accused. The stronger the entanglement, the higher the obligation of secrecy. Once public pressure becomes particularly high because of accusations, it increases the importance of the community as a permanent system of relationships. Compassion belongs to the brother who is suspected or belongs to the institution that is at risk. Compassion does not belong to the person concerned who clearly 'disturbs' the existing bonds with his accusations (Hallay-Witte and Janssen 2016, 129, 131). If perpetrators feel safe that as far as their acts of violence are not consistently reported to law enforcement authorities or are sanctioned by the enforcement of canon law but rather accepted and tolerated, then violence is legitimized as something that is part of the everyday life of an institution. For the psychiatrist and psychotherapist for children and adolescent Professor Jörg Fegert, the exclusive feeling of:

> being special, the desire not to endanger the institution threatened by society, the problem of getting qualified staff and a resulting network of personal dependencies [...] here and there is the matrix of sexual exploitation in the institutions. (Fegert 2019)

Social Pact of Silence

In male fraternities/alliances, there are often clear rules about when, where and to whom and who speaks or remains silent. These rules of silence are not always fixed but are sometimes lived tacitly. The cultural scientist Professor Aleida Assmann (2017) calls this the 'social pact of silence': silence bonds the social cohesion of a community essentially through 'discussion and silence, through rules on silence and discussion and de-thematisation'. What is addressed or not addressed in groups or communities is subject to historical changes.

Assmann (2017, 3) names tact and taboo as the central terms in which these codes of silence are summarized. She describes the 'social pact of silence' as follows:

> *Tact* is polite silence. It imposes restraint, which comes from an alleged consideration and serves the protection of the other. Lots must not be discussed in the presence of others, because it could burden them, blackmail them or otherwise put them into an embarrassing situation.
>
> *Taboos* concern topics that no one likes to talk about. The pressure that closes the mouth here is so deeply absorbed culturally that it does not even have to be translated into explicit prohibitions in order to be followed. Strong social feelings such as shame, guilt and revulsion are the main engines of taboos.

With the silence there are secrets which – according to Assmann (2017, 2) – separate between the internal community on the one hand and the external outside world of the public on the other. A secret in a community creates alliances and allies. The community appears as a place of familiar relationships, which have a lot to do with the construction of identity on the condition of establishing and maintaining loyalties. According to Assmann, the mystery of abuse divides the community into secret bearers, the initiated and the uninitiated as well as perpetrators and victims. The power of the secret then lies in enforcing a communal and common pact of silence (so-called silence cartel). The connection of the relationship systems is being strengthened by fear of loss of prestige, financial losses and resolution. The conjecture and (secret) co-knowledge of the violation of rules has an impact on the mutuality of the community. In connection to the rules of silence and secrecy, ominous alliances are formed, which quickly lead to insecurity and loneliness (so-called institutional captivity).

As, for example, the 'social pact of silence' and its effects: Sexuality is usually not discussed within church communities, partly because there is often a lack of openness and the ability to talk about one's own sexuality. Also a rigid sexual morality proves that talking about problems and questions in this area is afflicted with fear and loss of prestige. The idealization of celibacy leads to further prohibitions and subsequent violations. Homosexual-orientated men who feel attracted to the unmarried and male-alliance way of life must deny their sexual orientation. In addition, it can be a supposed 'hideout' for people with immature personality structures. Sexual abuse and psychological and physical violence are issues which are all the more silenced. Apparently legitimized lies and hypocrisy are not far and quickly grow into constancy.

17.4 The Defence of Responsibility

Another misconduct, which church leaders are accused of, is pointed out by the psychotherapist Bintig with the psychological concept of 'responsibility defence'. The defence of responsibility is then often expressed in the use of so-called perpetrator language, which is according to Bintig hardly noticeable, because it is used in the daily media by political and business leaders in a comparable way (Bintig 2017, 194). Denial and trivialization are coherent in sentences like: 'I wasn't aware of that'. 'That was before my time'. 'I was not informed'. 'I did not give orders to do so'. 'They were not authorized'. (Deegener 1995, 1999; Bintig 2001).

For many people responsible, including other areas, a personal assumption of responsibility through resignation is the 'last exit' (Dreßing 2019b). It will only be acknowledged what needs to be acknowledged under public pressure; it will only be made known to the public what must be admitted and what needs to be published (so-called salami tactics – Bintig 2017, 189). If, due to external authorities – for example, law enforcement media, the public and stakeholders' initiatives – officials have to admit more and more of what they have previously vehemently denied, their resistance and their defence of responsibility will become public. This will not stay without consequence for their credibility. The longer a crisis of confidence lasts, the stronger and more attention-seeking external authorities exercise social control; and the less the mechanisms of repelling responsibility prove to be effective (Bintig 2017, 189).

In 2002, 2010 and after the publication of the MHG-Study in 2018, church leaders spoke much of shame and guilt. There were apologies, but no church leader in Germany has taken on personal responsibility for the institutional failure and drew any active consequence.

17.5 Missing Liability

Over the past few years, the Catholic Church has sought to improve the protection of children and vulnerable adults by taking effective intervention and prevention measures. In some areas, this has also been successful. The church has set an example. Papers, rules and regulations have been prepared at the federal level and in all dioceses. The scope of the initiatives and measures that are still being planned outlines the extent of mistakes, errors and failures (Hackenschmied and Mosser 2017,

170). The preparation of the various measures happened at first very quickly. The haste was always due to great public pressure and demand, such as a distraught effort to regain lost credibility and trust. However, the implementation of the measures at the various levels was much more hesitant and not standardized. Initiatives at the federal level were only half-heartedly taken up, were not ultimately supported and quickly faded.

An example: The German Conference of Catholic Bishops was one of the first institutions to have GUIDELINES for dealing with sexual abuse of minors and of adult charges by clergy, religious and other staff within the domain of the German Bishops' Conference since 2002 and in 2010, 2013, 2018 has continued to update them. However, the outlined measures which are supposed to be taken do not have binding nature. They were only recommendations to the Bishops. They were not always comprehensively understood, installed and equipped with the necessary resources within each German diocese. In some cases they were only 'correctly copied for glossy brochures' (Fegert 2019). The 'independent' contact person of the so-called commission is in some dioceses not independent, because of being a diocesan employee (MHG-Study 2018, 7) and in some cases was even being a priest. Also the procedure for receiving financial benefits in recognition of the suffering inflicted on victims of sexual abuse or the FRAMEWORK REGULATION Prevention were implemented in different ways in each diocese (MHG-Study 2018, 11). As a result of the MHG - Study new Guidelines are being released as from January 2020 on, which will be compulsory for being enforced in each German diocese.

17.6 It Is a Mistake That...

Misconduct in dealing with sexual abuse and with those affected is based on serious errors made by church leaders. These errors are used and disseminated in an argumentative way to legitimize looking away, not listening and remaining silent. In the following list, some of the main errors should be named:

Error No. 1: It's going to be over. No. The conscious or unconscious hope that the public interest in the subject of sexual abuse in the Catholic Church could be forgotten again is an erroneous belief.

No matter which innovative measures will be initiated, the abuse scandal will always remain latent. With every new case of abuse that is disclosed, everything that has happened in the past will be at present again. It will never go away; see the USA, Ireland and so on (Janssen 2015, 233).

Error No. 2: These are all isolated cases. No. The MHG-Study speaks of the evidence of 3677 victims of sexual assault and 1670 accused priests, deacons and religious between 1946 and 2014 in Germany. The dark field is called large (MHG-Study 2018, 3).

Error No. 3: This does not happen with us. No. Sexual abuse can happen anywhere. It's not a problem of the others. Neither the 1968s, the nor the homosexuals in the church nor the devil are to blame. This is very clear in the MHG-Study. It is important to identify and consistently raise awareness about possible risks and to take action against them.

Error No. 4: Victims are free riders. No. The experience over decades shows that the vast majority of all allegations, in more than 95% of cases, is substantial (Rosetti 2012). Nobody wants to be identified being a victim and certainly not as a victim of sexual abuse. To deny a person being recognized as a victim of sexual abuse is far worse for the church than mistakenly believing a free rider. Affected parties generally wish for their dignity being restored and for the recognition of their legal rights ('We believe you'.). They want the institution to be responsible for its guilt and to be confronted with its own shame. This is supposed to be painful for the institution. This institutional pain is supposed to find its expression through high financial compensations, which have to be paid to the victims.

Error No. 5: The media is to blame ('media shaming'). No. The abuse scandal and the public debate are not 'anti-Catholic propaganda' nor 'primitive manipulation' or 'targeted popular stupidity' nor 'despicable slander campaign' of the media or the journalists who 'keep the truth so outrageously'. Church officials criticized media representatives, even though their own institution is facing massive accusations of crimes and mistakes (Hallay-Witte and Janssen 2016, 75). The media certainly do not always report fairly, but of course the problem of the Catholic Church is not the reporting media. It's not the media that harmed the church. The perpetrators, who abuse girls and boys, are responsible for the damage that has been done. The church leaders are responsible for ensuring the silence of victims and for not taking protective measures. The consequences of these acts and irresponsible behaviour must now be addressed (Hallay-Witte and Janssen 2016, 75). Courage and open communication are needed to absorb negative reporting and avert further damage. Whoever remains silent, rumours will quickly be circulating about him.

Error No. 6: Prayers will help. Prayers certainly do no harm, but will only help to a very limited extent in these cases: The renewal of the church only by 'personal conversion, devotion to God and through a life of faith and the sacraments' (domradio 2019), as could be heard, will certainly not be enough to deal with the continuing loss of confidence and to stop the downward spiral.

Error No. 7: Perpetrators are sick paedophiles. No. The MHG-Study (2018, 4) and the Leygraf Study (2012) show that only a small number of church perpetrators are paedophiles. The far greater number of perpetrators uses sexuality as a means of exercising power.

Error No. 8: (Only) prevention work, etc. is sufficient. No. Sanctioning individual accused, public regret, financial compensation to those affected, the publication of prevention concepts in brochures, etc. are not enough. With paste and copy alone – as some church institutions and communities have tried to do – prevention work cannot be successful. There must be an attitude behind it (Fegert 2019). This requires actively lived commitment – and taking on responsibility also for institutional failure. This also requires external advice and support in order to allow an independent review of structures and dynamics. The MHG-

Study (2018, 14) explicitly points out that, if this is not the case, such basic approaches are even appropriate to maintain clerical power structures, since they only affect the aiming for the symptoms of misdevelopment and prevent the confrontation with the fundamental problem of clerical power.

17.7 Willingness to Listen

The essence of any dispute resolution lies in the willingness of the opponents to listen to each other and not to articulate own positions, interests and emotions by rejecting and disqualifying what they have heard. Of course, people like to hear what corresponds with their own views. Their listening is limited to a quick comparison with familiar patterns, own experiences or beliefs. Things do not have any relevance for the individual at the time. They slip unreflected through the filter of the individual perception. If the other side cannot be convinced, walls will be pulled up, in order to isolate the individual from 'the other', to protect oneself and not to be touched by the others (Janssen 2019). One of the greatest failures of church leaders over the decades is not listening honestly to those affected and letting themselves be touched by their concerns and stories.

17.7.1 Listening Is a Leadership Issue

The letter in January 2010 from Fr. Klaus Mertes SJ, then director of the Canisius College, to 600 former students shows the power of listening. The letter brought change to the system. For decades, the responsibles of this elite school have not been listening and have looked away. In his letter, Fr. Mertes asks for forgiveness and promises to end – and listen – to the practice of cover-up and repression. The willingness of church representative to listen to those affected was new and has a 'domino effect' (Pörksen 2016): more and more people break their silence. They want to denounce the events within the church and possibly also demand compensation, even though they had long since concluded with their church. Those affected are no longer silent. Their aim was to name the mistakes, errors and failures of the past. They demand their concerns to be heard and taken seriously.

It is true that since the 2002 Guidelines, the recommendation has been made to appoint independent contact persons who 'listen' (Hallay-Witte and Janssen 2016, 190). Often, as volunteers, they would just receive the allegations of sexual abuse as a 'preceding letterbox' or a 'reception room'. Further discussions and dealing with the case would continue to be conducted by the head of human resources or the judicial officer of the diocese. Not all contact persons were able to relate to a victim in an appropriate professional manner and really listen nor were they able to ask 'What do you need?' 'What do I have to do, so you can trust me (again)?' (Janssen 2019).

Even still in 2019, there are reports of cases where the application form for a recognition of compensation is just sent to the victim. Once the form is returned completed, the recognition amount is transferred without offering a conversation or getting involved with the compensation-seeking person (MHG-Study 2018, 7). And precisely these erroneous behaviours are the ones that lead to justified criticism. The encounters which happen in an appropriate manner will hardly be discussed in public.

If the listener is authentically trying to perceive the positions and interests of his counterpart, listening does not just mean ‘listening’. It is a more complex process. If listening is supposed to have a constructive effect and generate trust, it demands empathy, great attention ability and concentration (Janssen 2019).

On the other hand, the ignorance of not wanting to perceive what does not suit the ecclesial worldviews leads to disturbances and scandals, which therefore will not be recognized and eliminated within the system. New solutions, which are being pursued decisively, can be developed in the form of church leaders who are willing to listen openly to those affected. This includes the principle of recognizing that sexual abuse can happen in the own institution and that there is no absolute protection against it. This attitude enables an encounter which is capable of meeting the person concerned on an equal footing and of corresponding to their dignity and rights. Many of those affected who did not feel heard by the Church were heard through the hotline of the Federal Government’s Independent Commissioners, as well as through the establishment of a council of affected persons and the establishment of a commission to discuss the possibilities for consultation. The Catholic Church begins to set up advisory councils with survivors in order to obtain the expertise of those persons who suffered sexual abuse in the preparation and revision of regulations. Participation and transparency can convey those affected that church representatives have understood and approach this subject through a relevant attitude, not only through norms and rules.

17.7.2 Listening Is a Theme of Faith

Many people do not feel that they are listened to, do not feel understood. Nevertheless they say that they have not yet completely turned away from the Church and describe their faith and spirituality as an important source of strength for survival. They hope that they (again) will be granted acceptable access to the church community and see this as an obligation of the church.

Still missing in the reappraisal to this extent is the theological discourse (Fegert 2019). Hans Zollner (2015), Member of the Pontifical Commission for Child Protection, drafted the following questions:

> What sort of theology could encourage abuse and cover-up within its own ranks for decades? What led to the institution being the focus, not the human being? What do you say to those affected? What does forgiveness or the possibility of reconciliation mean? What does this mean for the church? What does this mean for the accountability of the church?

Zollner sees this previous failure as a 'symptom of a certain blindness that has prevailed within the institution of the Church for too long'. For him, it is also a 'reflection of how we as a church as a whole and the authorities in the church have dealt with these questions for a long time, frankly by simply pushing them away, simply not thinking about them, not actually reflecting on them and not trying to answer them in anyway'.

The professor for fundamental theology Hildegund Keul (2017) focuses her research on theologically relevant answers through the interdisciplinary discourse on vulnerability. Her approach assumes that one often protects oneself against being wounded by leaving others to be wounded. As a result, she said, tension arises between vulnerability and security. This entails a high potential for violence. In this context, Keul raises the following questions:

> Where is it necessary to protect oneself and the own community (family, religion, state) from being wounded? Where is it necessary, for the sake of humanity – also as an institution – to risk one's own vulnerability?

17.8 Conclusion

Abuse in institutions can never be completely avoided. But church leaders can change the specific risk constellations of an institution. If they allow and encourage discussions about mistakes, errors and failures, new spaces of thinking can open up and new solutions can emerge. Willingness to change, participation and transparency are important prerequisites for a confidence-building process. Many of these men and women who became victims by clergy, religious and other church employees in the area of the German CCB certainly have a lot to say about their experiences with the institution and the representatives of the Catholic Church. However, it is no longer enough to 'only' discuss it: In order to allow sustainable change and taking on responsibility within the Catholic Church, it needs concrete objectives and a binding schedule for the active implementation of the necessary future steps on the basis of what has already been disclosed (Dreßing 2019b).

Developing a culture of mindfulness is a common learning and development process that requires not just medium-term but long-term attention and guidance. It is about a different attitude: to listen, to look and not to look away, to be able to act and to show moral courage.

The measures taken by the bishops following the publication of the MHG-Study 2018 will now be (further) developed, expanded and implemented at all levels of the Catholic Church. It requires the (sensitive) breaking down of the initiated measures down to the ground so that they can be accepted by all church staff. It is important that the process is supported by the responsible leaders as early as possible. The best measures and action concepts only work if as many as possible know and support them (paper alone is patient!). The consistent and continuous implementation and adherence to the self-commitments for work-up, intervention and prevention will (again) be the relevant touchstones, from which it can be read whether and what the Catholic Church in Germany learned from the deep crisis that emerged already in 2002 and later in 2010 (Hallay-Witte and Janssen 2016, 152).

References

Archdiocese of Hamburg. (2018). Arbeitshilfe. *Hinsehen – Handeln – Schützen.* Prävention im Erzbistum Hamburg. Fachstelle Kinder- und Jugendschutz im Erzbistum Hamburg. Retrieved July 25, 2019, from https://www.facebook.com/erzbistumhamburg/posts/10156443184406530.

Assmann, A. (2017). *Geheimnis, Schweigen, Reden.* Lecture on 31 January 2017 in Berlin the 1st Public Hearing ‚Kindesmissbrauch im familiären Kontext' of the Independent Commission for the Treatment of Child Sexual Abuse. p. 1–8 Retrieved July 25, 2019, from https://www.aufarbeitungskommission.de/wp-content/uploads/2017/05/Vortrag-Berlin-Hearing-Assmann.pdf.

Bintig, A. (2001). *Täterarbeit als Beitrag zum Opferschutz.* Leitlinien der Pro Familia NRW e.V. für die Arbeit mit Männern, die sexualisierte Gewalt ausüben. Edited by Pro Familia NRW. Wuppertal.

Bintig, A. (2017). Endbericht. *Sexueller Missbrauch, physische und psychische Gewalt am Collegium Josephinum Bad Münstereifel – Eine wissenschaftliche Aufarbeitung mit und für Betroffene.* to be done with Bundschuh, C. & Janssen, B. Retrieved July 25, 2019, from https://pro-cj.de.

Deegener, G. (1995). *Sexueller Missbrauch: Die Täter.* Weinheim: Psychologie Verlags Union.

Deegener, G. (Ed.) (1999). *Sexuelle und körperliche Gewalt.* Weinheim: Psychologie Verlags Union.

domradio May, 22, 2019. *Bishop Zdarsa. Not in the sense of the Catholic faith.* Retrieved July 25, 2019, from https://www.domradio.de/themen/reformen/2019-05-22/nicht-im-sinne-des-katholischen-glaubens-augsburger-bischof-zdarsa-hat-kein-verstaendnis-fuer-maria.

Dreßing, H. (2019a). *Die Täterorganisation kann keine Aufarbeitung machen. Interview with Christiane Florin.* Deutschlandfunk July 1, 2019.

Dreßing, H. (2019b). *Die Missbrauch-Studie ist keine Aufarbeitung. Interview with Daniel Deckers.* F.A.Z. May 20, 2019.

Dreßing, H., Salize, H. J., Dölling, D., Hermann, D., Kruse, A., Schmitt, E. & Bannenberg, B. (2018). Forschungsprojekt *Sexueller Missbrauch an Minderjährigen durch katholische Priester, Diakone und männliche Ordensangehörige im Bereich der Deutschen Bischofskonferenz.* Retrieved July 25, 2019, from https://www.zi-mannheim.de/fileadmin/user_upload/downloads/forschung/forschungsverbuende/MHG-Studie-gesamt.pdf.

Fegert, Jörg (2019). *Empathie statt Klerikalismus.* Stimmen der Zeit 03/2019, p. 189–204. Retrieved July 25, 2019, from https://www.herder.de/stz/hefte/archiv/144-2019/3-2019/empathie-statt-klerikalismus-chancen-und-grenzen-externer-unterstuetzung-bei-der-auseinandersetzung-mit-sexuellem-missbrauch/.

FRAMEWORK REGULATION *Prevention of sexualised violence against minors and adult charges within the domain of the German Bishops' Conference* (Note: In the current version of June 25, 2019). Retrieved July 25, 2019, from https://dbk.de/fileadmin/redaktion/diverse_downloads/presse_2012/2013-151b-en-Ueberarbeitung-Leitlinien_Rahmenordnung-Praevention_Rahmenordnung-englisch.pdf.

Galtung, Johan (2004): *Gewalt, Krieg und deren Nachwirkungen.* Über sichtbare und unsichtbare Folgen der Gewalt. Forum für interkulturelle Philosophie 5. Retrieved 25 July 2019, from www.them.polylog.org/5/fgj-de.htm.

Grant-Hayford, N. & Scheyer, V. (2016). *Strukturelle Gewalt verstehen.* Eine Anleitung zur Operationalisierung. Galtung-Institut für Friedenstheorie und Friedenspraxis. P. 1-9. Retrieved July 25, 2019, from galtung-institut.de/papers/ G-I-WP-2016-06-SG.pdf.

GUIDELINES for dealing with sexual abuse of minors and of adult charges by clergy, religious and other staff within the domain of the German Bishops' Conference (Note: In the current version of June 25, 2019). Retrieved July 25, 2019, from https://dbk.de/fileadmin/redaktion/diverse_downloads/presse_2012/2013-151a-en-Ueberarbeitung-Leitlinien_Rahmenordnung-Praevention_Leitlinien-englisch.pdf.pdf.

Hackenschmied, G. & Mosser, P. (2017). *Untersuchung von Fällen sexualisierter Gewalt im Verantwortungsbereich des Bistums Hildesheim* – Fallverläufe, Verantwortlichkeiten, Empfehlungen. Institut für Praxisforschung und Projektberatung. IPP-Arbeitspapiere Nr. 12. Retrieved July 25, 2019, from https://www.bistum-hildesheim.de/fileadmin/dateien/PDFs/Pressetexte/IPP_Muenchen_Gutachten_Bistum_Hildesheim.pdf.

Hallay-Witte, M. & Janssen, B. (2015). Forum – *5 Jahre danach. Der lange Weg des Perspektivenwechsels im Skandal des sexuellen Missbrauchs in der katholischen Kirche.* Lebendige Seelsorge 01/2015, p. 65–70.

Hallay-Witte, M. & Janssen, B. (2016). *Schweigebruch – Vom sexuellen Missbrauch zur institutionellen Prävention.* Eine perspektivische Dokumentation der Lern- und Entwicklungsprozesse der katholischen Kirche in Deutschland. Freiburg: Herder-Verlag.

Janssen, B. (2015). *Tatorte und Aspekte der Täter-Opfer-Institutionen-Dynamik*, in: Fegert, J./Wolff, M. (Hrsg.): Kompendium Sexueller Missbrauch in Institutionen – Entstehungsbedingungen, Prävention und Intervention. Weinheim und Basel: BeltzJuventa. p. 208–223.

Janssen, B. (2019). *Höchste Zeit, zuzuhören* – DIE MEDIATION Quartal II/ 2019, p. 12–15.

Keul, Hildegund (2017): Verwundbarkeit, Sicherheit und Resilienz – der Vulnerabilitätsdiskurs als Chance für eine gesellschaftsrelevante Theologie. *Stimmen der Zeit* (StZ) 142. Jg. Heft 9 (2017), 589–598.

Leygraf, N. & König, A. et al. (2012). Study '*Sexuelle Übergriffe durch katholische Geistliche in Deutschland – Eine Analyse forensischer Gutachten 2000–2010*'. Published on December 7, 2012. Retrieved July 25, 2019, from https://www.dbk.de/fileadmin/redaktion/diverse_downloads/presse/2012-198b-Analyse-forensisch-psychiatrische-Gutachten-Praesentation-Prof-Leygraf.pdf.

Pörksen, B. (2016). Kommunikation: Hört doch mal zu!. Retrieved 7 September 2019, from https://www.zeit.de/2016/34/kommunikation-zuhoeren-aufmerksamkeit-du-ohr-verdraengung-schweigen

Rosetti, St. J. (2012). *Learning from our mistakes: responding effectively to child sexual abusers.* In: Scicluna, C. / Zollner, H. / Ayotte, D. (Eds.): Toward healing and renewal: the 2012 Symposium on the Sexual Abuse of Minors held at the Pontifical Gregorian University. English Edition Mahwah, N.J.: Paulist Press. German Edition Munich: Don Bosco Mediaien.

Unabhängige Kommission zur Aufarbeitung sexuellen Kindesmissbrauchs (2019): Aufarbeitungsberichte zum Thema sexueller Kindesmissbrauch. Retrieved July 25, 2019, from https://www.aufarbeitungskommission.de/wp-content/uploads/2019/05/Aufarbeitungsberichte_Mai_2019.pdf.

Zollner, H. (2015). Kirche und Missbrauch: *Viele unbeantwortete theologische Fragen.* Interview. Vatican Radio June 24, 2015. Retrieved July 25, 2019, from http://www.vaticanhistory.de/wordpress/?p=10607.

Mary Hallay-Witte is a Dipl. Religious Pedagogue, Systemic Therapist for Individuals, Couples and Families (DGSF). In her current position, she is working at the 2019 newly founded Institute for Prevention and Appraisal of sexual abuse (IPA). As the managing Director of the Office for Child and Youth Protection in the Archdiocese of Hamburg from 2010 to 2018, she was responsible for the conceptual design and set-up of the office. Also she was commissioned for the prevention and the coordination of the intervention of sexual abuse of minors. Until her current position, she worked as a research assistant at the Medical School Hamburg (MSH). Since 2018, she is a member of the research group Vulnerability, Security and Resilience at the University of Würzburg. In her research work, she focuses on the institutional prevention of the sexual abuse of minors and vulnerable adults.

Dr. iur. Bettina Janssen is a self-employed lawyer and mediator (BM), who runs her own consultancy since 2004 in Cologne. For the past 10 years, she has also been professionally focusing on sexual, psychological and/or physical violence in institutions. From 2010 to 2014, she was the Head of the Office of the German Bishops' Conference on Issues of Sexual Abuse in Bonn. Recently (2015–2017) she has been responsible for the reappraisal project Collegium Josephinum Bad Münstereifel, Archdiocese of Cologne, in conjunction with Prof. Dr. Claudia Bundschuh. Since 2019 she is working on the reappraisal project Albertinum Gerolstein (district Vulkaneifel), Diocese of Trier, in conjunction again together with Professor Bundschuh.

Part IV
Mistakes, Errors and Failure in Education

Chapter 18
Failures, Errors, and Mistakes: A Systematic Review of the Literature

Amber Simpson, Adam V. Maltese, Alice Anderson, and Euisuk Sung

Abstract Terms such as failure, mistakes, errors, obstacles, and struggle are used interchangeably, but each carries different connotations and discipline-specific meanings. Reactions to experiencing a failure can range as well from being seen as having educative value to be debilitating. These reactions are based on criteria like environment, prior experiences, and individual characteristics, to name a few. The purpose of this chapter is to synthesize and clarify how these terms are articulated and utilized in research studies and commentaries published between 1970 and mid-2018. Through a systematic literature review, we will discuss similarities and differences in how researchers defined these terms, as well as how these definitions differ by cultural context, discipline, and age of participants. Next, we briefly highlight how our research findings on failure within making and tinkering contexts contribute to our current thinking on failure, mistakes, and errors. Our research included approximately 500 youths and 150 educators situated in a variety of settings that implement making and tinkering programs and/or activities including an informal educational setting (i.e., museum), a formal educational setting (i.e., public middle school), and a hybrid setting (i.e., science center running after-school programming at local school sites). We conclude with open questions and recommendations for the field to consider when conducting research around failures, errors, and mistakes in educational contexts.

Keywords Mistakes · Errors · Failures · Maker education

A. Simpson (✉)
Department of Teaching, Learning, and Educational Leadership, Binghamton University, Binghamton, NY, USA
e-mail: asimpson@binghamton.edu

A. V. Maltese · E. Sung
W.W. Wright School of Education, Indiana University, Bloomington, IN, USA
e-mail: amaltese@indiana.edu; sunge@iu.edu

A. Anderson
Minneapolis Institute of Art, Minneapolis, MN, USA
e-mail: aanderson@artsmia.org

E. Vanderheiden, C.-H. Mayer (eds.), *Mistakes, Errors and Failures across Cultures*, https://doi.org/10.1007/978-3-030-35574-6_18

18.1 Introduction

Our research team has been conducting research on the role of failure within making and tinkering contexts. Grounded in a prior study from a set of interviews with science, technology, engineering, and mathematics (STEM) professionals, we discovered that many pointed to the critical role of failures in their jobs (Simpson and Maltese 2017). One key finding from this work was that although these professionals discussed how failure and failure analysis were really important to them creating things or improving objects or processes, nearly all of them said that they were not given the chance to learn about the importance of revision before advanced schooling or entry into the workforce. Based on these interviews, we became interested in the opportunities that making and tinkering activities provided for youth to engage in failure and perhaps gain from it, in ways described by this sample of STEM professionals. We contend that experiences with making and tinkering in STEM spaces have the potential to expose and encourage youth to pursue STEM careers. We initiated a study to investigate how youth responded to failure when engaged in making experiences across a set of formal and informal environments. As such, educators are positioned to support or hinder youth through these occurrences and help them learn (or not) from their experiences with failure (Simpson et al. 2017; Maltese et al. 2018).

18.2 The State of Failure Use

One of the key challenges we experienced from the start of this work is around terminology. The first way this manifested was in talking with educators about the term "failure" and how they talked about it with their learners. While many educators we spoke with reported engaging their learners in experiences that included an outcome that differed from expectations, they often used terms other than failure because of the negative connotations they and/or their learners held by the term. Often educators reported using terms like mistakes, challenges, obstacles, and others to capture similar ideas but to avoid connecting failure in making or STEM activities with the traditional meanings associated with poor academic performance.

Such an avoidance of using the term failure to define youths' experiences have been documented by other researchers as well (e.g., Simpson et al. 2018; Lottero-Perdue and Parry 2017a). For example, the majority of teachers in the study by Lottero-Perdue and Parry (2017a) viewed failure as a negative event or behavior (e.g., giving up, not trying); therefore, they reported rarely using the term failure within their classroom setting but related failures to mistakes or errors. Educators are often concerned with students identifying themselves as failures, as well as experiencing negative behavioral and emotional states such as hopelessness, depression, embarrassment, and learned helplessness (e.g., Guler 2013; Lottero-Perdue and Parry 2017a). For those who avoid the word, it is grounded in the idea that failure does not capture the essence of creative and inventive progression toward reaching some goal (e.g., Maltese et al. 2018; Ryoo and Kekelis 2018).

This tension in using the term failure is also a debate within maker education (e.g., Clapp 2015). Consider the following quote by Martinez (2013), which highlighted how the negative connotation of failure is grounded in academic settings and, as such, may not translate well to making and tinkering contexts:

> Here's the problem. It's the word "failure." Failure means a VERY specific thing in schools. The big red F is serious. In school, failure is NOT a cheery message to "try, try, again!", it's a dead-end with serious consequences. Using this loaded word to present mistakes, hurdles, challenges, detours, etc. is confusing and unnecessary. Teachers cannot talk about failure as a challenge, when failure also mean judgment – the worst possible judgment.... Is this just silly semantics? I don't think so. (para. 5–6, 9)

Blikstein and Worsley (2017) too questioned the glorification and oversimplification of failure in making context. These sentiments are expressed by others (e.g., Thomas 2016).

18.3 The State of Failure Definitions

The second challenge related to terminology is possibly more of a critical problem in our work – the issue of a number of related threads of research that are not connected or informed by the others because they included different keywords or have origins in different areas of research (e.g., mathematics education, educational psychology, the role of failure in innovation). There are studies on productive failure and productive struggle (e.g., Kapur 2008; Kapur and Kinzer 2009; Lai et al. 2017). This is often disconnected from research on errors or mistakes (e.g., DeBrincat 2015; Tulis 2013). Beyond this, there are mentions of desirable difficulty (e.g., Bjork and Bjork 2011), gradual downward slumps (Zsigmond 2016), and unhappy eventualities (Fogle 1979) to name a few. Moreover, much of this research is an extension of the current rhetoric around growth mindset (Dweck 2006) and grit (Duckworth et al. 2007).

Additionally, failure, as well as mistakes and errors, have several meanings as defined in at least three unabridged dictionaries (e.g., Oxford, Random House, and Webster). For example, in the unabridged Random House dictionary (2019), errors have eight different definitions, some of which are distinguished based on a particular discipline (e.g., baseball, law, mathematics). Moreover, errors are defined in relation to mistakes – "a deviation from accuracy or correctness; a mistake, as in action or speech" (Random House 2019) or "something produced by a mistake" (Merriam-Webster 2019). The synonymous nature of these terms is illustrated in their use (or not) within formal and informal learning settings (e.g., Lottero-Perdue and Parry, 2017a).

Although this issue of related research being siloed within different scholarship, as well as being not being clearly defined, is not unique to the topic of failure, errors, and mistakes (e.g., McKnight and Chervany 2001/2002), we feel strongly that this reduces the efficiency in building on previous research, as well as having a shared meaning among researchers and between researchers and educators. This chapter builds out of our struggles with this issue and our hope to help others see similarities and differences among similar terminology within related research, "creating order out of chaos" (McKnight and Chervany 2001/2002, 39). As such, our purpose is to synthesize and clarify how these terms are articulated in research studies and commentaries, to make sense of the terminology chaos among three terms – failure, errors, and mistakes. Specifically, we address the following research question: How is failures, mistakes, and errors defined within the scholarship published between 1970 and mid-2018? Subsequently, we consider similarities and differences in how researchers defined these terms, as well as how these definitions differ by cultural context, discipline, and age of participants. Our findings are then situated within our current research regarding failure in making contexts.

18.4 Method

This study is situated within linguistics, specifically textual map analysis, as this analysis accounts for both words or concepts used within a given text, as well as the relationships between them (Carley 1993). For us, we holistically focused on how the words failures, errors, and mistakes were defined and used within scholarship across a range of disciplines, age groups, and cultural contexts and the similarities and/or differences among them. As such, this research is grounded within a pragmatist perspective as our systematic literature review is focused on the "vocabularies we use and how changes in words can affect how we think and act" (Noddings 2005, 58).

18.4.1 Search Process and Criteria

Our search for peer-reviewed journal articles, book chapter, and commentaries published between January 1970 to June 2018 were conducted using the following databases: Academic Search Complete, Education Source, ERIC, PsycINFO, and Social Sciences Full Text. Search terms within the abstract included fail∗ (i.e., fail or failure or failing), mistake∗, and error∗, in which the asterisk was used to capture similar wording (e.g., mistake and mistakes). Each of these abstract search terms was paired with the following subject search terms: education∗, informal∗, and learning∗. Articles were initially kept if the title and abstract seemed to meet the inclusion/exclusion criteria. This yielded 309 articles, 230 articles with a focus on failure, 51 articles with a focus on mistakes, and 128 articles with a focus on errors.

Studies were included if the following criteria were met: (1) full-text publication written in English; (2) set within an educational context (e.g., school, afterschool program, workplace); and (3) included individuals' experience as opposed to organizational, institutional, or national experiences with failure, mistakes, or errors. In addition, studies with a focus on failure did not include academic failure (e.g., not passing a class or a test) as these were typically focused on pass/fail or right/wrong and not well-defined. We also did not include studies examining attributions of achievement or academic failures.

Next, we extracted information from each article including location of study, age of participants, discipline, and definition. Simultaneously, we omitted studies that did not meet the criteria captured during our initial reading of the title and abstract. The most common reason for omitting a study was researchers did not clearly articulate how they defined failures, mistakes, or errors. This reduced our analysis to 201 articles. A list of articles (see Appendix A) is included within our systematic literature review located online at https://orb.binghamton.edu/education_fac/4[1].

18.4.2 Data Analysis

Our analysis began with descriptively coding each definition (Saldaña 2013). In other words, we used initial codes that summarized the essence of each definition. For example, entry failures, or children's unsuccessful "attempts to enter the play of peers" (Wilson et al. 2011, 377), were coded as social to signify individual's inability to establish and/or maintain relationships with others. We continued to refine the initial codes throughout the analysis. For instance, we collapsed a code identified as planning within the code process as both terms indicated a failure, mistake, or error as part of a series of actions toward a goal or end state. As another example, we divided our initial code of unawareness into unawareness and accidental slip as the first indicated lacking an understanding of consequences based on one's actions and behaviors, as the latter indicated a momentary lapse in thought. Lastly, we did not include codes when it was associated with fewer than five studies (e.g., entrepreneurial). See Appendix B in our online supplementary material for our codes, definitions, and example citations. For a few studies, more than one code applied (e.g., Aksu et al. 2016).

Next, to consider similarities and differences among the definitions of failures, errors, and mistakes, we descriptively compared the codes by age group (e.g., elementary/aged 5–12, postsecondary), discipline (e.g., science, second-language acquisition), and country(ies) in which the research was collected, or if a commentary, the country of the author.

[1] All online supplementary material (i.e., appendices) may be found at this website.

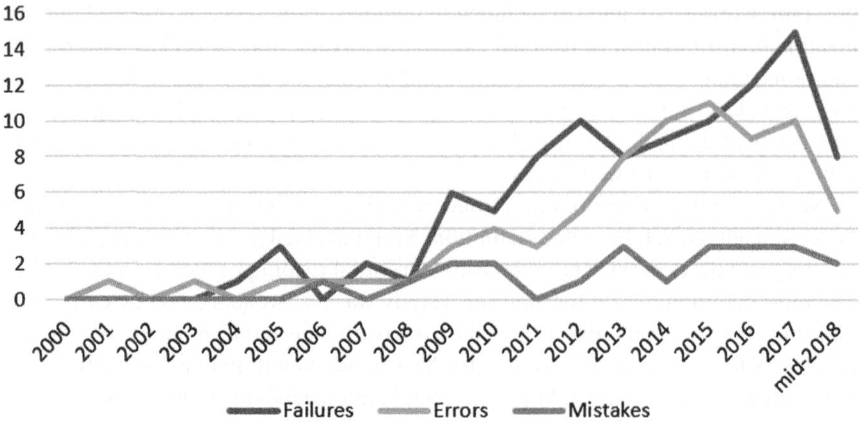

Fig. 18.1 Included studies by year and domain

18.4.3 Limitations

Several limitations should be acknowledged as part of this systematic review of failures, errors, and mistakes published between January 1970 and June 2018. One, we do not claim to have included every study and commentary that clearly defined one of these three domains within an educational setting. Two, our results based on location of study, discipline of study, and age range of participants were not complete in that some authors did not disclose this information. Yet, we contend that the results of this systematic literature review and our own research are timely as we have seen an increase of studies (see Fig. 18.1) regarding the three domains since the turn of the century as we came across few studies within our inclusion criteria prior to 2000.

18.4.4 Results

Below we address how failures, mistakes, and errors were defined within the scholarship published between 1970 and mid-2018 including examples from included studies. Next, we compare these definitions by country, discipline, and age group of participants.

Figure 18.2 visually illustrates how researchers defined the domains of failures, mistakes, and errors by code. In considering similarities and differences, we compared percentages as there were fewer included studies who based and defined their research within mistakes (12%) as opposed to failures (49%) or errors (39%).

Across the domains, the most common definition was stated as a deviation from a norm or standard way of being, acting, and/or behaving. For example, Andréassian, Perrin, Parent, and Bárdossy (2010) defined failure as monsters, "something

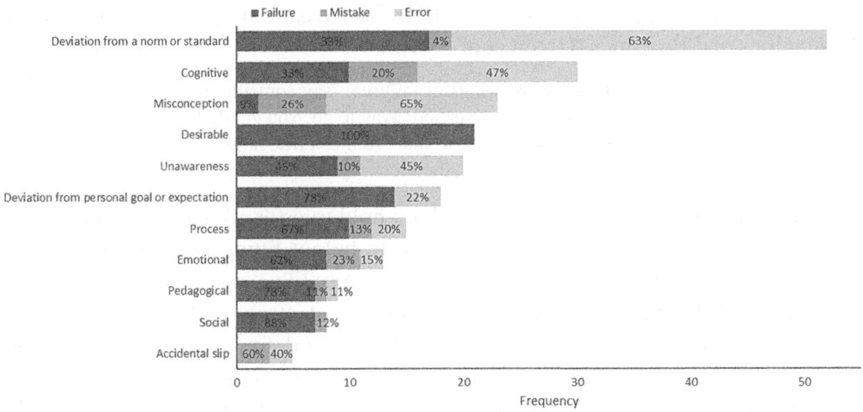

Fig. 18.2 Stacked bar plot of codes by failures, mistakes, and errors

incongruous, unexpected, deviating from the norm or unpredictable" (p. 851). We coded these definitions as deviations from a norm or standard to encompass a wealth of studies including deviations within second-language acquisition (e.g., Bao 2015), vocational education (Cattaneo and Boldrini 2017), the academic job search (Stein and Santa 1975), and physics (Omosewo and Akanbi 2013) to name a few. Similarly, there was a small percentage of studies across the three domains coded as unawareness, pedagogical, and process. For the latter, researchers were interested in failures, mistakes, and errors within a series of actions or steps toward some goal or end state, part of an iteration and means of learning. For example, Lottero-Perdue and Parry (2017b) defined failures as a "normal and expected outcome as a part of the iterative nature of designing solutions to problems, although the end goal is that the solution (hereafter, the 'design') is not intended to fail" (p. 1).

In comparing the percentages, there seems to be a difference in how mistakes and errors are framed in comparison to failures. To begin, researchers more often defined mistakes and errors in terms of lacking the mental capability and/or capacity to perform or execute an action (i.e., cognitive) and lacking a conceptual and/or procedural understanding (i.e., misconception) than the way in which researchers defined failures. For instance, Ashkenazi (2017) defined mistakes as containing a "certain faulty logic brought about by a lack of understanding of mathematical definitions or principles" (p. 306). Similarly, included studies within the failure domain did not consider failure an accidental slip or momentary lapse in thought, while a few included studies within the other two domains did consider mistakes and errors as a form of carelessness (e.g., Tarawneh and Almomani 2013). Together, these insights may imply that researchers do not view failures as associated with the mind or memory (i.e., cognitive structures).

On the other hand, definitions of failure seemed more often associated with one's self-worth (i.e., personal deviation, emotional) and social relations than errors and mistakes. In other words, failure was considered as "whatever [felt] like a failure to the person experiencing it" (Bishop 2017, 962). Consider the following definition of a "magnificent" failure offered from Katie, an assistant professor of Medical Humanities and Bioethics (Green et al. 2016):

> I'm a big fan of what I think of as beautiful failures—say something was ambitious and well-intentioned, and you're like, "That sucked! Way to go. You got that out of you!" But it had all kinds of great things behind it. I love that. To me, a true failure is a failure of spirit. It's a failure of integrity. It's a failure of authenticity. (p. 480)

Yet such a positive view of failure did not hold true for all definitions of failure. Chin (2015), for example, perceived failure to be not fitting in or belonging as a "real American" throughout her childhood and daily life experiences as an adult.

Another difference between the two domains of errors and mistakes and the domain of failures is the number of researchers that defined failures as desirable. The majority of these studies were grounded in Kapur's (2008) work around productive failure. In these studies, failure was intentionally planned as part of the environment for its potential to enhance individual's learning experiences provided that direct instruction was subsequently provided. As employed by Trueman (2013), "Productive failure (Kapur 2009) is an emergent pedagogical theory that argues learning activities must be designed so that students reach an impasse during their problem-solving activities" (p. 201). As such, researchers who examined mistakes and errors did not intentionally design opportunities for students to learn concepts and practices through making errors and mistakes through novel or ill-developed problems.

Next, we considered differences among codes by country as the included literature spanned 39 countries (see Appendix C). Studies within the United States was most frequent ($n = 75$), followed by scholarship in Germany ($n = 15$) and the United Kingdom ($n = 12$). In looking at the map of studies by codes, there are no clear patterns, which implies that studies regarding failures, mistakes, and errors are of a global concern and one perspective or code is not more prevalent in any particular region. For example, studies coded as cognitive were conducted in 17 different countries including the Czech Republic, Taiwan, Nigeria, Turkey, South Africa, Canada, and Germany.

In terms of discipline or subject area, mathematics was the most common across the three domains of failures, errors, and mistakes. More specifically, mathematics was most often considered in terms of students' misconceptions and cognitive discord (37% and 18%, respectively), as well as how to support students through intentionally designing for student failures (i.e., desirable; 35%). Second-language acquisition (SLA) studies were the second most common discipline examined within each domain. Particularly, SLA was often viewed as deviation from some norm of a second language (54%) and as having no awareness of one's failures, mistakes, and/or errors in speaking or writing (18%). Science, physics most often, was also a common discipline viewed within each of the domains. On the other hand, scholarship within the disciplines of medical and fine arts (e.g., music, art) was most often grounded in the domain of failure. In addition, there were few studies within the fields of engineering and technology as we expect that many studies in these two disciplines are not at the individual level but at an organizational level (e.g., start-up company) or on the failures, errors, and mistakes themselves.

Postsecondary students (i.e., undergraduates and graduates) were the most common age group to be examined across the three domains with 45% in the domain of failures and 43% in the domain of errors. Studies including an adult population most often considered the domain of failure (70%). Conversely, in considering students at the elementary (grades K-6; ages 5–12) and secondary (grades 7–12; ages 12–18) school levels, a higher percentage of studies examined students' errors (46% and 50%, respectively) within a particular discipline. In looking at similarities and differences by code, the highest percentage of studies for secondary and postsecondary students were coded as deviation from a norm, 31% for both age groups. Differences between the two age groups were noted in terms of the discipline as the majority of studies with secondary students were deviation from a norm in STEM-related fields such as mathematics (e.g., Makonye and Luneta 2014), while studies with postsecondary students were deviations from a norm in SLA (i.e., written and spoken language; e.g., Nuruzzaman et al. 2018). For studies with elementary-aged students, the majority of studies were in relation to misconceptions (31%) and cognitive dissonances (23%). Studies coded as pedagogy were only considered with the educational workforce. Similarly, a higher percentage of scholarship coded as process (six of nine) were examined with an adult population. Therefore, failures, errors, and mistakes may be analyzed as an end state in K-12 and postsecondary education settings as opposed to action and behaviors toward reaching an end state. Lastly, studies that considered the impact of designing for student failures (i.e., desirable) were situated more often with secondary-aged students (45%) than elementary-aged students (5%). This raises the question as to whether or not young children are able to developmentally handle failures or are we avoiding such instances to protect young children from what we perceive as negative experiences (Lottero-Perdue and Parry 2017a).

18.4.5 Our Research

Over the past 3 years, we have examined how youth aged 9–14 years of age and educators across a variety of educational contexts have experienced and discussed the role of failure through making and tinkering activities (i.e., tasks that encourage the creation of a digital and/or physical object for purposeful or playful means). We have collected (a) survey data from 107 educators, (b) interviews from 13 educators, (c) interviews from 133 youths (43 in public school setting, 46 in weeklong informal summer camp, and 44 in informal drop-in exploration), and (d) 336 point-of-view videos from youth (223 in public school, 49 in museum, and 54 in after-school program). Similar to the majority of researchers in this systematic review, we defined failure as an experience in which the intended or expected result of the maker deviates from the actual outcome (Simpson et al. 2019). We also contend there is a range of failure experiences in making from a miniscule failure (e.g., LED does not light up) to a global failure (e.g., product does not work in final presentation). In other words, failures are part of the making process and typically lead to informed or exploratory design changes (Simpson et al. 2017). From across this data set, we considered in what ways our findings contribute to our current understanding of how failures, mistakes, and errors have been defined and researched, as well as our working definition of failures in making and tinkering contexts.

One of our assumptions entering our exploratory study on youths' experiences with failures in making contexts was that youth would consider failures as detrimental or negative and to be associated with negative emotional states and diminished sense of belongingness (e.g., Heyd-Metzuyanim 2015). While in some instances this was the case, our cumulative research with youth showed otherwise (Simpson et al. 2018, 2019). Youth in our study were often resilient and not averse to failures and expressed how failures throughout a process of making typically led to opportunities to learn from their errors and mistakes; to make improvements; and to gain understanding of what works and does not work in particular situations. For example, at the conclusion of a coding project, Penny and Joan reflected upon their project – a piano slide:

> If we could redo it, we would switch our design around. First of all, the slide would have been all one piece instead of two. Secondly, we would not have used a golf ball. Lastly, we would have made stronger doors so that they would not bend. We were upset that this project did not work, but we know this is a really good learning experience.

Failure was often viewed by youth as giving up on a project and/or yourself, or as not trying hard enough (i.e., effort), which was rarely observed in our study. As stated by Juan:

> Mistake is when you go back, and fix it, and learn from it. Failure is where you make a mistake and give up on it. You don't try to fix it and you don't learn from it.

However, such views of failures may not have been expressed or experienced by all youth as we observed instances of failure avoidance or moments in which youth asked for help before trying any part of the making process (Simpson et al. 2019). This was often expressed as "Can you help me?" In constructing a car using LEGO and littleBits, Joseph asked for help prior to attempting a part of the design 16 times in about a 30-min time period. This equates to asking for help every 2 min. Dweck and Reppucci (1973) described this as learned helplessness, a perception of a situation that is beyond one's control. We hypothesize that instances of failure avoidance are associated with negative views of failures within academic contexts (e.g., failed a test) and the educator-youth power dynamic in that the educator is viewed as an "expert" and tends to "rescue" youths from experiencing failures (Lottero-Perdue and Parry 2017a). However, in the case of Joseph, his request for help was not always responded to by an educator; yet, Joseph continued constructing his car.

Within our video data, we considered types of failures within the process of making and tinkering. Consistent with our definition, we observed failures that we considered deviations from some norm. For example, while turning a crank of a music box, the generator did not seem to be producing sound waves. Cameron attended to this failure by stating "Why is this not working?" In other words, Cameron expected the music box to produce sound waves; thus, the failure was a deviation from this standard. Additionally, failures were noted as aesthetic failures or failures in which the look of the object did not meet students' expectations. This would be coded as a deviation from a personal norm or standard. We also observed instances of this code when youth verbalized failures as a personal experience. As an illustration, Chris was designing a 3D chess piece when he stated to the educator, "I'm doing the chess piece and every time I revolve it, it doesn't have the flat thing at the top and I've done it three times now." Note the use of I as we considered these to be attributing failure to one's self, a personal deviation.

Conversely, we witnessed youths' experiences of failure that did not align well with our definition, nor that of our codes from our systematic literature review. One was due to understanding how to use tools, materials, or resources appropriately (e.g., adhesives, software programs, yarn, and fabric), while another was lacking the strength and/or fine motor skills to be successful with tools, materials, and resources. For example, youth throughout our study had a difficult time with sewing projects as they lacked the skill to thread a needle, knot the end of the conductive thread, and/or insert the needle into the hole of a LilyPad. As another instance, as part of a tabling activity, youth struggled with punching a hole into a piece of tin. As a last example, this one of the former, Zeus attempted to cut off a piece of cardboard using a "pizza cutter" knife, which she finally determined was pointless in that the tool was not doing the job intended. We also witnessed failures due to the tools, materials, and resources available to youth. For instance, youths were asked to cut through tennis shoes using dull, kid-friendly scissors. After several attempts, Bob expressed frustration in his tone of voice. "I can't cut this [shoe]. Can someone help me?" Many youths within this activity noted, "we need better scissors."

In our work with educators, the survey indicated a balanced view of failure – positive (e.g., learning) and negative (e.g., frustrated) sentiments and outcomes. They acknowledge that such sentiments and outcomes are dependent on individual students, who they are and their previous experiences with failures in any context. Educators often reported not using the word failure but similar words such as challenges, obstacles, and setbacks and often framed failure as part of an iteration and an opportunity to improve (Maltese et al. 2018). Yet, educators in our study did consider where and how students would experience challenges and struggles during making contexts, but do not typically think of these moments as planning for failures (i.e., desirable). This is illustrated in the following quote by an educator who facilitated a summer camp at a science museum:

> I think I am often thinking about what are kids capable of, or likely capable of, and then keeping the activities right on the cusp of what they're able to do or not do, and knowing it's going to be really hard, and then building in supports within the lessons of like these are extra things that you can… . If you consider part of that struggle as failure, like on a really minor tiny scale, then I suppose maybe I had planned for it. But I guess I'd always thought about it more as making things challenging, or giving the kids a challenge. And thought about that as one broad category, rather than a series of failures.

This quote also highlights the complexity in terminology, here the difference in failures, challenges, and struggles.

Educators in our study also expressed obstacles (or failures) around students' knowledge of a particular tool or material and/or having the fine motor skills to use a tool appropriately, as well as moments when a tool and/or software itself did not work. As an example of the latter, "I think of blowing up the Arduino boards, which happens a few times. I guess I don't think of like kids' failure. I'm thinking of like the technology failure." Some educators expressed struggles more often with technological tools students are not familiar than with "crafty/recycled material" in which students are more likely to try to figure out how to fix an issue.

18.5 Conclusion and Recommendations

Taken together, we have realized the difficulty in defining failure within the context of making. This sentiment was shared by others (e.g., Carr 2013; Farrell and Hooker 2009; Simpson and Maltese 2017). As stated by Carr (2013), "failure is difficult, maybe impossible, to define" (p. 2). Through our research, we contend that our definition of failure should be broadened to include deviations largely – deviation from a norm such an end goal vocalized by an educator, the end goal established as a peer group, or deviation from a known use of tools, resources, and technological devices, as well as a deviation from a personal norm or standard. We have further contemplated our use of the term failures throughout the process because as stated by Lottero-Perdue and Parry (2017a), "failures are not mistakes … failure is negative" (p. 49). Would miniscule failures (i.e., deviations) be better termed as mistakes or errors, mistakes or errors that holistically lead to a global failure? Or should we consider if individuals experience moments of mistakes or errors prior to miniscule failures during making activities? As argued by Dahlin, Chuang, and Roulet (2018), failures "range from small technical *errors* and *mistakes* to product breakdowns to large-scale disasters" (p. 1) [emphasis added]. We further contemplate this shift in language from failures to mistakes or errors within the process of making as the term failure seems to be associated with one's self-worth more often that the term mistake or error, at least as identified within our literature review.

As such, in considering the similarities and differences among the three terms within the included research studies and commentaries, there appears to be a distinction between failures and mistakes, and errors in that failures are more often defined as more personal and self-defined while mistakes and errors as a deficit in one's cognitive ability. Failure is experienced and known by individuals (e.g., project does not meet self-imposed goals) and potentially others (e.g., code does not run during presentation), while mistakes and errors may be unknown or hidden to an individual but not to others (e.g., mathematical miscalculation). Moreover, there is much research on productive failure (e.g., Kapur 2008) in which designing for failure, and supporting individuals through this failure, is considered within the broader learning context. There is not a similar argument for productive mistakes nor productive errors. On the other hand, across the domains, they shared a common definition as a deviation from some norm or standard way of being, acting, and/or behaving and a deviation from what is expected as appropriate or "correct" as defined by society, an institution, a discipline, an authority figure, and so forth.

In terms of future research studies, one could expand upon our search to include additional terms such as obstacles, setbacks, and challenges as these seemed to be used more often by the educators in our study. Two, it is not clear whether planning for failures (i.e., productive failure; Kapur 2008) within making contexts is a common practice. As noted by our research, this is typically not something considered in designing activities. What might be the implications of ensuring that youth experience failure during making to then be supported through instruction? On the other hand, should this experience with failure be early in the experience and be followed by a discussion about appropriate ways to handle and move past these experiences? Of these two, which may lead to greater opportunities to learn from failures, mistakes, and/or errors within making contexts? Three, our research highlighted how lacking the necessary knowledge and skills of tools, resources, and materials are causes of youth's experiences with failure in making activities. We contend the difficult nature in planning such activities for youth specifically in informal spaces as educators do not have an understanding of youth prior to a program or drop-in session. How might knowledge of youth in such spaces change the nature of failure? We argue that experiences with failures should not be due to lack of the necessary knowledge and skills to be successful. Four, future research should continue to explore how use of various terms affect students' self-worth and motivation, and how this may differ based on discipline. Lastly, future studies should consider the role that errors and mistakes, particularly those grounded in individual's misconceptions and cognitive dissonance, may lead to experiences with failures. Does this occur within one activity or task, or does it span several weeks or months?

Funding This research is funded by the US National Science Foundation under Award DRL-1623452. Any opinions, findings, conclusions, or recommendations expressed in this material are those of the author(s) and do not necessarily reflect those of the National Science Foundation.

References

Aksu, Z., Ozkaya, M., Gedik, S. D., & Konyalıoglu, A. C. (2016). Mathematics self-efficacy and mistake-handling learning as predictors of mathematics anxiety. *Journal of Education and Training Studies*, 4(8), 65–71. doi:https://doi.org/10.11114/jets.v4i8.1533

Andréassian, V., Perrin, C., Parent, E., & Bárdossy, A. (2010). The court of miracles of hydrology: can failure stories contribute to hydrological science?. *Hydrological Sciences Journal*, 55(6), 849–856.

Ashkenazi, Y. (2017). Common mathematical mistakes and misconceptions among pre-academic Israeli students. *International Journal of Arts & Sciences*, 10(1), 305–320.

Bao, X. (2015). Senior high school students' errors on the use of relative words. *English Language Teaching*, 8(3), 137–154. doi: https://doi.org/10.5539/elt.v8n3p137

Bishop, K. (2017). Framing failure in the legal classroom: Techniques for encouraging growth and resilience. *Arkansas Law Review*, 70(4), 959–1006.

Bjork, E. L., & Bjork, R. A. (2011). Making things hard on yourself, but in a good way: Creating desirable difficulties to enhance learning. In M. A. Gernsbacher, R. W. Pew, L. M. Hough, & J. R. Pomerantz (Eds.), *Psychology and the real world: Essays illustrating fundamental contributions to society* (pp. 56–64). New York: Worth Publishers.

Blikstein, P., & Worsley, M. (2017). Children are not hackers: Building a culture of powerful ideas, deep learning, and equity in the maker movement. In K. Peppler, E. R. Halverson, & Y. B. Kafai (Eds.), *Makeology: Makerspaces as Learning Environments* (pp. 64–79). New York, NY: Routledge.

Carley, K. (1993). Coding choices for textual analysis: A comparison of content analysis and map analysis. *Sociological Methodology*, 23, 75–126.

Carr, A. (2013). In support of failure. *Composition Forum*, 27. Retrieved from http://compositionforum.com

Cattaneo, A. A., & Boldrini, E. (2017). Learning from errors in dual vocational education: video-enhanced instructional strategies. *Journal of Workplace Learning*, 29(5), 357–373. doi: https://doi.org/10.1108/JWL-01-2017-0006

Chin, C. (2015). Failure to be a "Real American"?→ challenging failure: An impetus to shape scholarship and teaching. *Journal of Social Theory in Art Education*, 35(1), 10–29.

Clapp, E. (2015, February 2). *Reconsidering failure in maker-centered learning*. [Blog post.] Retrieved from http://agencybydesign.org.s219538.gridserver.com/reconsidering-failure-in-maker-centered-learning/

Dahlin, K. B., Chuang, Y. T., & Roulet, T. J. (2018). Opportunity, Motivation, and Ability to learn from failures and errors: Review, synthesis, and ways to move forward. *Academy of Management Annals*, 12(1), 252–277. doi: https://doi.org/10.5465/annals.2016.0049

DeBrincat, D. (2015). Yes, no wait, what?: The benefits of student mistakes in the classroom. *The History Teacher*, 49(1), 9–34.

Duckworth, A. L., Peterson, C., Matthews, M. D., & Kelly, D. R. (2007). Grit: Perseverance and passion for long-term goals. *Journal of Personality and Social Psychology*, 92(6), 1087–1101. doi:https://doi.org/10.1037/0022-3514.92.6.1087

Dweck, C. (2006). *Mindset: The new psychology of success*. New York, NY: Ballantine Books.

Dweck, C. S., & Reppucci, N. D. (1973). Learned helplessness and reinforcement responsibility in children. *Journal of Personality and Social Psychology*, 25(1), 109–116.

Farrell, R. P., & Hooker, C. A. (2009). Error, error-statistics and self-directed anticipative learning. *Foundations of Science*, 14(4), 249–271. doi: https://doi.org/10.1007/s10699-008-9155-6

Fogle, D. O. (1979). Preparing students for the worst: The power of negative thinking. *The Personnel and Guidance Journal*, 57(7), 364–367.

Green, M. J., Myers, K., Watson, K., Czerwiec, M. K., Shapiro, D., & Draus, S. (2016). Creativity in medical education: the value of having medical students make stuff. *Journal of Medical Humanities*, 37(4), 475–483. doi: https://doi.org/10.1007/s10912-016-9397-1

Guler, D. M. P. (2013). Success and failure in science education: a focus on group study on Turkish students. *Journal of Baltic Science Education, 12*(6), 716–729.

Heyd-Metzuyanim, E. (2015). Vicious cycles of identifying and mathematizing: A case study of the development of mathematical failure. *Journal of the Learning Sciences*, 24(4), 504–549.

Kapur, M. (2008). Productive failure. *Cognition and Instruction*, 26, 379– 424.

Kapur, M., & Kinzer, C. K. (2009). Productive failure in CSCL groups. *International Journal of Computer-Supported Collaborative Learning*, 4(1), 21–46. doi: https://doi.org/10.1007/s11412-008-9059-z

Lai, P. K., Portolese, A., & Jacobson, M. J. (2017). Does sequence matter? Productive failure and designing online authentic learning for process engineering. *British Journal of Educational Technology*, 48(6), 1217–1227.

Lottero-Perdue, P. S., & Parry, E. A. (2017a). Perspectives on failure in the classroom by elementary teachers new to teaching engineering. *Journal of Pre-College Engineering Education Research* (J-PEER), 7(1), 47–67. doi: https://doi.org/10.7771/2157-9288.1158

Lottero-Perdue, P. S., & Parry, E. A. (2017b). Elementary teachers' reflections on design failures and use of fail words after teaching engineering for two years. *Journal of Pre-College Engineering Education Research* (J-PEER), 7(1), 1–24. doi: https://doi.org/10.7771/2157-9288.1160

Makonye, J. P., & Luneta, K. (2014). Mathematical errors in differential calculus tasks in the Senior School Certificate Examinations in South Africa. *Education as Change*, 18(1), 119–136.

Maltese, A., Simpson, A., & Anderson, A. (2018). Failing to learn: The impact of failures during making activities. *Thinking Skills and Creativity*, 30, 116–124. doi: https://doi.org/10.1016/j.tsc.2018.01.003

Martinez, S. L. (2013, December 17*). Failure is not an option.* Unless it is. [Blog post.] Retrived from https://sylviamartinez.com/failure-is-not-an-option-unless-it-is/

McKnight, D. H., & Chervany, N. L. (2001/2002). Trust means in e-commerce customer relationships: An interdisciplinary conceptual typology. *International Journal of Electronic Commerce*, 6(2), 35–59.

Merriam-Webster (2019). *Error.* Retrieved from https://www.merriam-webster.com/dictionary/error

Noddings, N. (2005). Perspective 2: Pragmatism. In J. L. Paul (Ed.), *Introduction to the philosophies of research and criticism in education and the social science*s (pp. 57–60). Upper Saddle River, NJ: Pearson/Merrill/Prentice Hall.

Nuruzzaman, M., Islam, A. S., & Shuchi, I. J. (2018). An analysis of errors committed by Saudi non-English major students in the English paragraph writing: A study of comparisons. *Advances in Language and Literary Studies*, 9(1), 31–39.

Omosewo, E. O., & Akanbi, A. O. (2013). Analysis of errors committed by physics students in secondary schools in Ilorin Metropolis, Nigeria. *Acta Didactica Napocensia*, 6(1), 55–60.

Random House, Inc. (2019). *Error*. Retrieved from https://www.dictionary.com

Ryoo, J. J., & Kekelis, L. (2018). Reframing "failure" in making" The value of play, social relationships, and ownership. *Journal of Youth Development*, 13(4), 49–67. doi: https://doi.org/10.5195/jyd.2018.624

Saldaña, J. (2013). *The coding manual for qualitative researchers* (2nd ed.). Los Angeles, CA: Sage.

Simpson, A., & Maltese, A. V. (2017). "Failure is a major component of learning anything.": The role of failure in the career development of STEM professionals. *Journal of Science and Technology Education*, 26(2), 223–237. doi: https://doi.org/10.1007/s10956-016-9674-9

Simpson, A., Burris, A., & Maltese, A. V. (2017). Youth's engagement as scientists and engineers in an after-school tinkering program. *Research in Science Educati*on. [Advanced Online Publication.] doi: https://doi.org/10.1007/s11165-017-9678-3

Simpson, A., Anderson, A., Maltese, A. V., & Goeke, M. (2018). "I'm going to fail": How youth interpret failure across contextual boundaries. In J. Kay & R. Luckin (Eds.), *Proceedings of the 13th International Conference of the Learning Science* (Vol. 2, pp. 981–984). London, United Kingdom: University College London.

Simpson, A., Anderson, A., & Maltese, A. V. (2019). Caught on camera: Youth and educators' noticing of and responding to failure within making contexts. *Journal of Science Education and Technology*. [Advanced Online Publication.] doi: https://doi.org/10.1007/s10956-019-09780-0

Stein, G. M., & Santa, J. L. (1975). The academic job hunt: Is it more frustrating than it has to be?. *American Psychologist*, 30(8), 861.

Tarawneh, R. T., & Almomani, I. M. (2013). The spoken errors and mistakes committed by senior English students at Princess Alia University College. *Theory and Practice in Language Studies*, 3(3), 497–502.

Thomas, A. M. (2016, February 20). *Why I don't embrace failure* (ED FOO lightening talk). Retrieved from https://annmariethomas.typepad.com/annmarie-thomas/2016/02/why-i-dont-embrace-failure-ed-foo.html

Trueman, R. J. (2013). Productive failure in STEM education. *Journal of Educational Technology Systems*, 42(3), 199–214.

Tulis, M. (2013). Error management behavior in classrooms: Teachers' responses to student mistakes. *Teaching and Teacher Education*, 33, 56–68. doi: https://doi.org/10.1016/j.tate.2013.02.003

Wilson, B., Petaja, H. S., Stevens, A. D., Mitchell, M. F., & Peterson, K. M. (2011). Children's responses to entry failure: Attention deployment patterns and self-regulation skills. *The Journal of Genetic Psychology*, 172(4), 376–400.

Zsigmond, A. (2016). The imagery of failure. *Social Research*, 83(3), 537–547.

Amber Simpson is an Assistant Professor of Mathematics Education in the Department of Teaching, Learning, and Educational Leadership, Binghamton University, Binghamton, NY. Her main topic of concern is the low number of individuals from traditionally underrepresented groups entering and persisting in pathways toward STEM careers. She conducts research on understanding the interplay of voices shaping and embodying individual's STEM identity, as well understanding the role of making in formal and informal educational settings with a particular focus on mathematical play. In addition, Amber is examining the role of family and community engagement as a way to support youth and adolescents in the development of practices and skills common to STEM professionals (e.g., critical thinking, creativity).

Adam V. Maltese is an Associate Professor of Science Education at Indiana University and Director of the MILL Makerspace housed in the School of Education. His current research involves collection and analysis of both quantitative and qualitative data regarding student experiences, performance, and engagement in science education from elementary school through graduate school. In addition, Adam currently teaches courses in secondary science methods and graduate seminars at the School of Education around making and the development of interest in STEM education. He also leads a seminar for doctoral students in STEM fields who plan to pursue academic careers and are interested in improving their teaching practices based on research.

Alice Anderson is the Manager of Audience Research and Impact at the Minneapolis Institute of Art (MIA), where she studies what people think, feel, and learn through informal learning experiences. At MIA she develops and implements program evaluation and audience research initiatives to understand MIA's audiences, educational programs, exhibitions, and social impact. She has led evaluations and research studies of digital media resources, maker education programs, and professional development programs and in formal and informal learning contexts. Guided by a background in art museum education, she is particularly interested in how the visual arts support dialogue-based and hands-on maker learning experiences. Alice holds an Ed.M. in Human Development and Psychology from the Harvard Graduate School of Education and a B.A. in Art History from Grinnell College.

Euisuk Sung (PhD) is a postdoctoral researcher at Indiana University. He studied computer science for his bachelor's degree at Chungnam National University, South Korea, and worked in a start-up company as a software engineer. Afterward, he decided to become an educator which was the most exciting and valuable work for him. He taught in public high schools for 9 years and wrote five technology education textbooks for South Korea K-12 national curriculum. He received a master's degree in career and workforce education from Seoul National University, South Korea, and completed his PhD degree in engineering and technology teacher education at Purdue University, IN. His research interest includes the maker movement, computational thinking, design thinking, and issues in the K-12 STEM pipeline.

Chapter 19
Low-Socioeconomic Status Students Turn Their Academic Failure to Success: A Synthesis of Qualitative Research

Naomi Takashiro and Clifford H. Clarke

Abstract Although many studies have examined how low-socioeconomic status (SES) individuals achieved academic success despite the odds, most of them focused on a few ethnic minorities. The purpose of our study was to include different ethnicities and identify what factors contributed to low-SES student academic success after failure with a systematic review of 19 qualitative studies, which were published between 2000 and 2018. Our findings revealed three themes: (a) family and others' support and influence, (b) motivation, and (c) learning strategies. As expected, a strong factor was that individuals received support and assistance from their family and extended family. By the same token, students also received help and encouragement from their teachers, tutors, peers, and school. Successful students also had strong motivation to achieve their educational goals. However, not all individuals had such sources of support. Even though some students received negative feedback from their own family and others, they used it as a source of motivation to succeed. We also found that some students experienced culture shock and cultural adaptation to new cultures as motivation. Learning strategies was not a dominant theme, but some students used effective time management and application to manage their schoolwork. The findings in our study would contribute to researchers, educators, and school officials who are interested in educating disadvantaged students who manage to achieve academic success despite adversity.

Keywords Mistakes · Errors · Failures · Low socioeconomic status · Academic success · Academic failure · Synthesis of qualitative research

N. Takashiro (✉)
Department of Global Tourism, Kyoto University of Foreign Studies, Ukyō-ku, Kyoto, Japan

C. H. Clarke (Retired)
Affiliated Graduate Faculty, University of Hawai'i, Mānoa, Hawaii

E. Vanderheiden, C.-H. Mayer (eds.), *Mistakes, Errors and Failures across Cultures*, https://doi.org/10.1007/978-3-030-35574-6_19

19.1 Introduction

Abundant previous literature showed evidence of the effect of individual socioeconomic status (SES) on students' academic achievement (e.g. Liu et al. 2006; Nonoyama-Tarumi 2008; Takashiro 2017; Tomul and Savasci 2012). It is well known that low-SES individuals are related to low academic achievement. The effects of low SES are not only limited to academic achievement. Low SES influences many other factors negatively, for example, developing basic learning skills, learning competencies, parenting-child development, motivation, aspirations, expectations, and study hours (Hoffman 2003; Kariya 2004, 2010; Kariya and Rosenbaum 2003; Orr 2003). That is, low SES could have detrimental influences on individuals in the long term.

Faced with poverty, violence, dysfunctional family life, physical living condition (Dass-Brailsford 2005), drugs, violence, and peer issues in school (Reis et al. 2004), low-SES individuals are more susceptible to academic struggles and failures. Despite such tremendous predicaments, some low-SES individuals manage to beat the odds and become academically successful. Scholars have examined the contributing factors for low-SES student academic achievement. However, extant literature has focused on how minority students, mainly African American and Latino students, in the USA achieved academic success despite obstacles. There is a gap in the literature explaining how other ethnicities, immigrant, and community college students achieved academic excellence despite academic adversity. Examining immigrant students and community college students is also important because community college students are more likely to be from low-SES backgrounds (Horn and Nevill 2006) and immigrants tend to fall into chronic low-income status compared to native-born populations (Picot and Lu 2017). That is, both groups are related to low SES. Investigating other ethnicities from low-SES backgrounds is also essential to understand how they achieve academic success in addition to Latino and African American students.

Further, how low-SES students experience academic difficulties and failures is not commonly discussed in the low-SES student academic success literature. Discussing how low-SES students' academic struggles and failures would be helpful in understanding how they turn academic failure into success. In addition, the number of qualitative, systematic synthesis studies on low-SES academic success is inadequate. More studies are needed to synthesize the existing studies not only of Latino and African American ethnicities but also other perspectives as well in order to understand what contributes to low-SES student academic success despite academic adversity.

The purpose of our study was to synthesize a collection of qualitative research from low-SES individuals' perspectives in order to understand how they achieved academic success despite the odds. Our research question was "What were contributing factors for low-SES students' academic success after experiencing academic failure?"

19.2 Literature Review

We summarized the current literature below on how low-SES student achieved academic success. Many studies examined how disadvantaged students, especially African American and Latino students, achieved academic excellence despite challenges from multiple adversities (e.g. Crisp et al. 2014; Turner and Juntune 2018; Williams and Bryan 2012; Williams et al. 2017).

A study done by Williams and Bryan (2012) revealed that several successful factors for African American college students were family (e.g. parents' support), school (e.g. teachers' support, good teaching, and extracurricular activities), and community factors (e.g. friends, neighbours' support).

In a similar vein, research conducted by Williams and his colleagues (2017) examined 24 culturally diverse, low-SES middle school students. The findings revealed that (a) peer social capital (e.g. good relationships with high-achieving peers), (b) teachers who care, (c) family and community assets (e.g. support from adults, outside school activities), and (d) multiple streams of motivation (e.g. to live a better life) were factors that led to successful academic results.

Research also suggested a model for four success factors for at-risk students (McMillan and Reed 1994). They were (a) individual attributes (e.g. high intrinsic motivation and self-efficacy), (b) positive use of time (e.g. involvement in school and outside school activities), (c) family factors (e.g. building trust with family), and (d) school factors (e.g. support from teachers and counsellors).

Similarly, Reis et al. (2004) conducted a qualitative, longitudinal study for 18 culturally diverse, economically disadvantaged, academically excellent, high school students to identify their success factors. The successful factors were that individual characteristics, such as self-belief, determination, motivation, and skills, such as strategies to deal with negative aspects of life, to build relationships with caring adults and other high-achieving friends, and to take part in advanced classes and extracurricular activities. Additionally, students' previous participation in a gifted programme was also helpful for their success.

Some studies have been conducted on minority students besides African American and Latino students. These studies added cultural uniqueness to their studies. Kumi-Yeboah (2016) conducted a qualitative research on 60 Ghanaian-born high school immigrants' academic achievement and identified several key themes: (a) self-regulation (e.g. I can manage my own learning.), (b) religious faith, (c) past personal experiences and goals (e.g. I do not want to repeat my life back home.), (d) the use of technology, (e) the availability of educational opportunities and resources (e.g. the Internet and teachers), and (f) parental support. Participants also reported that the negative influence, such as people's negative perceptions of Africa helped them be motivated to succeed in school.

In a similar vein, Dass-Brailsford (2005) reported how 16 low-SES African students in South Africa achieved academic excellence in college as follows: (a) individuals' attributes (e.g. goal orientation, self-motivation, and initiative), (b) support from families and role models, and (c) support from schools and communities. Dass-Brailsford also reported the role of spirituality (e.g. going to church and practising ancestral worship) was important for the participants.

Trieu and Jayakody (2018) conducted a study about ethnic minority's educational success for 10th to 12th grade students in Vietnam. From the qualitative part of the study, they found (a) individuals' positive attitude towards education and (b) various support from immediate and extended family, school, and peers from the same ethnicity. They also reported that some parents lived separately from children to make a better salary for upper secondary education.

Some scholars conducted research from single-factor perspectives, such as family influence and students' persistence. For example, a study done by Martin et al. (2014) examined common characteristics for 17 persistent community college graduates. Community college students were more likely from minority and low-SES backgrounds (Horn and Nevill 2006). Successful students had (a) clear goals, (b) strong motivation to succeed, (c) ability to manage external demands (e.g. managing school and work), and (d) self-empowerment (e.g. taking initiatives to solve problems).

By the same token, Hampton (2016) identified seven successful personal characteristics for African American students from Grades 4 to 10 to succeed in school. The findings revealed the successful factors were that (a) self-respect, (b) command of standard English, (c) goal-setting ability, (d) self-motivation, (e) time management skills, (f) consequence awareness (the ability to demonstrate a concern for outcomes), and (g) respect for others. He used students' actual grades and teachers' rating for each student's characteristics in their classes instead of students' own ratings for themselves.

Another study investigated nine impoverished Hispanic, Caucasian, and African American graduate students' home environments that led to academic success (Turner and Juntune 2018). The findings were as follows: (a) the importance of a broad support system (e.g. unwavering support from family and teachers) and (b) academics became an escape (e.g. academic activities were used to escape from poverty).

In summary, the past literature commonly found that support from family, peers, teachers, and community and positive personal attributes were positively associated with low-SES student academic achievement. Other studies reported that learning strategies, religious faith, negative stereotypes of a certain ethnicity, and engagement with extracurricular activities were related to student academic success.

What we identified from the review of literature was that (a) many studies have focused on Latino and African American and (b) there are inadequate numbers of qualitative research for low-SES student academic success with other ethnicities and (c) a scarcity of qualitative syntheses on low-SES student academic success.

More research is needed to understand multilayered successful factors for low-SES student academic achievement from different cultural backgrounds. Systematic qualitative studies would be ideal for synthesizing previous studies and to reflect low-SES students' real voices on their academic success after failure despite adverse predicaments. Results from such studies would contribute to educators, school officials, parents, and disadvantaged students for the goal of increasing their academic successes.

19.3 Method

19.3.1 Data Collection

We conducted systematic qualitative research on low-SES individuals' academic success by summarizing and synthesizing the data:

> Systematic reviews are a method of identifying and synthesising all the available research evidence of sufficient quality concerning a specific subject. (Victor 2008, p. 1)

We used the electronic databases of ERIC via EBSCO and Academic Search Complete in order to locate relevant articles. In addition, we relied on an Internet search in Google Scholar and relevant journals, for example, the *International Journal of Qualitative Studies in Education* and *International Journal of Educational Research*, in order to reduce selection bias and not to overlook any relevant articles.

We used combinations of keywords including socioeconomic status, academic achievement, educational resilience, and qualitative study to select articles based on the following criteria: participants were (a) from low-SES backgrounds, (b) had experienced academic failure, and (c) had achieved academic success. Additionally, we utilized criteria for identifying low-SES participants to select articles in which (a) participants had a parent who had educational backgrounds in high school or below, (b) participants attended low-SES schools, or (c) participants grew up in a poor, low-income, or working-class family. Academic failure was indicated as failing in school tests, receiving bad grades, or struggling in academic work, whereas academic success was indicated when participants achieved higher grades, passed tests, or graduated and/or attended postsecondary education.

According to our search results, articles on low-SES student academic success and contributing factors did not appear much before the 2000s; therefore, peer-reviewed articles published in English from 2000 to 2018 were included. Due to the lack of rigorous reviews and possible lack of quality of evidence, non-peer-reviewed articles were not included in our study. Although some of the reviewed articles did not highlight low-SES student academic failures, success, and successful factors, they were selected as reviewed articles as long as they met our selected criteria.

Studies included in our study had two types of data as follows: (a) research consisting of participants' responses, such as interviews, and (b) data consisting of general conclusions based on participants' data. Selected articles included (a) participants' perspectives on their academic success and failure and (b) participants' descriptions of their academic experience retroactively. Excluded articles included (a) parental perspectives on their children's academic success and failure and (b) participants with disabilities. Consequently, we selected 19 articles for review and the study characteristics of each are listed in the appendix.

19.3.2 Data Analysis

On the selected articles, we employed content analysis for our systematic qualitative research. Our analysis was guided by the research question "What are the contributing factors for low-SES student academic success after academic failure?". The first author read each article several times for familiarity and entered the relevant data in Word with annotations. Then she identified the similarities among the notes. She grouped these similarities together. Then she consulted with the second author about the grouping of the similarities and the relevancy of the data to the research question. The first author then named the groups in order to answer the research question. The first author again shared her groupings and tentative themes with the second author to seek his opinion. When we had disagreement during the grouping of notes according to their similarities and created themes, we discussed the issues until they were resolved.

19.4 Results

Succinct characteristics of the reviewed articles are described before presenting the results below. Most reviewed articles on low-SES student academic success and their contributing factors were written from North American perspectives. Researchers commonly studied Latino and/or African American in 70% of the articles. The reviewed articles included individuals who were in higher education or already had higher education degrees (90%). The analysed articles are using interviews and focus groups as a common data source approach (80%).

Before presenting the results, participants' academic struggles or failures are succinctly shown here. The examples of feelings that the participants had are shame, embarrassment, regret, and even trapped. Cabrera and Padilla (2004) reported that when a Mexican heritage individual misunderstood her class assignment and brought a bag of cherries by mistake, "My classmates laughed, and I was, needless to say, very embarrassed (2004, p. 157)". In a similar vein, students who took tests and failed a second time in Canada said, "I was pretty upset about it…" (Kearns 2011, p. 118) and a Jamaican student who also failed a test twice felt "regret, rebuke and rejection" (Dole 2014, p. 148). A Dominican student who was mistreated by her American co-workers in the workplace due to her inadequate English abilities felt "…like a slave" (Reynoso 2008, p. 405). Despite the negative experiences that the participants had gone through, they used contributing factors that led them to achieve academic success.

19.4.1 Contributing Factors Linked to Academic Success

Three themes emerged from our analyses as contributing factors for low-SES individuals' academic success as follows: (a) family and others' support and influence, (b) motivation, and (c) learning strategies.

19.4.1.1 Supportive Influence from Others

The first theme was family and others' support and influence. The theme had three subcategories: (a) family and extended family's support, (b) school support, and (c) community support. Thirteen articles indicated family and extended family's support.

19.4.1.1.1 Family and Extended Family's Support

Support from parents was most frequently described in the literature. Examples of family support were: "...my parents pushing me all the time" (Kenny et al. 2002, p. 172) and "My parents helped me; they told me to study, even if they could not help me" (Casanova 2012, p. 393). Support from mothers was more evident than fathers'. When a Taiwanese student was denied a graduate school's admission and did not want to try again, he said,

> ...my mother encouraged me to study... [My mother] asked me to study...Anyway, [she] just told me I must study. (Pan and Yi 2011, p. 377)

Most selected articles described parents who gave them emotional support, such as strong beliefs, inspiration, and high expectations. Two articles indicated parents' direct involvement with their children. An immigrant mother tried to create a good study environment for her daughter by telling family members to be quiet (Rezai et al. 2015). A Korean father's involvement in teaching math and how to think to his child was rewarded when his child later became a Science Olympian (Cho and Campbell 2010).

Another finding was that the presence of a child gave a parent support to succeed. A newborn daughter became an emotional support for a student-mother to develop a positive image and to earn degrees (Reynoso 2008). Some participants received support from their extended families, such as grandmothers and grandfathers (i.e. Dole 2014) for their commitment to religion.

19.4.1.1.2 School Support

Support from schools was identified in the selected literature. Support from teachers was reported in 11 articles. Teachers gave students strong beliefs, inspiration, encouragement, and praise and were role models. For example, a teacher made a great impact on a student's life as indicated in Dole's (2014) study. A Jamaican female student reported:

> It is because of the attitudes of these teachers, which influences who I am as a teacher today. (Dole 2014, p. 151)

High-quality instruction and high expectations from teachers were also identified. A high school student reported:

> …but if we were to do slum work, she would notice that and she would want more from us… we know not to do slum work and so we don't do it. And that will help us in college. (Tomlinson and Jarvis 2014, p. 203)

Sometimes teachers go beyond their roles and work on behalf of students. A teacher made an indigenous Chilean student change her easy choice of curricular, because such a track would not be helpful for her future (Webb 2018).

Tutorial assistance was reported by four studies. Tutors were described as helpful, skilful, accessible, and supportive. For example, a student in South Africa who participated in an accounting programme after tertiary education indicated:

> … [the tutors] were still accessible for us; we could call them if we were doing a course and, then [when] you struggled, you can still call them. (Barac 2015, p. 89)

Participants identified counsellors, advisors, and principals who helped. They were described as knowledgeable, dedicated, and empathetic. For example, a Mexican-descendent student studying at a community college had an advisor who had gone through the same negative experiences. The student reported about the advisor, "He comes up to me and says, you can do it, I don't want to see you leave" (Reyes III 2009, p. 113). A school principal raised an educational fund for an undocumented student going to college (Garcia and Tierney 2011).

Peers and friends were also identified as supportive, important, helpful, and encouraging in seven articles. A student described his peers from the same low socioeconomic backgrounds:

> …then I found others like me from peripheral neighbourhoods of Santiago, our social backgrounds united us… so we helped each other, supported each other. (Webb 2018, p. 13)

Some participants in five articles found that institutional support (i.e. orientations, financial aids, educational programmes, and student organizations) was helpful for their academic success, for example, the availability of financial support (Wirth and Padilla 2008).

19.4.1.1.3 Community Support

Support and inspiration from community (i.e. guest speakers, church, community, and workplace) was documented in seven articles. Some participants felt inspired, bonded, were encouraged and learned some skill sets. Some were inspired by role models who had similar backgrounds as they did. Listening to success stories from role models made them believe that they could also be successful (i.e. Barac 2015; Reyes III 2009). Another source of support was co-workers. A Dominican student who established rapport with her co-workers reported:

> I have established supportive relationships in the restaurant where I work as a waitress. They are my friends, and they encourage me to get a college education. (Reynoso 2008, p. 420)

19.4.1.2 Motivation

The second theme was motivation, and it had four subcategories: (a) self-motivation, (b) motivation from outside sources, (c) overcoming negative influence from others, and (d) adjusting to a new culture.

19.4.1.2.1 Self-Motivation

Self-motivation was frequently seen in the reviewed literature. The participants expressed determination (11 articles), confidence (9 articles), and enjoyment (2 articles). Determination was mostly seen, for example, in a study of a Dominican community college student:

> I have experienced many academic and personal difficulties. However, I am determined to achieve my dreams. (Reynoso 2008, p. 425)

Some students developed self-confidence in their academic abilities (Olive 2008). One study identified enjoyment that a Hispanic college student would spend his time reading encyclopaedias during the breaks in the workplace (Cavazos et al. 2010).

19.4.1.2.2 Motivation from Outside Sources

In addition to self-motivation, most participants expressed their motivation was influenced by external factors in 18 journals. The importance of education and school was frequently reported in the literature. Some participants identified the importance of education due to their family members' hardships in life. They learned that education was necessary by watching their parents engage in physical labours and that they did not want to repeat a similar life. A student indicated that:

> But I saw how my mama was. She was in the streets, had her baby young, and I was like, 'She's in jail, so not that path [for me].' That's how I got interested in school. (Reddick et al. 2011, p. 611)

Several participants indicated that their parents told them the importance of education and high expectation. A Taiwanese student mentioned:

> My father expects me to study harder. Otherwise, [I] will become a construction worker like him. That is hard and exhaustive work, so he doesn't want me to be like him. (Pan and Yi 2011, p. 378)

Some participants realized that education was essential in order to have a better job and a better life. Some expressed their desires to climb up the socioeconomic ladder. An African American female who had grown up in a low-SES family was motivated by "trying to get away from where I came from" (Griffin 2006, p. 391) and another Jamaican student mentioned:

> Did I want to continue living in the low socioeconomic group? Did I want to be jobless and hopeless? And the answers were no. (Dole 2014, p. 146)

Others were motivated to go to postsecondary education to take care of their family financially (e.g. Cabrera and Padilla 2004; Olive 2008).

Religious faith, helping others, and social responsibilities were reported as motivation by some participants. They were spiritually motivated. Some of the students sought guidance from God and church for their motivation (Dole 2014; Kenny et al. 2002; Reynoso 2008). Some individuals were motivated to help others by using knowledge gained in postsecondary education (Olive 2008; Reddick et al. 2011; Reynoso 2008), and others wanted to help people because they were helped in the past and had some altruistic attitudes (Cavazos et al. 2010; Dole 2014; Rezai et al. 2015; Wirth and Padilla 2008).

19.4.1.2.3 Overcoming Negative Influence from Others

Not all low-SES students had supportive family members and school staff. Some participants were discouraged from attending higher education from their own family, extended members (six articles), and others (four articles). Negative feedback from family and extended family members included a grandmother's disbelief about an African female participant's ability (Dole 2014) and a Latino father threatened to disown his daughter from his family for applying to college (Cavazos et al. 2010). Another Mexican-descendent first-year student was told by her extended family that education was a waste of time and that she should get married (Reyes III 2009). Morales (2018) explained that male figures in the family resisted their daughters or spouses' academic engagement because they were afraid that education might become an obstacle for their female roles and responsibilities.

Some students faced negative influences from outside of family members, including a teacher's disbelief, peer pressure, and co-workers' mistreatment (i.e. Dole 2014; Olive 2008; Reynoso 2008). Although negative influences tried to thwart their education, students used them as a source of motivation. The students praised their own previous academic excellence, ignored negativities, felt determined to succeed, and avoided negative parental disappointment (Casanova 2012; Dole 2014; Olive 2008; Reynoso 2008; Reyes III 2009) as strategies to turn family and others' negative attitudes into motivation for academic success.

Some minority students faced negative messages of being a certain minority, such as African American, African, and Latino. Despite the negative feedback from others, some were motivated to do well in school because they tried to disapprove stigmatizations of a certain ethnicity. A male student's quote clearly indicated:

> What motivates me more than wanting to, because I am not in it for the money, having grown up as a migrant farm worker I've been humbled, so it's not the money, it's mainly getting rid of that stereotype, showing what can come from [this area], what can come from the Mexican-American race. (Cavazos et al. 2010, p. 181)

19.4.1.2.4 Adjusting to a New Culture

Adjusting to a new culture was identified in three articles. For example, indigenous Chilean students expressed their struggles and efforts in adjusting to the cultural environment and high standards of an elite university (Webb 2018). One indigenous student adjusted himself to an elite university's culture by associating with his own low-SES peers but also with high-SES peers who had common interests with him. Although he initially felt out of place, the student managed to associate with high-SES students due to the possible advantages of working with them, which was recommended by his friends (Webb 2018).

Developing English proficiency and becoming familiar with a new culture was some immigrant students' source of motivation. A Dominican student came to the USA and made cultural adjustments and developed his language skills. The student mentioned:

> Although I have adapted to the American culture, I'm still very Dominican, very Dominican. (Reynoso 2008, p. 40)

19.4.1.3 Learning Strategies

The third theme was learning strategies, which were found in three articles. Although this theme was not as dominant when compared to the other two themes, learning strategies helped some individuals to have academic success in three articles. This theme had two subcategories: (a) time management and (b) applications.

19.4.1.3.1 Time Management

A student father mentioned time management:

> ...I leave the house at six in the morning, study on the [long] bus ride in, I don't lose time in social gatherings ... I organize my time... I work in a cooler storage, and I have a son so I have to give time to him too". (Webb 2018, p. 15)

The student seemed to manage with work, study, and family. He somewhat seemed to know how to allocate his time properly. Although he did not spend any time in social gatherings with his peers, he seemed to manage his busy life.

A community college student in Reynoso's (2008) study admitted that he was not good at balancing social, family, and school life and did not know how to manage his time. Due to stress and little rest, his health was deteriorating. He eventually learned how to allocate his time properly, the situation got better.

19.4.1.3.2 Applications

A student used an application learning strategy to study for her English classes. The community college student reported:

> I strongly believe that to learn English, one has to connect it to an academic discipline. (Reynoso 2008, p. 425)

The student further explained that she tried to learn English using her interests rather than learning just grammar. Through interests and other applications, the student attempted to learn a subject more effectively than by just memorizing and repeating things.

19.5 Discussion

We synthesized the existing qualitative studies to find out what contributed to low-SES students' academic success after failure.

Students from low-SES backgrounds experienced academic struggles but achieved academic success despite adversity. One can easily imagine that these students' academic success is extraordinary and they cannot easily obtain such accomplishments. According to McMillan and Reed (1994), successful at-risk students believe that their challenging surroundings, such as family, school, and neighbourhood, do not critically influence their academic successes or failures.

We found three contributing factors for low-SES student academic success. The contributing themes were (a) supportive influence from others, (b) motivation, and (c) learning strategies. The reviewed studies showed the evidence that these factors intertwined with one another. These factors seem to buffer the negative aspects of low-SES characteristics and to maximize student academic success.

19.5.1 Supportive Influence from Others

Family and extended family members' support and influence, especially parental support was found frequently in the reviewed articles. Among parents, maternal support was commonly identified. Low-SES parents' support and influence in relation to academic achievement are in line with other literature (e.g. Dass-Brailsford 2005; Kumi-Yeboah 2016; McMillan and Reed 1994). Most low-SES students described their parents as giving them high expectations, emotional support, strong beliefs, and inspiration.

Our study found that low-SES individuals appreciated such parents' support. Parents of successful at-risk students exercised pressure on their children in order for them to achieve academic success due to holding higher expectations for their children's education than their own. Establishing good rapport and caring attachment with parents seem to be successful academic factors for children (McMillan and Reed 1994). Dedicated parents provide support, informal counselling, and assistance to guide their children to succeed in school (McMillan and Reed 1994) although they had lower educational attainments and few educational resources. Mothers tend to be the primary caregivers for children, and their support is especially important for children.

Besides parents, the role of other family and extended family members should not be ignored. Turner and Juntune (2018) identified that supportive family members are necessary for their children from an early age to succeed academically. McMillan and Reed (1994) also argued that most successful at-risk students establish a close trusting relationship with any family member who gives them support and attention. This indicates that positive, supportive relationships with adults may mitigate the effect of low educational attainment of parents.

Although support from parents is essential for their children's academic success, parental support alone should not be overly emphasized, especially for grown-up children. Cabrera and Padilla (2004) found that parental aspiration for their children to go to higher education is insufficient. Even though a Mexican mother gave her child unwavering support, the child would not have gone to college without learning about college opportunities from her counsellors and tutors. Individuals who have such knowledge should provide and guide low-SES students through higher education.

School support such as teachers, counsellors, tutors, and peers was seen commonly in the selected literature. Most respondents described them as encouraging, supportive, and helpful. School support in our findings is consistent with others' (e.g. Crisp et al. 2014; McMillan and Reed 1994; Reis et al. 2004). Academically competent at-risk students appear to find support mostly in school (McMillan and Reed 1994) in addition to home. Professional competence and good interpersonal relations are essential qualifications as teachers and counsellors. Such individuals have higher expectations and provide support to students (McMillan and Reed 1994). Tutors also have similar roles to those of teachers and counsellors. Teachers, counsellors, and tutors gave low-SES students invaluable knowledge and support towards their academic achievement. They provide complementary support that low-SES parents cannot provide, such as tutoring and giving guidance on colleges.

Peers are also important because they provide different emotional support and guidance that parents may not be able to give. Especially associating with other high-achieving peers is essential for students to maintain their high standards. Reis et al. (2004) found that associating with high-achieving peers is one of the successful factors for high-achieving, low-SES high school students. It appears that students built a sense of trust when they interacted with teachers, peers

(McMillan and Reed 1994), and other school staff. Having good relationships with peers and school staff also seems to be important for low-SES students' academic success.

The institutional support found in our study was orientations, financial aids, educational programmes, and student organizations. Institutional support in our findings is also consistent with Crisp and her colleagues' (2014) systematic study. McMillan and Reed (1994) indicated that involvement with extracurricular activities at school creates opportunities for connecting with peers and may contribute to the growth of one's self-esteem.

Role models, church members, community members, and co-workers were found as community supporters and inspirations in our study. Such community support is also consistent with previous studies (e.g. Crisp et al. 2014; Dass-Brailsford 2005). Although some students never interacted with successful individuals, they perceived them as role models. Role models who achieve high educational goals were seen as inspirational especially for stigmatized and minority groups (Morgenroth et al. 2015).

19.5.2 Motivation

Self-motivation was frequently described in the reviewed studies. The findings in our study are congruent with others' (e.g. Dass-Brailsford 2005; McMillan and Reed 1994; Reis et al. 2004; Williams et al. 2017). The successful students in our study were motivated to succeed and felt responsible for their own achievement. Successful at-risk students accept their academic failure as their own fault rather than others. They take initiatives to succeed and give credit to their own performance. Despite the negative environments they are in, they are optimistic and confident about their future and have realistic long-term goals (McMillan and Reed 1994). In our study, we found some students valued the importance of education. They learned that from their own negative experiences or from family hardships. When these students faced such difficult experiences, these experiences strengthened the importance of education (McMillan and Reed 1994).

The students realized having higher education degrees would bear fruits in the future. It could bring a good job with income, knowledge, and various opportunities. Using the power of education, they were interested in helping others and family members financially. Growing up in a low-SES family, they saw having better education as a way to climb up the socioeconomic ladder.

Religious faith was commonly identified among African students in our study. Some participants used faith, which was influenced by their family members, and others took initiatives to use faith to cope with difficulties. Our findings are congruent with some studies (Dass-Brailsford 2005; Kumi-Yeboah 2016).

Dass-Brailsford (2005) found that faith was associated with high-achieving low-SES African students in South Africa. African Americans who actively practice religious faith accomplish higher socioeconomic status than those who do not (Hill 1993).

19.5.2.1 Overcoming Negative Feedback from Others

Several students turned negative experiences from their own family members and outside of family members to motivation to achieve in our study. Some students faced low expectation, discouragement, mistreatment, and disbelief from their family members and others. The findings are in line with other studies (Crisp et al. 2014; Kumi-Yeboah 2016; Reis et al. 2004). Reis et al. (2004) discussed how dealing with family hardships and their surrounding environments helped high-achieving low-SES students develop new strategies and strength to achieve despite these hardships. Some successful low-SES students have gone through difficulties in life and learned how to make sense of the world and perceived negative influence as not important but rather as opportunities (Dass-Brailsford 2005). Especially African American and Latino students faced negative stereotypes from others. However, they used the unfavourable feedback as a source of motivation. African American students used their ethnic background (Griffin 2006) and Latino students used pride (Cabrera and Padilla 2004) as contributing factors to their academic success.

19.5.2.2 Adjusting to a New Culture

We found that some students had adjusted to new cultures after experiencing cultural and language obstacles. One finding was a low-SES individual's cultural adjustment to a high-SES elite university. The other finding was immigrant students' cultural and language adaptation to new host cultures. It appears that these students experienced culture shock but eventually adapted to different cultures. Cultural adjustment is not commonly discussed in low-SES students' academic success studies because few authors examined this aspect. According to Winkelman (1994), when the participants entered different cultures, they felt various negative psychological reactions, such as confusion, fear, difficulty, and frustration, which are typical culture shock characteristics. Managing culture shock is a key for student success. The students in the reviewed studies seemed to manage culture shock through maintaining family and existing friendships and establishing new relationships with peers. These relationships were likely to have helped the students develop their self-esteem and characteristics that fulfilled personal and emotional needs (Winkelman 1994). Their new cultural adaptation skills served as success factors for their academic achievements.

19.5.3 Learning Strategies

Learning strategies was also found to be a contributing factor for low-SES student academic success although it was not a dominant theme in our study. Weinstein and Mayer (1986) wrote:

> …learning strategies, can be defined as behaviors and thoughts that a learner engages in during learning and that are intended to influence the learner's encoding process. (p. 315)

The findings of our study are in line with others' (Renzulli 2015; Robbins et al. 2004). Learning strategies are important skills for students. Renzulli's (2015) qualitative research revealed that college students who were on academic probation did not have good study skills and time management skills for learning. Given meta-analytic evidence by Robbins et al. (2004), academic-related skills, such as time management, and study skills were positively related to college students' GPA. Other research results found evidence that college students who set goals and priorities, made plans and schedules, perceived control of time, and preferred an organized workspace had higher academic achievement (Macan et al. 1990). Macan et al. (1990) also found that college students who perceived control of time and preferred an organized workspace and projects were less likely to feel stress. Successful students have time management skills, such that when they do feel stress, it is under their control. Since time is limited for busy students, the issue is how to use their time wisely. Utilizing good learning strategies and skills is important for college student academic success.

19.5.4 Academic Failure Turned into Success

Here are some examples of how low-SES individuals who experienced academic failures or struggles turned into academic success by using the contributing factors. Casanova (2012)'s case study of a female Mexican immigrant described such a story. Being a teenager immigrant from a low-SES family from Mexico to the USA, she faced embarrassment and low self-esteem about her Spanish accent and pronunciation. A new teacher helped her gain confidence by believing in her and placing her in the right track for her English level. Although her school counsellor discouraged her from attending a 4-year college, she interpreted that as an error of judgement. Her math teacher wrote a letter of recommendation and helped her write a financial aid application for college. She also established rapport with academically competent peers with diverse cultural backgrounds. She had been encouraged with unwavering support from her parents. She often thought about leaving high school but believed that would be a mistake. She felt that higher education would be able to reduce her family problems. After she became familiar with her host culture and developed language fluency, she became academically competent and graduated from a top-tier university. Her tenacity, support from home and school, and adaptation of language and culture changed her situation from potential failure to success.

Another story depicted a low-SES college student's academic and cultural struggle in Webb (2018). Attending an elite university in Chile, the student had tremendous academic and cultural difficulties. Being a top performer in his public secondary education, he must have expected to do well in higher education.

However, things were very different in the top-notch university. He realized that his public school education did not prepare him well enough to compete with his high-SES peers. They were from prestigious secondary schools and academically competent. He had not seen these types of bright students in his life. Feeling disadvantaged by growing up in a poor family, he felt incompetent. Although he studied a lot by himself, he was unable to handle both cultural and academic struggles initially, and he experienced failure. However, he found some of his peers in school were helping and supporting one another. Using his determination, peer support, and cultural adaption turned around the situation.

19.6 Limitations

There are three major limitations in our study. Because we used existing studies, some of the reviewed articles did not specify detailed information. For example, some studies did not specify socioeconomic status for each participant. Instead, they summarized the low-SES information for the whole group of participants. Another limitation was that some selected articles had mostly authors' interpretations of the results with only a few participants' quotations. Finally, there was a limitation of the availability of studies. Few studies have focused on low-SES students' academic success after failure in different cultural contexts.

19.7 Conclusion

It is overtly quite difficult for low-SES student to accomplish academic excellence despite the odds. However, some manage to shine. These students have positive and trusting relationships with family, friends, school staff, and others. They receive support from family members and people from all walks of life. They have optimistic views of life, long-term goals, a sense of personal responsibility, and strong motivations to accomplish their goals. Even when some of them face unfavourable judgement and feedback from their family members and others, they use them as a source of motivation to succeed. They also possess effective learning strategies and cultural adaptation skills. Despite our limitations, our findings should shed some light on the existing low-SES student academic achievement literature by adding some cultural aspects that are not commonly examined in the SES literature. More research is needed to understand how low-SES students utilize cultural adaptation and learning strategy skills. We hope that our results would contribute to educators, researchers, school officials, and parents by inspiring new policies and practices that support their low-SES students. Our study is dedicated to those who are disadvantaged but who are devoted to shine and accomplish academic success despite academic adversity.

References

Barac, K. (2015). Helping Disadvantaged Students: Findings from the Thuthuka Programme. *Accounting Education*, 24(2), 75–101. Retrieved from https://doi.org/10.1080/09639284.2015.1010171

Cabrera, N. L., & Padilla, A. M. (2004). Entering and succeeding in the "culture of college": The story of two Mexican heritage students. *Hispanic Journal of Behavioral Sciences*, 26(2), 152–170.

Casanova, S. (2012). The stigmatization and resilience of a female indigenous Mexican immigrant. *Hispanic Journal of Behavioral Sciences*, 34(3), 375–403.

Cavazos, Jr. J., Johnson. M. B., Fielding. C., Cavazos. A. G., Castro. V., & Vela, L. (2010). A Qualitative Study of Resilient Latina/o College Students. *Journal of Latinos and Education*, 9 (3), 172–188

Cho, S., & Campbell, J. R. (2010). Differential influences of family processes for scientifically talented individuals' academic achievement along developmental stages. *Roeper Review*, 33(1), 33–45.

Crisp, G., Taggart, A., & Nora, A.. (2014). Undergraduate Latina/o Students: A Systematic Review of Research Identifying Factors Contributing to Academic Success Outcomes. *Review of Educational Research*, 1–24.

Dass-Brailsford, P. (2005). Exploring resiliency: Academic achievement among disadvantaged black youth in South Africa. *South African Journal of Psychology*, 35(3), 574–591.

Dole, S. (2014). Voices of Resilience: Successful Jamaican Women Educators. *Journal of Ethnographic & Qualitative Research* 8, 144–156

Garcia, L. D., & Tierney, W. G. (2011). Undocumented immigrants in higher education: A preliminary analysis. *Teachers College Record*, 113(12), 2739–2776.

Griffin, K. (2006). Striving for success: A qualitative exploration of competing theories of high-achieving black college students' academic motivation. *Journal of College Student Development*, 47(4), 384–400.

Hampton, F. M. (2016). The seven secrets of successful urban school students: The evidence continues to grow. *Education and Urban Society*, 48(5), 423–443.

Hill, R. B. (1993). Supporting African American families: Dispelling myths and building strengths. *The Roundtable*, 7, 2.

Hoffman, L. W. (2003). Methodological issues in studies of SES, parenting, and child development. In Bornstein & Bradley (Eds.). *Socioeconomic status, parenting, and child development* (pp. 125–43), Mahwah, NJ: Lawrence Erlbaum Associates.

Horn, L., and Nevill, S. (2006). *Profile of Undergraduates in U.S. Postsecondary Education Institutions: 2003–04: With a Special Analysis of Community College Students* (NCES 2006-184). U.S. Department of Education. Washington, DC: National Center for Education Statistics.

Kariya, T. (2004). Gakuryoku no kaisosa wa kakudaishitaka [Did the differential student academic achievement among different social classes expand?]. In T. Kariya & H. Kariya, Shimizu (Eds.), *Gakuryoku no shakaigaku: chōsa ga shimesu gakuryoku no henka to gakushū no kadai* [Academic achievement in sociology: The changes in academic achievement and issues]. (pp. 127–151). Tokyo: Iwanami Shoten.

Kariya, T. (2010). From credential society to learning capital society: a re-articulation of class formation in Japanese education and society. In H. Ishida, & D. H. Slater,(Eds.), *Social class in contemporary Japan*. London: Routledge: 87–113.

Kariya, T., & Rosenbaum, E. (2003). Stratified incentives and life course behaviours. In J. T. Mortimer & M. J. Shanahan (Eds.), *Handbook of Life Course* (pp 51–78). New York: Kluwer academic/Plenum Publishers.

Kearns, L. (2011). High-stakes Standardized Testing and Marginalized Youth: An Examination of the Impact on Those Who Fail. *Canadian Journal of Education*, 34(2), 112–130.

Kenny, M. E., Gallagher, L. A., Alvarez-Salvat, R., Silsby, J. (2002). Sources of support and psychological distress among academically successful inner-city youth. *Adolescence*, 37(145), 161–182.

Kumi-Yeboah, A. (2016). Educational Resilience and Academic Achievement of Immigrant Students From Ghana in an Urban School Environment. *Urban Education* 1–30.

Liu, Y., Wu, A. D., & Zumbo, B. D. (2006). The relationship between outside of school factors and mathematics achievement: A cross-country study among the U.S. and five top-performing Asian countries. *Journal of Educational Research & Policy Studies*, 6(1), 1–35.

Macan, T. H., Shahani, C., Dipboye, R. L., & Phillips, A. P. (1990). College students' time management: Correlations with academic performance and stress. *Journal of Educational Psychology*, 82(4), 760–768.

Martin, K., Galentino, R., & Townsend, L. (2014). Community College Student Success: The Role of Motivation and Self-Empowerment. *Community College Review*, 42 (3), 221–241.

McMillan, J. H., & Reed, D. F. (1994). At-risk students and resiliency: Factors contributing to academic success. *The Clearing House*, *67*, 137–140.

Morales EK (2018) Exceptional female students of color: Academic resilience and gender in higher education. Innov High Educ 33:197–213. Retrieved from doi10.1007/s10755-008-9075-y

Morgenroth, T., Ryan, M. K., & Peters, K. (2015). The Motivational Theory of Role Modeling: How Role Models Influence Role Aspirants' Goals. *Review of General Psychology*. Advance online publication. https://doi.org/10.1037/gpr0000059

Nonoyama-Tarumi, Y. (2008). Cross-National Estimates of the Effects of Family Background on Student Achievement: A Sensitivity Analysis. *International Review of Education*, 54(1), 57–82.

Olive, T. (2008). Desire for higher education in first-generation Hispanic college students enrolled in an academic support program: A phenomenological analysis. *Journal of Phenomenological Psychology*, 39, 81–110.

Orr, J. E. (2003). Black-white differences in achievement: the importance of wealth. *Sociology of education*, 76(4), pp. 281–304.

Pan, L., & Yi, C. (2011). Constructing Educational Resilience: The Developmental Trajectory of Vulnerable Taiwanese Youth. *Journal of Comparative Family Studies*, Summer, 42(3), 369–383.

Picot, G., & Lu, Y. (2017). *Chronic Low Income Among Immigrants in Canada and its Communities.* Retrieved from https://www150.statcan.gc.ca/n1/pub/11f0019m/11f0019m2017397-eng.htm

Reddick, R. J., Welton, A. D., Alsandor, D. J., Denyszyn, J. L., & Platt, C. S. (2011). Stories of Success: High Minority, High Poverty Public School Graduate Narratives on Accessing Higher Education. *Journal of Advanced Academics* 22(4), 594–618

Reis, S. M., Colbert, R. D., & Hébert, T. P. (2004) Understanding resilience in diverse, talented students in an urban high school. *Roeper Review*, 27(2), 110–120, Retrieved from DOI https://doi.org/10.1080/02783190509554299

Renzulli SJ (2015) Using learning strategies to improve the academic performance of university students on academic probation. NACADA Journal 35(1): 29-41. https://doi.org/10.12930/NACADA-13-043

Reyes, III. R. (2009). "Key interactions" as agency and empowerment: Providing a sense of the possible to marginalized, Mexican-descent students. *Journal of Latinos and Education*, 8(2), 105–118.

Reynoso, N. A. (2008). Academic Resiliency Among Dominican English-Language Learners. *Community College Journal of Research and Practice*, 32:4–6, 391–434, DOI:https://doi.org/10.1080/10668920701884364

Rezai, S., Crul, M., Severiens, S., & Keskiner, E. (2015). Passing the torch to a new generation: Educational support types and the second generation in the Netherlands. *Comparative Migration Studies*, 3(12), 1–17.

Robbins, S. B., Lauver, K., Le, H., Davis, D., Langely, R., & Carlstrom. A. (2004). Do Psychosocial and Study Skill Factors Predict College Outcomes? A Meta-Analysis. *Psychological Bulletin*, 130(2), 261–288.

Takashiro, N. (2017). A multilevel analysis of Japanese middle school student and school socioeconomic status influence on mathematics achievement. *Educational Assessment, Evaluation and Accountability*, 29(3), 247–267.

Tomlinson, C. A., & Jarvis, J. M. (2014). Case studies of success: Supporting academic success for students with high potential from ethnic minority and economically disadvantaged backgrounds. *Journal for the Education of the Gifted*, 37(3), 191–219.

Tomul, E., & Savasci, H. S. (2012). Socioeconomic determinants of academicachievement. *Educational Assessment, Evaluation and Accountability*, 24, 175–187. Retrieved from DOI https://doi.org/10.1007/s11092-012-9149-3

Trieu, Q., & Jayakody, R. (2018). Ethnic minority educational success: Understanding accomplishments in challenging settings. *Soc Indic Res*, 1–39.

Turner, J. S., & Juntune, J. (2018). Perceptions of the home environments of graduate students raised in poverty. *Journal of Advanced Academics*, 29(2), 91–115.

Victor, L. (2008). Systematic reviewing. *Social research update*, 54, 1–4.

Webb, A. (2018). Getting there and staying in: first-generation indigenous students' educational pathways into Chilean higher education. *International Journal of Qualitative Studies in Education*, 1–19.

Williams, J. M., & Bryan, J. (2012). Overcoming Adversity: High-Achieving African American Youth's Perspectives on Educational Resilience. *Journal of Counseling & Development*, 91, 291–300.

Williams, J. M., Bryan, J., Morrison, S., & Scott, T. R. (2017). Protective Factors and Processes Contributing to the Academic Success of Students Living in Poverty: Implications for Counselors. *Journal of Multicultural Counseling and Development*, 45, 183–200.

Winkelman, M. (1994). Cultural shock and adaptation. *Journal of Counseling and Development*, 73(2), 121–126.

Winstein, C. E., & Mayer, R. E. (1986). The teaching of learning strategies, In M. C, Wittrock (Ed.), Handbook of research on teaching, (3rd ed) (pp. 315–327). New York: MacMillan.

Wirth, R. M., & Padilla, R. V. (2008) College Student Success: A Qualitative Modeling Approach. *Community College Journal of Research and Practice*, 32(9),688–711, DOI: https://doi.org/10.1080/106689207013809

Naomi Takashiro (PhD), Dr. Takashiro has a PhD in Educational Psychology and has been teaching English classes as adjunct faculty at the Kyoto University of Foreign Studies and its junior college in Kyoto, Japan. Growing up in a low-SES family in Japan, her academic interests are socioeconomic status, inequality, and motivation in education, and she has published several articles in the area. She lived in Hawaii for 20 years, taught Intercultural Communication at universities, and worked in multicultural organizations before coming back to Kyoto 4 years ago. In her spare time, she likes to read, walk, cook, and play with birds. She has been looking for a full-time job at a university. She remains grateful to God for his guidance in writing this paper.

Clifford H. Clarke (Retired) (ABD) Clarke was raised in Japan by second-generation expatriate parents, whose own parents first moved to Japan in 1898 when the USA forced the Queen to abdicate her crown in the Kingdom of Hawai'i. Since arriving in Japan at the age of 7, his favourite pastime has been exploring cultural assumptions, and at the age of 10, he was asked to become a bridge between cultures in Kyoto.

His higher education focused on the goal of becoming an effective "bridge person" by studying world religions and philosophies (B.A.), counselling across cultures (M.Div.), and studying interdisciplinary studies in the social sciences (ABD) at Stanford University's Graduate School of Education. His four careers have evolved through 11 years of counselling foreign students at Cornell and Stanford universities; 8 years of teaching intercultural communication at Stanford and the University of Hawaii; 30 years of intercultural business management consulting in 13 countries in Asia, Europe, and North America; and 6 years of educational programme design and evaluation in the State of Hawai'i public and charter schools. He also founded the Stanford Institute for Intercultural Communication (SIIC), Clarke Consulting Group (CCG), and cofounded SIETAR (1971) and SIETAR Japan (1984). Clarke has published 25 papers, chapters, or books in all of these areas, given 45 presentations at professional societies and universities, and been quoted by 25 newspapers and magazines in Japan, the USA, and Europe. Clarke retired from his Affiliated Graduate Faculty position in Hawaii to return home to Kyoto, Japan, 4 years ago.

Chapter 20
Errors and Mistakes in Foreign Language Learning: Drawing Boundaries from the Discourse of Argentine Teachers

Thalita Camargo Angelucci and María Isabel Pozzo

Abstract From a psychoanalytical perspective, we associate the subjective development of the human being with his/her appropriation of the environment language. This subject is hampered by words of others. In this way, we affirm that the subject is structured in and on a language. This issue takes an important place in the increasing migratory movements. In this study, we focus on the significance of error on the processes of teaching and learning languages. First, we present a theoretical review on the polysemy – plurality of meanings – of the concept of error in the field of foreign language teaching. Next, we discuss the first results of qualitative research, which analyzes the discourse of Argentine foreign language teachers about the theme. We adopt the sociolinguistic perspective of Marcos Bagno and the methodological approach of discourse analysis. The differences between error and mistakes were first systematized by the studies carried out during the 1970s, which considered that the errors should be corrected, whereas not necessarily the mistakes. Nowadays, the need for correction is being replaced by a positive view of learners' mistakes and errors. The discourse elicited in our interviewees shows a communicative vision of the errors and places the polysemy of the term in a secondary problem.

Keywords Mistakes · Error · Failure · Foreign language · Teaching and learning · Sociolinguistics

T. Camargo Angelucci (✉) · M. I. Pozzo
Rosario Institute of Research in Educational Sciences (Instituto Rosario de Investigaciones en Ciencias de la Educación – IRICE), National Scientific and Technical Research Council (Consejo Nacional de Investigaciones en Ciencias y Técnicas – CONICET), & National University of Rosario (Universidad Nacional de Rosario – UNR),
Rosario, Provincia de Santa Fe, Argentina
e-mail: angelucci@irice-conicet.gov.ar; pozzo@irice-conicet.gov.ar

E. Vanderheiden, C.-H. Mayer (eds.), *Mistakes, Errors and Failures across Cultures*, https://doi.org/10.1007/978-3-030-35574-6_20

20.1 Introduction[1]

Before a baby's birth, it is expected that the surrounding community gives him/her a name, not only a proper name but also many physical and symbolic attributes. Words mean before one's existence. Relying on authors' closed to psychoanalytic principles, we can affirm that the human being is constituted as a subject by/into a language (Revuz 1992; Kristeva 1994; Benveniste 1995; Celada 2004; Coracini 2007; Payer and Celada 2016). In subjective terms, one is because it says it is: today, here and now, I say that I am. In this way, the first language, or, as it is known, the mother tongue, provides the possibility of becoming a subject, while foreign languages made feasible to this subject become another one. From these premises, the acquisition of the first language is not only based on the embodiment – which literally involves mental and bodily changes, of a linguistic system – but also on the affections, own name and other symbolic attributes, provided from outside or, rather, from people who take care of this process of subjectivation. Because of this, the languages which would be learned later would be impregnated with these first and primary conditions of the subject constitution. The self belongs to itself and also to its language, and because we do not choose the language, we are likely to say "I only have one language; it is not mine" (Derrida 2012, 42). With this brief reflection, we want to underline the fact that there is not always a univocal relationship between one and one's languages or the languages one speaks.

From our psychoanalytic position, we also assume that the subjects resist changes. One way of showing this resistance is in the most genuine human expression: speech. In the case of speaking a foreign language, the self affirms its identity by marking the new language with features of its first language. Celada (2002) relates it to a narcissistic fissure that the subject tries to suture. A stranger accent could be interpreted as a resistance that the body offers into the processes of speaking a new language in an intention to keep an identity. This is just one event that is often linked with the production of errors. The following questions arise: What is considered a language error? Which are the differences between errors, failures, and mistakes in teachers' discourse? How could the teachers' treatment of learners' mistakes influence foreign language learning?

Research devoted to foreign language learning/acquisition errors generally focus on the analysis of the errors produced by the students or on the way teachers correct them (Alexopoulou 2006; Balcarcel 2006; Carcedo 2012; Miranda 2013; Sánchez Rufat 2015; Galindo Merino 2016; Amara 2018). The studies centered on teachers' beliefs about students' errors are few in number (Silva and Figueiredo 2006; Silva Guerra Vicente and Martins Ramalho 2009; Neves 2009; Gargallo and Chaparro 2014). Some studies have been carried out in Latin America, but the subject is still a vacancy area in Argentina.

[1]This chapter is part of an ongoing doctoral thesis in Educational Sciences, carried out at the National University of Rosario (Argentina), focused on the analysis of foreign language teachers discourse on learners' errors.

Thus, the aim of this chapter is to discuss Argentine teachers' conceptions of error in the field of foreign language teaching and how that contributes to the studies in the area. To achieve our goal, we have first implemented a bibliographical review on how the concept of error has been treated throughout specialized literature, which will be presented. Second, we carried out semi-structured interviews with ten teachers; among these, we selected four of them, which were transcribed and analyzed with the contributions of the discourse analysis' tools (Orlandi 2008; Pêcheux 2017). These initial results will be presented in Sect. 20.3, before the final considerations.

20.2 The Error Throughout the Literature of Foreign Language Teaching: A Polysemic Construct

First of all, there is a wide variation in the terminology used in the field of linguistic studies to refer to languages. To refer to "mother tongue," "first language," and "native language," we will simply use "L1," whereas to refer to "foreign language," "additional language," "second language," "third language," and "language of inheritance," we will use "L2." We decided to use these simpler signs since we focus on what it is conceived as an error in the processes of teaching new languages, without taking into account any specificity. Beyond the nomenclature, this conceptual decision relies on the most important difference for us to separate the two groups: the fact that the first language is in the order of subject constitution and the following ones rely on an order already structured (Revuz 1992; Angelucci 2017).

After clarifying our conceptual choices, we organized this section into two subsections. First, we present the polysemy of error's construct, that is, the main perspectives of classical studies on the acquisition of foreign languages from 1950 until today. Afterward, we show the contributions of Latin American Sociolinguistics Studies that demystify the place of the norm in language teaching, in which the conception of what an error is or is not plays a relevant role.

20.2.1 Errors, Failures, and Mistakes in Foreign Language Teaching

Dealing with students' mistakes is a key point in any educational activity, since it evidences characteristics of the teaching and learning processes involved therein. According to Fernández (1997), errors make up the most idiosyncratic aspect of language learning, and the teachers' choices to correct them determine the success or failure of their students.

Pit Corder is considered the founder of the investigations in second language acquisition, and his book, *The Significance of Learners' Errors*, published in 1967, deals precisely with the issue of errors. Until the mid-1960s, error was understood as an index of the learning process, where fewer errors meant better learning. In this sense, there were two schools of thought: one suggested that a correct teaching method does not lead to the production of errors, while the other was based on the assumption that if we live in an imperfect world, it is natural and expected that errors occur in the learning processes (Amara 2018). Both perspectives were influenced by the same logic: behavioral psychology and the Chomskyan school. The application of these reflections in the teaching of languages took form in the audio-lingual method. According to Fernández (1997), the error was, then, synonymous with no learning.

From a behaviorist perspective, linguistic processes were understood grosso modo as verbal behaviors. Language was considered a product of the formation of habits, in other words the repetitive association between stimulus and response, consolidated by positive reinforcements. In this way, acquiring an L2 involved training a substitution of forms: replace formulas of the L1 with those of the L2. To achieve these exchanges of forms, scientific systematization and confrontation between the languages of origin and those of destination were required. This resulted in the appearance of a contrastive analysis research line. In this perspective, the error was non grata, undesirable, and should be avoided from constant exercising.

The interest of the contrastive analysis in foreseeing and, therefore, avoiding the production of errors had little empirical support. In practice, the contrast of the two linguistic systems involved in the scheme did not guarantee the cataloging and anticipation of all possible errors. These difficulties, added to Chomsky's criticism in the 1960s[2], fostered the proliferation of new proposals toward error. Among these new proposals, we point out two specific ones which perspectives toward error sometimes diverge and others converge. One perspective characterizes the errors as interferences from L1, while the other perspective understands them as part of the students' learning strategies to form a hypothesis about L2.

Corder (1967) defends the thesis that some strategies adopted by the second language learner coincide with those by which the first language is acquired, which does not mean that the learning sequence is the same in both cases. The author supports the importance of errors in language learning from data on the acquisition of L1. The errors produced by children in an L1 environment follow certain learning stages. In this way, errors are the best evidence that the child is constructing grammatical rules, while the use of correct structures indicates, instead, that they are only repeating what they hear. This fact could also apply to the field of second language learning.

In this line, Corder (1967) proposes a theoretical differentiation between mistakes and errors with practical applicability. It is noticed that this precision of

[2] Chomsky (1959) presents a critical review in response to Skinner's book called *Verbal Behavior* (1957) and proposes that language is acquired through the internalization of rules, not through the formation of habits. These problems supported the famous controversy of Chomsky-Skinner about the generativity of language, which has not yet been closed. For more information, see Bandini and De Rose (2010).

concepts does not always appear at a discursive level, a topic that we will resume in the discussion of the results. The distinction, then, had as a basic criterion the systematicity of the error. The mistakes corresponded to performance errors, produced in moments of tension (lapses, failures, slips, or negligence), and, therefore, are non-systematic. In turn, errors themselves would be those of competence, the systematic ones. Therefore, the latter could be used by researchers and teachers to reconstruct the student's knowledge in the target language. The author called transient competence to this provisional knowledge in which the learner tests hypotheses about the new language. Later, Selinker (1972) characterized this linguistic stage as interlanguage, a term widely spread in the field. In summary, the mistakes belong to the order of chance; ergo, only the errors should be studied.

The possibility of revealing, through errors, students' performance in a certain period of their learning gives rise to the discipline known as error analysis (EA), which overcomes contrastive analysis. In the EA, the linguistic strategies that try to explain the origin of the errors are crucial. These are divided into intralingual and interlingual, depending on their relationship or not with the L1. Intralingual errors include both developmental errors – similar to those produced by children in the acquisition of L1 – and unique errors, produced only by L2 apprentices. In turn, interlingual errors respond to cases of interference from the learner's L1.

As a consequence, addressing the error implies different nuances that, in practice, overlap and cross each other. For this reason, researchers from different periods have agreed on the difficulty of delimiting one and the other to turn them into reliable study objects, or rather, with direct applicability to the didactics of languages. This vision broadens the horizon and reveals more critical theoretical perspectives, capable of coping with the complexity that the subject demands. Instead of questioning the role of the L1, the efforts shift to assume the errors as learning indicators and teaching guides. In this sense, it is relevant to recall Scovel's assertion (1988, 177, cited in Figueiredo 2004, 50) to understand the error as a "result of intelligence and not stupidity[3]." From this perspective, the learner becomes a central figure, who is considered capable to generate, test, and reformulate hypotheses about what he or she learns.

From this brief review, it can be noted that the concept of error in the 1960s was linked to the idea of correction, while in the 1970s, it became associated with the idea of learning, which implies both to state correct hypotheses and temporary hypotheses that are permanently modified (Ellis 1985). Finally, in the 1980s, communication studies were developed.

From the communicative approach, as the name itself evokes, the effectiveness of the communicative exchange is the focus and not the correct use of linguistic forms. In other words, the error is defined not by the incorrect linguistic production but by the failure in the transmission of the message. Cavalari (2008) recalls the distinction between what is called "Focus on formS" and "Focus on Form." The first

[3] In the original: "*resultado da inteligência e não da estupidez.*"

expression refers to the linguistic code, whereas the second one considers not only isolated linguistic elements but also their meaning in an act of communication.

However, to analyze the discourse of professors, it is convenient to recapitulate three current and general ideas systematized by Figueiredo (2004) regarding the polysemy of the concept of error defined as (a) that which does not follow the linguistic variety adopted for teaching, (b) that which does not reproduce linguistic forms produced by a native speaker in similar production situations, and (c) that which is an effect on communication that was not expected or adequate.

Finally, research in this area comprises approaches ranging from various error dimensions (morphosyntactic, semantic, phonetic, lexical, pragmatic, etc.) to concerns about how to deal with the error already produced: correction strategies, overcoming, etc. In Larsen-Freeman and Long (1994, 34), an extensive bibliography can be consulted in this regard. These studies highlighted the influence of teaching on the development of learners' errors. It is important to note that one of the most important discrepancies found was in the relationship of proximity between languages. While some studies promoted the belief that when the source and target languages are close, the acquisition is easier, later investigations asserted just the opposite. Thus, theorizations derived from the first studies were not always endorsed by subsequent ones, precisely because of a difficulty in specifying the concept of error and, due to that fact, making it possible to compare the results of each investigation.

Finally, the field of sociolinguistic presents new tools to think about the subject, and it is quite in vogue nowadays. For this reason, we present it in a separate section.

20.2.2 The Sociolinguistic Perspective: Linguistic Variation as the Natural State of Languages

As we have seen, there are different perspectives to interpret errors in foreign language teaching, but they are all linked with what error represents in our normative lifestyle. This means that everything –behavioral, personal, political decisions, etc. – that represents a deviation from the established order must be annihilated. This situation is made explicit, for example, in the struggle that the minority social movements that demand land, housing, equal rights, and/or gender identity have to face. Indeed, society is reflected in the language used. In this way, the same problem is reflected in the place given to the error in teaching in general. There is a tendency to associate error with deviation. The question is: deviation from what? Although the answer is clear – deviation from a standard norm – we have to ask ourselves: which standard? To think about this question in the field of language, we are going to take contributions from sociolinguistic studies, which deal with the relations between languages and society.

Bagno (1999, 2003) is a Brazilian linguist who takes the language as a system's basis to think of any linguistic manifestation as a deviation. In this sense, the standard norm is just another deviation. Therefore, the question about the right parameter for correction should always be accompanied by other questions: correct for what? for whom? and in what production situation? These pragmatic parameters will give us a guide on how to use the language in the most appropriate way. In this line, socio-discursive interactionism, for example, considers that the core of language teaching is in the teaching of some discursive genres (Bronckart 2010).

When interpellating languages from their constitutive heterogeneity (Authier-Revuz 2004), it is clear that their manifestation is intimately linked to the territories, to the relationships established between the speakers, to formal and informal registers, etc. It is scientifically proven that within the same language, there are ways of saying that involve relatively stable regularities depending on their context of use (Rotaetxe Amusategi 1990; Lippi-Green 1997; Bronckart 1999; Bajtín 2002; Calvet 2007; Mira Mateus and Cardeira 2007; Labov 2008). In technical terms, we make reference to the different discursive genres and diatopic (different geographic places), diastratic (different social classes), diametric (spoken versus written language), diaphasic (the way of speaking, i.e., the degree of discursive monitorization), and diachronic (stages of history) variations.

Then, if different linguistic variations inhabit the same language, why should we assume the norm as the crystallization of homogeneity, as the correct variety? The boundaries between what is normal, expected, and taught and what is not necessarily imply power relations. Bourdieu (2008) contributes with this study developing the concept of "symbolic power of language," which influences the way languages reach foreign nations. This is reflected in teaching materials, in the choice of which linguistic variety to impose, and in teachers' training. The symbolic power of language is explicit in situations such as the following: in March 2019, the President of Argentina – by the way, a politician, not a linguist – expressed in the opening speech of the VIII Congress of the Spanish Language, held in that country, that "the [Spanish] language is the best-distributed wealth of our [Latin American] community[4]" (Gigena, 2019). This affirmation serves to maintain the status quo of the language of the colonizer, as if it was homogeneous. The president ignores Latin American plurilingualism, precisely when the UN Organization (ONU 2017) celebrates 2019 as the International Year of Indigenous Languages.

For Bagno (2007), the construction of a norm pattern "represents a control of the inherent processes of variation and change[5]" (2007, 37). In this perspective, there are two highly conflictive and constantly interacting poles: that of the "cult" norm, which imposes an artificial model to neutralize dissent, and that of linguistic variation, which respects the unstable character of languages. Sociolinguistic proposes, then, to relate social heterogeneity with linguistic heterogeneity, where language errors can be understood as a social construction.

[4] In the original: "*[el español] es la riqueza mejor distribuida de nuestra comunidad.*"

[5] In the original: "*representa um controle dos processos inherentes de variação e mudança.*"

20.3 Development

Argentina is a majority Spanish-speaker country located in southern of South America, with approximately 40 millions citizens. In comparison to the attention received by the original languages and those of the ethnic minorities of the population, foreign languages attract the greatest efforts and resources in the educational system. The teaching of the latter – in their most common standard dialects – is part of the school curricula, where English is the first foreign language taught both formally and informally (Pozzo 2009).

20.3.1 Methodology

To carry out the proposed objective, a qualitative study was implemented framed in the fields of applied linguistics and educational sciences. Semi-structured interviews were conducted with ten Spanish-speaking Argentine teachers' trainers. Out of the ten, we selected four of them: two English professors (referred as I1 and I2) and two professors of French (F1 and F2). These professors work in two teacher training institutes with a degree in languages and two public national universities located in the city of Rosario (Argentina), the third most populated city in the country with an outstanding economic and cultural importance. The informants have had professional teaching and linguistic training and an average of 30 years of teaching experience. Each interview lasted about 30 min and were carried out in Spanish during February 2019. They were later transcribed and analyzed from the tools of discourse analysis of French and Brazilian origin (Pêcheux 2017; Orlandi 2008). In this chapter, we present excerpts of them translated into English.

By listening to the teachers' discourse, the focus was in recognizing the displacements of meaning that are invoked through the interdiscourses from different linguistic theories with respect to the categories "mistake" and "error." In Spanish, it is diffuse to differentiate the two concepts, since it tends to name both as "error." However, it is important to highlight their nuances in the discourses analyzed. In this sense, some Spanish-speaking authors refer to the aforementioned difference in the terms "error" and "equívoco" or "falla."

20.3.2 First Results

In order to analyze the teachers' discourse, it is also necessary to recall the conception of error that is present in the Curricular Guidelines of Oriented Secondary Education of the Province of Santa Fe (Ministerio de Educación de la Provincia de Santa Fe 2014), a document that frames the scope of professional performance of the interviewees. It was made explicit in this extract:

> Let's say there was an earlier conception that tended to resemble the native model, so any deviation that did not fit within that native standard foreign language was considered an error. At the moment, that is changing, especially in what is the legislation of the Province of Santa Fe in terms of learning a foreign language, and trying to be a foreigner who speaks a foreign language, let's say, and not to resemble the native's pattern. If we look at it from that last point of view, then the previous error would no longer be an error... (F1)

Santa Fe's document reveals a positive overview in which the error is considered a fundamental support and integral part of the learning process. A relationship between the error and the effectiveness of the message is revealed, based on the communicative approach, which is noted in the speech of all interviewers, as noted here:

> the error is part of the learning process [...] the presence of the error means that something is happening [...] I have a totally positive look towards the error [...] let's say that I look more negatively a student who does not dare to speak, and is not encouraged to make mistakes, than one who does. (I1)

Another English teacher assumes that it is more important to transmit the message than to obey the standard norm:

> in the phonological part, precisely, it has to do with the point where the sounds can interfere with the comprehension of the message. [...] what we are dealing with, although that is the parameter [received pronunciation English], what we are trying to do is to focus on those errors that interfere with communication. (I2)

Teachers agree, then, that in foreign language teachers training, there is a shift from a more rigid perspective – where the error is considered a serious fault – to a more flexible one, focused on the possibility of communication. However, it is evident that changes at the discursive level come untimely into practice, as it is often the case in other areas of scientific and sociocultural development. This is seen in the discursive materiality when the past perfect is used followed by an argumentative readjustment to the present continuous: "Now it has changed, that is, things are changing, there is more flexibility in many things" (I2) or through monitorial degree: "Yes, it has been changing for a while, not much..." (F1).

The informants made reference to different types of errors but did not indicate them at the level of the signifier. However, the theoretical review presented above functioned as a matrix to recall the small changes of meaning that arose during the interviews. In this sense, the misunderstanding has been assumed not only as unavoidable but also necessary to learn a language. Taking this phenomenon into consideration causes a change of perspective both in the attitude of the learner and in the dynamics of the classroom.

In her study, Fernández (1997) followed Spanish/L2 learners from different languages and levels, and she could reinforce the hypothesis that the increase in the number of errors is not a sign of regression but rather of progress, since it implies that a more creative process has been initiated, "in which the learners rehearse and risk more in the new language" (1997, 261). This statement coincides with the interviewed teachers' accounts about their experiences with first-year students:

In that case of first-year students, let's say, you let them become confident because the important thing is to encourage them to speak, to jump a little into that new language. Correcting some issues, but hey, there are things that... that are allowed to happen. [...] not just saying 'look, you made a mistake here', but 'go back to listen' or 'what did you say?' or some kind of ..., let's say, friendlier guideline. (F1)

Adding to this, too much correction can inhibit the student. A permissive attitude to errors can, then, encourage participation and contribute fairly to the reduction of errors produced in the future, that is, it would be a productive position:

what I notice is that if you, uh..., you mark the L2 student every time he makes the mistake, it's like you cut his intention to produce and start talking, I think that is counterproductive. (I2)

That perspective is also remarked by the French teacher:

in the first year we let them talk, no matter how, we do not interrupt them [...] the oral intervention is prepared, with just some guidelines, and we let them speak [...] I personally take notes, and it is also something that I ask my colleagues to do, I take notes of the good and the bad [...] And I always start saying they did this well, they did this well, they did this well, but we must pay attention to this mistake between *tu* and *vous* [...] I think that it makes the student not feel so bad facing the error, in the beginning, we would let it pass by so students would be encouraged to talk. (F2)

The informant F2 explained that, as the coordinator of a group of teachers of other languages, she agrees to make corrections more flexible in the oral productions of first-year students to encourage them to express themselves without fear, since fear is another issue which appears related to errors, as it is evident in the following statements: "I receive all these people with this fear and terror to English, they have terror, they are afraid to speak" (I2) and "I notice that in the oral presentations, they sprout, colored spots appear, and I worry and I think 'how can this happen in a French test?'"(F2).

It is clear from the teachers' speeches, moreover, that the type of error, the moment of learning, and the proposed objectives influence the characterization of them. In any case, the degree of distortion of the message as a priority criterion when defining or delimiting an error prevails as an undoubtedly common ground.

Inevitably, the discussion of error as a deviation from the norm has led to questioning, precisely, what norm is being discussed. This question was asked to the informants, and the answer was not simple in every case. However, we were able to confirm our assumption that the symbolic power of language imposes a normative model. In other words, the standard by which the deviation is measured as an error is, for English, England (the received pronunciation of London, a functional creation linked to the royalty), and for French, France (Paris). In this regard, three extracts are illustrative. The first one highlights the tendency to misjudge a linguistic variety in relation to others:

there are a lot of varieties and we tend to...to..., I do not know, to grant supremacy to certain..., certain places where Spanish is spoken, I do not know, well, 'Argentinian Spanish is the best and Colombian is not', and ..., that is, there is a tendency within the linguistic world to reject and stigmatize [...] There is linguistic variety, there are no better or worse. [...] that happens within the same mother tongue, imagine this in a second language. (2I)

The second extract shows an emerging perspective that includes "new" Frenchs. Let's see:

> We take France 'standard' French, as we call it. Now that is also being revised, because we are seeing that we have several French, or that French is that diversity of pronunciations. (F1)

Finally, in the context of the third extract, the informant F2 notices a change in the didactic materials. This can be seen, for example, in the presentation of characters from other Francophone countries, with names different from those that were customary in the books. In this case, we noticed some resistance from the teacher in having to deal with things for which she had not been prepared:

> For example, what happens at the most advanced levels is that there is a variety of French people, there is a Canadian, Belgian, Swiss, Senegalese variety, in the same handbooks, documents, eh..., they present a difficulty for the teacher, and a greater difficulty for the student, because we were not trained in that. We were not trained, we do not have the audio... it's not just a matter of pronunciation, there are structures, there are cultural issues, which I do not know about. (F2)

As noted, the symbolic power previously discussed is such that it is not only a matter of choosing a country among those who speak a certain language but choosing a specific variety, a prestigious one, which coincides with that used in the capital cities with the greatest economic power. These considerations are also derived from the didactic materials used to teach language courses in Latin America (for the case of teaching Portuguese in Argentina, see Scola in press).

In the next and last excerpt, the contradictions that language teachers face in their daily work teaching and evaluating subjects in an increasingly multinational world but with a monolingual political and economic horizon are represented. It corresponds to French teachers' trainer who is in charge of Haitian students, whose mother tongue is French. Related to what Bagno (2003) states, the choice of the prestige variety – in this case, French from Paris/France – is observed as a parameter of correctness. It is important to highlight that it is a compulsory decision, since the teacher's margin of action is limited, at least, by the teacher training she received and by the didactic materials that come from abroad. It is observed that the teacher has difficulties to raise the problem, in which she interpellates herself:

> we can not understand ourselves on certain topics, it has to do with their [Haitians] phonetics, with their way of speaking, that is..., very different. Eh..., many speak Creole, or most speak Creole, and then that Creole greatly influences the French with which they arrive. And there are phonemes that are different, uh..., and well, there's the question of phonology, or not, let's say. Do we accept it? If it's their French, why not? But we do not understand..., then, there is a problem. [...] We try to approximate certain phonemes, for example, some nasals are very different. Some aspire completely, then, you do not understand, and really..., it's hard, you know..., to be constantly telling them 'Can you repeat? Can you repeat?' There is a big problem with comprehension, then, well... As regards myself, I ask them to approximate the understanding. [...] There is another teacher who is perhaps a little more purist than..., well..., she intends some other more articulatory issue, we can say. I would like them to..., at least, to achieve that we understand each other... (F1)

From the corpus, we can affirm that French teachers speak predominantly L2 in the classroom, avoiding L1 use. They argue that the school environment is the only redoubt in which students are exposed to French. This is a matter of complaint on the side of secondary students. The use of L1 in L2 class is not pernicious. Miranda (2013) and Payer (2013) state the important role that L1 plays in the foreign language teaching and learning process; it means maintaining a close relationship between teacher and student, since becoming a subject in another language implies having confidence in the possibility of being someone else.

In this sense, what we noticed in these teachers' discourse coincides with the results of other works. Veríssimo and Andrade (2001), for example, analyzed the social representations of Brazilian primary school teachers regarding the errors of their students. The authors warned that although at a discursive level there is a positive view of error, understood as a natural way to achieve learning – a perspective associated with the constructivist approach – the same teachers attribute the error to non-learning and use the word misguided as its synonym, which highlights the traditional idea of opposing "error" to "success."

In turn, Carcedo (2012) reveals the way in which 26 Spanish/L2 teachers who work in 12 different countries define the error. From his sample, the author concludes: "The teachers point out that it [an error] is an incorrect use of the target language and a typical phenomenon of the acquisition process, at the point where a learner tests the hypotheses that he/she has previously generalized in a real attempt to communicate" (p 21). Finally, the author affirms that the respondents pointed out as more serious those errors that invalidate the communication, which coincides with the expression of our interviewees.

20.4 Final Considerations

What is understood as an error is configured in different ways according to the linguistic theory adopted for its examination and, in addition, by the symbolic power politically and historically imputed to each language. Language understood as a norm is reduced to one of its many characteristics. Knowing how to speak a language is rather to handle with solvency different discursive genres, to master a set of grammatical rules, or to adhere exclusively to one of its linguistic varieties. It is understood that, despite the mistakes and errors, people can communicate. This is the most relevant issue, although the degree of acceptability of certain linguistic forms can also be considered.

In conclusion, two possible ways regarding the polysemy of the concept of error are systematized: on the one hand, its difficulty for its apprehension as a study object in the scientific and didactic field; on the other hand, it means openness and potentiality. A restrictive vision of error, for example, circumscribed to normative grammar, crushes the communicative approach of language learning, in which errors are welcome, as they represent the learners' advances. Therefore, a dilemma is derived from the polysemy of the concept: in the end, does it work or not? What or who does each of these two possibilities serve to? Who creates them? Obviously, it is a social construct. Depending on the political intentions – individual or institutional – one or another way is kept.

The teachers' discourse shows that a new perspective of action is being installed in Argentina that seeks to value error and understand it as positive and profitable. However, we can see from these same voices that the discourse has not yet been installed in practice to the desired extent. Despite the reflections, the interviewees share the perception that it is difficult to produce more structural changes since education, in general, is still very traditional and conservative. In this sense, the motto "teaching as I was taught" prevails, since "it worked for me" hiding the fact that it does not necessarily work with everyone or, even, that there may be less stressful ways to go through it.

Furthermore, it was perceived that the choice of teaching varieties is related to political and economic interests. The belief that there is an ideal speaker model, which would be able to correctly manipulate any linguistic structure in different pragmatic contexts, is also supported by structuralist linguistic theories. This speaker, who considers themselves as the owner of their discourse, embodies the notions of their native, perfect, omniscient orality. Therefore, from this perspective, a teacher-to-be should strive for this model. It threatens the advances in linguistics that account for subjects traversed by history, who do not own what they say, which is dialogical and polyphonic, as Bajtín (2002) has proposed. In other words, L1 speakers daily experience situations permeated by constant communication misunderstandings, in which they must come to an agreement as regards the meanings they express. Now, if this happens in L1 itself, naturally, it also happens in L2. In this line, it is interesting to deepen the studies regarding the myth of the native speaker (Hernández 2012; Rajagopalan 1997; Schmitz 2013).

The contributions of the new studies in multilingualism also encourage the birth of new error-correction dynamics in order to destabilize in South America the cultural imposition of certain norms as a single model of acceptance, since this overvaluation of forms considered correct underlies a univocal conception of error.

Finally, the power of the discourses addressed in the general senses to which we are traversed is noted, although not always explicitly. The presented proposals are intended for new possibilities of professional work, in order to reduce the distances that damage social relations and to make them more human. To meet a language is to face and mirror with a culture, with others, an Other in capital letters; is to relate to each Other to become subjects. We talk about the encounter with an Other that subjectively lodges us with love, although it imposes a language that, paraphrasing Derrida (2012), is the only one we have even if it is not ours. By affirming this, we think about the regional context of ex-colonies in which the present study was developed. To reinforce and encourage this loving encounter in the teaching and learning of Other languages means to take charge of the ethical humanity that belongs to us as educators.

References

Alexopoulou, A. (2006). Los criterios descriptivo y etiológico en la clasificación de los errores del hablante no nativo: una nueva perspectiva. *Porta Linguarum*, 5, 17–35.
Amara, N. (2018). Correcting Students' Errors: Theory and Practice. *Current Educational Research, 1*(5), 45–57.
Angelucci, T. C. (2017). La lengua materna en la lengua extranjera: un arma de doble filo. In G. Cariello, G. Ortiz, J. Miranda, D. Bussola, F. Miranda (Comp.). *Tramos y Tramas IV: culturas, lenguas, literaturas e interdisciplina, estudios comparados* (pp. 167–174). Rosario: Laborde Editora.
Authier-Revuz, J. (2004). Heterogeneidade mostrada e heterogeneidade constitutiva: elementos para uma abordagem do outro no discurso. In J. Authier-Revuz, *Entre a transparência e a opacidade: um estudo enunciativo do sentido* (pp. 11–80). Porto Alegre: EDIPUCRS.
Bagno, M. (1999). *Preconceito lingüístico: o que é, como se faz*. São Paulo: Edições Loyola.
Bagno, M. (2003). *A norma oculta: língua & poder na sociedade brasileira*. São Paulo: Parábola.
Bagno, M. (2007). *Nada na língua é por acaso: por uma pedagogia da variação linguística*. São Paulo: Parábola.
Bajtín, M. M. (2002). El problema de los géneros discursivos. In M. M. Bajtín, *Estética de la creación verbal* (pp. 248–293). México: Siglo XXI Editores.
Balcarcel, G. (2006). La corrección del error en clases de inglés como lengua extranjera. *Letras, 48*(73), 349–363.
Bandini, C. S. M., & De Rose, J. C. C. (2010). Chomsky e Skinner e a polêmica sobre a geratividade da linguagem. *Revista Brasileira de Terapia Comportamental e Cognitiva, 12*(1/2), 20–42.
Benveniste, E. (1995). Da subjetividade na linguagem. In E. Benveniste, *Problemas de linguística geral I* (pp. 284–293). Trans. Novak, M. G., & Neri, M. L. Campinas: Pontes.
Bourdieu, P. (2008). *¿Qué significa hablar? Economía de los intercambios lingüísticos*. Madrid: Ediciones Akal.
Bronckart, J. P. (1999). *Atividade de linguagem, textos e discursos. Por um interacionismo sócio-discursivo*. São Paulo: Educ.
Bronckart, J. P. (2010). Gêneros de textos, tipos de discurso e sequências. Por uma renovação do ensino da produção escrita. *Letras*, (40), 163–176.
Calvet, L. J. (2007). *Sociolingüística: uma introdução crítica*. Trans. Marcionilo, M. São Paulo: Parábola.
Carcedo, V. B. (2012). ¿Cómo acertar en la corrección?: ventajas e inconvenientes de las técnicas de corrección de errores en la expresión oral. *Boletín de la Asociación para la Enseñanza del Español como Lengua Extranjera*, (46), 17–30.
Cavalari, S. M. S. (2008). O gerenciamento do erro em aulas de inglês como língua estrangeira: um estudo com foco na produção oral. *Trabalhos em linguística aplicada, 47*(1), 45–63.
Celada, M. T. (2002). *O espanhol para o brasileiro: uma língua singularmente estrangeira*. (Doctoral thesis). Brasil: Instituto de Estudos da Linguagem, Universidade Estadual de Campinas.
Celada, M. T. (2004). Lengua extranjera y subjetividad. Apuntes sobre un proceso. *Estudios Lingüísticos XXXIII*, 38–52.
Chomsky, N. (1959). A Review of B. F. Skinner's Verbal Behavior. *Language, 35*(1), 26–58.
Coracini, M. J. (2007). *A celebração do outro: arquivo, memória e identidade: línguas (materna e estrangeira), plurilinguismo e tradução*. Campinas: Mercado de Letras.
Corder, S. P. (1967). The significance of learner's errors. *IRAL-International Review of Applied Linguistics in Language Teaching, 5*(1–4), 161–170.
Derrida, J. (2012). *El monolingüismo del otro*. Trans. Pons, H. Buenos Aires: Manantial.
Ellis, R. (1985). *Understanding second language acquisition*. Hong Kong: Oxford University Press.

Fernández, S. (1997). *Interlengua y Análisis de Errores en el aprendizaje de español lengua extranjera*. Madrid: Edelsa Grupo Didascalia.
Figueiredo, F. J. Q. (2004). *Aprendendo com os erros: uma perspectiva comunicativa de ensino de línguas*. Brasil: Editora Universidade Federal de Goiás.
Galindo Merino, M. M. (2016). La corrección de errores en tareas de expresión oral en el aula de idiomas: qué, cómo y por qué. In P. Torresan (Ed.), *Favorecer el desarrollo de la expresión oral en el aula de idiomas*, (pp. 143–163). Lima: Instituto Italiano di Cultura.
Gargallo, I. S., & Chaparro, M. (2014). Análisis descriptivo de las creencias y actitudes de alumnos no nativos de español ante los errores y las técnicas de corrección en la interacción oral. *International Journal of Foreign Languages*, (3), 111–135.
Hernández, G. Z. (2012). El mito del "hablante nativo": dilemas en la apropiación del lenguaje del otro. In M. C. Contijoch Escontria, & K. B. Lusnia, *Investigación y enseñanza de lenguas: andanzas y reflexiones* (pp. 385–398). México: Editorial Universidad Autónoma de México.
Kristeva, J. (1994). *Estrangeiros para nós mesmos*. Trans. Gomes, M. C. C. Rio de Janeiro: Rocco.
Labov, W. (2008). *Padrões sociolingüísticos*. Trans. M. Bagno, M. M. P. Scherre, C. R. Cardoso. São Paulo: Parábola Editorial.
Larsen-Freeman, D., & Long, M. H. (1994). *Introducción al Estudio de la Adquisición de Segundas Lenguas*. Madrid: Gredos.
Lippi-Green, R. (1997). The standard language myth. In R. Lippi-Green, *English with an accent: Language, ideology, and discrimination in the United States* (pp. 53–62). London and New York: Routledge.
Ministerio de Educación de la Provincia de Santa Fe. (2014). *Diseño curricular. Educación secundaria orientada*. Argentina.
Mira Mateus, M. H., & Cardeira, E. M. D. C. M. (2007). *Norma e variação*. Lisboa: Ed. Caminho.
Miranda, J. D. V. (2013). *O Erro, uma análise necessária: sua implicação no ensino da Língua Portuguesa em Cabo Verde* (Master's thesis). Portugal: Universidade de Lisboa.
Neves, M. S. (2009). O processo identificatório na prática de assistência ao aluno com dificuldades de inglês como LE no curso de Letras. *Revista Brasileira de Lingüística Aplicada, 9*(2), 563–582.
ONU. United Nations Organizations. (2017, January 31). Derechos de los pueblos indígenas. Res. n° 71/178 aprobada por la Asamblea General el 19 de diciembre de 2016. Retrieved 10 September 2019, from https://undocs.org/es/A/RES/71/178.
Orlandi, E. P. (2008). *Discurso e texto: formulação e circulação dos sentidos*. 3ed. Campinas: Pontes.
Payer, M. O. (2013). Processos, modos e mecanismos da identificação entre o sujeito e a (s) língua (s). *Gragoatá, 18*(34), 183–196.
Payer, M. O., & Celada, M. T. (2016). *Subjetivação e Processos de Identificação: Sujeitos e línguas em práticas discursivas, inflexões no ensino*. Campinas: Pontes Editores.
Pêcheux, M. (2017). *Las verdades evidentes. Lingüística, semántica, filosofía*. Buenos Aires: Ediciones del CCC.
Pozzo, M. I. (2009) La enseñanza de lenguas extranjeras en Argentina. *Diálogos Latinoamericanos, 15*, 10–33. Aarhus Universitet. Aarhus, Denmark.
Rajagopalan, K. (1997). Linguistics and the myth of nativity: Comments on the controversy over 'new/non-native Englishes'. *Journal of Pragmatics, 27*(2), 225–231.
Revuz, C. (1992). A língua estrangeira entre o desejo de um outro lugar e o risco do exílio. Trans. Serrani-Infante, S. In I. Signorini, *Língua(gem) e identidade: elementos para uma discussão no campo aplicado* (pp. 213–230). Campinas: Mercado das Letras, 1998.
Rotaetxe Amusategi, K. (1990). *Sociolongüística*. Madrid: Editorial Síntesis.
Sánchez Rufat, A. (2015). *El verbo "dar" en el español escrito de aprendientes de L1 inglés: estudio comparativo entre hablantes no nativos y hablantes nativos basado en corpus*. (Doctoral thesis). España: Universidad de Extremadura.
Schmitz, J. R. (2013). The native speaker and nonnative speaker debate: What are the issues and what are the outcomes? *Calidoscópio, 11*(2), 135–152.

Scola, V. I. R. S. (in press). Políticas lingüísticas e integración regional: la enseñanza del portugués en Argentina (2003–2015). In E. N. Arnoux, & R. Bein. *Los peronismos desde la perspectiva glotopolítica en la educación y en las academias*. Buenos Aires: Biblos.

Scovel, T. (1988). *A time to speak: A psycho linguistic inquiry into the critical period for human speech*. New York: Newbury House/Harper & Row.

Selinker, L. (1972). Interlanguage. *IRAL-International Review of Applied Linguistics in Language Teaching*, *10*(1–4), 209–232.

Silva, S. V. D., & Figueiredo, F. J. Q. D. (2006). Erro e correção: as crenças de dois professores de escola pública e de alguns de seus alunos. *Revista Brasileira de Linguística Aplicada*, *6*(2), 113–141.

Silva Guerra Vicente, H., & Martins Ramalho, F. (2009). Uma visão pragmática de crenças de alunos sobre o ato de errar. *Revista Brasileira de Linguística Aplicada*, *9*(1), 225–243.

Skinner, B. F. (1957). *Verbal behavior*. New York: Appleton-Century-Crofts.

Veríssimo, D. S., & Andrade, A. S. (2001). Estudo das representações sociais de professores de 1ª a 4ª série do ensino fundamental sobre a motivação dos alunos e o papel do erro na aprendizagem. *Paidéia (Ribeirão Preto)*, *11*(21), 73–83.

Thalita Camargo Angelucci is a psychologist by the Federal University of São Carlos (UFSCar, Brazil), Bachelor in Portuguese from the National University of Rosario (UNR, Argentina), and PhD Student in Educational Sciences at the same university, where she serves as Assistant in the Chair of Portuguese Language and Grammar III. She holds a doctoral scholarship of the National Council of Scientific and Technical Research (CONICET) at the Rosario Institute for Research in Educational Sciences (IRICE), in the area of languages, cultures, and education. She is a member of the University Extension Project "Portuguese language and Integration," carried out at the Languages School of the Rosario National University, and of the Research Project "Teaching practices of postgraduate thesis writing: comparative study of experiences in face-to-face and virtual environments," selected by the National Agency for Scientific and Technological Promotion of Argentina.

María Isabel Pozzo (Dr.) is a Professor, Licentiate, and Doctor in Educational Sciences from the National University of Rosario (UNR, Argentina) and Master in Spanish as a Foreign Language Teachers Training from the University Barcelona (Spain). She works as a researcher at the National Council of Scientific and Technical Research (CONICET), at the Rosario Institute for Research in Educational Sciences (IRICE), where she coordinates the area of languages, culture, and education. She is a graduate and postgraduate Professor at different faculties, she has directed research projects related to intercultural education and ICT, she has been a speaker in several international conferences in different countries, and she has published articles in indexed journals. Lately, she has co-authored "Intercultural competence in synchronous communication between native and non-native speakers of Spanish," published in Language Learning in Higher Education (2017) and "Impact of a Remote Lab on Teaching Practices and Students Learning," in Computers and Education (2018).

Part V
Mistakes, Errors and Failure in Psychology, Therapy and Counselling

Chapter 21
Psychodynamic Therapy: A Cross-Cultural and Generational Failure

Kathryn Anne Nel and Saraswathie Govender

Abstract One of the main deficiencies in terms of using therapeutic and theoretical models in psychology on the African continent is the fact that it stems from individualistic theories with western philosophical underpinnings. It became clear to the authors that in a diverse, African cultural setting, because of its theoretical underpinnings, this type of therapy has little efficacy. In one institution in South Africa, the 'golden hour', where if the client does not speak, the therapist does not speak, is still taught as an element of psychodynamic therapy. This is all well and good for middle-aged to elderly persons from a western cultural background (baby boomers) but is doomed to failure in an African setting as their sociocultural history is not related to western historical traditions. However, it is taught in many institutions in the country and is widely practised, as until 25 years ago, the African majority was ruled (through Apartheid) by a small white minority, who held western practices in high esteem. Change in teaching psychologists has been slow; thus African culture is nominally or not utilised when teaching therapeutic principles. We would also assert that this is frequently true for many of the 'cut and paste' generation or postmillennials as well. There will be much criticism about these assertions; however, this chapter aims to show how failures and misunderstandings brought about by using psychodynamic therapy cause much confusion and typically doomed to failure. A brief overview of the key points in Klein's, Winnicott's and Fairbairn's work will be provided. This will be followed by an illustration of African collectivism and caregiving which relates to contemporary society and a sketch of millennial clients from other backgrounds and how these do not relate to psychodynamic concepts. Case study examples outlining how psychodynamic therapy failed in these settings will also be given.

Keywords Mistakes · Errors · Failure · African · Collectivism · Culture · Individualism · Psychodynamic · Western therapeutic and theoretical models in psychology on the African continent

---

K. A. Nel (✉) · S. Govender
University of Limpopo, Sovenga, Limpopo, South Africa

E. Vanderheiden, C.-H. Mayer (eds.), *Mistakes, Errors and Failures across Cultures*, https://doi.org/10.1007/978-3-030-35574-6_21

21.1 Introduction

Psychodynamic therapy is driven by individual's exploring their own patterns of behaviour, what they believe and how they think, which begin in infancy or childhood. The emotions that are felt in these early years are deemed important in the psychological maturity of adults. As individuals may not realise that their issues are related to their past, it is assumed that elements of their subconscious and unconscious minds need unpacking (Mcleod 2017). In other words, the individual needs to gain insight into self which requires long-term therapy. This can be lifelong but at the very least will last for 2 years. It is true that brief psychodynamic theory can be used in ten sessions. However, in disadvantaged countries, it is often difficult to see a client more than several times at state hospitals and clinics as he or she does not have the funds to get to the venue. It is also problematic dealing with 'medical aids' who often do not want to pay for this amount of sessions particularly if it is not for a specific traumatic event.

As one can determine, this is an expensive process which is difficult to undertake in developing countries such as South Africa. In state hospitals and clinics, psychologists do not have the time due to the sheer volume of clients, and private patients must have adequate economic means.

It is also postulated, as can be seen by the following necessarily brief explications of some of the major concepts of theorists out of which psychodynamic theory was born, that this kind of therapy is individualistic in nature and is arguably not suited to collectivist cultures or, arguably, the 'cut and paste' generation (those born after the turn of the century) which are also briefly explained. The concepts which are presented are explained in a simple fashion so that they can be understood by readers not acquainted with the notions. In-depth reading is required for a proper understanding of these concepts which, few in the new technological age, might pursue! This may seem a contentious statement but has been the observation of the authors who teach under- to post-graduate students.

This is followed by a rationale, using case studies, by the authors as to why psychodynamic therapy is often, in South Africa (and arguably all developing countries), a cross-cultural and generational failure. It must be noted that there are no concepts in psychodynamic theory, which is firmly based on Freudian thinking, that relate well to traditional African collectivist culture. It must be remembered that self-insight and reflection in this theoretical framework are soundly linked to Freudian premises which do not have a sounding board in collective African culture. The latter is likely in some developed countries as well.

21.2 A Brief Explanation of Key Points in Klein's, Winnicott's and Fairbairn's Work Which Is Used in Psychodynamic Therapy

These therapists were chosen as their concepts are commonly taught in South African higher education institutions and, as is suggested, do not relate to the psyche of the majority who have collective as opposed to western individualistic cultures.

21.2.1 Melanie Klein

Melanie Klein was arguably the first therapist who really explored the world of young children. She was born in Austria (1882–1960) of Jewish descent and thus lived through troubled times. Her first major publication was the *Psycho-Analysis of Children* (1932). She postulated that toys had a symbolic meaning for children. Her therapy with youngsters also looked at how anxiety and fear could be seen in their play and what kind of defence mechanisms they used. At the time she lived in Berlin where her work was not noted as credible however, in the United Kingdom her work was well received. Interestingly, during the 1950s, and beyond, her therapeutic approach was used on adults as Klein thought that strange and even bizarre adult behaviour was a result of withstanding terror that first manifested in childhood. Klein is best remembered for what she called the 'paranoid-schizoid' and 'depressive' positions which are still widely used in twenty-first-century therapy.

21.2.1.1 The 'Paranoid-Schizoid' and 'Depressive' Positions

The publication in 1946 of Klein's *Notes on Some Schizoid Mechanisms* was, and still is, a very influential work. Fundamentally, she hypothesised that 'splitting' is a primaeval defence mechanism which occurs when an individual is overcome with anxiety which defines the 'paranoid-schizoid' position. This overarching cognitive anxiety can further cause a 'depressive position'.

Fundamentally, in the 'paranoid-schizoid position' an infant experiences paranoid anxiety which is underpinned by contexts which are inconsistent, usually caused by the unreliability of others (and self) and splits objects (for instance, someone who praises (good object) or punishes (bad object) he or she finds it easier to cope. As the infant grows older, usually the 'splitting' often becomes unnecessary as the child becomes resilient. Problematically, the 'paranoid-schizoid position' is a dichotomy that must be managed throughout an individual's life as good and bad are found in different life situations with, for instance, significant others. It is associated with managing aggressive tendencies by projecting feelings of anger and hate onto the so-called bad object. If the infant does not understand that their own love is greater than their hate, which can happen even if the caregivers do their best, frustration and anger grow and are projected outwards to prevent feelings of self-hate. Challengingly, this type of psychological damage experienced in infancy can occur throughout life and needs to be properly managed. Unresolved feelings associated with this position lead an individual to experience symptomology associated with the 'depressive position'. These are linked to feelings of guilt and horror as he or she finds it difficult to integrate the love and hate he/she feels towards the person (object) that he/she desires to love and be loved by. Sometimes, the individual becomes dependent on the person (object); think of individuals trapped in physically abusive relationships who are unable to leave. The use of defence mechanisms where, for instance, an individual convinces himself or herself that he or she does not need the love of the desired object (person). This can happen when teenagers run away from home and are psychologically unable to return.

21.2.2 Donald Fairbairn

The Scottish psychiatrist/psychoanalyst William Ronald Dodds Fairbairn (1889–1964) served in World War I and began his medical training when he returned home. His war experiences left a lasting impression on his psyche (Burton 2016). It is likely that he saw what was then called 'shell shock' which much later (after the Vietnam War) became known as post-traumatic stress disorder (PTSD).

Although Fairbairn (1952) based his theories on the work of Melanie Klein, there were many differences. For instance, Klein thought of internal objects as 'fantasised' images existing in the child's psyche. Conversely, Fairbairn thought that objects were related to the unavailable part of a caregiver experience by the infant and occurred as a result of poor parenting (Mitchell and Black 1995).

Fairbairn also differed from Freud in his interpretation of the libido which suggests that people are pleasure seekers and avoid pain at all costs. However, although the libido is supposedly flexible, it is not able to overcome our inherent unhappiness. This infers that our patterns of behaviour are ultimately self-defeating, in that happiness is ultimately overwhelmed by our innate unhappiness. Fairbairn sought to overcome this conundrum by proposing the 'the object-seeking libido' (Mitchell and Black 1995).

21.2.2.1 The Object-Seeking Libido

Freud proposed that the libido was pleasure seeking, while Fairbairn suggested it was object seeking. This means that human beings do not seek gratification, using others for that purpose alone, but want to connect with others. He proposed that an infant is cognitively wired to make connections to others. Moreover, bonds from infancy and childhood to caregivers are what make up our overt patterns of behaviour throughout life; fundamentally this is a learned experience. If positive patterns of behaviour are observed and learned in infancy and childhood, then the adult repeats that type of interaction and vice versa (Mitchell and Black 1995).

21.2.2.2 Repression

His understanding of repression, as a defence mechanism, was also different from that of Freud who hypothesised that repression was used to control impulses and/or memories that are taboo and that should not be allowed into an individual's consciousness. Fairbairn believed that repression is associated with the inaccessibility (or dangerous aspects) of the caregiver which, in turn, is linked to the child's more positive understandings (Mitchell and Black 1995). Holistically, this is 'viewed aspects of the self's experience of itself and its world' (Rubens n.d.).

21.2.2.3 The Spitting of the Ego

As the child grows older and no parenting is perfect, they become more in touch (or absorbed) with themselves and grow apart from their parents both internally and externally. They may feel more comfortable with themselves but also more isolated unless they can befriend others (usually their peers). Moreover, Fairbairn suggested that this split in the ego happens to everyone; thus some part of the ego (self) is fixed on the caregiver(s) in the real world, while another part of the self is fixed on imagined caregiver(s) as internalised objects. After this the child's ego spits again they struggle to find what they want for instance, displays of affection (exciting object) while experiencing the emotional distance (rejecting object) that the caregiver has created. In this way the child's ego is linked to the exciting object (ever hoping) and the other part (rejecting object) that which is angry and forever frustrated. In real terms perceived (and real) poor parenting can cause anxiety, depression and numerous other psychological disorders (as the ego becomes more and more fragmented) which must be worked through.

21.2.3 Donald Winnicott

Donald Woods Winnicott (1896–1971) was an English medical doctor who became a paediatrician and then a psychoanalyst. He was a leading member of the British Psychoanalytical Society and twice its president. His interest in psychology stemmed from the mental illnesses his first wife had (he later divorced her and remarried a colleague he worked with in World War II). He also experienced what he termed oppression by his depressed mother, sisters and the 'nanny'; thus he was part of a very middle-class family (Rodman 2004). It is probable that his parents held the held the Victorian viewpoint that children should be seen not heard and thus were 'remote'.

His concept of the 'holding environment', 'transitional object' and 'true and false self' still plays a major, though controversial, role in those who practise psychodynamic/analytic therapy today.

21.2.3.1 The Holding Environment

The holding environment is created by the mother and how she displays love and attention to her baby (Winnicott 1958). Today, we suggest that some of Winnicott's theoretical underpinnings are controversial as he was a man of his times which were steeped in patriarchy which included the notion of the nuclear family, that is, husband, wife, two children (preferably boy and girl) and a white picket fence. He felt that if a child is to become a psychologically health adult then their first maternal experience must be one of security and love. Later the child expands that feeling to others, first in his/her family and then to friends and so on. If the holding environment and mother are not experienced positively, then psychological problems occur (Mitchell and Black 1995). The term 'holding environment' is used in psychodynamic therapy today to suggest that the therapist bonds with the client and effectively replaces the mother.

Winnicott (1958) postulated that the mother was not in her right mind as her only instinct was to protect her infant which, as the child grows, lessens. The infant becomes aware that his mother is becoming more interested in herself and others which is experienced as painful. In other words, the child realises that she/he is not the only thing in the mother's world (she/he is not omnipotent). If the infant and later child has experienced 'good enough' mothering, their subjective view of their world becomes more objective. During this phase the infant uses what Winnicott (1958) termed the 'transitional object'.

21.2.3.2 The Transitional Object

The transitional object is one that exists (for instance, a stuffed toy or a blanket) and one which the infants 'transfers' feelings to (although objectively aware the transitional object is not a person with emotions). Nonetheless, the infant and young child subjectively bestow the object with some of their feelings (Mitchell and Black 1995). For instance, both authors have children who as infants would throw their beloved object 'away' in the day but at night cry if it was not returned. This shows that there is some ambiguity in their attachment to the object, but for a proper transitional experience, it cannot be removed until the child is ready for relationships with others.

21.2.3.3 True and False Self

Fundamentally, Winnicott (1958) suggested that the true or authentic (real) self is one where individuals feel alive and imaginative and which allows them to interact and be close with other people. The 'good enough' mother fosters this in her child by being there in a positive way which helps the child feel secure and loved; thus she/he develops confidence in self. Individuals who have a false self have internal feelings of feeling empty although they can present a socially acceptable mask which is presented to others. He also suggested that the false self developed as an infant when the child did not experience 'good enough' mothering and felt alone or distressed for long periods of time (Mitchell and Black 1995). Today we would say that the child had not experienced good (enough) caregiving. Winnicott however, meant mothering not parenting or fathering, due to the patriarchal nature of the times he lived in, which is now open to feminist critique (Barlow 2004).

The infant dealt with not 'good enough' mothering by being 'compliant' which is often true of infants and children of addicts (of any kind). Furthermore, he suggested that by internalising their negative feelings, the 'false self' would essentially imitate them hence the saying, 'She's just like her mother'. This was used based on a Freudian concept called introjection (Mitchell and Black 1995). This concept was, as all psychodynamic notions are, individualistic in nature and not mirrored in African collectivism as described in the following paragraph.

21.3 African Collectivism

21.3.1 Collectivism Versus Individual Caregiving Systems

The collectivism/individual dichotomy has been used to classify people providing care to family members, particularly the elderly and the disabled (Pyke and Bengtson 1996). Reher (1998) maintains that collectivism is a cultural value in which the extended family is the central concept and the needs of an individual family member are subordinate to a sense of family responsibilities. Collectivistic families, and individuals in them, typically exhibit closeness and interdependence. In contrast the cultural values of individualism promote the need of the nuclear family over the extended family, and the key features are autonomy and independence (Reher 1998). Pyke and Bengtson (1996) contend that collectivists willingly provide informal care and do so out of affection for their family members, whereas individualists are less willing to provide informal care and do so out of a sense of necessity.

Several studies found that many collectivistic cultures prioritise social harmony over the desire to achieve or strive for personal goals (Aziz et al. 2012; Pharr et al. 2014; Reher 1998; Reyers 2018). Collectivistic culture promotes forbearance, which entails keeping problems to oneself and quietly accepting and enduring adversity, as a favourable coping mechanism because it sustains social harmony. The preservation of positive social relations is the forefront of concern for collectivistic individuals (Pharr et al. 2014). Collectivism is a cultural value in which the extended family is the central concept, and collectivistic families typically exhibit closeness (for instance, sense of responsibility rather than overt emotional expression towards others) and interdependence (Sampson and Roger 2014). Pharr et al. (2014) reported that to say no to caregiving and to place the responsibility of care in the hands of a stranger or institutions outside the family violated the values of collectivism and was turning one's back on the family. The concept of 'Ubuntu' is a widely held African philosophy, which highlights the collective nature of culture on the continent. It entails that a person can only be seen through others not alone. Lefa (2015, p. 1) states that:

> Ubuntu is a capacity in South African [African]culture that [also] expresses compassion, reciprocity, dignity, harmony and humanity in the interests of building and maintaining a community with justice and mutual caring.

Western countries have put the mental health recovery approach into practice since the 1980s, and other cultures have started to adopt into their service. While people with the individual value orientations place importance on personal goals, people with collectivistic value orientations see themselves and their goals as an inseparable part of a family or community. In South, people living in the urban areas adopt a more individualistic lifestyle and seek more western-aligned health-seeking practices. However, those that live in rural areas generally adhere to more collectivistic practices, as they pride themselves in their community - oriented, interdependent way of life. It is a culture in which people's concept of being human is anchored in meaningful relationships. Therefore, within this social context, care for the elderly and disabled would not be a cultural expectation but would also be perceived as a social responsibility not an individual one (for instance, a daughter or son deciding to place an aged parent into a care home without input from family, peers and community).

In the following paragraph, the postmillennial generation is discussed in broad terms to underpin our assertions that psychodynamic theory is not a psychological tool that works well in this context. Although some may find our assertions about this generation 'difficult', all generations have been given holistic characteristics often immortalised in academic works, for instance, Bejkovký (2016) discusses the different work ethics of baby boomers and generations X, Y and Z. Millennials, the generation before that discussed by the authors, have been described as both competitive in a good way but also as lazy and narcissistic (Main 2017)

21.4 The 'Cut and Paste' Generation (Postmillennials)

As both authors are professors with much experience with postmillennial students, we have decided that the 'cut and paste' generation is an appropriate name for those born on after 2000. Discussions with teachers, mentors and other educationalists have confirmed our view that this generation has very little idea about history and the present. Certainly, there are youngsters who are fighting for a 'green planet' which is commendable. However, when we asked some post-millenials who believed in saving the planet about the Holocaust, Idi Amin and/or the Rwandan genocide they knew little or nothing (immediate Google!) about them. Many (in fact most) cannot do simple arithmetic without their phones, and their assignments and work are 'cut and paste'.

This generation does not read; they skim and 'cut and paste;' thus their background knowledge about the world and origins of patriarchy, religion and politics are poor because they do not 'engage' with material. In cots today music is played on a smart phone, and the infant becomes used to being 'soothed' in this manner. It is not a transitional object however, because the child or toddler does not use his or her imagination and is thus unable to invest his or her feelings onto it. It is what it is, and the very young toddler (some at 9 months and perhaps younger) learns to play games on it which become imprinted on his/her psyche. As a result, we assert that they do not develop the ability or capability to really use their creativity and imagination. If they want to see something, they can – not like reading a book (or having it read to them) where they can 'see' and 'fantasise' about all manner of things. Some will say yes, but they can read and learn on smart phones – they can but it is learning that has no depth because they 'cut and paste' or 'skim' and many sites are poor or as a well know American would say 'Fake News'. With no depth to learning, psychodynamic therapy is difficult as will be shown in the 'cut and paste' generation case study.

The 'cut and paste' generation has also experienced more problems with mental health than previous generations, for instance, in the United Kingdom, girls were found to be more prone to depressive symptoms than boys and that there were dangers for mental health, associated with prolonged use, for both sexes (Kelly et al. 2018). In South Africa it has been found that 24% of school children are cyberbullied. It is also noted that suicide is the third largest cause of unnatural death in the country which in part is likely due to social media (The South African Depression and Anxiety Group [SADAG] 2017). The authors have also noticed that many of this generation (across all cultures in South Africa) seem to feel entitled, for instance, if they fail a test or assignment or have plagiarised or done no work in a group, they complain and try to justify why they should get passing marks. They also complain about being 'hurt' if given constructive criticism and show little resilience which may account for the upsurge in mental health issues. However, others see them as the most successful generation ever (Tabaka 2018). Stein (2013) does not agree and calls millennials the me-me generation.

> Millennials got so many participation trophies growing up that a recent study showed that 40% believe they should be promoted every two years, regardless of performance...They're so convinced of their own greatness that the National Study of Youth and Religion found the guiding morality of 60% of millennials in any situation is that they'll just be able to feel what's right...What millennials are most famous for besides narcissism is its effect: entitlement. (Stein 2013, p. 1).

21.5 Two Case Studies: Failures in Psychodynamic Therapy

21.5.1 Thato

Thato, a 25-year-old woman, was referred because her fiancé, who she had lived with for 3 years, had told her he was going to marry someone else because his parents did not think she was 'worthy'. They were very well off financially, and Thato's remaining family were very poor. Jabu, her fiancé, told her that she did not have a 'good' family as her mother had died (of an unspecified illness) when she was young and she did not know who her father was. She was brought up by her grandmother and her mother's two sisters. Thato was devastated as the payment of 'lobola' (bride price paid to the family of the intended bride) had already been discussed. However, Jabu packed his bags and left on the same day he informed her as he did not want to be 'cut out' of his father's will. She cried all the time and had not gone to work for 2 weeks, and thus her job was at risk. Thato was also embarrassed by what had happened as it had brought 'shame'. She also thought that Jabu had lied to her because she had been unable to have a baby, about which she felt guilty, and therefore he had left.

At her first session, she cried, was distressed and reported that she did not want to get out of bed and spent most days sleeping. Thato described that she felt unloved and sometimes did not want to go on. She mentioned that she had not known her father and her grandfather had died when she was young. Her aunts were unmarried (though they had children). On discussing her childhood, she noted it was strict and that she was hit with a belt when she was naughty. Moreover, when she was good, she was rewarded with sweets or extra food. It was considered appropriate to use psychodynamic therapy particularly Kleinian theory with reference to the 'paranoid-schizoid' and 'depressive' positions.

In the following two sessions, it was realised that Thato was not responding well to the therapy. Although its overall aim was for her to gain deeper insight and understanding of self, the 'tools' did not fit her experience and can be considered both an error and a failure. For instance, growing up in a home without a male role model did not produce any emotions, thoughts or beliefs that she felt were pertinent to her present situation. She told the therapist over and over that there were her aunts' 'boyfriends' and her 'uncles' and her friends' parents so she knew what relationships were. It became apparent that her sense of family extended to not only her close family but her community as well which she defined as 'close' to her. It was also found that 'holding' her emotions was different to what the therapist had expected. Thato stated that she wanted to discuss sessions with her close friends so they could help her work through her issues. This made it clear to the therapist that she needed more than a one-on-one session and she was asked if she would like to bring her best friend with her. She was very happy to do that (and did) and did so for two sessions, and at one session she brought her aunt. In western culture this would likely be interpreted as pathology and dependence on others (or issues in transference); however, in her cultural space, it worked. Although the therapist did not share Thato's culture and was asked if she would prefer someone who spoke her language, she stated she was quite happy to carry on with therapy.

One of the more interesting things was early life experiences; one example which the therapist had thought might prove a factor in how Thato interacted with others was the 'beating' with a belt she described by her grandmother and aunts (which tended to be inconsistent) that did not emerge. When asked about the 'beatings', she laughed, as did her aunt and best friend when the therapist repeated the question in different sessions. Fundamentally, they said it was quite okay and expected in their culture if a child was naughty. It was not seen as extreme or wrong. This was difficult to understand at first; however, on discussing it with colleagues (of Thato's culture), it was found that this was (and is) a common practice. Not taking this into account is a flaw in psychodynamic therapy where generally this type of behaviour would be a negative factor in an individual having a scarred psyche.

We make no assertions about this being correct but are reporting what was found. In South Africa corporal punishment is against the law, so over time, indubitably, this type of practice will cease.

When asked if she had a favourite toy, doll or blanket when she was young, her aunt said, 'No, she had whatever was spare…if there was anything'. The therapist asked the aunt if any of her children had toys or blankets they would let out of their possession, and she said, 'Of course not', which is much the same as the best friend's response. This, of course, may only be applicable to this family, but there was no 'transitional object' in Thato's experience. She was also not in denial or indeed repressing any 'unconscious' or 'subconscious' memories.

The therapist used an eclectic approach over the last three sessions and used Jungian play therapy which worked very well. One can of course state that this would trigger her unconscious, but as this type of therapy is bound to universal archetypes, it was more successful. When she last saw the therapist, she was positive about life and looked 'happier'. She had decided that she wanted to work on her career and take a break from relationships.

It was apparent that although emotions are universal thoughts, beliefs and early life experiences are language and culture bound which makes psychodynamic therapy using westernised individualistic theories inappropriate. This may not always be the case, but therapies designed for collectivist cultures need more investigation. For instance, the use of the concentric system framework which suggests that a self with many layers, the outer being, inner being and innermost being (Dalal 2001). However, in Africa an African psychological therapeutic framework needs developing as, at present, none exists. As noted there is the Afrocentric philosophy of Ubuntu (I see myself only through others) but no purely African psychology with clearly demarcated therapeutic guidelines. There is always much talk about adapting psychoanalytic and psychodynamic theory to fit into collectivist African culture, but the authors feel this is not appropriate. There is also much discussion about its development but as Makhubela (2016) controversially states, From Psychology in Africa to African Psychology: Going nowhere slowly. Nonetheless, the authors hope that 'all the talking' results in a new therapeutic model developed for collective African cultures specifically in this case for the South African context. Or it could be that the present status quo persists as Makhubela (2016, p. 15) states:

> A different politics of psychology that will involve more than just substituting Western individualisms with notions of persons and self in cultural contexts is necessary. As such, the current instigations by some, for a shift in the body politic from "psychology in Africa to African psychology" are, in my view, regrettably a call for a move from nothing to nothing else.

21.5.2 James

James is a postmillennial or as the authors prefer a member of the 'cut and paste' generation. He was referred because he didn't attend any lectures at post-graduate level in a humanities subject. When called in and asked why he did not attend, he stated that he did not need to as he could get all the information he required from the 'net'. It must be noted that the referral was in the latter half of the first semester and James had not failed any tests nor assignments. However, his assignments, although they passed the plagiarism software, had no depth and by his judicious rewording of sentences were not noted as plagiarised. His referral note stated that James did not understand that plagiarism was cheating and wrong.

James was indifferent to discussing any issues at all and did not turn his phone off (until told to which he did reluctantly). When the therapist tried to assess what he understood about the subject he was studying, it was apparent he had not fully engaged with it and had a limited understanding. James stated that he 'went onto the net' to search for essays for assignment and then re-worked them by changing a few words. He also noted that he had paid specific sites for some assignments which he had also changed a bit. James noted that he had done this through his matriculation year when studying Shakespeare (he had never actually read any of the plays) and other 'content' subjects. His parents were divorced when he was 13, and his mother reportedly drank (alcohol) quite heavily, but he said this was quite usual in his circle of friends. Although he had played some sport, he spent many hours using his PlayStation and on social media throughout his school (and university) life. He lived with his mother but did not interact much with her as he said she (nor he) was much interested in the other. Although 'not good enough mothering' was considered, questioning him using a psychodynamic format did not get anywhere. Getting him to discuss his youth revealed that he had felt happy and was not 'bothered' by his parents' divorce as he was 'friendly enough' with both. He stated he felt fine and showed no depressive symptomology, and a personality test did not reveal any psychopathy. In essence, using psychodynamic therapy revealed its flaws as James could not relate to its concepts. Thus, using the therapeutic mode in this instance was an error.

James said the use of technology was the 'way forward' in terms of education and said that most lecturing staff were either technophobes or had little understanding of anything since 'Facebook'. On discussion with colleagues, in the 35–60 year age range, this was confirmed. Many older lecturers (55 +) admitted being technophobes but used used Facebook or WhatsApp but did not for instance use, Instagram or more recent Apps. They also admitted that they did not 'keep up' with the latest technologies. He said that all his peers plagiarised in one way or another and that it was 'not that difficult' to cheat different plagiarism software programmes.

He reported that he had used a smart phone from a toddler and he found it easier to engage with people through social media than face to face. The authors have observed this when students sitting in a group are messaging one another rather than talking. James said this is usual, and there is nothing wrong with it. He was not happy about the lecturer who had picked up his lack of attendance and poor in-depth knowledge about his chosen post-graduate subject using the word 'dinosaur' in his description of that person. His beliefs, emotions and thoughts were as far as he was concerned normal as they related only to himself and others were not that important (me-me!). James presented himself as confident and articulate but could not engage through psychodynamic therapy as he could not relate to the questions. He said it was his 'bad', in other words his fault. James did not think his unconscious (or sub-conscious) thoughts needed 'unpacking' as he said he dealt with the 'here and now', and if he needed to know anything, he googled it. Nonetheless, it was apparent he lacked resilience to any form of criticism (constructive or otherwise).

It was an interesting experience for the therapist who realised that James had interacted with smart phones since he was a baby. He believed his smart phone (and other devices) could help him solve any life-problems he experienced that is social, emotional and/or academic. As he stated, "There's an App for everything". After several sessions he said he would read some more about his subject but was not going to use books – and he would read the abstract and conclusion of journal articles (he felt that was enough) to help him through. James also stated that he would attend 'some' lectures if it would make the 'dinosaurs' happy. It was apparent that the use of psychodynamic therapy was a failure in this case.

This case illustrated that it is likely that post-millenials, like James, often find it difficult to interact with therapists face-to-face as they do not like receiving criticism on a one-to-one basis. If, for instance, James received criticism through social media he could ignore it while in person he could not. James preferred using e-learning rather than sitting in a lecture hall which he reported was the same for many of his friends. It may be necessary to use mails or other forms of social media when connecting with some 'cut and paste' generation clients. This, of course, brings up ethical questions as most social media platforms are not 'safe'. Face-to-face video calling through WhatsApp is also difficult as James stated, 'I'd rather not see you'. He did say he was 'okay' with Instagram. The sessions were a limited success; however, they certainly made the therapist think about the current use of very old theoretical frameworks which form the basis of psychodynamic therapeutic interventions.

21.6 Conclusion

It is apparent from the case studies that psychodynamic therapy is not always useful with clients that are from collectivist cultures or from the 'cut and paste' generation. In South Africa therapy must be relevant to different groups; thus more up-to-date frameworks that interrogate African collectivism and postmillennials conceptions of self are needed. The authors state the need for a radical transformation, a 'sea change' or paradigm shift in the practice and teaching of psychology in Africa. As it is currently practised, it does not constitute a carefully crafted and functional blend of models drawn from both African collectivist and postmillennial culture. As psychologists and therapists, we need to be more proactive in developing such models not just talking about the need for them.

Psychodynamic concepts, used by different theorists, in the authors' opinion reflect archaic western notions inherent to psychology which evolved out of the late nineteenth- and early twentieth-century thinking and societal context. It is interesting how medical science has evolved, yet psychology still 'harks' back to previous eras that do not reflect the social, environmental and technological issues in contemporary and collective societies in terms of theoretical prescripts.

Fundamentally, the point is that psychodynamic theory is not useful with either collective cultures (as derived from individualistic western culture) or generations that do not understand allusions from different eras which require that they are well read and versed in literature, which this type of therapy requires. As a result errors, flaws and failures in psychodynamic therapy can be expected.

References

Aziz, R., Salam, A., & El-Soud, F.A. (2012). Caregivers burden from caring with impaired elderly: A cross-sectional study in rural Egypt. *Italian Journal of Public Health, 9(4)*, 1–10.

Barlow K. (2004). Critiquing the "Good Enough" Mother: A Perspective Based on the Murik of Papua New Guinea. *Ethos,* 32(4), 514–537.

Bejtkovy, J. (2016). The current generations: the Baby Boomers, X, Y and Z in the context of Human Capital Management of the 21st century in selected corporations in the Czech Republic. *Littera Scripta [online]* 9(2), 25–45

Burton, E.S. (2016). Ronald Fairburn. Retrieved from https://psychoanalysis.org.uk/our-authors-and-theorists/ronald-fairbairn

Dalal, A.S. (2001). A greater psychology. New York: NY: Library of Congress.

Fairbairn, W. R. D. (1952). An object-relations theory of the personality. New York: Basic Books.

Kelly, Y., Zilanawala, A., Booker, C., & Sacker, A. (2018). Social media use and mental health: findings from the UK millennium cohort study. *EClinical Medicine, 6,* 59–68.

Lefa, B.J. (2015). *Ubuntu in South African education*. Retrieved from https://www.researchgate.net/publication/274374017_The_African_Philosophy_of_Ubuntu_in_South_African_Education

Main, D. (2017). Who are the millennials? Retrieved from https://www.livescience.com/38061-millennials-generation-y.html

Makhubela, M. (2016). From psychology in Africa to African psychology: going nowhere slowly. *PINS, 52,* 1–18.

Mcleod, S. (2017). *Psychodynamic approach*. Retrieved from https://www.simplypsychology.org/psychodynamic.html

Mitchell, S.A. & Black, M.J. (1995). Freud and beyond. New York, N.J., Basic Books.

Pharr, J.R., Francis, C.D., Terry, C., & Clark, M.C. (2014). Culture, caregiving and health: Exploring the influence of culture on family caregiver experiences. *Journal of Public Health,* 1–8.

Pyke, K.D. & Bengtson, V. (1996). Caring more less: collectivistic systems of family eldercare. *Journal of Marriage and the Family, 58(2)*, 371–392.

Reher, D.S. (1998). Family ties in Western Europe. Persistent contrasts. *Population and Development Review, 24(2),* 203–234.

Reyers, M.L. (2018). Cultural moderators of the influence of environmental affordances and provisions on children's subjective well-being. *Research, 12 (1)*, 71–98.

Rodman, F.R. (2004). Winnicott life and work. USA: Da Capo Press.
Rubens, R.L. (n.d.). Fairburn's structural theory. Retrieved from http://www.columbia.edu/~rr322/FAIRBAIRN.html
SADAG (2017). Death by social media. Retrieved from http://www.sadag.org/index.php?option=com_content&view=article&id=2793:death-by-social-media&catid=58&Itemid=132
Sampson, T. & Roger, M. (2014). Applying a mental health recovery approach for people from diverse backgrounds: The case of collectivism and individualism paradigms. *Journal of Psychosocial Rehabilitation and Mental Health, 1(!)*, 7–13.
Stein, J. (2013). Millennials the me-me generation. Retrieved from https://time.com/247/millennials-the-me-me-me-generation/
Tabaka, M. (2018). Some see millennials as lazy and entitled: yet they may be the most successful generation of our time. Retrieved from https://www.inc.com/marla-tabaka/some-see-millennials-as-lazy-entitled-yet-they-may-be-most-successful-generation-of-our-time.html
Winnicott, D. W. (1958). Through paediatrics to psychoanalysis. London: Hogarth.

Kathryn Anne Nel (Prof. PhD) is a professor at the University of Limpopo (Turfloop Campus), Sovenga, Limpopo Province, South Africa. She acted as HOD industrial psychology at the University of Zululand for a period of 3 years before moving to the University of Limpopo in 2009. She has a National Research Foundation (South Africa) rating and broad research interests including gender issues, neuropsychology, social psychology, sport psychology and community psychology.

Saraswathie Govender is an associate professor at the University of Limpopo (Turfloop Campus), Sovenga, Limpopo Province, South Africa. She has acted as HOD psychology at the Department of Psychology at the University of Limpopo (Turfloop Campus). She is head of research at the department and serves on many of the institutions research committees. Her main areas of interest are neuropsychology, social psychology and indigenous knowledge systems (IKS).

Chapter 22
Transcultural Sensitivity: A Way to Prevent Mistakes, Errors, and Failures in Psychotherapeutic and Psychiatric Treatment of Migrants

Christine Bales, Josua Leibrich, Katja Brinkmann, Ibrahim Özkan, Umut Altunoz, Janina Wesolowski, and Maria Belz

Abstract "Agreement in misunderstanding" – what can we learn by treatment errors in transcultural psychiatry and psychotherapy? Agreement in misunderstanding is a phenomenon describing the agreement of the inability of treatment by both the patient and the therapist, based on misunderstanding of each other due to cultural differences. Such differences can, for example, arise from difficulties in the treatment of migrants, such as language barriers, different expressions of psychological stress, or feeling othered. Therapists' insecurities might inhibit not offering treatment to foreign appearing patients caused by the fear of making mistakes and resulting avoidance of migrants as patients. A possible explanation for this phenomenon is culturalization, resulting from categorizing the patient based on own stereotypes. This leads to the attribution of unreflected characteristics, intentions, and behavior (so-called Othering). Thus treatment errors can arise by wrong attribution, consequently causing, for example, a wrong diagnosis or choosing wrong treatment

C. Bales
Hochschule Magdeburg-Stendal, Stendal, Germany

J. Leibrich
Georg-August-Universität Göttingen, Göttingen, Germany

K. Brinkmann
Hochschule Fresenius Düsseldorf, Gladbeck, Germany

I. Özkan (✉) · M. Belz
Asklepios Fachklinikum Göttingen, Psychiatrische Institutsambulanz Schwerpunkt für Kulturen, Migration und psychische Krankheiten, Göttingen, Germany
e-mail: i.oezkan@asklepios.com; i.oezkan@asklepios.de; m.belz@asklepios.com

U. Altunoz
Wunstorf, Germany

J. Wesolowski
Göttingen, Germany
e-mail: janina.wesolowski@stud.uni-goettingen.de

E. Vanderheiden, C.-H. Mayer (eds.), *Mistakes, Errors and Failures across Cultures*, https://doi.org/10.1007/978-3-030-35574-6_22

strategies. Therapists' estrangement, automatically attribution, and treatment errors should be mindfully noticed to learn from these mistakes. Therefore the concept of transcultural mindfulness and the "diversity" approach offers assistance to avoid such mistakes. Following two case vignettes will give examples to describe this process.

Keywords Mistakes · Error · Failure · Therapy · Transcultural psychiatry and psychotherapy · Treatment errors · "Othering"

22.1 Introduction

In this chapter, we will look at the effects that migration has on a person. As in psychiatry/psychotherapy, when professionals come to terms with migrants, they become alienated. Due to erroneous application and culturalizing views, mistakes could be made. Here, mistakes – especially in psychotherapy – should not be seen as obstacles but rather as useful potentials to establish individual relationships.

22.2 Global Migration

Migration is a global phenomenon. There is no country without cross-border immigration (international migration) or inland migration (internal migration) (Angenendt 2019). An essential impulse in the issue of migration is globalization and global integration. We should keep in mind that people do not migrate only for economic reasons. A significant part of the global migration is attributed to refugees, who mostly do not leave their homes to improve economic conditions for themselves or their family but to seek protection from suppression and persecution (United Nations High Commissioner for Refugees [UNHCR] 2016). Refugees rarely leave their homes voluntarily. The flight is dependent on external constraints, including various factors, such as war, discrimination, persecution, poverty, and environmental disasters. Mostly, there is a mixture of such reasons as to why people leave their country of origin (Bundesamt für Migration und Flüchtlinge [BAMF] 2016a).

According to global statistics, in 2015, 24 people were displaced internally or externally every minute (UNHCR 2016). In total, more than 65 million people fled war, conflict, or persecution in 2015 (UNHCR 2016). Among those, about 51 percent of the refugees were children and adolescents under the age of 18 (Angenendt 2019). Most refugees are internally displaced people, who were expelled within their country, while about a third of the refugees have fled across the country's borders (UNHCR 2016). Nine out of every ten refugees are from developing countries (UNHCR 2016), and only a small number are reaching Europe. In 2016, about 280,000 asylum seekers came to Germany (BAMF 2016b). The majority of asylum seekers came from Syria, Afghanistan, or Iraq (Angenendt 2019), where there have been ongoing violent conflicts for years.

People with a migration background form a heterogeneous group regarding their country of origin, mother tongue, culture, and general health. New immigrants in general are often in a particularly good state of health, which is also called the "healthy migrant effect" (Razum and Saß 2015). However, as the length of the stay in a host country increases, unfavorable working conditions, as well as disadvantaged socioeconomic situations, can contribute to a worsening of the health situation (Knipper and Bilgin 2009). Importantly, people with a migration background and the non-migrated majority population share the same socioeconomic determinants of health (Razum and Saß 2015). However, migrants, especially refugees, may have experienced other risks during their lifetime (such as war, torture, and flight) and post-migratory living difficulties. Furthermore, for some populations, access to healthcare is restricted (Bolten 2007). This group includes refugees, asylum seekers, people without a residence permit, as well as the Romani people, who live in different European countries (Beauftragte der Bundesregierung 2014).

On the one hand, cultural and linguistic diversity contains valuable social enrichment. On the other hand, diversity also poses a challenge to healthcare. In the 1980s, at the first international World Health Organization (WHO) conference on health promotion, the Ottawa Charter was adopted, recommending that health promotion strategies should be adapted, oriented, and respectful to the patients' cultural backgrounds and social needs (1986).

22.2.1 The Power of the Migration Background

It is likely that many migrants can successfully manage the challenges of migration. In this context, individual and social resources are mentioned as particularly important (Belz and Özkan 2017). Discrimination can be detrimental to managing migration resulting in bad mental health and hindering integration processes. A critical aspect is the visibility of a migration background: For example, external features such as clothing characteristics (e.g., a headscarf), skin color, or language can be used as cues that guide the perception of a judging person (Belz and Özkan 2017). As a result, stereotypical assumptions are made, such as religiosity, gender roles, or education. The former can result in the formation of misjudgments, which can, in turn, lead to communication disturbances as well as exclusions. Accordingly, how specific languages and accents are perceived in society can be decisive (Wagner and Riehl 2013). Plewnia and Rothe (2011) reported mostly positive attitudes in Germany toward languages such as English, Spanish, French, or Italian and a negative attitude toward languages such as Russian or Turkish. In this regard, several studies have shown an adverse effect of such discrimination experiences on mental health (Keys et al. 2015).

22.2.2 Mental Effects of Migration

For those who migrate, migration does not only mean moving to another country but also the loss of the previous living environment (Bolten 2007). In this context, there are three types of stressors associated with migration, which are pre-migration stressors, peri-migration stressors, and post-migration stressors (Naydenova 2007). First, pre-migration stressors include reasons for migration, such as war, economic hardship or persecution, as well as preparations for the upcoming migration or farewell to home. Second, peri-migration stressors are difficulties on the journey or the migration process. Third, post-migration stressors occur after the actual migration and include language problems, cultural alienation, lack of a social network, legal problems, and other difficulties in terms of acculturation (Knipper and Bilgin 2009). Acculturation difficulties are associated with an increased vulnerability to mental illness (Sirin et al. 2013).

People who migrate face new challenges that can be indicated by a closer look at the migration process. The migration process can be divided into five stages (Sluzki 2010):

1. Preparatory phase
2. Act of migration itself
3. Phase of overcompensation
4. Phase of decompensation
5. Phase of intergenerational adaptation processes.

The first stage is the preparatory phase. The affected people are mentally concerned with the migration up to the concrete implementation. At this stage, for example, the entrance opportunities to another country are evaluated, and it may be that the new language is learned. During this phase, pre-migration stressors appear (Belz and Özkan 2017). The second stage is the act of migration itself and includes the path from the country of origin to the destination of the migration. The stage of the migration act may take a longer time, such as for people who have to stop off in different countries when fleeing wars. At this stage, peri-migration stressors appear (Naydenova 2007). The third stage is the phase of overcompensation, which is explained by the high adaptability of migrants following arrival at their destination (Belz and Özkan 2017). The fourth stage is the phase of decompensation. The goal of this phase is to create a balance between preserving own cultural identity and simultaneously orienting oneself toward the new cultural and social environment. Important stressors that can cause an increased risk for mental illness at this stage are fear and confrontation with the foreign as well as mourning for the loss (Knipper and Bilgin 2009). In such cases, some common patterns, such as somatic complaints or psychological problems, arise in migrants to cope with pain, conflict, grief, tension, and accumulated stress (Sluzki 2010, p. 117f). Particularly, severe stressors, associated with mental stress, are experiences of discrimination and exclusion (Leong et al. 2013). The fifth and final stage is the phase of intergenerational adaptation processes. If the phase of decompensation has not been completed before, the adaptation processes are reactualized in the interaction with the descendants (Belz and Özkan 2017). Consequently, conflicts between the generations can arise that can, in turn, lead to symptom formation.

To date, epidemiological findings on the relationship between migration background and physical health are contradictory (UNHCR 2016). Nonetheless, regarding the epidemiological outcomes of mental health, there is talk of an increased burden for people with a migration background. For instance, studies showed an increased psychosocial burden on people with a Turkish migration background living in Germany (Möskö et al. 2011). Additionally, regional studies showed increased stress levels among adolescents and low mental health measures among adults with a Greek and Turkish migration background in Germany (Fichter et al. 1988; Rogner et al. 2001). International research also showed increased levels of psychopathological burden in Turkish immigrants in the Netherlands and Belgium (Levecque et al. 2007; Van der Wurff et al. 2004).

At the beginning of treatment in psychosomatic rehabilitation, people with migration background in Germany show a significantly higher psychopathological burden than those without a migration background (Möskö et al. 2011). Moreover, the outcome of psychosocial treatment showed the lowest treatment success rates for migrant groups from former Yugoslavia and Turkish patients compared to German patients (Möskö et al. 2011). The treatment of people with a migration background can sometimes be more difficult because of difficulties in the diagnostic process, barriers in language communication, different cultural understandings in terms of disease and disorder concepts, and uncertainties of the practitioner in how to treat migrants (Al-Saffar et al. 2004; Penka et al. 2003; Yeo 2004. In addition, the encounter with the "foreign patient" is associated with the experience of negative feelings among employees of a psychiatric ward. Therefore, these negative feelings can complicate the relationship building and cause limited treatment success (Wohlfart et al. 2006).

These results illustrate the complexity and multiple challenges that have to be addressed in the context of psychosocial care for patients with a migrant background. Thus, migration is associated with an increased incidence of stressors and demands. As a result, there is an increased vulnerability to mental illness. However, it should be clearly emphasized that this does not mean that all migrants suffer from mental stress.

22.2.3 *The Issue of Differences in Expression, Comprehension, and Culture*

The first difficulties exist if the native language of a patient and therapist are not the same. The therapist and patient might, then, fall back on a third, common language, which has high possibility to not be as optimal as native languages in terms of self-expression. There might be different reasons for migrants why they may show inadequate proficiency in the migration country's language, for example, due to mental health problems and lack of necessary political and/or financial possibilities and support. For instance, the costs for German language courses in Germany are not refunded by social services for people with an ongoing procedure for their status of asylum. Language barriers frequently lead to the reduction of treatment quality. For example, some therapists simply use medication, as there would be an insufficient base of common language for psychotherapeutic approaches (Belz and Özkan 2017). Likewise, language barriers often go along with deficiencies in treatment of patients with migration background, since the treatment sometimes even can be avoided by the clinician (Özkan and Belz 2015).

In the case of patients with low linguistic proficiency, it is possible to use interpreters; however, this can be difficult due to political and/or institutional terms. Rarely do therapists speak the language of the foreign patient (Gün et al. 2010). Furthermore, the use of interpreter is not always recommended, especially when the interpreters are not specially trained for therapeutic settings. Different problems may arise in that context. Incorrect translations, for example, insufficient language proficiency of the interpreter, could lead to the loss of control of the therapist; there also might be a loss of information because of selective translation, which could result in underdiagnosed or wrongly diagnosed situations. Eventually, because of the presence of the interpreter in the therapy room, the therapist could feel judged, observed, disrupted, and even competed with. This may impair the therapy, for example, therapists may behave differently and not in an authentic way (Özkan and Belz 2015). In addition, the psychological situation of the interpreters is also of concern; they are especially vulnerable, since they are exposed to high emotional stress and have no background in psychotherapeutic training and psychohygiene (Özkan and Belz 2014).

Also, differences in cultural expressions can affect the therapeutic process. Cultural expressions of symptoms like "My liver is burning" (Bröhl 2010) are expressions for pain which actually means "being down in the dumps" for describing feeling depressed, which might be misinterpreted by doctors and therapists as a somatic illness. Somatization is often regarded as expressions of non-Western cultures to a suffering, psychological condition. Initially, it may seem to correlate with low knowledge about the human body and a low tolerance for psychological strain, resulting in a focus on somatic pain. However, it should be considered that such expressions are part of the interpersonal and social meaning of a language, because many patients are able to name psychological aspects when inquired more closely. Nevertheless, based on cultural differences, therapists may misinterpret these expressions, and such misunderstandings may lead to a wrong diagnosis, which also affects the treatment outcomes and, thus, critically, the health of the patient (Özkan and Belz 2015).

Not only expression and language might yield an aggravating contrast but also the understanding and perception of illness itself. Patients may have different assumptions about the etiology of the medical conditions. Assumptions can range from a magic, religious causality to a naturalistic conclusion. Important to mention is the shame for the suffering as well, due to the respective culture: For example, someone may not like to talk about one's distress, to preserve the reputation of the family and to avoid social contempt. As a result of shame and fear, diagnosis about the condition of a patient might be incomplete and unspecified. However, it must be taken into account that such beliefs can be found among native patients from western cultures too, such that the foreign culture or migration would not have to be the cause (Özkan and Belz 2015).

22.2.4 *Culturalization*

People seeking refuge and/or migrating to another country often experience a radical change of their life. Within a new environment, they first must learn, understand, and adapt to social aspects like cultural expression and other procedures. Besides these challenges, the escape means a great burden, as many leave their homelands unwillingly. Not only do they have to face the separation from their home and social environment, but also they might experience isolation in the new country based on cultural differences and language barriers (Özkan and Belz 2014). The new language and other post-migratory living difficulties in the new country display many challenges.

Sometimes some features such as traits and behaviors of a patient are stereotypically categorized by the therapist based on the common cultural features and characteristics of a certain culture. This is called culturalization wherein values and attitudes of a culture are attributed to the other person. Such ascriptions may be triggered already by external features (i.e., headscarf, accent); however, values and attitudes are hardly possible to determine just by the physical appearance. It can quickly lead to misunderstandings and misjudgments and the culture of a patient instead the patient as an individual would be brought into the focus. In addition, the perception of culture could be perceived differently by the therapist to what it actually is. Thus, the patient's individuality would be ignored and the patient perceived as a representative member of one homogenous group (Belz and Özkan 2016). This impedes identifying cultural similarities between patient and therapist, and the patient will be distinguished as subjectively strange or foreign. With the so-called othering (Reuter 2011), one focuses on the difference, resulting in exaggeration of differences and ignoring similarities. The therapist can feel uncertain and insecure in the treatment process of the "other" which can evoke consequences like strangeness of the therapist, rejection or referral to another therapist, cancellation of the therapy, or even misdiagnosis and mistreatment (Belz and Özkan 2016).

22.2.5 *Risk Factors for Migrants*

While the therapeutic interaction may contain mistakes in terms of culturalization and othering, risk factors also play an important role beforehand. Migration stress describes the correlation between an increased vulnerability for psychological disorders and a migration background. It is founded through migration as a process of critical life changes, including the planning to migration as an act, also adaptation and interaction in the new, cultural environment. Therefore, of relevance are different kinds of migrant stressors. For instance, in the face of language barriers and cultural differences, it is hard to build up a social network. Many have had to leave behind their social network; additionally they may experience isolation and cultural strangeness in the migrated country (Belz and Özkan 2017; Özkan and Belz 2014). In the so-called acculturation process, it leads to a change of the personal identity through migration. This includes learning and adaption to the new cultural context. However, trying to adapt to the new culture can conflict with their own cultural characteristics, which may lead to dissonances and acculturation stress. Besides the use of individual resources and received social support, perceived discrimination is also critical during that process. Again, possible stereotypes and discriminative attitudes of natives possibly lead to communication failures, racism, and/or isolation. Structural barriers such as limited residency permits or limited access to healthcare systems hinder the positive influence of the psychotherapy as well (Belz and Özkan 2017). Moreover, having a low socioeconomic status may aggravate the access to therapists, which additionally correlates with a higher experience of stress in general (Mösko et al. 2008; Özkan and Belz 2014; Razum and Saß 2015).

22.3 Case Studies

22.3.1 Case Study 1 Treatment Errors in Practice

A single young man from Afghanistan was brought to hospital by the police because he had previously behaved aggressively toward others. According to the staff of the residential facility, Mr. S. presented himself as friendly and reserved. However, after several weeks, his behavior suddenly changed.

Mr. S. could barely communicate in German language, and no interpreter was involved during the treatment. On the ward, the patient acted agitated and was quickly irritable, which, in addition to the language barrier, led to uncertainties when the treatment team contacted to the patient.

Given the situation, the frustration of the patient and the treatment team was increasing. Mr. S. was getting more and more demanding, and the situation was getting worse. At the same time, the patient presented himself intrusive toward the female patients and staff members. After addressing the issue, the patient showed little understanding and cooperation. Without further diagnostics, Mr. S. was diagnosed with an antisocial personality disorder. The staff had a negative attitude toward the patient and intended a fast discharge. A doctor expressed the need for a general discussion on how to "handle these aggressive young men who are constantly harassing women." Other staff members used the "culture" of the patient to explain the rude behavior.

Upon later admission of the patient to another ward of the same clinic, methylenedioxypyrovalerone (MDPV) consumption was detected, which explained his consipcuity. Among others, MDPV can trigger intense paranoia, hypervigilance, and increased mental arousal. After a detailed personality diagnostic was carried out, it became clear that the patient did not fulfill the criteria of an antisocial personality disorder. After treatment with a neuroleptic drug, the patient's overreacting behavior diminished.

In the case of Mr. S., failures occurred in the beginning of the treatment leading to mistakes in diagnostics and treatment. The treatment without an interpreter was already critical, because of his lack of proficiency in German. There might have been some misunderstandings because of a low language base and ways of expression, which led to the corresponding misdiagnosis. Additionally, Mr. S. received an inappropriate treatment for his situation. The communication regarding the behavior between staff and patient also might have been ineffective because of the mentioned language barriers. By using a trained interpreter, many aspects could have been clearly communicated and the treatment quality improved.

Culturalization and stereotyping play an important role for the diagnosis and treatment in general: Mistakenly, the behavior was overgeneralized and attributed to the culture, instead of considering the individuality of the case, which led to ignoring the patient's personal biography and situation. The consequences were in the form of the attitude of the staff toward Mr. S. and the absent culture-sensitive treatment: They categorized him as someone "other" and treated him in this way, which may have led to the increasingly negative attitudes and isolation of the patient.

In that case, it was important to consider the influence of MDPV on his behavior and symptoms. The statement of the clinician about "young men of his kind" implies such behavior was observed before elsewhere. Mr. S. was related to "other cases" in terms of hidden wrong assumptions based on his external features and cultural background, which caused recommendation of wrong treatment while ignoring relevant symptoms and causes.

22.3.2 *Potential Treatment Errors Regarding Trauma Patients*

As mentioned already, different languages and expressions can lead to misunderstandings, following incorrect diagnosis and treatment. Furthermore, the post-traumatic stress disorder (PTSD) symptoms by themselves can impede right diagnosis and treatment. When patients try to explain their symptoms related to a PTSD, for example, visual and acoustic flashbacks, some therapists, based on language difficulties, misinterpret these symptoms as schizophrenic hallucinations. In addition, avoidance behaviors harden the detection of a traumatization by making it difficult for patients to talk about their trauma and related symptoms.

Apart from the overlooking of the PTSD diagnosis, sometimes there is also a risk of overfocusing on traumatization, especially in refugees. Mental distress in refugees could also be a different, psychological disorder other than PTSD. In this regard, a comprehensive differential diagnostic evaluation is recommended, and attention should be strongly given to the biography and history of a patient.

22.3.3 Case Study 2: Treatment Errors Regarding Trauma Patients

Mrs. G. was a refugee from Afghanistan, who had been living in Germany for 2 years. She came to therapy because she had hardly slept for months and was anxious and frightened. She also said that she saw regular news reports about violence and terror in her home country. She was only able to describe in a few words that she was afraid that a man could take her away. The therapist asked about the fear more precisely, and he found that Mrs. G. often saw a man in front of her and was unable to do anything about that situation. He would suddenly stand in front of her, yelling at her, and then, just as suddenly, he would no longer be there. She felt a heavy burden, so that she often could not sleep, had nightmares, and was nervous during the day. When she had these thoughts, she often twitched, was sensitive to loud noises, and was often unresponsive. Especially after these moments, she remained nervous and frightened for a long time. Out of fear, she especially avoided long stays outside her home.

The therapist assumed that Mrs. G. was afraid of becoming a victim, based on the news from Afghanistan. Above all, he attributed the described impressions to the news reports, which actually would have nothing to do with Mrs. G personally. Because of the constancy and nature of the description, he assumed a psychotic disorder as diagnosis. He tried to explain that the terror was taking place in Afghanistan and not in the country she had fled to and that the danger was far away from her. The therapist assumed that Mrs. G. considered the appearance of the man to be real. He recommended antipsychotic medication in a psychiatric setting.

However, the therapist did not know that Mrs. G. herself was the victim of aggressive abuse in her home country. Out of shame, she did not talk about the intrusive experiences of abuse. The therapist limited the treatment to the current situation after the flight, neglecting the biography of Mrs. G as well as a sensitive approach. She tried to make the therapist realize that she knew that the impressions of the man could not be real, and she did not inevitably experience them as if they were. In that case, many of the therapist's direct questions were quite unpleasant. She gave up trying to further differentiate her descriptions to avoid talking about the abusive experiences of her past. Thus, the therapist overlooked possible PTSD symptoms.

Cases like Mr. S. and Mrs. G. are not uncommon. Even with available access to treatment options, quality of treatment is often lower for migrants and refugees compared to the majority of the population. Health-related interventions and health services often lack cultural sensitivity (Razum and Saß 2015).

22.3.4 Stereotypes

The cases of Mr. S. and Mrs. G. show that, had some factors during these treatment processes been taken into account, the treatment could have been positively influenced.

The attitude of the clinician is very important, especially in case of patients with a migration background. Prejudices and stigma are everywhere; they are essential for the brain to create categories, which enable us to make decisions which are crucial for survival. Moreover, they also make us act nonreflectively, and that can lead to phenomena such as culturalization. It is important to recognize and reflect our own prejudices and stigmata, because they influence our actions unconsciously, which affects facial expressions, gestures, and connotations of words, no matter how much effort is put in to put across an open-minded attitude. This can affect the way the practitioner deals with the problems of the patient and, ultimately, the course of the therapy.

Simply by reflecting our own prejudices and cultural imprints, the stereotyping of certain ethnic groups can be reduced. The encounter with "foreign patients" can trigger negative feelings, such as dissatisfaction, impatience, and frustration (Wohlfart et al. 2006), but these feelings of strangeness can be counteracted through the recognition and reflection of this information. The feeling of strangeness as a product of perception is not manifest because it results in the distinction of the self (Özkan 2011; Waldenfels 2006). The process of self-reflection enables the perception of our own life objectively and, consequently, the ability to improve the understanding of people's individual inner world and their diverse cultural backgrounds. Through interaction across cultural boundaries, self-reflection, acquisition of background knowledge, personal experience, and narrative empathy (Althaus et al. 2010), we can develop the so-called transcultural sensitivity.

22.3.5 Transcultural Sensitivity

The term transculturation describes a complex process regarding the interplay of different cultures, which interact to each other to consequently form a new cultural phenomenon. The interconnections between cultures result from migration processes and globalization (Welsch 1995).

Althaus et al. (2010) describe three main goals of transcultural sensitivity: The first goal is, as mentioned before, to improve the mind-set of the clinicians regarding cultural issues and reflections of the stereotyping and culturalization. The second goal is dealing with theoretical medical knowledge about the patient's concepts and perceptions of illness. There are a number of diverse influence factors, which are dependent on cultural background, and these can affect the development and expression of the disease. Social determinants can play a significant role for the expression of disease, which can be more body-related in eastern cultures when compared with western cultures. The last goal describes the development of a "know-how" concept for the practitioner, which is mainly acquired by improving communication skills. Scientific studies have shown a direct link between effective communication and health outcomes of the patient (Stewart 1995). Dealing with patients with diverse cultural origins and other languages can be quite challenging for clinicians. According to a study evaluating the intercultural opening of an outpatient psychotherapeutic care unit in Berlin, more than half (56.8%) of the psychotherapists in charge mentioned difficulties in the treatment of patients with limited German language skills. Furthermore, almost one-third of the psychotherapists (30.5%) indicated that they refused to carry out the treatment due to language barriers (Odening et al. 2013). In terms of language barriers, it is important to implement a professional interpreter to promote communication in a transcultural context, which leads to an effective treatment process (Stewart et al. 1999).

The sufficiency and efficiency of communication should always be monitored, especially when dealing with patients with a different linguistic background. Clinicians and interpreters should be trained in cooperation to ensure a good communication.

As mentioned before, the contact with patients with different cultural roots can initially initiate insecurity. An opportunity to carry out the treatment is to begin with joining, which is characterized by an opened curious contact with an interest in the patient's inner world. It is important to schedule plenty of time to create an opportunity to discuss different cultural views.

First, a meeting of two people takes place through interaction, which leads to finding out more about each other's cultural values and inner world. The resonance between the history of the patient and the clinician leads to transcultural connection (von Wogau 2003). Attributing Mr. S's behavior to his cultural background would not have been the case if empathetic asking about his inner world and perception of himself and his own culture had been employed. By means of this, his conspicuous behavior could have been assigned to signs of drug use. The aspect of no opportunity to communicate and clarify can be experienced as quite frustrating and overstraining for the patient and clinician. Therefore, it is important to work with a professional interpreter in such cases, to reduce challenges for both sides.

From the first moment on, the clinician should be sensitive and mindful about cultural differences. For instance, conventions of greeting can differ from culture to culture. In some cultures, the handshake is unusual and can be interpreted as inappropriate. During the session, it could be helpful if the clinician says something about himself in the form of self-disclosure (Baldwin 2013), to reduce anxiety related to psychotherapy and negative associations about its use. Every clinician should be attentive as to how much he is revealing about himself, since self-disclosure is not helpful for every patient. In sum, barriers can be reduced by an empathetic and open-minded clinician, who respects the individuality of every patient.

Also, maintaining an attitude as "knower not knower" (Anderson and Goolishian 1988; von Wogau 2003) may be useful. The clinician takes the position as a knower knowing about nothing. In this manner, he is able to find more understanding about the subjective inner world of the patient, even without much knowledge about their background. Generally, the subjective attitude of the patients to their culture is very important and not equal to universal aspects of the culture. The first step is to find out more about the belief systems, family structures, hierarchies, gender roles, religion, concepts of illness, and socioeconomic structure and how these elements influence the patient (von Wogau 2003). By an empathetic and respectful listening, the clinician is able to get an insight into the individual lifeworld of the patient. In this case, the patient is the expert of his own culture, and it is worthy to be open for new views and learning more about his personal culture. This approach has some characteristics in common with the client-centered therapy by Carl Rogers (Rogers 1981). To get an insight of the patient's inner world, it can be helpful to carry out a migration-focused narrative by questioning about the experiences before migration, reason of migration, the way of entry, separationss from important persons, and reunification (Falicov 1998; von Wogau 2003).

Acquiring competences in how to interact with patients having different cultural backgrounds can be accomplished in different ways. Self-reflection and self-awareness are vital in that process. Obtaining knowledge about different cultures is helpful to be capable quickly and acquire a certain degree of understanding. On the other hand, it is impossible to gain a deep insight for every culture in the world, and that would exceed the capacity of the clinician. Through self-awareness, self-reflection, and acquiring knowledge, the clinician can get a better awareness of one's own mind-set and improve one's transcultural sensitivity, which is applicable to every patient regardless of the cultural background.

22.4 The Göttinger Concept

Culture-sensitive therapy based on transcultural sensitivity is carried out in different institutions. As an example, the Göttinger concept was developed in 1998 at the state hospital in Göttingen and improved further in the Asklepios clinic, Göttingen, Germany (Özkan and Belz 2015; Tumani et al. 1999). The concept pursues the goal to integrate patients with migration background into the regular care system. This opportunity is not complementary to the present care system but, rather, regarded as a part of the regular care within the scope of psychiatric institutional outpatient units in Germany (Özkan and Belz 2014). An important component of that service is a culture-sensitive, disorder-focused, and resources-oriented individual therapy. Not only interpreters but also therapists with migration backgrounds who speak other languages are employed to ensure unproblematic communication with patients.

In addition, a specific group therapy, which is adapted to patients with low knowledge of the German language, is carried out. By this means, even patients with low language proficiency can be supported through group therapeutic interventions. Moreover, a holistic, multidisciplinary approach is practiced via interdisciplinary teams consisted of psychiatrists, psychologists, care professionals, and social workers. Cultural competence is ensured through training courses and seminars, across the disciplines in a culture-sensitive way. As mentioned before, interpreters are indispensable when needed. Specialized training for interpreters about the special requirements of the field is also provided. This is important to avoid excessive demands that can arise during the process of translation and possible psychological burden of the interpreters that can be triggered by the psychotherapeutic process.

Even if this concept is 20 years old already, there is still demand on awareness of culture-sensitive hospitals in Germany, which means that there is effort but not fully sufficient implementation.

In the long term, it is hoped that, through the transcultural opening of the whole health system in Germany, it would not be necessary to have specialized psychiatric units for migrants (Özkan and Belz 2014).

22.5 Summary

Working in a transcultural setting can be associated with different barriers and is not always uncomplicated for the clinician and the patient. There is lack of scientific data on patients with migration background, their access to qualified interpreters, and work conditions of clinicians who are dealing with that issue (Althaus et al. 2010). However, it is a fact that we live in a multicultural world and everybody has daily contact with diverse people. Additionally, people who are working in healthcare institutions often treat people with migration background, and deal with their individual needs, especially after the rising number of refugees in the western world. Although there are existing barriers in the healthcare system, some of them can be overcome through the effort of the clinician. Exploration of one's own stereotyping tendencies takes time but, at the same time, enables individual growth of the personality. Independent of whether the patient has a migration background or not, self-exploring and reflecting are crucial in treatment processes. In the long term, that approach delivers benefits in dealing with the understanding of the own inner world and developing open-mindedness toward any other culture. This can also reduce or resolve mutual misunderstandings. It is necessary to change structures of the health system, to enable equal therapeutic standards for all patients. In therapy with patients with migration background, integrative approaches are more effective than excluding concepts. Concepts which just include patients with migration background would not be supportive regarding integration strategies. That method can lead to exclusion and decline the visibility of some patients in the regular health system (Özkan and Belz 2014).

In contrast to that, a diversity-supportive healthcare system that pays regard to individual needs of the patients, no matter where they come from, opens the doors for patients with migration background and leads to decrease access barriers (Razum and Saß 2015).

Knischewitzky-Bohlen and Graef-Callies (2014) also support to decrease access barriers and determine three levels of intercultural competence in healthcare system:

1. Knowledge level: Consciousness and knowledge about existence of different living worlds and environment, which can be culturally shaped and find their results in presenting symptoms, illness concepts, and healing progresses.

2. Attitude and positioning: Openness, inquisitiveness, encouragement, appreciation, and respect for the individual biography should be present.
3. Attainments: Skills in shaping therapeutic processes. It is about skills in dealing with treatment difficulties or the perceived helplessness and also the ability to get professional advice in such cases.

By means of empathic, open-minded, and culture-sensitive therapeutic approaches, barriers between the clinicians and help-seeking patients with migration background can be overcome. Improving transcultural competencies of the care providers can definitely be helpful in meeting the demands of the patients and clinicians. In these approaches, mistakes should not always be considered as failures and result in helplessness in therapists but should be seen as possibilities by overthinking and solving them with the patient as an expert in his own culture to better approximate the individual needs of the patient.

References

Al-Saffar, S., Borgå, P. & Wicks, S. et al (2004). The influence of the patients' ethnicity, socio-demographic conditions and strain on psychiatric diagnoses given at an outpatient clinic. *Nordic Journal of Psychiatry*, 58, 421–427.

Althaus, F., Hudelson, P., Domenig, D., Greein, A. & Bodenmann, P. (2010). Transkulturelle Kompetenz in der medizinischen Praxis, Bedürfnisse, Mittel, Wirkung. *Schweiz Med Forum*. (5), 83.

Anderson, H., & Goolishian, H. A. (1988). Human systems as linguistic systems: preliminary and evolving ideas about the implications for clinical theory. *Family Process*, 27(4), 371–393.

Angenendt, S. (2019). Dossier Migration: Herausforderungen | bpb. Retrieved 5 September 2019, from https://www.bpb.de/gesellschaft/migration/dossier-migration-ALT/56667/herausforderungen

Baldwin, M. (2013). *The Use of Self in Therapy, Third Edition* (3rd ed.). Abingdon: Routledge

BAMF. (2016a). Schlüsselzahlen Asyl 2016. Retrieved 5 September 2019, from https://www.bamf.de/SharedDocs/Anlagen/DE/Publikationen/Flyer/flyer-schluesselzahlen-asyl-2016.html?nn=1694460.

BAMF. (2016b). IAB-BAMF-SOEP-Befragung von Geflüchteten: Überblick und erste Ergebnisse. Retrieved 5 September 2019, from http://www.bamf.de/SharedDocs/Anlagen/DE/Publikationen/Forschungsberichte/fb29-iab-bamf-soep-befragung-gefluechtete.pdf?__blob=publicationFile.

Beauftragte der Bundesregierung (2014). 10. Bericht der Beauftragten der Bundesregierung für Migration, Flüchtlinge und Integration über die Lage der Ausländerinnen und Ausländer in Deutschland. Berlin: Beauftragte der Bundesregierung.

Belz, M. & Özkan, I. (2016). Herausforderung Migration und Flucht. In Elgeti, H., Albers, M., & Ziegenbein, M. (Eds.). (2016). *Armut behindert Teilhabe: Herausforderungen für die Sozialpsychiatrie* (1st ed.). *Hart am Wind: Band 2*. Köln: Psychiatrie Verlag.

Belz, M., & Özkan, I. (2017). *Psychotherapeutische Arbeit mit Migranten und Geflüchteten* (1st ed.). *Psychodynamik* kompakt. Göttingen: Vandenhoeck & Ruprecht. https://doi.org/10.13109/9783666405785

Bolten, J. (2007). Internationalization and intercultural competence in the health sector. Internationalisierung und interkulturelle Kompetenz im Gesundheitssektor. *Kosmetische Medizin*, 1, 2–7.

Bröhl, D. (2010). Meine Leber brennt. In Müller-Schwefe, G. H. H. (Ed.), *Der Deutsche Schmerz- und Palliativtag 2010: Versorgung in der Breite* (pp. 3 – 6). Deutsche Gesellschaft für Schmerztherapie e.V. - DGS.

Falicov, C. J. (1998). Latino families in therapy: A guide to multicultural practice. The Guilford family therapy series. New York, London: Guilford Press. Retrieved from http://www.loc.gov/catdir/bios/guilford051/98002636.html

Fichter, M. M., Elton, M., Diallinal, M. et al. (1988). Mental Illness in Greek and Turkish Adolescents. *European archives of psychiatry and neurological sciences*, 237, 125–134.

Gün, A., Toker, M., & Senf, W. (2010). "… keine Lust, meinem deutschen Therapeuten zu erklären, dass ich kein Pascha bin …". *PiD - Psychotherapie Im Dialog*, 11(04), 352–356. https://doi.org/10.1055/s-0030-1265917

Keys, J. H., Burgos Minaya, R. Y., Foster, J. W., Kaiser, B. N. & Kohrt, B. A. (2015). Perceived discrimination, humiliation, and mental health: A mixed-methods study among Haitian migrants in the Dominican Republic. *Ethnicity & Health*, 20 (3), 219–240.

Knipper, M. & Bilgin, Y. (2009). Migration und Gesundheit. Berlin: Konrad Adenauer Stiftung.

Knischewitzky- Bohlken, V. & Graef-Callies, I. T (2014). Die interkulturelle Öffnung in der Therapie. In: Vanderheiden, E. & Mayer, C.-H. (Hrsg.), *Handbuch Interkulturelle Öffnung, Grundlagen, Best Practice, Tools* (S. 335–342). Göttingen: Vandenhock & Ruprecht.

Leong, F., Parks, Y. S. & Kalibatseva, Z. (2013). Disentangling immigrant status in mental health: Psychological protective an drisk factors among Latino and Asian American immigrants. *American Journal of Orthopsychiatry*, 83 (2, 3), 361–371.

Levecque, K., Lodewyckx, I. & Vranken, J. (2007). Depression and generalised anxiety in the general population in Belgium: A comparison between native and immigrant groups. *Journal of Affective Disorders*, 97, 229–239.

Mösko, M., Schneider, J., Koch, U., & Schulz, H. (2008). Beeinflusst der türkische Migrationshintergrund das Behandlungsergebnis? Ergebnisse einer prospektiven Versorgungsstudie in der stationären Rehabilitation von Patienten mit psychischen/psychosomatischen Störungen. Psychotherapie, Psychosomatik, Medizinische Psychologie, 58 (3–4), 176–182. https://doi.org/10.1055/s-2008-1067352

Mösko, M., Pradel, S. & Schulz, H. (2011). Die Versorgung von Menschen mit Migrationshintergrund in der psychosomatischen Rehabilitation. *Bundesgesundheitsblatt Gesundheitsforschung Gesundheitsschutz*, 54, 465–474.

Naydenova, V. (2007). Gesundheit und Stress bei osteuropäischen Bildungsmigranten in Deutschland. Veröffentlichte Dissertation. Bielefeld: Universität Bielefeld.

Odening, D., Jeschke, K., & Hillenbrand, D. & Mösko, M. (2013). Stand der interkulturellen Öffnung in der ambulanten psychotherapeutischen Versorgung in Berlin. *Verhaltenstherapie & Psychosoziale Praxis*, 45 (1), 53–72.

Özkan, I. (2011). Migrationsstress, Alter und Lernen: Betrachtung der Zusammenhänge sowie Implikationen für die Didaktik (Dissertation). Retrieved from: http://ediss.uni-goettingen.de/bitstream/handle/11858/00-1735-0000-0006-AEF9-5/oezkan.pdf?sequence=1

Özkan, I., & Belz, M. (2014). Das Fremde als Herausforderung in der Psychotherapie: Psychiatrisch-psychotherapeutische Regelversorgung von Migranten – Transkulturelle Psychotherapie nach dem Göttinger Konzept. In BDP (Ed.), *Quo vadis, Psychologie. Beiträge zum Tag der Psychologie 2014* (pp. 21 – 34). Berlin: Deutscher Psychologen Verlag..

Özkan, I., & Belz, M. (2015). Clinical Diagnosis of Traumatised Immigrants. In M. Schouler-Ocak (Ed.), *Trauma and Migration* (pp. 83–93). Cham: Springer International Publishing. https://doi.org/10.1007/978-3-319-17335-1_7

Penka, S., Krieg, S.& Hunner, C. et al. (2003). Unterschiedliche Erklärungsmodelle für abhängiges Verhalten bei türkischen und deutschen Jugendlichen: Bedeutung für Prävention und Behandlungsangebote. *Nervenarzt*, 74, 581–586.

Plewnia, A. & Rothe, A. (2011). Spracheinstellungen und Mehrsprachigkeit. Wie Schüler über ihre und andere Sprachen denken. In L. Eichinger, A. Plewnia & M. Steinle (Hrsg.), *Sprache und Integration. Über Mehrsprachigkeit und Migration* (S. 215–253). Tübingen: Narr.

Razum, O. & Saß, A.- C. (2015). Migration und Gesundheit: Interkulturelle Öffnung bleibt eine Herausforderung. *Bundesgesundheitsblatt*, 58, 513–514.
Reuter, J. (2011). Geschlecht und Körper. Studien zur Materialität und Inszenierung gesellschaftlicher Wirklichkeit. Bielefeld: transcript.
Rogers, C. R. (1981). Der neue Mensch. Konzepte der Humanwissenschaften. Stuttgart: Klett-Cotta.
Rogner, J. Bökli, E. & Bartram, M. (2001). Emotionales und körperliches Wohlbefinden türkischer Einwohner der Stadt Osnabrück. In Marschalck, P. W. & Wiedl, K. H. (Hrsg). *Migration und Krankheit*. Osnabrück: Universitätsverlag Rasch.
Sirin, S. R., Gupta, T., Rogers-Sirin, L. & Ryce, P. (2013). The role of acculturative stress on mental health symptoms for immigrant adolescents: A longitudinal investigation. *Developmental Psychology*, 49 (4),736–748.
Sluzki, C. E. (2010). Psychologische Phasen der Migration und ihre Auswirkungen. In T. Hegemann & R. Salman (Hrsg.), *Transkulturelle Psychiatrie. Konzepte für die Arbeit mit Menschen aus anderen Kulturen* (pp. 101–115). Bonn: Psychiatrie Verlag.
Stewart, M. A. (1995). Effective physician-patient communication and health outcomes: a review. *CMAJ: Canadian Medical Association Journal*, 152(9), 1423–1433.
Stewart, M., Brown, J. B., Boon, H., Galajda, J., Meredith, L., & Sangster, M. (1999). Evidence on patient-doctor communication. *Cancer Prevention & Control : CPC = Prevention & Controle En Cancerologie : PCC*, 3(1), 25–30.
Tumani, V., Özkan, I., Bremer-Faure, K., Faure, H., Kandulski, F., Sachsse, U. & Koller, M. (1999). Behandlungskonzepte für ethnische Minoritäten am LKH Göttingen – das Göttinger Konzept. *Psycho*, 25 (2), 111–120.
UNHCR. (2016). Global Trends. Forced Displacement in 2015. Retrieved 5 September 2019, from http://www.unhcr.de/service/zahlen-und-statistiken.html
Van der Wurff, F. B., Beekman, A. T. F. & Dijkshoorn, H. et al. (2004). Prevalence and riskfactors for depression in elderly Turkish and Moroccan migrants in the Netherlands. *Journal of Affective Disorders*, 83, 33–41.
Von Wogau, J., (2003). Looking through a cultural Lens: crosscultural competencies in different phases of therapie: A systemic reflection on therapeutic work with immigrants in germany. *Systeme*, 17(1/03), 66–83.
Wagner, K. & Riehl, C. (2013). Mehrsprachigkeit: gesellschaftliche Wahrnehmung und zukünftige Potenziale. In H. Brandl, E. Arslan, E. Langelahn & C. Riemer (Hrsg.), *Mehrsprachig in Wissenschaft und Gesellschaft. Mehrsprachigkeit, Bildungsbeteiligung und Potenziale von Studierenden mit Migrationshintergrund* (pp. 1–8). Bielefeld.
Waldenfels, B. (2006). Grundmotive einer Phänomenologie des Fremden (5. Auflage). Frankfurt am Main: Suhrkamp.
Welsch, W. (1995). Transkulturalität: Schwerpunktthema. *Zeitschrift Für Kulturaustausch*, 45.
Wohlfart, E., Hodzic, S.& Özbek, T. (2006). Transkulturelles Denken und transkulturelle Praxis in der Psychiatrie und Psychotherapie. In Wohlfart, E. & Zaumseil, M. (Hrsg.), *Transkulturelle Psychiatrie – interkulturelle Psychotherapie*. Berlin: Springer.
World Health Organization (1986). Ottawa charter for health promotion – First international conference on health promotion Ottawa.
Yeo, S. (2004). Language barriers and access to care. *Ann Rev Nurs Res*, 22, 59–73.

Christine Bales studies rehabilitation psychology B.Sc. in the sixth semester. Before that, she trained as an occupational therapist. While studying in Stendal, she completed an internship in the psychiatric institute ambulance of Asklepios in Göttingen with the focus on culture, migration, and mental diseases. In particular, her interests are transcultural psychotherapy and neuropsychology, especially language.

Josua Leibrich studies psychology B.Sc. in the fifth semester. He absolved his internship in the psychiatric institute ambulance of Asklepios in Göttingen with the focus on culture, migration, and mental diseases. His main interest lies in psychotherapy in general and additional skills, e.g., transcultural psychotherapy and subjects like cultural influences in diseases.

Katja Brinkmann studies applied psychology B.Sc. in the sixth semester. She passed an internship in the psychiatric department of Asklepios in Göttingen with the focus on culture, migration, and mental diseases. Notably her interests are psychotherapy in general, transcultural psychotherapy, eminently cultural influences in diseases, and health psychology. Moreover, from the year 2015 to 2017, she worked for Caritasverband Gladbeck in a volunteering project, taught language courses for the introduction to the German language, and helped in a clothing store, especially for refugees.

Ibrahim Özkan (Dr.) is a Graduated psychologist and certified psychological psychotherapist, works as main employment in the outpatient department of the psychiatric hospital "Asklepios Fachklinikum Göttingen," Rosdorfer Weg 70, 37081 Göttingen, Germany. Here he is the supervisor of the clinical expert team for culture, migration, and mental illness. He works as medical psychologist and is a scientific employee at the department for social science, and he has a teaching assignment at the center for key competences at the art department of the Georg-Augusta-University of Göttingen. Core subjects are a.o. migration, migration and mental health, psychotrauma, refugees, intercultural work in mental healthcare, practice management, and psycho-oncology.

Umut Altunoz, MD, currently works as a senior psychiatrist and psychotherapist at the Wunstorf Psychiatric Clinic, Hannover Region Clinics, Wunstorf, Germany. He is a member of Research Group Social and Transcultural Psychiatry and Psychotherapy, Department of Psychiatry, Social Psychiatry and Psychotherapy, Hannover Medical School, Hannover, Germany.

Field of interest: Cultural psychiatry, psychiatric trauma, PTSD, dissociation, anxiety disorders, dementia.

Janina Wesolowski, B.Sc., is a master's student of psychology and completed an internship in the Research Group Social Psychiatry and Psychotherapy of Hannover Medical School in Germany. She is mainly interested in transcultural psychotherapy, primarily in improving the mental healthcare situation for refugees.

Maria Belz (Dr.) is a psychologist and in training to become a certified behavioral psychotherapist; she works in the outpatient department of the psychiatric hospital "Asklepios Fachklinikum Göttingen," Göttingen, Germany. She is employed in the focus group for culture, migration, and mental illness. As a certified trainer, she is holding diversity seminars.

Chapter 23
The Success and Failures of Michael Jackson. A Psychobiography Through the Lens of the Trickster Archetype

Claude-Hélène Mayer

> *Such a man knows that whatever is wrong in the world is in himself,*
> *and if he only learns to deal with his own shadow*
> *he has done something real for the world.*
>
> *He has succeeded in shouldering at least*
> *an infinitesimal part of the gigantic, unsolved social problem of our day…*
>
> *How can anyone see straight*
> *when he does not even see himself*
> *and the darkness he unconsciously carries*
> *with him into all his dealings.*
>
> C.G. Jung

Abstract Jung's archetypes have been subject to numerous research studies. The trickster is an aspect of the shadow archetype in its negative traits, representing the shadowy sides of flexibility, fluidity, wit and ingenuity. The trickster is viewed as an embodiment of contradictions and dualities and is associated with a force which serves as a balancing agent, challenging convention. The author reflects on the trickster archetype and its implications in the life of Michael Jackson, an American leader in the music industry, who became one of the most famous pop icons in the world, the "King of Pop". By reflecting on his life development and on selected outstanding events, the author explores the way in which the trickster archetype affected the success and failure of the star. This chapter offers an analysis of the moves of Michael Jackson within the context and expression of the trickster archetype and his appeals to overcome boundaries of race, gender, generation and culture

C.-H. Mayer (✉)
Department of Industrial Psychology and People Management, University of Johannesburg, Johannesburg, South Africa

Institut für Therapeutische Kommunikation und Sprachgebrauch, Europa Universität Viadrina, Frankfurt (Oder), Germany
e-mail: claudemayer@gmx.net

E. Vanderheiden, C.-H. Mayer (eds.), *Mistakes, Errors and Failures across Cultures*, https://doi.org/10.1007/978-3-030-35574-6_23

flexibly and fluidly with ingenuity, creativity and positive leadership. In the end, however, it is assumed that the strength and power of the trickster archetype active in this celebrity's life led to failures and ultimately to his premature death. It is argued that the trickster archetype needs to be recognised, seen, acknowledged and understood in its depth to maintain the success of the leader or to transform leadership stories from those of failure to stories of success.

Keywords Mistakes · Error · Failure · Jung · Archetype · The trickster · Success · Boundary · Convention · Acknowledgement · Transformation · Crossover

23.1 Introduction

Jung's archetype theory has been subject to numerous research studies in the context of psychology and related disciplines (Jung 1969, 1971; Snider 2009; Azaria 2017). Archetypes are defined as images, themes and symbols of the collective consciousness. They can be both positive and negative and always contain the potential for the opposite of their (positive) central characteristic and their positive potential. Usually the shadow represents "the negative side of the personality, the sum of all those unpleasant qualities we like to hide, together with the insufficiently developed functions and the contents of the personal unconscious" (Jung 1971, 103). Every person carries a shadow, and the less it is embodied in the individual's conscious life, the denser it is.

The trickster is usually seen as an aspect of the shadow in its negative traits, representing flexibility, fluidity, wit and ingenuity, being either an individual or archetypal shadow. The trickster archetype might appear in disguise, for example, as an animal or as someone who changes shape. It is viewed as an embodiment of contradictions and dualities and is associated with a force which serves as a balancing agent, which challenges convention.

This chapter discusses the trickster archetype and its expression and application in the context of leadership. Therefore, a psychobiographical approach is chosen, and the life and specific life events of Michael Jackson, as a leading artist in the twenty-first century, are analysed. Findings are presented and discussed in the context of Jung's archetype theory, particularly that of the trickster. Based on theoretical approaches, the usefulness of comprehending the success and failure in Michael Jackson's artistic leadership is proposed. Selected life events, his life development and stories of his leadership in local, regional and global affairs are analysed, and his success and failure are viewed in the context of the trickster archetype. It is argued that the trickster archetype needs to be recognised, seen, acknowledged and understood in its depth to maintain success in leadership and/or to transform leadership from failure to success.

In the next section, a short introduction to archetype theory is provided, followed by a closer view of the trickster archetype from a research perspective. Further on, a theoretical background on leadership is given in terms of success and failure. Based on this theoretical foundation, one artistic leadership story is analysed from a psychobiographical perspective. Finally, conclusions are drawn and recommendations given, while it is assumed that understanding the life of the "King of Pop" could lead to an increased understanding of the archetypal forces at play in contemporary societies and global affairs.

23.2 Archetype Theory

Discourses on archetypes have evolved in science ever since Carl Gustav Jung developed the concept. According to Jung (1971), archetypes are culturally and generationally transmitted and often unconsciously present in the life of individuals. They are universal patterns, found across cultures (Hall 1989). They build the content of myths and mythology, legends, fairy tales and stories and can also be found in spiritual or religious texts (Hall 1989). They are bipolar, meaning that they contain the potential for the opposite of their central characteristic (Snider 2009). Stein (2009, 85) explains that for Jung, "the archetype is a primary source of psychic symbols which attract energy, structure it, and lead ultimately to the creation of civilization and culture". Archetypes are stored in the collective unconscious (Rosen et al. 1991) and are described by Jung (1936) as pre-existent form of motifs and images which reproduce themselves repeatedly and which are originated through repeated human experiences. Reason and Marshall (2001) observe that individuals tell stories about themselves and they "re-story" their lives by drawing on myths, imaginal forms and collective motifs to do this. Reason and Marshall (2001, 317) argue that if individuals draw on these archetypal forms to define themselves within the world, they express the collective unconscious and reach out to an "essential source of creativity and to the reality of our imagination" which integrates the soul and psyche as well as the intellect and experience.

23.2.1 The Trickster Archetype

The trickster archetype can be found in many stories, across time and across various cultures (Azaria 2017; Den Uijl 2010; Lock 2002) and has been described as being a hero of different cultures (Radin 1956/1971; Hyde 1998). The trickster archetype is often viewed as an embodiment of contradictions and dualities. It is associated with being a liminal and transitional archetype which recreates boundaries and edges and stimulates transition (Hyde 1998). According to Azaria (2017), it is also a force which serves as a balancing agent, challenging convention. Reason and Marshall (2001, 317) suggest that the trickster archetype represents a pattern in which the character "flits from idea to idea, moves between upper and lower worlds, is a bearer of new ideas, [and] loves to give others the ideas or tools to do a job, and then leave them to do the dirty work". Hyde (1998, 7) defines the trickster as "the mythic embodiment of ambiguity and ambivalence, doubleness and duplicity, contradiction and paradox", while Radin (1956) states that it is not clear whether the trickster is a human or a subhuman. Further, the author maintains that the trickster is a very unconscious character who always displays his ambiguity without being aware of it (Radin 1956). In their writings, Reason and Marshall (2001) point out that living the trickster archetype can bring amazing positive, as well as very negative experiences which can be painful, but also helpful to move from one transition in life to another.

Snider (2009) emphasises that the trickster can appear in various guises, such as in the form of a fool, a vampire, a charlatan or, in its more positive way, a clown. Tricksters are usually unconsciously possessed by archetypal forces or figures which lead them to compensate for their psychic split by persecuting others (Snider 2009). Often, the trickster archetype, if active in a leader or powerful and influential person, can either cause harm for the in-group or for members of other groups who are perceived as the out-group (Snider 2009). These "others" are then described as enemies or they are demonised. Snider (2009) concludes that the trickster archetype—for example, Satan, the coyote, the raven (trickster might often change in narrations or myths into animals), the Winnebago trickster in Native American mythology,[1] as well as world leaders such as Hitler or Stalin—can play havoc with the hyperrational personality and community.

Hynes and Doty (1993) define six characteristics of the trickster which might be unified in the trickster figure or else occur in another way within this mythological figure: (a) ambiguity, anomaly and polyvalence; (b) trickery; (c) metamorphosis and ability to change; (d) being a motivator, revolutionary and changer of a situation; (e) being a messenger and imitator of gods; and (f) a bricoleur. The trickster figure can be very violent in reaching its aims without taking the consequences into account (Jung 1969).

In view of the global trends of increasing violence, destruction, ambivalence and terrorism—but at the same time increasing revolutionary thoughts, creativity, progressive ways of living, transculturality and individual ways of expression—it is assumed in this chapter that the trickster archetype is active in many individuals and sociocultural contexts. Michael Jackson is seen as an individual who strongly used the archetype of the trickster in his life and his career. Azaria (2017) argues that if one aims at understanding and balancing meaning and action "in the currently duplicitous cultural and political climate in which we find ourselves", one has to take a closer look at the dynamics of the archetype of the trickster. The trickster archetype usually represents someone or something which challenges the status quo (Lock 2002). However, it has been noted that to understand the trickster archetype

[1] The Winnebago trickster is a figure represented in the myth of the Winnebago (Siouan people of Wisconsin, USA). This trickster occurs in tales and stories in human or animal form and represents anarchy, disorder and chaos (Velie 1991).

is in itself challenging, since it appears to be dubious and ambiguous (Lock 2002). Often, it is not clearly defined whether the trickster is human or divine, female or male, or which ethnic origin it has. Tricksters usually cross, bend, break and redefine borders and often derive intelligence by acting on their desires and learning from the consequences (Garrison 2009). This can be interpreted as positive, because the trickster archetype may create new insights and openings into closed structures and thereby reveal hidden potentials and innovations. The trickster can, however, also be interpreted as negative in the way that it displays characteristics of an individual's "shadow", characteristics which are paradoxical, ironic and ambiguous and which create this kind of effect in an unsettling atmosphere (Beebe 1981). The trickster has a loosening function which compensates for the disposition to rigidity in the collective consciousness, thereby approaching the irrational depths and keeping entry open to the world of the instincts and the archetypal realities (Jung and von Franz 1985). The trickster figure is a rebel, constantly changing the rules, and is usually described as a male figure which temporarily changes into that of a female (Lock 2002).

In post-modern societies, the trickster archetype is displayed, for example, in hackers who are described as "tricksters of the digital age", bringing creativity and innovation to organisations and societies on one hand while threatening them on the other hand, not least at the level of digital security (Nikitina 2012). Lock (2002) points out that the contemporary figure of the trickster seems to be well aware of its trickery, while the ancient archaic type of the trickster is rather unconscious. The post-modern trickster is then further characterised as playful, manipulating the language, ambiguous regarding the truth and conscious of its influence. Jung (1969) shows that the trickster, if evolving to be conscious on a higher level, is able to reflect on and meta-communicate about its role. Edward Snowden, for example, displays a post-modern trickster figure, simultaneously a hero and a villain, who is breaking conventions (Azaria 2017). The trickster archetype is present when individuals experience unpredictability and doubt, when breaking out of categories, confronting risk, having "mixed feelings", for example, joy and sorrow. The archetype represents an "inner split" which occurs in transition stages and appears to be an "immature yet tremendously powerful individual" (Azaria 2017).

Archetypal theory has been strongly criticised (Den Uijl 2010). However, while such criticism is acknowledged, in the present chapter, it remains unexamined. Further information can be found in Den Uijl (2010).

23.3 Leadership, Leadership Stories, Success and Failure

Leadership has become a highly recognised research area globally and in terms of interdisciplinary research (Gupta and Van Wart 2015; Northouse 2013). It is defined as the ability of an individual, a leader, to motivate others to reach the aims of the system, for example, the organisation (Amos 2012). Rost (1994) emphasises that several leadership definitions involve the mobilising of a group. Leaders have to influence their followers to follow and perform (Northouse 2016). Often, they are required to resolve complex problems and find solutions for complex phenomena occurring in ambiguous situations (Reiter-Palmon and Illies 2005). A successful leader needs creativity, intelligence and wisdom—and uses the interplay of these three characteristics (Sternberg 2003, 2006). Knowledge and a desire to think in novel and original, innovative ways are also characteristic of leaders (Sternberg and Lubart 1995).

Leadership resides in the leader's ability to create a story of successful leadership (Sternberg 2005). This leadership story needs to address the followers' needs; it should be authentic and carry parts of the leader's life story (Avolio et al. 2004). In addition, it should correspond to the leader's action and support the leader's behaviour. Leadership should be perceived as authentic and stable; it should provide followers with an idea of reality and with emotional connection and commitment (Bennett 2016), as well as meaningfulness (Stephens and Carmeli 2016). All of this can be established by successful leadership stories.

According to Sternberg (2008, 103), leadership stories which succeed are those which fit their followers, are communicated in a compelling way, are implemented to give the impression that they are succeeding and persuade followers to believe that the story accomplished its aim. Leadership stories which fail are usually those which do not fit the followers' needs, fail to communicate their story, fail to implement the story and do not persuade followers that the stories manage to accomplish what they promised. They fail to be coherent and allow a story of successful leadership to be replaced by stories of personal failure.

23.4 Research Methodology

Psychobiographies aim to analyse the lives of extraordinary individuals across their lifespan, through the lens of a psychological theory (Runyan 1988; Mayer 2017) by using either single case study approaches or comparative case studies (Schultz 2005). The focus in this chapter is on the person, Michael Jackson, his life and selected life events in the context of the trickster archetype theory.

23.4.1 Sampling

The study used purposive non-probability sampling (Oliver 2006), based on primary and secondary data analysis. Michael Jackson was one of the most extraordinary musicians in the world at the beginning of the twenty-first century. He was purposefully chosen according to the following criteria: He was a US citizen and a twenty-first-century leader in the world of music and the music industry. He is described as extraordinary and discussed as a controversial figure. In terms of the primary analysis, Michael Jackson displays the trickster archetype and therefore seems to be suitable for the analysis based on the chosen theory (primary and secondary data).

23.4.2 *Data Collection and Analysis*

The data collection was based on first-person and third-person documents (Allport 1961), including autobiographical accounts, internet sources, journal and newspaper articles, interviews, video documentaries, personal statements and creative works. These documents were sourced from literature and Internet analysis through various search engines (Google scholar, Eric, Sabinet) using keywords such as "Michael Jackson", "King of Pop" and music titles.

The various forms of data were analysed through content analysis based on a five-step process described by Terre Blanche et al. (2006, pp. 322–326). The process involves familiarisation and immersion (researchers familiarise themselves with the first- and third-person documents), inducing themes (the trickster archetype), coding (with regard to the theme trickster), elaboration (data is elaborated and reconstructed) and interpretation and checking (findings are described, analysed, interpreted). During the last process phase, findings are reconstructed (Yin 2009) into the form presented below. Ethical considerations for psychobiographical research were followed (Ponterotto 2014), and qualitative research criteria were used (see Northcote 2012).

23.5 The Trickster Archetype in Michael Jackson's Life

Michael Jackson (1958–2009) is said to be the most iconic and influential contemporary artist of his time (Vogel 2011): an innovative singer, composer, dancer and choreographer but also a messenger of peace and a spiritual revolutionist (Risi and Pade 2017). Besides his musical talent, Michael Jackson also expressed himself in other creative ways, such as drawings (Artlima 2015).

The trickster archetype manifested in Michael Jackson's life from an early age, not necessarily in a shadowy form, but rather in a positive way: he displayed flexibility and fluidity in his performances as a child, with a certain wit, and was known for his ability to learn new dance steps faster than all of his brothers. However, the often negatively associated aspects of the archetype of the trickster, such as the embodiment of contradictions and dualities and the challenging of convention, started to play out during his adolescence.

The artist was born on 29 August 1958 in Gary, Indiana, in the USA, as the seventh of nine siblings to his father Joseph (Joe) Jackson and his mother Katherine Scruse (Sullivan 2012). Both parents were very musical and exposed their children to music from an early age through singing, playing instruments and music lessons (Sullivan 2012). When his parents heard Michael sing at a kindergarten concert, they became aware of his talent and brought him into the family-based music group which had consisted of his four brothers, until Michael joined as lead singer of the "Jackson 5". His father coached the singing boy band to perform at local concerts and talent shows, where they won most of the competitions entered (Sullivan 2012). Michael's early career as a child star was later, during and following adolescence, associated with stereotypes and clichéd images of black masculinity anchored in blackface minstrelsy[2] (Warwick 2012), and constructions of blackness including the idea of black male hypersexuality which—according to Manning (2014) in an interview—led to later accusations of his "strange sexual activities".

It is clear that culturally and generationally transmitted collective images and symbols were personally inherited (Jung 1971) in Michael Jackson. As a child, he became the image of the "sweet, black young boy and child star", carrying the images of the Hollywood child stars from the 1930s (Manning 2014). During adolescence and in adulthood, however, he turned to subverting blackface minstrelsy stereotypes (Manning 2014). He then enacted the white stereotypes of "in your face" blackness, exposing gender and sexuality "under the mask" and defined in terms of "the norm": white and straight (as the "norm"), with different, black and gay being the opposed "other", or even oversexed, violent and sexually aggressive (Manning 2014). Michael used the blackface minstrelsy tradition in terms of dance steps (e.g. standing on his toes as opposing the image of black slaves' flapping feet) but also in terms of clothing (white socks, white gloves) by parodying the images of black artists or servants in the eighteenth- and nineteenth-century USA. According to Manning (2014), the main black minstrelsy character is mad, bad and dangerous; Michael opposed this image of self-ridicule and disgust of re-enactment of blackface minstrelsy stereotypes (Manning 2014), thereby playing out the trickster archetype. He constructed his own identity in a fluid, flexible way, undermining the traditional racist constructions, thereby taking in the dualistic, controversial meaning of the trickster archetype. By parodying the blackface minstrelsy tradition, Michael tricked the often unconscious historical images and collectively suppressed and unconscious stereotypes of black slavery and black parody, enacting it in his personalised, parodied way, thereby combining black and white images of the performer and the audience at the same time.

Michael combined and broke the stereotypes of race (turning from a black boy who moves masses of white audiences to "being white"), gender (from a boy to an "androgyne adult") and generation (developing from a boy into an adult and maintaining a boyish approach to the world). He also constructed his own "vocal signature": a personal creative use of different vocalisations and sounds, combining historical types, roles and styles of popular music with a contradictory generic coding, code-breaking new authenticity and a newly established artistic persona based on race, ethnicity, sex and gender (Johansson 2012).

---

[2] Blackface minstrelsy is the white theatrical parody of black dance, music and gesture, a tradition which dominated pop culture throughout the 1800s in the UK and the USA and which parodied race, gender and sexuality (Manning 2014).

In his autobiography, Michael describes his childhood as being full of work: school, church and rehearsals and as including the love of his mother and her Christian belief (Jackson 1988). In *Dancing the Dream* (Jackson 1992/2009), he publishes poems and reflections on soul issues such as the environment, nature and animals, personal development and feelings. He thereby contradicts the societal trend of environmental destruction and opposes the traditional images and stereotypes of the blackface minstrelsy which are associated with violence, destruction and amoral behaviour. He plays the bipolar aspects of his publicly viewed and recognised bipolar character as a black-male, white-female artist with a revolutionary message criticising the white mainstream culture of environmental destruction, violence against animals and egoism, by screaming out for the "healing of the world" (1991). In this manner, Michael plays with powerful archetypal images and dualism of death and survival, construction and destruction, healing and sickness, reproducing humankind's collective experiences on a meta-level consciousness and in parallel at a subliminal, unconscious level.

Michael represents the trickster archetype, calling for healing and a spiritual revolution in the world of materialistic destruction, egoism and power (as, e.g. shown in the music video *Earth Song*), thereby "re-storying" his life, his power, creative ideas and enactment as a form of a modern trickster, integrating the soul and the intellect (see Reason and Marshall 2001). The archetypal images and their oppositions unify in Michael as a person. In his creative works (body, voice, personal presentation, dances) for the audience, he draws unconsciously on extremely powerful images, stereotypes and myths (Stein 2009) and provides structure for the future vision and future enactment of revolutionised ideas and their implementation. Michael's images draw on conventional stereotypes of blackface minstrelsy through parodied artefacts, symbols and acts and thereby play the trickster archetype criticising mainstream culture, materialism and conventions in a subliminal, unconscious rather than conscious way. However, it is assumed that a majority of his audience is not aware of this subliminal, double bind connection of parodying the historical blackface minstrelsy.

According to the strict routines applied by his father, Michael was always under pressure to perform at his best (Anderson and Shaw 2002) and to assume the brotherly group and family values. When Michael was 12 years old, the Jackson 5 performed on TV shows and released several singles which became chart-toppers. One year later, aged 13, Michael released his first singles and the family moved to California into an upgraded estate (Taraborelli 2009). During adolescence, Michael was teased by his father about the way he looked and he isolated himself, full of fear of failure (Sullivan 2012). Aged 18, Michael met Quincy Jones and pursued his solo career, moving away from his father's influence but remaining a perfectionist (Jackson 1988). His concern about his external appearance increased (King 2009); however, the public loved him, and he won eight Grammys for his album *Thriller* (Sullivan 2012), after the release of his first album *Off the Wall* (1979) had generated four top ten hits in the USA. His brother Jermaine describes, in his autobiographical book, how the Jackson 5 learned from their mother to focus on positive thinking and positive affirmations to become the success they were (Jackson 2012). He explains how Michael wrote an affirmation "Thriller – 100 million sold" in 1982 on his mirror, which later turned "magically" into reality (Jackson 2012).

Michael continued with his success, won awards, produced two films (*Thriller* and *Moonwalker*) and bought a farm in California which he called "Neverland", containing exotic animals and an entertainment park (Taraborelli 2009). He was ascribed a "Peter Pan complex" by the public (Sullivan 2012), which describes the idea of not wanting to grow up and the image of a lonely, lost, obsessed and anxious self (Brunner 2013). In an interview (Winfrey 1993), Michael stated "I am Peter Pan", and he developed his Neverland Ranch with much fantasy and secret pathways. Nunn (2009) highlights the fact that Michael wanted to play Peter Pan on stage on Broadway and that he idealised the story, as if he never wanted his childhood dream to end. It is possible that he wished to protect his inner self through this idealised figure, aimed at escaping his sad and painful reality (Pinsky and Young 2009). The Peter Pan complex suggests a type of dualistic nature which might be connected to a representation of the trickster archetype: the idea of not wanting to grow up, of living childhood dreams in adulthood. Building the Neverland Ranch represents the ambiguity of the trickster (Radin 1956) of wanting to stay a child while being an adult. The act of developing the childhood (dream) world during adulthood might have helped Michael to progress into adulthood, managing his personal transition, as described by Reason and Marshall (2001).

Michael's success is strongly based on the creation of his individual style and change over the years of his career (Mercer 1993, 93). The change in his physical appearance, moving from an African American child towards a "paragon of racial and sexual ambiguity" and from a boy towards an image of androgyny (Mercer 1993, 94), creates a huge mystification around him. Snider (2009) comments that the trickster archetype is known for changing forms and being flexible in changing its outward appearance, which can be seen in Michael turning from black to white, from male to androgyne, and playing on various generational lines. Michael uses the trickster archetype to cross boundaries, to shake up conventions and to bring change and transformation to the world.

He shows characteristics of the trickster as defined by Hynes and Doty (1993) in terms of ambiguity, anomaly and polyvalence, in the ability to change in terms of crossing music genres and artistic disciplines (musician, dancer, singer, composer), and as a motivator, revolutionary and changer of situations in that he aimed to change and heal the world. However, he also presented himself as a messenger and an imitator of gods (Hynes and Doty 1993) by reaching beyond the limits, by making a career possible which was not possible for any African American singer before him and by moving huge audiences across cultural, racial and gender lines. He also carried the characteristic of a bricoleur (Hynes and Doty 1993), being a person who constructs bricolages and new things using whatever material is available. Michael used many characteristics of the trickster (Hynes and Doty 1993); he fascinated his audiences and the world by moving beyond the norm, calling out for positive change, displaying huge amounts of creativity, revolutionary thoughts and ideas, progressive ways of living, with transcultural and interpersonal ways of expressing himself. He showed many positive aspects of the trickster archetype as a world-leading artist. At the same time, he carried negatively ascribed aspects of the archetype of the trickster, by displaying strong ambivalences in terms of race and gender, health and sickness and the psychic splits within himself. Further aspects which are often ascribed to the archetype of the trickster are those of destruction and violence (Azaria 2017). These are partly seen in terms of the artist's self-destruction (changes in his body leading to pain, the need for constant reconstruction of his nose and the intake of pills and medication). His videos usually show violent acts towards him which he counteracts with softness (as expressed in dance or alternate methods of conflict resolution). However, he was repeatedly accused of violence, in repeated child molestation trials.

Michael's parents, particularly his father, claimed Michael's success for himself (King 2009), while the media described him as freaky, quirky and weird without recognising—according to Brunner (2013)—his serious mental health problems which seemed to be connected to his narcissism (Pinsky and Young 2009). Boteach (2009) describes Michael's life as painful, unhappy and a tragedy. However Risi and Pade (2017) emphasise its dualistic nature: the accusations and denial of child molestation; his idea to heal the world and create a media imperium that is built of light rather than darkness; his confidence in aiming to create something healing and huge, while fighting his pain and sicknesses; the dark powers of the entertainment industry and media systems; and his riches and his losses.

Viewing these dualities, Taraborelli (2009) emphasises both sides of Michael's life, "the magic, the madness"—describing the archetype of the trickster in its essence as a double bind, dubious and ambiguous (Lock 2002). Wiesner (2015) explains that at the time of his death, but also long before, Michael was driven by the surrounding media and music production industry systems which did not care for him as a person, but rather used him in one way or another. Risi and Pade (2017) observe that Michael's spiritual message and his detailed plans to change the world into something better became a disturbing threat to the "dark systems", their power, money and influence. If Michael is viewed as a spiritual messenger, challenging the status quo of the music industry, he displays part of the trickster archetype, as described by Lock (2002).

According to Garrison (2009), tricksters usually cross, break and redefine borders and often derive intelligence by acting on their desires and learning from the consequences of such actions. Michael's skin colour change was much debated (Brunner 2013; Risi and Pade 2017; Wiesner 2015), and the question of why his skin colour changed remains open (Brunner 2013). Michael himself attributed it to a rare skin disease called vitiligo, explaining also that he had only two operations to his nose to advance his breathing to improve his singing (Anderson and Shaw 2002; Risi and Pade 2017).

According to Marx (in Mercer 1993, p. 94), Michael's image became a "social hieroglyph", a kind of social image that needs to be decoded by, for example, the audience. Others, such as Brunner (2013), claim that Michael suffered from a narcissistic personality disorder. This is a serious mental health disorder which is accompanied by a body dysmorphic disorder—a co-morbid condition leading the afflicted person to alter their bodily features and to anorexia nervosa, a form of self-starvation (Brunner 2013). The public debate on Michael's operations and body changes is ongoing and unresolvable in terms of clarifying why these surgeries were conducted and to what extent. The entire situation remains unknown and incomprehensible, as is often the case in trickery.

Michael's sexuality and sexual preferences became the focus of attention in the press, while he never made a public statement about it since he believed this to be his private issue (Mercer 1993). In 1993, Michael was accused of child molestation, and he settled the case out of court (Erni 1998). This incident was followed by the announcement of his marriage to Lisa Marie Presley in 1994. However this marriage appears to have been a publicity stunt to restore his reputation; he seems to have chosen her because she was Elvis Presley's daughter (Sullivan 2012). In an interview after his death, Presley described Michael as "the master of manipulation" to survive in the world as a superstar (Winfrey 2010). They divorced in 1996, and he married Debbie Rowe a few months later. They had two children, Prince Michael Joseph Jr. Jackson (1997) and Paris Jackson (1998). They divorced in 1999, and Michael gained full custody of their two children (Sullivan 2012). In 2002, Michael's youngest child, Prince Michael Jackson II, called "Blanket" was born. It is assumed that this son was birthed by a surrogate mother, but the circumstances are not clear.

His career was overshadowed by his eccentric behaviour (Sullivan 2012). Over the years, Michael was accused of further child molestation. Although he was acquitted of these charges in 2005, his finances were depleted, and he turned to the Prince of Bahrain for financial help (Adams 2008). Jones (2005) describes the difficulties in establishing whether Michael was a child molester, owing to varying statements and entanglements of the individuals and families involved. Therefore, the discourse on what really happened stays unresolved. Others interpret the child molestation trials as stigmatising acts with queer configurations through which queer culture became pervasive in the media. Fast (2010) points out that Michael Jackson's "difference" exceeded the understanding of the public in terms of racial, generational and gender discourses and made him unknowable and untouchable, thereby creating fear, anxiety and fascination. Brackett (2012) explains how Michael lived the idea of "crossover", crossing boundaries of music genre divides, but also racial divides, holding a vision of crossed-over racial relations. Fast (2012) comments on the way in which Michael, as an outsider to the genre of rock music, plays with rock conventions in an unusual way in the sound of his music, in selected video narratives, in live performances and in the choice of artists to perform with.

All of the information gathered here suggests confusion, great complexity and difficulty of interpreting and understanding Michael as a person, his actions and interactions around his personal changes, ideas, wishes, accusations, ascribed preferences and visions, which is typical of the impact of the trickster archetype as emphasised by Lock (2002). As a result of experiences of a dubious nature surrounding Michael's actions in the topics mentioned above, he created an unsettling atmosphere (Beebe 1981) which is typical of the trickster archetype. By breaking taboos on topics and overcoming conventions and boundaries, Michael dove into the world of archetypal realities (as discussed by Jung and von Franz 1985), being seen as the rebel who changes the rules of the world (Lock 2002) and turning sex and gender (as a trickster) from male into female (Lock 2002).

During the court case in 2005, Michael was mainly supported by his family; all of his business friends had left him (Jackson 2012). His brother Jermaine, with whom Michael had shared a room during childhood and adolescence, writes about his brother and the suffering he experienced regarding the accusations (Jackson 2012). However, other writers, such as Michael's long-term public relations correspondent Bob Jones, claim that Michael hated his family and would do anything to keep them small and dependent on his wealth, not upstaging his success, while manipulating people and contracts in the music industry to keep success to himself without competition from his family (Jones 2005). The siblings, says Jones (2005), were involved in strong rivalry, and Jermaine criticised him openly for turning white. Manning (2014) points out that often black male individuals who do not uphold the racial and gender-related stereotypes of the blackface minstrelsy—such as Barack Obama or Michael Jackson—are attacked for behaving "too white" and crossing racial boundaries, as does the trickster archetype. However, Manning (2016) also notes that Michael should not have been understood from a personalised racial perspective but should have rather been seen as a revolutionary who managed to free himself from the "black mask", enhancing the perception of remixing and reimagining the self through "self/other sublimation" and the recreation of boundary. His arts are a social critique from the Black American working class, a parody of Black minstrelsy. He might be described as a "modern trickster", being aware of his trickery with regard to the music industry, the manipulation of the media, his play with boundaries, stereotypes and confusion regarding self-presentation (Azaria 2017; Lock 2002).

In 2008, Michael announced that he would be doing 50 last concerts in London, England. He died on 25 June 2009 while preparing for his final tour. Reports show that he died from acute propofol intoxication, an overdose of several prescribed drugs (Sullivan 2012); however other publications maintain that Michael died as the result of a conspiracy of manipulation and intrigues (Tyrasa 2015). Wiesner (2015) emphasises that Michael died at a time when he had lost control of his life and was tricked by his managers and the music industry to prepare for the "This is it" tour. Wiesner (2015) claims that if he had not died prematurely, Michael would have developed new business models and become a "new Michael". Up to his death, Michael left the public with a kind of unpredictability, doubt, the breaking of categories, the confronting of risks, mixed feelings and experiences of the in-between which is, according to Azaria (2017), typical when the trickster archetype is at play.

Michael was described as "magic" by Beyoncé (Jackson, 2009, back cover) when putting himself into a scene, by appearing somewhere out of nowhere (Wiesner 2015), by creating music and dance and by playing with the atmosphere of the unsettling (Beebe 1981). Michael (Jackson 1992/2009) describes himself and his dance as "magic" when he becomes the dance itself, changing his body into the music and dance movement and becoming "everything that exists" (Jackson 1992/2009).

In the social media, responses to Michael's death expressed grief, empathy, God's blessings and condemnation (Sanderson and Cheong 2010). After his death, however, he was mainly celebrated as a modern hero (Wiesner 2015) and compared to his idol, Nelson Mandela, for working for his charities and good causes (Coda 2012).

23.6 Acknowledging the Trickster in Michael Jackson's Artistic Leadership: Success and Failure

It is argued in this chapter that the active application of the trickster archetype played an outstanding role in the success and failure of Michael Jackson. On one hand, the positive aspects of the trickster archetype, which loosen tight conventions, display creativity, open new topics and new horizons and support the crossing of boundaries, helped Michael Jackson to portray himself in a specific and particular light which reached out to fans across various music genres and to people of different sociocultural backgrounds and origins. It thereby contributed to his unlimited success. On the other hand, the trickster archetype showing itself in terms of a shadow, of a dubious, manipulating, incomprehensible and unbounded subject might have contributed to the failure of Michael Jackson. He can be described as a contemporary, modern trickster who played consciously with conventions, who broke the parodies of the blackface minstrelsy with a subliminal ironic and parodied break with convention in a conscious and well-arranged, rather than an unconscious way. Millions of fans around the world followed him and his ideas and visions to find new solutions for the world in a creative, intelligent and wise way (Sternberg 2003, 2006). It is assumed—since leadership often requires leaders to find solutions for highly complex and ambiguous situations (Reiter-Palmon and Illies 2005)—that Michael probably learned from an early age to deal with ambiguity in a way that might even be ambiguous itself, as well as original and innovative (Sternberg and Lubart 1995).

Undoubtedly, Michael Jackson was a leader in his crossover genres, as an artist and musician. He had the ability to move masses of individuals and groups with his music and actions, with his art to spread his message of change and healing across the world (as described in Amos 2012; Rost 1994). Over many years, he managed to create leadership stories which appeared to be authentic in that they met the needs of the audience (Avolio et al. 2004) to see an African American child star displaying characteristics of child stars from the 1930s. His leadership in music appeared to be "continuous and stable" (Avolio et al. 2004) in terms of portraying the rise of an African American child and superstar and drawing on blackface minstrelsy concepts and their parodies which are still part of the collective unconscious in the USA and the UK. It appears that the audiences could connect to what he presented, while he was able to connect to the emotions (Bennett 2016).

From his childhood onwards, Michael managed to successfully create an authentic leadership story (see Sternberg 2005), by representing aspects of blackface minstrelsy with the Jackson 5. Later on, he became an image of the American dream: a working-class African American individual who pursued his personal career. In both regards, Michael met the needs of the audience (Avolio et al. 2004), fulfilling African American stereotypes and the development of living the American dream of success through hard work, talent and original ideas as well as creativity and wit. Particularly during the first years of success, Michael managed to persuade his followers to believe that the story of leadership accomplished its aim, as he became one of the most famous and most sold artists in the global music industry.

The leadership story began to fail—as described in Sternberg (2008)—when Michael, in an attempt to build his own individualised, authentic identity, failed to address the need of the audiences. By changing his skin colour, becoming an androgynous person, and wanting to live his childhood dream in adulthood, Michael's behaviour no longer suited the aim of the audience, which was to watch an ascending African American star who is viewed as socially and culturally well-adjusted. Perhaps even these factors would not necessarily have led to failure. What truly brought him down from the leadership pedestal was the fact that he failed to implement and communicate his leadership story, that he failed to explain himself in a stable, continuous and comprehensible, authentic way. The audience seemed to struggle to believe the varying stories of his changing identity, expressed in change of skin colour, his sexuality and gender and his living on a childhood dream. Although he sang, "It don't matter if you're black or white", it obviously did matter, and his stories were not acknowledged as authentic, comprehensible, stable and fitting for a leading artist in the music industry. These stories which showed his inner ambiguity and ambivalences, his insecurities, and which failed to be coherent finally led to the decrease in his success and the taking over of scandals about his sexual preferences, child molestation, change of racial features and move towards androgyny. He failed to make his story comprehensible.

The trickster archetype—which supported Michael in terms of being perceived as creative, talented, extraordinary, original, going against convention and breaking open music genres, black and white stereotypes, gender and sexuality—finally led to his failure. When the positive aspects of the archetype were outnumbered by the negative, shadowy images of violence, confusion, dubiousness and fluidity, his leadership failed. The archaic trickster archetype is reflected in the psychic split which could not finally be contained by the audience, either seeing him as the King of Pop or condemning him (Sanderson and Cheong 2010).

23.7 Conclusions and Recommendations

Analysing the life of extraordinary individuals, their leadership, success and failure by taking archetypical influences into account, can bring new aspects of understanding to failure and success in leadership. Viewing the trickster archetype in action can broaden the understanding of ambiguous processes. This chapter aims to contribute to increasing awareness of these largely unconsciousness images, figures and symbols. Doing so, by seeing them manifested in an individual, extraordinary person, might increase the comprehensibility of the ambiguous and ambivalent thoughts, emotions and behaviours which occur in contemporary societies.

For future research, it is recommended that studies in psychobiography should take Jung's archetypal theory increasingly into consideration when analysing the life of extraordinary individuals. Archetypes active within the thoughts, emotions and actions of an individual's life should be analysed by taking the individual's sociocultural background into account. This could lead to an increased understanding of success and failure of extraordinary individuals in selected cultural or even global contexts.

References

Adams, W.L. (2008, November 24). Michael Jackson settles out of court with Sheik. *Time.* http://content.time.com/time/arts/article/0,8599,1861497,00.html.

Allport, G.W. (1961). *Pattern and growth in personality.* New York, NY: Holt, Rinehart & Winston.

Amos, T.L. (2012). The dynamics of leadership. In D. Hellriegel, J. Slocum, S.E. Jackson, L. Louw, G. Staude, T.L. Amos, H.B. Klopper, M.J. Louw, T.F.J. Oosthuizen, S. Perks, & S. Zindiye (Eds.), *Management* (pp. 370–401). Cape Town: Oxford University Press Southern Africa.

Anderson, J. (Producer), & Shaw, J. (Director). (2002). *Living with Michael Jackson* (Documentary). United Kingdom: Granada Television.

Artlima (2015). *Kunstwerke von Michael Jackson: Die unbekannte Seite eines Weltstars.* Basel, Switzerland: Reinhardt Verlag.

Avolio, B.J., Gardner, W.L., Walumbwa, F.O., Luthans, F. & May, D.R. (2004). Unlocking the mask: A look at the process by which authentic leaders impact follower attitudes and behaviors. *The Leadership Quarterly*, 15, 801–823.

Azaria, T. (2017). Trickster: Archetype of Changing Times. *Depth Insights. Seeing the world with Soul*, 10. http://www.depthinsights.com/Depth-Insights-scholarly-ezine/issue-10-fall-2017/#.

Beebe, J. (1981). The Trickster in the Arts. *The San Francisco Jung Institute Library Journal*, 2(2), 21–54. doi: https://doi.org/10.1525/jung.1.1981.2.2.21.

Bennett, M. (2016). Relational Leadership, storytelling, and narratives: practices of local government chief executives. *Public Administration and the Disciplines*, 77(4). https://doi.org/10.1111/puar.12680.

Boteach, S. (2009, October 29). The myth that Michael Jackson was healthy and happy. *Huffington Post.* http://www.huffingtonpost.com/rabbi-shmuley-boteach/the-myth-that-michael-jac_b_338196.html.

Brackett, D. (2012). Black or White? Michael Jackson and the idea of crossover. *Popular Music and Society*, 35(2), 169–185.

Brunner, S. (2013). Was he the man in the mirror? *Journal of Integrated Studies*, 4(1). http://jis.athabascau.ca/index.php/jis/article/view/101/109.

Coda. (2012). Michael Jackson – A troubled genius (OV). Dublin, UK: Coda International.

Den Uijl, S. (2010). The trickster "Archetpye" in the Shahnama. *Iranian Studies*, 43(1), 71–90.

Erni, J.N. (1998). Queer figurations in the media: Critical reflections on the Michael Jackson sex scandal. *Critical Studies in Mass Communication*, 15(2), 158–180.

Fast, S. (2010). Difference that exceeded understanding: Remembering Michael Jackson (1958–2009). *Popular Music and Society*, 33(2), 259–266.

Fast, S. (2012). Michael Jackson's Queer Musical Belongings. *Popular Music and Society*, 35(2), 281–300.

Garrison, J. (2009). Teacher as prophetic trickster. Educational Theory, 59(1). https://doi.org/10.1111/j.1741-5446.2009.00307.x.

Gupta, V., & Van Wart, M. (2015). *Leadership across the globe.* New York, NY: Routledge.

Hall, J.A. (1989). *Jung: Interpreting your dreams—A guidebook to Jungian dream philosophy and psychology.* New York: St. Martin's Press.

Hyde, L. (1998). *Trickster makes this world; Mischief, myth and art.* New York, NY: Farrar, Straus, & Giroux.

Hynes, W. J. & Doty, W.G. (Eds.). (1993). *Mythical Trickster Figures. Contours, Contexts, and Criticisms*. Tuscaloosa and London: University of Alabama Press.

Jackson, M. (1988). *Moonwalk*. New York: Doubleday.

Jackson, M. (1992/2009). *Dancing the Dream*. New York: Doubleday.

Jackson, J. (2012). *You are not alone – Mein Bruder Michael Jackson*. Höfen: Hannibal Verlag.

Johansson, M. (2012). Michael Jackson and the expressive power of voice-produced sound. *Popular Music and Society*, 35(2), 261–279.

Jones, B. (2005). *Michael Jackson: The man behind the mask: An insider's story of the king of pop*. New York: SelectBooks.

Jung, C.G. (1936). *The concept of the collective unconscious*. Collected Works, 9(1).

Jung, C.G. (1969). On the Psychology of the Trickster-Figure in *The Archetypes and the Collective Unconscious*. 2nd edition. Trans. R.F.C. Hull. Princeton, NJ: Princeton University Press, 1969. Vol. 9, part I of *The Collected Works of C. G. Jung*. (pp. 255–272).

Jung, C.G. (1971). *Psychological types*. Princeton, NJ: Princeton University Press.

Jung, C.G. & von Franz, M. (1985). *The Grail legend*. Boston: Sigo Press.

King, L. (2009, July 20). Interview with Joe Jackson. CNN *Larry King Live*. New York, NY: CNN Network.

Lock, H. (2002). Transformations of the Trickster. *Southern Cross Review*. https://southerncross-review.org/18/trickster.htm.

Manning, H.J. (2014). Manning in Interview. Michael Jackson: Subverting Blackface Stereotypes. https://dancingwiththeelephant.wordpress.com/2014/01/02/michael-jackson-and-the-blackface-mask/.

Manning, H.J. (2016). *Michael Jackson and the Blackface Mask*. London: Routledge.

Mayer, C.-H. (2017). *The life and creative works of Paulo Coelho. A Psychobiography from a Positive Psychology Perspective*. Cham, Switzerland: Springer.

Mercer, K. (1993). Monster metaphors: Notes on Michael Jackson's Thriller. In S. Frith, A. Goodwin, & L. Grossberg (Eds.), *Sound and Vision. The Music Video Reader* (pp. 93–108). London: Routledge.

Nikitina, S. (2012). Hackers as Tricksters of the digital age: creativity in hacker culture. *The Journal of Popular Culture*, 45(1). https://doi.org/10.1111/j.1540-5931.2011.00915.x.

Northcote, M.T. (2012). Selecting Criteria to Evaluate Qualitative research. In M. Kiley (Ed.), *Narratives of Transition: Perspectives of Research Leaders, Educators & Postgraduates*. (pp. 99–110). Paper presented at the 10th Quality in Postgraduate Research Conference, StamfordGrand, Adelaide, 17–20 April. Canberra, Australia: The Centre for Higher Education, Learning and Teaching. The Australian National University. http://www.qpr.edu.au/wp-content/uploads/2015/09/QPR_2012_proceedings-1.pdf.

Northouse, P.G. (2013). *Leadership: Theory and practice*. 6th edition. Thousand Oaks, CA: Sage.

Northouse, P.G. (2016). *Leadership: Theory and practice*. 7th edition. Thousand Oaks, CA: Sage.

Nunn, T. (2009, July 5). Michael Jackson's Peter Pan obsession. *The Sunday Times*. http://www.thesundaytimes.co.uk/sto/culture/arts/theatre/article176195.ece.

Oliver, P. (2006). Purposive sampling. In V. Jupp (Ed.), *The Sage Dictionary of Social Research Methods* (pp. 244–245). London: Sage.

Pinsky, D. & Young, M. (2009). *The mirror effect: How celebrity narcissism is seducing America*. New York: HarperCollins Publishers.

Ponterotto, J.G. (2014). Best practices in psychobiographical research. Ethical considerations and publishing. *Qualitative Psychology,* 1(1), 77–90. doi: https://doi.org/10.1037/qup0000005.

Radin, P. (1956/1971). *The Trickster: A Study in American Indian Mythology*. New York: Schecken.

Reason, P. & Marshall, J. (2001). On working with graduate research students. In P. Reason & H. Bradbury (Eds.), *Handbook of action research: Participative inquiry and practice* (pp. 413–419). Thousand Oaks, CA: Sage.

Reiter-Palmon, R. & Illies, J.J. (2005). Leadership and creativity: understanding leadership from a creative problem-solving perspective. *The Leadership Quarterly*, 15(1), 55–77.

Risi, A. & Pade, S. (2017). *Make that change: Michael Jackson.* Botschaft und Schicksal eines spirituellen Revolutionärs. Rheinau: Govinda.
Rosen, D.H., Smith, S.M., Huston, H.L. & Gonzalez, G. (1991). Empirical study of associations between symbols and their meanings: evidence of collective unconscious (archetypal) memory. *Journal of Analytical Psychology*, 36, 211–228.
Rost, J.C. (1994). Spirit at work: discovering the spirituality in leadership. *The Journal of Leadership Studies*, 2(2), 158–160.
Runyan W.M. (1988). *Psychology and historical interpretation.* Hoboken, NJ: Oxford University Press.
Sanderson, J., & Cheong, P.H. (2010). Tweeting prayers and communicating grief over Michael Jackson online. *Bulletin of Science, Technology & Society*, 20(5), 328–340.
Schultz, W.T. (2005). Introducing psychobiography. In W.T. Schultz (Ed.), *Handbook of psychobiography* (pp. 3–18). New York, NY: Oxford University Press.
Snider, C. (2009). *The stuff that dreams are made on: A Jungian interpretation of literature.* Illinois: Chiron Publications.
Stein, M. (2009). *Jung's map of the soul.* Peru, Il: Open Court Publishing Company.
Stephens, J.P., & Carmeli, A. (2016). Relational Leadership and Creativity: The Effects of Respectful Engagement and Caring on Meaningfulness and Creative Work Involvement. In S. Hemlin & M.D. Mumford (Eds.), *Handbook of Research on Creativity and Leadership.* Cheltenham, UK: Edward Elgar Publishing.
Sternberg, R.J. (2003). Creative thinking in the classroom. *Scandinavian Journal of Educational Research*, 47, 325–338. doi:https://doi.org/10.1080/00313830308595.
Sternberg, R.J. (2005). *The WICS model of organizational leadership.* https://dspace.mit.edu/bitstream/handle/1721.1/55937/CPL_WP_05_06_Sternberg.pdf
Sternberg, R.J. (2006). The nature of creativity. *Creativity Research Journal*, 18(1), 87–98.
Sternberg, R.J. (2008). The WICS approach to leadership: Stories of leadership and the structure and processes that support them. *The Leadership Quarterly*, 19(3), 360–371.
Sternberg, R. J., & Lubart, T.I. (1995). *Defying the crowd: Cultivating creativity in a culture of conformity.* New York, NY: The Free Press.
Sullivan, R. (2012). *Untouchable: The strange life and tragic death of Michael Jackson.* Great Britain, UK: MPG Books Group.
Taraborelli, J.R. (2009). *Michael Jackson: The magic, the madness, the whole story.* New York, NY: Pan Books.
Terre Blanche, M., Durrheim, K., & Kelly, K. (2006). First steps in qualitative data analysis. In M. Terre Blanche, K. Durrheim, & D. Painter (Eds.), *Research in practice: Applied methods for the social sciences* (pp. 321–344). Cape Town, South Africa: University of Cape Town.
Tyrasa, J. (2015). *Pans letztes Lied – Die Michael Jackson Verschwörung.* Chicago: One World Production.
Velie, A.R. (1991). *American Indian Literature. An Anthology.* Revised Edition. Oklahoma: University of Oklahoma Press.
Vogel, J. (2011). *Man in the Music. The Creative Life and Work of Michael Jackson.* New York: Sterling.
Warwick, J. (2012). "You can't win, child, but you can't get out of the game": Michael Jackson's transition from child star to superstar. *Popular Music and Society*, 35(2), 241–259.
Wiesner, D. (2015). *Michael Jackson: Die wahre Geschichte.* Berlin: Artlima
Winfrey, O. (1993, February 10). The Michael Jackson Interview. Video file. http://www.youtube.com/watch?v=WZpnmpP2TlQ.
Winfrey, O. (2010, October 21). Lisa Marie Presley talks about Michael Jackson. https://www.youtube.com/watch?v=_iQt3bPuwAk.
Yin, R.K. (2009). *Case study research: Design and methods.* 4th edition. Thousand Oaks, CA: Sage.

Claude-Hélène Mayer, (Dr. habil., PhD, PhD) is a professor in Industrial and Organisational Psychology at the Department of Industrial Psychology and People Management at the University of Johannesburg, an Adjunct Professor at the European University Viadrina in Frankfurt (Oder), Germany, and a Senior Research Associate at Rhodes University, Grahamstown, South Africa. She holds a PhD in Psychology (University of Pretoria, South Africa), a PhD in Management (Rhodes University, South Africa), a Doctorate (Georg-August University, Germany) in Political Sciences (socio-cultural anthropology and intercultural didactics), and a Habilitation (European University Viadrina, Germany) in Psychology with focus on work, organizational and cultural psychology. She has published several monographs, text collections, accredited journal articles and special issues on transcultural mental health and well-being, sense of coherence, shame, transcultural conflict management and mediation, women in leadership in culturally diverse work contexts, constellation work, coaching and psychobiography.

Chapter 24
The Cognitive Bias in Cross-Cultural Design

Pei-Luen Patrick Rau, Zhi Guo, Nan Qie, Xin Lei, and Andong Zhang

Abstract Cognitive biases are often treated as cognitive constraints or flaws in the design of the mind that were not overcome. But in an evolutionary perspective, they do make a lot of sense as they were evolved and not eliminated. This chapter provides an original and positive perspective to view cognitive bias. The outline includes the theoretical framework and empirical research on the cognitive bias in the cross-cultural design and the integrative framework of design processing with the consideration of the cognitive bias. The first section reviewed the foundations of cognitive bias in cross-cultural design and discussed the relationship between cognitive bias and user-centered design. The second and third sections summarized the empirical researches on the cognitive bias in cross-cultural design. In the last section, we addressed handling cognitive bias would link design processing with innovation outcomes for the system design in cultural contexts and design team.

Keywords Mistakes · Errors · Failure · Cognitive bias · Cross-cultural design · Cultural difference · User-centered design

24.1 Introduction

In industry, cross-cultural cooperation is more prevalent with the globalization of information technology and economy. But practitioners did not take the interaction of human, machine, and environment into account and were not aware of the significance of culture as a dimension during the localization process. System failures or mistakes caused some business failure, critical crashes, and disasters. For example, the radical reason for Korean Air Flight 801 crash in Guam International Airport is related to the obedience to the authority specific in Asian cultures such as Chinese, Japanese, and Korean cultures (Murata 2017). Badre (2002) introduces the term

P.-L. P. Rau (✉) · Z. Guo · N. Qie · X. Lei · A. Zhang
Department of Industrial Engineering, Tsinghua University, Beijing, China
e-mail: rpl@mail.tsinghua.edu.cn; jennyguo@mail.tsinghua.edu.cn; qienan14@mails.tsinghua.edu.cn; lei-x16@mails.tsinghua.edu.cn; zad17@mails.tsinghua.edu.cn

E. Vanderheiden, C.-H. Mayer (eds.), *Mistakes, Errors and Failures across Cultures*, https://doi.org/10.1007/978-3-030-35574-6_24

culturability to stress the importance of the interrelatedness of culture and usability. The differences are embodied in attentional allocation, contextual sensitivity, spatial cognition, processing of persuasion messages and decision-making, and other cultural factors, which must be taken into account during localizing the product or service besides language. These factors are often neglected during design localization and result in poor user experience.

The cultural inconsistencies on human cognition or cultural biases in human cognition might be regarded as human errors by designers and practitioners. Actually in the evolutionary perspective, it is a kind of cognitive bias resulting from the trade-off between information processing time and accuracy in different environments and is a kind of genuine bias and biased response pattern to adaptive problem due to various cultural norms. Therefore, the connection between cultural bias and human-machine interfaces is not negligible.

24.2 Cognitive Bias

Due to bounded rationality (Loewenstein et al. 2001; Miller 1956; Pfister and Böhm 2008; Simon 1955; Wang et al. 2001), an individual systematically misperceives objective reality and predictably does not conform to standards, the laws of logic, and mathematical accuracy of probability theory when making a judgment (Hilbert 2012; Johnson et al. 2013; Kahneman and Tversky 1973). The occurrence ranged from observation (objective information) to decision-making (subjective estimate) of human information processing (Haselton et al. 2015; Hilbert 2012). These phenomena are called cognitive biases and are basic features of human cognition.

Generally, cognitive biases are often treated as cognitive constraints or flaws in the design of the mind that were not overcome. It would indeed cause some disastrous consequences for society. For example, investors overestimate or underestimate risk, which is embodied in the worldwide economic crisis of 2008 (Ariely 2008; Greenspan 2008). On the other hand, cognitive biases could help to predict individual behavior. Furthermore, the human mind does not develop and evolve for perfection or even theoretical optimization, but simply for fitness in a specific environment (Haselton et al. 2015; Johnson et al. 2013) and a rational trade-off between time and accuracy (Lieder et al. 2018).

24.2.1 The Type and Mechanism

Cognitive biases comprise biases in attention, perception, memory, representation of mental model, and prediction or interpretation. In the process of attention, the biases contain those ones such as attentional biases toward threat, eating disorders, smoking, alcohol use, etc. (Hakamata et al. 2010; McNally 2019). For example, threat-related attentional biases refer to the tendency of humans to protect them from threats to safety and health (Haselton et al. 2015) and are almost associated with the anxiety emotion (Hakamata et al. 2010). As to perception (Hubbard 2018), listeners tend to consistently respond at an average of 500 ms before the arrival of the real approaching sound source, namely, auditory looming. Although the arrival time of visually approaching sound source would not be underestimated when the whole approaching process of the looming object was observed, it would be underestimated when the visual approaching object disappears before arriving the observer. In the memory process, the recall for the first and end items of the list is always easier than that for the middle items, namely, primacy and recency effects (Glanzer and Cunitz 1966; Kelly and Risko 2019; Murdock Jr 1962). In addition, for example, the recency effect is more obvious when the list is displayed via speech than writing (Degelder 1994), items displayed in pictures are more easily remembered than those displayed in words (Curran and Doyle 2011; Shepard 1967), and in-context items are much easier to recall than the out-of-context items (Hupbach et al. 2011). As to representation, frequency is more understandable and easier to reduce the error rate than probability (Mellers et al. 2001). For example, research suggests medical doctors would likely misinterpret the meaning and application of survival rate (Gigerenzer and Wegwarth 2013). In motivated reasoning, human would seek or interpret the evidence in the ways related to existing beliefs, expectations, or a hypothesis, namely, confirmation bias (Oswald and Grosjean 2004).

The mechanism of cognitive bias generally includes two types of explanations. One explanation is that cognitive bias is the result of limited information processing capacity and time (Lieder et al. 2018; Miller 1956). It could explain the occurrence of all heuristic and shortcuts (i.e., adjustment and anchoring, primacy and recency effects, frequency bias). It relates to the priming stimuli (first stimuli that come to mind and the first thought) and the mental model in memory. If the design is not consistent with the mental model, it will cause new biases or errors. For example, confirmation bias is motivated by the dissonance with the mental model or previous cognition (Stone and Wood 2018). The other explanation is the results of emotional and social influence and motivational factors. It is also called the results of adaption (Haselton et al. 2015; Pfister and Böhm 2008; Wang et al. 2001). This kind of cognitive bias is a genuine bias and biased response pattern to adaptive problems. It is related to threat, social exchange, interpersonal interaction, and self-evaluation (Haselton et al. 2015). It is useful to reduce error costs than unbiased response patterns. As humans are not the truth seekers but adaptation executors, they would trade off the cost of taking unnecessary action and the cost of failing to take action. For example, group thinking is that a group of people is easier to lead to an irrational or dysfunctional decision-making outcome due to pursuing harmony or conformity (Janis 2008). If not, potential ostracism would happen. The cost is very high, especially in collectivism culture.

24.2.2 The Connection with User-Centered Design

The user-centered design approach is proposed to make the design of everyday things and complex systems intuitive (Norman and Draper 1986). As mentioned above, if the design is not consistent with the human mind, it would make human error. Therefore, cognitive biases as design features need to take into account in user-centered design. For example, humans tend to avoid or reduce inconsistencies between what they hope to be true and what they observe. It is called cognitive dissonance and would trigger motivated reasoning and then lead to confirmation bias and further cause future cognitive dissonance (Stone and Wood 2018). IKEA and Lego's self-assembly service design is taking advantage of the process range from cognitive dissonance to confirmation bias (Stone and Wood 2018). As consumers participated in the production, they evaluated a higher value of the goods they assembled than that of fully assembled goods before purchase. Also, cognitive bias shows that human-centered decision-making approaches would take a risk, especially in the safety field (i.e., aviation). The introduction of information system promotes data-driven decision-making to reduce the risk of disastrous consequence for a society (O'Driscoll et al. 2019).

No matter the cognitive bias is the design feature or purpose, the information process is influenced by culture due to top-down information processing. For example, the mental model is different as the concept formation is influenced by cultures (Kövecses 2010). Time orientation is also affected by cultures. People in polychromic time culture (i.e., Chinese) are more likely to do many things at once and focus more on relationships, but people in monochromic time culture (i.e., German) do one thing at a time and focus more on tasks (Benabou 1999; Rau et al. 2011). It might be influence the choice of humans due to time management and bounded rationality. These characteristics would further influence the appearance and navigation in design. Furthermore, culture is evolved by generations and is a kind of biased response patterns in the evolutionary perspective. For example, the self-concept and interpersonal relationship are different in cultures (Bochner 1994; Gudykunst et al. 1988). So the cognition about these dimensions affects the human-computer interaction.

24.3 Cross-Cultural Influence in Human Cognition

Generally, researchers grouped people from China and the countries influenced by Chinese culture, like Japan and South Korea together as "East Asians" and people from European culture as "Westerners." According to Hofstede's country theory, East Asians tend to be more collectivistic, whereas Westerners tend to be more individualistic (Hofstede and Hofstede 2004). The thinking process has been proved to be closely linked to the individualism-collectivism cultural background (Ju 2015), namely, holistic thinking and analytic thinking. As an example of holistic thinking culture, East Asians consider themselves as a part of the whole society and place

Table 24.1 Cross-cultural cognitive process (Nisbett et al. 2001)

Dimension	Descriptions
Attention and perception	East Asians tend to pay more attention to environmental factors and more likely to figure out relationships among events, whereas Westerners tend to focus more on a salient object.
Attribution	East Asians tend to explain events more with respect to the field (contexts and situations), while Westerners tend to explain events more with respect to object's inner properties.
Control	East Asians believe less in controllability than Westerners.
Prediction	East Asians tend to take into account more potential factors, and their predictions have vast candidates. They also tend not to be surprised by any particular outcome, as they are ready to find explanations in the complex circumstances of potentially relevant factors.
Habits of organizing the world	East Asians emphasize relationships, while Westerners prefer categories.
Logic thinking	Westerners have a stronger tendency to logical reasoning, while East Asians tend to have more empirical inferences.
Dialectical approaches	East Asians tend to look for middle way when confronted with contradictions, while Westerners insist on the correctness of one belief vs. another.

more emphases on their relationships with other parts (i.e., other people, environmental factors) than Westerners (Heine et al. 1999; Nisbett et al. 2001). On the contrary, Westerners are more likely to view themselves as self-contained and autonomous, thus leading them to be analytic thinkers (Heine et al. 1999; Nisbett et al. 2001).

Nisbett et al. (2001) summarized that culture affects cognitive processing in the following seven dimensions (shown in Table 24.1): (1) attention and perception, (2) attribution, (3) control, (4) prediction, (5) habits of organizing the world, (6) logic thinking, and (7) dialectical approaches.

In summary, we can categorize these cognitive biases into four steps of cognitive processes: attention, perception, interpretation, and action selection. In the following parts, we will explain how culture affects these aspects of the cognitive process.

24.3.1 Attention

As to attention, Nisbett et al. (2001) claimed East Asians are inclined to pay more attention to environmental factors and more likely to detect relationships among different parts, whereas Westerners tend to focus more on a salient object. For instance, in a usability study of in-vehicle information systems (IVIS), Chinese drivers preferred extra information of environment to support their driving, while Swedish drivers regarded the same interface as a distraction in urgent situations (Wang et al. 2016). Evidence from eye movement indicated Japanese paid more attention to surrounding people and environment when recognizing facial expressions compared to Americans (Matsumoto 1992). The difference can be explained by the holistic and analytic thinking as East Asians always consider target and environment as a whole (Nisbett et al. 2001).

24.3.2 Perception

It has been shown that culture unconsciously affects one's perception in verbal texts, images, music, etc. (Ju 2015; Nisbett et al. 2001). A cross-cultural study of American and Japanese showed that Japanese perceptions of emotion would be influenced surrounding people's emotions, while Americans viewed people as autonomous (Matsumoto 1992). East Asians and Westerners also showed differences in music perceptions as well. Individuals from America (Western countries, the system of analytic thinking) tend to perceive music independent of context (i.e., music story), while individuals from Korea (East Asians, the system of holistic thinking systems) tend to rely on context when perceiving music (Ju 2015). Another study on spontaneous attention to word content and emotional tone across cultures suggested that Japanese (East Asians) showed greater difficulty in ignoring vocal tone than Americans in Stroop tasks (Ishii et al. 2010).

24.3.3 Interpretation

As to interpreting progress, the cross-cultural study shows that cultural-specific factors like language, history, and religion are supposed to affect people's understanding of colors, icons, symbol, and pictures (Bourges-Waldegg and Scrivener 1998). Boor and Russo (1993) also discussed the use and understanding of colors used in websites across countries. Their findings were summarized in Table 24.2 and suggested the same color may have different meanings across culture and should be carefully used in website design.

Table 24.2 The color-culture chart (Russo and Boor 1993)

	China	Japan	Egypt	France	USA
Red	Happiness	Anger Danger	Death	Aristocracy	Danger Stop
Blue	Heavens Clouds	Villainy	Virtue Faith Truth	Freedom Peace	Masculine
Green	Ming Dynasty Heavens	Future Youth Energy	Fertility Strength	Criminality	Safety Go
Yellow	Birth Wealth Power	Grace Nobility	Happiness Prosperity	Temporary	Cowardice Temporary
White	Death Purity	Death	Joy	Neutrality	Purity

Also, Dasen (2018) suggested culture will influence people's spatial interpretation. There are three frames of reference which can be used to describe the spatial location of objects, intrinsic (object-centered), egocentric (observer-centered), and geocentric (environment-centered) (Levinson 2003). In the intrinsic frame, objects are described in reference to each other (i.e., next to, near, inside, etc.). In the egocentric frame, objects are described from the view of the observer (i.e., right, left, etc.). The egocentric frame is preferred in many language systems, including Arabic, Bantu languages, Indo-European, and Japanese (Levinson 2003) (Dasen 2018). Geocentric frame describes objects with distant geographic features and coordinates (i.e., to the mountain, toward the sea, north, east, etc.). Dasen (2018) stated that two cultures showed different preferences toward spatial frames even if they used the same language.

Another important aspect of the interpretation is attribution. Nisbett et al. (2001) believed that cultural differences between East Asians and Westerners in the sense of attribution could be tracked to Ancient China and Ancient Greek. For instance, Ancient Chinese people associated cosmic events (e.g., comets) with important occurrences in history, while Ancient Greeks believed that there was a fundamental nature of the world. For instance, they tried to find out regularities behind the world (i.e., the regularity of cosmic events). As a result, East Asians tend to explain events, with respect to the field (contexts and situations), while Westerners tend to explain events more with respect to the object's inner properties (Nisbett et al. 2001). A study on self-serving attribution bias indicated Westerners presented a higher level of self-serving bias than East Asians. In other words, Westerners are more likely to attribute success to their own abilities and efforts but attribute failure to external factors (Mezulis et al. 2004).

24.3.4 Action Selection

As to a very simple action, saying yes or no, a younger person in high power-distance culture (i.e., Japan) will consider it's improper to say "no" to a senior person (Hofstede and Hofstede 2004). When it comes to user behaviors in human-computer interaction, people from high uncertainty avoidance and strong task orientation culture (i.e., German) preferred to use less mouse movement or mouse clicks than culture with lower uncertainty avoidance and task orientation (i.e., China). Web structure should be customized to fit the target culture according to the concept of structure congruity. For instance, users from China preferred websites with a hierarchical structure, while a search-based structure may be preferred in Germany (Luna et al. 2002). High-context and low-context culture could affect people's interaction style. Further studies on cross-cultural studies showed Chinese users preferred instant and affective communication than are German students when using social networks (Raue 2008). It is because instant and affective messaging can provide nonverbal information (i.e., typing speed) to help users in a high-context culture communicate with each other. As China is a polychronic time-oriented culture, Chinese drivers can deal more tasks at the same time than English and German drivers when driving (Heimgärtner et al. 2007). It is because Westerners are monochronic time-oriented, prefer to do things one at a time, and divide time into precise, small units (Heimgärtner et al. 2007).

24.4 Cross-Cultural Design

In human-computer interaction, "user" actually refers to a group of users with more or less homogeneous languages and mental models (Dix 1998). Therefore, interaction design should put more emphasis on the cognitive aspects of user groups from different cultures. Culture is supposed to influence users' cognitive process in attention, perception, interpretation and action selection, and affect users' attitudes and behaviors through the following four manifestations: values, heroes, rituals, and symbols (Hofstede and Hofstede 2004; Luna and Gupta 2001).

This section pays attention to the cross-cultural design from the perspective of the website design because websites are an important vehicle for spreading opinions to people in global contexts. It has been proven that Internet behavior varies with both national culture and level of economic development (Barnett and Sung 2005), but the impact of cultural differences on website design has been ignored (Kim et al. 2009).

Windl and Heimgärtner (2013) developed a cultural model to expand the concept of usage-centered design (Table 24.3). It involves appearance, navigation, metaphors, mental models, and interaction. The goal of culture-centered design and cross-cultural study is to assure that users will not be offended or confused by the interface addressing him/her not only in his/her own language but in the language of his culture (Rimondi 2015).

24.4.1 *Appearance*

Nowadays, a website is a conglomerate of images, multimedia, interactive features, animated graphics, and sounds (Würtz 2005). Cross-cultural website design requires considering many factors, including culture-specific color connotations, animation, sounds, and other effects.

Table 24.3 Content of the cultural model about the usage-centered design (Windl and Heimgärtner 2013, pp. 5)

Dimensions	Examples
Appearance	Color, layout, font, density, etc.
Navigation	Hierarchy, menu tree, structure, etc.
Metaphors	Sound, icons, symbols, etc.
Mental models	Context, cognitive style, metaphysics, etc.
Interaction	Speed, frequency, etc.

When it comes to graphic interface, the cross-cultural design should pay attention to the graphical elements such as icons, colors, and symbols because there may be some problems of understanding and interpretation due to cultures but not limited to language (Russo and Boor 1993). For instance, users may not be able to associate the image of icon to the intended concept correctly. The images of icons may not be acceptable to some users. Additionally, the use and understanding of colors also vary across countries (see Table 24.2). For example, red represents danger in the USA but happiness in China. Green means safety in the USA but criminality in France. Besides, as regards symbols, it is not effective to use a red "X" as a forbidden symbol in Egypt because red does not mean forbiddance, and "X" is not interpreted as prohibitive (Garland 1982; Russo and Boor 1993).

Würtz (2005) conducted a cross-cultural, qualitative analysis of websites from nine countries: the USA, Germany, Denmark, Sweden, Norway, Finland, Japan, China, and Korea. It is found that websites in Asian countries highly employ animation and images of moving people in particular. In the North American and European countries, however, websites use fewer animation and are mainly reserved for highlighting effects of the text. Another study also supports this finding. Kim et al. (2009) found more animation, more splash pages, more clickable images, and more streaming videos of South Korean websites than those of American websites.

Also, websites in Asian countries employ images describing products used by individuals, while North American and European websites employ images portraying lifestyles of individuals without a direct emphasis on the use of products (Würtz 2005). Similar results are found in other studies. Information of products and purchasing products is provided in American apparel websites, whereas information about consumers' relationship to their community appeared on Korean apparel websites (Sook Lee et al. 2007). Such a difference is reflected not only in the website design but also in the web advertisements. It's noted that the USA and the UK emphasize consumer-message and consumer-marketer interactivity, while South Korea and Japan emphasize consumer-consumer interactivity (Cho and Cheon 2005).

24.4.2 Navigation

Würtz (2005) analyzed websites from nine countries including Asian, European, and North American countries. It is found that websites in Asian countries are more process-oriented, while those in Europe and America are more goal-oriented. The former promotes an exploratory way of website navigation, while the latter provides clear and redundant cues of navigation to ensure that users can find the target. More sidebars and menus are used in Asian websites. Besides, Asian websites open new browser windows for each new page, whereas Western websites constantly open the same browser window. Asian websites are more likely to use images to convey information regarding navigation elements. For example, hyperlinks on Japanese websites were represented by images, but they were displayed in the text on Scandinavian websites.

Table 24.4 Ranking of preferred navigation tools in four countries (Seidenspinner and Theuner 2007)

Navigation tools	Germany	Egypt	China	USA
Navigation bars	1	5	3	1
Hyperlinks in text	2	4	4	3
Graphics/pictures	3	2	1	2
Search mask on website	4	6	2	4
Sitemaps	5	7	5	5
Mouse-over links	6	1	5	6
Pop-up windows	7	3	3	7

The perceived effectiveness of design features in website navigation varies a lot from culture to culture. Seidenspinner and Theuner (2007) summarized several common navigation tools: navigation bars, hyperlinks in text, graphics/pictures, search mask on the website, site maps, mouse-over links, and pop-up windows. They invited web users from Germany, the USA, China, and Egypt to rank these navigation tools according to their personal preference. Table 24.4 presents the ranking of preferred navigation tools by users. On the whole, navigation bars, graphics/pictures, and hyperlinks in the text were ranked high, whereas site maps were ranked low in all the four countries. Differences still existed. For example, pop-up windows were ranked high by Egyptian users and Chinese users but low by German and American users. Mouse-over links were ranked first by Egyptian users but low by users from other countries.

Although navigation bars were ranked high by users from different cultures as the most preferred navigation tools (Seidenspinner and Theuner 2007), cultural differences were found by Kim et al. (2009). Two common kinds of navigation bars are pull-down and rollover. According to Badre (2002), the pull-down bars are arranged linearly and organized as plain textual information, whereas the rollover bars are more colorful and differently shaped. Among the Korean websites surveyed, 53% used rollovers and 43% used pull-downs. As for the American websites surveyed, 20% used rollovers and 19% used pull-downs.

24.4.3 Metaphor

Metaphor is a way to directly refer to one thing by mentioning another. All interfaces are to some extent metaphoric (Preece et al. 1994). For example, the desktop of the Windows operating system is a metaphor of the desktop in the real world. A metaphor can help users quickly map the related concept onto the system. Once the user understands the concept of desktop, it becomes natural to use files and file folders in the system.

Except for the worldwide accepted metaphor such as desktop and file folders, there are metaphors that are possibly understood differently among cultures. To learn about the cultural differences in understanding of specific vocabulary, sound, icon, or symbol is necessary for cross-cultural interface design.

The same label or symbol may be perceived differently across cultures. For example, people from different cultures perceive hazard at different levels regarding the same warning label. When the relative level of word strength was similar, the Chinese participants tended to perceive less hazard than the US participants. Evers et al. (1999) found perception difference in understanding of campus-related metaphor between Dutch and English participants. Designers should pay attention to these differences during icon and interface design.

24.4.4 Mental Model

In the HCI field, the designer's or the user's mental model can be described by a network structure that consists of the whole set of concept elements and the connections between them. The mental model cannot be observed directly by the designers and can only be inferred through the user's behaviors. The wrong mental model may reduce the user's performance (Allen 1997). The structure is highly related to a person's cognitive style (Qian et al. 2011).

East Asian people are considered more field-dependent, thus tending to pay more attention to the context than Western people (Witkin et al. 1974). Masuda et al. (2008) found that when participants were asked to watch a cartoon depicting a person with a certain kind of emotion surrounded by other people showing a different emotion from the central person, Japanese participants' judgments of the central person's emotion were more influenced by the surrounded people's emotions, while Western participants' judgments were not. During interface design, designers for Eastern users should consider more on the consistency of the main contents and the context, and designers for Western users should put all information in the main contents.

The thinking style of Eastern people is holistic, synthetic, concrete, and parallel, while the thinking style of Western people is analytic, abstract, imaginative, and linear (Rau et al. 2004). Kim and Lee (2005) indicated that Korean participants performed significantly better in recognizing concrete icons, while American participants performed abstract icons. The finding is in line with that Eastern people have a more concrete thinking style, while Western people have a more abstract thinking style. In another experimental study on cultural differences in computer performance, for Chinese people in both mainland China and Taiwan, computer performance error rate is lower when information is in thematic structure (Rau et al. 2004).

24.4.5 *Interaction*

Interaction refers to the way people get, understand, and give feedback to the information provided by the system. Interaction designers should consider how the system should provide information.

The researchers found that people in high-context culture prefer to trust and follow the information given implicitly, while people in low-context culture prefer the explicit way. In human-robot interaction, when robots suggested a different idea, Chinese people changed their decisions more when collaborating with robots that communicated implicitly, while American people do so when collaborating with robots that communicated explicitly (Wang et al. 2010). Chinese people, compared to German people, were more inclined to accept implicit recommendations (Rau et al. 2009). In intercultural collaborating teams, Chinese participants showed higher level of trust satisfaction, and future collaboration intention on an implicit advisor, compared to American and German participants (Li et al. 2014).

People from a different cultural background not only prefer a different way of information presentation, but they also understand the same outcome in different ways. When a service failure happens, Americans (versus Chinese) are more disappointed with an outcome failure but less dissatisfied with a process failure. When they express their dissatisfactions, Americans prefer voice response, but the Chinese prefer private response (Chan and Wan 2008).

24.5 Cross-Cultural Design Process Based on Cognitive Bias

In the cross-cultural design process, besides the cross-cultural design feature of the web mentioned above, the design team could also treat cognitive bias as a design purpose to help humans correct the bias by system design. It involves two aspects: debiasing design and reduction bias among the design team.

24.5.1 *The Consideration of Users' Cognitive Bias in Design Processing*

Bias could cause disastrous consequences in safety management. Therefore, debiasing design in the cross-cultural design of safety management is indispensable. It includes the prevention of artifacts due to inappropriate design based on the cultural influence in human cognition. For example, individuals in Western countries think a knob on an electrical appliance increases the appliance's output when turned clockwise, but the system design a water or gas tap or faucet (Murata 2017). The faucet operation is totally in contrast to that of a knob. It also should involve culture dimension in the development of safety management culture and human-machine system (Murata 2017) as it is a biased response pattern. Taking Korean Air Flight 801 crash as an example, the absolute obedience to authority in high power-distance culture leads to subordinate who did not correct the captain's misunderstanding of VHF Omnidirectional Range (VOR). Therefore, Asian countries with power distance need to take an open culture without authority or the qualified responsibility of authority into account for the design of human-machine system.

24.5.2 The Reduction of Designers' Cognitive Bias in Design Processing

Design processing involves not only the user's cognition but also the designer's cognition. Therefore, it is necessary to consider reducing the possible cognitive biases of the design team. Liedtka (2015) listed the following flaws in cognitive processing for the design team: the projection bias, the egocentric empathy gap, the hot/cold gap, the focusing illusion, the say/do gap, the planning fallacy, the hypothesis confirmation bias, the endowment effect, and the availability bias. They could be divided into three types. The first type relates to decision-makers' limitation of their experience (projection bias, hot/cold gap) and preference (egocentric empathy gap) and attention bias toward specific factors (focusing illusion). Its remedies could be like improved perspective-taking, metaphor, and storytelling skills of the designers and build a diverse multidisciplinary and cross-cultural team. The second type concerns to user's limitation of accurate expression of future needs and feedback on new ideas (say/do gap). The remedies could be like tools like journey mapping and job-to-be-done analyses for users and field observation for designers. The third type relates to the designer's tendency to confirm the hypotheses they proposed. They are unimaginative (availability bias), overly optimistic (planning fallacy), and wedded to initial (endowment effect) and preferred (hypothesis confirmation bias) solutions. The design's hypothesis-driven approach like prototyping, the market feedback through field experiments to stimulate after-event review, and the conduction of reflections on the results of real experiments would improve the accuracy of testing.

24.6 Conclusion

The same stimulus is responded inconsistently by people from different cultural backgrounds. The cultural inconsistencies on human cognition or cultural biases in human cognition are often treated as cognitive constraints or flaws in the design of mind and sometimes cause human errors. Actually in the evolutionary perspective, it is believed that the bias results from the trade-off between information processing time and accuracy in different environments and is a kind of genuine bias and biased response pattern to adaptive problems due to various cultural norms. The cultural influences on human cognition are embodied in the dimensions of attention, perception, interpretation, and action selection and indeed have an impact on the aspects of appearance, navigation, metaphors, mental models, and interaction in user-centered design. Therefore, it is necessary to consider the cultural bias in cognition as a design feature in cross-cultural design and to reduce the potential cognitive biases generated from design team in cross-cultural design process.

We summarized the findings of empirical researches in cross-cultural website design. It would provide the profounding insights in the cross-cultural interface design. Actually, the cross-cultural design is not limited to the website design or interface design; the service design should also be included and thoroughly reviewed in the future. In addition, the more specific cultural bias in cognition should be illustrated, demonstrated, and reviewed more specifically in the fields involving safety management, like aviation, automotive manufacturing, and other industrial manufacturing, because the decision bias would cause disastrous consequences.

References

Allen, R. B. (1997). Mental models and user models. In *Handbook of human-computer interaction* (pp. 49–63). North-Holland: Elsevier.

Ariely, D. (2008). The hidden forces that shape our decisions. New York: Harper Collins.

Badre, A. (2002). *Shaping Web usability: interaction design in context*: Boston: Addison-Wesley Professional.

George A. Barnett, Eunjung Sung, (2005) Culture and the Structure of the International Hyperlink Network. Journal of Computer-Mediated Communication 11 (1):217–238

Benabou, C. (1999). Polychronicity and temporal dimensions of work in learning organizations. *Journal of Managerial Psychology, 14*(3/4), 257–270.

Bochner, S. (1994). Cross-cultural differences in the self concept: A test of Hofstede's individualism/collectivism distinction. *Journal of cross-cultural psychology, 25*(2), 273–283.

Boor, S., & Russo, P. (1993). How fluent is your interface? Designing for international users. *In Proceedings of the INTERACT'93 and CHI'93 conference on human factors in computing systems (pp. 342–347). ACM.*

Bourges-Waldegg, P., & A. R. Scrivener, S. (1998). Meaning, The Central Issue in Cross-Cultural HCI Design. *Interacting with computers, 9*(3), 287–309.

Chan, H., & Wan, L. C. (2008). Consumer responses to service failures: a resource preference model of cultural influences. *Journal of International Marketing, 16*(1), 72–97.

Cho, C. H., & John Cheon, H. (2005). Cross-cultural comparisons of interactivity on corporate web sites: the United States, the United Kingdom, Japan, and South Korea. *Journal of advertising, 34*(2), 99–115.

Curran, T., & Doyle, J. (2011). Picture superiority doubly dissociates the ERP correlates of recollection and familiarity. *Journal of Cognitive Neuroscience, 23*(5), 1247–1262.

Dasen, P. R. (2018). Cross-cultural research on spatial concept development. *Cognitive Processing, 19*(1), 93–99.

Degelder, B. (1994). Memory for consonants versus vowels in heard and lipread speech. *Journal of Memory and Language, 33*(6), 737–756.

Dix, A. (1998). *Human-Computer Interaction*. New York: Springer US.

Evers, V., Kukulska-Hulme, A., & Jones, A. (1999). Cross-cultural understanding of interface design: A cross-cultural analysis of icon recognition. In: *Designing for Global Markets: 1st*

International Workshop on Internationalization of Products and Systems (Prahbu, G.V. and del Galdo, E.M. eds.), New York: Rochester, pp. 173–182.
Garland, K. (1982). *The use of short term feedback in the preparation of technical and instructional illustration*. Paper presented at the Research in Illustration: Conference Proceedings Part II (pp. 63–80).
Gigerenzer, G., & Wegwarth, O. (2013). Five year survival rates can mislead. *BMJ: British Medical Journal (Online), 346*.
Glanzer, M., & Cunitz, A. R. (1966). Two storage mechanisms in free recall. *Journal of verbal learning and verbal behavior, 5*(4), 351–360.
Greenspan, A. (2008). The Financial Crisis and the Role of Federal Regulators. Hearing before the US House of Representatives Committee on Oversight and Government Reform, 23 October. In.
Gudykunst, W. B., Ting-Toomey, S., & Chua, E. (1988). *Culture and interpersonal communication*: Washington: Sage Publications, Inc.
Hakamata, Y., Lissek, S., Bar-Haim, Y., Britton, J. C., Fox, N. A., Leibenluft, E., … Pine, D. S. (2010). Attention bias modification treatment: a meta-analysis toward the establishment of novel treatment for anxiety. *Biological psychiatry, 68*(11), 982–990.
Haselton, M. G., Nettle, D., & Murray, D. R. (2015). The evolution of cognitive bias. *The handbook of evolutionary psychology*, 1–20.
Heimgärtner, R., Tiede, L. W., Leimbach, J., Zehner, S., Nguyenthien, N., & Windl, H. (2007). *Towards Cultural Adaptability to Broaden Universal Access in Future Interfaces of Driver Information Systems*. In International Conference on Universal Access in Human-Computer Interaction (pp. 383–392). Springer, Berlin, Heidelberg.
Heine, S. J., Lehman, D. R., Markus, H. R., & Kitayama, S., (1999). Is there a universal need for positive self-regard? *Psychological Review, 106*(4), 766–794.
Hilbert, M. (2012). Toward a synthesis of cognitive biases: How noisy information processing can bias human decision making. *Psychological bulletin, 138*(2), 211.
Hofstede, G., & Hofstede, G. J. (2004). *Cultures and Organizations. Software of the Mind* (Vol. 2). New York: Mcgraw-hill.
Hubbard, T. L. (2018). *Spatial Biases in Perception and Cognition*: Cambridge: Cambridge University Press.
Hupbach, A., Gomez, R., & Nadel, L. (2011). Episodic memory updating: The role of context familiarity. *Psychonomic bulletin & review, 18*(4), 787–797.
Ishii, K., Reyes, J. A., & Kitayama, S. (2010). Spontaneous attention to word content versus emotional tone: differences among three cultures. *Psychological Science, 14*(1), 39–46.
Janis, I. L. (2008). Groupthink. *IEEE Engineering Management Review, 36*(1), 36.
Johnson, D. D., Blumstein, D. T., Fowler, J. H., & Haselton, M. G. (2013). The evolution of error: Error management, cognitive constraints, and adaptive decision-making biases. *Trends in ecology & evolution, 28*(8), 474–481.
Ju, M. (2015). *Music Perception and Two Systems of Thoughts (Holistic and Analytic Thinking)*. University of California, Berkeley.
Kahneman, D., & Tversky, A. (1973). On the psychology of prediction. *Psychological review, 80*(4), 237.
Kelly, M. O., & Risko, E. F. (2019). Offloading memory: Serial position effects. *Psychonomic bulletin & review*, 1–7.
Kim, J. H., & Lee, K. P. (2005). Cultural difference and mobile phone interface design: Icon recognition according to level of abstraction. In *Proceedings of the 7th international conference on Human computer interaction with mobile devices & services* (pp. 307–310): ACM.
Kim, H., Coyle, J. R., & Gould, S. J. (2009). Collectivist and individualist influences on website design in South Korea and the US: A cross-cultural content analysis. *Journal of Computer-Mediated Communication, 14*(3), 581–601.
Kövecses, Z. (2010). Metaphor and culture. *Acta Universitatis Sapientiae, Philologica, 2*(2), 197–220.

Levinson, S. (2003). *Space in Language and Cognition: Explorations in Cognitive Diversity* (Vol. Vol. 5).
Li, H., Rau, P.-L. P., Salvendy, G., Chen, C., Huebner, D., & Frey, D. (2014). Effects of communication styles on acceptance of recommendations in intercultural collaboration. *Journal of International Business and Cultural Studies Volume*.
Lieder, F., Griffiths, T. L., Huys, Q. J., & Goodman, N. D. (2018). The anchoring bias reflects rational use of cognitive resources. *Psychonomic bulletin & review, 25*(1), 322–349.
Liedtka, J. (2015). Perspective: Linking design thinking with innovation outcomes through cognitive bias reduction. *Journal of Product Innovation Management, 32*(6), 925–938.
Loewenstein, G. F., Weber, E. U., Hsee, C. K., & Welch, N. (2001). Risk as feelings. *Psychological bulletin, 127*(2), 267.
Luna, D., & Gupta, S. (2001). *An integrative framework for cross-cultural consumer behavior* (Vol. 18).
Luna, D., A. Peracchio, L., & De-Juan-Vigaray, M. (2002). *Cross-Cultural and Cognitive Aspects of Web Site Navigation* (Vol. 30).
Masuda, T., Ellsworth, P. C., Mesquita, B., Leu, J., Tanida, S., & Van de Veerdonk, E. (2008). Placing the face in context: cultural differences in the perception of facial emotion. *Journal of personality and social psychology, 94*(3), 365.
Matsumoto, D. (1992). American-Japanese Cultural Differences in the Recognition of Universal Facial Expressions. *Journal of Cross-Cultural Psychology, 23*(1), 72–84.
McNally, R. J. (2019). Attentional bias for threat: Crisis or opportunity? *Clinical psychology review, 69*, 4–13.
Mellers, B., Hertwig, R., & Kahneman, D. (2001). Do frequency representations eliminate conjunction effects? An exercise in adversarial collaboration. *Psychological Science, 12*(4), 269–275.
Mezulis, A., Y Abramson, L., S Hyde, J., & Hankin, B. (2004). Is There a Universal Positivity Bias in Attributions? A Meta-Analytic Review of Individual, Developmental, and Cultural Differences in the Self-Serving Attributional Bias. *Psychological bulletin, 130*(5), 711.
Miller, G. A. (1956). The magical number seven, plus or minus two: Some limits on our capacity for processing information. *Psychological review, 63*(2), 81.
Murata, A. (2017). Cultural difference and cognitive biases as a trigger of critical crashes or disasters—Evidence from case studies of human factors analysis. *Journal of Behavioral and Brain Science, 7*(09), 399.
Murdock Jr, B. B. (1962). The serial position effect of free recall. *Journal of Experimental Psychology, 64*(5), 482.
Nisbett, R., Peng, K., Choi, I., & Norenzayan, A. (2001). Culture and Systems of Thought: Holistic Versus Analytic Cognition. *Psychological review, 108*(2), 291.
Norman, D. A., & Draper, S. W. (1986). *User centered system design: New perspectives on human-computer interaction*: Florida: CRC Press.
O'Driscoll, M., Kiely, G., & McAvoy, J. (2019). Special issue on cognitive bias–the data-driven pilot and the risk of personal sensitivity to a negative outcome. Journal of Decision Systems, 1–19.
Oswald, M. E., & Grosjean, S. (2004). Confirmation bias. In: *Cognitive illusions: A handbook on fallacies and biases in thinking, judgement and memory* (Pohl, R eds.), New York: Psychology Press, pp. *79*.
Pfister, H.-R., & Böhm, G. (2008). The multiplicity of emotions: A framework of emotional functions in decision making. *Judgment and decision making, 3*(1), 5.
Preece, J., Rogers, Y., Sharp, H., Benyon, D., Holland, S., & Carey, T. (1994). *Human-computer interaction*: Essex: Addison-Wesley Longman Ltd.
Qian, X., Yang, Y., & Gong, Y. (2011). The art of metaphor: a method for interface design based on mental models. In *Proceedings of the 10th International Conference on Virtual Reality Continuum and Its Applications in Industry* (pp. 171–178): ACM.

Rau, P.-L. P., Choong, Y.-Y., & Salvendy, G. (2004). A cross cultural study on knowledge representation and structure in human computer interfaces. *International journal of industrial ergonomics, 34*(2), 117–129.

Rau, P. L. P., Li, Y., & Li, D. (2009). Effects of communication style and culture on ability to accept recommendations from robots. *Computers in Human Behavior, 25*(2), 587–595.

Rau, P., Liu, J., Verhasselt, S., Kato, T., & Schlick, C. M. (2011). *Different time management behaviors of Germans, Chinese and Japanese.* Paper presented at the Proceedings of the ACM 2011 conference on Computer supported cooperative work.

Raue, N. (2008). *Factors influencing online sociability: A cross-cultural study.* Lehrstuhl und Institut für Arbeitswissenschaft.

Rimondi, R. (2015). Intercultural aspects of Web Design: approaches to Culture-Centred Design *PsychNology Journal, 13*(1), 101–120.

Russo, P., & Boor, S. (1993). *How fluent is your interface?: designing for international users.* Paper presented at the Proceedings of the SIGCHI conference on Human factors in computing systems - CHI'93, Amsterdam, The Netherlands.

Seidenspinner, M., & Theuner, G. (2007). Intercultural aspects of online communication a comparison of mandarin-speaking, US, Egyptian and German user preferences. *Journal of Business Economics and Management, 8*(2), 101–109.

Shepard, R. N. (1967). Recognition memory for words, sentences, and pictures. *Journal of Learning and Verbal Behavior, 6*(1), 156–163.

Simon, H. A. (1955). A behavioral model of rational choice. *The Quarterly Journal of Economics, 69*(1), 99–118.

Sook Lee, M., Geistfeld, L. V., & Stoel, L. (2007). Cultural differences between Korean and American apparel web sites. *Journal of Fashion Marketing and Management: An International Journal, 11*(4), 511–528.

Stone, D. F., & Wood, D. H. (2018). Cognitive dissonance, motivated reasoning, and confirmation bias: applications in industrial organization. In *Handbook of Behavioral Industrial Organization*: Edward Elgar Publishing.

Wang, Simons F., & Brédart, S. (2001). Social cues and verbal framing in risky choice. *Journal of Behavioral Decision Making, 14*(1), 1–15.

Wang, L., Rau, P.-L. P., Evers, V., Robinson, B. K., & Hinds, P. (2010). When in Rome: the role of culture & context in adherence to robot recommendations. In *Proceedings of the 5th ACM/IEEE international conference on Human-robot interaction* (pp. 359–366): IEEE Press.

Wang, M., Duan, L., Xin Wang, J., Li, L., Sun, D., & Chen, F. (2016). *Drive Advisory System: Do Swedish and Chinese Drivers Appreciate It in the Same Way?* (Vol. 8).

Windl, H., & Heimgärtner, R. (2013). *Intercultural Design for Use – Extending Usage-Centered Design by Cultural Aspects.*

Witkin, H. A., Dyk, R. B., Faterson, H. F., Goodenough, D. R., & Karp, S. A. (1974). *Psychological Differentiation: Studies of Development (Potomac, Md*: Lawrence Erlbaum Associates)(originally published 1962.

Würtz, E. (2005). Intercultural communication on web sites: A cross-cultural analysis of web sites from high-context cultures and low-context cultures. *Journal of Computer-Mediated Communication, 11*(1), 274–299.

Pei-Luen Patrick Rau, professor at the Department of Industrial Engineering and vice dean of Global Innovation Exchange Institute at Tsinghua University, is interested in the research areas of human factors engineering, human-computer interaction, cross-cultural design, and user experience.

Zhi Guo, a research fellow at Tsinghua University, mainly focuses on psychology, human factors, and human-computer interaction.

Nan Qie, is a doctoral candidate at Tsinghua University. Her research interests include cross-cultural interaction and cultural intelligence.

Xin Lei is a doctoral candidate focusing on human-robot interaction, augmented reality and virtual reality.

Andong Zhang is a doctoral candidate focusing on social web of things and cross-cultural research.

Part VI
Mistakes, Errors and Failure in Law, Justice and Crime

Chapter 25
Errors and Failures in Forensic Practice

Wayne Petherick

Abstract Failures and errors occur in a variety of settings and for a variety of reasons. In some practices, errors present a good learning opportunity with little (or minimal) impact to the lives of those concerned. However, in other areas, errors have disastrous or catastrophic consequences, such as the explosion at the Chernobyl nuclear reactor on April 26, 1986. In any given number of forensic disciplines (forensic science, forensic psychology/psychiatry, and forensic criminology among others), such failures can have a profound negative impact on the life or liberty of any or all parties involved. This can occur when experts do not avail themselves of all available evidence, when they are oblivious or unaware of evidence that exists, when experts are not aware of their own shortcomings, or where bias or cognitive distortion taint the expert's opinion, even in cases where the evidence may be pristine or voluminous.

This chapter examines error from the perspective of forensic practice, followed by a discussion of two forms of cognitive errors: metacognition and patternicity. Some examples will be used throughout to highlight areas of discussion. These will mostly be drawn from the area of forensic science as these are perhaps the most documented and accessible. Finally, some recommendations for reducing error and failure will be offered through the lens of culture.

Keywords Mistakes · Errors · Failure · Forensic · Metacognition · Patternicity · Confirmation bias

25.1 Introduction

Failures occur for a variety of reasons. Some of these occur "inside the room", while some are the result of forces "outside the room". These two broad distinctions are contextual identifiers the author has used in incident management theory and practice to describe the direction or flow of error either away from or towards the expert. Factors inside the room include pressure from management to make decisions

W. Petherick (✉)
C/- Criminology Department, Faculty of Society and Design, Bond University, Robina, QLD, Australia
e-mail: wpetheri@bond.edu.au

E. Vanderheiden, C.-H. Mayer (eds.), *Mistakes, Errors and Failures across Cultures*, https://doi.org/10.1007/978-3-030-35574-6_25

before they are appropriate, pressure from peers in group situations, the level of training or knowledge of the individual involved, cognitive distortions, and any other factors that impact decision-making. Factors outside the room include the quality and quantity of evidence provided to decision-makers, the quality of the investigation or the amount of evidence collected, when bias affects the quality or quantity of information provided to the analyst, and others.

Sometimes mistakes can be made and lessons learned providing a bedrock for future action. In low-stakes environments, such mistakes constitute little more than a minor inconvenience at worst or a training opportunity at best. In high-stakes environments, such as in the forensic disciplines, mistakes and failures can see an individual lose their life or liberty. This chapter examines forensic practice, specifically what feature makes something forensic. Metacognition is then discussed, which relates to knowing when one is in error and the subsequent ability to realise why (Kruger and Dunning 1999). Patternicity will then be discussed which refers to the finding of patterns in meaningless noise (Shermer 2008), which can lead to confirmation bias. Some recommendations for reducing error and failure in forensic practice are provided at the chapter's close.

25.2 What Is "Forensic"?

Virtually any discipline can be a forensic discipline providing a certain condition is met, with some belonging to the so-called "hard" sciences while some are "soft" sciences. Hard sciences typically include the biological or elemental sciences such as geology, biology, and medicine, while the soft sciences typically include psychology, criminology, and sociology. This distinction is somewhat arbitrary and may be interpreted as the hard sciences being more scientific in approach, while the social sciences adopt a "soft science" approach. Nothing could be further from the truth, however, with the main difference being how experiments or hypothesis testing is carried out. In the hard sciences, variables under study usually belong to discrete categories, and there may be devices used to aid in the analysis or interpretation (such as when running a DNA test). In the social sciences, however, variables are usually less discrete or concrete and may therefore be harder to measure or monitor (such as measuring thoughts and feelings). Because of this, it could be said that in the social sciences, the scientific method becomes more critical, though this is not to downplay the role of the scientific method in the natural or physical (i.e. hard) sciences.

The term forensic comes from the Latin *forensus* which means "of the forum" (Thornton 1983). Prior to modern criminal justice systems, trials in Roman times were a public affair where charges were presented to assembled masses who voted on the culpability of the accused. In modern times, forensic has replaced forensus and refers to "the study and practice of applying natural and physical sciences to the just resolution of social and legal issues" (Thornton 1983, p. 289). While Thornton refers specifically to forensic science, his definition applies equally to any branch of the natural or social sciences, as would Blackburn's (1996, p. 309) discussion on forensic psychology where it is noted that forensic practices are distinguished by their application, and not by theory or methodology.

Regardless of the specific application of the science, the defining criterion that makes something forensic is the expectation that the practitioner's work will be used to educate investigators, attorneys, judges, and jurors (Petherick and Turvey 2010). This is explained in more detail by Thornton and Petersen (2002, p. 148):

> What of the forensic scientist? The single feature that distinguishes forensic scientists from any other scientist is the expectation that they will appear in court and testify to their findings and offer an opinion as to the significance of those findings. The forensic scientist will, or should, testify not only to what things *are*, but to what things *mean*. Forensic science is science exercised on behalf of the law in the just resolution of conflict. It is therefore expected to be the handmaiden of the law, but at the same time this expectation may very well be the marina from which is launched the tension that exists between the two disciplines.

Practitioners in any discipline can be specialists or generalists. Because specialisation usually requires a broad-based education and career track, this usually requires starting as a generalist. However, while this is a good general rule, as with anything, there will always be exceptions. This is discussed by Chisum and Turvey (2007, pp. ix–xx) in relation to forensic science:

> A forensic generalist is a particular kind of forensic scientist who is broadly educated and trained in a variety of forensic specialties. They are "big picture" people who can help reconstruct a crime from work performed with the assistance of other forensic scientists and then direct investigators to forensic specialists as needed. They are experts not in all areas, but in the specific area of evidence interpretation.
>
> …
>
> Specialization occurs when a forensic scientist has been trained in a specific forensic subspecialty, such as an area of criminalistics, forensic toxicology, forensic pathology, or forensic anthropology. Specialists are an important part of forensic science casework, with an important role to fill. Traditionally, forensic specialists provide the bricks, and forensic generalists have traditionally provided the blueprints.

As noted, the above relates to forensic science, though the concept is universal. In criminology, for example, a generalist may know a little about crime prevention, the causes of crime, and victimology, though they may not be an expert in any one specific area. A criminological specialist may know a lot about all of the above areas, but specialise in carrying out forensic victimological assessments.

25.3 What Is Error?

Error is a relatively vaporous term. In common usage, error refers to being wrong in thought or conduct, though this chapter utilises the definition of error given by Du (2017, p. 140) who defines error as "the degree that measurement results deviate from the true value". Being able to accurately identify error when it is encountered is vital as it will not only inform us about the degree to which examinations can be trusted, but it will also enable us to know how often a particular practice or practitioner "gets it wrong". This is known as the error rate, which became particularly important in forensic examinations in the United States of America following *Daubert vs Merrell Dow Pharmaceuticals* where error rates are one criterion as to whether to allow certain types of expert evidence (Risinger et al. 2002).

Forensic practices of any flavour are complex endeavours and require not only a healthy grasp of the theoretical and practical limitations of the discipline but also how theory and practice intersect with the law. That is, forensic disciplines operate at the crossroads of science and the law. This complexity and the issues of error are explicated by Christensen et al. (2014, p. 123):

> The concept of error has been problematic, and too often, the courts as well as forensic practitioners misunderstand the meaning of error as it relates to forensic science research, procedures, and techniques. Error can be defined in a number of ways including the following: an act, assertion, or belief that unintentionally deviates from what is correct, right, or true; the condition of having incorrect or false knowledge; the act or an instance of deviating from an accepted code of behaviour; or a mistake. Mathematically and statistically, error may refer to the difference between a computed or measured value and a true or theoretically correct value.

Errors are inevitable in any system and can mostly be controlled for but never completely eliminated. The presence of fail-safe and redundancy mechanisms in critical systems are evidence that mistakes, errors, and failures can and do happen. This is summed up by Du (2017, p. 139) who states that:

> systematic errors, such as invalid science, stemming from operating such a forensic analytical system are inevitable...Alternatively, from the perspective of the system, both systematic and random errors are inevitable. The problems of which types of errors should be recognised and how to control them arise.

According to Christensen et al. (2014), there are four potential sources of error including practitioner error, instrument error, statistical error, and method error. Obviously, these apply in a somewhat different fashion across disciplines as there is some degree of variability, say, in the instrumentation used. Within the forensic sciences, instrumentation refers to any machine or automation process that performs an analysis in whole or in part. Examples include any number of machines for the analysis of DNA. However, in the social sciences, machines are not typically employed in analysis or interpretation, and so instrumentation may refer to tests or questionnaires used by mental health professionals in order to gather data on psychological functioning, as but one example.

Each type of error is discussed further below.

25.3.1 Practitioner Error

Practitioner error refers to mistakes or human error, which may be related to negligence or incompetence (Christensen et al. 2014). Practitioner error can be the result of a simple mistake such as an incorrect value entered into the data, though incompetence or negligence can occur when experts are unable to make judgements because they lack appropriate skill sets (Dror and Charlton 2006) and are therefore unable to know when they are in error and why (and thus, a metacognitive failure). While negligence certainly can be related to a lack of metacognitive ability, it is often the result of carelessness, which is a failure to apportion the appropriate attention to a task.

Practitioner errors are not limited to any one discipline as they are related to training – or perhaps a lack of it – and training should be relatively ubiquitous in most professional endeavours. This will be discussed more as a recommendation at the end of this chapter.

A good example of practitioner error is contamination of physical evidence. For example, during an interview, an expert lets slip a key piece of information to a witness that police were withholding, thereby contaminating the eyewitness' recall. An example from the area of forensic DNA analysis is provided by Walter (2012):

> A forensics error has led to an innocent man being held for five months on a charge of rape in the UK. The DNA sample from the rape victim was contaminated during a routine DNA extraction procedure, although this is thought to have been an isolated incident.
>
> Adam Scott was wrongly accused of raping a woman in Manchester, solely on the basis of the faulty DNA evidence. However, phone records indicated that he was in Plymouth at the time the assault took place.
>
> A report from the UK forensic science regulator, Andrew Rennison, said that the error was the result of 'avoidable contamination'. Record keeping and procedures at the lab were singled out for criticism.
>
> The cross-contamination event occurred at the privately run LGC Forensics lab in Teddington. In October 2011 a saliva sample sent in by the British Transport Police was being processed after an alleged 'spitting incident' in Exeter. At the same time, swabs from the woman who was attacked in Manchester were also sent to the lab.
>
> It appears that the contamination occurred when DNA was extracted from the saliva sample for further analysis. The plastic tray that contained the saliva DNA samples was then reused when the samples from the rape victim were also run for DNA extraction.
>
> Once Scott's DNA was isolated from the contaminated sample tray it was run through the UK's DNA database producing a partial match. As a result, LGC's forensic report concluded that the chance of the DNA being from someone unrelated to Scott was 'approximately one in one billion'.

Of the three types of error, practitioner error is most related to metacognition and patternicity discussed in the coming sections.

25.3.2 *Instrument Error*

Instrument errors occur when instruments or technologies fail. As machines cannot exercise judgement in analytical procedures, failures at this level are the province of the machine's operator. These failures will be related to metacognition when there is error that results from the failure to properly care for, maintain, or calibrate the testing equipment because one simply does not know how to or understand why such actions are critical to proper functioning and measurement.

An example of instrument error is from the *Houston Chronicle* regarding the efficacy and accuracy of breathalysers used in drink-driving prosecutions (Mcvicker 2002):

> One night last December, a Houston man drove away from a downtown bar and had an accident. After taking a breath test, he joined 98,000 other Texans charged that year with driving while intoxicated.
>
> The case's outcome was far from routine, however.
>
> In September, a judge threw out the charge after a defense lawyer raised questions about not only the scientific integrity of the machine that gauges sobriety, but about the state's breath-alcohol testing program, too.
>
> Those questions – sparked by the discovery that Texas disregards the manufacturer's guidelines for operating the machine – potentially could affect thousands of cases throughout the state as authorities and defense lawyers debate the credibility of breath tests.
>
> Attorney Troy McKinney argued in a Harris County court last month that the program lacks adequate quality controls for calibrating breath-test devices, which compute a DWI suspect's breath-alcohol level.
>
> Results are critical in determining whether a driver is legally drunk.
>
> …
>
> McKinney became suspicious after looking at the Intoxilyzer 5000, the machine used throughout Texas in a DWI program overseen by the state Department of Public Safety. He said records indicated the machine in his client's case was operated with its voltage meter registering a current outside that recommended by the manufacturer, CMI Inc. of Owensboro, Ky.
>
> Questioned about the discrepancy in a hearing without the jury present, HPD breath test training chief Rick Viser, who also performs maintenance on the machines, testified that DPS guidelines on an acceptable voltage range for the Intoxilyzer differ from the manufacturer's – although he could not say exactly how.
>
> Viser, who has a Bachelor of Science degree in biology from Prairie View A&M University, declined to speak with the Chronicle for this story. He took on more responsibilities in the HPD breath test program after the October 2003 ouster of Pauline Louie, who retired after being suspended as head of the crime lab's toxicology division, which tests blood and urine for alcohol and drugs.
>
> The Police Department also briefly closed that division and announced a review of 1300 cases, including evidence retests in nearly 400.

25.3.3 Statistical Error

The third type of error relates to more fundamental methodological factors such as an error in the algorithms used by the apparatus providing the measurement (Dror and Charlton 2006). This may be the result of the programmer's lack of skills in the related domain, an error in the algorithm, or an error in the analyst's interpretation. Statistical errors can also occur where the analyst fails to recognise erroneous output because they lack the proper skills to do so or simply because they do not care. In some cases, statistics may be overstated because the analyst is convinced of the suspect's guilt despite the results of tests. In these instances, the result may be "noble cause corruption", also known as a noble cause miscarriage of justice, where it is believed that the end justifies the means (Sorochan 2008).

While a vast amount of error was identified, there was widespread evidence of statistical error on the part of Fred Zain, a serologist with the West Virginia State Police Crime Laboratory. Numerous exonerations resulted from inquiries into Zain's conduct, and it is widely recognised that his errors resulted from fraud including falsifying or exaggerating his credentials. A summary of many problems is cited by Ross and Castelle (1993, p. 1):

> The acts of misconduct on the part of Zain included: (1) overstating the strength of results; (2) overstating the frequency of genetic matches on individual pieces of evidence; (3) misreporting the frequency of genetic matches on multiple pieces of evidence; (4) reporting that multiple items had been tested when only a single item had been tested; (5) reporting inconclusive results as conclusive; (6) repeatedly altering laboratory records; (7) grouping results to create the erroneous impression that genetic markers had been obtained from all samples tested; (8) failing to report conflicting results; (9) failing to conduct or to report conducting additional testing to resolve conflicting results; (10) implying a match with a suspect when testing supported only a match with the victim; and (11) reporting scientifically impossible or improbable results.

While an initial investigation exonerated Zain, subsequent findings would see a more in depth probe in which numerous catastrophic errors were found, with Zain performing poorly in training activities, as discussed by Giannelli (2010, pp. 1317–1318):

> A 1985 investigation of the serology department raised further questions of Zain's competence. The investigating officer contacted the FBI about Zain's performance in FBI serology courses. The FBI responded by noting that Zain" 'apparently doesn't like to do things by the book.' " A crime lab director "recalled being told by [an] FBI instructor that Zain ' 'did well below the class average.' "

25.3.4 Method Error

An example of method error is the difference between nuclear DNA and mtDNA (mitochondrial DNA) (Christensen et al. 2014), with the former offering much greater levels of sensitivity of detection than the latter. According to Giannelli

(2010) method errors relate to limitations that have nothing to do with practitioner error and thus would seem unrelated to cognitive errors such as metacognition. It is the view of this author that method error incorporates or is related to practitioner error, where the analyst is robbed of the ability to understand the flaws in the methods they are using. One such example is CBLA or comparative bullet-lead analysis. At a fundamental level, CBLA involves the comparison of the composition of bullets found at a crime scene to those found in the possession of a suspect. If there is a metallurgical match between these two projectiles, it follows that the bullet found at the crime scene (the forensic sample) must have therefore been fired by the individual in whose possession the other bullets were found (the reference sample).

While such a comparative analysis may sound good in theory, it is based on significantly flawed assumptions and unsupported subjective belief (Tobin 2004) about the degree to which bullets were "analytically indistinguishable" (Giannelli 2011, p. 1). Not only is this term problematic, the science on which CBLA is based is significantly flawed and relies on determinations of the degree to which something is individuating (can identify an item from every other item of its type in the known universe). As far as CBLA is concerned, individuation is problematic because projectiles found at a crime scene may also be a metallurgical match to reference samples in completely different parts of the country (for an excellent analysis on CBLA, the interested reader should consult 60 min, 2008). This is because different manufacturers source raw components for their bullets from the same suppliers, and a given batch of potentially millions of bullets will all have the same metal composition based on the presence and balance of seven elements – arsenic, antimony, tin, copper, bismuth, silver, and cadmium (Giannelli 2011).

It is impossible to completely eliminate error of any type, though understanding how errors happen can help establish good quality assurance practices (Budowle et al. 2009) and thus minimise the number of errors and the impact they have. Regular proficiency testing, which measures how accurate and competent someone is at their job, is also vital as are reviews of failures so that the contributions, causes, and impacts can be understood and rectified where necessary.

25.4 Metacognition

In a seminal paper on metacognition, Kruger and Dunning (1999, p. 1121) open with an amusing and equally chilling story involving a bank robber too bereft of wit to understand that lemon juice was not an effective guard against CCTV:

> In 1995, McArthur Wheeler walked into two Pittsburgh banks and robbed them in broad daylight, with no visible attempt at disguise. He was arrested later that night, less than an hour after videotapes of him taken from surveillance cameras were broadcast on the 11 o'clock news. When police later showed him the surveillance tapes, Mr. Wheeler stared in incredulity. "But I wore the juice", he mumbled. Apparently, Mr. Wheeler was under the impression that rubbing one's face with lemon juice rendered it invisible to videotape cameras.

Kruger and Dunning use this robber's folly as an example of metacognition, which broadly speaking refers to the ability to identify when one is in error and why (Kruger and Dunning 1999). More specifically, metacognition refers to "the kinds of processes involved, and the self-knowledge gained, in thinking about, and in controlling, one's own thinking" (Proust 2010, p. 989) or "the ability to know how well one is performing, and when one is likely to be accurate in judgement, and when one is likely to be in error" (Kruger and Dunning 1999, p. 1121). The study of metacognition is traced to the work of developmental psychologist John Flavell who noted its importance in oral and reading comprehension, attention, memory, problem-solving, and self-control among numerous other areas (Flavell 1979).

While early investigations into metacognition revolved around children and their ability at cognition about cognitive processes (Flavell 1979; Livingston 2003), more recent work has focused on the role of metacognition in a vast number of contexts such as sports ability, comedic talent, chess ability, and the role of metacognition in criminal profiling (Woodhouse and Petherick 2014). In a study testing the original hypothesis of Kruger and Mueller (2002) found that those who performed poorly vastly overestimate their own performance and are deficient in metacognitive skill, while top performers have a tendency to underestimate their ranking comparative to others.

Metacognition is related to the "better than average" (BTA) effect which is the tendency to view yourself as exceptional and unique rather than as average and common (Brown 2012). BTA is in turn related to confidence, more specifically, overconfidence, where one believes themselves to be more adept than they actually are. The relationship between confidence and competence can best be understood as a plot with knowledge on the X (horizontal) axis and confidence on the Y (vertical) axis. When knowledge is low, confidence tends to be high as the individual lacks an understanding of exactly how much they do not know. As knowledge increases, confidence tends to decrease as one begins to comprehend the scope of the problem and to develop an appreciation of how little they know about the domain of inquiry. As knowledge increases yet again, confidence increases slightly as one begins to develop a sense of mastery. Ideally, confidence should not never exceed knowledge though this can and does happen, and this will be discussed in the recommendation section.

Ignorance tends to increase a person's confidence (Staub and Kaynak 2014), rather than decreasing it, likely a result of a failure to understand complexity. That is, the less one knows about an area, the simpler that area seems to them. This has been stated elsewhere in another, more simple form, as "to the ignorant the world looks simple" (Dörner 1997). Of the four types of error discussed above, metacognitive failures relate mostly to practitioner error as they reside within the individual, that is, their cognitive and critical thinking facilities though metacognition can play a role in all of the types of error discussed.

25.5 Patternicity

As discussed, errors in forensic practice are related to many different factors. One major error in thinking that leads to errors and failures is metacognition: not knowing when we are wrong and why. This relates to a lack of domain-specific skills and may therefore be prone to repetition because lessons are not learned from mistakes that are made. These differ from honest mistakes wherein the practitioner understands the error and appropriately corrects for course in future endeavours to reduce the likelihood of repetition. That does not mean that the same or different mistakes will not occur again, only that their likelihood is reduced. However, other errors are equally likely to afflict the competent as well as the incompetent, for different reasons, though the outcome will be the same. It may be that higher performers who should be more competent are more conscientious (Liao and Chuang 2004) and therefore more prone to patternicity errors because they have a greater investment in the work product or the outcome. That is, they are not lazy or apathetic in the process.

Because of this, a thinking error that can lead to mistakes is the tendency to find patterns in data where no patterns exist. This may or may not be related to a lack of knowledge or competence and is referred to as patternicity (where apophenia is the technical term for this tendency). This is introduced by Shermer (2008, p. 1) with examples of common identified patterns given:

> Why do people see face in nature, interpret window stains as human figures, hear voices in random sounds generated by electronic devices or find conspiracies in the daily news? A proximate cause is the priming effect, in which our brain and senses are prepared to interpret stimuli according to an expected model. UFOlogists see a face on Mars. Religonists see the Virgin Mary on the side of a building. Paranormalists hear dead people speaking to them through a radio receiver. Conspiracy theorists think 9/11 was an inside job by the Bush administration. Is there deeper ultimate cause for why people believe such weird things? There is. I call it "patternicity", or the tendency to find meaningful patterns in meaningless noise.

Patternicity is not necessarily a cognitive deficit, though it may result from the reduction of complex pattern information into simple forms or explanations. This tendency is an adaptive mechanism assisting with survival where, from an evolutionary perspective, our chances of escaping harm or death reduce if we over interpret patterns that do not exist rather than under interpret ones that do. In short, for survival, it is better to be safe than sorry. Shermer (2008, p. 1) in fact goes on to explain patternicity not as a fault in cognition but as a computer primed to find meaning:

> Traditionally, scientists have treated patternicity as an error in cognition. A type I error, or a false positive, is believing something is real when it is not (finding a non-existent pattern). A type II error, or a false negative, is not believing something is real when it is (not recognising a real pattern – call is "appaternicity")…our brains are belief engines: evolved pattern-recognition machines that connect dots and create meaning out of the patterns we see in nature.

Regardless of the fact that patternicity is adaptive, errors will still be the occasional outcome. A worse situation and potential outcome though is when patternicity occurs in conjunction with other cognitive distortions. Perhaps one of the most problematic pairings is where the discovery of non-existent patterns leads to a bias wherein evidence supporting a hypothesis is chosen over that which refutes the hypothesis. This is called confirmation bias, also referred to as "cherry picking" in the language of logical fallacies.

25.5.1 Confirmation Bias

Simply put, confirmation bias is a cognitive shortcut where we tend to overemphasise evidence that supports our view while ignoring evidence that does not. Put another way, people tend to "seek and interpret in ways that are partial toward existing beliefs", and this is a well-documented phenomenon playing a role in every aspect of human cognition (Ask and Granhag 2005, p. 45). As falsification is the cornerstone of science, any work product that fails to falsify and seeks only to confirm would therefore be less than scientific. This may especially plague forensic work where the result of confirmation bias can be life or liberty. Perhaps most insidious is that even when there is no personal reason to confirm a hypothesis, people seem to favour confirmation as the default reasoning strategy (Rassin et al. 2010).

Of all the flaws in critical thinking and reasoning, confirmation bias is perhaps among the most important for consideration (Nickerson 1998). This is perhaps because humans tend to be "satisficers", coming to conclusions once a minimally satisfactory evidentiary threshold is reached (Heuer 1999), which becomes more likely when we have an idea in mind while we are still working through the evidence trying to understand its meaning. This is what Hans Gross referred to as a preconceived theory (Gross 1924). The observer sees what they want or expect rather than what is actually there (Langenburg et al. 2009). This may be particularly problematic when the confirmation aspect is actually a stage of the analytic method, as evidenced in the use of ACE-V fingerprint methodology in the case of Brandon Mayfield (Kassin et al. 2013, p. 42):

> On March 11, 2004, a coordinated series of bombs exploded in four commuter trains in Madrid. The explosions killed 191 people, wounded 1800 others, and set into motion a full-scale international investigation. On the basis of a latent fingerprint lifted from a bag containing detonating devices, the U.S. Federal Bureau of Investigation (FBI) positively identified Brandon Mayfield, an American Muslim from the state of Oregon. Subsequent to 9–11, Mayfield had been on an FBI watch list. Following standard protocol, a number of FBI fingerprint examiners independently concluded that the fingerprint was definitely that of Mayfield. After being arrested and appearing in court, Mayfield requested to have a fingerprint examiner on the defense team examine the prints. That fingerprint examiner concurred with the judgment that the print was Mayfield's. Soon thereafter, however, the Spanish authorities matched the prints to the real Madrid bomber, an Algerian national by the name of Ouhnane Daoud.

A later review of the case found that the problem with the fingerprint identification was that it resulted from confirmation bias (Kassin et al. 2013) or context and confirmation bias (Langenburg et al. 2009), and the result was a $2m USD payout for Brandon Mayfield.

Both of these problems can be found in forensic practice but are far more common in every day [il]logical thinking such as that seen in 9/11 conspiracy theories, the anti-vaxxing movement, and global warming denial. The tendency for conspiracy theorists to vigorously acquire supporting evidence is noted by Clarke (2002, p. 135):

> Because conspiracy theorists almost always wish to see conspiracies exposed, they are typically quite dedicated in their search for evidence relevant to their favourite conspiracy theory and are usually able to overwhelm you with a deluge of evidence in favour of that theory.

25.6 Improving Practice and Reducing Error

There are many ways to improve practice and reduce error. This would be another work in itself, and there is simply no room in this chapter to do the area full justice. Instead, a few select ways forward have been chosen because they are fundamental and/or relatively easy to implement and enforce, as well as targeting some core and largely preventable causes of failure. These factors have been identified as cultural solutions, though it is admitted that culture is used in a slightly different form than its traditional usage. According to Eagleton (2016, p. 1), culture "can mean

(1) a body of artistic and intellectual work;
(2) a process of spiritual and intellectual development;
(3) the values, beliefs and symbolic practices by which men and women live; or
(4) the whole way of life".

For this chapter, the meaning of culture is most aligned to (3) above regarding values, beliefs, and symbolic practices.

25.6.1 A Culture of Scientific Thinking

A vital part of science is the scientific method, which is in itself designed to protect against error. The scientific method is a systematic process for obtaining knowledge through hypothesis generation and falsification (Petherick and Rowan 2015). While the number of steps or stages in the scientific method differs between authors, the goal of the process is the same. To identify a logical understanding of how something operates and then trying to show how, with the available evidence, it may be wrong (referred to as falsification). The process usually follows as such:

- Observations are made about a phenomenon or event.
- We collect evidence or information about that even. This can be virtually anything including all types of physical and testimonial evidence.
- The evidence must be examined for themes, patterns, and associations.
- From this examination, we develop a range of hypotheses that account for every possibility or probability.
- Attempts are then made to test each hypothesis against the available facts with a view to disproving rather than proving each one.
- Once we have eliminated all but one (the best-case scenario but not always realistic), this remaining hypothesis become the working hypothesis about what occurred.

Having only one hypothesis remain is not always possible and may happen for a variety of reasons. One is a lack of education and training, and another is when evidence used to inform the hypothesis generation stage is lacking. In such instances, every attempt must be made to secure further information and, if available, return to the themes, patterns, and association stage to develop further hypotheses for falsification.

If the analyst finds themselves in a position where they have a number of hypotheses, many of which cannot be definitely ruled out, a useful tool is the analysis of competing hypothesis (ACH). ACH is a powerful tool that "requires an analyst to explicitly identify all the reasonable alternatives and have them compete against each other for the analyst's favour, rather than evaluating their plausibility one at a time" (Heuer 1999, p. 95). While an eight-step process in practice, the ACH matrix is relatively easy to prepare. First, the analyst identifies each of the hypotheses generated during the appropriate stage of the scientific method. These are then allocated to columns in a spreadsheet. On the left-hand side, each row is given to a piece of information or evidence available in the case. The analyst then works through each hypothesis giving consideration to whether the hypothesis is supported by that evidence or not. Those that are supported are marked with a plus (+) and those that are not supported with a minus (−). Once the matrix is complete, a tally of evidence that supports or refutes each hypothesis is performed, where the hypothesis with the most support (as indicated by the most (+)) is adopted as the working hypothesis in the case.

25.6.2 A Culture of Education and Training

Education and training can take a variety of forms, though all have one relatively common goal: to further society through knowledge. Education and training provide the requisite skills and information one needs to do their job properly and in the most efficient and effective manner possible. Having a well-developed and reasonable understanding of the world around us allows us to better understand what is happening and why and provides us with an understanding of cause-and-effect relationships. Critically, having more information and knowledge at hand will be a guard against metacognitive failures, patternicity, and confirmation bias. Ideally, this education should start before individuals begin their respective career pathways, beginning in the primary and secondary schooling years, as promoted by Paris and Winograd (2013, p. 15):

> The central message is that students can enhance their learning by becoming aware of their own thinking as they read, write, and solve problems in school. Teachers can promote this awareness directly by informing students about effective problem-solving strategies and discussing cognitive and motivational characteristics of thinking. The twin benefits of this "consciousness-raising" are: (a) it transfers responsibility for monitoring learning from teachers to students themselves, and (b) it promotes positive self-perceptions, affects, and motivation among the students. In this manner, metacognition provides personal insights into one's own thinking and fosters independent learning.

Tertiary and continuing education must be well rounded and ideally involves not only material relevant to the subject matter but also a more liberally based platform with a focus on epistemology. This would ideally include subjects or courses on logic, reasoning, and critical thinking, and equally important, on report writing and communication. This is vital because understanding the basic principles and precepts of one's discipline will only get the practitioner so far if the results of analysis cannot be accurately and clearly communicated. A valid method for teaching good critical thinking skills through assessment items analogous to job tasks is known as case-based reasoning. Not only does this provide domain relevant skills, it is also engaging for students and has been getting significant traction in education sectors for many years. As discussed by Aamodt and Plaza (1994, p. 1):

> Case-based reasoning is a problem solving paradigm that in many respects is fundamentally different from other major AI approaches. Instead of relying solely on general knowledge of a problem domain, or making associations along generalized relationships between problem descriptors and conclusions, CBR is able to utilize the specific knowledge of previously experienced, concrete problem situations (cases). A new problem is solved by finding a similar past case, and reusing it in the new problem situation. A second important difference is that CBR also is an approach to incremental, sustained learning, since a new experience is retained each time a problem has been solved, making it immediately available for future problems.

As noted above and elsewhere (Kolodner 1992), past situations similar to the current one are used to help reasoners solve a new problem. In the forensic domain, this can be accomplished by giving students case material to evaluate (past situations) in a similar fashion to that they will undertake in their future careers (a new problem). Not only can the case be assessed on whether they have performed well in the analysis (as measured through the accuracy of their assessment), they can also be monitored and given feedback on their process (logic, reasoning, and critical thinking), as well as their ability to master the technical aspects of report writing (conveying their opinion/s in the clearest and most economical way possible). Providing students with feedback will be a critical part of this process, and research has tended to show that something as simple as providing feedback can help mitigate some metacognitive failures (Ryvkin et al. 2012).

25.6.3 A Culture of Evidence Not Belief

Evidence and not belief should be the cornerstone of forensic inquiries. An effective way to guard against error and failure is to be guided by the evidence – what you have and do not have – and what that means for the case and any subsequent conclusions, specifically, what this means about how this will limit the analysis. It would seem contradictory to identify the source of some forensic errors as metacognitive deficiencies while simultaneously arguing that an important role of the practitioner is to explain the nature and limitations of the information on which the analysis is based. Surely if an analyst is incompetent, they will be unable to identify the meaning and importance of the evidence? The remedy to this problem is based on two related propositions that stem from the notion that *all* forensic work be accompanied by a written report detailing the analyst's findings.

The first is that writing down our conclusions helps us identify flaws in thinking and reasoning. If errors still plague the practitioner's work, then these will likely be found in the peer review stage of report writing (it is the author's advice that unless strictly prohibited by issues of confidentiality that all reports be peer-reviewed). If nothing else, this provides an additional line of defence, and this could succinctly be summed up as explaining our thought processes to ourselves.

The second is based on the idea that writing opinions down for the purpose of educating others may similarly help identify flaws in thinking and reasoning. This could succinctly be summed up as explaining our thought processes to others. A good litmus test for whether we have not only performed a competent and thorough analysis and communicated this through a written report is if another can understand what we have done, why we have done it, and the results of our analysis.

To sum up, if we can understand our own processes and others can understand them also, this is can be a guard against error or failure.

In order to assist this process, the author and a colleague developed a set of guiding principles for applied crime analysis (ACA) which aims to provide a holistic understanding of a crime or crime series (Petherick 2015). ACA is a social science approach to understanding crime, criminals, and victims, and while related to other types of crime analysis, it is more investigative in focus. These three principles are known as validity, reliability, and sufficiency (Petherick and Rowan 2015) and relate to any and all kinds of evidence or information that is to be used for analytic purposes.

Validity refers to whether the evidence represents a reality (Petherick and Rowan 2015). That is, whether the evidence paints an accurate picture of the facts. In a case involving bloodstains, it needs to be determined whether the deposit is human blood, whether it belongs to the victim, and whether it is the result of some criminal action or simply the product of accident of environmental interaction. It should be obvious that we do not want to introduce superfluous information of any kind into analysis and anything that does not accurately represent a reality needs to be excluded, or at least identified as potentially extraneous, and given the appropriate weighting.

Reliability equates to trust, that is, whether we can trust the evidence or information (Petherick and Rowan 2015). Any given statement is only useful insofar as it is an accurate account of what happened, and then whether we can accept information from that source. A statement given by a neutral third party is likely more trustworthy than that given by a suspect in a crime.

Information can be both a valid representation of reality and come from a reliable source. However, if there is not a lot of information, then this may still have a negative impact on how far we can take our opinion or conclusion, as there may not be sufficient information to act upon (Petherick and Rowan 2015). The impact of this may be mitigated if the validity and reliability of the evidence are high, though sufficiency will also be a problem if there is not much information where it has low validity and low reliability.

Each of these three elements is judged according to [an admittedly arbitrary] standard of low, medium, and high. The best situation for the analyst to find themselves in is to be dealing with information that is highly valid, highly reliable, and sufficient. On the other end of the spectrum, opinions and conclusions may be rendered more speculative should all three be judged as low. Whatever the combination is deemed to be for any evidentiary item, the weight of this must be clearly communicated in the final report so that the client is fully aware of the strengths and limitations of the report, which translates equally to the probative (i.e. forensic) value of the report.

The benefit of accounting for the evidentiary weight in terms of validity, reliability, and sufficiency is that it makes the analyst stop and account for their opinion rather than providing it without qualification. If they cannot adequately do so, this can signal a skills deficit that can be corrected with education, training, and guidance. Of course, this does beg the question of what they are doing writing reports in the first place, but that reality is beyond the purview of this chapter.

25.7 Error as a Resource

Despite the range of issues in error and failure, including various influences on human error, the situation may not be as dire as it would appear. There are many ways to harness errors as a resource, which include but are not limited to an opportunity for personal growth, changes in institutional and organisational policy and procedure, and discipline-wide reforms promoted and implemented through various professional organisations' codes of conduct and practice standards. These provide a valuable learning tool for students, academics, practitioners, managers, and others.

Piggybacking on the above discussion of case-based reasoning (CBR), I suggest that the best way to utilise error and failure as a resource for personal, organisational, and discipline growth is to utilise examples in instruction at various levels of education for students and for professionals through continuing professional development. There are two styles of case-based reasoning which serve as a platform for growth and a reduction in factors that lead to error and failure and thus potentially contribute to a lower number of overall events. The first style is problem-solving and the second is instructive. In the first "solutions to new problems are derived using old solutions as a guide. Old solutions can provide almost-right solutions to new problems and they can provide warnings or potential mistakes or failures" (Kolodner 1992, p. 6). The second style of CBR is interpretive where "new situations are evaluated in the context of old situations. A lawyer for example, uses interpretive case-based reasoning when he uses a series of old cases to justify an argument in a new case" (Kolodner 1992, p. 6).

Both styles are useful in instructional environments, where the case provides the learning resource and the structure of the discussion provides the learning opportunity. Educators can modify the case as required to meet different goals, and they can provide different questions or problems to different student groups. In this way, learners identify the salient features of the case, identify the problematic aspects that lead to the error, apply the appropriate theoretical frameworks, and then apply the problem-solution-relevance framework (What is the problem? What is the solution? What is the relevance of this problem and of the solution to the situation as a whole?). At an individual level, there are a variety of ways in which these examples can be harnessed including at least the following:

- Learners can be tasked with finding the relevant theories that explain the error or failure, for example, metacognition, patternicity, confirmation bias, groupthink, etc.
- Learners can be tasked with finding the relevant theories that provide a solution to the problem.
- Where the example involves a violation of an ethical code of conduct, learners can identify the relevant aspects of the case and match it to a specific code of ethics to identify specific ethical violations.
- Learners can be asked to find vulnerabilities in systems which can lead to error or failure in the future.
- Learners can be asked to identify ways in which the errors or failure can be used to motivate change in individual practice, organisational culture, or society at large.
- Learners can be tasked with identifying the appropriate mechanisms or fail-safes that could have prevented the error or failure in the first instance.
- Where a catastrophic event was avoided by the action of an individual or group, learners can identify those things that were done which prevented an escalation of the failure or error.

Error and failure at all levels are part of the human condition. In complex systems, those comprised of many moving, interconnected, and interdependent parts, such outcomes are not necessarily inevitable or predictable, but they are certainly a possibility and even a probability. Their occurrence can certainly be mitigated by the implementation of certain measures, including education and training, and Christensen et al. (2014) suggest that educational programmes for practitioners address error and error analysis. I suggest that this be broadened out to include individuals at all levels of organisation and practice which is one of the best hopes we have of avoiding errors and failures. As a concluding comment for this chapter, I will leave the reader with a comment spoken at the end of every subject every semester: strive diligently to be the best you can be so you do not end up as a case study.

25.8 Conclusions

Forensic disciplines are those that address investigative or legal questions in order to educate investigators, attorneys, judges, jurors, and others. According to John Thornton, a forensic practitioner is identified by the expectation that they may testify in court. Like virtually all other professionals, forensic professionals are prone to error and failure though they operate in a high-stakes environment where these errors and failures can result in the loss of life or liberty for those accused of crimes. This chapter has discussed metacognition which results in error because practitioners do not have the skills to know they are wrong and why. Patternicity or apophenia, where individuals find meaning in meaningless data, was also discussed along with the related issue of confirmation bias. Ways to address error were provided at the chapter's conclusion, including the use of the scientific method, education and training, and validity, reliability, and sufficiency.

References

60 Minutes. (2008, November 18). *Evidence Of Injustice*. Retrieved from https://www.cbsnews.com/news/evidence-of-injustice/

Aamodt, A., & Plaza, E. (1994). *Case-Based Reasoning: Foundational Issues, Methodological Variations, and System Approaches*. *7*(1), 39–59.

Ask, K., & Granhag, P. A. (2005). Motivational sources of confirmation bias in criminal investigations: The need for cognitive closure. *Journal of Investigative Psychology and Offender Profiling*, *2*(1), 43–63. https://doi.org/10.1002/jip.19

Blackburn, R. (1996). *The Psychology of Criminal Conduct: Theory, Research and Practice*. Chichester: Wiley.

Brown, J. D. (2012). Understanding the Better Than Average Effect: Motives (Still) Matter. *Personality and Social Psychology Bulletin*, *38*(2), 209–219.

Budowle, B., Bottrell, M. C., Bunch, S. G., Fram, R., Harrison, D., Meagher, S., … Stacey, R. B. (2009). A Perspective on Errors, Bias, and Interpretation in the Forensic Sciences and Direction for Continuing Advancement. *Journal of Forensic Sciences*, *54*(4), 798–809. https://doi.org/10.1111/j.1556-4029.2009.01081.x

Chisum, W. J., & Turvey, B. E. (2007). *Crime Reconstruction* (1st ed.). San Diego: Elsevier Science.

Christensen, A. M., Crowder, C. M., Ousley, S. D., & Houck, M. M. (2014). Error and its Meaning in Forensic Science. *Journal of Forensic Sciences*, *59*(1), 123–126. https://doi.org/10.1111/1556-4029.12275

Clarke, S. (2002). Conspiracy Theories and Conspiracy Theorizing. *Philosophy of the Social Sciences*, *32*(2), 131–150.

Dörner, D. (1997). *The Logic of Failure: Recognising and Avoiding Error in Complex Situations*. New York: Basic Books.

Dror, I. E., & Charlton, D. (2006). Why Experts Make Errors. *Journal of Forensic Identification, 56*(4), 600–616.

Du, M. (2017). Analysis of errors in forensic science. *Journal of Forensic Science and Medicine, 3*(3), 139. https://doi.org/10.4103/jfsm.jfsm_8_17

Eagleton, T. (2016). *Culture* (1st ed.). New Haven, CT: Yale University Press.

Flavell, J. H. (1979). Metacognition and Cognitive Mointoring: A New Area of Cignitive-Developmental Inquiry. *American Psychologist, 34*(10), 906–911.

Giannelli, P. C. (2010). Scientific Fraud. *Criminal Law Bulletin, 46*(6), 1313–1333.

Giannelli, P. C. (2011). Comparative Bullet Lead Analysis: A Retrospective. *Criminal Law Bulletin, 47*, 1–10.

Gross, H. G. (1924). *Criminal Investigation: A Practical Handbook for Magistrates, Police Officers, and Lawyers*. 1002. https://doi.org/10.2307/1147310

Heuer, R. J. (1999). *Psychology of intelligence analysis*. Washington, D.C.: Center for the Study of Intelligence, Central Intelligence Agency.

Kassin, S. M., Dror, I. E., & Kukucka, J. (2013). The forensic confirmation bias: Problems, perspectives, and proposed solutions. *Journal of Applied Research in Memory and Cognition, 2*(1), 42–52. https://doi.org/10.1016/j.jarmac.2013.01.001

Kolodner, J. L. (1992). An introduction to case-based reasoning. *Artificial Intelligence Review, 6*(3), 3–34.

Krueger, J., & Mueller, R. A. (2002). Unskilled, Unaware, or Both? The Better-Than-Average Heuristic and Statistical Regression Predict Errors in Estimates of Own Performance. *Journal of Personalityand Social Psychology, 82*(2), 180–188. Retrieved from https://oce-ovid-com.ezproxy.bond.edu.au/article/00005205-200202000-00003/HTML

Kruger, J., & Dunning, D. (1999). Unskilled and Unaware of It How Difficulties in Recognising One's Own Incompetence Lead to Inflated Self Assesments. *Journal of Personality and Social Psychology, 77*(6), 1121–1134. Retrieved from http://ovidsp.tx.ovid.com.ezproxy.bond.edu.au/ovftpdfs/FPDDNCMCLHDHLD00/fs047/ovft/live/gv024/00005205/00005205-199912000-00002.pdf

Langenburg, G., Champod, C., & Wertheim, P. (2009). Testing for Potential Contextual Bias Effects During the Verification Stage of the ACE-V Methodology when Conducting Fingerprint Comparisons∗. *Journal of Forensic Sciences, 54*(3), 571–582. https://doi.org/10.1111/j.1556-4029.2009.01025.x

Liao, H., & Chuang, A. (2004). A Multilevel Investigation of Factors Influencing Employee Service Performance and Customer OUtcomes. *Academy of Management Journal, 47*(1), 41–58.

Livingston, J. A. (2003). Metacognition: An Overview. *Institute of Education Sciences*, 2–9.

Mcvicker, S. (2002, October 26). Accuracy of sobriety testing machine challenged. *Houston Chronicle*. Retrieved from https://www.chron.com/news/houston-texas/article/Accuracy-of-sobriety-testing-machine-challenged-1953036.php

Nickerson, R. S. (1998). *Confirmation bias: A ubiquitous phenomenon in many guises*. https://doi.org/10.1037/1089-2680.2.2.175

Paris, S. G., & Winograd, P. (2013). How Metacognition can Promote Academic Learning and Instruction. In B. F. Jones & L. Idol (Eds.), *Dimensions of Thinking and Congitive Instruction* (pp. 15–47). New Jersey: Routledge.

Petherick, W. A. (2015). An Introduction to Applied Crime Analysis. In *Applied Crime Analysis: A Social Science Approach to Understanding Crime, Criminals, and Victims* (1st ed., pp. 1–13). Waltham: Academic Press.

Petherick, W. A., & Rowan, A. (2015). Physical Evidence and the Crime Scene. In W. A. Petherick (Ed.), *Applied Crime Analysis: A Social Science Approach to Understanding Crime, Criminals, and Victims* (1st ed., pp. 39–61). Waltham: Anderson Publishing.

Petherick, W. A., & Turvey, B. E. (2010). Cognitive Ethos of the Forensic Examiner. In W. A. Petherick, B. E. Turvey, & C. E. Ferguson (Eds.), *Forensic Criminology* (1st ed., pp. 81–129). San Diego: Academic Press.

Proust, J. (2010). Metacognition. *Philosophy Compass*, *5*(11), 989–998. https://doi.org/10.1111/j.1747-9991.2010.00340.x

Rassin, E., Eerland, A., & Kuijpers, I. (2010). Let's find the evidence: An Analogue Study of Confirmation Bias in Criminal Investigations. *Journal of Investigative Psychology and Offender Profiling*, *7*(3), 231–246. https://doi.org/10.1002/jip.126

Risinger, D. M., Saks, M. J., Thompson, W. C., & Rosenthal, R. (2002). The Daubert/Kumho Implications of Observer Effects in Forensic Science: Hidden Problems of Expectation and Suggestion. *CALIFORNIA LAW REVIEW*, *90*, 56.

Ross, A., & Castelle, G. (1993, November 4). Matter of W. Va. State Police Crime Lab., 438 S.E.2d 501 – CourtListener.com. Retrieved June 30, 2019, from CourtListener website: https://www.courtlistener.com/opinion/1252942/matter-of-w-va-state-police-crime-lab/

Ryvkin, D., Krajč, M., & Ortmann, A. (2012). Are the unskilled doomed to remain unaware? *Journal of Economic Psychology*, *33*(5), 1012–1031. https://doi.org/10.1016/j.joep.2012.06.003

Shermer, M. (2008). Patternicity. *Scientific American*, *299*(6), 48–48. https://doi.org/10.1038/scientificamerican1208-48

Sorochan, D. (2008). Wrongful Convictions: Preventing Miscarriages of Justice and Some Case Studies. *TEXAS TECH LAW REVIEW*, *41*, 25.

Staub, S., & Kaynak, R. (2014). Is an unskilled really unaware of it? *Social and Behavioural Sciences*, *150*, 899–907. Retrieved from https://ac.els-cdn.com/S1877042814051489/1-s2.0-S1877042814051489-main.pdf?_tid=spdf-f5c0d58f-578d-4115-9b86-57f380ae279d&acdnat=1519518541_f19f9b3b08438c85cf9eb07148fb7d78

Thornton, J. (1983). Use and Abuses of Forensic Science. *American Bar Association Journal*, *69*, 288–292.

Thornton, J., & Petersen, J. (2002). The General Assumptions and Rationale of Forensic Identification. In D. L. Faigman, D. H. Kaye, M. J. Saks, & J. Sanders (Eds.), *Modern Scientific Evidence: The Law and Science of Expert Testimony.* (Vol. 3). St. Paul: West Publishing Company.

Tobin, W. (2004). Comparative Bullet Lead Analysis: A Case Study in Flawed Forensics. *The Champion*, (July), 12–21.

Walter, P. (2012, October 5). Forensic lab error led to miscarriage of justice. *Chemistry World*. Retrieved from https://www.chemistryworld.com/news/forensic-lab-error-led-to-miscarriage-of-justice-/5503.article

Woodhouse, B., & Petherick, W. A. (2014). Metacopgnition in Criminal Profiling. In W. A. Petherick (Ed.), *Profiling and Serial Crime: Theoretical and Practical Issues* (3rd ed., pp. 185–206). San Diego: Anderson Publishing.

Wayne Petherick (PhD) is a Forensic Criminologist and is currently Associate Professor of Criminology at Bond University on the Gold Coast, Queensland, Australia. Wayne has taught at Bond for 21 years and teaches Criminal Profiling, Applied Crime Analysis, Criminal Motivations, Crime and Deviance, Forensic Criminology, and Profiling and Crime Analysis (the latter two taught at the postgraduate level). His research interests include serial crimes such as stalking and murder, criminal profiling, self-esteem and crime, criminal motivations, and victim precipitation.

Wayne is also Principal of Forensic Analytic, offering training and consultancy in serial crime, applied crime analysis, stalking, risk assessment and threat management, arson, false reports, victimology, and human factors in incident management. In this capacity he has worked in Queensland, New South Wales, Victoria, South Australia, and the United States.

He has authored over 70 book chapters and journal articles and is the Editor or Coeditor of *Forensic Criminology*, *Profiling and Serial Crime: Theoretical and Practical Issues*, *Applied Crime Analysis: A Social Science Approach to Understanding Crime, Criminals, and Victims*, and *The Psychology of Criminal and Antisocial Conduct: Victim and Offender Perspectives.*

Chapter 26
Failures in Wildlife Crime Eradication and Strategies Forward

Claude-Hélène Mayer

Abstract The chapter describes the common attempts to combat and eradicate wildlife crime. It provides examples of wildlife crime in different national contexts and explores the sociocultural circumstances which need to be considered when fighting international, regional, national and local wildlife crime. Strategies to combat wildlife crime successfully are described. The aim is to present failures to combat wildlife crime in general and in different societies, to reflect on errors and mistakes conducted at different levels and to discuss successful strategies to transform wildlife crime into wildlife protection on international, regional, national and local levels.

Keywords Mistakes · Errors · Failure in wildlife crime combat · Wildlife crime eradication · Sociocultural context · Global and local crime investigations and combat · Asia · Africa · Australia · Russia · China

26.1 Introduction

Wildlife crime has become a serious criminal offence at international, national, regional and local levels of societies. Several authors have pointed out that the situation with regard to wildlife crime has moved beyond a global environmental crisis which causes huge environmental, financial, social and cultural damage on an international level (see Nellemann et al. 2014; World Wildlife Fund [WWF] 2012). It has further been stressed that wildlife crime and crimes against nature have advanced to become the most threatening crimes in present and future years (White and Heckenberg 2014).

C.-H. Mayer (✉)
Department of Industrial Psychology and People Management, University of Johannesburg, Johannesburg, South Africa

Institut für Therapeutische Kommunikation und Sprachgebrauch, Europa Universität Viadrina, Frankfurt (Oder), Germany
e-mail: claudemayer@gmx.net

E. Vanderheiden, C.-H. Mayer (eds.), *Mistakes, Errors and Failures across Cultures*, https://doi.org/10.1007/978-3-030-35574-6_26

Not only has the international community started to fight wildlife crime, but also regional, national and local communities and associations have begun to combat wildlife crime through legal frameworks and organised crime combat structures and networks in different parts of the world (Wilson-Wilde 2010). However, wildlife crime still increases across the world and appears to be strongly resistant to crime combat strategies (Ayling 2013).

Wildlife crime has been defined by the WWF (2012) as an "environmental related crime that involves the illegal trade, smuggling, poaching, capture or collection of endangered species, protected wildlife (including animal and plants that are subject to harvest quotas and regulated permits) derivatives or products thereof". It threatens the integrity and sustainability of ecosystems and their services and usually impacts negatively on the economy with loss of income, as well as government revenue (Salum et al. 2018).

According to various authors, wildlife crime might occur in various forms, such as wildlife trafficking, poaching or consuming of wildlife (Moreto 2016), but also trading of illegal animal skins, leather goods, souvenirs or live pets (Sonia 2013). It usually affects the environment and causes loss of biodiversity, environmental destruction, loss of habitat and problems with the protection of endangered species (Ayling 2013). Gede (2014) emphasises that illegal wildlife trade is a multibillion-dollar business on one hand, but brings huge losses for governments on the other hand. Therefore, many stakeholders, government representatives and NGOs have increased their efforts to combat wildlife crime.

Previous literature has pointed out that failures in combatting wildlife crime are manifold (Kumarathunga et al. 2016). Failures are understood as a particular communicative and relationship-building activity (modelled after Lingard et al. 2004) which lacks success in communicating and/or building relationships with regard to a specific topic or content. In this chapter, failure is defined as lacking success in the combatting of wildlife crime owing to complex situations and circumstances.

This chapter analyses the failures of wildlife crime combat on global, regional, national and local levels. Based on this analysis, the author explores sociocultural circumstances which need to be considered when fighting wildlife crime at all levels. The question which arises is: why do international wildlife crime combat efforts fail to fight wildlife crime successfully and effectively? The aim here is to present common failures in combatting wildlife crime in selected sociocultural and national settings and to discuss successful strategies to transform wildlife crime into wildlife protection.

26.2 Failures in Wildlife Crime Combat in Different National and Cultural Contexts

Various failures in wildlife crime combat have been highlighted for different sociocultural areas and can be explored within the literature on wildlife crime eradication (Bräutigam and Knack 2004; Kisingo 2013; Kumarathunga et al. 2016; Salum et al. 2018; WWF 2015).

In her article on the failure of law enforcement systems to save endangered species, Bennett (2011) comments that humankind in general is failing to save these species from illegal hunting. The illegal business is controlled by well-organised international criminal syndicates which operate through countries with high levels of corruption (Bennet 2009). The WWF (2015) emphasises that different forms of corruption can lead to failures of prosecution of wildlife crime, such as in deliberately losing records; delaying cases; losing, contaminating or failing to gather evidence; failing to investigate suspected instances of wildlife crime; providing tip-offs about investigations to suspects of wildlife crimes; coercing witnesses, investigators, prosecutors or judges; bribing prosecutors, investigators or judges; or improper influence of senior officials or politicians over investigators, prosecutors and the judiciary.

According to Bennett (2011), success necessitates a complete change of how governments and wider societies deal with wildlife crime. Often, it seems to be the idea that wildlife crime is not a serious offence, which leads law enforcement agencies, such as customs and police, to being negligent with following up on wildlife crime. Not only are institutions often negligent with follow ups, but specific investigative techniques and other investigative tools such as anti-money laundering legislation are frequently not mobilised in connection with wildlife crime (CITES Secretariat 2013). Additionally, techniques such as intelligence-driven operations, risk-profiling, controlled deliveries, overt operations, forensics and the sharing of forensic evidence are not taking place, and financial flows are not monitored (Shaw and Reitano 2013).

Kurland and Pires (2016) stress that in the US context, specifically regarding the US Fish and Wildlife Services, analytical techniques and risk assessment strategies from criminology need to be utilised, and resources should be allocated and prioritised accordingly. Akella and Allan (2012) recommend that influential nation states such as the USA – which are one of the biggest consumers of legal and illegal wildlife products – should recognise their potential influence in the world in combatting wildlife crime; transform the demand for wildlife products; enhance intelligence and information-sharing; strengthen interdiction, investigations and prosecution; and build international capacity, cooperation and partnerships.

Illegal wildlife crime is often linked to African countries, because many of the wildlife products which are in demand in other parts of the world are exported from African countries. In *South Africa*, wildlife parks are often surrounded by local communities and previously disadvantaged groups whose socio-economic needs are not taken into account by governmental institutions. As long as these communities are not supported in securing a sustainable and stable future, poaching by community members will scarcely be prevented, and the protection of wildlife in the parks will not happen (The National Agricultural Marketing Council [NAMC] 2006). In the South African context, the country's history of apartheid is highly relevant in terms of wildlife crime and its prevention. Most of the wildlife laws and environmental legislation have not been adjusted since the end of apartheid (Snijders 2015). Mainly white European immigrants ran wildlife parks and game farming parks, and the ownership of wildlife has become a strongly debated political issue since ownership is still racially untransformed and often claims to land by, for example, traditional owners, clash with conservation areas (Mayer 2019).

Wildlife products for the Asian markets are usually shipped from East African countries, mainly Tanzania or Kenya, to Asia. Wildlife crime combat in *Tanzania*, according to Salum et al. (2018), fails due to weak governance. In Tanzania, this failure in governance often leads to unlawful possession of government trophies, failure to report these possessions, unlawful hunting of wildlife and specified animals, unlawful possession of weapons and unlawful capture of wildlife animals. Failure to successfully combat wildlife crime relates to a weak rule of law, bureaucracy, absence of accountability and high levels of corruption which are closely linked to weak governance (Bräutigam and Knack 2004). The failure in wildlife crime fighting is also related to weak conservation agency structures, corruption, lack of accountability and transparency in policy-making and administrative incompetency (Kisingo 2013). Corruption, as the abuse of entrusted power for private gain in the context of wildlife crime, is rife, when there is a lack of transparency and accountability mechanisms (such as measures for tracking, reporting performance and conduct), lack of effective deterrents, social stigma and low irregular pay (WWF 2015). Mabele (2017) stresses that Tanzania needs diversified strategies to combat wildlife crime and poaching rather than militarised tactics. This is particularly important, since the Tanzanian president announced his intention in 2015 to fight poaching with special paramilitary "anti-poaching" units. However, military war – "green militarisation" (Lunstrum 2014) – cannot be the final solution for conserving wildlife (Bluwstein 2018), particularly since wildlife areas have become "spaces of exception" (Mabele 2017, 488) in which violence is widespread and human rights abuses and killings are common.

Van Uhm and Moreto (2017) describe the failures in defining and living moral and ethical enterprises and relationships in the social world of wildlife contexts and emphasise that unscrupulous behaviour is fundamental to wildlife crime. Therefore, legal and illegal actors usually engage in antithetical relationships (van Uhm and Moreto 2017). It has further been argued that governments, but also other stakeholders, have greatly underestimated the social actors active in the relationships between legal and illegal wildlife trade (Raxter 2015) which has probably contributed to the failure of combatting wildlife crime and challenged the resource system's resilience.

In the context of *Uganda*, Picho et al. (2018) explain that efforts to combat wildlife crime often fail because of the failure to have mechanisms in place to detect wildlife products at ports of entry and exit and at borders. However, Mabele (2017) also notes that the dialogues among policy-makers, conservationists, academics and citizens are not sufficiently effective to improve strategies to combat wildlife crime and still fail to a large extent in terms of implementation. Failures to understand the competitive nature of illegal trade, the consumer preferences of wildlife crime products and the biological feasibilities need to be eradicated, or at least minimised (Mabele 2017).

Other authors, focusing on other countries on the African continent such as *Ethiopia*, highlight that prosecution rates for illegal ivory trade and trafficking need to increase to reduce wildlife crime (Ethiopian Wildlife Conservation Authority

[EWCA] 2014). Success and failure of court cases related to wildlife crime need to be communicated transparently (EWCA 2014).

Particularly in *Southeast Asia*, illegal wildlife trade is growing, since it is a hub for the consumption of wildlife and a key supplier of wildlife products. However, data is insufficient and unavailable (van Asch 2017), and law enforcement fails to decrease smuggling and trafficking (Wyatt 2016) since the ways and ideas of how to smuggle and traffic wildlife are becoming more sophisticated. In Vietnam, for example, bear parts have been smuggled in fake ambulances and military vehicles (World Bank 2005). Duffy et al. (2015, 2016) ascribe the failing of African wildlife protection to the rapidly rising wealthy population in Southeast Asia, particularly China, Vietnam and Taiwan, while Schroeder (2008) attributes the failure of wildlife crime combatting to failed promises of prioritising wildlife protection. This is also true for *Russia* and the *Far East* where wildlife crime mainly refers to fur trading of endangered animals and the illegal falcon trade (Wyatt 2009). Wyatt (2009) observes that here, the illegal wildlife markets need to be understood in depth, to fight wildlife crime in the region by establishing structural frameworks of understanding of these illegal markets so as to eventually destroy them. Wyatt (2011) points out that wildlife crime combat has failed to minimise wildlife trafficking, illegal raptor trade in Russia, the cruelty to animals and the threat to national and human security in connection to dangerous illicit activities.

Kumarathunga et al. (2016) find in their research study that wildlife crime is a serious offence in *Sri Lanka*. Approximately 43% of the cases of wildlife crime refer to entering and being in wildlife-protected areas without prior permission. Failure to combat wildlife crime is connected to the absence of a separate officer responsible for raids at field offices; weaknesses of initial investigations; not keeping accurate and complete records of crime incidences; errors in bail bonds, reports and charge sheets; absence of relevant officials before the courts; evidence-handling errors; and conflicting evidence as the major reasons for failures in wildlife crime investigations and bringing offenders before the courts.

Stimulation of the demand for ivory products in *China* greatly contributes to the failure of minimising wildlife crime globally (Cao 2016), although the Chinese government is reported to have raised the enforcement to combat wildlife crime to top political levels (Nowell 2012). Rhino horn trading has a long tradition in China dating back to 2600 BC (Ayling 2013). The trading of tiger parts shares this long tradition, with strong cultural and medical influences in China which maintain the demand for tiger parts (Moyle 2009). Within China, smuggling of tiger parts along Chinese and across international borders has led to small operating, highly effective criminal groups (Moyle 2009). Very little data and information exists about these groups, which makes it difficult to eradicate the crime (Moyle 2009). In 2018, however, it was reported that China has shut down the illegal ivory trade which, in recent years, contributed to the killing of thousands of African elephants (Southerland 2018). The demand for wildlife products, however, grows in China.

Vietnam and *Thailand* used to be only transit routes for wildlife products but have now developed a huge demand for these products (Felbab-Brown 2011). China, as well as Vietnam, has failed to reduce crime related to illegal rhino horn trade, and Southerland (2018) reports that, particularly in Myanmar, the mistreatment and killing of elephants continues since several body parts of elephants are reported to have medicinal effects. Although the government of *Myanmar* has reacted to the high number of elephant killings, their released trafficking ban is widely ignored, and the trafficking across the Myanmar–Chinese border continues. A relatively new phenomenon is "elephant skinning" which is spreading in *China*, *Thailand*, *India*, *Laos*, *Cambodia* and *Malaysia*. Elephant skin is used in pharmaceutical products to reduce illnesses and diseases, and elephant-skin tracking is in high demand. Nowell (2012) argues that particularly China and Vietnam should prioritise the development and implementation of well-researched and culture-specific demand reduction campaigns. In this context, methods to effectively monitor compliance and enforcement should be introduced to reduce the failing of wildlife crime combat. This has hardly happened (Nowell 2012).

The authorities in Australia report that wildlife crime in that country occurs mainly with reptiles, birds and native plants and that the fines given in the years 1998–2007 were usually below the black market value of the seizure itself (to a maximum of 30,000 Australian dollars) (Alacs and Georges 2008). The trend in globalisation of commerce continues and the restrictions on trade relax, which increases wildlife crime on the Australian continent (Alacs and Georges 2008).

Often wildlife crime is described as a problem of developing countries and of failures in governance. However, it has been pointed out that the *European Union* is strongly involved in the problems and failures to contain wildlife crime (Ruiz 2017). Within the European Union, the position of Spain as a gateway to and from the African continent makes it a relevant entry point to Europe for wildlife crime (Directorate General for Internal Policies 2016). In recent years, many operations have started to tackle a wide spectrum of wildlife-related crimes in *Spain*, focusing on stopping the illegal trade of birds of prey, snakes and lions, but also fish and specific plants and wood, such as illegally logged timber. Spanish failures to combat wildlife crime relate to the way that Spanish criminal law depends on administrative law, and often judges do not take both laws into account. Further, it has been criticised that judges have adopted questionable decisions in the past, in the way that they have not taken all facts into account or in the way that they have been lenient with penalties for wildlife crime offences (Directorate General for Internal Policies 2016). Generally, the most problematic situation is that there is a high rate of dismissal and acquittals because of insufficient evidence. The main failure therefore often occurs with regard to providing sustainable evidence for the case (Directorate General for Internal Policies 2016).

Several authors such as van Asch (2017) and Ford (2017) point out that in remote areas in which wildlife crime occurs, the crime often stays undetected, and these authors recommend that strategies, models and computer-based programmes should be developed to detect crime more frequently. These models could also help to define the failures and successes of wildlife crime combat more realistically since usually these statistics are estimated rather than defined in numbers. Often, organisations and models to combat wildlife crime act on statistics, the origin of which is uncertain or unclear (van Asch 2017). Knowledge of organised crime syndicates

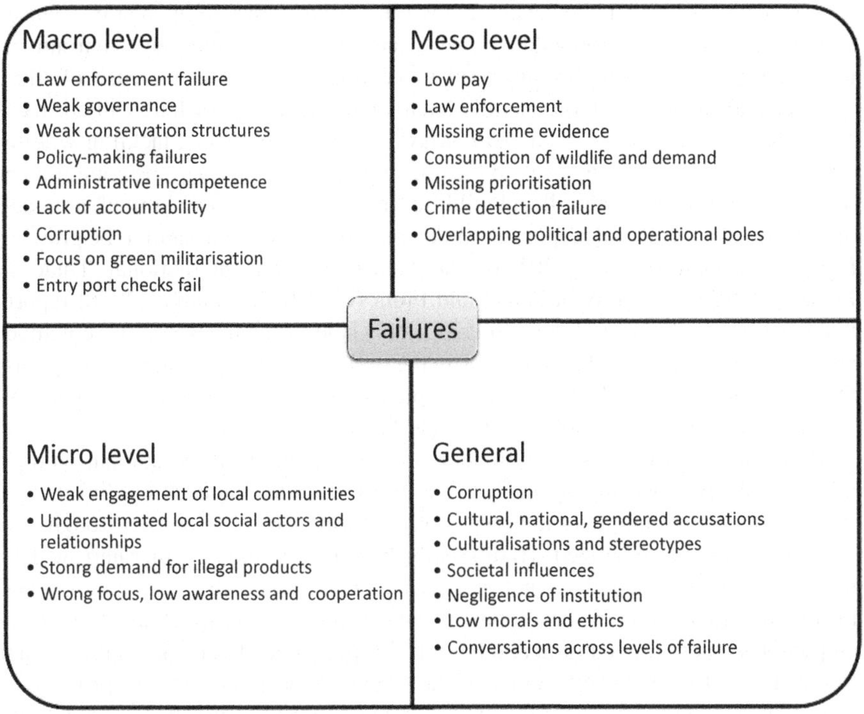

Fig. 26.1 Wildlife crime combat failure. (Author's own construction)

which are active in wildlife crime is still very limited and is only slowly growing (Ayling 2013, 59).

Figure 26.1 provides an overview of the areas in which wildlife crime combat and eradication often fails.

26.3 Strategies to Transform Failures in Combatting Wildlife Crime

Failures in wildlife crime combat need to be addressed urgently on global, regional, national and local levels. Guille (2010) proposes that to address wildlife crime effectively and efficiently, the layers of how to tackle wildlife crime need to be integrated; macro, meso and micro levels need to coordinate their data, actions and plans, while organisations and stakeholders on each level need to decide if they want to be political or operational and in which way. In this section of the chapter, strategies will be presented which should be taken into account when addressing failures in combatting wildlife crime in order to actively transform crime into wildlife protection.

When exploring strategies to combat wildlife crime, areas of interest in sciences which particularly focus on wildlife crime, such as green criminology, environmental or conservation criminology, need to be highlighted. The increase of these research and study areas has generally led to an increase in knowledge, interest and research in the field (van Asch 2017; Mayer 2019). The idea of tackling wildlife crime seems to be growing, even in the operational field; however, the commitment to tackle wildlife crime and illegal wildlife trade still seems to be limited, although diplomatic efforts, global responses and increased enforcement seem to be growing (US Department of State 2012). The Convention on International Trade in Endangered Species of Wild Fauna and Flora (CITES) Secretariat (2016) reports that the 17th Conference of the Parties (CoP17) held in Johannesburg in September and October 2016 showed major shifts in the protection of wild animals and against the overexploitation and illegal trade of plants and that international cooperation would increase and law enforcement would become more strict.

Researchers, as well as practitioners, often focus on efforts to combat wildlife crime instead of focusing on the prevention of wildlife crime. According to van Uhm (2018), new and alternative ways of eradicating wildlife crime through prevention need to be developed. Traditionally, criminology uses a rather narrow definition of crime which does not necessarily incorporate the sociocultural and historical influences on the development and combatting of crime. Van Uhm (2018) emphasises that social, cultural and historical aspects need to be taken into account to develop a deeper understanding of the crime, its development and process, as well as the networks it uses. This is particularly true for fulfilling the aim of wildlife crime prevention.

In many countries in which wildlife crime is rife, government, stakeholders, NGOs and other major players do not put an emphasis on the topic of wildlife crime, but rather focus on other burning topics such as poverty eradication or human trafficking (Snijders 2015). In countries which trade in curios, luxury foods and wildlife-based products such as medicine based on horn, ivory and other high-value species, awareness needs to be created of the problems connected to the demand for these products (Challender and MacMillan 2014). Wildlife crime eradication should not only be a central topic for the public and for operational and practically acting stakeholders; it also needs to be a central topic in the context of studies in criminology and crime sciences. Research and lectures on green criminology and particularly in wildlife crime and its combat should be increased internationally but also in these national contexts in which wildlife crime is a major concern (Mayer 2019). Strategy plans of the SADC (2016–2021), for example, further suggest to readjust wildlife laws and anti-poaching strategies and law enforcement. Policies need to be adjusted and the topic strengthened and reinforced across disciplines. Multidimensional aspects of wildlife crime combat need to be taken into account (Ramutsindela 2016).

26.3.1 International Level

Internationally, wildlife crime combat needs to take the following considerations into account. On international levels, organisations need to increase international cooperation to combat wildlife crime. International investigators, researchers and crime combat specialists need to increase their cooperation to combat wildlife crime more effectively (Wilson-Wilde 2010). Contextual aspects of wildlife crime need to be taken into account from various cultural perspectives which then need to lead into internationally planned actions (see Lunstrum 2014). This means that not only the elites of a country or the individuals and groups focusing n wildlife need to be taken into consideration, but also that cultural groups need to gain a voice in combatting wildlife crime. Cultural groups are usually under-represented in the national and international discourses. This could bring new perspectives, ideas and integrated approaches to the table and thereby lead to a multi-perspective approach in wildlife crime combat. In South Africa, for example, the representatives of previously disadvantaged groups need to be taken into the discourse along with white key players who run wildlife parks, to disentangle wildlife protection topics and historical racial debates in connection with agency.

Since most of the seizures of ivory and horn have occurred in China, Russia and the USA (Biggs et al. 2013; Taylor et al. 2016), international stakeholders need to work on decreasing the demand for wildlife hunting through education and training in these countries.

During recent years, several stakeholders have worked on increasing the strength of networks regarding law enforcement to define wildlife crime as a serious offence, such as the United Nations Office on Drugs and Crime (UNODC) and the International Consortium on Combating Wildlife Crime (ICCWC) who signed themselves into effect (Interpol 2010). International law seems to work towards addressing "the failures of human behaviour through the development of rules, institutions and other modalities of international governance" (van Asch 2017, 39).

In countries with a high demand for wildlife crime products, wildlife crime needs to be established as a serious international crime, because only then it will be treated effectively by law. Only then, more resources of wildlife crime conduct will be allocated (Bennett 2011; Mayer 2019). Based on these newly allocated resources, operational practices as well as new investigation tools and wildlife crime combat tools can be developed and applied. The newly developed investigative tools should be used in various global contexts and also in rural areas in which technological and professional standards might be less advanced than in industrialised urban areas. The tools need to be operational and practical and should be able to be operated with a minimum expertise of forensic investigation.

On international levels, research and operational networks need to be established, and investigation tools and techniques need to be expanded and opened for international exchange of information and sharing of criminal investigation tools. In addition, analysis and evaluation of effective research data and investigation tools should be made available internationally, and databases should be established.

International and national law enforcement practices can then be established along with the investigation processes. These processes must be established not only in the countries in which wildlife crime takes place but also along the chain of trade routes of wildlife crime (Bennett 2011). Particularly in these countries along the trade routes, judiciaries need to be informed and must to be prepared to give sentences to criminals active in wildlife crime.

Within this international cooperation, culturalisations (cultural group ascriptions) and intercultural stereotyping should be minimised and reduced (Griffiths 2018; Lambrechts and Goga 2016; Liddick 2011; Vázquez 2018) to foster cooperation which is based on a common aim to combat crime, not to be distracted by cultural stereotypes and accusations. In South African contexts, for example, wildlife crime is often considered the fault of Chinese markets, the huge Chinese demand of wildlife products and the Chinese wildlife crime mafia (Conservation Action Trust 2017). This shifts the focus from the complexity of the problem, as well as from the local criminal networks and their internal strategies, and externalises the problems and failures of local crime combat networks. The difficulty of such a shift in focus is that, then, crime is not viewed as being part of the failures or problems within the countries where it takes place and the complexity of crime and its countering is minimised. On a related note, Liddick (2011) comments on the assumption that the Neapolitan Mafia from Italy is behind illegal trading in China, Australia, Canada and South Africa. Although this may be partially true (Liddick 2011), the accusation and externalisation of criminal networks bear the risk that crime is not viewed as an internal problem but rather as an external problem. This might lead to wrong accusations and cultural stereotyping.

Griffiths (2018) observes that wildlife crime has a strong cultural impact in terms of ethnic groups in societies who define their own identity based on the relationship with nature and wildlife. The author points out that wildlife crime might even be interpreted as a form of cultural victimisation and has therefore a huge cultural impact on certain ethnic and cultural groups, which is often underestimated (Griffiths 2018).

In the context of 87 elephant cadavers found in the Okavango Delta in Botswana in September 2018, Sahba (2018), the UN environmental director of communication points out that the eradication of wildlife crime is failing, in part, because of missing cross-cultural communication. An urgent change in strategy is needed to save the world's wildlife. Wildlife crime is often attributed to certain indigenous groups stereotyped as being driven by poverty and cultural values and norms to commit wildlife crime (Duffy 2010). Instead of being stereotyped, indigenous people need to be understood in terms of their relationship with natural resources and wildlife.

In conclusion, at an international level, it can be seen that culture, nationhood, and gender play important roles in crime trials and crime combatting efforts. "Cultural others" often represent a threat to the nation if they fail to live up to the collective ideal and inclusiveness of the receiving society. In this case, culture, nationhood and gender are used to explain behaviour or even to justify it. Vázquez (2018) provides an example of this, in which a court operator explains that East

Europeans are accustomed to killing wildlife and would not know that it is a crime in their receiving country; therefore, they are involved in wildlife crime owing to their cultural background. Culturalisation processes are often racialised and gendered processes in court cases (Vázquez 2018), and this is true for wildlife crime cases as well. However, intersectionalities such as race, culture, gender and nationhood should be researched more frequently and in more depth to improve the understanding of their impacts on success and failure in combatting wildlife crime.

26.3.2 National Level

At national levels, national laws need to be established to combat wildlife crime effectively. Legal economic trade needs to be fostered and promoted and be used to combat illegal trade. Strategies need to take the national and local circumstances into account. In most of the countries in which wildlife crime is widespread, the eradication of wildlife crime needs to be made a key political issue (Mayer 2019). If this is not the case, law enforcement and operational practices will struggle to implement wildlife crime protection. Only when public concern is built, can long-term change be maintained in protecting against wildlife crime. Public concern can be built further by governmental subsidies which are landowner-friendly and which support them to protect their wildlife. Additionally, laws, for example, taxation laws, could help wildlife owners to protect their wildlife (Cloete et al. 2015).

National governmental wildlife parks need to increase ideas and actions of ownership and agency. If necessary, privately and governmentally owned wildlife conservation areas might need to be restructured to combat wildlife crime effectively. On national levels, governmental and national forces need to be unified to protect wildlife. In the Mokolodi Game Reserve, in Botswana, for example, the privately owned reserve cooperates effectively with the national military defence force to protect their wildlife in the park (Personal Communication Mokolodi 2018).

In countries in which corruption is high, different stakeholders should be included and networks built to prevent corrupt structures which might counteract wildlife protection. Individuals working in professions to protect wildlife (such as police, security, conservationists and rangers) should be paid well, and the risks they take should be appreciated. Civil society in countries battling with wildlife crime needs to become active and allocate their resources to destroy "sophisticated, well-funded, globally linked criminal operations" (Bennett 2011, 478). Further, historically grown political and economic frameworks – for example, with regard to land ownership as in South Africa or Zimbabwe – need to be taken into account, understood in their complexity and redefined.

New models and computer programmes could be used on national and local levels to combat wildlife crime. For instance, Ford (2017) evaluates various types of adversary attack prediction models. The models attempt to predict the likelihood of different targets being attacked, providing predictions of poacher attacks in a specific area. Ford (2017) identifies a new and advanced adversary behaviour modelling application which, when tested in real-world conditions, leads to greatly improved numbers of findings of wildlife crime in remote areas compared to the average historical observation rate. The improvement and wider use of attack protection models could help to detect criminal activity more frequently.

These kinds of adversary behaviour model applications, however, have been criticised for being limited to certain regions in which the park rangers usually patrol (Gholami et al. 2018). In Uganda, only 60% of the parks are usually controlled, and the attack protection models are limited to these areas (Gholami et al. 2018). Because the remote areas in which wildlife crime occurs are too huge to be patrolled, patrols are limited to certain posts, and areas are understaffed. This means that real crime data is always limited to the conditions of the regional and patrol activities and therefore might only reflect part of the reality of crime activities (Gholami et al. 2018). Failures in crime prevention when using adversary behaviour modelling software can occur owing to insufficient patrol activities. Predictions also fail as a consequence of annual crime analysis, while the actual trends in wildlife crime change more frequently and fluently. Further, the software equipment and techniques used are expensive and cannot be used effectively in low resource output areas. Data from different areas is often not integrated, and law enforcement agencies fail to use the modelled data (Gholami et al. 2018). These failures can lead to unreliable predictions and misleading information in wildlife crime prevention. Gholami et al. (2018) suggest a new model (aWare) which improves accuracy and runtime of algorithms and allows fine-grained patrols, which allows for improved patrol planning, based on improved predictions and in combination with lower cost equipment over multiple protected areas (Gholami et al. 2018).

26.3.3 Local Level

Particularly at local levels, the training of professionals to increase competencies and expertise to combat wildlife crime needs to increase (Snijders 2012). Local staff members such as rangers, private security guards and natural conservation specialists need to create ownership and agency within local communities and in wildlife habitats to cooperate to protect wildlife. Trained specialised social workers could support the establishment of tight cooperation structures at local levels across communities, with operational specialists (wildlife protection units, investigators, operational experts) and local inhabitants. Within the local community, specific key persons such as elders, community spokesmen, local decision-makers or municipal representatives should be called upon to inform local inhabitants about wildlife protection.

Information on wildlife protection should be provided not only in national languages but also in the languages of the local inhabitants. Different ways of distributing information, such as written information, oral presentations, panel discussions, scientific seminars, workshops and theatre plays, should be implemented to reach out for local inhabitants across ethnic and cultural groups, language groups, generational and gender lines. Training programmes for different stakeholders (police, security, rangers, conservation experts) need to be provided to prepare individuals professionally to use forensic investigation tools. If at all possible, training centres in combatting wildlife crime should be established in remote area where they are really needed, and programmes of volunteering could support the running of these trainings in decentralised centres. These centres would also need to have essential equipment such as forensic investigation tools (Mayer 2019) and would require the use of culture-specific didactical approaches (Henson et al. 2016). In Sri Lanka, researchers Kumarathunga et al. (2016) conclude that providing a sound training in legal court practices, employing legal committed officers, providing uniforms and weapons, and accelerating reward processes and appreciation of commitments would positively affect and decrease the failures in wildlife crime eradication. Besides the training programmes in rural areas, higher education institutions should expand their criminology and crime science departments to advance wildlife crime fighting with regard to local structures and develop interesting career development paths for local professionals (Mayer 2019).

Summarising, strategies to combat wildlife crime should include more monitoring of wildlife crime activities and an increased global awareness of wildlife crime as an environmental concern and threat to humankind, a critical evaluation of green militarisation and increased military patrols, increase of proactive law enforcement action with intelligence-led detection mechanisms and a well-established system to punish the perpetrators. Successful prosecutions and appropriate penalties need to be defined and standardised at local, national and international levels. The critical evaluation of behaviour modelling applications and their abilities to contribute to investigations needs to be explored further. To implement strategies successfully, loopholes and leakages need to be closed through a meaningful and collaborative multi-agency collaboration across social, cultural and organisational boundaries, while creative, innovative and effective strategies to reduce the demand for wildlife products need to be implemented in socioculturally specific ways.

Figure 26.2 provides an overview of overall strategies to counter failures in wildlife crime combat in the different areas and levels described above.

26.4 Conclusions

Wildlife crime is a huge threat to the global, regional, national and local environment and to the basis of existence for humankind. On all levels of cooperation, wildlife crime combatting needs to use bottom-up and top-down approaches simultaneously to minimise wildlife crime effectively. During the past few years, research on wildlife crime prevention and its failures in different contexts has increased, with the aim to develop effective, operational and practical tools, turning wildlife crime into wildlife protection.

Persistent challenges and failures exist with regard to the effective fighting of wildlife crime, such as weak international cooperation and too little data exchange,

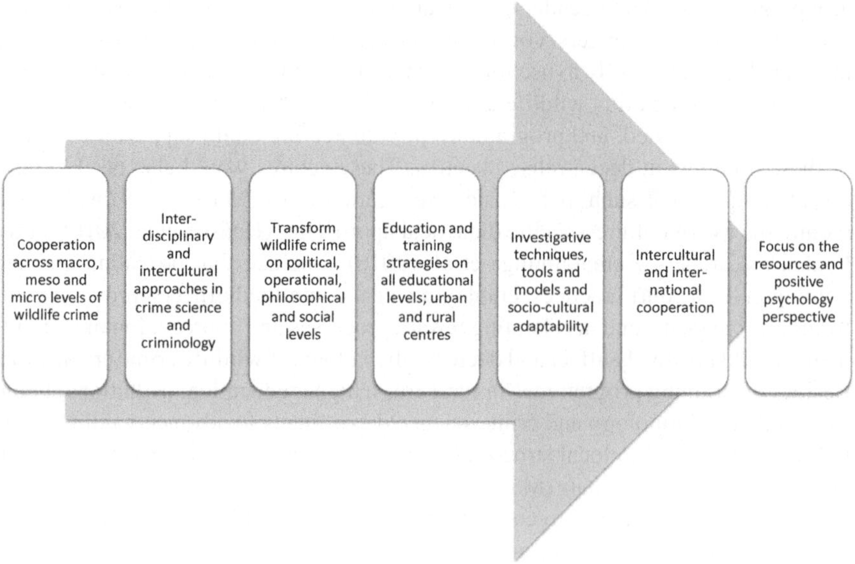

Fig. 26.2 Areas of strategies of wildlife crime combat. (Author's own construction)

a lack of political and governmental will at national and local levels, lack of resources on all three levels, as well as a lack of capacity and interagency cooperation, a lack of transparency and performance monitoring, as well as insufficient educational forces at all levels. Further, erroneous communication, analysis, interpretation and judgement of facts may have led to false decision-making in terms of wildlife crime combatting and its eradication. However, these failures, errors and mistakes can be transformed into worthwhile direction posts and resources when they are analysed and evaluated openly, critically and in cooperation across cultural and agency lines. Then, past and present failures in stemming the flow of wildlife crimes can turn into opportunities for future success in diminishing wildlife crimes across cultural lines.

References

Akella, A.S., & Allan, C. (2012). *Dismantling wildlife crime: Executive summary*. Washington, DC: World Wildlife Fund. https://www.traffic.org/site/assets/files/7385/dismantling-wildlife-crime_2.pdf.

Alacs, E. & Georges, A. (2008). Wildlife across our borders: a review of the illegal trade in Australia. *Australian Journal of Forensic Sciences,* 40(2), 147–160.

Ayling, J. (2013). What sustains wildlife crime? Rhino horn trading and the resilience of criminal networks. *Journal of International Wildlife Law & Policy*, 16, 57–80.

Bennet, E.L. (2009). Social dimensions of managing hunting in tropical forests. In M.J. Manfredo, J.J. Vaske, P.J. Brown, D.D. Decker & E.A. Duke (Eds.), *Wildlife and Society: The Science of Human Dimensions* (pp. 289–300). Washington, DC: Island Press.

Bennett, E.L. (2011). Another inconvenient truth: the failure of law enforcement systems to save charismatic species. Fauna & Flora International, *Onyx,* 45(4), 476–479.

Biggs, D., Courchamp, F., Martin, R., & Possingham, H.P. (2013). Conservation. Legal trade of Africa's rhino horns. *Science,* 339,1038–1039.

Bluwstein, J. (2018). Problematizing debates on wildlife conservation and the war on poaching. *Conservation Biology,* 30(4), 692–693.

Bräutigam, D.A. & Knack, S. (2004) Foreign aid, institutions, and governance in Sub-Saharan Africa. *Economic Development and Culural Change,* 52(2), 255–285.

Cao, D. (2016). Wildlife crimes and legal protection of wildlife in China. Animal Law and Welfare—*International Perspectives*, 263–278.

Challender, D.W.S., & MacMillan, D.C. (2014). Poaching is more than an Enforcement Problem. Conservation letters. *A Journal of the Society for Conservation Biology,* 7(5), 484–494.

Cloete, P.C., van Der Merwe, P., & Saayman, M. (2015). *Game ranch profitability in South Africa.* 2nd edition. Pretoria: Caxton.

Conservation Action Trust. (2017). *Chinese underworld exposed (Namibia)* https://conservation-action.co.za/recent-news/chinese-underworld-exposed-namibia/.

Convention on International Trade in Endangered Species (CITES) Secretariat. (2013). *Chair's Summary of ICCWC Roundtable on Combatting Transnational Organised Wildlife and Forest Crime for Ministers and High-level Representatives.* Document CoP16 Inf.54 prepared for the 16th meeting of the CITES Conference of the Parties, 3–14 March. http://www.cites.org/eng/cop/16/inf/E-CoP16i-54.pd.

Convention on International Trade in Endangered Species (CITES) Secretariat. (2016). *Largest ever World Wildlife Conference hailed as a 'game changer'*. 4 October 2016. https://cites.org/eng/news/pr/Largest_ever_World_Wildlife_Conference_CoP17_-hailed_as_a_game_changer_04102016.

Directorate General for Internal Policies. (2016). *Wildlife Crime in Spain.* http://www.europarl.europa.eu/RegData/etudes/IDAN/2016/578962/IPOL_IDA(2016)578962_EN.pdf.

Duffy, R. (2010). Your role in wildlife crime. *New Scientist*, 207 (2777), 28–29. https://doi.org/10.1016/S0262-4079(10)62197-5.

Duffy, R., St John, F.A.V., Büscher, B., & Brockington, D. (2015). The Militarization of Anti-poaching: Undermining Long-term goals? *Environmental Conservation*, 4 (4), 345–348.

Duffy, R., St John, F.A.V., Büscher, B., & Brockington, D. (2016). Toward a New Understanding of the Links between Poverty and Illegal Wildlife Hunting. *Conservation Biology*, 30 (1), 14–22.

Ethiopian Wildlife Conservation Authority (EWCA). (2014). *National Ivory Action Plan for Ethiopia*. Addis Ababa, Ethiopia. https://www.cites.org/sites/default/files/common/prog/niaps/E-Ethiopia-NIAP-2014.pdf.

Felbab-Brown, V. (2011). *The Disappearing Act: The Illicit Wildlife Trade in Asia.* Brookings Institution, Washington, DC, USA.

Ford, B. (2017). Real-world evaluation and deployment of wildlife crime predication models. Doctoral thesis. University of Southern California, US. http://teamcore.usc.edu/papers/2017/BenFord_thesis.pdf.

Gede, M. (2014). A tale of two species: Habitat conservation plans as bounded conflict. *Journal of Wildlife Management*, 68(4), 743–761.

Gholami, S., McCarthy, S., Dilkina, B., Plumptre, A., Tambe, M., Driciru, M., Wanyama, F., Rwetsiba, A., Nsubaga, M., Mabonga, J., Okello, T. & Enyel, E. (2018). Adversary models account for imperfect crime data: forecasting and planning against real-world poachers. Session 21: Engineering multiagent systems 1. *AAMAS*, July, 10–15, 2018, Stockholm, Sweden.

Griffiths, M. (2018). Heritage lost: the cultural impact of wildlife crime in South Africa. *South African Crime Quarterly*, 60. https://doi.org/10.17159/2413-3108/2017/v0n60a1728.

Guille, L. (2010). Policing in Europe: An Ethnographic Approach to Understanding the Nature of Cooperation and the Gap between Policy and Practice. *Journal of Contemporary European Research*, 6(2), 257–271.

Henson, D.W., Malpas, R.C., & D'Udine. (2016). *Wildlife law enforcement in sub-Saharan African protected areas. A review of best practices.* Cambridge, UK: International Union for Conservation of Nature and Natural Resources.

Interpol. (2010). *Powerful Alliance to Fight Wildlife Crime comes into Effect.* http://www.interpol.int/Public/ICPO/PressReleases/PR2010/PR098.asp, 1 November 2018.

Kisingo, A.W. (2013) *Governance of Protected Areas in the Serengeti Ecosystem*, Tanzania. Doctor of Philosophy dissertation, University of Victoria, Canada. Retrieved 10 September 2019, from https://dspace.library.uvic.ca/bitstream/handle/1828/4931/Kisingo_Alex_PhD_%202013.pdf?sequence=1&isAllowed=y.

Kumarathunga, U., Supun Lahiru Prakash, T.G., & Perera, P. (2016). *Reasons for Failures in Wildlife Crime Investigations and Court Procedures of the Department of Wildlife Conservation in Polonnaruwa Assistant Directors' Region of Sri Lanka (Qualitative Study).* 21st International Forestry and Environment Symposium 2016, Department Of Forestry and Environmental Science, University of Sri Jayewardenepura, 21.

Kurland, J., & Pires, S.F. (2016). Assessing U.S. Wildlife trafficking patterns: How criminology and conservation science can guide strategies to reduce the illegal wildlife trade. *Deviant Behaviour,* 38(4), 375–391.

Lambrechts, D., & Goga, K. (2016). Money and marginalisation: the lost war against Abalone poaching in South Africa. *Politikon*, 43(2), 231–249.

Lunstrum, E. (2014). Green Militarization: Anti-poaching efforts and the spatial contours of Kruger National Park. *Nature and Society*, 104(4), 816–832.

Liddick, D.R. (2011). *Crimes against nature. Illegal industries and the global environment.* Santa Barbara, CA: ABC-Clio Corporate.

Lingard, L., Espin, S., Whyte, S., Regehr, G., Baker, G.R., Reznick, R., Bohnen, J., Orser, B., Doran, D. & Grober, E. (2004). Communication failures in the operating room: an observational classification of recurrent types and effects, *BMJ Quality & Safety*, 13(5), 321. doi: https://doi.org/10.1136/qhc.13.5.321.

Mabele, M.B. (2017). Beyond forceful measures: Tanzania's 'war on poaching' needs diversified strategies more than militarised tactics, *Review of African Political Economy*, 44(153), 487–498. doi: https://doi.org/10.1080/03056244.2016.1271316.

Mayer, C.-H. (2019). *Combating wildlife crime in South Africa – Using gelatine lifters for forensic trace recovery*. Springer Briefs in Criminology. Cham, Switzerland: Springer Briefs.

Moreto, W.D. (2016). Occupational stress among law enforcement rangers: Insights from Uganda. *Oryx*, 50(4), 646–654.

Moyle, B. (2009*).* The black market in China for tiger products. *Global Crime*, 10(1–2), 124–143.

NAMC: The National Agricultural Marketing Council. (2006). *Report on the Investigation to Identify Problems for Sustainable Growth and Development in South African Wildlife Ranching*. Pretoria, South Africa: NAMC.

Nellemann, C., Henriksen, R., Raxter, P., Ash, N., & Mrema, E. (2014). *The environmental crime crisis: threats to sustainable development from illegal exploitation and trade in wildlife and forest resources*. Nairobi, Kenya: UN Environment. Programme.

Nowell, K. (2012). *Wildlife Crime Scorecard*: Assessing compliance with and enforcement of CITES commitments for tigers, rhinos and elephants. World Wildlife Fund for Nature Report, 1–36. http://awsassets.panda.org/downloads/wwf_wildlife_crime_scorecard_ report.pdf.

Personal Communication Mokolodi (2018). Mokolodi Game Reserve. Gaborone, Botswana.

Picho, E.O., Musinguzi, J. & Basheka, B.C. (2018). *The nature of management of wildlife trade in Uganda.* http://dir.muni.ac.ug/bitstream/handle/20.500.12260/244/Picho_Article_2018.pdf?sequence=1&isAllowed=y

Ramutsindela, M. (2016). Wildlife crime and state security in South(ern) Africa: An overview of developments. *Politikon: South African Journal of Political Studies*, 43(2), 159–171.

Raxter, A. (2015). *Wildlife crime and other challenges to resource system resilience*. Doctor of Philosophy (PhD) dissertation, International Studies, Old Dominion University, doi: 10.25777/8dxn-x142. https://digitalcommons.odu.edu/gpis_etds/3.

Ruiz, I.B. (2017). Europe, a silent hub of illegal wildlife trade. Deutsche Welle. https://www.dw.com/en/europe-a-silent-hub-of-illegal-wildlife-trade/a-37183459.

Salum, J., Eustace, A., Malata, P.F., & Mbangwa, O.F. (2018). Wildlife crime promoted by weak governance. *African Journal of Ecology*, 56(1), 101–108. https://onlinelibrary.wiley.com/doi/epdf/10.1111/aje.12424.

Schroeder, R.A. (2008). Environmental Justice and the Market: The Politics of Sharing Wildlife Revenues in Tanzania. *Society & Natural Resources*, 21(7), 583–596.

Shaw, M. & Reitano, T. (2013). *The Evolution of Organized Crime in Africa: Towards a New Response*. Institute for Security Studies, Paper 244.

Sahba, N. (2018, October 8). The missing link: communication to combat wildlife crime. *Independent*. https://www.independent.co.uk/voices/campaigns/GiantsClub/Botswana/the-missing-link-communication-to-combat-wildlife-crime-a8574946.html.

Snijders, D. (2012). Wild property and its boundaries—on wildlife policy and rural consequences in South Africa. *The Journal of Peasant Studies*, 39(2), 503–520.

Snijders, D. (2015). *Shifting Species in South Africa. Wildlife Policy, Rural Consequences*. Doctoral dissertation, University of Amsterdam. http://www.rhinoresourcecenter.com/pdf_files/142/1422583600.pdf.

Sonia, D. (2013). *National Survey of fishing, hunting, and Wildlife associated recreation: National overview*. Washington, DC: US Department of the Interior.

Southerland, D. (2018). China shuts down ivory trade, wildlife trafficking continues. Commentaries. *Radia Free Asia*. https://www.rfa.org/english/commentaries/wildlife-05042018154949.html.

Taylor, A., Lindsey, P., & Davies-Mostert, H. (2016). *An assessment of the economic, social and conservation value of the wildlife ranching industry and its potential to support the green economy in South Africa. Green Economy Research Report*. Johannesburg: The Endangered Wildlife Trust. http://www.the-eis.com/data/literature/Taylor%20et%20al%20%202016%20An%20assessment%20of%20the%20economic%20social%20and%20conservation%20value%20of%20the%20wildlife%20ranching%20industry%20and%20its%20potential%20to%20support%20the%20green%20e.pdf.

US Department of State. (2012). [Media Release] A Call to Action. 8 November. Retrieved 10 September 2019, from http://www.state.gov/r/pa/prs/ps/2012/11/200355.htm.

van Asch, E. (2017). *Exploring the effectiveness of international cooperation to combat transnational organized wildlife crime: lessons learned from initiatives in Asia*. Doctoral thesis, the University of Sheffield, School of Law, Department of Criminology. http://etheses.whiterose.ac.uk/19161/1/van%20Asch%2C%20E%20%282017%29%20Exploring%20Effectiveness%20of%20International%20Cooperation%20to%20Combat%20Transnational%20Organized%20Wildlife%20Crime%20Lessons%20Learned%20from%20Initiatives%20in%20Asia.%20PhD%20thesis%2C%20University%20of%20Sheffield.pdf.

van Uhm, D.P. & Moreto, W.D. (2017). Corruption within the illegal wildlife trade: a symbiotic and antithetical enterprise. *British Journal of Criminology*. doi:10.1093/bjc/azx032.

van Uhm, D.P. (2018). The social construction of the value of wildlife: A green cultural criminological perspective. *Theoretical Criminology*, 22(3), 384–401.

Vázquez, Y. (2018). Enforcing the politics of race and identity in migration and crime control policies. In M. Bosworth, A. Parmar, & Y. Vázquez (Eds.), *Race, criminal justice and migration control. Enforcing the boundaries of belonging*. Oxford, UK: Oxford University Press.

White, R., & Heckenberg, D. (2014). *Green Criminology. An introduction to the study of environmental harm*. Oxon, OX: Routledge.

Wilson-Wilde, L. (2010). Wildlife Crime: a global problem. *Forensic Science, Medicine and Pathology*, 6, 221–222.

World Bank. (2005). *Going, Going, Gone: The Illegal Trade in Wildlife in East and Southeast Asia, (English)*. Environment and Social Development Department, East Asia and Pacific Region discussion paper series. Washington, DC: World Bank.

World Wildlife Fund (WWF). (2012). *Fighting illicit wildlife trafficking: a consultation with governments. Retrieved 10 September 2019, from* http://www.cites.org/common/news/2012/Dalberg-Report-on-Fighting-Illicit-Wildlife-Trafficking.pdf.

World Wildlife Fund (WWF). (2015). *Strategies for fighting corruption in wildlife conservation: a primer*. Gland, Switzerland: WWF.

Wyatt, T. (2009). Exploring the organization of Russia Far East's illegal wildlife trade: two case studies of the illegal fur and illegal falcon trades. *Global Crime,* 10 (1–2), 144–154.

Wyatt, T. (2011). The illegal trade of raptors in the Russian federation. *Contemporary Justice Review*, 14(2), 103–123.

Wyatt, T. (2016). The uncharismatic and unorganized side to wildlife smuggling. In L. Elliot & W.H. Schaedla (Eds.), *Handbook of Transnational Environmental Crime*. Cheltenham, UK: Elgar Publishing.

Claude-Hélène Mayer (Dr. habil., PhD) is a Professor in Industrial and Organisational Psychology at the Department of Industrial Psychology and People Management at the University of Johannesburg; an Adjunct Professor at the European University Viadrina in Frankfurt (Oder), Germany; and a Senior Research Associate at Rhodes University, Grahamstown, South Africa. She holds an M.A. (his-phil) degree in Sociocultural Anthropology, Intercultural Didactics and Socio-economics of Rural Development (Georg-August University, Germany) and an M.Sc. degree in Crime Science, Investigation and Intelligence (University of Portsmouth, UK). She further holds a PhD in Psychology (University of Pretoria, South Africa) and in Management (Rhodes University, South Africa), a Doctorate (Georg-August University, Germany) in Political Sciences (Sociocultural Anthropology and Intercultural Didactics) and a Habilitation (European University Viadrina, Germany) in Psychology with focus on work, organisational and cultural psychology. In Crime Science, she has focused on wildlife crime combat, as well as on concepts and interventions in positive criminology/positive victimology as well as crime and shaming.

Part VII
Mistakes, Errors and Failure in Medicine

Chapter 27
Safety 3.0 and the End of the Superstar Clinician

Chris P. Subbe and Paul Barach

'Every system is perfectly designed to get the results it gets'.

Paul Batalden

Abstract Training of clinicians in both nursing and medicine is often focused on improving their individual competencies in the hope to reduce error and patient harm rates to a negligible level. Medicine attracts the brightest students in most countries through a highly competitive selection process. Despite this, 5–10% of patients admitted to hospital continue to suffer complications with significant morbidity and mortality. Disappointingly error rates in many areas have not significantly changed for decades.

The dominant philosophies of error reduction are 'Safety 1' and 'Safety 2'. The principle of 'Safety 1' focuses on measurement and understanding of errors. 'Safety 2' is looking for resilient systems in which we seek to understand how people manage to create safety despite system weaknesses and endeavour to better appreciate successful safe working practices.

In this chapter in build on Safety 1 and 2, and introduce the concept of Safety 3.0. In contrast to the principles applied to reducing errors in hospitals, the high-reliability industries have used another approach to assure reliable, reduction of failures and to enhance safety: modular redundancy. This approach assures that safety-critical parts of technical systems exist in triplicate or quadruplicate backups and the failure of individual parts does not lead to catastrophic system failures and fatal outcomes. This might be the key to reliable safety of complex social-technical systems such as aviation, nuclear power, space travel and more.

The application of this principle is still rare in healthcare, but acceptance of the need for a robust safety management system based on redundancy of safety-critical

C. P. Subbe (✉)
Bangor University, Bangor, UK

P. Barach
Wayne State University, Detroit, MI, USA

E. Vanderheiden, C.-H. Mayer (eds.), *Mistakes, Errors and Failures across Cultures*, https://doi.org/10.1007/978-3-030-35574-6_27

steps in medical processes and distributive models of governance might improve error rates, reduce patient harm and enhance clinical outcomes. Patient involvement is essential as an equal partner in the co-design of robust safety in healthcare and key to achieving the triple aims goals of safe, effective and patient-centred care.

Keywords Mistakes · Errors · Failures · Patient safety · Patient-centred · Healthcare · Hierarchy · Co-production

27.1 The Ecosystem of Clinical Safety

27.1.1 Medicine as the Noble Profession

The framework of healthcare delivery is shifting rapidly across the world. Healthcare is in a political, social and financial crisis that is fuelling dramatic action and reform. Chronic disease is shortening our lifespan, destroying our quality of life, bankrupting governments, and threatening the health of future generations. Unfortunately, conventional medicine has failed to adequately address this challenge, and the prevalence of most chronic health problems continues to rise. The systems that will thrive will focus on cost-efficiency, quality of care, innovative healthcare delivery and alignment of incentives with payers and other participants in the healthcare equation (Barach and Kleinman 2018).

Medicine continues to attract the greatest minds and an exploding array of technologies investigating the creation of life, the structures underlying our existence and the reasons why these might or might not fail. In no other field of science has progress been more closely linked to the expectations and fantasies of the human mind, and in no other field is change felt in the same way. Diseases that were un-survivable even 20 or 30 years ago are now routinely managed if not treated successfully. The scourges of human history have in many areas been beaten back or at least contained such as with HIV AIDS where one can expect in 2019 to live a long and productive life (Gapminder Foundation n.d.; Griffiths et al. 2018). Infectious diseases such as leprosy and plague are now treatable, nutritional diseases such as scurvy and rickets have been all but eliminated in Western countries, and even many cancers are today survived thanks to a combination of better understanding of their aetiology, genetics and vulnerabilities.

Investment into new technologies has been relentless with the medical-industrial complex taking on a larger and larger proportion of the economic output so that in the USA, for example, nearly 1/5 of the GDP is consumed by healthcare (Sisko et al. 2019).

At a time when diagnostic tests are becoming more insightful and treatments more powerful, a more sinister narrative has however started to emerge. These highly qualified specialists that modern medicine produces, are being undermined by complex and dysfunctional systems that are generating a significant number of errors, abetted by powerful technologies, and directly contributing to patient harm.

27.1.2 Challenged by Increasing Complexity of Care

The exploding complexity of modern medicine (Braithwaite et al. n.d.) has challenged providers, while the autonomy of the medical profession has been under threat all while maintaining or increasing work productivity and profitability. A single hospital might create the same amount of data as a globally operating bank – but have only a fraction of the systems expertise and analytic frameworks to understand and respond to this data and its implications. A single patient who is admitted for a hospital stay will have vital signs captured four to eight times per day depending on local policy. The majority of patients who require hospital admission will suffer from a number of pre-existing conditions and will take medications usually several times per day. At the same time, nurses will chart fluid intake and output, bowel movements, status of the skin, and other observations. As a conservative estimate, an average-sized clinical unit looking after up to 30 patients will generate 1500 data points per day of which half are dynamic and constantly changing and often interacting; administering a blood pressure tablet will lower blood pressure but might also affect heart rate and blood tests indicating renal function or urine output and require a system to check for these daily and over several days.

Changes in epidemiology have added an additional layer of complexity. Frailty is a clinical syndrome of accumulated deficits that can affect every single organ system but will affect individual patients in different ways (Jones et al. 2004). Patients who are frail might or might not respond to usually successful treatments, and importantly they might also hold beliefs about what treatments might or might not be appropriate for them. The increasingly frail inpatient population is more vulnerable and adds a layer of risk and complexity to individual and organizational risk and clinical decision-making. It is hence clear that the amount of data creates a cognitive load that simply overwhelms clinical systems and clinicians (Harry and Sweller 2016).

27.1.3 Organizational Culture: An Important Context for Addressing and Improving Error Rates in Patient Care

Aspects of organizational culture, or how providers 'do things here', are increasingly appreciated as essential in understanding how best to improve the quality of healthcare (Boan and Funderburk 2003; Schein 2010). We define organizational culture as the social-organizational phenomena, in terms of behaviour or attitudes, that emerge from a common way of sense-making, based on shared values, beliefs, assumptions and norms (Bolman and Deal 1997; Scott et al. 2003). Evidence suggests that organizational culture may be relevant for successful and sustained improvement efforts, especially in training years, and to better define key problems and formulate hypothesis to test models of change (Spencer-Oatey n.d.; Vohra et al. 2007).

The culture of the world of clinical medicine has some characteristics that might have made it more susceptible to the safety challenges outlined below. Healing has been associated for millennia with divine powers. Those undertaking the healing have therefore often been associated with these powers. Medicine has in the last two centuries acquired a renewed status by association with the knowledge and belief systems underlying modern science that has replaced in many areas religious value systems. Science offers a perspective to use rational analysis of data as a way to understand and frame problems and then devise solutions to 'fix' them. When this type of thinking is used in areas that are closely related with life and death, it is difficult to not ascribe those who lead it with quasi-religious powers.

Rapid advances in specific technologies, breakthroughs in transplant surgery, understanding of our genome and fertility treatments have inspired the public imagination and made pioneering clinicians and researchers into superstars of popular culture. Furthermore, until fairly recently this culture was overwhelmingly male dominated. While few doctors would these days want to be described as 'half-gods in white', the religious context of medicine is part of its heritage and unlikely to foster insight, reflection and humility. The seminal study, *Boys in White* (Becker et al. 1976), remains a remarkable and relevant ethnographic study of how highly impressionable young men in medical school lived their schedules, their efforts to find out what professors wanted from them in tests and exercises, their 'latent culture' (the division into alphas and betas, fraternity and non-fraternity men), their slow assimilation of medical professional values through peer pressure and example, their learning how to negotiate a hospital or clinic in all its complexity and their perspectives on what they must do to guarantee their futures.

27.2 The Safety Challenges of Modern Medicine

Studies from the United States, Australia (Wilson et al. 1995), the Netherlands (Zegers et al. 2009), New Zealand (Davis et al. 2002, 2003), Canada (Baker et al. 2004) and the United Kingdom (Vincent et al. 2001; Hogan et al. 2012) show that a significant proportion of patients who enter the 'healthcare cathedrals' of the (twentieth and) twenty-first century will suffer adverse events as a result of the diagnostic and therapeutic interventions they receive (Kohn et al. 2000).

Safety is defined as freedom from accidental injury (Kohn et al. 2000). Harm is defined through morbidity or death not related to the initial disease or the need for additional resources (Nebeker et al. 2005). Harm can be caused by errors of commission or omission. Some of the errors might well be unavoidable and the result of unexpected variation in patients' physiology and vulnerabilities. But in today's understanding of medical harm caused by medical errors, there is a broad understanding that around a half of the charted harm is probably preventable (Panagioti et al. 2019).

At the same time, there is an understanding that the 'culture' of hospitals is intimately linked to the safety of its operations; in a number of studies using questionnaire-based tools or direct observations, investigators have found that strong hierarchies, bullying, working in professional silos and disruptive and poor communication directly impact the chances of patients to survive (Weaver et al. 2013). A deeper understanding about the relationships between patient outcomes, organizational structure, and their underlying cultural barriers is needed because they may provide a better understanding of the harm when staff and management are diengaged and lack psychological safety (Bruback et al. 2019). This has resulted in a number of training programmes that target the culture of teams to improve safety such as the team training program TeamSTEPPS (Barach 2007; Siassakos et al. 2013; Wakeman and Langham 2018).

Why has the safety and quality movement been slow to improve care (Phelps and Barach 2014)? To examine the topic, an illustrative example might be helpful.

27.2.1 Safety Case Study: Cardiopulmonary Arrests and Avoidable Admissions to Critical Care

Modern hospital medicine deals with increasingly complex conditions: patients present with a multitude of previous conditions, treated with powerful medications, and present to the hospital often at a late stage of their illness or life when physiological reserves to combat acute illness might be partially depleted. The combination of frail elderly patients who are suffering from serious illness and are being treated with one or often several powerful treatments results in an explosive combination. In patients where survival is expected, the deterioration and death are usually not what patients, families or clinicians expect. The sudden stop of the heart and or breathing, the 'cardiopulmonary arrest', is therefore often seen as the worst-case-scenario and an unexpected catastrophe.

Cardiopulmonary arrests are however not as uncommon as one would expect. Cardiopulmonary arrests rates are between 0.2 and 2 per 1000 patients admitted to a given hospital (Santamaria et al. 2010). The more challenging aspect is that the overwhelming number of these cardiopulmonary arrests is predictable. Researchers have found that over 80% of patients had clearly documented signs of worsening vital signs, in particular breathlessness and changes in level of consciousness, before they arrested, and were often missed by staff (Schein et al. 1990). 66% of patients who subsequently suffered cardiopulmonary arrests had documented deterioration over 6 h or more (Franklin and Mathew 1994). Similarly a large study examining patients admitted to UK intensive care units showed significant abnormalities in patients' vital signs as early as 72 h before they were moved from their general ward to intensive care (Cullinane et al. 2005). So how can a system that employs so many highly motivated and talented staff with cutting edge technology lead to such preventable harm?

27.3 Frameworks for Continuous Systems Improvement

Safety 1 and Safety 2 are approaches to learning systems that were first described by Hollnagel and Braithwaite (Hollnagel et al. 2015). Safety 1 starts with an adverse event and tries to deduct the reasons and mechanisms that led to this outcome but undertaking an analysis of root causes that can then be the target for efforts to improve the system and prevent future mishaps (Cassin and Barach 2012). Many adverse events follow patterns, and analysing events and near miss events in some detail might therefore help to prevent many future events (Barach and Small 2000).

The weakness of this approach is that while the identified route causes might have contributed to disasters, more often they don't because individuals and teams find ways to improvise, mitigate against them and work around them. Understanding these workarounds and using them to make systems more reliable is hence the basis of thinking behind 'Safety 2' (Halbesleben et al. 2008).

Safety 2 starts with the observation that the majority of episodes of care don't end in disaster despite being performed in the same environment by the same people and the same equipment in which the care that went wrong. Understanding the human and systems conditions under which things go right, is therefore another route to create safer systems (Amalberti et al. 2005a, b).

The principles of Safety 1 and Safety 2 can be applied to the problem of preventable catastrophic deterioration leading to cardiac arrests and unplanned admissions to intensive care units. The root causes of analysis of failure to rescue has revealed a number of mechanisms by which deterioration can be missed (Subbe and Barach 2017a): incomplete measurements of vital signs, lack of training in the interpretation of abnormal signs and problems to escalate to senior staff (Subbe and Barach 2017b). These can in part be addressed by introducing standards for acquisition and reporting such as the United Kingdom's National Early Warning Score (NEWS) (Jones 2012). NEWS (Fig. 27.1) and comparable systems have helped hospitals to reduce rates of cardiac arrests (Winters et al. 2013) and death from severe infections (Hancock 2014). The systems required to drive safety in this group of patients with the learning from Safety 1 have been described as 'rapid response systems', and their structures, processes and expected safety outcomes have been reported in international consensus statements (Devita et al. 2006; Subbe et al. 2019).

The systems that are required to achieve safety have hencde a transparent philosophy of care – a chain of survival where the analysis of vital signs leads to staff recognition of patient deterioration, escalation to a more senior clinician and direct changes in treatment (Fig. 27.2).

At the same time, team training (Guidry et al. 2011) communication (Stead et al. 2009) and staffing levels (Aiken et al. 2002) are factors that a Functional Resonance

	Physiological Parameters	3	2	1	0	1	2	3
A	Respiratory rate (bpm)	≤8		9-11	12-20		21-24	≥25
B	O_2 Saturations (%)	≤91	92-93	94-95	≥96			
	Any supplemental Oxygen		Yes		None			
C	Systolic BP (mmHg)	≤90	91-100	101-110	111-219			≥220
	Pulse (bpm)	≤40		41-50	51-90	91-110	111-130	≥131
D	AVPU score				Alert			VPU
E	Temperature (°C)	≤35.0		35.1-36.0	36.1-38.0	38.1-39.0	≥39.1	
Concern about a patient should lead to escalation, regardless of the score.								

Fig. 27.1 Scoring card provided by NHS Wales for the National Early Warning Score

Fig. 27.2 Mechanism of a rapid response system (Subbe & Welsh)

Accident Model (FRAM) (Hollnagel and Goteman 2015) would suggest are as important conditions for the safe functioning of a system through a Safety 2 lens.

27.4 Safety of Complex Systems

27.4.1 Understanding Interdependencies

While Safety 1 assumes causality of variation and error, Safety 2 assumes causality of functioning, and both systems accept that multiple factors will affect failure or system functioning; the philosophy of these models is largely linear in assuming a

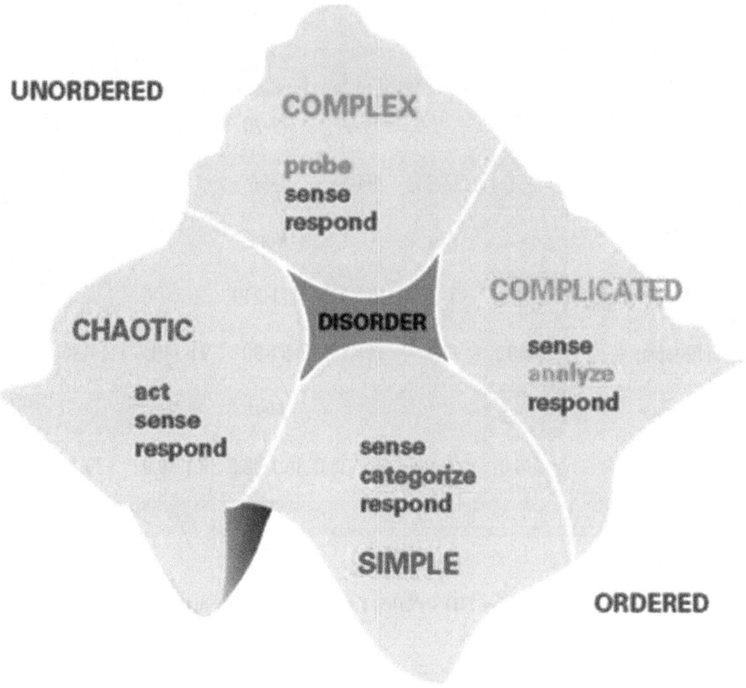

Fig. 27.3 Cynefin Framework – Image Harvard Business Review

certain logical and chronological order of events (Cassin and Barach 2012). This is true for many processes in medical care and beyond but might be usefully complemented by understanding more fully the performance elments and degradation of complex, social-technical systems.

27.4.2 The Cynefin Framework as a Way to Understand and Manage the Terrain

David Snowdon has developed a framework for understanding of complex processes that was initially applied to management theory and offers an attractive model to explain medical dilemmas and potential strategies to resolve them (Snowden and Boone 2007). The Cynefin framework (Fig. 27.3) distinguishes between four main types of problems: simple, complicated, complex and chaotic. Simple and complicated problems have a logical solution that is either obvious in the case of simple problems or can be deducted through rational analysis using available data in the case of complicated problems. Complex problems have no obvious solution, but by testing out interventions and analysing system responses, it is possible to find solutions. Chaotic systems have no solution and no coherent system by which a solution can be achieved and moving out of the system is the preferred strategy.

Cynefin has relevance to the choice of strategies individuals and systems can choose in creating safe care which can be illustrated with the example of surgical checklists (Table 27.1) used by clinical teams to manage simple (Haynes et al. 2009), complicated (Arriaga et al. 2013), complex (Subbe et al. 2017a) and chaotic (ALS – Advanced Life Support course n.d.) care problems.

Table 27.1 Application of Cynefin framework for physiological problems and safety of organizations

Cynefin category	Application to clinical problem – individual patient	Application to hospital safety – healthcare strategy
Simple problem	A young fit person dehydrated after a short run will require a limited amount of fluid to recover wellbeing	Checklists like those used prior to sending a patient to theatre: check of name, date of birth, hospital number (Bognár et al. 2008)
	Simple measurements of heart rate and urine output can guide treatment	
Complicated problem	An elderly person with the same illness and being treated with the same number of medications, can greatly influence urine output, blood pressure and heart rate	For complicated problems such as potential complications during a long surgical procedure, the checklist of the World Health Organization that is used in the presence of the whole team that is involved in the operation provides a mechanisms to improve safety (Chaplin 1985)
	A step-wise approach with monitoring of impact for each fluid intake by measuring blood pressure, heart rate, urine output and basic blood tests to gauge the correct amount of fluid required to restore wellbeing	
Complex problem	An elderly person with multiple medical conditions including a weakness of the heart and serious infection with fluid loss through infectious diarrhoea	For complex problems such as unstructured emergencies on general wards in patients with multiple problems of unclear aetiology, our group has established checklists with questions rather than answers as a potential strategy that allows less experienced practitioners to enhance safety of care in simulated environments (Kolb 2014)
	Weakness of the heart usually requires a restriction of fluids; serious infection requires generous application of fluid. Admission to intensive care and application of advanced ways to monitor the functioning of large blood vessels, the pump strength of the heart and hourly urine output measurement would guide treatment with a combination of small fluids boluses and heart strengthening medications with continuous measurement of parameters to assure that the treatment fits this particular unique patient and his or her response	

(continued)

Table 27.1 (continued)

Cynefin category	Application to clinical problem – individual patient	Application to hospital safety – healthcare strategy
Chaotic problem	Septic shock, the most severe form of infection with changes to tone of blood vessels, contractility of the heart and permeability of blood vessels	Airway-Breathing-Circulation-Disability-Exposure system for cardio-pulmonary arrests to identify and resolve sequential potentially unrelated problems and gain control (Knowles 1990)
	Septic shock management has changed little after 20 years inspite of much research including using invasive blood pressure monitoring and many randomized controlled trials, which have not shown more than a marginal benefit with newer treatment modalities (Franklin and Mathew 1994)	

The failure of clinical teams to understand in which zone of the framework they are operating can lead to a flawed mental model, misjudgement of risk and the choice of the wrong strategy to support patients. Given that there are no simple demarcations between the four zones, it is often the pattern recognition of experienced staff that translates into choosing the most-suitable correct strategy.

27.4.3 Triple Modular Redundancy as a Technological Model for Working of Teams

The basic underlying construct behind most efforts to improve medical safety is the concept that better training of individuals and improved processes will mitigate against medical error. This however, turns out be over simplistic and fails to translate to helping staff learn to better manage and care for patients.

This system contrasts with a model of safety that has been developed for complex technology, most notably in aviation and the Apollo spaceflight programme (Apollo Guidance Computer and the First Silicon Chips I National Air and Space Museum 2015). The underlying philosophy is important: a single unit will always have a failure rate, and by combining several independent units, the risk that both fail at the same time is reduced. Safety-critical parts of the process are provided in modular and redundant fashion (Fig. 27.4).

Despite the widespread use of the principle of modular redundancy in the hi-tech world, it is virtually unheard of in the world of medical safety. Only a few systems have redundant parts; administration of powerful drugs such as cancer treatments, blood products or pain killers is often undertaken by two healthcare professionals – this is to assure that accidental errors, 'slips', don't go unnoticed (Amalberti et al. 2005a, 2005b).

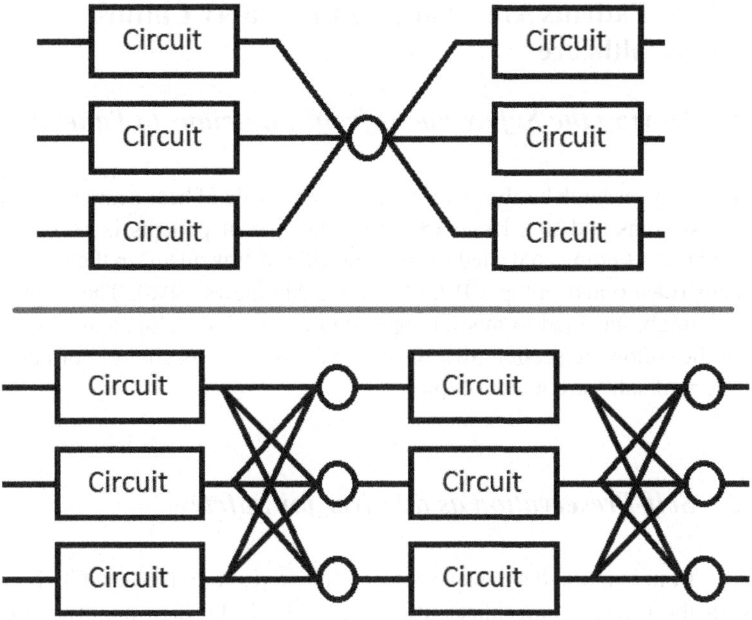

Fig. 27.4 Triple modular redundancy – with one voter (top) and three voters (bottom) (Wikipedia): the three-voter system means that even the voting mechanism is not dependent on a single fallible item (Wikipedia)

Another potentially modular system is the usage of checklists by multiple users in operating theatres (Haynes et al. 2009). Checklists have however important social determinants which when not appreciated can greatly limit their impact (Dixon-Woods et al. 2011; Urbach et al. 2014).

Technology can be used to create this modular redundancy even in healthcare. Our group has tested a technology-supported solution to allow distribution of safety-critical data to multiple responders. Vital sign measures were summarised in values of the National Early Warning Score (Jones 2012) and transmitted in real time to a large graphic board at the nursing station, the senior duty doctor and a member of the rapid response team – a group of nurses with critical care skills. Implementation in a study with over 4000 patients led to a significant reduction in adverse events by a third, and the cardiopulmonary arrests by 80% as well as better survival of patients requiring admission to intensive care (Subbe et al. 2017b). The ability of several responders to support a deteriorating patient would negate the variability in performance of individuals, flatten hierarchical patterns of communication and facilitate a transparent and truthful culture of shared safety.

27.5 How Patients Are Changing the Safety Culture in Healthcare

27.5.1 *Moving the Safety Focus from Clinicians to Patients*

Much of safety research has however focused on the role of healthcare professionals and their systems and to a lesser extent on the role of patients in system safety. These and other findings have led to an accusation of 'tokenism' in the involvement of patients (Ocloo and Fulop 2012; Ocloo and Matthews 2016). The emphasis on clinicians might have led to missed opportunities in the development of safer systems. In the following section, the rational and evidence for the role of patients in the delivery of safe care will be explored.

27.5.2 *Self-Preservation as a Driver for Safety*

Examples from aviation have inspired many initiatives to improve safety in healthcare with the usage of checklists (Ziewacz et al. 2011), high-fidelity simulation (Streufert et al. 2001; Barach 2003), reporting systems and national learning structures like the UK's Healthcare Safety Investigation Branch (Stewart et al. 2018).

One mechanism of safety that is distinct from safety of systems in healthcare has however not been sufficiently highlighted, and this oversight might explain in parts the lack of progress in system safety in healthcare. Pilots and their teams are on board of the airplane, and 'the pilot is always the first person at the site of the accident'. Self-preservation might be a driver for safety in aviation and other high-reliability industries (Sanchez and Barach 2012).

27.5.3 *Agency and Ownership Facilitating Change*

Behavioural psychology offers another model to support patient involvement. Behavioural economist Dan Ariely from Duke University and his colleagues describe the attribution of value to goods based on the involvement of individuals (Norton 2011). Ariely has labelled this the 'IKEA effect' and compares it to the satisfaction that customers of the Swedish furniture chain IKEA experience if they build their flat-packed units (Norton et al. 2012). Participation promotes ownership and agency. Participation of patients in their own healthcare in general and aspects of safety in particular might therefore be legitimate drivers for improvement (Hanson and Barach 2012). Ownership of healthcare data and agency to act are transformative as illustrated by the rise in personal health records (Leveille et al. 2012; Bell et al. 2015) and self-management programmes for patients with chronic diseases (Franek 2013; Haslbeck et al. 2015). It is likely that these very mechanisms of behavioural economics underlie some of the successes of projects using co-production (Dineen 2014).

27.5.4 Human Sensors and the Importance of a Personal 'Normal'

Medical textbooks describe commonly 'normal' physiology based on data that is often historic and derived from young healthy individuals – often students. It is arguable that these normal values are only present in a minority of patients who would, for example, be admitted to a modern hospital. Attempts to restore 'normal physiology' to the numbers reported in healthy students would be impossible and potentially outright dangerous. Observations from patients and those close to them acting as 'human sensors' are likely to provide the best approximation of what a future state of successful restauration of health might look like. The 'normal' status of a patient is therefore owned by patients.

27.5.5 Examples for Patient Powered Safety in Management of Chronic Illness

Many medical safety incidents are related to 'high-risk medications'(Nebeker et al. 2004) such as drugs used for the treatment of diabetes and blood-thinning medications used for the prevention of strokes in patients with an irregular heartbeat or artificial heart valves (Sanduende Otero et al. 2019). While the drugs have obvious risks, these are being handled near exclusively by the patients using them with sporadic input from their professional colleagues in primary care.

Inflammatory bowel disease is a group of disorders that leads to diarrhoea with blood and mucus and complications in many other organs outside the bowel. Introduction of patient registries, patient portals and other forms of personal health records has allowed patients to chart their symptoms online, link to results from blood tests and then adjust the dosage of medications such as steroids that modify their immune system. Data from a number of international studies shows that this approach by patients managing their own disease leads to less complications than treatment that is solely directed by healthcare professionals (Crandall et al. 2011; Price et al. 2015; Carlsen et al. 2017).

Training of patients in the management of long-term conditions through their peers has similarly shown to positively impact outcomes that are usually linked to safety of care (Horton et al. n.d.).

Changes in vital signs are commonly linked to the potential of deterioration. The technology required to monitor vital signs used to be the prerogative of healthcare professionals, but devices that can remotely record vital signs such as blood pressure, heart rate, temperature, oxygen saturations or respiratory rate are now available to consumers (Koshy et al. 2018).

27.5.6 Patient Powered Safety Applications in Hospital

The participation of patients in their own safety while being in hospitals is an area with significantly less evidence. There is strong evidence from multiple case examples that patients and those close to them often 'know that something just isn't right'. Patient safety campaigners such as Helen Haskell from 'Mothers Against Medical Errors' and the World Health Organisation's Patient Safety programme have used this evidence successfully to introduce legislation that requires hospitals to make mechanisms available to patients and families to directly alert teams specialising in the diagnosis and treatment of life-threatening illness (Haskell and Lord 2017). This type of intervention has again not been studied in large interventional studies, but the underlying rational that patients need to be able to 'safe their own life, even if in hospital', is difficult to challenge on ethical grounds and can foster a culture of safety in hospitals that are using this care model (Odell et al. 2010). This has been recommended as a quality metric for hospitals worldwide (Subbe et al. 2019). Additionally it might be possible for patients and families to actively take part in the routine reporting of safety incidents (Lopez et al. 2017).

Acute kidney injury (AKI) is an often fatal complication of acute illness. About half of all patients at risk in hospital are able to monitor their own fluid intake and indicate the colour of their urine (Fig. 27.5) with significant improvements in the way that nurses record urine output (Subbe 2015).

Parents in some neonatal intensive care units are now presenting the symptoms of their child and its progress on official ward rounds – this facilitates better insights of progress and allows clinicians to benefit from the knowledge of parents about their child (Voos et al. 2011).

These examples indicate that patients and those close to them might be able to play a more active and meaningful role in their own safety even while in hospital.

27.6 Building a Safety Culture Fit for Complex Challenges Through Distributive Networks: Safety 3.0

This chapter summarizes the safety challenges of medical practice supporting patients with increasingly complex circumstances. Error rates and misadventures are common, and medicine as an industry is struggling with its cultural heritage and the unreliability of its practices. The model of omnipotent superstar clinicians in this context is drawing to a close.

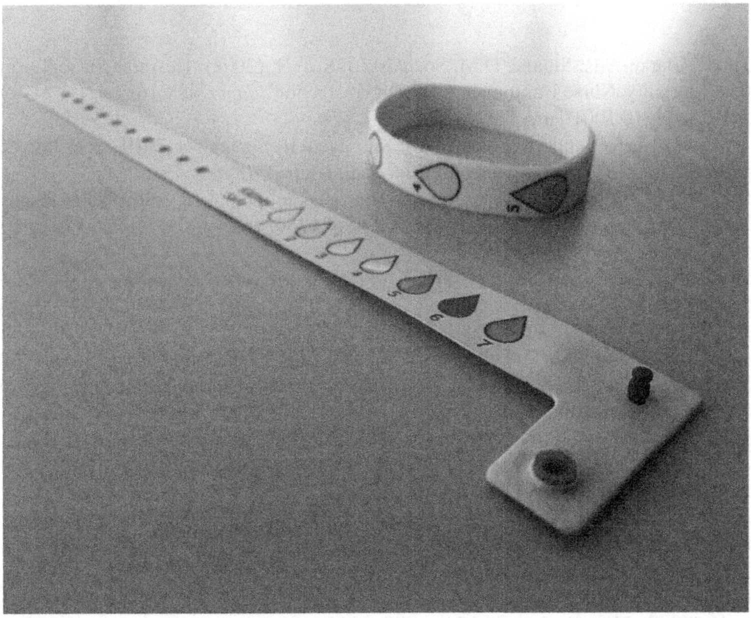

Fig. 27.5 KidneySafe Bracelet from NHS Wales – following an electronic alert, patients are given the bracelet and instructed to let nurses know when they have passed urine and what colour of the bracelet the urine colour corresponds to

The case study of cardiopulmonary arrests illustrates causes of errors and solutions through the lenses of Safety 1 and Safety 2. At the same time, it clarifies the limitations of current approaches. Examples from other industries might support the use of modular system architecture for safety-critical information and actions. We define 'Safety 3.0' as a system with modular redundancy where patients are actively involved and engaged in managing their care in a reliable and transparent manner. There are a number of examples from clinical practice that support a deeper understanding of the mechanisms by which this might be effective.

Redesigning the safety systems of healthcare is challenging and critically necessary and probably unavoidable. Faced with the challenges of complexity, uncertainty and the difficulty to increase reliability of human actors, innovative non-linear solutions will require further exploration using experimental studies and clinical trials. Networks including healthcare professionals, patients and their social environments might open new opportunities to reduce errors and improve the experience of safety in those requiring healthcare and those providing it. These models of 'distributive safety' are likely to have different properties than the models described as Safety 1 and Safety 2 and might be therefore be best described as models of 'Safety 3.0'.

References

Aiken, L.H., Clarke, S.P., Sloane, D.M, Sochalski J, S. J. H. (2002) 'Hospital Nurse Staffing and Patient Mortality, Nurse Burnout, and Job Dissatisfaction', *Jama*, 288(16), pp. 1987–1993. doi: https://doi.org/10.1001/jama.288.16.1987.

ALS - Advanced Life Support course (n.d.). Retrieved 10 September 2019, from https://www.resus.org.uk/information-on-courses/advanced-life-support/

Amalberti, R *et al.* (2005a) 'Five system barriers to achieving ultra safe health care, *Annals of International Medicine*, 142, pp. 756–764. doi: https://doi.org/10.1016/S0271-7964(08)70407-5.

Amalberti, René *et al.* (2005b) 'Five system barriers to achieving ultrasafe health care.', *Annals of internal medicine*, 142(9), pp. 756–64. doi: https://doi.org/10.7326/0003-4819-142-9-200505030-00012.

Apollo Guidance Computer and the First Silicon Chips | National Air and Space Museum (2015). Retrieved 10 September 2019, from https://airandspace.si.edu/stories/editorial/apollo-guidance-computer-and-first-silicon-chips.

Arriaga, A. F. *et al.* (2013) 'Simulation-based trial of surgical-crisis checklists.', *The New England journal of medicine*, 368(3), pp. 246–53. Retrieved 10 September 2019, from http://www.ncbi.nlm.nih.gov/pubmed/23323901.

Baker, G. R. *et al.* (2004) 'The Canadian Adverse Events Study: the incidence of adverse events among hospital patients in Canada.', *CMAJ : Canadian Medical Association journal = journal de l'Association medicale canadienne*. Canadian Medical Association, 170(11), pp. 1678–86. doi: 10.1503/CMAJ.1040498.

Barach, P. (2007) 'A team-based risk modification programme to make health care safer.', *Theoretical Issues in Ergonomics Science*. Taylor & Francis, 8(5), pp. 481–494. doi: 10.1080/14639220701193116.

Barach, P. and Kleinman, L. C. (2018) 'Measuring and improving comprehensive pediatric cardiac care: Learning from continuous quality improvement methods and tools', *Progess in Pediatric Cardiology*, 48, pp. 82–92. doi: https://doi.org/10.1016/j.ppedcard.2018.02.010.

Barach, P. and Small, S. D. (2000) 'Reporting and preventing medical mishaps: lessons from non-medical near miss reporting systems.', *BMJ (Clinical research ed.)*, 320(7237), pp. 759–763. doi: https://doi.org/10.1136/bmj.320.7237.759.

Barach, P. (2003) The end of the beginning: Lessons learned from the patient safety movement. Scand Journal Trauma Emergency Medicine 11:79–80.

Becker, H. S. *et al.* (1976) *Boys in white : student culture in medical school*. Transaction Books.

Bell, S. K. *et al.* (2015) 'Partnering with patients for safety: The opennotes patient reporting tool', *Journal of General Internal Medicine*, 30, p. S220. Retrieved 10 September 2019, from: http://www.embase.com/search/results?subaction=viewrecord&from=export&id=L71877824

Boan, D. and Funderburk, F. (2003) 'Healthcare quality improvement and organizational culture', *November*, 3, p. 2003.

Bognár A, Barach P, Johnson J, Duncan R. Woods D, Holl J, Birnbach D, Bacha E. (2008) Errors and the Burden of Errors: Attitudes, Perceptions and the Culture of Safety in Pediatric Cardiac Surgical Teams. Ann Thoracic Surgery 4:1374–1381

Bolman, L. G. and Deal, T. E. (1997) *Reframing organizations : artistry, choice, and leadership*. Jossey-Bass Publishers.

Braithwaite, J. *et al.* (n.d.) 'When complexity science meets implementation science: a theoretical and empirical analysis of systems change'. doi: 10.1186/s12916-018-1057-z.

Bruback K et al (2019) Associations between Work Satisfaction, Engagement, and 7-day Patient Mortality; a Cross-Sectional Survey, BMJ Open.

Carlsen, K. *et al.* (2017) 'Self-managed eHealth Disease Monitoring in Children and Adolescents with Inflammatory Bowel Disease', *Inflammatory Bowel Diseases*, p. 1. doi: https://doi.org/10.1097/MIB.0000000000001026.

Cassin B, Barach P. (2012) Making Sense of Root Cause Analysis Investigations of Surgery-Related Adverse Events. *Surg Clin North America*, pp. 1–15. doi: https://doi.org/10.1016/j.suc.2011.12.008.

Chaplin J. (1985) Dictionary of Psychology [Internet]. 2nd Revised Edition. Laurel Books [cited 2019 Jul 10].

Crandall, W. *et al.* (2011) 'ImproveCareNow: The development of a pediatric inflammatory bowel disease improvement network', *Inflammatory Bowel Diseases*, 17(1), pp. 450–457. doi: https://doi.org/10.1002/ibd.21394.

Cullinane, M. *et al.* (2005) *NCEPOD 2005 Report: An Acute Problem?* London. Retrieved 10 September 2019, from https://www.ncepod.org.uk/2005report/

Davis, P. *et al.* (2002) 'Adverse events in New Zealand public hospitals I: Occurrence and impact', *New Zealand Medical Journal*, 115(1167).

Davis, P. *et al.* (2003) 'Adverse events in New Zealand public hospitals II: Preventability and clinical context', *New Zealand Medical Journal*, 116(1183), pp. 1–11. doi: https://doi.org/10.1097/00002030-199311000-00016.

Devita, M. A. *et al.* (2006) 'Findings of the First Consensus Conference on Medical Emergency Teams*', *Crit Care Med*, 34(9), pp. 2463–2478. doi: https://doi.org/10.1097/01.CCM.0000235743.38172.6E.

Dineen, R. (2014) 'Co-producing prudent healthcare: putting people in the picture', *Making prudent healthcare happen / Welsh Government*. Retrieved 10 September 2019, from http://www.prudenthealthcare.org.uk/coproduction/.

Dixon-Woods, M. *et al.* (2011) 'Explaining Michigan: Developing an Ex Post Theory of a Quality Improvement Program', *Milbank Quarterly*, 89(2), pp. 167–205. doi: https://doi.org/10.1111/j.1468-0009.2011.00625.x.

Franek, J. (2013) 'Self-management support interventions for persons with chronic disease: an evidence-based analysis.', *Ontario health technology assessment series*, 13(9), pp. 1–60. Retrieved 10 September 2019, from http://www.ncbi.nlm.nih.gov/pubmed/24194800

Franklin, C. and Mathew, J. (1994) 'Developing strategies to prevent inhospital cardiac arrest: analyzing responses of physicians and nurses in the hours before the event.', *Critical care medicine*, 22(2), pp. 244–7. Retrieved 10 September 2019, from http://www.ncbi.nlm.nih.gov/pubmed/8306682.

Gapminder Foundation (n.d.) *Gapminder Tools*. Retrieved 10 September 2019, from https://www.gapminder.org/tools/#$state$time$value=2018;&marker$axis_x$which=life_expectancy_years&domainMin:null&domainMax:null&zoomedMin:null&zoomedMax:null&scaleType=linear&spaceRef:null;;;&chart-type=bubbles

Griffiths, P. *et al.* (2018) 'Nurse staffing, nursing assistants and hospital mortality: retrospective longitudinal cohort study.', *BMJ quality & safety*. BMJ Publishing Group Ltd, p. bmjqs-2018-008043. https://doi.org/10.1136/bmjqs-2018-008043.

Guidry, M., Rothwell, W. and Conkerton, B. (2011) 'Integrated multidisciplinary training and practiced coaching of TeamSTEPPS improves reporting of teamwork in code blue and rapid response performance', *Journal of Hospital Medicine*, 6(4), p. S32. Retrieved 10 September 2019, from http://onlinelibrary.wiley.com/doi/10.1002/jhm.920/pdf.

Halbesleben, J. R. B., Wakefield, D. S. and Wakefield, B. J. (2008) 'Work-arounds in health care settings', *Health Care Management Review*, 33(1), pp. 2–12. doi: https://doi.org/10.1097/01.HMR.0000304495.95522.ca.

Hancock, C. (2014) 'A national quality improvement initiative for reducing harm and death from sepsis in Wales', *Intensive and Critical Care Nursing*, 24 March.

Hanson C, Barach P. (2012) Improving cardiac care quality and safety through partnerships with patients and their families. Progress in Pediatric Cardiology, 33:73–79.

Harry, E. and Sweller, J. (2016) 'Cognitive Load Theory and Patient Safety', in Ruskin, K., Stiegler, M., and Rosenbaum, S. (eds) *Quality and Safety in Anesthesia and Perioperative Care*. Oxford: Oxford University Press. doi: https://doi.org/10.1093/med/9780199366149.003.0002.

Haskell, H. and Lord, T. (2017) 'Patients and Families as Coproducers of Safe and Reliable Outcomes', in *Surgical Patient Care*. Cham: Springer International Publishing, pp. 101–120. doi: https://doi.org/10.1007/978-3-319-44010-1_8.

Haslbeck, J. *et al.* (2015) 'Introducing the chronic disease self-management program in Switzerland and other German-speaking countries: findings of a cross-border adaptation using a multiple-methods approach.', *BMC health services research*. BioMed Central, 15, p. 576. doi: 10.1186/s12913-015-1251-z.

Haynes, A. B. *et al.* (2009) 'A surgical safety checklist to reduce morbidity and mortality in a global population.', *The New England journal of medicine*, 360(5), pp. 491–499. doi: https://doi.org/10.1056/NEJMsa0810119.

Hogan, H. *et al.* (2012) 'Preventable deaths due to problems in care in English acute hospitals : a retrospective case record review study', (July). doi: 10.1136/bmjqs-2012-001159.

Hollnagel, E. and Goteman, O. (2015) 'The functional resonance accident model (FRAM)', (January 2004).

Hollnagel, E., Wears, R. L. and Braithwaite, J. (2015) *From Safety-I to Safety-II: A White Paper*. Retrieved 10 September 2019, from https://www.england.nhs.uk/signuptosafety/wp-content/uploads/sites/16/2015/10/safety-1-safety-2-whte-papr.pdf

Horton, J. *et al.* (n.d.) *Patient driven solutions to common problems: Educational Programmes for Patients*. Swansea. doi: ISBN: 978-1-912334-11-7.

Jones, M. (2012) 'NEWSDIG: The national early warning score development and implementation group', *Clinical Medicine, Journal of the Royal College of Physicians of London*, pp. 501–503.

Jones, D. M., Song, X. and Rockwood, K. (2004) 'Operationalizing a frailty index from a standardized comprehensive geriatric assessment', *Journal of the American Geriatrics Society*, 52(11), pp. 1929–1933.

Knowles, M. S. (1990). The adult learner: A neglected species. Houston, TX: Gulf Publishing.

Kohn, L. T., Corrigan, J. M. and Molla, S. (2000) *To Err Is Human, Medicine*. doi: https://doi.org/10.1017/S095026880100509X.

Kolb, D. A. (2014). Experiential Learning: Experience as the Source of Learning and Development. New Jersey: FT Press.

Koshy, A. N. *et al.* (2018) 'Smart watches for heart rate assessment in atrial arrhythmias.', *International journal of cardiology*, 266, pp. 124–127. doi: https://doi.org/10.1016/j.ijcard.2018.02.073.

Leveille, S. G. *et al.* (2012) 'Evaluating the impact of patients' online access to doctors' visit notes: designing and executing the OpenNotes project.', *BMC medical informatics and decision making*, 12, p. 32. Retrieved 10 September 2019, from http://www.pubmedcentral.nih.gov/articlerender.fcgi?artid=3351950&tool=pmcentrez&rendertype=abstract.

Lopez, C. *et al.* (2017) 'Improving communication with families of patients undergoing pediatric cardiac surgery', *Progress in Pediatric Cardiology*. Elsevier Ireland Ltd, 45, pp. 83–90. doi: https://doi.org/10.1016/j.ppedcard.2016.11.001.

Nebeker, J. R., Barach, P. and Samore, M. H. (2004) 'Clarifying Adverse Drug Events: A Clinician's Guide to Terminology, Documentation, and Reporting', *Annals of Internal Medicine*, 140(10), p. 795. doi: https://doi.org/10.7326/0003-4819-140-10-200405180-00009.

Nebeker, J., Samore, M., Barach, P. (2005) Clarifying Adverse Drug Events: A Clinicians guide to Terminology, Documentation, and Reporting. Annals of Internal Medicine, 142:77–78.

Norton, M. I. (2011) 'Norton, Mochon & Ariely - 2011 - The Ikea effect, When Labor Leads to Love.pdf'. Retrieved 10 September 2019, from https://www.hbs.edu/faculty/PublicationFiles/11-091.pdf

Norton, M. I., Mochon, D. and Ariely, D. (2012) 'The IKEA effect: When labor leads to love', *Journal of Consumer Psychology*. No longer published by Elsevier, 22(3), pp. 453–460. doi: https://doi.org/10.1016/J.JCPS.2011.08.002.

Ocloo, J. E. and Fulop, N. J. (2012) 'Developing a "critical" approach to patient and public involvement in patient safety in the NHS: learning lessons from other parts of the public sector?', *Health expectations : an international journal of public participation in health care and health policy*, 15(4), pp. 424–32. doi: https://doi.org/10.1111/j.1369-7625.2011.00695.x.

Ocloo, J. and Matthews, R. (2016) 'From tokenism to empowerment: progressing patient and public involvement in healthcare improvement.', *BMJ quality & safety*, 25(8), pp. 626–32. doi: https://doi.org/10.1136/bmjqs-2015-004839.

Odell, M., Gerber, K. and Gager, M. (2010) 'Call 4 Concern: patient and relative activated critical care outreach', *British Journal of Nursing*, 19(22), pp. 1390–1395.

Panagioti M, Khan K, Keers RN, Abuzour A, Phipps D, Kontopantelis E et al (2019) Prevalence, severity, and nature of preventable patient harm across medical care settings: systematic review and meta-analysis. BMJ 366:l4185

Phelps, G. and Barach, P. (2014) 'Why has the safety and quality movement been slow to improve care?', *International journal of clinical practice*. WILEY-BLACKWELL, 111 RIVER ST, HOBOKEN 07030-5774, NJ USA, 68(8), pp. 932–5. Retrieved 10 September 2019, from http://apps.webofknowledge.com.librweb.laurentian.ca/full_record.do?product=WOS&search_mode=CitingArticles&qid=9&SID=1BXmOeJYrpejITftuXv&page=1&doc=1.

Price, T., Lithgo, K. and Johnson, M. (2015) 'PWE-062 The outcomes and benefits of moving stable inflammatory bowel disease patients from a paper based self management system to an supported, self help and management programme (ibd-sshamp) with specialist overview', *Gut*. BMJ Publishing Group, 64(Suppl 1), p. A238.3-A239. doi: https://doi.org/10.1136/gutjnl-2015-309861.511.

Sanchez J, Barach P. (2012) High Reliability Organizations and Surgical Microsystems: Re-engineering Surgical Care. Surgical Clinics of North America, February 2012, 92(1):1–14. https://doi.org/10.1016/j.suc.2011.12.005.

Sanduende Otero Y. *et al.* (2019) A Ten Year Review of Adverse Medication Incidents in a National Incident Reporting System, British Journal of Anesthesia, https://doi.org/10.1016/j.bja.2019.10.013.

Santamaria, J., Tobin, A. and Holmes, J. (2010) 'Changing cardiac arrest and hospital mortality rates through a medical emergency team takes time and constant review∗', *Critical Care Medicine*, 38(2), pp. 445–450. doi: https://doi.org/10.1097/CCM.0b013e3181cb0ff1.

Schein, E. H. (2010) *Organisational Culture and Leadership (eds), Jossey-Bass*. doi: https://doi.org/10.1136/jcp.10.4.354.

Schein, R. M. H. *et al.* (1990) 'Clinical antecedents to in-hospital cardiopulmonary arrest', in *Chest*, pp. 1388–1392.

Scott, T. *et al.* (2003) 'Does organisational culture influence health care performance? A review of the evidence', *Journal of Health Services Research & Policy*, 8(2), pp. 105–117. doi: https://doi.org/10.1258/135581903321466085.

Siassakos, D. *et al.* (2013) 'What makes maternity teams effective and safe? Lessons from a series of research on teamwork, leadership and team training.', *Acta obstetricia et gynecologica Scandinavica*, 92(11), pp. 1239–43. doi: https://doi.org/10.1111/aogs.12248.

Sisko, A. M. *et al.* (2019) 'National Health Expenditure Projections, 2018–27: Economic And Demographic Trends Drive Spending And Enrollment Growth', *Health Affairs*, 38(3), pp. 491–501. doi: https://doi.org/10.1377/hlthaff.2018.05499.

Snowden, D. J. and Boone, M. E. (2007) 'A Leader' s Framework for Decision Making', *Havard Business Review*. Retrieved 10 September 2019, from www.hbr.orgorcall800-988-0886.www.hbrreprints.org

Spencer-Oatey, H. (n.d.) *Core Concepts What is Culture? What is Culture? What is Culture? A Compilation of Quotations Compiled by*. Retrieved 10 September 2019, from http://www.warwick.ac.uk/globalpadintercultural.

Stead, K. *et al.* (2009) 'Teams communicating through STEPPS.', *The Medical journal of Australia*, 190(11 Suppl), pp. S128–32. Retrieved 10 September 2019, from http://www.ncbi.nlm.nih.gov/pubmed/19485861

Stewart, K., Macrae, C. and Toff, N. (2018) 'Safety investigation practices can be adapted from aviation for use in healthcare.', *BMJ (Clinical research ed.)*, 361, p. k2822. doi: https://doi.org/10.1136/bmj.k2822.

Streufert, S., Satish, U. & Barach, P. (2001) 'Improving Medical Care: The Use of Simulation Technology', *Simulation & Gaming*. Sage PublicationsSage CA: Thousand Oaks, CA, 32(2), pp. 164–174. doi: https://doi.org/10.1177/104687810103200205.

Subbe, C. (2015) *Safety=Design: BCUHB Shine 2014 final report*.

Subbe, C.P. & Barach, P. (2017a) *Failure to rescue and failure to perceive patients in crisis, Surgical Patient Care: Improving Safety, Quality and Value*. doi: https://doi.org/10.1007/978-3-319-44010-1_37.

Subbe, C.P. & Barach, P. (2017b) 'Failure to Rescue and Failure to Perceive Patients in Crisis', in *Surgical Patient Care*. Cham: Springer International Publishing, pp. 635–648. doi: https://doi.org/10.1007/978-3-319-44010-1_37.

Subbe, C. P. *et al.* (2017a) 'Crisis checklists for in-hospital emergencies: expert consensus, simulation testing and recommendations for a template determined by a multi-institutional and multi-disciplinary learning collaborative', *BMC Health Services Research*, 17. doi: https://doi.org/10.1186/s12913-017-2288-y.

Subbe, C. P., Duller, B. & Bellomo, R. (2017b) 'Effect of an automated notification system for deteriorating ward patients on clinical outcomes.', *Critical care (London, England)*. doi: 10.1186/s13054-017-1635-z.

Subbe, C. P. *et al.* (2019) 'Quality metrics for the evaluation of Rapid Response Systems: Proceedings from the third international consensus conference on Rapid Response Systems.', *Resuscitation*, 141, pp. 1–12. https://doi.org/10.1016/j.resuscitation.2019.05.012.

Urbach, D. R., Govindarajan, A. & Saskin, R. (2014) 'Introduction of surgical safety checklists in Ontario, Canada', *NEJM*, 370(11), pp. 1029–38. doi: https://doi.org/10.1016/j.jvs.2014.05.036.

Vincent, C., Neale, G. and Woloshynowych, M. (2001) 'Adverse events in British hospitals: preliminary retrospective record review.', *BMJ (Clinical research ed.)*, 322(7285), pp. 517–519.

Vohra, P. D. *et al.* (2007) 'Housestaff and medical student attitudes toward medical errors and adverse events.', *Joint Commission journal on quality and patient safety*, 33(8), pp. 493–501. Retrieved 10 September 2019, from http://www.ncbi.nlm.nih.gov/pubmed/17724946.

Voos, K. C. *et al.* (2011) 'Effects of implementing family-centered rounds (FCRs) in a neonatal intensive care unit (NICU).', *The journal of maternal-fetal & neonatal medicine : the official journal of the European Association of Perinatal Medicine, the Federation of Asia and Oceania Perinatal Societies, the International Society of Perinatal Obstetricians*, 24(11), pp. 1403–6. doi: https://doi.org/10.3109/14767058.2011.596960.

Wakeman, D. and Langham, M. R. (2018) 'Creating a safer operating room: Groups, team dynamics and crew resource management principles.', *Seminars in pediatric surgery*, 27(2), pp. 107–113. doi: https://doi.org/10.1053/j.sempedsurg.2018.02.008.

Weaver, S. J. *et al.* (2013) 'Promoting a Culture of Safety as a Patient Safety Strategy: A Systematic Review HHS Public Access', *Ann Intern Med*, 158(2), pp. 369–374. doi: https://doi.org/10.7326/0003-4819-158-5-201303051-00002.

Wilson, R. M. *et al.* (1995) 'The Quality in Australian Health Care Study', *Medical Journal of Australia*, 163(12), p. 754. Retrieved 10 September 2019, from pm:7476634%5Cn http://www.mja.com.au/public/issues/misc/wilson.pdf%5CnPM:8668084.

Winters, B. D. *et al.* (2013) 'Rapid-response systems as a patient safety strategy: A systematic review', *Annals of Internal Medicine*, pp. 417–425. doi: https://doi.org/10.7326/0003-4819-158-5-201303051-00009.

Zegers, M. *et al.* (2009) 'Adverse events and potentially preventable deaths in Dutch hospitals: results of a retrospective patient record review study.', *Quality & safety in health care*, 18(4), pp. 297–302. doi: https://doi.org/10.1136/qshc.2007.025924.

Ziewacz, J. E. *et al.* (2011) 'Crisis checklists for the operating room: Development and pilot testing', *Journal of the American College of Surgeons*, 213(2).

Christian P. Subbe is a senior clinical lecturer at Bangor University and a Consultant in Acute, Respiratory and Critical Care Medicine working at the Ysbyty Gwynedd in Bangor, North Wales and an Improvement Science Fellow with The Health Foundation in London.

He has studies in Münster and Cologne and completed an MD in Respiratory Pathophysiology at the University of Cologne. He trained in England, Germany, and Wales and has complemented this with work for Médecins Sans Frontières in Angola and fellowships in France and the US.

He published the first peer-reviewed paper on Early Warning Scores, and his research focuses on pragmatic solutions to enhance safety of care in hospital (http://www.ncbi.nlm.nih.gov/pubmed/?term=subbe).

Dr. Paul Barach is deeply committed to translating research into strategies for systems strengthening, health protection and population health. Paul Barach, MD, MPH, is a double-boarded anaesthetist, critical care physician-scientist and clinical professor at Wayne State University School of Medicine and Children's Hospital of Michigan. He is visiting faculty at Jefferson College of Population Health and Sigmund Freud Univeristy, Vienna, Austria. He trained at the Massachusetts General Hospital affiliated with Harvard Medical School. Paul is an elected member of the lead honorary society the Association of University Anesthesiologists. Theories and ideas he has helped shape and provided research findings for are now in common use as a result of his work: TeamSTEPPS; surgical team training; human factors tools; multi-method, triangulated approaches to research; governance of health systems; and interprofessional learning and culture change to achieve safe and reliable outcomes. He has published more than 300 scientific papers and 5 books.

Chapter 28
Empowerment: Error Management Through Cultural Change in Medicine

Jan S. Brommundt

Abstract This chapter illustrates that any error management system, its techniques and its structures need to be embedded in a broader error management culture in a hospital in the Netherlands. Non-innovative and overly hierarchical structures are incompatible with such a culture, and the empowerment of personnel traditionally in the lower echelons of hierarchical systems (nurses, air hostesses) is a necessary, efficient and cost-effective precondition and cornerstone for such a system.

Empowerment is the promise of greater responsibility and participation towards the individual employee. It was developed as a management concept during the 1980s and 1990s. Its modern origins lie in American community psychology.

In accordance with the author's background, most examples and experiences described are from the medical field.

Keywords Mistake · Error · Failure · Medical contexts · Empowerment

28.1 From Research to Policy: Origins of Error Management in Medicine

The acknowledgment of the magnitude of medical error is relatively recent. In 1999 the Institute of Medicine published a landmark study that concluded that in the United States between 44,000 and 98,000 people die each year as a result of preventable medical errors (Kohn et al. 2000) (see also introduction to this book). The report was a meta-analysis based on various studies by a range of organisations. The report reconfirmed that medicine is a high consequence industry. The degree to which reverse outcomes in medicine can be attributed to human error was a new insight. For comparison, in the same year, only 17,000 died of illicit drug use (Mokdad et al. 2004). Remarkably the report suggested that the knowledge to

J. S. Brommundt (✉)
University Medical Centre Groningen, University of Groningen, Groningen, The Netherlands
e-mail: j.s.brommundt@umcg.nl

E. Vanderheiden, C.-H. Mayer (eds.), *Mistakes, Errors and Failures across Cultures*, https://doi.org/10.1007/978-3-030-35574-6_28

prevent these fatal errors already existed and that the challenge was to consequently translate this knowledge into clinical practice.

To do that, cultural change was needed within the medical community.

28.2 A Successful Example: Saving 28,000 Lives

Central venous catheters (CVCs) are lines that are essential to deliver intravenous drugs to severely ill patients. They are also used to draw blood samples and measure the central venous pressure from which doctors draw therapeutic conclusions. CVCs are used in most intensive care patients. Doctors advance them through the skin, via larger venous blood vessels in the groin or the neck towards the heart.

Unfortunately CVCs can get infected, and these infections can cause sepsis, multi-organ failure and death.

Peter Pronovost is a professor at the Johns Hopkins School of Medicine and professor of Healthcare Management at the Carey Business School. He studied hospital-acquired infections and concluded that adhering to a simple five-point checklist while inserting CVCs would significantly reduce infections (Pronovost et al. 2006).

1. Wash hands with soap.
2. Clean the patient's skin with chlorhexidine antiseptic.
3. Put sterile drapes over the entire patient.
4. Wear a sterile mask, hat, gown and gloves.
5. Put a sterile dressing over the catheter site (Pronovost's five-point checklist).

One hundred three intensive care units (ICUs) participated in the study. By strictly adhering to the five-point checklist, the infection rate of CVCs was reduced from 2.7/1,000 patients to zero. In the first 18 months after implementation, 1500 lives and US$ 100 million were saved.

When calculated for the entire United States, the resulting numbers were stunning: CVCs cause 80,000 catheter-related bloodstream infections and 28,000 deaths annually. If it was possible to reproduce the results through the implementation of the five-point checklist, 28,000 lives would be saved every year. With costs of US$ 45,000 per case, up to US$ 2.3 billion would be saved annually!

Nothing about the five-point checklist was extraordinary. Every healthcare provider would have agreed that those five points made sense and were essential when inserting CVCs. As suggested in the 1999 Institute of Medicine Report, the knowledge existed within the medical community. Policy was easily written down. The crux was to successfully implement the compliance with the policy.

28.3 From Policy to Implementation: The Role of Empowerment

Intrinsic motivation correlates with being goal-directed and enjoying challenges according to Csikszentmihalyi (1990). When the challenging level of a task meets a person's highest skill level, the best state of intrinsic motivation is reached.

If this is not the case and despite intellectual insight into the data, physicians were unlikely to feel motivated to be governed by checklists. Some might feel insulted that professionals with their training and wisdom need to be governed by checklists in a workplace that is already consumed by too much bureaucracy.

The success of the five-point checklist was based on the truly innovative step to empower nurses. Nurses were supposed to monitor doctors when putting in CVCs: did the doctors apply all rules of the checklist? Did they work perfectly sterile? Did they wash their hands before getting started? The nurses were empowered to speak up and force the doctors comply with the rules of the checklist. This was a substantial cultural change within the medical community.

For Pronovost's study, at least one doctor and one nurse per hospital had been assigned as team leaders for the implementation of the checklist. They had received special training and coaching by research stuff. Three months had been the necessary time to implement the cultural change of implementing the five-point checklist and empower nurses.

Nurses felt intrinsically motivated with the empowerment and saw the new challenges as job enrichment and fulfilment of their core mission to take care of patients. It is very beneficial that nurses are well trained and deeply care about the outcome of their work: the health of the patient.

Leading executives needed to be on board for the implementation of checklists and cultural change and were easily convinced by the financial indications of the figures.

This development offers opportunity for research: traditionally more exciting types of research into new therapies and drugs have been favoured by the medical research establishment. But scientifically measuring if therapies are effectively delivered and decrease mortality can be very rewarding and brings extra motivation to nurses and doctors involved in the research.

Depending on country and medical traditions, giving nurses power is a real revolution. Obstacles will vary depending on country and culture. But as the numbers show, the empowerment of nurses makes a lot of sense and saves lives!

28.4 The Success of Checklists

Surgery is a crucial part of healthcare systems (Rose et al. 2015). The estimated need for surgical procedures is huge and addresses an extensive range of diseases such as injuries, obstructed labour, malignancy, infections and cardiovascular disease.

The World Health Organization (WHO) estimates that 312.9 million surgical procedures were performed worldwide in 2012 (Weiser et al. 2016).

Looking at other high-risk industries like aeronautics and construction, Haynes et al. theorised that the successful implementation of a 19-item Surgical Safety Checklist intended to improve team communication, and consistency of care would reduce complications and death associated with surgery. They studied mortality and complication rates in eight hospitals in eight countries of different income levels. 3733 patients were included before and 3955 patients after the introduction of the Surgical Safety Checklist. The death rate decreased by 47%, the complication rate by 36% (Haynes et al. 2009)

In a by-now familiar pattern, the Checklist did not suggest any innovative policies or standards but rather aimed to reassure the proper, timely and consequent use of established treatment standards.

The success of the study made the WHO adopt and promote its use worldwide. The Checklist can be freely downloaded and used from the WHO website (World Health Organization 2019). The WHO provides teaching material and insights on how to implement the Checklist in a hospital. Users are encouraged to adapt the Checklist to the reality of their setting and to their needs, thus giving room to include the institutional memory built from specific conditions and errors that have occurred (Fig. 28.1).

The Checklist distinguishes three phases of an operation. Before induction of anaesthesia, it is checked that the right patient is receiving the right operation on the correct side of the body. As in aeronautics before takeoff, the correct function of needed technical gear is confirmed.

After induction of anaesthesia and before the incision by the surgeon, communication issues play the major role in the second part of the Checklist: is every team member known by name and function to the others? What are the expectations of the different disciplines (anaesthesia, surgery, nursing) for complications or specific concerns in this patient?

It is interesting to note that unlike in aeronautics where team members of cabin and cockpit have different depths of similar training backgrounds and similar cultures, the operating room (OR) teams are always multidisciplinary with different role-specific expectations and cultures. Typically the surgeon is focused on the operation itself and needs to be in the moment, while the anaesthetist through his training is focused on potentially occurring complications in the near future and tries to avoid their manifestation. An example would be giving pain killers to the patient before the expected pain manifests in order to avoid it altogether. Thus typi-

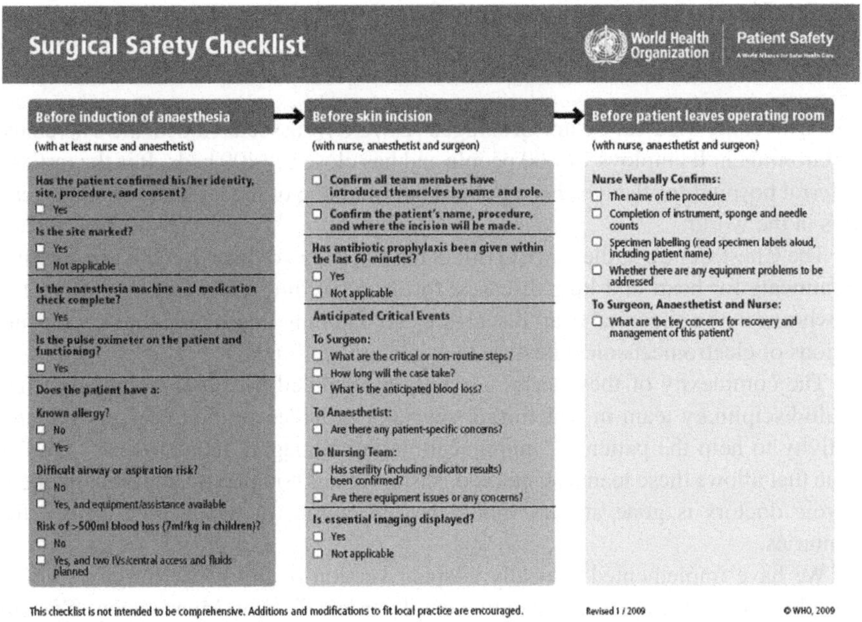

Surgical Safety Checklist

World Health Organization | Patient Safety

Before induction of anaesthesia → **Before skin incision** → **Before patient leaves operating room**

Before induction of anaesthesia

(with at least nurse and anaesthetist)

Has the patient confirmed his/her identity, site, procedure, and consent?
- ☐ Yes

Is the site marked?
- ☐ Yes
- ☐ Not applicable

Is the anaesthesia machine and medication check complete?
- ☐ Yes

Is the pulse oximeter on the patient and functioning?
- ☐ Yes

Does the patient have a:

Known allergy?
- ☐ No
- ☐ Yes

Difficult airway or aspiration risk?
- ☐ No
- ☐ Yes, and equipment/assistance available

Risk of >500ml blood loss (7ml/kg in children)?
- ☐ No
- ☐ Yes, and two IVs/central access and fluids planned

Before skin incision

(with nurse, anaesthetist and surgeon)

- ☐ **Confirm all team members have introduced themselves by name and role.**
- ☐ **Confirm the patient's name, procedure, and where the incision will be made.**

Has antibiotic prophylaxis been given within the last 60 minutes?
- ☐ Yes
- ☐ Not applicable

Anticipated Critical Events

To Surgeon:
- ☐ What are the critical or non-routine steps?
- ☐ How long will the case take?
- ☐ What is the anticipated blood loss?

To Anaesthetist:
- ☐ Are there any patient-specific concerns?

To Nursing Team:
- ☐ Has sterility (including indicator results) been confirmed?
- ☐ Are there equipment issues or any concerns?

Is essential imaging displayed?
- ☐ Yes
- ☐ Not applicable

Before patient leaves operating room

(with nurse, anaesthetist and surgeon)

Nurse Verbally Confirms:
- ☐ The name of the procedure
- ☐ Completion of instrument, sponge and needle counts
- ☐ Specimen labelling (read specimen labels aloud, including patient name)
- ☐ Whether there are any equipment problems to be addressed

To Surgeon, Anaesthetist and Nurse:
- ☐ What are the key concerns for recovery and management of this patient?

This checklist is not intended to be comprehensive. Additions and modifications to fit local practice are encouraged.

Revised 1 / 2009

© WHO, 2009

Fig. 28.1 The WHO surgical safety checklist. (WHO 2019)

cally (and stereotypically), the anaesthetist will be a bit more hesitant and thoughtful, while the surgeon will have a rather goal-orientated mind-set.

It is not surprising that these different mind-sets can be the cause for disagreements, negative sentiments and errors. This makes communication essential and relevant for the outcome of the patient! Good communication is very fruitful and interlinks two well-trained, differently thinking human brains for the safety of the patient. It is reminiscent of Daniel Kahnemans (2017) System 1 and 2, with the two systems talking to each other and being housed in two heads.

The last part of the Checklist is used at the end of the operation and focuses on technical issues: Were all sponges and instruments accounted for? Were there technical problems that need to be addressed before the next patient is operated?

Progressive hospitals have added an extra Checklist item to this phase to focus on meta-communication: did we communicate clearly with each other? Were there hints of aggression that should be addressed now?

In order to improve high-performing teams, it is essential to also address these communication errors. Bad feelings within the team and between different specialties can easily become chronic and hinder future performances. I will give an insight on how we address these issues in our institution.

28.5 Error Management and Communication Tools Used in Our Institution

The University Medical Centre Groningen (UMCG) is associated with the University of Groningen. It employs 17,000 people and has close to 1400 beds. It is the tertiary referral hospital for the Northern Netherlands and one of the largest transplant centres in the world.

The Chest Centre at the UMCG offers the full range of invasive and noninvasive treatments for heart and lung diseases, for example, multiple-stage operations for newborns with congenital heart diseases, heart and lung transplantations or implantations of electromechanical devices to assist cardiac function.

The complexity of these cases can only be handled by a well-communicating multidisciplinary team in which each specialty provides a unique perspective and activity to help the patient. Communication and managing human factors are the glue that allows these teams to succeed. Vis-à-vis this complexity, the area of single heroic doctors is gone and so should be the culture in which they thrived for centuries.

We have implemented a locally adapted version of the WHO Surgical Safety Checklist that is implemented into our electronic Patient Management System (PMS). As stated above, the continuous professional, friendly and efficient communication is considered to be of utmost importance in our institution. We strive to solve communication problems and issues of negative emotions or aggression between team members immediately. We believe that not doing that can easily become chronic and endanger the safety of our patients.

Thus during the last part of the Checklist, the sign-out, each team member has the possibility to ask for a debriefing. If a debriefing is asked for, the elective surgical programme of this team is put on hold. After finishing the current case, the team comes together to talk about the miscommunication or the negative emotions. The debriefing is led by the surgeon and the aim is to resolve the issue. If the team does not achieve this, a professional mentor and team builder can be added, and the team will continue the debriefing within a couple of days.

We have had this construct in place for 5 years. In practice the pure possibility of a debriefing seems to make the major effect: people talk more thoughtful to each other, and the sign-out is used for quick apologies or clarifications. It is not more often than once per year that somebody asks for a debriefing.

There is another aspect to it that is essential: with the introduction of the debriefing, we have agreed with each other that if somebody is overheard bad mouthing another team member in the corridors or the coffee room, he or she is supposed to be addressed with the question why they did not initiate a debriefing.

Either you have a concern and speak about it at the right moment and towards the people involved or you keep silent. It was a way to teach people to communicate assertively.

The implementation of these rules had very positive effects on our team climate.

Other error management tools we use include Incident Reporting. Every team member at any moment has the possibility to report an incident. An incident can be anything that might have an influence on the outcome for the patient: perceived miscommunication with other parts of the hospital, unprofessional behaviour of somebody, technical problems or changed processes.

An incident is not reported anonymously so that clarifications can be given and a threshold is created to not use this tool for backstabbing in an emotional moment. We have a multidisciplinary incident committee in which each specialty and group of the OR is represented. The incident committee meets twice per month and looks at the reported incidents to determine if we can learn as an institution from the perceived incident and improve processes or if other actions are needed. If so, a recommendation is made to the responsible entity. The person that reported receives a written feedback within 14 days of reporting.

Another tool to improve and maintain good communication is the faculty hour. We reserve the first work hour of every Tuesday for communication. Different formats exist. One Tuesday per month, we meet with the specialists of our department; on another Tuesday of the month, we meet with the multidisciplinary within the area in which we work. Faculty hours are normally run without agenda and are a place to ventilate perceived shortcomings or to share experiences and insightful anecdotes. It is the formalised contemporary replacement for the shared beer at the pub on Friday after work. While there is nothing per se wrong with the pub approach for exchange and communication, it is a too informal setting and does often not include every team member. By dedicating work time for communication, an employer demonstrates the importance they give to these soft skills.

After 1 year of implementing the faculty hour, we assessed its effect on our OR productivity and found that it had no significant negative influence. It seems that the positive impact it has on team performance compensates for the time needed.

In medicine some complications happen with a certain probability and frequency. For example, an immobile patient can develop a blood clot (thrombosis) in a blood vessel despite prophylaxis. Complications like that are documented in our PMS, and they are openly discussed in a meeting once per month. In our institution, this meeting happens during a faculty hour. Complication can contribute to institutional learning:

- If a specific complication occurs too frequently
- If it is a very rare and extraordinary complication
- If medical research has suggested a new and more efficient way to fore come this complication.

In all of these cases, the complication meeting will make a recommendation to the responsible entity – for example, suggest an increase of dose of a drug against thromboses.

Aeronautics has historically been at the forefront of error reporting. One tool we are using to increase performances of our high reliable teams and to detect communication and other failures is *crew resource management* (CRM). Once per month, one of our ORs will start with a simulated case. The simulated scenario will include complications of some sort. While the team takes care of the simulated patient and works together to get on top of the complication, they are filmed and observed by our specially trained CRM coaches. After the scenario is finished, the team comes together and debriefs. Watching parts of the recorded video can be very helpful and insightful.

Debriefing, incident reporting, faculty hour, complication meeting, CRM – all of these vehicles improve our performance, make us learn from mistakes and empower the individual healthcare provider.

A more serious category of error we define is a *calamity*. A calamity has the potential for compensational payments to the patient and personal consequences for the doctors and nurses involved. Any event that has the potential of being a calamity needs to be reported as such. We have an extra senior person on-call for calamities. Documentation and communication with the patient's family become paramount in such a situation.

There are two factors that make these very complicated and often extremely sad situations bearable in our setting: the first one is the fact that all doctors of our institution are sufficiently insured via the hospital. In our part of the world, potential compensation payments to patients are adequate and not excessive. It is possible to maintain an open communication culture during these events.

The second factor is that after calamities, we aim to retrain the involved personnel rather than to just blame and fire them. Thereby we stick to a fair-blaming culture. Obviously there are limits to the possibility of forgiving and retraining, surely at the point where national criminal law kicks in.

But a person who has caused a calamity and has been retrained and rehabilitated can become a resource: a strong stakeholder and leading example into the culture of learning from mistakes.

28.6 The Role of Cultural Change: How to Implement

Over the last years, we have been trying to be at the front of the insights into the concepts of learning from failure and errors.

The essential component to make this possible is to truly change the culture of an institution and its people to not only implement a new error management tool but also to sustain the use of it. "Culture eats strategy for breakfast" is the correlating famous management quote attributed to Peter Drucker.

How was it possible to implement these cultural changes in our institution that are far from the traditional medical command and control ways of organising?

Our way was to invest time and resources in the implementation processes. To do this, the top management needs to be on board with the envisioned changes.

Typically a train-the-trainers approach is chosen for implementation with the help of an external expert. The trained trainers need to come from all disciplines of the workplace involved. Training own trainers increases compliance and is cost-effective. Two trainers from different disciplines will group up to teach multi-disciplinary teams during working hours. An implementation process decreases our OR productivity by 10% and takes a total of 3 months.

After 6 weeks when 50% of the group has been trained, we start using the tool. For example, when we introduced the sign-out procedure with the possibility of a debriefing, in average, 50% of the people had not been trained yet. We have good experience with this timing. Waiting too long can have negative effects.

As stated above, nurses are very likely to enjoy empowerment and job enrichment. Doctors are the more likely professional group with some adjustment problems. Training, time and scientific insights can be helpful. Accepting that there is a new type of leadership style required is important. This style needs insight and courage and works with coaching and guiding. It is open to feedback, asks questions and invites answers. It communicates on eye level. Leading by example and being open with own mistakes are essential. Transforming personally into this type of new leader can be a rewarding experience.

Some people might not be ready for cultural change and stuck in old ways. At some point of the change process, these people might need to be let gone.

28.7 Reaching the Second Half of the Chessboard

With the achieved technical medical sophistication, focusing on nontechnical skills like communication and culture has become a way of improving outcomes in medicine, but medicine continues to be at the forefront of technical developments.

We are at a point where technical developments happen at a breathtaking speed. Moore's law implies that every 2 years or so, computing power will double (Encyclopaedia Britannica 2019). So far humans have mostly kept on top of this development. But we have reached a point that Ray Kurzweil, director of development at Google, calls "reaching the second half of the chessboard" (Friedman 2017).

The story goes that the inventor of the game of chess was granted a wish. He wished for rice: one grain of rice on the first square of a chessboard, two on the second, four on the third and so forth. When reaching the end of the first half of the chessboard, the amount of rice extends to the production of some acres, but when reaching the 64th square, the pile of rice would expand to the size of Mount Everest – more than our planet produces.

Reaching the second half of the chessboard technologically will transform our society and the way we work and interact. It will have a huge impact on medicine, on our culture and on how we deal with errors. Eric Topol (2019) believes that patients will be empowered through technology to run many tests at home, have a better understanding of their disease and meet doctors on eye level. Doctors will gain lots of time and will be able to use it for being with their patients: to treat them more individually and more empathically.

That is a very positive vision, and it is up to the society and the medical community to work towards it. It will be paramount to empower the patient and not the technology.

References

Csikszentmihalyi, M. (1990). *Flow: The psychology of optimal experience*. New York: Harper & Row.

Encyclopaedia Britannica. (2019). *Moore's law*. Retrieved 8 September 2019, from https://www.britannica.com/technology/Moores-law.

Friedman, T.L. (2017). *Thank You For Being Late*. New York: Picador/Farrar Straus & Giroux.

Haynes, A., Weiser, T., Berry, W., Lipsitz, S., Breizat, A., & Dellinger, E. et al. (2009). A Surgical Safety Checklist to Reduce Morbidity and Mortality in a Global Population. *New England Journal Of Medicine*, *360*(5), 491–499. doi: https://doi.org/10.1056/nejmsa0810119

Kahneman, D. (2017). *Thinking Fast and Slow*. New York: Farrar Straus & Giroux.

Kohn, L., Corrigan, J., & Donaldson, M. (2000). *To err is human*. Washington, DC: National Academy Press.

Mokdad, A., Marks, J., Stroup DF, & Gerberding, J. (2004). Actual Causes of Death in the United States, 2000. *JAMA*, *291*(10), 1238. doi: https://doi.org/10.1001/jama.291.10.12383

Pronovost, P., Needham, D., Berenholtz, S., Sinopoli, D., Chu, H., Cosgrove, S., Sexton, B., Hyzy, R., Welsh, R., Roth, G., Bander, J., Kepros, J., Goeschel, C. (2006). An Intervention to Decrease Catheter-Related Bloodstream Infections in the ICU. *New England Journal of Medicine*, 355, 2725–2732.

Rose, J., Weiser, T., Hider, P., Wilson, L., Gruen, R., & Bickler, S. (2015). Estimated need for surgery worldwide based on prevalence of diseases: a modelling strategy for the WHO Global Health Estimate. *The Lancet Global Health*, 3, S13-S20. doi: https://doi.org/10.1016/s2214-109x(15)70087-2

Topol, E. (2019). *Deep Medicine*. New York: Ingram Publisher Services US.

Weiser, T., Haynes, A., Molina, G., Lipsitz, S., Esquivel, M., & Uribe-Leitz, T. et al. (2016). Size and distribution of the global volume of surgery in 2012. *Bulletin Of The World Health Organization*, 94(3), 201–209F. doi: https://doi.org/10.2471/blt.15.159293

World Health Organization. (2019). WHO Surgical Safety Checklist. Retrieved 8 September 2019, from https://www.who.int/patientsafety/safesurgery/checklist/en/

Jan S. Brommundt (Dr.) is medical doctor in anaesthesiology as well as international, humanitarian and disaster medicine. His background is in management in high-performing multidisciplinary, multicultural medical teams at the Netherland's largest academic hospital, the University Medical Center Groningen.

Chapter 29
Humorous Handling of Mistakes: A Personality or Culture-Specific Trait to Combat Adverse Health Effects?

Florian Fischer, Franziska Carow, and Hannah Eger

Abstract Mistakes, errors and failures offer opportunities for further development, as long as you talk about and work with them. However, there are fears of making mistakes, because a mistake or failure is seen as a threat to self-esteem in individualistic-oriented societies. Consequently, there are more and more discussions about the topic of error culture in society. An open error culture contributes to safety and to health: Mistakes are no longer concealed but conceived and used as learning opportunities. In this context, the handling of errors is of interest, because people from different cultures and within a culture react very differently towards negative experiences. The handling of errors is particularly dependent on individual personality traits. It has been shown in positive psychology that the interpretation of negative events is a key to adequate information processing. This is relevant for making suitable judgements based on the mistakes and, simultaneously, for protecting self-esteem.

This contribution will focus, on a theoretical level, on the effects a humorous handling of errors has in relation to health. This is based on the hypothesis that humour, as a personality trait, is a health-promoting resource. The article will take the perspective of public health, a genuinely interdisciplinary field of research and application, to illustrate the relationship between humorous handling of mistakes and health and well-being.

Keywords Mistakes · Errors · Failure · Humour · Culture · Coping

F. Fischer (✉) · F. Carow · H. Eger
Department of Population Medicine and Health Services Research, School of Public Health, Bielefeld University, Bielefeld, Germany
e-mail: f.fischer@uni-bielefeld.de; franziska.carow@uni-bielefeld.de; hannah.eger@uni-bielefeld.de

E. Vanderheiden, C.-H. Mayer (eds.), *Mistakes, Errors and Failures across Cultures*, https://doi.org/10.1007/978-3-030-35574-6_29

29.1 Introduction

We all make mistakes and we do so regularly. Mistakes and errors may occur in everyday life and in every setting in which we are living or working. Some errors are small, some are bigger or might even be crucial, but the appraisal of these mistakes depends on various factors. However, individual appraisal of these errors and mistakes may lead to negative emotions and stress (King and Beehr 2017). This is where public health comes into play: As one source of stress, these appraisals are related to ill health (Rybowiak et al. 1999; WHO 2018). Stress has effects on the development and progression of cardiovascular disease (Kivimäki and Steptoe 2017). Additionally, the excess risk of stress on various cancer entities has been debated in the scientific community (Coyne et al. 2010; Nielsen et al. 2007; Sawada et al. 2016). However, the most profound adverse effects of stress have been found relating to mental health. Depression and stress, for example, are highly associated (Plieger et al. 2015). Additionally, psychological, behavioural and biological factors impacting on mood and the sense of well-being are related to stress (Schneiderman et al. 2005). These effects seem to have already started in childhood (Toussaint et al. 2016). Furthermore, these results also have a cultural component due to differences in the stress appraisal and mental health-related symptoms. According to the concept of cultural consonance, individuals approximate the prototypes for belief and behaviour encoded in shared cultural models (Balieiro et al. 2011). Cultural consonance is related to concepts such as "status inconsistency" that identify contradictions in social life and the stresses associated with those incongruities. It identifies the contradictions that can arise between shared cultural models and individual attempts to apply those models in their own lives (Dressler 2004). It has been shown that higher cultural consonance in the cultural domains of lifestyle and social support was associated with lower psychological distress (Dressler 2012; Dressler et al. 2007).

Due to increasing disease burden related to psychological disorders, such as depression (WHO 2018), within the last few decades, research has started focusing on examining the potential causes of mental disorders, the coping strategies of healthy and non-healthy individuals and the potential therapy approaches.

But what has humour got to do with it? Firstly, humour functions as a distraction by interrupting the chain of thought that results in stress. Secondly, effective humour also results in laughter, which is a physical release of tension. Thirdly, humour shifts the focus of attention away from oneself. Fourthly, humour often helps people to recognize that however bad their situation might be, there is always a way to form it into positive emotions or, at least, in a way, to cope with it. This contribution introduces the use of humour as a coping strategy in the handling of errors, mistakes and failures and, thereby, relieving of stress. The main questions are: Is using humour a health-promoting factor related to the handling of mistakes, for whom and what kind of humour? But before we think about this, we need to know how far people use humour as a coping strategy to understand how a humorous handling of mistakes may influence our daily life.

29.2 Mistakes, Emotions and Stress

When trying to define mistakes and errors, one can find many different meanings in different languages and different cultures. Mistakes and errors generally refer to something which was done incorrectly or improperly. More precisely, mistakes can be understood as the most general term used in everyday situations, whereas error is more suitable for formal contexts. In addition, the term "error" might even be considered as more severe than a "mistake". Within this contribution, "mistakes" are thought of as accidental happenings, while "errors" are made due to a lack of knowledge, for example, not knowing the fitting answer to a question or the way of performing adequately. A "failure" is simply defined as a lack of success, which might even be due to the neglect or omission of an expected or required action (Oxford Dictionary 2014).

29.2.1 Mistakes and Errors in Daily Life

The connotation of the terms is predominantly negative in many cultures. We learn to avoid mistakes and errors from early childhood, simply because we learn it is wrong to make them. We often even fear making mistakes and errors, especially in groups and interpersonal contact, as we are consequently "punished" with bad grades and humiliation. We feel the need to "perform correctly" in many situations and, by doing so, fulfil our own and other people's expectations. There are cultural differences in error orientation, because culture influences what individuals learn across different aspects of socialization (Zotzmann et al. 2019).

Frese and Keith (2015) claim that every error may affect social relationships. Depending on the level of failure perceived and the people surrounding us, expectations can lead to pressure and often end as an assault on self-esteem and, therefore, in an even less correct performance and insecurity.

The educational scientist Weingardt (2014) states that the opposite should be the case: If you stop making mistakes, you will stop learning. He suggests that in mathematics, for example, the Scandinavian way of learning – encouraging pupils and students to make mistakes and errors and discussing them openly – is decisive for adult life as an exploring way of learning.

Additionally, he claims that there are many different types of mistakes which need further distinction (Weingardt 2014). One would expect that the judgement of mistakes would consider these variations. However, the result of making either a major or minor mistake is the same in German, American and other Western societies and error cultures: You are wrong, and you fail. You can fail a bit, more than a bit or very much – but you fail.

Error culture is also highly relevant at the workplace. Mistakes cannot be avoided, particularly due to the rising complexity of work. A workplace culture of learning from mistakes may allow for effective learning experiences (Harteis et al. 2008). There is a lack of discussion and acceptance in several cultures, societies and many organizations when it comes to mistakes and failures. This prohibits learning from those mistakes. Instead, failures are actually neglected, or mistakes are manipulated in the hope of being forgotten and never noticed. Aspiring towards perfection, linked with the fear of making mistakes, not only hinders daring and taking risks to progress but also puts pressure on individuals. Instead, error orientation has the potential to act as an enhancer of learning which may lead to better performances in the future (Dormann and Frese 1994). Error competence and learning from errors are related to self-efficacy as well as plan and action orientation. In addition, error strain is related to ill health, as it is negatively correlated with self-efficacy and self-esteem but positively associated with control rejection, psychosomatic complaints, depression and negative affectivity (Rybowiak et al. 1999).

Error orientation is also dependent on cultural values: Current research suggests that people scoring high in "collectivism" have a significantly higher score on error orientation than participants scoring high in "power distance" (Zotzmann et al. 2019). Collectivism is defined as the "principle of giving a group priority over each individual in it" (Oxford Dictionary 2014). We find collectivism typically in Asian and eastern countries. Power distance means the extent to which the lower-ranking individuals of a society accept and expect that power is distributed unequally, which we, for example, find in America or Germany. A possible explanation for this phenomenon might be a higher "common sense" in societies living collectivistic. Further research is necessary to find out about the exact reasons.

Apart from that also masculinity plays a role. Societies with "masculine" orientation (e.g. America) scored significantly lower in error orientation. The reason might be that being masculine also means being strong and making mistakes and errors is considered "weak". Apart from these cultural aspects, error orientation is related to personality traits. Although positively related to both personality and culture, error orientation cannot be explained entirely yet (Zotzmann et al. 2019).

The handling of errors is of interest, particularly, because people from different cultures and within a culture react very differently towards negative experiences. What we do know so far is that an open error culture contributes to safety and success, because mistakes are no longer concealed but conceived and can be used as learning opportunities. This has been shown in the setting of the school (Wuttke and Seifried 2012) and in the capital markets (AFM 2017). Errors and mistakes may even be conducive, as empirical research has shown that making errors is more helpful for learning than error avoidance and detailed guidance, especially in difficult tasks (Frese and Keith 2015).

29.2.2 A Closer Look: The Connection of Mistakes and Emotions

Everyone makes mistakes in daily life from time to time. However, the degree of appraisal can vary depending on the extent to which people undergo negative experiences while making mistakes. If you are being laughed at, for example, for something you apparently did wrong, you will assess it in a different way than you would have done if you had received encouraging feedback. Knowing you will be dismissed can make you work harder, on the one hand, or make you react aggressively or feel sad, on the other hand. Making a mistake in the company of family members might be different than making the same mistake when your superior is around, especially when you fear them. Putting it on the record, these examples show that emotional appraisal differs from situation to situation and mistake to mistake but also from culture to culture. However, the more emotionally an individual reacts, the stronger the appraisal and learning effect is (Frese and Keith 2015). The appraisal is negative when you feel uncomfortable or the mistake/error you have made is dealt with in a way that makes you feel uncomfortable. Consequently, negative appraisals can lead to distress and, thus, have an influence on our future mistake and error behaviour and, as a result, on our overall behaviour (Reif et al. 2018).

Being judged a failure, a mistake might be accompanied by a variety of emotions and uncomfortable feelings, such as embarrassment, anxiety, anger or sadness. People are likely to do anything they can to escape feeling emotional discomfort, but the question is: Which kind of actions should be taken? An oversimplification of potential responses towards a mistake may distinguish between the two most familiar actions:

- Accepting the responsibility – fully or at least partly – for the mistake.
- Pushing back against the facts and denying either the mistake itself or one's own action.

The reasons for choosing either to accept or deny the mistake are related to psychological characteristics, such as self-esteem, and cultural background. As admitting one is wrong is unpleasant, it takes a certain amount of emotional strength and courage to deal with the situation.

29.2.3 Effects of Humour on Emotions and Stress

As humour is effective in reducing afflicting or unpleasant feelings, it might be conducive in the appraisal of mistakes and coping with failures. Humour is more than just laughter, because humour can be understood as a quite broad and multifaceted psychological phenomenon that encompasses several components, such as cognitive, emotional and interpersonal aspects (Martin 2016). Finding something to laugh at supports the feeling of being more in control. Humour provides an opportunity for individuals to shift perspective regarding a stressful situation, which might be caused by a mistake, and to reappraise it from a new and less threatening point of view (Dixon 1980). Rim (1988) pointed to the fact that the stress-buffering effects of humour can be seen either in a mode of "minimization", for example, looking on the bright side of things, or "reversal", for example, trying to find something funny in a distressing situation. This indicates that humour offers the benefit of coping with unpleasant experiences as it appears as a buffer for an individual against the adverse effects of stress (Abel 1998; Labott et al. 1990). This positive effect may be explained by the role of humour in the cognitive appraisal of stressful situations and its function as a coping strategy in general (Abel 2002). For that reason, it was claimed more than two decades ago that more research about the effects of humour on cognitive appraisals was needed (Kuiper et al. 1995; Lefcourt and Thomas 1998).

The current evidence indicates that humour produces a cognitive-affective shift or a restructuring of the situation, leading to a concomitant release of emotion (Dixon 1980; Martin et al. 1993) associated with the appraisal of mistakes and feeling of having failed. This cognitive-affective shift is related to the transactional model of stress, which illustrates that stress depends upon a person's cognitive appraisal of events and circumstances and the ability to cope (Lazarus and Folkman 1984). Two different coping mechanisms using humour can be distinguished: (1) the emotion-based coping strategy, applying a defensive measure by reducing negative emotional reactions due to humour, and (2) the problem-focused coping, using humour to alter the stressful situation itself (Lefcourt et al. 1997).

The particular relevance related to mistakes can be seen in the fact that an increased sense of humour supports a more positive and growth-oriented handling of these challenging situations and circumstances. This enables the process of constant learning from mistakes, as it also increases the likelihood of conscious efforts at seeking alternative perspectives to problems (Kuiper et al. 1995).

29.3 Coping Associated with Humour

The way one deals with mistakes is highly important for health and well-being. The concept of salutogenesis, first introduced by Aaron Antonovsky (1979), although not explicitly focused on the handling of mistakes, contains a theoretical foundation for factors supporting human health and well-being – in contrast to the perspective of pathogenesis, which emphasizes those factors causing a disease. Within this theory, the dichotomous view on health vs. illness is rejected. Instead, Antonovsky (1979) describes the relationship between health and illness as a continuous variable.

The so-called continuum of health describes three components that influence one's behaviour while dealing with a situation: comprehensibility, manageability and meaningfulness. Altogether, this coping mechanism is called "sense of coherence". The understanding of a problem, a "way out" and the answer to the question whether life makes sense to an individual define how he or she can handle a situation and how ill he or she feels (Antonovsky 1979). His theoretical approach has remained applicable until today and shows major effects, as it enables both individuals and societies to deal with problems (Eriksson and Lindström 2007) and as the appraisal of individual life situations plays a major role in the subjective feeling of health. However, the relationship between salutogenesis and humour has not been explicitly researched until now.

In the context of the handling of mistakes, it can be summarized that the appraisal of a mistake is related to coping strategies, which are dependent on different components. For example, cross-cultural differences of coping have been observed, although research on coping has been conducted predominantly in individualistic (Western) cultures and rarely in collectivistic cultures. Therefore, our understanding of coping is based mainly on Western views and concepts (See and Essau 2010). However, coping style is affected not only by the individual's appraisal of the situation he or she is faced with but also by the resources available, the use of which may be approved of or prohibited by cultural values and norms (Lazarus and Folkman 1984). In addition, cultures may differ with respect to environmental demands, political and economic systems, social structure, resources and cultural norms, which may influence coping patterns (See and Essau 2010). For that reason, cultural issues determine whether more problem- or emotion-focused strategies are chosen. This also applies to the tendency of using either primary control (attempts to influence objective conditions) or secondary control (attempts to adjust oneself to objective conditions) in coping (Essau 1992; Haynes et al. 2009).

The coping strategies, in turn, affect the subjective health status. As humour (as a personality trait) may impact on the appraisal of a mistake or act as an independent variable impacting on the coping strategy, direct and indirect effects of humour in the context of the handling of mistakes can be assumed. However, the appraisal of and coping with a potentially stressful situation, which may be caused by a mistake, is dependent on further personality traits. Furthermore, it also needs to be mentioned that several personality traits themselves are predictors of humour (Mendiburo-Seguel et al. 2015). For that reason, humorous coping (of mistakes) is dependent on cultural issues and personality traits.

29.3.1 Humour and Culture

Although humour is a universal human experience, people of different societies and with different cultural backgrounds perceive and use humour differently (Martin 2007). Humour can, of course, be used gently or aggressively and for good or ill. In Western countries, fun, humour and nonsense are perceived as being more benevolent ("laughing with") than satire, cynicism, sarcasm and irony, which carry connotations of bad-humoured "laughing at" (Beermann and Ruch 2009). The distinction between good and bad types of humour is also found in other cultures, but attitudes and tastes in humour differ, depending on circumstances (such as the political, social and cultural environment) and personal preferences (Davis 2013).

Each society and culture has found a different pattern of response to the problems of social life and, therefore, also specific ways of use and perception of humour (Yue et al. 2016). Research has shown that basic tendencies to deal with central issues of social life are stable across the generations in societies due to socialization (Hofstede 2005). Alharthi (2016) argues that we share the same concept of what humour is and how we respond to it. However, despite the recognition of this phenomenon, each society and culture have unique techniques for making jokes and provoking laughter which, in many instances, distinguish them from other societies and cultural backgrounds. As human beings, we may find the same topics humorous, but we still have something exclusive and special when utilizing these topics in our daily interactions and something that reflects our own lifestyle, beliefs and traditions (Alharthi 2016).

Socialization is a process through which a culture's rules are learned but also through which personality is developed. For that reason, the way how humour is used is related to cultural issues and personality traits.

29.3.2 Humour Embedded in Personality Traits

Sense of coherence, the core of the salutogenic model, is related to several further personality traits and is highly relevant in terms of coping (Kase et al. 2018). Evidence suggests that the sense of coherence and self-esteem are highly correlated (Moksnes and Lazarewicz 2016), as it is the case for the relationship between sense of coherence and self-efficacy (Trap et al. 2016). Self-esteem is a term used in psychology to describe a person's overall sense of self-worth or personal value. It is often seen as a personality trait and, therefore, tends to be stable and enduring. Self-esteem can involve a variety of beliefs about oneself, such as the appraisal of one's own appearance, beliefs, emotions and behaviours. It is an important factor for motivation, as Abraham Maslow (1943) described in his hierarchy of needs, which depicts self-esteem as one of the basic human motivations. Low self-esteem may hold one back from succeeding, because people do not believe that they are capable of success. By contrast, having a healthy self-esteem can help one to navigate life with a positive, assertive attitude, and it strengthens the belief that one can accomplish one's own goals. Therefore, self-esteem can lead to individual growth as a person and achieving self-actualization (Maslow 1943).

Self-efficacy is understood as the belief in one's own abilities, specifically the ability to meet the challenges ahead and complete a task successfully (Maddux 2009). While self-esteem is focused more on "being" (e.g. feeling that you are perfectly acceptable as you are), self-efficacy is more focused on "doing" (e.g. feeling that you are up to a challenge). Although both stand as separate constructs, they are highly interlinked.

Personality psychology also deals with styles of humour. In this regard, humour can be understood as a personality trait, because people of all ages and backgrounds engage in humour, but the style of humour can vary greatly. Although small variations in styles of humour depending on the situation are possible, they tend to be relatively stable personality characteristics among individuals (Ruch 1998). Martin et al. (2003) distinguished between four types of humour:

- *Affiliative humour*: enhancing one's relationships with others in a benevolent, positive manner

- *Self-enhancing humour*: having a good-natured attitude towards life and the ability to laugh at yourself, your circumstances and the idiosyncrasies of life in a constructive, non-detrimental manner
- *Aggressive humour*: use of sarcasm, teasing, criticism and other types of humour at the expense of others in a potentially detrimental manner
- *Self-defeating humour*: use of potentially detrimental humour towards the self in order to gain approval from others

More recent research distinguishes between nine styles to assess individual differences in humour more accurately. Heintz and Ruch (2019) provided empirical evidence on these nine styles, which are based on the four types of humour described by Martin et al. (2003) and further comic styles (Ruch and Heintz 2016), in some cases with overlaps: fun/affiliative, benevolent/self-enhancing, sarcasm/aggressive, nonsense, wit, irony, satire, cynicism and self-defeating (Heintz and Ruch 2019).

29.3.3 Humour and Coping: Empirical Evidence

Humour, as such, can lead to resilience, which is understood as the ability of humans to spring back from stressors in the environment. By not taking oneself too seriously, one is able to let go of excessively perfectionistic expectations, while remaining motivated to achieve realistic goals. For that reason, humour can enable us to encounter stress, which may be provoked by errors or mistakes, and to return to previous levels of functioning (Lefcourt and Thomas 1998). The positive styles of humour (affiliative and self-enhancing) are positively associated with error competence, learning from errors, error risk-taking and error communication, whereas negative styles of humour (aggressive and self-defeating) are associated with error strain, error anticipation and the covering up of errors (Csonka and Scheel 2012).

This emphasizes the relationship between humour, personality and handling of mistakes. But how can humour be used for coping? The example of the "7 Humour Habits Program" (7HHP) developed by McGhee (2010) may provide a first explanation. The effectiveness of this program related to boosting sense of humour, improvements in daily mood, optimism and the ability to cope with stress is widely accepted (Goldstein and Ruch 2018). The 7HHP itself consists of seven core habits (McGhee 2010):

- Surround yourself with humour.
- Cultivate a playful attitude.
- Laugh more often.
- Create your own verbal humour.
- Look for humour in daily life.
- Laugh at yourself.
- Find humour in the midst of stress.

All these habits are either directly or indirectly related to coping strategies which may be used to deal with mistakes and failures in everyday life. Beneficial effects of coping have been described, with better outcomes among people with active coping (engagement), such as active confrontation seeking social support, reassuring thoughts and expressing emotions, in contrast to avoidance behaviour (disengagement), characterized by passive reaction patterns (Dijkstra and Homan 2016).

It has been shown that the selection of coping strategies is not only dependent on cultural issues but also on personality, although several further factors seem to be more influential on coping. The most widespread instrument used to assess personality traits in psychology is the Big Five taxonomy (John et al. 2010). According to this taxonomy, one can distinguish between five broad dimensions describing the human personality:

- *Openness to experience*: inventive/curious vs. consistent/cautious.
- *Conscientiousness*: efficient/organized vs. easy-going/careless.
- *Extraversion*: outgoing/energetic vs. solitary/reserved.
- *Agreeableness*: friendly/compassionate vs. challenging/detached.
- *Neuroticism*: sensitive/nervous vs. secure/confident.

A meta-analysis tested moderators of the relationships between the Big Five personality traits and coping using 2653 effect sizes drawn from 165 samples and 33,094 participants. According to these results, extraversion, openness to experience, conscientiousness and agreeableness are positively associated with problem-solving coping, whereas neuroticism is associated with disengagement, withdrawal and negative emotion focus (Connor-Smith and Flachsbart 2007). This has been confirmed by a study which indicated that problem-solving (e.g. feedback) and cognitive restructuring (particularly humour) were related to higher levels of extraversion, conscientiousness and openness to experience. Withdrawal and negative emotion focus as coping styles were related to higher levels of neuroticism and lower levels of agreeableness (Geisler et al. 2009).

In the context of coping with daily failures, it has been shown that a positive reframing supports the achievement of a higher level of satisfaction. In this regard, humour, as a strategy of positive reframing, showed positive effects on satisfaction and managing stress effectively (Stoeber and Janssen 2011). Humour-oriented individuals have shown greater coping efficacy, which led to increased reports of life satisfaction (Wanzer et al. 2009). A study on the role of coping humour among older adults indicated that coping humour is significantly associated with social support and self-efficacy (Marziali et al. 2008). By contrast, a study conducted among older adults residing in assisted living facilities found no clear results of humour as a means of coping, although humour coping was positively related with the health status, particularly emotional health (Celso et al. 2003).

Therefore, one might expect a complex interwoven relationship between humour, coping strategies related to errors and health outcomes. A study by Deaner and McConatha (1993), for example, focussing on the relationship between depression and humour showed that individuals who scored lower on the depression inventory tended to score higher on the Coping Humour Scale, which measures the degree to which respondents make use of humour in coping with stress in their lives on a 7-item scale (Martin and Lefcourt 1983). In addition, individuals who scored higher on extraversion also scored higher on the humour scales, whereas individuals who scored higher on introversion scored higher on the depression scale. Emotional stability was significantly associated with higher scores on the sense of humour scale, which means that individuals who were less dependent were more likely to use humour as a coping mechanism (Deaner and McConatha 1993).

29.3.4 Humour and Positive Psychology

Humour may not only be a mean of coping but can also be understood as a resource – taking the perspective of health promotion. This is related to the ideas of positive psychology, which began as a new domain of psychology, studying what makes life most worth living. Positive psychology interventions have also been linked to the education sector (White 2016), which is of relevance in the context of learning from errors. Related to health outcomes, an intervention follow-up study (2374 participants before the intervention and 622 participants at the last follow-up after 6 months) aimed to investigate how far 9 different interventions from positive psychology can influence happiness and depressive symptoms. One of the interventions was called "Three funny things". In this intervention, participants were instructed to write down the three funniest things they had experienced or done. In addition, they should write down an explanation why those things happened to them on every day for 1 week. This intervention is a slight variation of "Three good things", where participants were asked to do the same, but with a focus on good instead of funny things. Small to medium effect sizes were observed, although the "Three good things" did not show a significant effect regarding an increase in happiness and a decrease in depressive symptoms in comparison with the baseline for all observation periods as it was for the "Three funny things" (Gander et al. 2013). This illustrates the relevance of humour as a mechanism to promote well-being.

A placebo-controlled online intervention study with a follow-up (n = 632) indicates that all five 1-week interventions using humour-enhanced happiness for 3 even up to 6 months (i.e. Three funny things, Applying Humour and Counting funny things) showed only short-term effects on depression (Wellenzohn et al. 2016). It has been observed that increases in sense of humour during and after the intervention were associated with the interventions' effectiveness. The humour-based interventions were equally suited for humorous and non-humorous people (Wellenzohn et al. 2018). Furthermore, it has been shown that extraversion plays a role in the effectiveness of a humour-based positive psychology intervention, as it was robustly positively correlated with happiness and negatively correlated with depression (Wellenzohn et al. 2016, 2018).

29.4 Conclusion

There is evidence about the positive effects of humour on both coping and positive health outcomes. However, until now, there has been no research available investigating the relationship between humour and dealing with errors and the resulting health consequences. The modes of action of both cultural factors and personality traits on use and perception of humour need further investigation in the future. Within this contribution, we have tried to shed some light on this issue. As humour can regulate emotions, it may also be supportive in dealing with critical situations which may occur due to mistakes and failures. Personality traits and coping strategies, which may both be linked with humour, can play an important role in error management, because cultural values, psychological appraisals and coping processes are essential in determining whether or not a potentially stressful life experience results in adverse health outcomes. Humour, as such, can, therefore, be used as a resource which promotes the appraisal and handling of mistakes as well as coping with stressful events. However, one might expect heterogeneity of effects related to personality traits and cultural factors which need further emphasis in future research.

References

Abel, M. H. (1998). Interaction of humor and gender in moderating relationships between stress and outcomes. *The Journal of Psychology, 132*, 267–276. https://doi.org/10.1080/00223989809599166

Abel, M. H. (2002). Humor, stress, and coping strategies. *Humor – International Journal of Humor Research* 15:365–381. https://doi.org/10.1515/humr.15.4.365

AFM. (2017). *Learning from errors; towards an error management culture: Insights based on a study in the capital markets*. Amsterdam: The Dutch Authority for the Financial Markets.

Alharthi, A. (2016). Humour and culture. *International Journal of Humanities and Cultural Studies, 1*, 119–130.

Antonovsky, A. (1979). *Health, stress, and coping* (The Jossey-Bass social and behavioral science series). San Francisco: Jossey-Bass.

Balieiro, M. C., Dos Santos, M. A., Dos Santos, J. E., & Dressler, W. W. (2011). Does perceived stress mediate the effect of cultural consonance on depression? *Transcultural Psychiatry, 48*, 519–538. https://doi.org/10.1177/1363461511418873

Beermann, U., & Ruch, W. (2009). How virtuous is humor? Evidence from everyday behavior. *International Journal of Humor Research, 22*, 395–417. https://doi.org/10.1515/HUMR.2009.023

Celso, B. G., Ebener, D. J., & Burkhead, E. J. (2003). Humor coping, health status, and life satisfaction among older adults residing in assisted living facilities. *Aging & Mental Health, 7*, 438–445. https://doi.org/10.1080/13607860310001594691

Connor-Smith, J. K., & Flachsbart, C. (2007). Relations between personality and coping: a meta-analysis. *Journal of Personality and Social Psychology, 93*, 1080–1107. https://doi.org/10.1037/0022-3514.93.6.1080

Coyne, J. C., Ranchor, A. V., & Palmer, S. C. (2010). Meta-analysis of stress-related factors in cancer. *Nature Reviews Clinical Oncology, 7*, 296. https://doi.org/10.1038/ncponc1134-c1

Csonka, M., & Scheel, T. (2012). *Humorously dealing with errors: pros and cons,* Oral presentation at the 48th Congress of the German Psychological Society, July 24, 2012, Bielefeld.

Davis, J. M. (2013). Humour and its cultural context. In J. M. Davis & J. V. Chey (Eds.), *Humour in Chinese life and culture: Resistance and control in modern times* (pp. 1–22). Hong Kong China: Hong Kong University Press.

Deaner, S. L., & McConatha, J. T. (1993). The relation of humor to depression and personality. *Psychological Reports, 72*, 755–763. https://doi.org/10.2466/pr0.1993.72.3.755

Dijkstra, M. T. M., & Homan, A. C. (2016). Engaging in Rather than Disengaging from Stress: Effective Coping and Perceived Control. *Frontiers in Psychology, 7*, 1415. https://doi.org/10.3389/fpsyg.2016.01415

Dixon, N. F. (1980). Humor: A cognitive alternative to stress. In C. D. Spielberger & I. G. Sarason (Eds.), *Anxiety and stress* (pp. 281–289). Washington, D.C.: Hemisphere.

Dormann, T., & Frese, M. (1994). Error training: Replication and the function of exploratory behavior. *International Journal of Human-Computer Interaction, 6*, 365–372. https://doi.org/10.1080/10447319409526101

Dressler, W. W. (2004). Social or status incongruence. In N. B. Anderson (Ed.), *Encyclopedia of health & behavior*. Thousand Oaks, Calif.: Sage Reference.

Dressler, W. W. (2012). Cultural consonance: Linking culture, the individual and health. *Preventive Medicine, 55*, 390–393. doi:https://doi.org/10.1016/j.ypmed.2011.12.022

Dressler, W. W., Balieiro, M. C., Ribeiro, R. P., & Santos, J. E. D. (2007). Cultural consonance and psychological distress: examining the associations in multiple cultural domains. *Culture, Medicine and Psychiatry, 31*, 195–224. https://doi.org/10.1007/s11013-007-9046-2

Eriksson, M., & Lindström, B. (2007). Antonovsky's sense of coherence scale and its relation with quality of life: a systematic review. *Journal of Epidemiology and Community Health, 61*, 938–944.https://doi.org/10.1136/jech.2006.056028

Essau, C. A. (1992). *Primary-secondary control and coping: A cross-cultural comparison.* Regensburg: Roderer.

Frese, M., & Keith, N. (2015). Action errors, error management, and learning in organizations. *Annual Review of Psychology, 66*, 661–687. https://doi.org/10.1146/annurev-psych-010814-015205

Gander, F., Proyer, R. T., Ruch, W., & Wyss, T. (2013). Strength-Based Positive Interventions: Further Evidence for Their Potential in Enhancing Well-Being and Alleviating Depression. *Journal of Happiness Studies, 14*, 1241–1259. https://doi.org/10.1007/s10902-012-9380-0

Geisler, F. C. M., Wiedig-Allison, M., & Weber, H. (2009). What coping tells about personality. *European Journal of Personality, 23*, 289–306. https://doi.org/10.1002/per.709

Goldstein, J., & Ruch, W. (2018). Paul McGhee and humor research. *International Journal of Humor Research, 31*, 169–181https://doi.org/10.1515/humor-2018-0031

Harteis, C., Bauer, J., & Gruber, H. (2008). The culture of learning from mistakes: How employees handle mistakes in everyday work: Organisational and Personal Contributions to Workplace Learning Environments. *International Journal of Educational Research, 47*, 223–231. https://doi.org/10.1016/j.ijer.2008.07.003

Haynes, T. L., Heckhausen, J., Chipperfield, J. G., Perry, R. P., & Newall, N. E. (2009). Primary and Secondary Control Strategies: Implications for Health and Well-Being Among Older Adults. *Journal of Social and Clinical Psychology, 28*, 165–197. https://doi.org/10.1521/jscp.2009.28.2.165

Heintz, S., & Ruch, W. (2019). From four to nine styles: An update on individual differences in humor. *Personality and Individual Differences, 141*, 7–12. https://doi.org/10.1016/j.paid.2018.12.008

Hofstede, G. J. (2005). Cultures and organizations: software of the mind. New York: McGraw-Hill.

John, O. P., Naumann, L. P., & Soto, C. J. (2010). Paradigm Shift to the Integrative Big Five Trait Taxonomy. In O. P. John, R. W. Robins, & L. A. Pervin (Eds.), *Handbook of personality: Theory and research* (pp. 114–117). New York, NY: Guilford Press.

Kase, T., Ueno, Y., & Oishi, K. (2018). The overlap of sense of co-herence and the Big Five personality traits: A confirmatory study. *Health Psychology Open, 5*, 2055102918810654. https://doi.org/10.1177/2055102918810654

King, B. S., & Beehr, T. A. (2017). Working with the stress of errors: Error management strategies as coping. *International Journal of Stress Management, 24*, 18–33. https://doi.org/10.1037/str0000022

Kivimäki, M., & Steptoe, A. (2017). Effects of stress on the development and progression of cardiovascular disease. *Nature Reviews Cardiology, 15*, 215. https://doi.org/10.1038/nrcardio.2017.189

Kuiper, N. A., McKenzie, S. D., & Belanger, K. A. (1995). Cognitive appraisals and individual differences in sense of humor: Motivational and affective implications. *Personality and Individual Differences, 19*, 359–372. https://doi.org/10.1016/0191-8869(95)00072-E

Labott, S. M., Ahleman, S., Wolever, M. E., & Martin, R. B. (1990). The physiological and psychological effects of the expression and inhibition of emotion. *Behavioral Medicine, 16*, 182–189. https://doi.org/10.1080/08964289.1990.9934608

Lazarus, R. S., & Folkman, S. (1984). *Stress, appraisal, and coping*. New York, Springer.

Lefcourt, H. M., Davidson, K., Prkachin, Kenneth, M., & Mills, D. E. (1997). Humor As a Stress Moderator in the Prediction of Blood Pressure Obtained during Five Stressful Tasks. *Journal of Research in Personality, 31*, 523–542. https://doi.org/10.1006/jrpe.1997.2191

Lefcourt, H. M., & Thomas, S. (1998). Humor and stress revisited. In W. Ruch (Ed.), *The Sense of Humor: Explorations of a Personality Characteristic* (pp. 179–202). Berlin/New York: Mouton de Gruyter.

Maddux, J. E. (2009). Self-Efficacy: The Power of Believing You Can. In C. R. Snyder & S. J. Lopez (Eds.), *Oxford handbook of positive psychology* (2nd ed., pp. 334–344, Oxford library of psychology). New York: Oxford Univ. Press.

Martin, R. A. (2007). *The psychology of humor: An integrative approach*. Amsterdam: Elsevier.

Martin, R. A. (2016). Sense of humor. In S. J. Lopez (Ed.), *Positive psychological assessment* (pp. 350–353). Washington, D.C.: American Psychological Association.

Martin, R. A., Kuiper, N. A., Olinger, L. J., & Dance, K. A. (1993). Humor, coping with stress, self-concept, and psychological well-being. *International Journal of Humor Research*. 6:89–104. https://doi.org/10.1515/humr.1993.6.1.89

Martin, R. A., & Lefcourt, H. M. (1983). Sense of humor as a moderator of the relation between stressors and moods. *Journal of Personality and Social Psychology, 45*, 1313–1324. https://doi.org/10.1037/0022-3514.45.6.1313

Martin, R. A., Puhlik-Doris, P., Larsen, G., Gray, J., & Weir, K. (2003). Individual differences in uses of humor and their relation to psychological well-being: Development of the Humor Styles Questionnaire. *Journal of Research in Personality, 37*, 48–75. https://doi.org/10.1016/S0092-6566(02)00534-2

Marziali, E., McDonald, L., & Donahue, P. (2008). The role of coping humor in the physical and mental health of older adults. *Aging & Mental Health, 12*, 713–718. https://doi.org/10.1080/13607860802154374

Maslow, A. H. (1943). A theory of human motivation. *Psychological Review, 50*, 370–396. https://doi.org/10.1037/h0054346

McGhee, P. E. (2010). *Humor as survival training for a stressed-out world: The 7 Humor Habits Program*. Bloomington: Author House.

Mendiburo-Seguel, A., Páez, D., & Martínez-Sánchez, F. (2015). Humor styles and personality: A meta-analysis of the relation between humor styles and the Big Five personality traits. *Scandinavian Journal of Psychology, 56*, 335–340. https://doi.org/10.1111/sjop.12209

Moksnes, U. K., & Lazarewicz, M. (2016). The association between self-esteem and sense of coherence in adolescents aged 13–18years—The role of sex and age differences. *Personality and Individual Differences, 90*, 150–154. https://doi.org/10.1016/j.paid.2015.10.049

Nielsen, N. R., Strandberg-Larsen, K., Grønbaek, M., Kristensen, T. S., Schnohr, P., & Zhang, Z.-F. (2007). Self-reported stress and risk of endometrial cancer: a prospective cohort study. *Psychosomatic Medicine, 69*, 383–389. https://doi.org/10.1097/PSY.0b013e31804301d3

Oxford Dictionary. (2014). *The Oxford dictionary of synonyms and antonyms* (3rd ed., Oxford paperback reference). Oxford: Oxford Univ. Press.

Plieger, T., Melchers, M., Montag, C., Meermann, R., & Reuter, M. (2015). Life stress as potential risk factor for depression and burnout. *Burnout Research, 2*, 19–24. https://doi.org/10.1016/j.burn.2015.03.001

Reif, J., Spieß, E., & Stadler, P. (2018). *Effektiver Umgang mit Stress: Gesundheitsmanagement im Beruf.* Gesundheitsmanagement im Beruf (Die Wirtschaftspsychologie). Berlin: Springer.

Rim, Y. (1988). Sense of humour and coping styles. *Personality and Individual Differences, 9*, 559–564. https://doi.org/10.1016/0191-8869(88)90153-5

Ruch, W. (1998). *The Sense of Humor: Explorations of a Personality Characteristic*. Berlin: De Gruyter Mouton.

Ruch, W., & Heintz, S. (2016). The German Version of the Humor Styles Questionnaire: Psychometric properties and overlap with other styles of humor. *Europe's Journal of Psychology, 12*, 434–455. https://doi.org/10.5964/ejop.v12i3.1116

Rybowiak, V., Garst, H., Frese, M., & Batinic, B. (1999). Error orientation questionnaire (EOQ): reliability, validity, and different language equivalence. *Journal of Organizational Behavior, 20*, 527–547. https://doi.org/10.1002/(SICI)1099-1379(199907)20:4<527:AID-JOB886>3.0.CO;2-G

Sawada, T., Nishiyama, T., Kikuchi, N., Wang, C., Lin, Y., Mori, M., et al. (2016). The influence of personality and perceived stress on the development of breast cancer: 20-year follow-up of 29,098 Japanese women. *Scientific Reports, 6*, 32559. https://doi.org/10.1038/srep32559

Schneiderman, N., Ironson, G., & Siegel, S. D. (2005). Stress and health: psychological, behavioral, and biological determinants. *Annual Review of Clinical Psychology, 1*, 607–628. https://doi.org/10.1146/annurev.clinpsy.1.102803.144141

See, C. M., & Essau, C. A. (2010). Coping Strategies in Cross-Cultural Comparison. In B. Mayer & H.-J. Kornadt (Eds.), *Psychologie – Kultur – Gesellschaft* (pp. 161–173). Wiesbaden: VS Verlag für Sozialwissenschaften.

Stoeber, J., & Janssen, D. P. (2011). Perfectionism and coping with daily failures: positive reframing helps achieve satisfaction at the end of the day. *Anxiety, Stress, and Coping, 24*, 477–497. https://doi.org/10.1080/10615806.2011.562977

Toussaint, L., Shields, G. S., Dorn, G., & Slavich, G. M. (2016). Effects of lifetime stress exposure on mental and physical health in young adulthood: How stress degrades and forgiveness protects health. *Journal of Health Psychology, 21*, 1004–1014. https://doi.org/10.1177/1359105314544132

Trap, R., Rejkjær, L., & Hansen, E. H. (2016). Empirical relations between sense of coherence and self-efficacy, National Danish Survey. *Health Promotion International, 31*, 635–643. https://doi.org/10.1093/heapro/dav052

Wanzer, M. B., Sparks, L., & Frymier, A. B. (2009). Humorous communication within the lives of older adults: the relationships among humor, coping efficacy, age, and life satisfaction. *Health Communication, 24*, 128–136. https://doi.org/10.1080/10410230802676482

Weingardt, M. (2014). Wer aufhört Fehler zu machen, lernt nicht mehr dazu. *Lernen und Lernstörungen, 3*, 23–38. https://doi.org/10.1024/2235-0977/a000056

Wellenzohn, S., Proyer, R. T., & Ruch, W. (2016). Humor-based online positive psychology interventions: A randomized placebo-controlled long-term trial. *The Journal of Positive Psychology, 11*, 584–594. https://doi.org/10.1080/17439760.2015.1137624

Wellenzohn, S., Proyer, R. T., & Ruch, W. (2018). Who Benefits From Humor-Based Positive Psychology Interventions? The Moderating Effects of Personality Traits and Sense of Humor. *Frontiers in Psychology, 9*, 821. https://doi.org/10.3389/fpsyg.2018.00821

White, M. A. (2016). Why won't it Stick? Positive Psychology and Positive Education. *Psychology of Well-being, 6*, 2. https://doi.org/10.1186/s13612-016-0039-1

WHO. (2018). Mental disorders. World Health Organization. Retrieved 10 September 2019, from https://www.who.int/news-room/fact-sheets/detail/mental-disorders.

Wuttke, E., & Seifried, J. (Eds.). (2012). *Learning from errors at school and at work.* Opladen, Berlin, Farmington Hills, MI: Verlag Barbara Budrich.

Yue, X., Jiang, F., Lu, S., & Hiranandani, N. (2016). To Be or Not To Be Humorous? Cross Cultural Perspectives on Humor. *Frontiers in Psychology, 7*, 1495. https://doi.org/10.3389/fpsyg.2016.01495

Zotzmann, Y., van der Linden, D., & Wyrwa, K. (2019). The relation between country differences, cultural values, personality dimensions, and error orientation: An approach across three continents – Asia, Europe, and North America. *Safety Science, 120*, 185–193. :https://doi.org/10.1016/j.ssci.2019.06.013

Florian Fischer is a PostDoc researcher at Bielefeld University with expertise in issues related to public health. His research focusses, among others, on the quantification of disease burden by using methods of evidence-based public health and epidemiology. Research topics cover a broad area: humour and health, health communication, environmental health hazards and digitalization and health.

Franziska Carow is studying health communication and is employed as a student assistant at the Department of Population Medicine and Health Services Research at Bielefeld University, School of Public Health. Her main research interests are related to humour and health and global health.

Hannah Eger obtained a bachelor's degree in health communication at Bielefeld University, School of Public Health. She is interested in topics related to global health as well as migration and health.

Part VIII
Mistakes, Errors and Failure in Traffic and Aviation

Chapter 30
Mistakes, Errors and Failures: Their Hidden Potential in Cultural Contexts – The Power of a Professional Culture

Jaco van der Westhuizen, Matita Tshabalala, and Karel Stanz

Abstract Improvement of aviation safety systems by learning from errors depends heavily on whether, how well and how frequently adverse events are reported. Most such events emanate from multiple systemic failures, the final failure of which often comes back to human operators. This chapter focusses on the perceptions of air traffic controllers in a local Air Navigation Service Provider in South Africa as an example of such human operators.

Human failure, also called human error, may even be criminalized after an aircraft accident, or perceptions of failure may be skewed through inappropriate measures of a safety system's performance. However, capturing human errors by means of an effective reporting system can reveal the vulnerabilities of the system and help managers/staff to prepare better for the next adverse event through training, learning and/or system improvements. The International Civil Aviation Organization recognizes this potential benefit and has published a recommended practice, a "Just Culture", to promote error reporting.

This chapter reports that in a local Air Navigation Service Provider in South Africa's multi-cultural arena, the professional culture of air traffic controllers trumped regional, local ethnic and organizational cultures when it came to error reporting for the sake of safety. The authors applied a culture lens to existing data from a qualitative study on error reporting as a social construct and found that learning does not occur in isolation or purely because an error is reported. Error reporting depends largely on how an industry publicly reacts to human error and how well organizations frame error as learning opportunities. We also show that a safety management system (SMS) needs to develop its knowledge management capability to transform error reports into learning opportunities and material at an individual, team and organizational (system) level.

J. van der Westhuizen (✉) · K. Stanz
Department of Human Resource Management, University of Pretoria, Pretoria, South Africa
e-mail: Karel.Stanz@up.ac.za

M. Tshabalala
Department of Industrial Psychology, University of South Africa, Pretoria, South Africa

E. Vanderheiden, C.-H. Mayer (eds.), *Mistakes, Errors and Failures across Cultures*, https://doi.org/10.1007/978-3-030-35574-6_30

Keywords Mistakes · Errors · Failure · Human error · Error reporting · Air traffic control · Professional culture · Safety culture

30.1 Introduction

In the aviation industry, the safety system has to rely heavily on the reporting of adverse events in order to counter system failure and learn from adverse events. Frequently such events emanate from multiple systemic failures, the final one of which is often an error by frontline operators (Fairbanks et al. 2014), for example, air traffic controllers, who were studied in the research reported in this chapter.

Internationally, the aviation industry, and notably the International Civil Aviation Organization (ICAO), has invested years of remarkable work in unifying and guiding the aviation industry across the globe towards establishing international standards and recommended practices to achieve better management of aviation safety. This concerted effort has led ICAO to realize that in most cultures, error is not accepted. Many societies turn to litigation when there is human error that has escalated into an accident, attempting to prove negligence by a single individual, instead of recognizing the fallibility of human stakeholders in the system (Solomon and Relles 2011). In other words, when there is an error, the public response is to litigate, and there is a widespread expectation that errors can and should be punished. The punishment usually takes the form of a monetary penalty or even a jail sentence (Dekker 2009).

In safety-critical industries (e.g. aviation, medicine or nuclear energy generation), adherence to rules and procedures is vital. There is a place for rules and regulations, but the complexity of the system at large in such industries is too great to allow strict adherence to the kind of rules that were prevalent in the early industrial era to ensure a required level of consistency in production. According to Hollnagel (2009), if a system is underspecified, situations will arise for which it is impossible to provide a detailed description of tasks and activities. In such situations, adjustments or compromises must be made; in other words, performance must be variable.

Definitions of what constitutes an "error" continue to be based on the premise that rules or regulations are incorrectly applied or executed, especially in an industry that is considered highly regulated. Errors are thus defined as deviations that are competence based and occur as a result of a lack of knowledge (Nassaji 2018). Mistakes, by contrast, are performance related and may occur even though a learner has the knowledge (Nassaji 2018). From a system safety perspective, it is important to report and learn from both errors and mistakes.

It is therefore a matter for concern that general intolerance of error discourages responsible error reporting (the reporting of adverse critical events). To address this disincentive to reporting, ICAO requires states and organizations to establish a "Just Culture" where operators are protected from disciplinary action and, in rare cases, even litigation, when they voluntarily report an incident – usually caused by their own mistake or error (ICAO 2016). The aviation industry, through the International Civil Aviation Organization (ICAO), has prescribed the notion of a "Just Culture" where managers and staff can report human mistakes, human and system errors and system failures into a safety management system with the promise of amnesty, provided that gross negligence or sabotage is not present (ICAO 2016). Reason (1997) defines a "Just Culture" as an atmosphere of trust in which people are encouraged for providing essential safety-related information but in which they are also clear about where the line must be drawn between acceptable and unacceptable behaviour. When adverse events are reported in such a "Just Culture" safety management system, it allows for a window onto the vulnerabilities of the system (Staender 2011) that enables managers and staff to prepare better for future adverse events through training, learning and/or system improvements.

The qualitative study discussed in this chapter examined the error reporting behaviour of frontline operators (air traffic controllers) and managerial staff across organizational levels dedicated to dealing with such reports in an Air Navigation Service Provider (ANSP) in the multi-cultural arena of South Africa with its 11 official languages and diverse cultures. This ANSP had a Just Culture defined in its SMS, although the definition was not actively promoted and implemented at the time of the study. The study found that the professional culture of air traffic controllers was stronger than national, regional and ethnic cultures when it came to self-reporting for the sake of safety. We discovered that local subcultures of a specific airport were stronger than the corporate culture. These subcultures differed from airport to airport and were considered effective by the local frontline operators in most cases, although the question whether locally based subcultures should be embraced for their uniqueness or rather opposed to fit into a corporate culture mould is posed. According to complexity theory of Cilliers (1998), these sub-cultures should be embraced instead of opposed. We found that the criteria set for assessing the performance of the system can have unintended effects on how operational staff define, report and investigate their errors. Lastly, the hidden potential of learning in a cultural context was embedded in the local learning rituals, where groups of professionals created their own practices of meaning creation through group engagement.

In this chapter, the Oxford Dictionary's definition of a subculture is applied as it refers to a cultural group within a larger culture, often having beliefs or interests at variance with those of the larger culture. Defining a professional culture, or what Schein (2004) refers to as an occupational culture, seems more allusive. Therefore, a working definition was crafted from observations offered by Schein (2004). A professional culture in this chapter is thus a culture that has strong assumptions about quality of work that is based on an experience base of what is safe and what is not. In addition, a professional culture has strong norms and values about guarding the profession that, in turn, often overrides new requirements imposed by an organization or industry.

30.2 Identifying a Local Professional Culture

In a prior study, as reported by van der Westhuizen and Stanz (2017), in 2015 to 2016, van der Westhuizen conducted purposive sampled interviews and random sampled focus groups with air traffic controllers, line managers, middle-level managers and executive managers at 7 of the 20 airports served by a South African Air Navigation Service Provider (ANSP) in order to explore the social construction of reporting across organizational levels. The aim of this prior study was to gain a better understanding of behaviour associated with the underreporting of safety-related errors and incidents. Data were initially coded and then analysed by means of thematic analysis, using Atlas.ti to identify themes within each data group, namely, operational staff, operational staff exposed to investigations of their errors, line managers as recipients of these reports and senior-level managers as strategic managers of safety.

For the purposes of this chapter, the authors of this chapter have re-examined the data from these interviews and focus group sessions by delving into the transcript text and recoding the data of the prior study with a culture lens by means of inter-researcher consensus. We combed the data for differences and similarities that may be informed by any cultural phenomenon or local custom of refraining from speaking up about safety matters or respecting elders or seniors when observing safety risks. This included an active reconsideration of the demographics of the focus groups and interviews as depicted in Table 30.1. We found a prominent theme that suggested that the professional culture of safety in this particular aviation domain was stronger than the national, regional and local ethnic cultures. In fact, the local safety culture – a culture of safety (see Sect. 3) – was found to have a stronger influence over reporting behaviour than the expected corporate culture. Local subcultures and the professional culture incessantly dictated responses from Xhosa-, Zulu-, Ndebele-, Sotho-, Afrikaans- and English-speaking respondents in the following ways:

> I don't know about in the whole of [the ANSP] but certainly here, it's pretty good, I mean people are supportive of each other and there's no finger pointing or …the culture's pretty good that we're all supportive and understanding to each other.
>
> …it's the, let's call it the voluntary ones [error reports], the ones that the Policies and Procedures don't specifically say I have to report, those ones will now depend on our culture here rather than the policies and procedures on whether they will report on them
>
> …next time around I will not file what has happened, because of the reaction or the results I'm getting back after filing the incident.

These responses may be considered remarkable, given that South Africa is noted for its multiple cultures, languages and history of racial and cultural difference. This finding offers hope for enhanced safety outcomes, provided that, as complexity theory teaches (see Cilliers 1998), the ANSP embraces local subcultures instead of enforcing a corporate mould onto a complex system.

At a local subculture level, represented by each of the seven specific airports' air traffic control staff, it emerged from the air traffic controllers' and line managers'

Table 30.1 Demographic representation of respondents

	Race and gender[a]								
	Black		White		Indian		Coloured		
Respondent type	Female	Male	Female	Male	Female	Male	Female	Male	Total
Senior management	–	1 (25%)	–	3 (75%)	–	–	–	–	4
Line management	–	1 (14.29%)	2 (28.57%)	4 (57.14%)	–	–	–	–	7
Focus groups	5 (17.24%)	7 (24.14%)	4 (13.79%)	8 (27.59%)	2 (6.89%)	1 (3.45%)	1 (3.45%)	1 (3.45%)	29
Investigated reporters	1 (14.29%)	2 (28.55%)	1 (14.29%)	1 (14.29%)	–	1 (14.29%)	–	1 (14.29%)	7

[a]The percentage in brackets below each race and gender number is expressed as a percentage of the total amount of respondents that participated in each data set.

responses that the reporting of error appeared very different from the way it was portrayed at a corporate level by senior managers. Local cultures varied. In some instances, dominant senior peers dictated group decisions regarding the reporting of human error, whether these were their own errors or those of junior controllers. The corporate culture of the organization held a fallibility view that allowed local cohesiveness. At one airport, operators felt that they could discuss the extent of an incident and the necessity to report such an error or what impact this incident will have on the individual/team. In other words, the team would caucus and decide whether an error/incident is reportable. Thereafter, the safety implications of such an incident were discussed in the context of personal errors committed in an air traffic control environment. However, at a different airport, the air traffic control staff were observed to be cynical, and individuals would merely keep to themselves, unwilling to share their experiences of an error because they feared being judged by their peers.

Our findings resonated with research in other safety-critical industries, such as the medical and maritime spheres, where error reporting is also deemed to be of great importance. We draw on research in these domains to enrich our conclusions. In the medical domain, Anderson et al. (2002) and Williams et al. (2015) found that underreporting was fuelled by a fear that the media might hear of the incident and publish the error, the absence in the local workplace of a tradition of raising and discussing incidents, not wishing to appear to be an incompetent professional, a fear of being reprimanded and the potential negative consequences for future employment or career progression. In the shipping industry, social and economic factors affect frontline operators' decision not to report personal errors. For example, although error reporting is critical to the system to enable safety improvement, social and economic reasons outside of the safety domain, such as job insecurity or being the only breadwinner for a family, inhibit Chinese mariners from reporting errors (Xue et al. 2019). Xue et al. (2019) argue that the system attracts such behaviour when error reporting managed at a systems level morphs into the management of error numbers instead of the management of safety.

In the aviation industry, error reporting is mostly managed through regulations that make error reports mandatory, although such regulation does not necessarily curb underreporting. It may be argued that in complex systems, many error-related incidents are still open to interpretation and context (Van der Westhuizen and Stanz 2014). Or perhaps error reporting is inhibited by the complexity of the operation, as Shi et al. (2017) found to be the case for aviation, where errors are created in the complex interactions of human operators, aircraft systems, airports, weather and a multitude of other interdependent factors. This is an undesirable state, where frontline operators of any safety-critical industry may become more fearful of committing errors, to the point where their fear leads to even more errors. Alternatively, such a fear may cause frontline operators to stop reporting errors altogether and hide critical information that may prevent accidents.

30.3 A Culture of Safety

There has been a long-standing debate in academia regarding the definition of culture. The same applies to a safety culture. For the purposes of this chapter, we accept the definition of Farsaraei et al. (2017, 290), who describe a safety culture as "the set of attitudes, beliefs and values of employees determining the necessity of the safety management practices of the organization".

Perhaps safety-critical industries are inaccurate when they incorrectly refer to a safety culture, because a safety culture cannot exist separately from an organizational culture. Therefore, we prefer to speak of a culture of safety in an organization, so that the term is not limited only to those who operate at the coalface of a safe operation. We see a culture of safety as a specific kind of organizational culture, usually within an industry where the safety of an operation is paramount to the survival of the organization. Where that situation pertains, the organization must ensure that its organizational culture embraces the delivery and support of safety practices. The organization should inculcate that culture into the very fibre of the organization, regardless of the function of a particular department. Moreover, such an organizational culture actively embraces error and incident reporting as a safety-critical ability to maintain a window into the system's safety vulnerabilities.

30.4 Can an Organization Inculcate the Wrong Safety Culture?

Regulation obviously has implications for organizational culture and, in turn, for a culture of safety within an organization or, indeed, in an industry. When an organization focusses on error-counting, in the form of adverse critical incidents (errors), regarding the number of incidents as reflecting the safety of the system, this approach becomes part of the fibre of the organization (Billings 1998; Van der Westhuizen 2018). Then the prevailing culture may (unintentionally) construe an error as unacceptable from a human being, creating the perception that it is not human to err and that humans have control over all errors. The greatest impact this had on the ANSP from which the secondary data was obtained was that respondents experienced associated corporate communication as an exaggerated focus on frontline operator error. The measure of error also led to an attempt management to reduce human error by constraining human/operator resilience (Van der Westhuizen 2018). This breeds a culture of perfection that is unachievable and creates localized cultures where frontline operators learn to hide safety information (Anderson et al. 2002; Wagner et al. 2012; Van der Westhuizen 2018). Hence, organizational leaders have to be attentive to their actions, decisions and communication as these shape and influence the organizational view of error and subsequently the organizational culture that should depict a culture of safety.

30.5 Applying the "Just Culture" Construct to Encourage Error Reporting

The notion of a "Just Culture" (ICAO 2016; Reason 1997) as a component of a culture of safety in an ANSP, for example, has been applied mainly by organizations in the aviation industry. ICAO's intention in requiring states and therefore companies and institutions to foster a "Just Culture" is to promote reporting and especially error reporting. However, it is up to each industry and organization to delineate the range and depth of its "Just Culture". According to EUROCONTROL (2017), a "Just Culture" is a culture in which frontline operators and others are not punished for their actions, omissions or decisions taken which are commensurate with their experience and training but where gross negligence, wilful violations and destructive acts are not tolerated. Nor does the construct apply to adverse events that have reached a litigation stage (Solomon and Relles 2011).

Determining and defining malicious or deliberate intent when it comes to safety is a complicated topic that usually favours the person charged with the responsibility to evaluate the behaviour of another – however, where a fatal accident has occurred, the primary drivers are media sensation and societal calls for justice and litigation benefits (Isaac and Ruitenberg 1999). The topic has been dealt with in detail in the work of Sidney Dekker (Dekker 2007, 2016).

Woods et al. (2010) pose important questions around human error. For example, they explore when precisely an act or omission constitutes an error. They ask how labelling some acts as human error advances our understanding of why and how complex systems fail, as well as how to respond to incidents and errors to improve the performance of complex systems. According to Woods et al. (2010), it is not an academic or a theoretical question regarding the human nor the system, because the issue at stake is intersecting bureaucratic, professional and legal conflict. Such conflict emanates from safety expressed as a single number that everyone pursues but that holds no value for learning and safety improvement.

At a pragmatic level, even if corporate policy stipulates the presence or perhaps desire for a "Just Culture", the actual application of organizational justice is fluid and changes shape every time that a manager or investigator changes in a particular organization. For overall safety to be enhanced and to counter such shifts, active calibration of a moral attentiveness is required to set the parameters for ethical judgment (Mihelic and Culiberg 2014).

In this context, it was noticeable from our review of the codes and themes produced from the previously mentioned study of reporting behaviour how local subcultures at each airport constructed its own definition of a "Just Culture". These variances led to organizational disparities; the display of a "Just Culture" by various managers across organizational levels caused prominent differences in operators' experiences of a "Just Culture". A shared understanding of a "Just Culture" and therefore how error is treated according to a corporate philosophy is critical for effective reporting and for a learning platform, as it pertains to human error.

30.6 Complexity of the System as a Factor in Making and Learning from Errors

Based on their experience of many years in the human factors domain, we, as the authors of this chapter, have come to realize that a "root cause" approach to incidents is far removed from the reality of complex sociotechnical systems. As Card (2017) has argued, in a complex system, focusing on one or on only a few indiscriminately determined "root causes" is not a reliable method to improve the performance of the system. This approach also distracts from the usefulness of a reported error and the subsequent learning that can occur. In other words, although the human factor may be the final safety filter in a safety management system that fails occasionally, in the majority of cases, a whole range of contributory factors also play a role in some way or another in creating the conditions in which an incident occurs or an operator makes a mistake (Dekker 2014).

Given the complexity of the system, it is important that organizations such as ANSPs and airlines recognize that humans are fallible. This reality does not seem to apply in safety-critical industries such as aviation, medicine and nuclear plants, perhaps because the stakes are seen to be too high to accept human error. Conversely, in these complex domains, there is seldom any acknowledgement of how many times the people at the frontline of safety actually save the day due to the flexibility and adaptability of a frontline operator and his/her line manager, allowing for a deviation from policy and procedure to achieve a safe outcome in a complex system that cannot be managed by merely following procedures and regulations.

As already indicated in the introduction, in a safety-critical industry such as aviation, rules and regulations are essential, but the system is too complex to function effectively without occasionally making adjustments or compromises, allowing for variability in performance. This is especially true, as Hollnagel (2009) points out, if a system is underspecified and situations occur where a detailed description of tasks and activities cannot be provided. From a system safety perspective, operators need to report and learn from both errors (incorrect applications of rules and regulations because of a lack of competence or knowledge) and mistakes (which may occur even though the operator has the knowledge) (Nassaji 2018).

In our study, in analysing various incident reports as secondary data to the social construction of error reporting, we found that the complexity of a sociotechnical system is fluid. In many instances, the operator (in our case, the air traffic controller) has to deal with unusual and unpredictable scenarios. These scenarios are affected by multiple contextual conditions that range from the weather to unexpected traffic demand or emergencies, apart from phenomena that have an impact on the behaviour and decision-making of multiple stakeholders in the broader industry (pilots, adjacent airspace sectors, airlines, general aviation).

It has to be acknowledged that things do go wrong from time to time, and as a result, mistakes and errors will be made. In a complex system such as the aviation industry, the system has to rely on incident reports to uncover performance concerns. These reports can stem from either errors or mistakes, as both relate to a learning opportunity to improve the system. In the context of this chapter, an error, mistake or failure in the bigger system can lead to a critical incident.

30.7 Incident Reports

Staender (2011, 209) describes a critical incident as follows:

> …every non-routine situation can have its origin in the processes, the technique, the environment and the human/team or in any combination of all these factors. An incident can either return to normal operations (if primary defences, such as Standard Operating Procedures, are in place and function sufficiently) or develop into a critical one when these defences fail. If there are no recoveries available or it is not working for a specific critical incident, an accident can occur. Should a recovery be functioning, the situation will end in a near-miss [incident].

This definition describes a critical incident in the medical domain, but the definition applies equally well to the aviation domain.

Two crucial points need to be noted in this definition when it comes to error reporting in complex systems. Firstly, the complex systems within which a medical or aviation service (and most other safety-critical industries) operate are required to make provision for offering a safe service, depending on the contextual factors or the environment within which the service is provided, because there are elements that can contribute to an error (Dekker 2011). Secondly, human error can be reported and recorded before the safety parameters are exceeded, while lessons can still be derived even though no incident occurred.

In the aviation industry, or at least in the ANSP that participated in the study, an error report is not required if a human error does not exceed the safety parameters. However, this does not mean that an error did not occur or that nothing can be learned from the scenario. Therefore, defining safety as well as errors is of paramount importance for each institution that seeks to invite reports on human error and wants to learn from errors to become better at what it does. In other words, the manner in which the parameters are set and defined, for safety, for example, may well skew how error is observed, reported and learned from. For example, in air traffic control, management may only be interested in incidents where an air traffic controller made a mistake to the point that the separation standard was infringed, although no risk of collision may have existed. The opposite is also relevant, where no infringement of the separation standard occurred but two aircraft missed each other without any control exercised by pilots or controllers to actively separate the two aircraft. In the latter case, no inaction or error of omission is reported because by corporate definition no incident occurred although a safe control was not achieved and no lesson is captured.

The problem can be demonstrated in the medical domain, as another safety-critical industry. Rochlin (1999) and Jafree et al. (2016) found that medical practitioners had a distorted view of their own proneness to error; hence, reporting of personal error was limited, or rather inhibited, by societal expectation. The other side of the coin is shown by Gawande (1999) and Chiang et al. (2019), who point out that the public and even peers hold a perception that medical error is only committed by "bad" physicians, who are referred to as "incompetent" and "negligent", and believe that those who make errors should be punished accordingly. These findings show that skewed perceptions of human error do no favours to a professional or societal culture that wishes professionals to become better at what they do. The outcome is a professional that merely become better at hiding errors to protect themselves and those closest to them – including the image of their profession (Salviz et al. 2016).

In our study, revisiting the codes in the original data from the study reported by van der Westhuizen and Stanz (2017) with a cultural lens found that frontline operators were willing to report their own errors where these contributed to critical incidents because of their safety mindedness. We discovered that incident reporting is socially constructed and is sensitive to the nuances of the environment in which these errors and subsequent incidents occurred. The participants focussed on error reporting by definition, in other words, on events where the human operator failed to recover the service/system in time. In some instances, the outcome dictated whether an error or mistake (as an incident) was deemed reportable or not, confirming Dekker's (2007) argument, and not the fact that there might be something to be learned from the incident ("let everybody know about this so they don't make the same mistake that I did"). This finding took us back to setting criteria – what constitutes an error, mistake or failure? The answer to this question is that criteria are usually based on objectives that will make the "boss look good" because the system is performing well – because no errors appear to be committed. This finding is in line with that of Williams et al.'s (2015) study of 596 pharmacists in the north-west of England, which reported that the outcomes, in the form of the factual history of patients' not coming to harm, informed the underreporting of errors in their study.

We found that in the ANSP in our study, a critical incident triggered the submission of a report of an error that would otherwise have been ignored. We found that in certain situations, there may be a useful lesson to be learned that can benefit the system, but the parameters set for an incident was seen as the only trigger for reporting. In most instances, the human may make a mistake, or the system may create an undesirable state that is recovered by the frontline operator, and then nothing is reported because the boundaries set by the parameters of what constitutes an incident dictate what is reportable or not.

Reporting behaviour about errors is influenced in subtle ways by corporate phenomena that can reside within or outside of the safety management domain. Our study found that every day various practices and corporate changes (even within reason) can have unintended consequences for safety reporting behaviour. One of the most prominent of these practices is corporate communication about safety performance statistics. In the case of this study, the ANSP's communication usually centred on a single indicator used to express the safety of the system, namely, the safety ratio or number of incidents per 100,000 aircraft movements. Although this is a useful yardstick that allows for comparison of safety data across a multitude of other ANSPs, its use skews the corporate focus, which becomes the imperative to drive down this safety ratio, instead of learning from these incidents.

Johnson (2003) rightly argues that it is important to move away from repeated reminders to be "careful" if one wants to preserve the confidence of those who contribute to such a system. Constant reminders can only appeal to the conscious mind, but neuroscientists estimate that about 95 per cent of what humans do is actually subconscious (Sylvestre 2017). In essence, people are conscious of what they are doing, but they do not necessarily make active, conscious decisions about each step. Reminding people of what they have already been trained to do cannot be used as the sole intervention to improve system performance.

30.8 Counting Errors Is Not Enough

Counting errors is a dangerous way of expressing business or system safety, because humans are error-prone. Such numbers skew the corporate view of what is really important in safety management: understanding what happened so that operators can counter such incidents or improve for the next time one occurs. Corporate or senior management communication can easily adopt an attitude of "driving down the numbers", and the actual safety intent of such reporting of errors and failures then falls by the wayside. Although this is not the intention of safety ratios, the number of errors becomes the focus, rather than learning/improvement. Safety then becomes a numbers game in the organization.

This kind of error focus may result in a corporate focus that does not show an active interest in systemic failures and learning from mistakes but rather privileges eliminating human error – conveniently forgetting that the human is the single solution within the complex system that can deal with the variability of unusual high-risk situations. The prominence afforded to the safety ratio echoes the message that human error and reporting of such error are undesirable. This side effect is promoted by the text that usually accompanies the regular release of the safety ratios, usually by senior management in the organization, stating that everyone's effort to keep the ratio down is appreciated or that recent incidents have been responsible for a rise in the ratio and efforts should be directed at reducing the ratio again.

The unintended result of this approach is underreporting, because the safety ratio is constructed purely from the number of incidents reported showing the number of errors that frontline operators made to a point where the minimum separation standard was infringed (even between aircraft that did not risk colliding). In other words, the way in which criteria to measure errors or incidents are set should be carefully considered and tested for unintended consequences before they are merely applied as a blanket approach, because of the impact the criteria themselves may have on error reporting.

One way in which organizations and industries try to counter this unintended effect of using a safety ratio is by promulgating regulations that make incident reporting mandatory. When mandatory reporting is coupled with disciplinary actions for failure to report, the essence of safety and learning from errors is diluted. What stood out clearly in our data was that most safety professionals would prefer to report for the sake of improving safety but will only do so freely if the reporting system accommodates personal errors, as well as systemic failures, beyond simple incident-like definitions.

30.9 Self-Preservation May Deter Error Reporting

When professionals hide information or do not self-report on errors/incidents, their decisions may stem from a deep-seated need for self-preservation that may be as human as committing errors (Van der Westhuizen and Stanz 2014). As long as mistakes are penalized by an industry or an organization, usually tied to how the entity has set up its primary performance criteria, a fair number of frontline operators will apply their local dominance in deciding whether an error is reportable or not. In any safety environment, there are obvious errors that can be directly linked to an incident and that are therefore clearly reportable, depending on how the criteria or parameters have been designed. In a complex work environment, there are also errors that do not lead to critical incidents (where an accident is averted), as well as errors that are considered borderline cases and that may not be reported, especially if a frontline operator deems it necessary to protect himself/herself against potential queries or investigations. Safety is unlikely to be enhanced, as nobody learns from such underreporting.

Our review of our data from the interviews and focus groups highlighted how prevalent self-preservation was across organizational levels. Even a manager who receives a report first-hand might attempt to downplay an incident if a safety ratio or similar statistic is attached to his/her own performance contract. At the higher levels in the organization, we found that even senior-level managers' behaviour is dictated by the consequences of incidents at the operational level. In other words, the responses and decisions of senior management regarding errors and incidents and their reporting are dictated by how these senior managers think they will be judged, for either responding or not responding in a positive or negative manner, for example, instituting a disciplinary hearing for an error for the sake of being able to report upwards that the matter has been dealt with.

At an organizational level, disciplinary action seems to be the ultimate sanction, and it inhibits error reporting. Dekker (2007, see also Dekker and Breakey 2016) has written extensively about this reality. He raises the question of who gets to draw the line between a violation (which is penalized) and an error (which should be addressed and learned from but is not punished). This is especially relevant in complex sociotechnical systems, where rules and regulations cannot prescribe for every scenario. Hence, an error can easily be misconstrued as a violation. This is not to say that violations do not occur or that all errors should be condoned; it is important for the aviation industry to align itself with what ICAO recommends. ICAO's guidelines are intended to eradicate gross negligence, recklessness and sabotage, but errors and deviations from the norm due to contextual factors are understood and acted upon in order to prevent future occurrences and improve the safety performance of the system.

Nevertheless, even if the focus is safety, underreporting may still be prevalent due to people's desire for self-preservation (Top and Tekingündüz 2015). According to van der Westhuizen and Stanz (2017), when participants indicated that they refrain from reporting minor or non-incident-related errors, this mostly goes hand in hand with a desire for self-preservation that originated from the judgemental language that is usually used in investigation reports. Even where the ANSP's intention was to improve safety, we found that frontline operators had internalized their human error at an extreme level as safety professionals. This also created acute sensitivity to the language used in investigation reports, which in turn has a negative impact on error reporting behaviour when investigations focus only on the frontline operator where error occurred and fail to recognize contextual and systemic factors that contribute to the incident.

Self-preservation can be countered by feedback that includes a systemic view of errors, as opposed to an individual view (Benn et al. 2009; Dekker 2007). This in turn can underpin the development of a safety-consciousness and "Just Culture" in an organization that is likely to promote the future reporting of errors and other system failures in safety-critical systems. In a similar vein, Adler-Milstein et al. (2009) also recommend visible management commitment to illustrate the focus on the recognition of risk and subsequent learning value to improve error reporting. In this manner, the focus on the individual is redirected towards the system, and this greatly increases the associated safety and behavioural benefits.

30.10 A Knowledge Management System Enabling Error Learning

Learning is not automatic. Nor does it occur merely because a lesson learned from an error or the investigation report is shared. The sociotechnical system is much more attuned to environmental conduits, bottlenecks and obstacles. Based on the descriptions of safety management from the van der Westhuizen and Stanz (2017) study, it was clear that the means of capturing what is learnt from errors and mistakes is crucial. However, from our experience, it seems that most safety-critical industries miss the important necessity of a knowledge management system that can enable organizational learning. Having a knowledge management system allows for robustness in capturing reports in formal and informal ways and enabling learning in various forms. In other words, there is no single reporting platform or lessons sharing means that is superior. It is clear, however, that a complex system requires multi-faceted capabilities to create optimal learning value.

This implies that it is one thing to have a reporting system that accepts the incident report, but that it is quite another thing to have the capability also to accept human error that did not culminate in an incident. Any error may well result in learning for the specific individual or frontline operator, but the systemic failures that constitute a breeding ground for more errors and that can contribute considerably to organizational learning that can lead to a safer or more efficient environment are often overlooked. Learning is expanded to reach its greatest potential only when the error lesson is adjusted or crafted for each audience in the organization. Our review of the data from the previously mentioned study indicated that the lesson to be learned from an error has a different meaning or lesson embedded in it for the local operational team than for an adjacent air traffic control sector, a safety manager at a mid-level in the organization and a manager of finances or executive manager of human resources.

Furthermore, in recognizing the "socio"-element of the complex sociotechnical systems in these safety-critical domains, we found that it is greatly beneficial to apply complexity system characteristics to the design of a knowledge management system (Van der Westhuizen 2018). Learning is created through patterns and feedback loops, which a knowledge management system should establish and emphasize as error information becomes available. Respondents to our study, especially frontline operators, overwhelmingly indicated the importance of focusing on the contextual conditions of the incidents as these factors also stress the context in which a particular error may occur.

Part of what is important to learning and improving safety at a systems level is to identify the local learning rituals and to harness these to become even more effective locally so that they benefit the corporate safety system (Niemiec 2017).

30.11 So What Are the Benefits of an Error?

A systemic view of errors in complex sociotechnical systems, especially the aviation industry, suggests that human error holds the potential to make a valuable contribution to the system. Unfortunately, if anyone dies because of an accident, most societies tend to want to blame a particular person (Dekker 2007; Hollnagel 2014) and to punish him/her without considering the bigger picture of what contributed to the error. This attitude is a sure way to disable a reporting system, because it discourages the self-reporting of errors. From a legal counsel point of view, underreporting may even be encouraged to limit the potential risk of litigation (Top and Tekingündüz 2015).

Blaming others is an easy way out. Reason (1997) argues that people are often ready to blame because people, especially in Western cultures, attach great value to the belief that they are free agents, the drivers of their own behaviour and fate. In line with this belief, when something goes wrong, they attribute the mishap to the behaviour of an individual. This argument is borne out by the way in which, after rail accidents in South Africa and the recent aviation accident surrounding the Boeing 737 MAX, blame has been apportioned to the frontline operators for making mistakes that culminated in these accidents (Cordle and McGregor 2019). In this context, Dekker (2014) rightly points out the fallacy underlying this attitude when he says that errors are consequences, not causes. Errors have a history, and discovering an error is the beginning of a search for causes, not the end. Only by understanding the circumstances of an error can an organization hope to limit the chances of a recurrence.

Dekker (2014) describes accidents as failures of risk management, which implies that they are neither random nor uncontrollable. It is not about an individual or a group of individuals responsible for an adverse outcome. Nor will understanding and learning from error result in progressive learning and improvements if blame is merely apportioned to a person higher up, or elsewhere in the system, who may have committed an error that contributed to an adverse event. In his description of the Safety II approach, Hollnagel (2014) recommends that to harness errors and error reporting to its full potential, organizations should apply a systems approach and explore multiple narratives/angles to understand the complexity of the system and what went wrong while realizing the difference between work as imagined and work as done. This argument is based on an acknowledgement of the fact that failure and success stem from the same sources and their interpretation lies in people's narratives. In addition, humans should be seen as a useful recourse for system flexibility and resilience that should and can continuously try to anticipate developments and events.

Therefore, learning from errors is paramount for any safety-critical institution or industry. However, there are pertinent aspects that have to be taken cognizance of to unlock the potential benefits that can arise from errors. These are the emotional labour of reporting, the reporting platform, competing demands and incentives. These aspects are discussed below.

30.11.1 Emotional Labour of Error Reporting

Reporting one's own error is no simple matter. Apart from the seriousness involved in a safety matter and the potential safety improvement lessons that can be learned or affected, there is also emotional labour associated with reporting personal error. Our study found that this emotional labour applies to the frontline operator who self-reports an incident, as well as to the manager receiving the report, especially if he/she has to escalate the report to higher authorities. The finding that many participating line managers internalized incident reporting of their staff was interesting. Their response was, however, mostly driven by the participating ANSP's objective setting, which established a safety target (the number of air traffic controller-related incidents/errors per annum) and allocated the target to a specific team to measure their safety performance. This emotional labour causes staff and line managers to avoid the vulnerability that a personal error may introduce into the operational context. Therefore, effective reporting cannot be expected if there is a failure to acknowledge that error reporting is a delicate social activity that demands more than just a well-designed reporting platform.

30.11.2 Reporting Platform

Nicholson and Tait (2002) found that practical inhibitors of reporting could range from the availability of printed report forms and the effort associated with searching for a form to the personal motivation required for completing and submitting a report after a long shift. Their study, in a medical setting, showed that where electronic report forms were branded to such an extent that they would be highly visible in a hospital ward's public area, this would discourage the completion of a report. In addition, these authors found that organizations' punitive response to multiple errors, for example, if incorrect medication was administered on several occasions by the same medical practitioner, also discouraged medical personnel from reporting to avoid any possible stigma.

In other words, the way in which a reporting platform deals with multiple errors reported by the same operator should be carefully crafted and embedded. The reason for this is that the system's response must continue to invite future reporting while also enabling alternative preventative changes for a reporter to improve on the work style that contributed to the incidents (provided the error-based behaviour was similar).

30.11.3 Competing Demands

Another factor that has a negative impact on error reporting is competing demands in the wider system or supersystem. The downside of this reality is that people do not go into the context of the problem, where errors can be prevalent as a result of what is created in the system. In one sense, it is easier to merely end with a "root cause" of human error and leave it at that. In many ways the system creates demands that become irreconcilable within the same time frame by expecting optimal safety and efficiency (see Hollnagel 2009).

The competing demands that a reporter faces, even in a mandatory reporting system, are the predominant contributors to underreporting of human error and associated incidents. They might make a decision because of the dominant narrative around the competing demands they have to face, not just in the act of reporting but also in the broader safety system. Their bounded system consists of everyday service delivery within set rules. However, they face far greater expectations from the system, beyond the written regulations, and in our data, that led to anecdotes that revealed competing demands. As previously reported, the focus groups in the study painted a picture of competing demands that range from the noble intent to report incidents for the benefit of the system to dealing with emotional impact, saving face or managing personal fears (Van der Westhuizen and Stanz 2014).

This says something about the competing demands from the organization, in other words, finding a balance between efficiency and safety. The safety ratio was the principal measure of system safety; the second was air traffic controller-attributed delays. These two measures are incorporated into the corporate as well as the individual performance contracts. The competing demand is therefore "do you want to be safe or be on time?"

When safety and learning from error become the focus, stakeholder conflict would dissipate because there would no longer be competing demands, and demands without a good reason and the need for self-preservation would disappear, because safety would become a common goal. Local, corporate and industry norms for safety would overlap.

30.11.4 Incentives

On the positive side, the focus groups raised comforting themes on the wider reality that operators still see reporting as an inherent part of the job – no incentive required. This may not apply to all safety-critical environments, but in the aviation industry, this phenomenon has been observed on multiple occasions where pilots and ATCs submit reports willingly because of their vested interest in safety (Van der Westhuizen 2018). However, the same did not always apply to personal error as extensively as with general safety risks.

According to our data, only line managers and respondents that had been exposed to an investigation following an error that contributed to a critical incident raised the theme of incentivized reporting. Line managers saw a reporting behaviour benefit in actively and consciously searching for success stories that will promote reporting and act as a driver to a purpose-driven system. Sadly, reporters who had been exposed to investigations displayed cynicism towards a corporate incentive scheme which they experienced as distorted because of its monetary implications linked to safety reporting. The focus groups stated that they perceived reporting as an inherent part of the job, but the themes that emerged from our study rather illustrated that incentivized reporting had unintended and even uncontrollable negative implications for reporting behaviour.

The natural outflow of such incentivized reporting is incentivized underreporting. This outcome appears to be unintentional but can quickly escalate to an organizational problem. This phenomenon was already identified by Reffett et al. (2014) for the financial industry. They note that systematic underreporting in the financial industry sets in where seniors create an expectation that misreporting can cover up mistakes. In cases like these, displacing of responsibility occurs, where a supervisor may induce misreporting of data. This is arguably similar to the underreporting of personal error in the aviation industry. Moreover, Mayhew and Murphy (2014) found that where such an expectation is created by seniors, it also serves as a mitigation for the emotional cost or labour of misreporting. As many as 49% to 72% of their respondents demonstrated a desire for misreporting, claiming that they were merely doing what was expected from seniors. Therefore, senior staff in safety-critical organizations have a paramount role to play in creating an environment that is conducive to healthy error reporting that benefits the system. There is evidence that shows that employee reward schemes based on reductions in safety occurrences are inherently flawed, since many causal factors of safety occurrences are not within the employees' control (Hopkins and Maslen 2015).

We found that for the system to benefit from effective error reporting practices, a potential reporter has at least to be set at ease. An atmosphere of acceptance has to be created in which there is an understanding for the fact that some human error (as opposed to negligence) is accepted as normal. The alternative is an incentivized reporting system where human error is demonized and inhumane expectations of perfection exist, but this has been shown to give rise to underreporting.

The bottom line is that incentivized reporting has a host of socially constructed influences with unintended consequences that affect reporting behaviour at a corporate and local level (Van der Westhuizen and Stanz 2017). Dekker (2014) notes that underreporting resulting from the implementation of safety incentive programmes where employees receive rewards for meeting safety targets (for not making mistakes or rather, in many cases, for not reporting their own mistakes) is counter-productive and is antithetical to mature safety management practices. It is therefore vital that organizations test new reporting practices or incentivized reporting initiatives on a test group rather than implement a fully fledged roll-out at an organizational level without ascertaining and being prepared for how organizational behaviour in the complex system might respond to such changes. Error reporting, and therefore healthy reporting behaviour, is a vital component of a safety management system, which requires dedicated attentiveness.

30.12 Conclusion

The sobering reality is that the aviation industry, as a complex sociotechnical system, like others in safety-critical industries, cannot exist without error reporting. The publication of the "Just Culture" concept by ICAO for the aviation industry offers great potential for reporting errors on a global scale.

The qualitative study discussed in this chapter on reporting behaviour of safety personnel across organizational levels in a local Air Navigation Service Provider (ANSP) in the multi-cultural arena of South Africa found that the professional culture of air traffic controllers was stronger than national, regional and ethnic cultures when it came to self-reporting for the sake of safety. Moreover, we discovered that local subcultures of a specific airport were stronger than the corporate culture. These subcultures differed from airport to airport and should be embraced for their uniqueness, rather than being forced into a corporate culture mould. We found that the criteria set for assessing the performance of the system may have unintended effects on how operational staff define, report and investigate their errors. Lastly, the hidden potential of learning in a cultural context was embedded in the local learning rituals, where groups of professionals created their own practices of meaning creation through group engagement.

Given system complexity, our findings suggest that local professional cultures seem to be best suited to enable learning from errors. However, a corporate culture of safety is necessary to create a platform for learning. Learning from errors is also dependent on how an organization frames error and whether it can avoid turning reporting into a numbers game, instead of establishing a comprehensive knowledge management system. Errors can only be transformed into opportunities for growth and improvement when a corporate knowledge management system acknowledges the emotional labour associated with error reporting, can position error reporting amongst other competing demands and can guard against inappropriate and often unintentional incentivization of safety reports or corporate performance target setting – in short, if it can develop a professional culture of safety that pervades the local organizational culture.

References

Adler-Milstein, J., Singer, S.J., & Toffel, M.W. (2009). Operational failures and problem solving: an empirical study of incident reporting (Working paper 10-017, Harvard Business School, Boston, Massachusetts). Retrieved from https://www.academia.edu/2857230/

Anderson, H.B., Madsen, M.D., Hermann, N., Schioler, T., & Ostergaard, D. (2002). Reporting adverse events in hospitals: a survey of the views of doctors and nurses on reporting practices and models of reporting. In C.W. Johnson (Ed.), Investigation and reporting of accidents (pp. 127–136). Glasgow: Department of Computing Science.

Benn, J., Koutantji, M., Wallace, L., Spurgeon, P., Rejman, M., Healey, A., & Vincent, C. (2009). Feedback from incident reporting: information and action to improve patient safety. Quality & Safety in Health Care, 18, 11–21.

Billings, C.E. (1998). Some hopes and concerns regarding medical event-reporting systems: Lessons from the NASA aviation safety reporting system. Archives of Pathology & Laboratory Medicine, 122(3), 214–215.

Card, A.J. (2017). The problem with '5 whys'. BMJ Quality & Safety, 26, 671–677. https://doi.org/10.1136/bmjqs-2016005849.

Chiang, H., Lee, H., Lin, S., & Ma, S. (2019). Factors contributing to voluntariness of incident reporting among hospital nurses. Journal of Nursing Management, 27(4), 806–814.

Cilliers, P. (1998). Complexity theory and postmodernism. Oxford: Routledge.

Cordle, V., & McGregor, D. (2019). The Boeing 737 MAX 8 crashes: The case for pilot error. Retrieved from https://www.linkedin.com/pulse/boeing-737-max-8-crashes-case-pilot-error-vaughn-cordle-cfa/

Dekker, S. (2007). Just culture: Balancing safety and accountability. Farnham, England: Ashgate Publishing.

Dekker, S.W.A. (2009). Prosecuting professional mistake: secondary victimization and a research agenda for criminology. International Journal of Criminal Justice Sciences, 4(1), 60–78.

Dekker, S. (2011). Drift into failure: from hunting broken components to understanding complex systems. Farnham, England: Ashgate Publishing.

Dekker, S. (2014). The field guide to understanding human error (3rd ed.). Farnham, England: Ashgate Publishing.

Dekker, S. W. A., & Breakey, H. (2016). Just culture: Improving safety by achieving substantive, procedural and restorative justice. Safety Science, 85, 187–193.

Eurocontrol. (2017). Just culture. Retrieved from http://www.eurocontrol.int/articles/just-culture

Fairbanks, R.J., Wears, R.L., Woods, D.D., Hollnagel, E., Plsek, P., & Cook, R.I. (2014). Resilience and resilience engineering in in Health Care. Joint Commission Journal on Quality and Patient Safety, 40(8), 376–383.

Farsaraei, A., Aghazadeh, A.M., Lotfi, M., & Sheikhalipour, Z. (2017). Patient safety culture from the perspective of emergency nurses. World Family Medicine, 15(10), 289–295.

Gawande, A. (1999, February 1). When doctors make mistakes. The New Yorker. Retrieved from https://www.newyorker.com/magazine/

Hollnagel, E. (2009). The ETTO Principle: Efficiency-thoroughness trade-off. Farnham, England: Ashgate Publishing.

Hollnagel, E. (2014). Safety-I and Safety-II: The past and future of safety management. Farnham, England: Ashgate Publishing.

Hopkins, A., & Maslen, S. (2015). Risky rewards: How company bonuses affect safety. Farnham, England: Ashgate Publishing.

ICAO. (2016). *Annex 19 to the Convention on International Civil Aviation: Safety management* (2nd ed).Montreal, Canada: ICAO.

Isaac, A.R., & Ruitenberg, B. (1999). Air traffic control: human performance factors. Farnham, England: Ashgate Publishing.

Jafree, S.R., Zaka, R., Zakar, M.Z., & Fischer, F. (2016). Nurse perceptions of organizational culture and its association with the culture of error reporting: a case of public sector hospitals in Pakistan. BioMed Central Health Services Research, 16(3).

Johnson, C.J. (2003). Failure in safety-critical systems: handbook of incident and accident reporting. Glasgow, Scotland: University Press.

Mayhew, B.W., & Murphy, P.R. (2014). The impact of authority on reporting behavior, rationalization and affect. Contemporary Accounting Research, 31(2), 420–443.

Mihelic, K.K., & Culiberg, B. (2014). Turning a blind eye: a study of peer reporting in a business school. Ethics & Behavior, 24(5), 364–381.

Nassaji, H. (2018). Errors versus Mistakes. Yeditepe University, Istanbul, Turkey. https://doi.org/10.1002/9781118784235.eelt0059

Nicholson, A.N., & Tait, P.C. (2002). Confidential reporting: from aviation to clinical medicine. Clinical Medicine, 2(3), 234–236.

Niemiec, R.M. (2017). Character strengths interventions: A field guide for practitioners. Boston, MA: Hogrefe Publishing.

Reason, J. (1997). Managing the risks of organizational accidents. Farnham, England: Ashgate Publishing.

Reffett, A., Eaton, T.V., & Gannod, G. (2014). An experimental examination of underreporting of time. Journal of Managerial Issues, 26 (2), 112–129.

Rochlin, G.I. (1999). Safe operation as a social construct. Ergonomics, 42(11), 1549–1560.

Salviz, E.A., Edipoglu, S.I., Sungur, M.O., Altun, D., Buget, M.I. & Seyhan, S.Ö. (2016). Critical incident reporting system in teaching hospitals in Turkey: A survey study.

Schein, E. (2004). Organizational culture and leadership (3rd ed). San Francisco, CA: Jossey-Bass.

Shi, D., Guan, J., Zuruda, J., & Manikas, A. (2017). A data-mining approach to identification of risk factors in safety management systems. Journal of Management Information Systems, 34(4), 1054–1081.

Solomon, E.D., & Relles, D.L. (2011). Criminalization of air disasters: What goal, if any, is being achieved. Journal of Air Law and Commerce, 76(3), 407–456.

Staender, S. (2011). Incident reporting in anaesthesiology. Best Practice and Research Clinical Anaesthesiology, 25, 207–214.

Sylvestre, C. (2017). Third generation safety: The missing piece. Parramatta: Habitsafe.

Top, M., & Tekingündüz, S. (2015). Patient safety culture in a Turkish public hospital: A study of nurses' perceptions about patient safety. System Practice and Action Research, 28, 87–110.

Van der Westhuizen, J. & Stanz, K. (2014). Critical incident reporting systems: perceived competing social consequences considered by reporters. Ergonomics SA, 26(1), 19–30.

Van der Westhuizen, J., & Stanz, K. (2017). Critical incident reporting system: A necessary multi-level understanding. Safety Science, 96, 198–208.
Van der Westhuizen, J. (2018). Reporting for safety: towards a complexity framework informing the social construction of reporting by multi-level stakeholder behaviour (Doctoral thesis, University of Pretoria). Retrieved from https://repository.up.ac.za/handle/2263/67930?show=full.
Wagner, L.M., Harkness, K., & Gallagher, T.H. (2012). Nurses' perceptions of error reporting and disclosure in nursing homes. Journal of Nursing Care Quality, 27(1),63–69.
Williams, S.D., Phipps, D.L., & Ashcroft, D. (2015). Examining the attitudes of hospital pharmacists to reporting medication safety incidents using the theory of planned behavior. International Journal for Quality in Health Care, 27(4), 297–304.
Woods, D.D., Dekker, S., Cook, R., Johannesen, L., & Sarter, N. (2010). Behind human error (2nd ed). Farnham, England: Ashgate Publishing.
Xue, C., Tang, L., & Walters, D. (2019). Occupational health and safety indicators and underreporting: Case studies in Chinese shipping. Industrial Relations, 74(1), 141–161.

Jaco van der Westhuizen is an ex-Air Traffic Controller by profession that now works as a Human Factor Specialist. His passion is safety management and his interest is in understanding safety behaviour within complex socio-technical systems and associated pragmatic solutions to complex problems that aims to improve safe operations from a complexity theory perspective. He holds a Master's degree in Business Leadership and a PhD in Organisational Behaviour that focussed on error reporting behaviour in the aviation safety domain.

Matita Tshabalala is an Industrial Psychologist registered with the Health Professions Council of South Africa (HPCSA). His interest is in cognitive psychology, complexity/chaos theory and systems thinking. He is registered with the European Association of Aviation Psychology (EAAP) as an Aviation Psychologist. His focus in human factors amongst other things was to measure and document improvements of system efficiency and safety as well as human productivity, performance and well-being as a result of human factor interventions.

Karel Stanz is a Professor in Industrial Psychology at the University of Pretoria currently managing the Human Resource Department of the University. He is also a registered Master HR Practitioner with the South African Board of People Practices that started his academic qualifications in the Military Sciences. His research interests include organizational behaviour, leadership development and talent learning.

Chapter 31
Leader Inquiry as a Method for Open Error Communication in Aviation and Beyond

Jan U. Hagen

Abstract There have been multiple aircraft accidents in the aviation industry resulting from a lack of error communication. Even though cultural differences have been cited as contributing factors, many accidents have happened due to the hierarchical status of the first and second officers and the reluctance of the latter to speak up during critical situations.

This is why, three decades ago, crew resource management (CRM) was developed in the aviation industry. Its goal was to reduce the hierarchy gradient on the flight deck and achieve open, factual error communication to ensure the safe operation of flights. This meant creating an environment in which lower-ranking crew members would feel comfortable speaking up when observing an error made by their superiors. Today, CRM is a mandatory element of flight crew training in civilian and military flight operations worldwide. Since its introduction, accident rates have declined tremendously.

However, even after three decades, the human factor continues to be the main cause of accidents. When talking to flight crews, we observe that lower-ranking crew members are still hesitant to speak up. We therefore suggest that – on top of training people to speak up more – we should start focusing on the leadership behavior involved. This requires leaders to include subordinates through active inquiry when making decisions in critical situations, thereby creating a flat hierarchy that allows them to speak freely.

Keywords Mistakes · Errors · Failure · Communication · Aviation · Management · Leadership

J. U. Hagen (✉)
ESMT Berlin, Berlin, Germany
e-mail: jan.hagen@esmt.org

E. Vanderheiden, C.-H. Mayer (eds.), *Mistakes, Errors and Failures across Cultures*, https://doi.org/10.1007/978-3-030-35574-6_31

31.1 Introduction

On the evening of February 6, 1996, the Turkish Birgenair Boeing 757–200 prepared for takeoff from Puerto Plata, Dominican Republic, to Berlin, Germany (Flight Safety Foundation 1999; Gröning and Ladkin 1999; Hagen 2013). The pilot in command and flying the aircraft was Captain Ahmet Erdem (62), who had built up almost 25,000 flying hours in the course of his career. He had been flying the Boeing 757 for 4 years. His copilot was 34-year-old Aykut Gergin. With 3500 flying hours, he also had a fair amount of experience under his belt. However, he had only just completed his training for the Boeing 757 and had flown a mere 75 hours in this particular model. Because of the length of the flight, there was also a third pilot in the cockpit, Muhlis Evrenesoglu (51). Like the copilot, he had only recently completed his training for the Boeing 757 and had accrued just 121 flying hours. Nonetheless, with 15,000 flying hours overall, he was also experienced.

The first indication that something was not normal appeared during takeoff: When the aircraft had reached a speed of 80 knots, Gergin called out "80." Erdem confirmed this information with "checked," which is a normal procedure. That should have meant that his display was also showing a speed of 80 knots.[1] Yet, 2 seconds later, he said to Gergin, "My airspeed indicator is not working. You tell me [the speeds]."[2] They continued the takeoff and the plane left the ground.

Shortly after takeoff, Gergin noticed that the captain's airspeed indicator now matched his own and commented, "It began to operate."[3] Everything seemed to be going smoothly.

Apart from the brief failure of the captain's airspeed indicator, the flight seemed to be routine. The crew made no further mention of the earlier problem. However, unnoticed by the crew, the captain's and copilot's airspeed indicators began to show different values as the plane gained altitude, while the third indicator – a small backup indicator in the center console – matched the copilot's. Whereas Erdem's airspeed indicator showed the rate of climb specified by the flight management computer,[4] those of Gergin and the backup instrument indicated the plane's speed was decreasing.

At 11:44 p.m., 3 min after takeoff, the upper screen on the center console flashed the Engine Indication Crew Alerting System warnings "rudder ratio" and "mach speed trim."[5] Upon spotting these, Erdem read the alerts out loud and said, "There

[1] Among other things, this check is supposed to ensure that the airspeed indicator is working properly for both pilots.

[2] According to regulations, there must be three working airspeed indicators on each flight. Erdem should have aborted takeoff immediately (Flight Safety Foundation 1999).

[3] In fact, the airspeed indicator was simply reacting to the pressure change in the pitot tube caused by the climb (Gröning and Ladkin 1999). Consequently, the airspeed indicator only displayed the correct speed for a brief moment. As the plane climbed higher, the speed shown was increasingly higher than the actual speed.

[4] Due to the blockage in the pitot tube, the airspeed indicator exaggerated the actual speed as the plane gained altitude.

[5] This warning – which the pilots would not have been expecting at this point – refers to the posi-

is something wrong. There are some problems." Gergin, however, was busy. He was still in radio contact with the departure controllers in Santo Domingo. Again, Erdem remarked, "Okay, there is something crazy, do you see it?" At this point, the plane was supposedly climbing at a pitch angle of 15° at a speed of 327 knots. These were contradictory values. At that pitch angle and with the engine thrust set to climb mode, the speed shown should have been far lower.

Just after this, Gergin also noticed that the values displayed did not tally and commented, "There is something crazy there at this moment. Two hundred [knots], only, is mine and decreasing, Efendim." Captain Erdem replied, "Both of them are wrong. What can we do? Let's check their circuit breakers."

In such situations, the normal procedure is to resolve the issue using the quick reference handbook of the aircraft. This handbook contains emergency procedures, checklists, and instructions for all imaginable faults and alerts. It is designed to ensure the flight can continue safely despite the problem. It is the job of the pilot not currently flying the plane to read out the information from the quick reference handbook. In this particular case, one of the first things the crew should have done was compare all three indicators. This would have revealed that one of the indicators was showing a different value – and was therefore supposed to be the defective one. Even if all three airspeed indicators were to have failed completely, there is a specific emergency procedure that would have enabled the crew to continue flying the plane based on precisely defined settings for engine power and pitch angle.

Crucially, the Birgenair crew failed to check the quick reference handbook. Instead, Erdem made the completely arbitrary decision that Gergin's airspeed indicator as well as the backup instrument was incorrect and decreed, "Both are wrong." Gergin did not intervene; he just followed the captain's decision. He then switched his airspeed indicator to "alternate" to ensure he would continue to see the values from the backup instrument. What Gergin obviously did not know was that, in this type of plane, switching to "alternate" meant he would see the (incorrect) values from the captain's airspeed indicator. The backup airspeed indicator, in contrast, continued to show the decreasing (correct) speed. Meanwhile, the autopilot was trying to compensate for Erdem's values by increasing the climb angle. The excessive pitch angle was now clearly visible on the attitude director indicator (ADI). By this time, alarm bells should have started ringing for Erdem, if not the others.[6] Yet, all he did was simply state, "As aircraft was not flying and on ground, something happening is usual, such as elevator asymmetry and other things. We don't believe them [the instruments]." Neither Gergin nor the relief pilot, Evrenesoglu, contradicted him. Evrenesoglu merely asked if he should pull the circuit breakers to reset the airspeed indicators. He obviously thought the problem was computer-related and hoped to resolve it by switching the indicators off and on. Captain Erdem agreed he

---

tion of the rudder on the tail and/or the elevator trim. It provides an initial indication that the rudder position is not consistent with the plane's speed.

[6]Volume 3 of the Birgenair quick reference handbook contains clear instructions for pilots flying with unreliable airspeed indicators. In particular, it lists recommended angles of attack and engine powers for a range of flight attitudes (climb, cruise, descent, and approach), depending on the gross weight. This should enable the flight to continue even without the primary airspeed indicator.

should try it. All this time, the autopilot was flying the plane in a climb based on data from the captain's airspeed indicator. This also meant the pitch angle was constantly increasing.

The first acoustic warning went off at 11:45 p.m. The loud clacking noise indicated that the plane had exceeded the maximum permissible speed. At an altitude of 6700 feet, the captain's airspeed indicator was reading 352 knots. Given that the pitch angle was now almost 15°, the power was set at normal climb mode, and the plane was nearly fully loaded; this speed was technically impossible. Although he knew that, Erdem said, "Okay, it's no matter. Pull the airspeed [circuit breaker], we will see." Pulling and reinstalling the circuit breaker deactivated the loud warning alarm. Copilot Gergin asked doubtfully, "Now it is three hundred and fifty, yes?"

Neither Erdem nor Gergin bothered to look at the backup airspeed indicator in the center instrument panel. It was currently reading just under 200 knots. Still believing that the plane was going up too fast, Erdem cut back the engine power to idle thrust. The pitch angle of the plane was now 18°, more than twice as high as specified in the flight profile.

Nearly 5 min after takeoff, events suddenly snowballed. The automatic stall alarm went off, as did four other alarms. Captain Erdem must have been faced with an incredibly confusing picture. According to his indicator, the plane was going too fast and seemed virtually impossible to slow down. At the same time, the shaking of the control column indicated that a stall was imminent, caused by the plane going too slow. In addition, the autopilot had reached the limits of its steering capabilities and duly deactivated itself at a pitch angle of 21°.

It was only when the plane rapidly began to lose altitude that Evrenesoglu reported the extreme pitch angle – clearly visible on the attitude direction indicator – saying simply, "ADI." Gergin reacted immediately and ordered, "Nose down," and a moment later, "Thrust." In pilot training, both these actions are among the basic maneuvers pilots are taught to regain control of a plane after a stall. At this moment, it should still have been possible to bring the plane back to a manageable altitude. Erdem ordered Gergin to deactivate the autopilot. Gergin answered, "Already disconnected, Efendim." In the meantime, the plane had dropped around 1000 feet. Evrenesoglu said again, "ADI." Erdem, however, still seemed convinced the plane was going too fast, whereas the plane was decelerating and losing altitude rapidly. "Not climb?" asked Erdem. "What am I to do?" Even at this point, the crew could still have regained control.[7]

Gergin made an attempt to get the plane back under control using the autopilot. "You may level off, altitude okay," he said. "I am selecting the altitude hold. Altitude hold, okay, five thousand feet." Gergin had obviously forgotten that the autopilot was now deactivated. Meanwhile, the plane continued to lose altitude.

[7]This was demonstrated as part of tests in a flight simulator. Furthermore, Boeing reported that, during a test flight, a B757 flying at a comparable altitude had gone into an unplanned stall. In this case, the crew had been able to regain control using standard maneuvers (nose down, rudder and ailerons neutral, increase power) (Flight Safety Foundation 1999).

Suddenly, at 11:45 p.m., captain Erdem finally made the connection between the idle engines and the stall. He shouted, "Thrust levers, thrust, thrust, thrust, thrust!"

Although the power levers were pushed for full thrust, it was too late. As the right engine spooled up faster than the left, the already unstable plane now rolled to the left until the wings were perpendicular to the ground at an angle of almost 99°. The nose of the plane was pointing steeply downward (−58°).

Fifteen miles northeast of Puerto Plata, the plane smashed into the Atlantic. All 176 passengers and the 13 crew members were killed instantly.

The investigation of the Dominican Republic's Dirección General de Aeronautica Civil, supported by the US National Transportation Safety Board,[8] revealed that the airspeed indicator on the captain's console had been faulty because of a blocked pitot tube.[9] The probable cause of the crash was the crew's failure to correctly interpret the stall warning. As a result, they were unable to take the necessary steps to regain control of the plane. The crew had become confused due to the contradictory readings on their indicators and the way events had accelerated. Their flying skills also proved inadequate in this crisis situation, and they showed limited knowledge of this particular type of plane. However, the key factor behind the crash was the lack of proper communication between the crew members.

It may become easier to understand Erdem's behavior – which was largely responsible for the crash – if we remember that he was an experienced pilot. For him, this flight posed no particular challenge. He was not even worried by the first alerts. After all, he was familiar with the redundancies built into the systems of the Boeing 757, and the flight appeared to be progressing as expected. When the first system errors were triggered as the plane began its climb, the aircraft nevertheless seemed to be flying normally. Erdem thus saw no reason to worry and slipped into a mindset that is common to us all. By telling himself everything was "normal," he created the framework of explanations for everything that was to follow. As a result, he saw what he expected to see: namely, a scenario familiar to him from his many years of experience. All of us have experienced this form of cognitive distortion. Given that it happens subconsciously, it probably happens more often than we think. Initially, even the contradictory information could not disrupt Erdem's fixed mental image. He only became concerned when what he saw no longer fit his set of expectations. But even then, any feelings of uncertainty were absorbed by his mental attitude, and anything not normal was termed "crazy" and "wrong" and therefore unbelievable. "As aircraft was not flying and on ground, something happening is usual [...]. We don't believe them [the instruments]."

However, the striking element in this tragedy was the behavior of first officer Gergin. He had the correct airspeed indication on his side of the instrument panel, which was in line with the backup speed indicator. Why did he not clearly state his

---

[8] Extracts translated into German and English (Gröning and Ladkin 1999; Flight Safety Foundation 1999).

[9] It was not possible to identify the exact cause of the blockage in the pitot tube, which was never found after the crash. The blockage had caused the faulty readings on the airspeed indicator and was probably due to an insect nest or dirt particles (Flight Safety Foundation 1999).

observation and correct his captain – which in hindsight seems so obvious? A possible answer can be seen in the culturally based high power distance in the cockpit (Hofstede 1983). However, accidents in cultures with lower power distances, such as those in Western Europe and the United States, show similar behavior on flight decks.[10] Looking at accident statics, we can observe higher accident rates for Asian countries and countries of the former Soviet Union that are associated with higher power distances (International Air Transport Association 2018). However, if we look more closely at accidents involving jets and turboprop aircraft, the picture changes. Regional differences can be found only for turboprop aircrafts, but not for jets that are operated by larger airlines.

In aviation, hierarchies played a major role, no matter to which culture the crews on the flight deck belonged. In the Birgenair case, we saw a young copilot subordinating his views and opinions to those of his captain. If the two had been of equal status, they might have used a "check and balance" system; Gergin would have compared the captain's indicator with the other two and raised the matter of the contradictory values. As it was, he quietly accepted Erdem's assertion that everything was fine. If there was a problem, it was due to a computer error, not an error by the captain.

Following this accident, "crew resource management" (CRM), which was first developed starting in the early 1980s in the United States and Europe, became a mandatory training requirement for flight crews globally (Helmreich et al. 1999). CRM demands that the crew works as a team throughout a flight. This does not mean that CRM questions the captain's abilities. It simply pays tribute to the fact that controlling a modern-day aircraft is beyond the skills of a single person and that everyone on the flight deck has the ability to speak up (Edmondson 1999). Hence, the rest of the crew are liberated from their roles as subordinates and are actively integrated into the flight's workflows and decision-making processes. The previous hierarchy on the flight deck is flattened, and crews follow a different behavioral scheme. Communication is accorded a special role in this process. The aim is to achieve open, factual exchanges of information and thought processes in order to ensure the safe operation of flights.

31.2 How Effective Is CRM Teamwork in Practice?

Teamwork on the flight deck can be observed during simulator training. Commercial aircraft pilots complete these training sessions every 6 months. These cover the pilots' command of an aircraft's systems and standard procedures, as well as the effectiveness of the collaboration between the crew in difficult and dynamic emergency situations.

---

[10] The accidents of KLM 4805 in 1977 (Roitsch et al. 1979; Comisión de Investigación de Accidentes e Incidentes de Aviación Civil 1979; Netherlands Aviation Safety Board 1977) and United Airlines 173 (National Transportation Safety Board 1979) showed similar crew behaviors.

From February 2010 to May 2013, my colleague Zhike Lei and I observed commercial flight crews during simulator training in a study of how teams collaborate and communicate. Among other things, pilots were required to handle emergencies such as the failure of speed sensors or an unexpected drop in cabin pressure. They had to solve the associated problems and complete the flight safely. Each task called for teamwork among those involved.

We established that the teams worked well together to solve acute emergency problems (Lei et al. 2016). However, we observed varying performance levels as the flights continued. Without exception, this was linked to the captain's communication behavior. Crews performed best when the captain involved the copilot in the decision-making process by asking questions such as: "How do you evaluate the situation?" "What options do you have in mind?" "What do you suggest?"

In a second project, which Zhike Lei, Avner Shahal, and I conducted in 2016 and 2017, we wanted to ascertain whether crews knew what the method of "leading with questions" actually meant. At the same time, we expected the answers to provide us with an overview of the status of CRM. In this case, we interviewed military aircraft pilots from the German and Israeli air forces – all of them experienced commanders, copilots, weapon systems officers, and technical loadmasters.

31.3 CRM: A Lot Has Been Achieved

The German military commanders in our study reported that, before CRM, the copilot was a marginal figure on the flight deck. Commanders would let them carry out their work while observing and assessing them. Some commanders even made copilots look foolish, and occasionally a repeatedly humiliated copilot took revenge – that is, waited for a good opportunity to let the commander trip himself up.

Even though situations like these can still be found today, our interviews showed that pilots are well aware of the CRM code of conduct by now. "Things are much better these days than they were," said one of the interviewees. "Communications are better. This enables the other person to contribute to the best of their ability." The reported improvements stem partly from CRM training itself and partly from the workload in increasingly complex aircraft – a workload that piles up significantly in high-pressure military situations. All of this is no longer manageable by one pilot alone.

The demands that both military and commercial pilots have to meet – above and beyond the regular task of flying – are described in the British Civil Aviation Authority's Flight-crew Human Factors Handbook (Civil Aviation Authority 2016) as follows:

> These might include concentrating, paying attention, calculating, trying to remember something, being careful, maintaining awareness, doing an unfamiliar or novel task, doing a challenging task, making a decision, assessing evidence, reviewing a situation, looking for something, listening to something or someone.

If additional external factors (i.e., stressful or emergency situations) then require pilots to carry out the abovementioned steps simultaneously or in rapid succession, anyone expecting to accomplish this on their own is destined for failure.

Take the example of Qantas Flight 32 in 2010 (Australian Transport Safety Bureau 2013). When an engine exploded during this flight, there were 36 warning messages that occurred within 20 s. In a situation such as this, even the most experienced pilot might overlook something, act too hastily, or lose their focus. Our brains can only process a limited number of stimuli at one time, and as soon as we focus on one thing, we lose sight of the other.

A number of the military commanders we interviewed concurred with this observation. One of them said:

> A team functions better than a single person. If I have a crew member who supports me, I will complete my mission better. Or when he pulls me out of a place I got myself into unintentionally, or when he suggests something I hadn't thought of.

Other pilots were keen to point out that their teamwork commences during the briefing, where the aim is to bring everyone involved in the mission "on board." We repeatedly heard that crews have to be cooperative and work as a team. They must also complement, listen to, and respect one another.

However, the key to CRM is communication. If we do not inform the other person with whom we are working about our take on a situation but rather assume – in silence, and all too often incorrectly – that they see things the way we do, we may end up with a misunderstanding. Therefore, the atmosphere on the flight deck has to be open so that no copilot is discouraged from asking the captain/commander how they are interpreting a situation and vice versa. Rather the entire crew has to be encouraged to inquire rather than simply assume.

One of the commanders we interviewed summed things up well. At the same time, he addressed the risk that arises if one of the pilots feels excluded.

> If he [the copilot] thinks differently and does not tell me because I did not ask him, then I may not have done the right thing; it could be that he doesn't feel comfortable and won't be with me 100 percent.

A "good commander" – whose characteristics are among the factors we wanted to identify – asks questions. "He inquires: 'How would you tackle this?' without it sounding as if they are testing the copilot. They may add: 'This is the solution I have in mind.'" A good commander must also "not be afraid to admit if there is something they don't know." We will come back to this point later on, as "not knowing something" may be held against a commander in a different scenario.

31.4 What Comes First?

However, despite the much-cited benefits of CRM, we found that its status represented a recurring issue. Most of the statements we collected portrayed CRM as a training element, but not as a fixed, integrated part of pilots' procedures for increasing safety and reducing the rate of errors on the flight deck. Our interviewees seemed to consider it rather as an add-on that ranked below carrying out their mission, safety, and standard operating procedures (SOPs). The following statement from a commander, or "pilot in command" (PIC), is representative.

> My responsibility is to see that things get carried out the way they should and the way I think is right, which is, first of all, the mission, followed by safety. If it simply happens and not much needs to be done because the copilot pushes ahead, then it's easy and comfortable, which is also good for teamwork. But I am careful with the way I speak to the copilot. In the end, the atmosphere in the crew is also somewhat the PIC's responsibility.

The communication between the commander and the copilot – which we consider to be instrumental to the success of the mission – crops up as an afterthought. Teamwork is deemed to have functioned properly if the "mission" is completed without difficulties and the copilot does what the commander wants. Basically, all actions fall under the responsibility and decision-making power of the commander. Unfortunately, this state of affairs bears little relation to CRM.

"Copilots are being involved at an earlier stage nowadays," said one of the commanders, who spoke in favor of CRM. However, if he and his coworkers had completely adopted CRM, there would be no "earlier" or "later," nor anyone deciding when the subordinate is involved, but rather a crew working together from the start.

Even in the examples that sound almost ideal, the teamwork was reliant on the good will of the commander. "The idea is to empower the copilot as much as possible, to give him a feeling that we are together." The fact is that, under CRM, the other crew members should not be given the "feeling" of inclusion, but rather they should be involved as a matter of course. However, our interviews painted the picture that even CRM-conscious commanders were unable to consider the second man as their equal.

> When to ask questions [one commander said], I see two options. One is to say what you think is the right thing to do and then ask him [the copilot] for his opinion. The second is to give him a moment to say what he thinks and then speak. In the beginning I started by asking and then making the decision. That can make the copilot uncomfortable if he said something else. That's why I hint as to what I think is the right direction. I don't have a problem changing my decision if the copilot convinces me of his opinion. If they don't, I'll say, 'Okay, I understand, but I think we should do x.' So I think it is better at least to hint.

These are not the words of an old-style commander who completely ignores the copilot as someone way down in the ranks but rather those of a new model of commander who sees himself more as a father figure. However, in this constellation, the opinions of copilots still do not carry equal weight, and they must make a special effort to get themselves heard. In fact, they must be able to convince a commander of their opinions. If they do not succeed, they discover that – although the commander can follow their train of thought – their opinions are not taken on board. We generally perceive this kind of reaction as belittling and insulting. The same applies if the commander suggests the "correct" opinion before the copilot even speaks.

It also seems to be the copilots' task to edit their own thought processes in advance and distinguish between important and superfluous inputs. We were only seldom able to identify the same with regard to the commanders, as if their statements were bound to be correct.

> I expect my copilot to provide what he was asked to do and not offer everything he thought of. A good captain will say, 'Aside from everything we mentioned just now, is there anything else important that you thought of?'

Although one or two of the commanders recognized the abovementioned potential for unwittingly insulting the second man, this does not in any way change the view that they themselves set the tone. The nonhierarchical communication envisaged in CRM does not occur. This paternalistic relationship is also fundamentally entrenched in the quotation below.

> I just let things get done and interfere if I see that it isn't done the way I think it should be done. I give some kind of guidance, something general, with the hope that I won't have to comment too much. If I give a lot of comments to someone, it ends up hurting him.

The following statement comes closest to the CRM mindset, but even then the relationship is not ideal. The rules of both military and civil aviation state that the captain/commander has the say in cases where there are any doubts; the copilot will not question this. Having said that, this does not mean the two cannot make joint decisions.

In the next example, the father figure is lurking again, clearly setting the boundaries. The copilot can speak when invited to, but the commander retains the right to inform him that his comments will go unheeded.

> I invite his opinion. I say, 'Monitor me, notice if I miss anything.' If something is unsafe, I expect him [the copilot] to intervene and I will listen. I tell the copilot that the most that can happen to him is that I tell him that we are not going to deal with what he said at the moment.

31.5 Ranks Are a Problem

The examples presented above are just a small selection, but they are representative of the broader picture. On the left sits the man with all the say. On the right sits his subordinate, who has to choose his words carefully.

Of course, this problem is inherent in all hierarchies and begins with the allocation of titles and the different roles associated with the commander, the PIC, the pilot flying the plane, the monitoring pilot, and the copilot. However, this does not blend well with CRM principles. CRM refers to crews, by which it means units. This unit envisages an almost flat hierarchy. In other words, in cases of doubt, it means that the decision-making power lies with the captain/commander. In all other cases, both pilots complete their tasks as colleagues, in accordance with CRM. Indeed, military forces would undoubtedly benefit from a more "collegial" concept being emphasized in the cockpit. As long as the ranks and the associated steep hierarchy remain embedded in people's minds, the aforementioned attitudes that run contrary to CRM will remain part of this system.

Changing these kinds of attitudes is difficult, but not impossible, as we have seen in civil aviation. Such a change would not only redress the hierarchical perception of roles, but it would also put an end to behavior that sometimes reaches bizarre role-playing heights. "When I am flying," one military pilot said, "I try to be more authoritative. When I am monitoring, then I try to be as attentive as possible." Why, an outside observer has to ask, are both crew members not equally "attentive"?

"My role as a PIC," another said, "is to ensure that the mission is carried out as safely as possible." No, the outsider thinks, that is the role of both people – the role of the crew.

31.6 Hierarchy Comes Before Safety

Giolito and Verdin have identified the unspoken precedence of "hierarchy first" over "safety first" in their work (Giolito and Verdin 2018). Most of the crews we observed also seemed to uphold this priority, whether consciously or not. If this is really the case, it suggests that the "safety first" rule constantly cited by our interviewees serves, among other things, to cover up a concealed need for authority and to shield anyone who hides behind this mantra from criticism.

The "hierarchy first" rule means that the copilot completes the tasks and is generally permitted to speak only when invited to do so by the commander – as outlined above. However, this dismantles the CRM approach and reinstates the former image of the all-knowing commander. It also resurrects the problem that originally prompted the development of CRM: the fact that copilots retreat inwardly and subordinate themselves to the commander's decisions. At its extreme, this leads to a situation that one of the commanders we interviewed described thus: "... that the copilots can neglect to think for themselves. They rely on the commander." This attitude presents a danger in a non-normal situation or an emergency.

31.7 The Role of the Commander

The strict hierarchy in the cockpit, the tone-setting or paternalistic role of the commander, the unequal weighting of input to communications – all this does not stem solely from the commander. Copilots frequently share this view and sometimes go as far as to magnify the commander's role even further, insisting that there needs to be someone in the cockpit who can do everything, which is to say, from the copilot's point of view, the other person is not a colleague, either.

Almost all the copilots interviewed said they expect the following characteristics from their commanders: "Someone who knows where this thing is headed. Someone who is calling the shots and makes decisions." The commander must be capable of making decisions and remaining calm under pressure. They must be able to assert themselves and must be solid as a rock in a crisis. They must always command respect. They must also be able to assert themselves with their superiors. Apart from this, they must be able to summarize situations and justify their decisions in the cockpit. They must also be able to feed the copilot with the information they require and ensure that "everyone is on board." They must not ride roughshod over others, nor make them look foolish, but they must ensure that "the crew members feel comfortable so that they say what they think." They must not take others' comments personally. They have to know how to get the best out of their copilot, no matter what their capabilities. They have to make the copilot part of all decisions and keep them informed about what is happening during the flight. They must ask the copilot for their opinions, listen to them, and ask, "Do we want to do it this way?" They must not be an alpha male. They should never act alone, for a poor commander "feels in control and does not communicate with the copilot."

This scenario complements the previous one because it represents a childlike definition of a benevolent father figure who knows everything, can do everything, is also loving, and takes the child's stage of development into consideration. We see the same kind of thing in supervisory roles in industry, by the way; this defect is not unique to military forces.

31.8 Decision-Making

So far, we have determined that the decision-making authority in the cockpit remains with the commander, even if they listen to and involve their copilot. None of the interviewees gave us the impression that decisions are based on proper discussions. As previously stated, this partly stems from both sides placing the commander figure on a pedestal. The commander believes in their own ability to make the right decision, and the copilot – despite also being a trained pilot – shares this view.

However, CRM offers a different approach to the decision-making process and emphasizes that, when it comes to major and complex decisions, we are not capable of considering all the necessary criteria by ourselves.

With reference to the conclusions drawn by Tversky and Kahneman from their cognitive-psychological research, the CRM handbook states: "When assessing information and making decisions, high workload can lead to complex decisions being taken more rapidly than normal, possibly without considering some factors, options, and complexities" (Kahneman and Tversky 1979).

Based on the research presented above, the CRM approach also offers solutions for the cognitive traps that can crop up during the decision-making process. One example is the way freshly absorbed information disproportionately influences our decisions. This can lead us to forget or ignore equally important information received beforehand. It is also possible for us to base our decisions on explanations that seem plausible without necessarily being correct. We are satisfied with partial information, yet we persuade ourselves that we know all the necessary facts. The well-known "confirmation bias" (i.e., our tendency to select information that supports our hypothesis of a situation and to reject any contradictory evidence outright) is also referred to in CRM. It is just as mistaken to rely on past experiences. Of course, it is tempting to say, "The last time I was in this situation, I did this and that and it worked, so I will do just the same again." However, when decisions need to be made quickly, we do not have the time to check whether the criteria really are the same as before, or if some difference means that what we learned from the previous experience is useless or requires modification.

Tools such as FORDEC exist that lay down the decision-making process and subdivide this into an analysis of facts, options for action, and the identification of the risks and benefits of each option before the decision is made, implemented, and put to the test. However, stressful situations do not grant the time it takes to use tools of this kind. It therefore makes sense, as a principle, to go through the steps in pairs, to compare the two different viewpoints, and to ensure that the combined expertise goes into reaching, carrying out, and checking the best possible decision.

A vital element of this approach is for both pilots to consider themselves as colleagues who continuously share information with one another – without one of them thinking alone, suggesting what the other should think, or considering the other's opinion as being inferior or a nuisance CRM obligation.

Our military interviewees are a long way off from an equal exchange of opinions. "Decisions need to be carried out quickly. You tell the copilot what to do," explained one commander. The copilots see things exactly the same way. "You can try as much as you can to help during a flight, but eventually he makes the decisions and you carry them out." Or: "I share my opinion, but in the end, the PIC is the one who decides. Or I wait until he asks me."

31.9 Emergencies

It is interesting to note that commanders and copilots actually agree that they work well together, even in accordance with CRM guidelines. They believe that exceptions only arise in emergency situations, during which the copilot usually withdraws from the decision-making process as a matter of course and leaves this to the commander.

Let us refer once again to what the aforementioned Flight-crew Human Factors Handbook has to say about this subject: "The combination of circumstances and options (often accompanied by an emergency) are unlikely to be the same as previously practiced due to situational complexity. Hence, although expertise can be factored into such circumstances, large elements are effectively new and unpracticed on every occasion. […] This means a process close to rational decision-making." Rational decision-making, as we have seen above, means that someone can overlook "factors, options, and complexities." The same applies to the commander.

Furthermore, the CRM strategy indicates quite explicitly that a stressful situation – which an emergency situation undoubtedly represents – can exceed the capabilities of a single person. "[I]f excessive demands are placed on an individual, it is possible to exceed the individual's capacity to meet them. This results in the deterioration of the individual's ability to cope with the situation."

Apart from that, CRM authors are conscious of potentially extreme reactions to stressful situations – our "fight or flight" mechanism or "freezing" – and warn about them. "Hypothetically and anecdotally, during flight or fight pilots can get mentally stuck within a situation (unable to interpret or resolve a situation, and unable to move on, even if that situation would present no problems under normal circumstances). […] The ultimate response to extreme levels of stress is to give up or freeze."

For the other crew members, the CRM instruction for situations like these is very clear: "Speak up when you see situational awareness (SA) breaking down." The one who is literally "paralyzed" with shock must be snapped out of a stupor, and this can only be achieved by talking to them in order to restore collaboration and consider the options for action.

Some of our interviewees had adopted the rules of CRM for emergency situations. "In situations like these," one said, "each keeps an eye on the other. The ball is passed back and forth. […] The commander must be able to delegate."

Elsewhere, the point was made that "the commander should exude calm and security and not become frantic. If anyone freezes, the others have to intervene." Whereas someone else stated: "The commander ensures calm and collection. Nonetheless, both must also work through the problem and be aware of what the other is doing."

Otherwise, the behavior corresponds with the way roles are generally perceived, as outlined above: "I, as the captain, will present the alternatives and say what the advantages and disadvantages of each option are. I ask the copilot's opinion so that I don't make a decision without taking something into account. If he thinks differently, I check myself and explain to him why we are going to do x." If the correct CRM procedures were being followed, the commander would have said: "We, as the crew, discuss the alternatives …"

However, it is a fact that most commanders and copilots abandon CRM in emergency situations. "I, as a PIC, begin by calming the other person, give him the right perspective, show him that it is an abnormal situation, and bring it to a normal situation."

Elsewhere, again, the point was made that "[t]he hierarchy only emerges when something happens, when decisions need to be made. Then it is clear that there is someone who provides information and there is someone making decisions." That distorted image of task-sharing appears again here, as it is not both who compare information and make a decision together, but rather that one "supplies" and the other decides.

Or, as one copilot said: "During an emergency, you need to have tact, because there are things that are urgent and your opinion doesn't always matter." It is interesting to learn that, although copilots do not wish to be "ridden over roughshod," they can do precisely this to themselves in an emergency. This is also reminiscent of the father-child scenario, in which the father "must not be disturbed" because he is working or has something "important" to do. However, as we have seen above in relation to extracts concerning CRM approaches, it is precisely in emergency situations that it is vital for both crew members to work on reaching a solution, with one being able to assist the other, if necessary.

This means avoiding the following attitude: "The situation in the cockpit has to be calm. When there is a loaded and complex situation, the setting for introducing a differing opinion is more dangerous."

The following statements from interviewees point in the same perilous direction:

> In an abnormal situation, you will be busy with SOP. Things need to be done quickly and you don't have time to express your opinion. [...] If it is urgent, I do what the captain says. There is no time for debates. You do what the captain says.

If you did not know any better, you would really believe that a child were sitting in the copilot's seat and not a trained pilot.

31.10 Aviation Culture

As already addressed above, hierarchical role allocation alone hinders collegial collaboration on the military flight deck. Another problem lies in the elevated status of the commander, which still incorporates elements of the solitary hero. The authors of the CRM handbook also address this: "It is common for an individual to believe that admitting to suffering from pressure is an admission of failure of ability to meet the demands of the job. It has long been an accepted culture in aviation that flight crews and others should be able to cope with any pressure of any situation."

We spoke above about the workload and numerous interlocking steps that have to be performed in the cockpit. We pointed out that one person alone cannot handle the complexities of the tasks and technologies involved, least of all in critical situations. The image of the heroic, all-knowing lone fighter was never the reality but rather a myth from the very beginning that someone should have consigned to history by now – something both commander and copilot should welcome.

One of the copilots explained that, in emergency situations, the commander is not allowed to express their concern and say "Oh my God," to which I would like to respond: Actually, it is high time they should be able to say that. It is also high time for copilots to not just metaphorically wrinkle their noses at commanders in situations like these but to respond, "We are going to make this."

31.11 The Creative Problem-Solver

Overall, we had the impression that the interviewees often pay lip service to CRM. Yet, although people are aware of its advantages, they do not know exactly how to apply CRM in their behavior and communications. We repeatedly heard the same statement from commanders and copilots alike that they should be – and wanted to be – “on board the same boat,” that the commander should ask the copilot’s opinion, and that the copilot, in turn, should indicate anything they feel is not right. There was also talk of the “assertiveness” that the copilots needed to develop. This prompted those commanders who wanted to integrate the copilots to consider whether they should first ask their opinion so as not to influence them. They then considered whether it would offend the copilot if they went on to enforce their own opinion, and that it would therefore be better to state their opinion to start with, or whether this would then deter the copilot from offering a different opinion.

Apart from the abovementioned status gap and its negative effects on CRM, we also came across helplessness in handling CRM. After all, how are you supposed to implement CRM without an adequate understanding of the behavioral psychological aspects of working together in both small and larger teams? How can you if you do not know which behavior has a damaging effect? How can you if there is insufficient training in what we now call “emotional” and “social” intelligence? How can you if you do not know the effect of your body language, facial expressions, and words and you cannot read the signals sent out by someone else? How can you if you are not aware of your own prejudices and do not know how these affect your behavior toward others? How can you if you have not learned how to talk to and negotiate with others in a situation of conflict?

The interviews showed that, despite extensive CRM training in military aviation, the focus remains on the commander. Thus, it would make sense for commanders to change their behavior first. This means involving the second man as an equal partner in tasks by asking him questions – a form of leadership that Edgar Schein terms “humble inquiry” (Schein 2013). It also means that the lead person does not ask questions for the sake of it (i.e., not the kind that require only yes/no answers) but rather gathers information, opinions, and proposals for action, which are subsequently discussed.

This approach taps into the other person’s expertise, calls up information, and reveals new perspectives and options. In the study we conducted during simulator training, we observed captains in commercial aviation who, in critical circumstances and under intense time pressure, still asked their copilots for their takes on problems and received constructive answers. Crews with this type of captain performed consistently better than those with captains who gave orders and who, at best, asked the copilot, “Do you agree?” or “Or do you see things differently?” These questions always resulted in the copilot backing up the captain’s opinion.

A culture of open communication provides the copilot with the chance not only to get involved in tasks but also to volunteer questions and to query a commander or captain’s decision without worrying how they will react. If captain Erdem from the introductory case would have simply asked his copilot for an analysis of the situation instead of (wrongly) stating about the indicators, “Both of them are wrong,” he and the 188 passengers and crew might still be alive.

There is one thing that captains, commanders, and other leaders do not need to worry about: questions do not mean a loss of authority. Amy L. Fraher outlines the types of leaders our times require (Fraher 2011). She calls them “creative problem-solvers.” We would go one step further and describe them as “collegial and creative problem-solvers." However, Fraher also makes it clear that the corresponding skills are not simply lying in wait but must always be taught.

> Today's leaders need: cultural awareness; an understanding of authority issues and how both overt and covert group processes can impede team performance, often in fatal ways; comprehension of the impact of technology on the pace and complexity of team operations; and sophisticated sense-making skills in order to manage team learning, evolve operations and incorporate new information as it emerges. To support these developments, even technical and professional fields, such as aviation, firefighters, law enforcement, maritime, medicine, military, nuclear power, offshore oil rigs, and railroads, must become more flexible and collaborative than ever before. And the leadership and teambuilding training programs for groups operating in these high-risk environments must follow suit, developing the creative problem-solvers our complex, evolving systems require. (Fraher 2011)

It has been 35 years since CRM was developed as a means of improving aviation safety. That initial attention to the necessity of communications between captain and copilot already improved upon prevailing conditions. The same can be said about incorporating the findings of modern-day cognitive psychology into CRM guidelines. However, as long as this is only being written on paper and not constantly being taught and practiced, CRM will not be properly implemented and remain merely a pleasant embellishment.

It is therefore high time for a change of perspective for creating the first framework that gets the most out of others by engaging them with the "leading with questions" approach. Despite having become an established cliché, leaders do not have to be heroes and know everything – even though we sometimes wish that.

References

Australian Transport Safety Bureau (2013). *ATSB transport safety report, aviation occurrence investigation – AO-2010-089, final investigation – In-flight uncontained engine failure overhead Batam Island, Indonesia, 4 November 2010, VH-OQA, Airbus A380-84.* Canberra: Australian Transport Safety Bureau.

Civil Aviation Authority – Safety Regulation Group (2016). *CAP 737, Flight-crew human factors handbook.* Gatwick Airport South.

Comisión de Investigación de Accidentes e Incidentes de Aviación Civil (1979). *A-102/1977 y A-103/1977 Accidente Ocurrido el 27 de Marzo de 1977 a las Aeronaves Boeing 747, Matrícula PH-BUF de K.L.M. y Aeronave Boeing 747, matrícula N736PA de PANAM en el Aeropuerto de los Rodeos, Tenerife (Islas Canarias).* Retrieved 10 September 2019, from http://www.fomento.gob.es/MFOM/LANG_CASTELLANO/ORGANOS_COLEGIADOS/CIAIAC/PUBLICACIONES/HISTORICOS/A-102–103–1977/.

Edmondson, A. (1999). Psychological safety and learning behavior in work teams. *Administrative Science Quarterly*, 44(2), 350–383.

Flight Safety Foundation (1999). Erroneous airspeed indications cited in Boeing 757 control loss. *Accident Prevention*, 56(10), 1–8.

Fraher, A.L. (2011). *Thinking through crisis: Improving teamwork and leadership in high-risk fields*. New York, NY: Cambridge University Press.

Giolito, V., & Verdin, P.J. (2018). Executive perspectives on strategic error management. In J. U. Hagen (Ed.), *How could this happen?* (pp. 59–80). Cham: Palgrave Macmillan.

Gröning, M., & Ladkin, P. (1999). *Bericht der Direccion General de Aeronautica Civil über die Untersuchung des Unfalles mit dem Flugzeug Boeing B-757 am 06. February 1996 bei Puerto Plato (in der Übersetzung vom Luftfahrtbundesamt).* Bielefeld: Universität Bielefeld, Technische Fakultät, AG Rechnernetze und Verteilte Systeme. Retrieved 10 September 2019, from http://www.rvs.uni-bielefeld.de/publications/Incidents/DOCS/ComAndRep/PuertoPlata/bericht.html.

Hagen, J. (2013). *Confronting mistakes: Lessons from the aviation industry when dealing with error.* Basingstoke: Palgrave Macmillan.

Helmreich, R.L., Merritt, A.C., & Wilhelm, J.A. (1999). The evolution of crew resource management training in commercial aviation. *International Journal of Aviation Psychology*, 9(1), 19–32.

Hofstede, G. (1983). The cultural relativity of organizational practices and theories. *Journal of International Business Studies*, 14(2), 75–89.

International Air Transport Association (2018). Safety report 2017. Montreal: IATA.

Kahneman, D., & Tversky, A. (1979). Prospect theory: An analysis of decision under risk. *Econometrica*, 47, 263–291.

Lei, Z., Waller, M.J., Hagen, J., & Kaplan, S. (2016). Team adaptiveness in dynamic contexts: Contextualizing the roles of interaction patterns and in-process planning. Group & Organization Management, 41(4), 491–525.

National Transportation Safety Board (1979). *Aircraft accident report. United Airlines, Inc., McDonnell-Douglas, DC-8–61, N8082U.* Portland, Oregon, December 28, 1978. NTSB–AAR-79–7. Washington, DC: NTSB.

Netherlands Aviation Safety Board (1977). *Final report and comments of the investigation into the accident with the collision of KLM Flight 4805, Boeing 747–206B, PH-BUF and Pan American Flight 1736, Boeing 747–121, N736PA at Tenerife Airport, Spain on 27 March 1977.* ICAO Circular 153-AN/56.

Roitsch, P.A., Babcock, G.L., & Edmunds, W.W. (1979). *Human factors report on the Tenerife accident.* Washington, DC: Airline Pilots Association.

Schein, E.H. (2013). *Humble inquiry: The gentle art of asking instead of telling.* San Francisco, CA: Berrett-Koehler Publishers.

Jan U. Hagen (Prof. Dr.) is an associate professor at ESMT European School of Management and Technology in Berlin. Jan's research and teaching focus is on leadership. He is particularly interested to understand how teams and organizations deal with errors. Apart from articles in academic journals, he published the book *Confronting Mistakes – Lessons from the Aviation Industry when Dealing with Error* (Palgrave Macmillan) in 2013 and his new book *How could this happen – Managing error in organizations* in summer 2018. His research received media coverage in international outlets like the Financial Times and The Economist.

Jan directs the ESMT open enrollment program *Leadership under Pressure* and is the host of the biennial ESMT Error Management Conference. He teaches in executive education programs and human factors training of the German Federal Armed Forces. In addition to his academic work, he has been active in consulting companies.

Chapter 32
Cultural Differences-Induced Mistakes in Driving Behaviour: An Opportunity to Improve Traffic Policy and Infrastructure

Václav Linkov and Petr Zámečník

Abstract Driving a vehicle is a complex task influenced by many factors, including cultural differences. When a driver with a certain cultural background drives in a foreign environment, their natural reaction to traffic situations might be unsuitable, so they can make a mistake in the comprehension of a traffic situation or in their reaction. In this chapter, we review theories of cultural differences, differences in driving behaviours in various cultures, and examples of driving mistakes induced by foreign cultural backgrounds. People in different countries are used to driving with a different level of aggressiveness, traffic signs that are positioned in different ways, and some specific-to-their-country traffic signs. These mistakes might inspire governments to change policies regarding traffic rules and improve infrastructure so that foreign drivers more easily adapt to the new environment. Such changes might include making traffic signs easier to comprehend, the usage of special traffic signs for foreigners, and governmental campaigns to educate foreign drivers.

Keywords Mistakes · Errors · Failure · Driving behaviour · Driving mistakes · Traffic infrastructure · Traffic signs · Cultural differences

32.1 Introduction

Transferring driving skills from one environment to another, as well as poor knowledge of local traffic rules, leads to worse driving performance (Zhang et al. 2010). This leads to the higher probability of a traffic accident for foreign drivers

V. Linkov (✉) · P. Zámečník
CDV – Transport Research Centre, Brno, Czech Republic
e-mail: vaclav.linkov@cdv.cz

E. Vanderheiden, C.-H. Mayer (eds.), *Mistakes, Errors and Failures across Cultures*, https://doi.org/10.1007/978-3-030-35574-6_32

(Castillo-Manzano et al. 2018). The risk increases with increased cultural differences – Yannis et al. (2007) showed that foreign drivers in Greece have a higher accident risk and the risk is higher for non-EU nationals than for EU nationals. It is, therefore, useful to know which cultural differences are responsible for traffic accident vulnerability and how they influence driving. The research concerning cross-cultural variability in driving behaviour usually focuses on universal concepts, like aggressive driving, or specific violations of traffic laws, like speeding. Some studies target more focused issues, like the problems of a certain cultural group in a specific foreign environment. The aim of this chapter is to review both universal and specific research regarding cultural differences in driving and to present some governmental actions which can help reduce the risk of traffic accidents.

In this chapter, we focus on driving behaviour mistakes that happen due to cultural differences. Defining culture is a difficult task (Jahoda 2012); we consider culture to be the set of rules, typical behavioural patterns, decision styles, and opinions for how people should behave within a certain society. By behaviour mistake, we mean a behaviour which is wrong in the current cultural environment and circumstances. In the context of driving, this means that the driver drives and decides differently than the accepted local traffic rules, driving customs, or opinions.

Differences in driving in various countries are caused by general cultural differences and by specific driving cultures. The first part of this chapter concerns general cultural theories and their impact on driving. The second part is about the differences in aggressive driving customs and traffic offences. The third part concerns driving mistakes caused by different traffic cultures, with various examples. Finally, we provide examples for how governments and NGOs might reduce the risks of accidents with campaigns and infrastructure changes.

32.2 Hofstede's Dimensions of Culture and Their Impact on Driving Behaviour

The most famous classification of cultural differences is that of Geert Hofstede (1980). His original research described four dimensions of culture, all which can be related to driving. Hofstede conducted factor analysis on questionnaire data collected from employees of the IBM corporation and derived dimensions of individualism/collectivism, power distance, masculinity/femininity, and uncertainty avoidance. Masculinity was defined as the importance of earnings, recognition, and advancement and femininity as the importance of good relationships and cooperation with other people (Minkov et al. 2019). Countries with high masculinity are Slovakia and Austria, and countries with high femininity are Sweden and Denmark (Hofstede Insights 2019). People in individualist societies care only about their own goals, while people in collectivist societies are loyal to others and care about them (Vollero et al. 2019). Countries with high individualism are the United States and Australia, while countries with high collectivism are Ecuador and Korea (Hofstede

Insights 2019). In cultures with low power distance, people view others as equal, while in cultures with high power distance, an unequal distribution of power is accepted (Vollero et al. 2019). High power distance cultures are Slovakia and Malaysia, while low power distance cultures are Israel and Ireland (Hofstede Insights 2019). In cultures with high uncertainty avoidance, people do not like changes, while in cultures with low uncertainty avoidance, people tolerate ambiguity and prefer innovation (Vollero et al. 2019). Countries with high uncertainty avoidance are Greece and Japan, and countries with low uncertainty avoidance are Jamaica and Bhutan (Hofstede Insights 2019). In the following paragraphs, we try to suggest the ways that these dimensions might relate to the differences in driving culture.

Power distance is related to the acceptance of the unequal distribution of power in society. In high power distance cultures, people with high social status show this status more and respect those with lower status less. Also, people with lower status respect the hierarchy more than in cultures with low power distance. Power distance might be connected to driving behaviour in two ways. First, it can be connected to behaviour related to higher status. In China, some drivers with expensive cars show their status by driving aggressively in order to force other drivers to move out of their way (Huang et al. 2006). Drivers showing higher status might cause serious traffic accidents. Problems might also arise with the acceptance or ignorance of a lower social position. Drivers coming from a culture with a higher power distance might expect that weaker people on the road (e.g. bicyclists) will get out of the way. Bicyclists from a culture with a lower power distance might expect that car drivers would show respect and slow down. The resultant situation might lead to an accident because of a mistake made by the driver or the cyclist.

People from individualistic cultures define themselves by their own characteristics, wishes, and abilities, while people from collectivistic cultures think about themselves in terms of their social roles and their relationships and pay more attention to the wishes and expectations of other people than those from individualist cultures. This distinction makes it important to watch the behaviour of other drivers (Huang et al. 2006). Individualism is related to speeding (Üzümcüoglu et al. 2018). People from collectivist cultures might drive slower to be able to concentrate on others, and they might be more sensitive towards other drivers' gestures. Risk perception and attitudes about traffic safety have an impact on driving behaviour in Norway and Russia, but not in Africa and Middle East (Nordfjærn et al. 2014a, b). Nordfjærn et al. think that this difference is due to the fact that people from individualistic cultures behave more according to their attitudes. The relationship between attitude and behaviour is lower in collectivistic countries, where people behave according to their perceived expectations of others.

Uncertainty avoidance expresses a preference for familiar situations. People in cultures with higher uncertainty avoidance have a lower tolerance for the unknown, which is related to speaking a more formal language (Giebels et al. 2017) or searching for more information about places to which to travel (Quintal et al. 2010). Nordfjærn et al. (2014a, b) think that uncertainty avoidance is related to maintaining traffic rules: Indians, who are higher in uncertainty avoidance, drive more safely than Africans, who are lower in uncertainty avoidance.

Cultures that are higher in masculinity are focused on performance, whereas feminine cultures regard good relationships and life quality as more important. People from masculine cultures might be prone to speeding, risky driving, overtrust in their driving skills, and driving in bad weather conditions, which all can decrease traffic safety.

32.3 Other Theories About Cultural Differences and Driving

Other theories of cultural differences related to behaviour are specific to certain regions and include the phenomena of face and holistic thinking. The phenomenon of "face" and "losing face" exists in East Asian cultures. Face is the way people present themselves to other people (Chen and Hwang 2016). The person tries to look good and persuade others to trust them. Losing face might be a serious social threat. This could have influence on traffic safety when a person tries to save face or make themselves look better by taking more risk than necessary. There is a low percentage of seatbelt usage in the population of Chinese drivers (Fleiter and Watson 2016). In China, a driver may not use a safety belt because, by using it, they would show that they do not trust their own driving skills and that they think that a traffic accident is possible. Losing face is based on social interaction, so these situations are more probable in areas with higher population density.

Holistic thinking is a cognitive style where people focus on the whole and relationships among different parts of the whole. Analytical thinking is focused on details and making the whole by assigning categories to its parts (Nisbett et al. 2001; Li et al. 2018a, b). Holistic thinking is more common in Eastern cultures, and analytical thinking is more common in Western cultures. A higher focus on detail might be useful when it is necessary to perceive specific details in the surroundings of the vehicle (e.g. barely visible traffic lights). Focus on the whole might be useful when it is necessary to perceive more objects at once (e.g. inside a traffic jam). People from holistic cultures might have problems with driving in analytical countries where the traffic infrastructure is designed for people with this type of thinking and vice versa (e.g. they might need some information to be repeated).

Cross-cultural differences in driving might also be explained by the theory of planned behaviour (Ajzen 1991; Grilli and Notaro 2019), which states that actions might be explained by attitudes towards specific behaviours, subjective norms, and the belief that a person might really change their behaviour. When a person thinks that some behaviour is correct and acceptable, they will behave that way. For example, Swedish drivers speed less than Turkish drivers. This difference might be because Swedish drivers consider following speed limits to be more important and perceive it as a social norm (Warner et al. 2009).

The driving behaviour of people who are learning to drive in a new driving culture is dependent on their level of acculturation to the driving cultures of both their country of origin and the new country. The more a person is acculturated to the new culture, the more they follow the culture driving customs. The more the person is acculturated to the original driving environment, the larger the effort necessary to adapt to the new environment. Shinohara and Nishizaki (2018) found that experienced Japanese drivers concentrate on their surroundings less in the United States than in Japan, while for less experienced Japanese drivers, there is no difference. They think that experienced drivers should concentrate more on driving in unknown environments than less experienced drivers because they have already developed driving habits in the native environment and, therefore, should allocate more cognitive skills for the driving itself to counteract these habits (Shinohara and Nishizaki 2018). For example, traffic signs are used more often in Europe than in Canada, so Canadians recognize the signs slower than Europeans (Shinar et al. 2014).

32.4 Differences in Driving Behaviour Between Various Cultures

A huge amount of research has focused on aggressive driving behaviour and the following of traffic rules in various cultures. Less wealthy European countries have more traffic accidents than more wealthy European countries. Among the less wealthy, those with a larger percentage of Roman Catholics have more traffic accidents than those with a lower percentage (Melinder 2007). Traffic accidents are fewer in countries with more roundabouts and more intersections with good visibility (Marshall 2018). Sârbescu et al. (2014) found that Serbians drive more aggressively than Romanian drivers. They think that this difference is caused by the different levels of development in the countries and because the behaviour of Serbian drivers was affected by military conflicts and the resulting economic difficulties of the country. The worsened economic situation in Serbia might have caused a lowering of mental capacity of drivers, because they are focused on unrelated issues. The economic situation also creates worse technical conditions for both cars and infrastructure, lowering the effectivity of social mechanisms that control safe driving and lowering the amount of social intervention in road safety (Sârbescu et al. 2014).

Greek and Turkish drivers engage in aggressive driving and violations of traffic rules more often than Swedish and Finnish drivers (Warner et al. 2011). Greek and Turkish drivers experience a traffic accident more often than Swedish and Finnish drivers. Swedish drivers think that they drive less safely in comparison with the self-opinion of Greek, Turkish, and Finnish drivers. Finnish drivers think they have worse driving skills than Swedish, Turkish, Greek (Warner, et al. 2013), and Australian drivers (Lajunen et al. 1998). People from Nordic countries also admit that they break traffic rules more often than Turkish drivers, especially speeding on a highway, which might be caused by the fact that Turkish drivers are used to regularly speeding and, therefore, do not consider it to be a serious offence (Özkan et al. 2006).

Turkish drivers consider driving to be more dangerous than Norwegian drivers. Norwegian drivers consider speeding to be a serious offence more often than do Turkish drivers, but Turkish drivers consider drunk driving to be a more serious offence than Norwegians. Turkish drivers are more willing to take risk when driving than Norwegian drivers. Turkish drivers also speed more often than Norwegian drivers (Simsekoglu et al. 2012).

Chinese, Japanese, and American driving cultures were compared by Atchley et al. (2014). Chinese drivers fight for the right of the way, so there is high number of traffic accidents in China. Despite this, the Chinese government focuses on increasing traffic flow more than on increasing traffic safety (Atchley et al. 2014). The driver's emotional control is related to safer driving style in China (Wu et al. 2018). Japanese drivers persist on safety and are willing to follow traffic rules, so the number of accidents is low, and they accept high penalties for breaking traffic rules. For American drivers, the car is a symbol of freedom, which leads to more risky behaviour and a higher number of traffic accidents (Atchley et al. 2014).

The tendency to make mistakes in preparation for driving properly might also vary across groups with different cultural origins. Timmermans et al. (2019) found that professional drivers from South Asia working in Qatar are more prone to driving while feeling sleepy than drivers with other cultural origins. Elias et al. (2016) worked with the hypothesis that such proneness to the violations of traffic laws by minority groups might be caused by their disregard for any laws based on discrimination by majority-group institutions and the distrust of laws issued by these institutions.

32.5 Driving Mistakes Related to the Traffic Environment

While driving, drivers constantly make decisions about their next steps. They should choose their speed, their direction, and their distance to other vehicles, bicycles, and pedestrians. Also, they decide how careful they should be and how much attention they should pay to ensure their safety. All these decisions are made according to expectations that the drivers have regarding the behaviour of other people on the road, the infrastructure, and the overall environment. These expectations might be wrong, and this could lead to a mistake in driving behaviour. They can make a bad decision regarding their speed, direction, or behaviour towards other people, and an accident might happen. Such mistakes could be classified as follows:

- Mistakes because of the incorrect anticipation of people's behaviour
- Mistakes because of confusion about the meaning of traffic signs
- Mistakes because of wrong estimation of the traffic environment (like traffic density)

We give examples for these types of mistakes in the following subchapters.

32.5.1 Driving Mistakes Because of the Incorrect Anticipation of People's Behaviour

Drivers in cultures where people do not follow traffic rules consider this to be an important issue in traffic safety. Iranian drivers think that the non-following of rules is caused by excessive Iranian individualism, the car as a status symbol, and bad law enforcement, which is perceived as unjust, inconsistent, and arbitrary (Banakar and Fard 2012). All of these lead to fatalistic orientation towards road traffic accidents (Nordfjærn et al. 2014a, b). Ignoring traffic rules by drivers might be expected by pedestrians. Iranian pedestrians expect less than Pakistani pedestrians that they will be respected by drivers (Nordfjærn and Zahadeh 2016). When a driver from a country with a traffic culture where pedestrians do not expect respect travels to a country where pedestrians expect to receive space from drivers, they might make mistake and ignore a pedestrian who – expecting respect – will enter the road and might be hit by the car.

Chinese drivers in the United States think that, when compared with their American counterparts, Chinese pedestrians and bicyclists more often ignore the potential danger from cars, so car drivers encounter more unexpected traffic situations with pedestrians and bicyclists. Sometimes there are no barriers between opposite-direction lanes on Chinese highways, so pedestrians may cross highways in the countryside (Huang et al. 2006). Not being prepared for pedestrian behaviour in countries where pedestrians follow the rules less than in the driver's home country might lead to results similar to those described above.

German drivers perceive situations where a motorcycle or a wild animal gets onto the road as more severe than Chinese drivers. Chinese drivers have a longer reaction time than German drivers in dangerous situations, because they do not believe that these situations need a reaction as quickly as do Germans. The illegal and dangerous behaviours of people on the roads are more common in China than in Germany, so Chinese drivers do not think that such a situation is abnormal and do not react immediately (Wang et al. 2019). Drivers from cultures with faster reactions to dangerous situations (like Germany) might make mistake and expect the driver from a culture with slower reaction (like China) to brake quickly, which can lead to an accident.

Driving cultures differ in driving styles. Chinese drivers, by comparison to British drivers, display greater variability in headway, lane position, and speed. They also spend a larger percentage of time looking at in-vehicle devices and away from the road (Large et al. 2019). This larger behavioural variability for Chinese drivers means that they might be less focused on driving. The larger variability in Chinese drivers' behaviours is also manifested in moped drivers more often changing lanes in multiple-lane roads, which is seen less often in Europe and America (Glaser et al. 2017). Such variable behaviours might lead to situations where a driver from a culture with less variable behaviours might make mistake and expect other drivers to keep their speed and direction.

Foreign drivers have problems with comprehending traffic situations and understanding unwritten local traffic rules. Yoh et al. (2017) studied the types of traffic violations made by drivers of different nationalities in Japan. Asian drivers violate the priority rule more often than others. North and South Americans violate speed limits, Southeast Asians have more problems with comprehension than other foreigners, and Koreans tend to violate traffic light rules and engage in drunk driving. Taiwanese drivers fail to stop at traffic lights, stop signs, and railway crossings. Korean and Taiwanese drivers tend to harm pedestrians more than foreigners of other nationalities. Filipino drivers tend to fail to yield to pedestrians. Failing to stop at traffic lights might be due to the longer cycle than in the country of origin, so the driver is used to running red lights rather than wait a long time for the green light (Yoh et al. 2017). All these differences might lead to a behaviour that does not fit the local traffic customs and results in an accident.

People in various cultures have different customs according to how much effort they put into watching whether the road is safe. Malaysian drivers perceive it to be safer to pull out in front of approaching vehicles than UK drivers (Lee et al. 2015). Crundall et al. think that this might be responsible for the higher fatality rates on Malaysian roads. Both UK and Malaysian drivers think that it is safer to pull out on Malaysian roads than on British roads. When British drivers in Malaysia do not expect a neighbouring car to pull out, it might lead to collision.

Chinese cars are more often overloaded, so they have a longer breaking distance (Huang et al. 2006). A dangerous situation might arise when a foreign driver expects a Chinese driver to be able to brake as quickly as would be possible with the less-loaded cars in their home country. Using flashing lights in the United States means that the driver will let the other driver go, but in China it means that the other driver should let him or her go (Huang et al. 2006). An American driver might make mistake, think that the Chinese driver is allowing him to go, and then run into the second car.

Not being aware of the increased risk of the inappropriate behaviour of specific types of vehicles with which a driver is not familiar might lead to a driving mistake. Tricycle drivers often disregard traffic rules and regulations in Nigeria (Uzondu et al. 2019). When the driver does not know this, they might not drive with special care in presence of a tricycle, and an accident might happen more often than with an informed driver.

32.5.2 Driving Mistakes Because of Confusion About the Meaning of Traffic Signs

When the foreign driver is not yet acculturated to local traffic culture and does not know the system for local traffic signs, it might result in a traffic accident. Summala (1998) describes cultural misunderstandings which happen to US-American drivers in Europe. Drivers in the United States are used to the fact that crossroads have signage to define the right of the way. Americans assume that a road without a right of the way sign means that they have the right of way and they continue driving. Yet, in Europe, many crossroads do not have a sign to tell the driver to yield. On such a road, the driver does not have the right of the way, but they should give this right to the car coming from the right. The American driver, believing that the other driver sees a "give right of the way" sign and will yield, is wrong. If such a driver continues, he might cause a traffic accident, because the second car might run into him from the right. There are no traffic signs to decide right of the way on many Chinese roads as well (Huang et al. 2006), so a similar situation might also happen in China.

Drivers in a foreign country have problems comprehending foreign traffic signs (Ward et al. 2004). Texts in the local language could create comprehension problems for foreign drivers (Bartłomiejczyk 2013). Research by Liu et al. (2019) provided some examples from Chinese drivers who were asked to describe German traffic signs. The Chinese subjects, who had never visited Germany, were asked to describe the meaning of traffic signs, some of which are not used in China. The "right of way on the main road" traffic sign, which has a cross with a thinner horizontal line, was judged to mean "go ahead" or "rocket" by 82% of participants, while only 6% knew the correct meaning. Nearly all of the participants did not know the meaning of the "end of priority road" traffic sign, while 5% thought it meant "turn right" (Liu et al. 2019). Sign comprehension difficulties might even arise for similar cultures – Ng and Chan (2007) asked Hong Kong Chinese to recognize traffic signs from Mainland China and found that the comprehension for those that were different from those used in Hong Kong was 10% lower than those that were similar. The most difficult traffic signs to comprehend were "farm trailer prohibited" and "tricycle with goods prohibited", because such vehicles are not present on Hong Kong roads. When a foreign driver does not know the meaning of a traffic sign – like "the right of the way" – he might make behave as if such sign has not been there.

32.5.3 Driving Mistakes Because of Not Fulfilling Expectations of Others

There is a cultural difference in choosing who the driver will try to save in the moments before an unavoidable accident. Awad et al. (2018) made people to decide who an autonomous car would kill, either the passengers by driving into a wall or pedestrians. People from individualistic cultures tended to spare more human lives, while people from collectivistic cultures spared older people. People from poorer countries spared pedestrians who were breaking the law more than people from countries with better institutions. People in Latin American and French-speaking countries spared women and young people more often. When a driver in a dangerous situation has to choose among several alternative reactions that would endanger a child or an old person, they might choose differently than the local population, and the local population would consider it to be his driving mistake.

People in various cultures have different attitudes to the usage of in-vehicle technologies. Chinese drivers consider in-vehicle technologies to be more important than German drivers (Li et al. 2018a, b), and Austrians are more reserved when compared to Americans and Koreans (Jeon et al. 2012). Not using in-vehicle technologies where expected (e.g. automatic mode on highway) might lead to a dangerous situation. The risk of such situations might increase with the presence of semi-autonomous vehicles in the future.

32.6 How to Decrease the Mistakes Induced by Driving Culture Differences: Infrastructure Changes and New Policies

Given the difficulties described above, governments should work to implement policies to minimize driving mistakes that arise from cultural differences and misunderstandings. This could be accomplished by improving infrastructure or instituting campaigns to educate foreign drivers about the specific features of the local driving culture.

The traffic safety of foreign drivers might be increased by creating special traffic signs for these drivers. Such signage might be useful at the border of countries where on one side, the flow of traffic is on the right and on the other side, the flow of traffic is on the left. Signs would remind drivers that it is necessary to keep the change in mind. These signs could be placed at roads where an accident caused by a foreign driver on the wrong side of the road had already happened.

Authorities might also improve foreigners' driving by changing standard traffic signs to contain easily comprehensible pictures. Such signs should be specific, because people in some cultures (e.g. Chinese) prefer to see specific information instead of abstract information (Ng and Chan 2007). Drivers in different countries have different mental representations of road infrastructure. For roundabouts, British drivers refer to exits in terms of whole numbers – the third exit – while Malaysian drivers use a clock metaphor, exit at 9 o'clock (Large et al. 2017). Instructions used for the navigation of drivers from different cultural backgrounds should be based on prior understanding and the kind of mental representation that works for the specific cultural group.

According to the theory of planned behaviour, driving behaviour might be affected by the changing attitudes of the drivers. This might happen through governmental information campaigns. Campaigns might be launched by private institutions or governments. One campaign aimed at influencing foreign drivers was launched by the Royal Automobile Club of Queensland (2019) in Australia. Drivers were encouraged to drive on the left, use a seat belt, obey stop signs and traffic lights, overtake safely, not drink and drive, respect the speed limit, not use a cell phone while driving, drive according to the conditions, and plan the trip because driving distances are long in Australia.

Another campaign was launched by the UK government for British drivers abroad. Foreign and Commonwealth Office (2013) informs British drivers about different traffic rules in foreign countries to prepare them for specific situations, like the fact that it is compulsory to carry additional eyeglasses for drivers with bad vision in Spain and that it is illegal to pick up hitchhikers in Russia.

The New Zealand government also launched a campaign for visiting drivers. According to the project website (Safer Journeys 2019), the most frequent nationalities of foreign drivers involved in fatal or injury crashes are Australian, Chinese, German, Indian, British, and American. The government uses billboards, posters, and social media to spread information about road safety in New Zealand. The messages were tested in the six countries whose nationals were most often involved in traffic accidents in New Zealand. The warnings included encouragement to drive on the left and take photos only from safe places (Beehive.govt.nz 2016).

Governmental campaigns should be designed to fit the cultural specifics of the country. What works in one culture does not necessarily work in another. For example, in collectivistic cultures, it might be less effective to persuade people to change their attitudes through information campaigns; it may be more effective to influence their perception of what other people expect from them – e.g. Chinese drivers change their travel behaviour when people in their social network do so (Habich-Sobiegalla et al. 2019). Traffic safety campaigns might be successful only in some cultures. As Lund and Rundmo (2009) note, the connection between attitudes and behaviour might be different in various cultures. When changes in attitude do not influence the behaviour, the safety campaign cannot be successful. Also, campaigns might be less successful in countries where driving is a basic habit and therefore less influenced by personal values (Orru et al. 2019).

32.7 Conclusion

Cultural differences might bring difficulties and dangerous situations to the traffic environment. Nevertheless, they might also serve as an opportunity to improve certain aspects of traffic culture, which might also be problematic for locals. For example, some traffic signs in China contain excessively complex Chinese characters, which are difficult to read when visibility is low (Huang et al. 2006). This is a problem for Chinese natives and difficult for foreigners. Changes to the infrastructure could benefit everyone, not just foreigners. Studying mistakes made by drivers in some countries due to their foreign cultural background might help to improve traffic safety in the country.

Research about cultural differences in driving behaviour provides several recommendations for how to improve the traffic safety of foreign and local drivers. Campaigns could be targeted at drivers who come from more culturally different environments, like American drivers in Europe or European drivers in China, because these drivers are vulnerable to mistakes. The governments of areas where local drivers often cross the border to countries or areas with specific traffic signs (like Hong Kong drivers going to Mainland China) should provide information about these signs to citizens.

The majority of information about driving behaviour variations among cultures comes from quantitative research that used international scales. Nevertheless, this research is unable to capture culture-specific behaviour nor the meanings of traffic signs and infrastructure for drivers of specific cultural backgrounds. The vulnerabilities of the local traffic culture for foreigners are likely to be captured by qualitative studies asking foreign drivers which problems they perceive while driving on local roads. We suggest more such studies should be conducted to give governments information for launching targeted campaigns.

Acknowledgments This chapter was produced with the financial support of the Ministry of Education, Youth and Sports within National Sustainability Programme I, a project of the Transport R&D Centre (LO1610), on a research infrastructure acquired from the Operation Programme Research and Development for Innovations (CZ.1.05/2.1.00/03.0064).

References

Ajzen, I. (1991). The theory of planned behavior. *Organizational Behavior and Human Decision Processes*, 50, 179–211.

Atchley, P., Shi, J., & Yamamoto, T. (2014). Cultural foundations of safety culture: A comparison of traffic safety culture in China, Japan and the United States. *Transportation Research Part F*, 26, 317–325. https://doi.org/10.1016/j.trf.2014.01.004

Awad, E., Dsouza, S., Kim, R., Schulz, J., Heinrich, J., Shariff, A., Bonnefon, J.-F., & Rahwan, I., (2018). The moral machine experiment. *Nature*, 563, 59–64. https://doi.org/10.1038/s41586-018-0637-6.

Banakar, R., & Fard, S.N. (2012). Driving dangerously: Law, culture, and driving habits in Iran. *British Journal of Middle Eastern Studies*, 39(2), 241-251.

Bartłomiejczyk, M. (2013). Text and image in traffic signs. *Linguistica Silesiana*, 34, 111-131.

Beehive.govt.nz (2016). New safety campaign focuses on visiting drivers. Retrieved 10 September 2019,fromhttps://www.beehive.govt.nz/release/new-safety-campaign-focuses-visiting-drivers.

Castillo-Manzano, J.I., Castro-Nuño, M., López-Valpuesta, L., & Vassallo, F. (in press). An assessment of road traffic accidents in Spain: the role of tourism. *Current Issues in Tourism*. https://doi.org/10.1080/13683500.2018.1548581.

Chen, R., & Hwang, K.-K. (2016). Nation, Face, and Identity: An Initial Investigation of National Face in East Asia. *Frontiers in Psychology,* 7:1557.

Elias, W., Blank-Gomel, A., Habib-Matar, C., & Shiftan, Y. (2016). Who are traffic offenders among ethnic groups and why? *Accident Analysis and Prevention*, 91, 64–71.

Fleiter, J.J., & Watson, B. (2016). Addressing the road trauma burden in China: Exploring attitudes, behaviours, risk perceptions and cultural uniqueness. *Accident Analysis and Prevention*, 95, 326–333.

Foreign and Commonwealth Office (2013). Foreign Office launches road safety Campaign for living abroad. Retrieved 10 September 2019, from https://www.gov.uk/government/news/foreign-office-launches-road-safety-campaign-for-driving-abroad.

Giebels, E., Oostinga, M.S.D., Taylor, P.J., & Curtis, J.L. (2017). The cultural dimension of uncertainty avoidance impacts police-civilian interaction. *Law and Human Behavior*, 41, 93–102. https://doi.org/10.1037/lhb0000227.

Glaser, Y.G., Guo, F., Fang, Y., Deng, B., & Hankey, J. (2017). Investigate moped-car conflicts in China using a naturalistic driving study approach. *Journal of Safety Research*, 63, 171-175.

Grilli, G., & Notaro, S. (2019). Exploring the influence of an extended theory of planned behaviour onpreferences and willingness to pay for participatory natural resources management. *Journal of Environmental Management*, 232, 902–909.

Habich-Sobiegalla, S., Kostka, G., & Anzinger, S. (2019). Citizens' electric vehicle purchase intentions in China: An analysis of microlevel and macro-level factors. *Transport Policy*, 79, 223–233.

Hofstede, G. (1980). *Culture's Consequences: International Differences in Work-Related Values.* Beverly Hills: Sage.

Hofstede Insights (2019). Online at https://www.hofstede-insights.com/product/compare-countries/.

Huang, Y.-H., Zhang, W., Roetting, M., & Melton, D. (2006). Experiences from dual-country drivers: Driving safely in China and the US. *Safety Science*, 44, 785–795. https://doi.org/10.1016/j.ssci.2006.05.002.

Jahoda, G. (2012). Critical reflections on some recent definitions of "culture". Culture *& Psychology*, 18, 289–303.

Jeon, M., Riener, A., Lee, J.-H., Schuett, J., & Walker, B.N. (2012). Cross-cultural differences in the use of in-vehicle technologies and vehicle area network services: Austria, USA, and South Korea. *Proceedings of the 4th International Conference on Automotive User Interfaces and Interactive Vehicular Applications (AutomotiveUI '12)*, New York, ACM, pp. 163–170.

Lajunen, T., Corry, A., Summala, H., & Hartley, L. (1998). Cross-cultural differences in drivers' self-assessments of their perceptual-motor and safety skills: Australians and Finns. *Personality and Individual Differences*, 24, 539–550.

Large, D.R., Burnett, G., Crundall, E., Lawson, G., Skrypchuk, L., & Mouzakitis, A. (2019). Evaluating secondary input device to support an automotive touchscreen HMI: A gross-cultural simulator study conducted in the UK and China. *Applied Ergonomics*, 78, 184–196.

Large, D.R., Burnett, G., & Mohd-Hasni, Y. (2017). Capturing cultural differences between UK and Malaysian drivers to inform the design of in-vehicle navigation systems. *International Journal of Automotive Engineering*, 8, 112–119. https://doi.org/10.20485/jsaeijae.8.3_112.

Lee, Y.M., Shepard, E., & Crundall, D. (2015). Cross-cultural effects on the perception and appraisal of approaching motorcycles at junctions. *Transportation Research Part F*, 31, 77–86. https://doi.org/10.1016/j.trf.2015.03.013.

Li, Ch., Wang, W., Guo, H., & Dietrich, A. (2018a). Cross-cultural analysis of young drivers' preferences for in-vehicle systems and behavioral effects caused by secondary tasks. *Sustainability*, 10, 4083. https://doi.org/10.3390/su10114083.

Li, L.M.W., Masuda, T., Hamamura, T., & Ishii, K. (2018b). Culture and Decision Making: Influence of Analytic Versus Holistic Thinking Style on Resource Allocation in a Fort Game. *Journal of Cross-Cultural Psychology*, 19, 1066–1080.

Liu, J., Wen, H., Zhu, D., & Kumfer, W. (2019). Investigation of the contributory factors to the guessability of traffic signs. *International Journal of Environmental Research and Public Health*, 16, 162, https://doi.org/10.3390/ijerph16010162.

Lund, I.O., & Rundmo, T. (2009). Cross-cultural comparisons of traffic safety, risk perception, attitudes and behaviour. *Safety Science*, 47, 547-553.

Marshall, W. E. (2018). Understanding international road safety disparities: Why is Australia so much safer than the United States? *Accident Analysis and Prevention*, 111, 251–265. https://doi.org/10.1016/j.aap.2017.11.031.

Melinder, K. (2007). Socio-cultural characteristics of high versus low risk societies regarding road traffic safety. *Safety Science*, 45, 397–414. https://doi.org/10.1016/j.ssci.2006.07.004.

Minkov, M. Dutt, P., Schachner, M., Jandosova, J., Khassenbekov, Y., Morales, O., et al. (2019). What would people do with thein money if they were rich? A search for Hofstede dimensions across 52 countries. *Cross Cultural & Strategic Management*, 26, 93–116.

Ng, A.W.Y., & Chan, A.H.S. (2007). Culture issues in traffic sign usability. In Aykin, N. (2007, ed.): *Usability and Internationalization, Part I, HCII 2007, LNCS 4559*. Berlin Heidelberg, Springer-Verlag, pp. 379–387.

Nisbett, R.E., Peng, K., Choi, I., & Norenzayan, A. (2001). Culture and systems of thought: holistic versus analytic cognition. *Psychological Review*, 108, 291–310. https://doi.org/10.1037/0033-295X.108.2.291.

Nordfjærn, T., Simsekoglu, Ö., & Rundmo, R. (2014a). Culture related to road traffic safety: A comparison of eight countriesusing two conceptualizations of culture. *Accident Analysis and Prevention*, 62, 319–328. https://doi.org/10.1016/j.aap.2013.10.018.

Nordfjærn, T., Simsekoglu, Ö., Zavareh, M.F., Hezaveh, A.M., Mamdoohi, A.M., & Rundmo, R. (2014b). Road traffic culture and personality traits related to traffic safety in Turkish and Iranian symplex. *Safety Science*, 66, 36–46.

Nordfjærn, T., & Zahadeh, M.F. (2016). Individualism, collectivism and pedestrian safety: A comparative study of young adults from Iran and Pakistan. *Safety Science*, 87, 8–17.

Orru, K., Poom, A., & Nordlund, A. (2019). Socio-structural and psychological factors behind car use: Comparing Northern and Eastern Europe. *Transportation Research Part A*, 119, 113–125.

Özkan, T., Lajunen, T., Chliaoutakis, J.E., Parker, D., & Summala, H. (2006). Cross-cultural differences in driving behaviours: A comparison of six countries. *Transportation Research Part F*, 9, 227–242. https://doi.org/10.1016/j.aap.2006.04.006.

Quintal, V.A., Lee, J.A., & Soutar, G.N. (2010). Tourists' information search: The differential impact of risk and uncertainty avoidance. *International Journal of Tourism Research*, 12, 321–333. https://doi.org/10.1002/jtr.753.

Royal Automobile Club of Queensland (2019). Top 10 driving tips for visitors in Australia. Retrieved 10 September 2019, from https://www.racq.com.au/cars-and-driving/safety-on-the-road/driving-in-australia.

Safer Journeys (2019). Overseas licences crash statistics questions and answers. Retrieved 10 September 2019, from https://www.saferjourneys.govt.nz/assets/Uploads/15-239-Safer-Journeys-visiting-driver-crash-stats2.pdf.

Sârbescu, P., Stanojevic´, P., & Jovanovic´, D. (2014). A cross-cultural analysis of aggressive driving: Evidence from Serbia and Romania. *Transportation Research Part F*, 24, 210–217. https://doi.org/10.1016/j.trf.2014.04.002.

Shinar, D., Dewar, R. E., Summala, H., & Zakowska, L. (2014). Traffic sign symbol comprehension: A cross-cultural study. *Ergonomics*, 1549–1565. https://doi.org/10.1080/001401303200 0121615.

Shinohara, Y., & Nishizaki, Y. (2018). Where Do Drivers Look When Driving in a Foreign Country? In R. Lee (ed.), *Software Engineering, Artificial Intelligence, Networking and Parallel/Distributed Computing*, Studies in Computational Intelligence 721, Springer, 151–163. https://doi.org/10.1007/978-3-319-62048-0_11.

Simsekoglu, Ö, Nordfjærn, T., & Rundmo, R. (2012). Traffic risk perception, road safety attitudes, and behaviors among road users: a comparison of Turkey and Norway. *Journal of Risk Research*, 15, 787–800. https://doi.org/10.1080/13669877.2012.657221.

Summala, H. (1998). American drivers in Europe: Different signing policy may cause safety problems at uncontrolled intersections. *Accident Analysis & Prevention*, 30(2), 285–289.

Timmermans, Ch., Alhajyaseen, W., Reinolsmann, N., Nakamura, H., & Suzuki, K. (in press). Traffic safety culture of professional drivers in the State of Qatar. *IATSS Research*, https://doi.org/10.1016/j.iatssr.2019.03.004.

Uzondu, Ch., Jamson, S., & Lai, F. (2019). Investigating unsafe behaviours in traffic conflict situations: An observational study in Nigeria. Journal of Traffic and Transportation Engineering. https://doi.org/10.1016/j.jtte.2018.06.002.

Üzümcüoglu, Y., Özkan, T., & Lajunen, T. (2018). The relationships between cultural variables, law enforcements and driver behaviours across 37 nations. *Transportation Research Part F*, 58, 743–753.

Vollero, A., Siano, A., Palazzo, M., & Amabile, S. (2019). Hofstede's cultural dimensions and corporate social responsibility in online communication: Are they independent constructs? *Corporate Social Responsibility and Environment Management.* https://doi.org/10.1002/csr.1773.

Wang, W., Cheng, Q., Li, Ch., André, D., & Jiang, X. (2019). A cross-cultural analysis of driving behavior under critical situations: A driving simulator study. *Transportation Research Part F*, 62, 483–493.

Ward, S.J., Wogalter, M.S., & Melcer, A.W. (2004). Comprehension and training of international road signs. *Proceedings of the Human Factors and Ergonomics Society Annual Meeting*, 48, 2104–2108.

Warner, H. W., Özkan, T., & Lajunen, T. (2009). Cross-cultural differences in drivers' speed choice. *Accident Analysis and Prevention*, 41, 816–819. https://doi.org/10.1016/j.aap.2009.04.004.

Warner, H. W., Özkan, T., Lajunen, T., & Tzamalouka, T. (2011). Cross-cultural comparison of drivers' tendency to commit different aberrant driving behaviours. *Transportation Research Part F*, 14, 390–399. https://doi.org/10.1016/j.trf.2011.04.006.

Warner, H. W., Özkan, T., Lajunen, T., & Tzamalouka, T. (2013). Cross-cultural comparison of driving skills among students in four different countries. *Safety Science*, 57, 69–74. https://doi.org/10.1016/j.ssci.2013.01.003.

Wu, Ch., Chu, W., Zhang, H., & Özkan, T. (2018). Interactions between Driving Skills on Aggressive Driving: Study among Chinese Drivers. *Transportation Research Record: Journal of the Transportation Research Board*, 2672 (31), 10–20.

Yannis, G., Golias, J., & Papadimitriou, E. (2007). Accident risk of foreign drivers in various road environments. *Journal of Safety Research*, 38, 471–480. https://doi.org/10.1016/j.jsr.2007.01.014.

Yoh, K., Okamoto, T., Inoi, H., & Doi, K. (2017). Comparative study on foreign drivers' characteristics using traffic violation and accident statistics in Japan. *IATSS Research*, 41, 94–105. https://doi.org/10.1016/j.iatssr.2017.06.004.

Zhang, X., Xiang, H., Wheeler, K. K., Smith, G. A., & Stallones, L. (2010). Road traffic injuries to foreigners in the People's Republic of China, 2000-2008. *Journal of safety research*, 41(6), 521–523. https://doi.org/10.1016/j.jsr.2010.09.003.

Václav Linkov (PhD) works as a researcher in transportation psychology in CDV – Transport Research Centre. He received master degrees in discrete mathematics and psychology and PhD. in Social Psychology from Masaryk University. He spent 5 years studying East Asian languages and cultures at universities in Seoul, Taipei, and Wuhan. His research interests are traffic psychology, cultural psychology, theoretical psychology, and East Asian cultures.

Petr Zámečník is the head of Department of Traffic Psychology, CDV – Transport Research Centre. He received master degrees in sociology and psychology from Masaryk University. His research interests are traffic psychology, drunk driving, rehabilitation programmes for drivers, and first aid education in driving schools.

Epilogue: Errors, Mistakes and Failures in Anticipation of the Fourth Industrial Revolution

Elisabeth Vanderheiden and Claude-Hélène Mayer

The contributions in this book show that although much has been done in recent years to explore errors, mistakes and failures as a resource, there is still much to be discovered in multiple approaches and different cultural perspectives on this topic.

The examples in this book have been able to demonstrate, in many different scientific contexts, how strongly the perception of what is failure or error is shaped, above all, by cultural context. Here, more intensive inter-, cross- and transcultural research could contribute not only to avoiding misunderstandings (see e.g. Clarke & Takashiro; Mayer & Mayer; Rau, Guo, Nan, Lei & Zhang, Linkov & Zamecnik in this book) but also to cooperating on ways to make mistakes and errors useful as resources. More research could also clarify situations where mistakes and errors should be avoided as far as possible because of their negative to catastrophic consequences, for example, in criminological contexts (see Mayer and Petherick in this book) or in the context of transport and aviation (Hagen, Linkov & Zamecnik, van der Westhuizen, Tshaba-lala & Stanz in this book) or in relation to medicine (see Brommundt, Subbe & Barach in this book). It is essential that this takes place to a greater extent than hitherto in terms of appreciative use of cultural diversity (see Mayer wildlife).

Further research needs to arise from the rapidly advancing Fourth Industrial Revolution (4IR) to include topics such as digitalisation, which bring progress and simplification in many respects. Nevertheless, there are many risks associated with

E. Vanderheiden
Catholic Adult Education of Germany, Römerberg, Germany
e-mail: ev@keb-rheinland-pfalz.de

C.-H. Mayer
Department of Industrial Psychology and People Management, University of Johannesburg, Johannesburg, South Africa

Institut für Therapeutische Kommunikation und Sprachgebrauch, Europa Universität Viadrina, Frankfurt (Oder), Germany
e-mail: claudemayer@gmx.net

E. Vanderheiden, C.-H. Mayer (eds.), *Mistakes, Errors and Failures across Cultures*, https://doi.org/10.1007/978-3-030-35574-6

errors, mistakes and failures, such as artificial intelligence (AI) and its related algorithms. Six phenomena are briefly outlined here as examples of the need for adjusted contemporary and future research on errors, mistakes and failures.

Error Scenario 1

Digitalisation, especially the use of AI, is generally associated with the idea that using technical applications should lead to improvements and optimisations, as people already depend so much on technology. This is also in connection with the assumed constitutive defectiveness of human beings. Already at the beginning of the 1980s, author Elaine Rich emphasised:

> Artificial Intelligence is the study of how to make computers do things which, at the moment, people are better [at doing]. (Charts of Humanity 2019)

In human resource management, for example, this focus has led to a drastic increase in the number of decisions that are no longer made by people but by systems. This applies to the selection, development and administration of personnel as well as to proposals for the release of personnel, to people analytics and, in some cases, to the analysis of private data in employees' social networks, so that with the help of AI, probable statements can be made about impending sick days, imminent dismissals and similar topics (Gesellschaft für Informatik e.V., GI 2019). This situation can potentially lead to mistakes, in view of the fact that people present themselves in the social media less with the intention of providing data for their employer, than to be in contact with family and friends, to find a partner, to connect with like-minded people and much more.

It is becoming increasingly clear that not only people but also the digital systems they create, manage and control are flawed. AI systems are likely to reflect the individual, cultural prejudices and attributions of the people who develop the systems and enter the data and thus create errors and mistakes by reproducing implicit racial, gender or ideological prejudices (O'Neil 2017; IBM Research 2019; Buolamwini 2019). Two examples: In 2018 it became apparent that Amazon was using an AI-based recruiting tool that showed bias towards women (Agarwal 2019). Self-driving cars are trained to perceive white people as road users to be aware of and therefore do not take humans with brown and black skin colour as humans (Agarwal 2019; WDR Fernsehen 2019).

This should ideally be avoided in both humans and machines in order to prevent discrimination. Such mistakes and failures in the AI system typically occur primarily in the data or in the algorithmic model (IBM Research 2019). IBM is one company that assumes most AI applications are currently prejudiced and that prejudiced AI applications will also spread rapidly in the coming years (IBM Research 2019).

This is all the more alarming as people's trust in AI is growing enormously. In Germany, for example, a representative survey of 1000 people was conducted in

2018. The question was: "When you think about your private life, in which of the following situations would you accept the decision of an artificial intelligence rather than that of a human being?" (Bitcom Research 2018). The results suggest that a majority of Germans have high confidence in AI and would even let AI decide on their behalf in certain situations:

- 15% would rather accept the decision of an AI than that of a person when applying for a loan from a bank.
- 10% would rather bow to the judgement of an AI than a human judge in court after a traffic accident.
- 9% would prefer an AI to their boss when determining a salary increase.
- 9 % of respondents consider the decision of an AI in a dispute with their partner to be useful if the partners cannot agree on a conflict, for example, on a larger purchase (Bitcom Research 2018).

Against the background of the biases that we can observe in AIs, these are frightening scenarios.

Error Scenario 2

A recent survey in Germany (Society for Informatics e.V., GI 2019) revealed that although a majority of Germans do not yet assign AI a gender, around one fifth of respondents perceive AI machines as "rather male" (19.3%). This is almost six times as many people as those who classify AI as "more female" (3.5%). This represents an imbalance that affects the entire population, whether old or young, man or woman, East or West. The data shows only one exception: the number of science fiction fans who classify AI as "more female" is 7.2%, twice as high as in the total population.

Error Scenario 3

Prejudice, stereotypes and attributions can also lead to momentous misjudgements in other fields, such as in the criminological context, illustrated by examples from predictive policing. Previous experience with predictive policing has shown that it has very far-reaching and serious consequences, both in terms of a massive increase in surveillance, an increase in the amount of data, the systematic surveillance of an unprecedentedly large number of people and also of people who have had no prior direct police contact and who experience massive consequences in terms of social inequality (see Brayne 2017; Hielscher and Heeder 2017; Oswald et al. 2017). Predictive policing is associated with a paradigm shift in police work, which in the past was primarily of a reactive nature, but in the future should be given a preventive proactive orientation (Brayne 2017). However, this can be based on erroneous assumptions and consequently lead to mistakes in implementation. It can be seen, for example, that residents of certain disadvantaged urban districts are more likely than others to be the focus of such surveillance, men more likely than women, people with darker skin tones more likely than people with lighter skin and poorer people more than wealthier ones, and people who have already attracted attention in the system of law enforcement authorities are more likely be judged than those who have not (Brayne 2017; Hielscher and Heeder 2017). Wachter et al. (2017) have pointed to a number of potential errors that can result from the use of algorithms in police work:

1. Inconclusive evidence leading to unjustified actions
2. Opaque evidence leading to opacity
3. Misleading evidence leading to bias
4. Unfair results leading to discrimination
5. Transformative effects leading to challenges for autonomy and data protection.

Oswald and her colleagues (2017) have already identified several such errors in connection with the implementation of the HART model in the United Kingdom. Brayne (2017) was able to prove similar errors in a policing system used in Los Angeles.

Error Scenario 4

The year 1997 represented a decisive milestone for AI in that Hochreiter and Schmidhuber (1997) published a method of providing the neural networks of AI with memory (known as long short-term memory) and thus ensured that the error rate during learning in the neural network could be systematically reduced. For example, self-propelled cars have been produced successfully since 2009. Since 2010, AI has been increasingly researching autonomous robots that learn on their own.

The neuronal network functions analogously to the human brain and generally consists of three levels. Data is recorded in the input layer. The data is processed in one or more intermediate layers, and output is a result in the third layer. AI programmes improve through continuous training. In contrast to humans, however, they have to process significantly more examples in order to achieve learning progress, requiring millions or even billions of training examples until it has developed a model that reliably recognises regularities. In addition, the data must be "clean", and patterns must remain unchanged over time. The weakness of AI in learning is also its strength. It requires more data than a human being, but it can also process and store information faster and to a much greater extent. AI has a distinct memory. Another important advantage is that AI programmes are able to filter out complex patterns and non-linearities from huge amounts of data. Machines are free of emotions, never get tired or unfocused in their work. But all of this requires human control to prevent errors and mistakes. This situation is made more difficult by the fact that learning performance is inextricably linked with constantly increasing computing capacities, which increases the speed at which AI learns independently. People can scarcely keep up with this speed and scope, and the question arises whether it is possible to control this pace and avoid mistakes.

Error Scenario 5

Another consideration related to error avoidance and "big data" is the disclosure of algorithms (Zweig et al. 2017; Trute 2018). How can it be ensured that AI works error-free—in the sense of freedom from discrimination in predictive policing and protection of fundamental rights such as personal rights, for example—if the corresponding algorithms are not disclosed? This situation makes it impossible to control, uncover and constructively deal with errors.

Error Scenario 6

In 2020, the People's Republic of China will introduce social scoring for all its citizens and companies, which is currently being tested in 40 districts and 20 cities in China (Botsman 2017; Krauter and Welchering 2019). Within the framework of this social scoring, every citizen will receive positive scores for every good performance, while every misbehaviour and failure will be subject to corresponding deductions which regulate access to certain resources such as education and consumer goods for them and, if applicable, for family members. At the same time, however, predictions are to be made about future behaviour, so that people are potentially deterred from committing crimes, and conformity with the politically dominant system is ensured (Krauter and Welchering 2019). Digital monitoring of public and private spaces plays just as important role as social control in the immediate vicinity of the workplace or living space.

Assuming that failure and making mistakes are constitutive parts of being human—and that they are resources, to the extent that they are opportunities to change perspectives and deepen new insights, individual and collective processes of recognition, learning and development—the question arises what the medium- and long-term psychological, social and political effects will be, especially since everyone's scoring results are publicly available at any time (Botsman 2017). The question also arises—independent of many other ethical questions—of who controls the control, in this case the communist system and eight private companies commissioned to develop the algorithms, collect and evaluate the data (Botsman 2017; Erling 2019). This could result in a variety of exciting research questions dealing with mistakes, errors and failures in certain cultural contexts.

The Way Forward

Having addressed and reflected on six selected errors, mistakes and failures in contemporary societies and cultures, as well as in future world and 4IR scenarios, we would like to emphasise that a positive and constructive view of errors, mistakes and failures will support individuals, organisations and societies to transform for the better. Undoubtedly there are several machine–machine, machine–human and human–human interactions in which errors, mistakes and failures should be minimised and avoided. However, since this is only possible to a limited degree, the transformation of errors, mistakes and failures into positive health resources and impactful agents is what we are aiming for in publishing this book.

References

Agarwal, R. (2019). Six Important Steps to Build a Machine Learning System. Retrieved 3 October 2019, from https://towardsdatascience.com/6-important-steps-to-build-a-machine-learning-system-d75e3b83686

Bitcom Research. (2018). Lieber Künstliche Intelligenz als menschliche Dummheit?. Retrieved 23 August 2019, from https://www.bitkom.org/Presse/Presseinformation/Lieber-Kuenstliche-Intelligenz-als-menschliche-Dummheit.html

Botsman, R. (2017). *Big data meets Big Brother as China moves to rate its citizens*. [online] wired.co.uk. Available at: http://www.guicolandia.net/files/expansao/Big%20data%20meets%20Big%20Brother%20as%20China%20moves%20to%20rate%20its%20citizens.pdf [Accessed 22 Aug. 2019].

Brayne, S. (2017). Big Data Surveillance: The Case of Policing. *American Sociological Review, 82*(5), 977–1008. doi: https://doi.org/10.1177/0003122417725865

Buolamwini, J. (2019). How I'm fighting bias in algorithms | Joy Buolamwini. Retrieved 23 August 2019, from https://www.youtube.com/watch?v=UG_X_7g63rY

Charts of Humanity. (2019). Artificial Intelligence – Definitions. Retrieved 12 August 2019, from http://www.chartsofhumanity.com/artificial-intelligence-1/

Erling, J. (2019). *Social Scoring: So absurd ausgefeilt ist Chinas Überwachungssystem*. [online] DIE WELT. Available at: https://www.welt.de/wirtschaft/article192029849/Social-Scoring-So-absurd-ausgefeilt-ist-Chinas-Ueberwachungssystem.html [].

Gesellschaft für Informatik e.V. (GI). (2019). Umfrage: Wenn KI ein Geschlecht hätte, wäre sie männlich. Retrieved 13 August 2019, from https://www.hrperformance-online.de/blog/detail/sCategory/209/blogArticle/3315

Hielscher, M., & Heeder, M. (2017). PRE-CRIME. Retrieved 12 August 2019, from https://kloosundco.de/pre-crime/

Hochreiter, S., & Schmidhuber, J. (1997). Long Short-Term Memory. *Neural Computation, 9*(8), 1735–1780. doi: https://doi.org/10.1162/neco.1997.9.8.1735

IBM Research. (2019). AI and bias - IBM Research - US. Retrieved 12 August 2019, from https://www.research.ibm.com/5-in-5/ai-and-bias/

Krauter, R. and Welchering, P. (2019). *Social Score - Wie China die digitale Überwachung vorantreibt. Peter Welchering im Gespräch mit Ralf Krauter*. [online] Deutschlandfunk. Available at: https://www.deutschlandfunk.de/social-score-wie-china-die-digitale-ueberwachung-vorantreibt.676.de.html?dram:article_id=442872 [Accessed 22 Aug. 2019].

O'Neil, C. (2017). *Weapons of math destruction*. Danvers: Broadway Books.

Oswald, M., Grace, J., Urwin, S., & Barnes, G. (2017). Algorithmic Risk Assessment Policing Models: Lessons from the Durham HART Model and Experimentall Proportionality. *SSRN Electronic Journal*. doi: https://doi.org/10.2139/ssrn.3029345

E. Vanderheiden, C.-H. Mayer (eds.), *Mistakes, Errors and Failures across Cultures*, https://doi.org/10.1007/978-3-030-35574-6

Trute, H. (2018). Rechtliche Herausforderungen der Digitalisierung. *Digitalisierung Im Spannungsfeld Von Politik, Wirtschaft, Wissenschaft Und Recht*, 313–330. doi: https://doi.org/10.1007/978-3-662-56438-7_22

Wachter, Sandra and Mittelstadt, Brent and Russell, Chris, Counterfactual Explanations Without Opening the Black Box: Automated Decisions and the GDPR (October 6, 2017). Harvard Journal of Law & Technology, 31 (2), 2018. Available at SSRN: https://ssrn.com/abstract=3063289 or https://doi.org/10.2139/ssrn.3063289

WDR Fernsehen. (2019). Video "Angeklickt: Diskriminierung durch künstliche Intelligenz" - Aktuelle Stunde. Retrieved 3 October 2019, from https://classic.ardmediathek.de/tv/Aktuelle-Stunde/Angeklickt-Diskriminierung-durch-künstl/WDR-Fernsehen/Video?bcastId=7293524&documentId=61779392

Zweig, K., Deussen, O., & Krafft, T. (2017). Algorithmen und Meinungsbildung. *Informatik-Spektrum*, *40*(4), 318–326. doi: https://doi.org/10.1007/s00287-017-1050-5

The manufacturer's authorised representative in the EU is Springer Nature Customer Service Centre GmbH, Europaplatz 3, 69115 Heidelberg, Germany. If you have any concerns regarding our products, please contact ProductSafety@springernature.com

Printed and bound by CPI Group (UK) Ltd, Croydon, CR0 4YY
30/09/2026
02225460-0020